MW00776525

A COMMENTARY ON

PROVERBS

PETER A. STEVESON

BJU PRESS
Greenville, South Carolina

Library of Congress Cataloging-in-Publication Data
Steveson, Peter A. (Peter Allan), 1934-
    A commentary on Proverbs / Peter A. Steveson.
        p. cm.
    Includes bibliographical references and index.
    ISBN 1-57924-455-6
    1. Bible. O.T. Proverbs--Commentaries. I. Title.

    BS1465.3 .S74 2000
    223'.7077--dc21   00-062622

The fact that materials produced by other publishers may be referred to in this volume does not constitute an endorsement by Bob Jones University Press of the content or theological position of materials produced by such publishers. The position of Bob Jones University Press, and the University itself, is well known. Any references and ancillary materials are listed as an aid to the student or the teacher and in an attempt to maintain the accepted academic standards of the publishing industry.

PROVERBS
Peter A. Steveson, Ph.D.

© 2001 Bob Jones University Press
Greenville, South Carolina 29614

Printed in the United States of America
All rights reserved

ISBN 1-57924-455-6

15 14 13 12 11 10 9 8 7 6 5 4 3 2 1

To Sue,
the "worthy woman"
(Proverbs 31:10)
given me by God
to share my life.

TABLE OF CONTENTS

PREFACE

This book is the culmination of many years of concentrated study in the Book of Proverbs. My personal interest in the book goes back even further, primarily due to my desire to know biblical principles that relate to the family. I have preached and taught these principles down through my years in the ministry. The full study of the book was a natural expansion of this interest.

Proverbs is the "wisdom" book of the Bible. Those who master the principles taught here gain something of the mind of God for daily living. Whether we think of the family, the employer-employee relationship, personal finances, friendship, speech, or a host of other matters, the book gives guidance. Despite this practicality, it is often a neglected book for serious study. We skim the cream off the top but omit to look deeper for those subtle points that can help us live pleasing to God.

As with all of the Bible, mere conformity to Scripture is not enough. There must as well be a personal relationship to God gained by accepting Jesus Christ as Savior. Man's sinful nature will keep him from the consistent practice of godly principles. It is the recognition of one's own sinfulness and the trust that Christ's sacrifice at Calvary atones for sin that allows one to build a godly life. Only then will one be able to be consistent in following the principles of wisdom given in this book.

Let me thank those who have helped me. Mrs. Jackie Eaves, Mr. Rob Loach, and Drs. Robert Bell, Terry Rude, and Mike Barrett, my colleagues in the ministry, have made helpful comments. The library staffs at Bob Jones University, Furman University, the University of Chicago, Emory University, and Wheaton College have assisted in finding research materials. The editors at Bob Jones University Press—especially Dr. Dan Olinger, Suzette Jordan, and Martin Grove—have given helpful guidance in the preparation of the book. Finally, I appreciate the kindness of Bob Jones University in giving me the sabbatical year that let me complete my preparation of the book.

ABBREVIATIONS

AB	Anchor Bible
AJSL	*American Journal of Semitic Languages*
ANET	James B. Pritchard, ed., *Ancient Near Eastern Texts* (1969)
AV	Authorized Version (King James Version)
BASOR	*Bulletin of the American Schools of Oriental Research*
BDB	Francis Brown, S. R. Driver, and Charles A. Briggs, eds., *Hebrew and English Lexicon of the Old Testament* (1974 rpt.)
BH	Rudolf Kittel, Biblia Hebraica
BibSac	*Bibliotheca Sacra*
BT	*The Bible Translator*
CBQ	*Catholic Biblical Quarterly*
CPTOT	James Barr, *Comparative Philology and the Text of the Old Testament* (1968)
DOTT	D. Winton Thomas, ed., *Documents from Old Testament Times* (1961)
EBC	Frank E. Gabelein, ed., *The Expositor's Bible Commentary* (1991)
ET	*The Expository Times*
ETL	*Ephemerides Theologicae Lovaniensium*
G.K.	E. Kautzsch, ed., Hebrew Grammar (1970)
GTJ	*Grace Theological Journal*
HUCA	*Hebrew Union College Annual*
IB	Interpreter's Bible
JAOS	*Journal of the American Oriental Society*
JBL	*Journal of Biblical Literature*
JCS	*Journal of Cuneiform Studies*
JJS	*Journal of Jewish Studies*
JNES	*Journal of Near Eastern Studies*
JNSL	*Journal of Northwest Semitic Languages*
JQR	*Jewish Quarterly Review*
JRAS	*Journal of the Royal Asiatic Society*
JSS	*Journal of Semitic Studies*

JTS	*Journal of Theological Studies*
KD	Franz Delitzsch, *Biblical Commentary on the Book of Proverbs* (1978 rpt.)
LXX	Septuagint
MT	Massoretic Text
NASB	New American Standard Bible
NEB	New English Bible
NET	God's Word to the Nations New Evangelical Translation
NIV	New International Version
NT	New Testament
NTS	*New Testament Studies*
OT	Old Testament
OTMS	H. H. Rowley, *The Old Testament and Modern Study* (1951)
OTTP	A. R. Hulst, *Old Testament Translation Problems* (1960)
PC	W. J. Deane and S. T. Taylor-Taswell, *Pulpit Commentary* (n.d.)
PNWSP	Mitchell Dahood, *Proverbs and Northwest Semitic Philology* (1963)
RSV	Revised Standard Version
SPCK	W. H. Phillott, *The Proverbs* (1880)
TB	*Tyndale Bulletin*
TOT	Walther Eichrodt, *Theology of the Old Testament* (1953)
TWOT	R. Laird Harris, *Theological Wordbook of the Old Testament* (1980)
TZ	*Theologische Zeitschrift*
VT	*Vetus Testamentum*
VTS	*Vetus Testamentum Supplements*
WBC	Charles F. Pfeiffer, ed., *Wycliffe Bible Commentary* (1962)
WIP	R. N. Whybray, *Wisdom in Proverbs* (1965)
ZAW	*Zeitschrift für die Alttestamentliche Wissenschaft*
ZPBD	Merrill C. Tenney, ed., *Zondervan's Pictorial Bible Dictionary* (1976)

INTRODUCTION

By the very nature of the Bible, different emphases occur in different sections. The opening pages reveal fundamental themes such as the omnipotence of the Creator and His requirement of holiness in His servants. Eschatological truths, on the other hand, generally develop later, in the prophetical portions. While the authors do not make sharp distinctions, it is still true that various sections of God's Word emphasize different doctrinal themes.

In keeping with this characteristic, the Book of Proverbs is the book of ethics and practical wisdom. It focuses on everyday life in a way not found in other parts of the Bible. Typical of this emphasis, the book deals with man's relationship with others, both in and away from work, family relationships, economic principles, and guidance for civil areas of life.[1]

Despite this focus, we should not think of Proverbs in purely secular terms. Rather, it joins religious beliefs to everyday life. The proverbs express religious philosophy as applied to the pragmatic demands of life. As such, the book is intensely practical and well worthy of close study.

All too often, theological studies include such topics as inspiration, anthropology, soteriology, and eschatology as subdivisions. This process often loses sight of the fact that theology includes the total relationship between God and man. It is important in studying Proverbs to keep a balanced view of theology. Theological studies include not only the characteristics of God knowable by man but also the requirements of God involving man. Theological studies therefore must be not only doctrinal; they must be also practical. For this reason, the study of OT theology involves the application of Bible principles to the believer's everyday life.

---

[1]Derek Kidner, *Proverbs* (1964) (hereafter cited as Kidner), p. 35, has well caught the nature of the book: "We should do Proverbs a poor service if we contrived to vest it in a priestly ephod or a prophet's mantle, for it is a book which seldom takes you to church. Like its own figure of Wisdom, it calls across to you in the street about some everyday matter, or points things out at home. Its function in Scripture is to put godliness into working clothes; to name business and society as spheres in which we are to acquit ourselves with credit to our Lord, and in which we are to look for His training."

Proverbs suits itself well to this approach. There is general agreement about the pragmatic nature of the book. We can describe its message as "Christianity in overalls," religious activity extended to everyday life. More familiar themes, such as God, inspiration, or salvation, receive only incidental emphasis. Doctrinal matters are subordinate to more practical themes.

Need for This Commentary

A survey of the available literature relating to the Book of Proverbs shows that this is one of the neglected fields of OT study. A small number of commentaries deal with the Hebrew text. Most of these come from the early years of the twentieth century.

To further complicate matters, the greater part of the literature comes from theologically liberal men. The inspiration and inerrancy of the original manuscripts and the authority of the book for today's believers do not concern these men. They often emend the text to support their views. They readily emend the thought of the text by using Semitic parallels. They consider the Hebrew proverbs to be mere copies of wisdom literature like those from other countries of the biblical world.

Their approach to Proverbs is confusing. The average Christian does not have the tools to refute a liberal commentary. Like a blind man following a blind leader, he reads without knowing that what he reads can harm him spiritually.

The present author approaches Proverbs from a Fundamentalist stance. As will be seen, every attempt has been made to follow the traditional text. This does not mean the rejection of scholarly methods. It means rather that a high view of inspiration governs scholarship so that one must avoid promiscuous changes in the text. The suggestions of contemporary scholarship have been considered and, where justified, reemphasized in the discussion.

Authorship

The Book of Proverbs claims multiple authorship. It names such individuals as Solomon (1:1; 10:1; 25:1), Agur (30:1), and Lemuel (31:1). The largest part of the book comes from Solomon, a man who elsewhere receives credit for producing three thousand proverbs, I Kings 4:32.

Despite this claim to Solomonic authorship, there is no agreement today among scholars as to the author of the book. At one position stands a man such as Kenneth A. Kitchen, who attributes the bulk of the book to Solomon, excluding only the appendices of chapters 30-31. He suggests that the form of the book, including a prologue (c. 1-9) followed by the major body of exhortations (c. 10-29), parallels the wisdom litera-ture of this period in OT history. Solomon could therefore have authored the book.[2] Far removed from this position is that of R. B. Y. Scott, who considers the connection between Solomon and the Book of Proverbs "a tenuous one." He suggests that Solomon was "the patron saint of the Wisdom movement" and that his name became associated with wisdom writing "by literary convention."[3] Within these extremes, there are a wide variety of other positions. Most attribute at least part of the book to Solomon but recognize that others also contributed, either by writing or editing the material.

As noted before, the book itself states that other men contributed to the writing. The appendices at the end (30:1-33; 31:1-31) were authored, respectively, by Agur and Lemuel. Older commentators sometimes made these names allegorical, representing Solomon.[4] These attempts, how-ever, were highly subjective and therefore suspect. It is natural to recog-nize these men as supplementary authors whose writings found a place alongside the collections of Solomon's writings. This same practice exists elsewhere in the OT (Deut. 34:1-12; Josh. 24:29-33; Isa. 38:9-20).

The acrostic poem that closes the book (31:10-31) does not name an author. It may be an extension of Lemuel's work in vv. 1-9. In form,

---

[2]Kenneth A. Kitchen, *The Bible in Its World* (1977) (hereafter cited as Kitchen), p. 106.

[3]R. B. Y. Scott, "Proverbs, Ecclesiastes," in Anchor Bible Commentary, ed. W. F. Albright and D. N. Freedman (1965) (hereafter cited as AB), p. 13. See also "Solomon and the Beginnings of Wisdom in Israel," in *Wisdom in Israel and the Ancient Near East, Vetus Testamentum Supplements*, ed. M. Noth and D. Winton Thomas (1960) (here-after cited as *VTS*), III, 262-79, in which Scott attempts to show that the attributing of Proverbs to Solomon was a part of Hezekiah's plan "to restore the vanished glories of Solomon's kingdom."

[4]Aaron Rothkoff, "Solomon," *Encyclopedia Judaica* (1971), XV, 106. Louis Ginzberg, "Agur ben Jakeh," *The Jewish Encyclopedia* (1901), I, 276. Franz Delitzsch, *Biblical Commentary on the Book of Proverbs*, in *Commentary on the Old Testament*, (rpt. 1978) (hereafter cited as KD), II, 260, likewise refers to older commentators who attempted to prove that Agur was another name for Solomon.

however, it differs from the earlier verses of the chapter. It too stands as an appendix to the book. The lack of an author's name does not detract from the beauty and practicality of the passage.

Within the book are a series of collections of proverbial wisdom. Aside from the material in 25:1–29:27, collected by the "men of Hezekiah" under the king's direction, there is nothing to tell how the various proverbs came together. Evidently, the wise sayings of Solomon circulated in Israel until some scribes collected them and wrote them down.

The opponents of Solomonic authorship make inconclusive arguments to support their claims. The following discussion summarizes the problems suggested by those who try to disprove Solomon's authorship.

Solomon's Moral Character. Some claim that the proverbs reflect views that go contrary to the character of Solomon's reign. Supposedly, he would not have deprecated wealth (cf. 11:28; 15:16; 16:8). He would not have implied weakness in his own government (cf. 28:2, 12; 29:4). Considering the Solomonic harem, he would not have praised monogamy (cf. 18:22; 19:14).

This objection carries little weight. It can be answered in either of two ways. (1) Solomon learned from his mistakes. This made his instruction more valuable since it rested upon personal experience rather than theory only. (2) He wrote the book during the middle period of his life before he had apostatized. In this case his instruction is doubly valuable since it shows what will happen when one takes truth lightly.

Commentators have adopted both of these positions. Matthew Henry suggests that "in his latter end [he] turned aside from those good ways of God which in this book he had directed others in."[5] The old rabbinical teaching held that Solomon wrote the Song of Songs as a young man, Proverbs during the middle period of his life, and the Book of Ecclesiastes as he neared the end of his days.[6]

---

[5]Matthew Henry, *Commentary on the Whole Bible* (rpt. 1935) (hereafter cited as Henry), III, 790.

[6]*Dictionary of Judaism in the Biblical Period*, ed. Jacob Neusner, II, 593. Julius Greenstone, *Proverbs* (1950) (hereafter cited as Greenstone), p. xviii, notes that some rabbis thought that the Book of Proverbs was written first, before Ecclesiastes and the Song of Songs. Another rabbinic tradition states that Hezekiah and his wise men edited

Taking the other view, Joseph Parker comments: "The man who has been in the pit can speak most vividly about its depth and darkness. He who is bruised in every limb can best tell how strong is the foe with whom the young man has to deal in the conflict incident to opening life."[7] Nora Irwin concludes that "Solomon left us some of his greatest proverbs to keep us from making mistakes he made."[8]

Form and Style. A second objection notes the form and style of the book and relates it to other wisdom literature. The common literary style shows that Proverbs follows the same format as much of the wisdom literature from other countries.[9] Because of this, authors see various relationships. These range from the suggestion of direct copying to the idea that Israel adopted the literary style of its wisdom writings from the style found in other countries of the area.

We cannot deny that Israel interacted with other nations of the Near East. Through travel, trade, and cultural interchange, the surrounding nations influenced Israel. This was especially true during the times when Israel involved itself with the worship of heathen gods. On several occasions, God judged His people by allowing them to come under the dominion of other nations. This contact certainly influenced Israel.

When we look at the literature of Israel, we see parallels with the wisdom literature of other nations. The writings of the Sumerians, Babylonians, and Assyrians, for instance, often take the form of collections of short proverbs and pithy sayings, much the same as occurs in the Book of Proverbs. In both Egyptian and Mesopotamian literature, we see instruction given by a father to his son. Frequent use of the imperative mood occurs. The authors normally address their instruction to individuals rather than to the nations.

---

the Book of Proverbs, Yehosua M. Grintz, *Encyclopedia Judaica*, p. 454. See also Rothkoff, p. 107.

[7]Joseph Parker, *The People's Bible* (1891), XIII, 3.

[8]Nora Irwin, *Solomon and Proverbs* (1973) (hereafter cited as Irwin), p. 11.

[9]The Egyptian work *Instruction of the Vizier Ptah-hotep* (c. 2450 B.C.) contains father-to-son instruction, comparable to that found in Proverbs. The Babylonian writing *Counsels of Wisdom* (dated before 700 B.C.) contains moral exhortations, often similar to the Book of Proverbs. The Assyrian *Words of Ahiqar* (probably dating to the seventh century B.C.), a collection of wisdom sayings preserved in a fifth century B.C. Aramaic text, is similar to the Book of Proverbs. *The Teaching of Amen-em-opet* (dated variously between the tenth and sixth centuries B.C.), an Egyptian writing, and Prov. 22:17–24:34 have several similar sayings.

Despite these similarities, there is no reason for assuming a direct relationship between the Book of Proverbs and the other wisdom literature that has come down to us. Even in those passages with similarities, there are no verbatim quotations. The similarities involve isolated phrases or verses arranged in juxtaposition and freely edited to give them a distinctive Israelite character.

For instance, Proverbs 22:22 reads, "Rob not the poor, because he is poor: neither oppress the afflicted in the gate." This compares with *The Teaching of Amen-em-opet*, chapter 2, lines 1-2: "Guard thyself against robbing the wretched and against being puissant over the man of broken arm."[10] The similarity here is vague, yet the passage represents what is supposedly a direct influence upon the Bible by a foreign writing. Proverbs 25:15 reads, "By long forbearing is a prince persuaded, and a soft tongue breaketh the bones." This is compared to *The Words of Ahiqar*, vii: "Soft is the tongue of [a king], but it breaks a dragon's ribs."[11]

The Book of Proverbs also maintains a distinctly Israelite character. It refers to the law, (28:4, 9; 29:18). The book likewise mentions religious ceremonies (7:14). References to *šǝʾôl* exist (e.g., 1:12; 15:24). The covenant name of Yahweh occurs throughout the book (e.g., 1:7; 20:12). There are allusions to life after death (15:11; 27:20).

Further, the monotheistic tone of Proverbs is in stark contrast with the writings of the biblical world. *The Teaching of Amen-em-opet* mentions two gods of fortune, Shay and Renent (c. 7, 1. 2). The Babylonian *Counsels of Wisdom* refers to the god Shamash as well as the Anunnaki, the underworld gods (ll. 60, 147). *The Legend of Aqhat*, from Ras Shamra, mentions Baal and El in several places. Despite a polytheistic influence on every hand, Proverbs is monotheistic.

The vague nature of the similarities and the substantial nature of the differences indicate that there is no *direct* dependence of the biblical writers upon the secular literature that *may* have been available to them. There may well have been an oral body of gnomic observations upon

---

[10]Trans. J. M. Plumley, *The Teaching of Amen-em-opet*, in *Documents from Old Testament Times*, D. Winton Thomas, ed. (1958) (hereafter cited as *DOTT*), p. 176.

[11]J. B. Pritchard, ed., *Ancient Near Eastern Texts Relating to the Old Testament* (1969) (hereafter cited as *ANET*), p. 429.

life that circulated. This may have served to influence the written body of Scripture. This, however, is a far cry from direct influence.

As a matter of fact, wisdom writings were common during OT times. Evidence shows that this style of literature pervaded the nations of the Bible. The Bible itself speaks of wisdom as characterizing groups of men in various countries: Egypt (I Kings. 4:30; Acts 7:22); Edom (Jer. 49:7; Obad. 8); Babylon (Isa. 47:10; Jer. 50:35; Dan. 1:4, 20); Phoenicia (Ezek. 27:8; Zech. 9:2); Persia (Esther 1:13; 6:13); Israel (II Sam. 14:2; Isa. 29:14). It is natural that the biblical writers would adopt a similar style. This would agree with the common cultural heritage they shared with that part of the world. There is no reason, however, to assume that the biblical writers adapted their material from the writings of other nations.

Within the Bible itself, many indications show that wisdom practitioners were a part of Israel. Jotham's fable (Judg. 9:8ff); Samson's riddle (Judg. 14:14); David's quote of the ancients (I Sam. 24:13); Nathan's parable (II Sam. 12:1ff); the woman of Tekoa (II Sam. 14:2ff); the claim of the town of Abel (II Sam. 20:16ff); and the counselors at the king's court (I Chron. 27:32-33) all illustrate this. It is logical, then, that the wisdom writings would parallel the writings of other nations. Dealing with the same general themes and following the same poetical style, it is reasonable that there would be similarities.

Lack of Evidence for Solomonic Wisdom. A third objection to Solomonic authorship claims that no serious evidence supports Solomon's literary ability. The statements of I Kings 4:29-34 and 10:1-9, 23-24 that refer to his wisdom and literary accomplishments are improbable.[12] The references in Proverbs to Solomon's authorship are meaningless apart from other evidence to show his literary interest.[13]

---

[12]For instance, Scott, *VTS* III, 264, 267, calls these "fanciful accounts" and "but one element in a cycle of folktales of the glory of Solomon." In AB, pp. 11-12, Scott adds the thought that the passage in I Kings "cannot be dismissed as wholly legendary, simply because one writer's imagination has run riot in describing them." He then goes on to explain that Solomon's success as a ruler was the basis upon which he was considered wise, not any literary ability.

[13]T. Henshaw, *The Writings* (1963), p. 137, adopts a typical position by taking 1:1-6 as an introduction to the whole book, added by some unknown compiler. This leaves only

This *a priori* reasoning assumes the conclusion, then argues its way to it. It is typical of the thinking often adopted by those who presuppose the Bible to be merely a natural book, not inspired by God.

R. B. Y. Scott does advance two arguments to support his contention. He suggests (1) that evidence from Hebrew proves the lateness of the passages in I Kings, and (2) he dismisses the reference to wisdom as descriptive of Solomon's ability as a successful ruler.[14] These arguments carry little weight. The Hebrew terms cited prove nothing since no one claims that the books of Kings are early. While they record early history, the author wrote during the Captivity. The books record Israel's history up to this time. Evidence that shows that parts of the book were written later than Solomon is what we would expect. Nevertheless, though the book was written late, the internal evidence supports the accuracy of its early history. First Kings 11:41 refers to "the book of the acts of Solomon," and over thirty references show that the author also consulted "the book of the chronicles of the kings of Israel" and "the book of the chronicles of the kings of Judah" (e.g., 14:19, 29; 22:39, 45). Thus, the references to Solomon's wisdom rest upon earlier witnesses to this fact.

The argument that Solomon's wisdom refers only to his success as a ruler is weak. First Kings 4:29-34 specifically mentions literary accomplishments and scientific interests. Ecclesiastes 12:9 likewise mentions his interest in proverbial wisdom. The titles of Psalms 72 and 127 show that the unknown rabbis who added these accepted Solomonic authorship. The fact that the "men of Hezekiah" collected proverbs of Solomon, 25:1, shows that Solomon's authorship was openly accepted by Hezekiah's time. To deny this today goes against the evidence.

The statements in Proverbs supporting the authorship of Solomon are reasonable in view of the literary production attributed to him elsewhere. For one who accepts the inspiration of the Bible, the statements are not simply reasonable: they are authoritative. There is no reason to deny Solomon's authorship.

---

two of the collections as attributed to Solomon, and he concludes, "It cannot be definitely proved that these two collections are from his hand."

[14]Scott, AB, pp. 266-74.

Date

We must associate the date of the writing and editing of the book with its authorship. Many critics hold that Israel's religious thought evolved over a long time. It follows, then, that Proverbs was written after the wisdom literature that it resembles from the neighboring countries.[15]

Those with this view generally assign the authorship of Proverbs to unknown individuals, members of a wisdom caste. These men possibly served at the court during the monarchy, acting as the king's advisors. By the time of Isaiah (ca. 760-680 B.C.) the class was firmly established in Israel (Isa. 29:14). A century later, in the days of Jeremiah (ca. 635-580 B.C.), the group still influenced the land (Jer. 18:18). These men compiled and edited proverbial sayings into several collections. With the passage of time, the present book developed. While Solomon may have encouraged the work of this wisdom caste, he was not the principal author of the book.

At least two strong arguments weigh against this line of reasoning. In the first place, evidence shows that the proverb style is of ancient origin. Semitic writings from Babylon, Assyria, and Egypt demonstrate a proverbial style of writing, dating back as far as the late third millennium B.C.[16]

Kenneth A. Kitchen conducted a thorough analysis of the form of Proverbs. He compared it to other wisdom writings. This conclusively showed that a date in the early seventh century B.C. is reasonable for the book's final editing. Rather than a late date, the style of the book suggests an early date, in the time of Hezekiah, ca. 700 B.C. The book itself states this (25:1). The two appendices of Agur (c. 30) and Lemuel

---

[15]The following men represent the position. W. Baumgartner, "The Wisdom Literature," in *The Old Testament and Modern Study,* ed. H. H. Rowley (1951) (hereafter cited as *OTMS*), p. 212, dates c. 1-9 in the fourth century to late third century B.C. Otto Eissfeldt, *The Old Testament: An Introduction,* trans. Peter Ackroyd (1965), p. 473, concludes, "It cannot have come into being before the fourth century." He argues both from form and from supposed Greek influence upon the portrayal of wisdom and folly. J. H. Hayes, *Introduction to Old Testament Study* (1979), pp. 352-53, admits the existence of similar style writing in other early Semitic cultures but tentatively suggests a date in the fourth century B.C.

[16]E.g., *A Pessimistic Dialogue Between Master and Servant* (ca. 2280-2000 B.C., Assyria); *The Instruction for King Meri-ka-Re* (ca. 2150-2080 B.C., Egypt); *Akkadian Proverbs and Counsels* (ca. 1800-1600 B.C., Babylon).

(c. 31) could well be this early although their actual date cannot be known.[17]

In the second place, the relationship of the text to Ugaritic literature indicates that portions of the book must be old. Cullen I. K. Story showed that more than three hundred Ugaritic words occur in the book. This was over one-half of the Ugaritic vocabulary available to Story at the time of the study. In addition, the irregular meter, parallelism, and structure of Proverbs parallel Ugaritic grammar.[18] Thus, an irregular style in itself is not an adequate basis for attributing the Massoretic Text to the mixing of different poetical writings.

There is no basis, then, for concluding that the aphoristic style of writing developed late. Israel could well have used this style during the time of Solomon. Further, it is difficult to see how Solomon could have acquired his reputation for wisdom if there were not some basis in fact. To say that Solomon's name was retrospectively associated with the wisdom literature of the OT is arbitrary. This theory ignores the evidence.

It is reasonable to accept the biblical claim as accurate. With Solomonic authorship claimed three times (1:1; 10:1; 25:1), it is logical to place the date during his life (ca. 1000-930 B.C.). This is the historical position, and it is the position that fits best into the nature of the book. We recognize the existence of additional editing (25:1) and the addition of appendices (30:1-33; 31:1-31). These do not exclude the possibility of Solomonic authorship for the bulk of the book. In the absence of evidence, we accept the biblical claim for Solomon's authorship.

The Text of Proverbs

Where possible, I have chosen to follow the traditional Massoretic Text. In the discussion of the individual verses, I have summarized many of the suggested emendations. Most of these are highly subjective and therefore unnecessary. Where the MT makes sense, there is no need to adopt other readings.

---

[17] Kenneth A. Kitchen, "Proverbs and Wisdom Books of the Ancient Near East," *TB* 28:69-114. Kitchen examined the structure of books concerning the title/preamble, prologue, subtitles, the address to sons, type of text (unitary as opposed to sectioned), length of line units, and identification of authors. In each case, he identifies the periods of history in which the different types of sections occur.

[18] Cullen I. K. Story, "The Book of Proverbs and Northwest Semitic Literature," *JBL* 64:319-37.

There is often disagreement between the early translations into other languages. The Latin Vulgate, the Syriac, the Greek (LXX), and so forth, sometimes suggest a Hebrew that differs from the MT. There are reasons for this. Translation is not an exact science. A person's background and vocabulary, his theological views, and his translation philosophy affect his translation. For example, notice the difference in translations of the phrase *taʾawat ʾadam ḥasdô*, 19:22. William McKane translates this "A man's *productivity* is his loyalty."[19] The Anchor Bible translates, "It is human to desire gain" (p. 22). Gunther Plaut renders, "The lust of a man is his shame."[20] Many other translations exist as well. Each of these translations reflects the commentator's understanding of the phrase. The translations are not authoritative. They are, however, something to consider when trying to understand the phrase.

The ancient translations were no different. The translators struggled with the difficulty of capturing the thought of the Hebrew in different languages. Sometimes they succeeded; sometimes they failed. For this reason, the mere fact that a translation suggests a Hebrew text that differs from the MT does not mean that we should abandon the MT. The translation is simply a piece of evidence that we should consider. It is not conclusive in itself.

I have chosen to adopt the *kətîb,* the written word of the MT, where possible. When the *kətîb* was not sensible, I have adopted the *qərê,* the marginal suggestion of the Massoretic scribes. Their respect for the written text was such that they would not change it, even when they felt that it had been incorrectly passed down by earlier scribes. The *kətîb,* occasionally modified by the *qərê,* reflects the earliest text available to us. While I have considered suggestions to modify the text, in most cases I have rejected them as unnecessary.[21]

---

[19]William McKane, *Proverbs* (1970) (hereafter cited as McKane), p. 240.

[20]Gunther W. Plaut, *Book of Proverbs* (1961) (hereafter cited as Plaut), p. 205.

[21]I have used a simplified transliteration system to indicate most of the Hebrew vowels. The *a* indicates both the *qames* and the *pathah,* the *e* indicates both the *segol* and the *sere,* the *o* indicates both the *holem* and the *qames hatup,* and the *u* indicates the *qibbus.* I have indicated the *šawa* with the *ə.* I have used *î* to represent the *hireq yod,* *ê* to represent the *sere yod,* and *â* to represent the *qames he.* The *ô* indicates the *holem waw* and the *û* the *šureq.*

Structure and Use of the Book of Proverbs

There is widespread agreement on the overall structure of the Book of Proverbs, although disagreement exists on the details of this structure. R. B. Y. Scott, for example, arranges the book as follows:

Preamble 1:2-7
Introduction 1-9
Solomonic proverbs 10:1–22:16
Words of wise men 22:17–24:22; 24:23-34
More Solomonic proverbs 25-29
Four appendices 30-31

He further divides the introduction into ten discourses, all beginning with a call to attention, "my son." These begin at 1:8, 2:1, 3:1, 3:21, 4:1, 4:10, 4:20, 5:1, 6:20, and 7:1.[22]

Kitchen argues on the basis of parallel wisdom literature from other Semitic countries that the book follows this pattern:

Title/preamble 1:1-6
Prologue 1:7–9:18
Main text 10:1–24:34
Second collection 25-29
Two appendices 30, 31

---

[22]AB, pp. 14-15. R. N. Whybray, *The Book of Proverbs* in *The Cambridge Bible Commentary*, ed. P. R. Ackroyd, A. R. C. Leaney, and J. W. Packer (1972) (hereafter cited as Whybray), p. 12; and Plaut, p. 12, generally agree with this division excepting that both close the book with three appendices, combining all of chapter 30 into a single composition. Greenstone, pp. xii-xiv, agrees with Whybray and Plaut except that he divides the introduction into twelve discourses. He obtains this when he divides chapter 6 into three sections instead of one. Robert L. Alden, *Proverbs* (1983) (hereafter cited as Alden), pp. 9-10, likewise takes chapter 30 as a unit. In addition, he divides chapters 1-9 into eight divisions, following the prologue. Patrick W. Skehan, "The Seven Columns of Wisdom's House in Proverbs 1-9," *CBQ* 9:190-98, attempts to arrange chapters 1-9 into seven fairly symmetrical columns, with chapters 1, 8-9 as a framework for the "building." To accomplish this, he makes wholesale changes in the order of the text, e.g., moving 3:13-24 to the head of chapter 4; omitting 6:1-19 as an intrusion; moving 3:35 to follow 4:18, which is transposed after 4:19. In a later article, "Wisdom's House," *CBQ* 24:468-86, Skehan develops a structure for 22:17–31:31 by dividing it into fifteen columns of roughly twenty verses each. This arrangement calls for radical changes in the order of the text. Older commentators often arrange the book to differ from the above suggestions.

He maintains the unity of the main text and of the two closing appendices, comparing them with similar writings found among the wisdom writings.[23]

Within the broader sections of material, there is an apparent lack of unity in the teachings. In the first nine chapters, Solomon introduces the theme of wisdom and develops it to a limited degree. Elsewhere, however, most of the teaching consists of isolated proverbial sayings. Here and there, a few connected proverbs will center on the same topic: e.g., 16:20-23 (wisdom); 24:30-34 (slothfulness); 26:4-5 (folly). For the most part, however, the book consists of collections of randomly distributed proverbs. These touch on a variety of practical topics in an unorganized manner. No visible bond joins them to form a logical array of teaching.

This lack of unity is a surface phenomenon only. In reality, a spiritual unity pervades the book. The teachings of Proverbs find a common denominator in their application. The authors apply the test of "wisdom or folly" to actions in every sphere of life. Wise conduct will always reflect godly behavior, and godly behavior will always be wise. Conversely, foolish conduct will always reflect wicked behavior, and wicked behavior will always be foolish. The unity of the book lies in this principle. The proverbial sayings of the book integrate godliness with everyday life. They guide man as to how he should live.

To develop the teachings of the book, we must work within the apparent randomness of the proverbs. Many of the maxims deal with identical subjects. By grouping the individual proverbs by subject, we find order and structure in the book. This grouping of specific proverbs makes it possible to isolate the many subthemes in the book. When taken together, these themes provide a firm basis for the dominant teaching that wise conduct requires godly behavior.

Many of the themes in the book almost force themselves upon us. The repetition of thought in the individual proverbs highlights these themes. The extent of the repetition allows us some objectivity. This organization is essential to determine the thematic teachings of Proverbs.

The organized framework of a subject study reveals the full teaching of the book on a single subject. When we consider the individual

---

[23]*TB*, 28:70-71.

proverbs, they give us single ideas, restricted in scope. But when we systematically order the proverbs, they give a fuller teaching on the broad range of a subject. Aspects of a particular theme come into the open as we carefully organize the topical teaching. This fully developed teaching forcibly emphasizes the message of Proverbs.[24] The subject studies in this book sample the teaching given in Proverbs.

Necessarily, this organization must be individual, reflecting personal insight into the teaching. For this reason, the organization of this book is traditional. The discussion of the individual proverbs is sequential. Nevertheless, as individuals wrestle with the organization of a subject study, the following pages will help in reaching the final product. The diligence of the student as he explores the available information and develops the final form of the topic will bring rich blessings from God.

---

[24]Kidner has contributed some helpful work in this area by including a series of subject studies in his work, pp. 31-56. Plaut has included a topical guide in his commentary, a series of brief outline studies, pp. 21-25. Greenstone includes a listing of topics, pp. 341-54. Earle B. Cross, in a brief but excellent survey, discusses several practical topics in Proverbs, *The Abingdon Bible Commentary,* ed. F. C. Eiselen, E. Lewis, and D. C. Downey (1929), pp. 605-13. W. O. E. Oesterley, *The Book of Proverbs,* in *Westminster Commentaries,* ed. Walter Lock and D. C. Simpson (1929) (hereafter cited as Oesterley), pp. lvi-lxxxvii, briefly describes several more traditional theological topics, e.g., God, repentance. Kitchen develops the theology of the book in an excellent summary, including the topics of "God, Man, Wisdom," "Personal Conduct," and "Society," in *The Biblical Expositor,* ed. Carl F. H. Henry (1960), II, 460-72.

PROLOGUE TO THE SOLOMONIC PROVERBS

PROVERBS

1:1–9:18

1 The proverbs of Solomon the son of David, king of Israel;
2 To know wisdom and instruction; to perceive the words of
understanding;

PROVERBS 1

PROLOGUE 1:1-7

1 The opening verse introduces the collection of Solomon's proverbs
(1:1–24:34).[1] The first word (*mišlê*) gives us the Jewish title of the book.
Here translated "proverbs," it comes from the verb *mašal*, "to represent,
to be like." The word has a broad meaning. It does not simply refer to a
short, pithy saying such as our English word suggests. The brief sen-
tences in 10:1–29:27 approximate the proverb in our English sense.
There, short word-pictures give profound lessons from life. The use of
mašal in longer passages such as I Kings 9:7-9; Ezekiel 17:2-24; and
24:3-14 shows that it is more than a terse saying. In all of its contexts,
the *mašal* refers to instruction of some kind—an object lesson, an extended teaching, a parable, and so forth. The word occurs in this sense
here. It introduces the weighty lessons of the opening part of the book.

2 Following the title, a preamble (1:2-7) sets forth Solomon's goal. A
series of infinitives introduces the purpose—to convey wisdom to the
readers. The description shows the desirable nature of wisdom. To a certain extent, the major synonyms for "wisdom" occur in free variation in
the book. Nevertheless, they keep their distinctive shades of meaning.

In all of its forms, the major word for "wisdom" (*ḥokmâ*) occurs over
one hundred times. Logically, *ḥokmâ* is primarily an attribute of God.
This idea occurs briefly in 3:19. Other Scripture more clearly reveals
this (Job 12:13, 16; Isa. 31:2; Jer. 10:12). The lack of emphasis in
Proverbs on wisdom's relationship to God comes from the greater emphasis on practical day-by-day life. Nevertheless, wisdom is firstly a divine attribute.

---

[1]Alden, p. 19, and McKane, p. 262, both refer the title to the whole book of Proverbs.
Kitchen, *TB,* 28:69-114, however, shows that the form of the first collection (c. 1-24) is
like that of other wisdom literature. These have a title, prologue, and main text (with optional subtitles). Kitchen refers to fifteen other works from both Egypt and western Asia
that have this structure. These span three millennia B.C. For this reason, it is better to
limit the title to the first major section of Proverbs.

For this reason, one gets wisdom only as a gift from God (2:6-7). This accounts for equating godliness with wisdom (9:10; 15:33). Only one who accepts the ways of God can be truly wise. At the same time, one who is wise will turn from evil (14:16).

This touches an important principle of wisdom. In the Bible, there is only one kind of wisdom—that which comes from God. There is not a secular wisdom that man follows in his everyday life and a religious wisdom that man follows in his relationship with God. All wisdom that divorces itself from God is false wisdom. It therefore cannot adequately guide man.

This background shows the significance of wisdom. Above all else, wisdom lets a man deal properly with basic principles of life and eternity. Given the practical nature of Proverbs, it is natural that wisdom touches routine activities of life. By wisdom a man learns to work (6:6-11), chooses wise friends with whom to associate (13:20), displays personal humility (11:2), and gains a greater measure of wisdom (19:20). A strong emphasis relates wisdom and speech (10:13, 31; 12:18; 14:3; 15:2, 7; 16:23; 25:12; 31:26).

Wisdom likewise guides man in choices concerning eternal matters. "Righteous" men are wise in their daily lives (9:9; 10:31). They try to convince other individuals of their philosophy of life (11:30). At the end, wisdom gives them eternal life (8:35; 15:24).

The second word developing the idea of wisdom is "instruction" (*mûsar*). The AV sometimes translates this "correction," e.g., 7:22; 15:10. The noun *mûsar* has a broader meaning than this. Although the word occurs widely, it is primarily a word of the wisdom and prophetic literature. Almost 70 percent of the occurrences are in the wisdom literature. Sixty percent are in Proverbs. In these, the underlying thought of chastisement appears. This happens directly, as in 13:24, where chastening parallels "rod." The word *mûsar* refers to the chastisement of one who has broken some standard of conduct (15:10). The word can parallel the thought of reproof (5:12; 10:17; 13:18). In these cases, the sense of chastisement includes admonition or correction.

The word *mûsar* also refers to instruction. The word relates to teaching of a moral nature (4:13; 6:23; 15:33). It may also refer to neutral teaching (24:32). It may embrace all kinds of instruction (13:1). When used

*3 To receive the instruction of wisdom, justice, and judgment,
and equity;*

in this sense, the word has the idea of the mental discipline that goes
with the pursuit of wisdom. The root idea of chastisement still is the
major component in the word's meaning.

The next synonym for wisdom is "understanding," *bînâ.* This comes
from the verb *bîn,* "to understand" or "to discern." The verb describes
an ability to distinguish between opposites, the good from the evil
(I Kings 3:9), the right from the wrong (Isa. 32:4), and honor from dishonor (Job 14:21). It can refer to an understanding of facts or a situation
(Dan. 9:23; Hos. 14:9). The meaning of "understanding" or "insight"
expresses the sense.

3 A fourth word (*haśkel*) refers to "wisdom." More precisely, we
should phrase this "wise behavior." The word *śakal* occurs widely. It
often parallels other words that express various facets of wisdom. The
word *śakal* implies the mental process that leads to wise activity, to prudent and successful behavior.

Solomon expands briefly on this wise behavior. He states that it will
involve "justice [or 'righteousness,' *ṣedeq*], and judgment [or 'justice,'
mišpaṭ], and equity [*mêšarîm*]." In other words, wise behavior is moral.
Righteousness, justice, and uprightness mark it.[2] These words describe
our relationship to others in a moral sense. To Solomon, wise conduct
must be moral; a wise man is a good man. His behavior is characterized
by *ṣedeq, mišpaṭ,* and *mêšarîm.*

The word *ṣedeq* occurs widely. It is conforming to an ethical or moral
standard. This standard may involve the Word of God. It may also refer
to human relationships that rest upon the Word of God, i.e., love for
one's neighbor. Also occurring broadly is *mišpaṭ.* This often involves the

---

[2]F. Renfroe, "The Effect of Redaction on the Structure of Prov 1, 1-6," *ZAW* 101:290-
93, argues that the phrase is a "moralizing insertion." He arrives at the conclusion from
a "colometric analysis" of the passage. This involves counting the number of consonants
in each phrase. It is astounding that he should change the text on the basis that a line is
two consonants longer than nearby lines. This approach is arbitrary. It forces the passage
to fit into a given structure. It gives the author no literary freedom, an unwarranted assumption.

4 To give subtilty to the simple, to the young man knowledge and discretion.

process of justice, the administration of the legal system. The third word, *mêšarîm,* comes from *yašar,* "to be straight" (see 3:6). Metaphorically, it refers to ethical uprightness.

4 Still another characteristic of wisdom is "subtilty" (*ʿormâ*), or "prudence." The verb *ʿarom* has a sense of shrewdness (see Gen. 3:1). Here, that quality has a desirable sense that agrees with the regular use of the word in Proverbs. In other words, a prudent person shrewdly evaluates advice (15:5), circumstances (27:12), and experience (12:16). By letting these influence him, he gains the wisdom that produces a satisfying and successful life.

Even a "simple" child can acquire prudence. His character is not fixed. If he will receive guidance, he can grow away from his simpleness of mind, his naiveté, and will become noted for his prudence.

Solomon parallels two terms to develop *ʿormâ* further. The young man will gain "knowledge" (*daʿat*) and "discretion" (*məzimmâ*). The word *daʿat* is a characteristic word of the book. It occurs forty-one times, mostly in a general sense as here. When used of man, *daʿat* is knowledge gained by experience while *məzimmâ* refers to the thoughts of a person. These thoughts often develop into some sort of plan. The word itself is neutral, referring both to good and evil thoughts. In Proverbs, there is a clear relationship between wisdom and the good plans of a man (cf. 1:4; 2:11; 3:21; 5:2; 8:12). Wisdom thus influences a man by guiding his thoughts to please the Lord.

It is interesting to note that wisdom leads the "young man"[3] to gain knowledge and good thoughts, rather than knowledge and good thoughts leading him to wisdom. This thought supports the idea that the book presents only one kind of wisdom—that which comes from God. A man who has this valuable gift will grow intellectually and in his ability to develop wholesome plans.

---

[3] Among others, D. Winton Thomas, "Textual and Philological Notes on Some Passages in the Book of Proverbs," *VTS* III, 280, suggests *naʿar,* "young man," should be read as a plural. He cites the Targum and the Peshitta in support. Although this would bring about parallelism with the first clause, there is no need for the change. It does not materially improve the meaning of the verse.

5 A wise man will hear, and will increase learning; and a man of un-
derstanding shall attain unto wise counsels:
6 To understand a proverb, and the interpretation; the words of the
wise, and their dark sayings.
7 The fear of the Lord is the beginning of knowledge: but fools despise
wisdom and instruction.

5 The Hebrew marks a new paragraph by shifting away from the use
of the infinitive. The wise man will hear words of instruction. These increase his "learning" (*leqaḥ*) and "wise counsels" (*taḥbulôt*). The noun
leqaḥ comes from the verb *laqaḥ*, "to take, receive." The point of connection lies in the receiving of truth with the mind, thus "learning."

The term *taḥbulôt* occurs six times in the OT, all in the plural. Five of
these are in Proverbs (also at 11:14; 12:5; 20:18; 24:6). The word comes
from the verb *ḥabal*, "to bind, tie." The notion of pulling a rope, as in
the steering of a ship, gave rise to the idea of guiding, or directing. From
this, metaphorically, we get "counsel," or "guidance."

6 To conclude the list of synonyms, Solomon returns to the use of the infinitive in v. 6. This develops the thought of v. 5. The wise man increases
in knowledge with the result that he understands proverbial sayings
(*mašal,* cf. v. 1), "interpretation" (*məlîṣâ*), the words of wise men (*dibrê
ḥəkamîm*), and "dark sayings" (*ḥîdotam*). These terms refer to the form of
wise sayings, expressed in ways that require thought to understand.

The *mašal* has already been discussed with v. 1. The *melîṣâ* is a scornful saying, a taunt. It has the sense of satire. The word occurs again only
in Habakkuk 2:6, where it refers to a "taunt." The phrase *dibrê ḥəkamîm*
occurs again only at Proverbs 22:17 and Ecclesiastes 9:17 and 12:11. It
refers to the words of men who have a reputation for wisdom. Such men
capture the sense of an issue in capsule form. Their words are brief yet
profound. The final word, *ḥîdâ,* indicates an enigmatical saying, a riddle,
or a difficult question. By receiving wisdom, man gains the capacity to
understand such instruction.

7 Solomon has urged the pursuit of wisdom. Now he turns to the starting point, a wholesome fear of Yahweh (*yirʾat yəhwah*).[4] This is an important theological concept. The phrase "fear of the Lord" describes a

---

[4]Crawford H. Toy, *The Book of Proverbs*, in *The International Critical Commentary*,
ed. S. R. Driver, A. Plummer, and C. A. Briggs (1970) (hereafter cited as Toy), pp. 8, 10,

reverential attitude of submission to the Lord, not an intense feeling of terror. The "fear of God" might call forth dread as one thinks of standing before an omnipotent being of absolute holiness. But the "fear of the Lord" uses the covenant name of Yahweh. This is the one who shows Himself in mercy to mankind. This revelation calls forth a worshipful response from mankind.[5]

The "fear of the Lord" has both positive and negative characteristics in Proverbs. The father commands his son to walk in a way that shows his "fear of the Lord" (24:21). This is an upright way (14:2). This is the beginning of knowledge (1:7; 2:5) and wisdom (9:10; 15:33).

On the other hand, the "fear of the Lord" keeps one from evil (3:7; 16:6), including the emotion of envy (23:17). A man who truly fears the Lord will "hate evil." This includes pride, arrogance, an evil manner of life, and perverted speech (8:13). No man who rejects the "fear of the Lord" can find true wisdom (1:28-29).

This godly way of life brings good results to one who maintains his relationship to the Lord. He will be confident about the future (14:26). The "fear of the Lord" is a "fountain of life" to sustain and nourish the godly person (14:27). It rewards him with riches, honor, and a full life (22:4). He enjoys tranquility (15:16; 19:23). His life reaches the full measure of days that God intends for it (10:27).

---

suggests that vv. 5, 7 are insertions by an editor of the book. He feels that v. 5 breaks the metrical rhythm of vv. 2-6. He gives no evidence to support the suggestion for v. 7. The suggestion to delete v. 5 denies the author literary freedom. The broad range of metrical rhythm elsewhere shows that Solomon used variety. The suggestion regarding v. 7 ignores the entire context leading up to the verse. There is no direction to the passage without the comment of v. 7.

[5]The book uses five separate words to convey the emotion of fear. Three of them occur only once each. In each case the context calls for an emotion of dread or terror: *məgôrat*, 10:24; *ʾêmâ*, 20:2; *ḥaradâ*, 29:25. The fourth word, *paḥad*, indicates an attitude of dread when used in the *qal* (1:26, 27, 33; 3:24, 25). Only the *piʿel* occurs in a desirable sense. Even here, the sense of the word is still dread (of sin), 28:14. The word *yirʾat*, which occurs in the expression "fear of the Lord," does not require the intensive emotion of "fright or terror." In Proverbs, *yareʾ* occurs four times apart from the phrase "fear of the Lord" (3:25; 13:13; 14:16; 31:21). Twice it refers to a lack of dread (3:25; 31:21). The two remaining times both denote the reverential trust in God that causes a wise man to turn from evil (14:16) and follow God's commands (13:13). Elsewhere in the OT, the word ranges from reverential awe to dread. In connection with the "fear of the Lord," the sense of reverence more correctly conveys the meaning.

8 My son, hear the instruction of thy father, and forsake not the law of thy mother:

This, then, is the "beginning [*re²šît*] of knowledge." The word *re²šît* occurs some fifty times elsewhere, normally meaning "first" or "best." It is not merely a starting point, but rather a foundation to build upon.[6] By way of contrast, "fools despise wisdom and instruction." The "fool" (*²əwîlîm*) is a morally wicked individual who does not fear the Lord. The word *²əwîl* occurs over forty times in Proverbs. It regularly indicates a morally corrupt person who is therefore foolish. Fools therefore "despise" (*bazû*) wisdom. The word *bûz* has a sense of belittling. This is the attitude held by fools toward *ḥokmâ* and *mûsar,* precious possessions to the wise man.

WARNING AGAINST CRIMINALS 1:8-19

Appeal to the Son 1:8-9

8 The opening words challenge the son to accept the instruction of his parents. Solomon speaks to a "son," but the principle also holds true for a daughter. The book emphasizes the son since wisdom literature normally involves statements made to sons.[7] The authors of Proverbs do not mention the daughter except metaphorically (30:15) and in connection with the worthy woman (31:29). Nevertheless, the principles stated for sons also hold true for daughters.

The son should keep the "instruction" (*mûsar,* see 1:2) and the "law" (*tôrâ*) of his parents. In the book, *tôrâ* denotes moral guidance. It refers to the Mosaic law only at 28:4, 9 and 29:18. The word parallels parental commandments (3:1; 6:20; 7:2) and instruction (4:2). It gives spiritual light (6:23) and guidance day and night to one who follows it (6:20-22).

---

[6]Henri Blocher, "The Fear of the Lord As the 'Principle' of Wisdom," *TB* 28:14-15, argues that the word *re²šît* should be understood in the sense of "principle." He rightly rejects the meanings of "chief part" or "substance, essence," pointing out that the parallel word in 9:10, *tehillat,* can be understood only as "beginning." Then, having accepted "beginning" as the correct sense, he reinterprets this as "principle," holding that one can leave behind his first step. Kidner, p. 59, likewise interprets "beginning" as "the first and controlling principle." In opposition, most commentators accept "beginning" as the correct sense.

[7]This form of address occurs widely in wisdom literature, e.g., *The Instruction of the Vizier Ptah-hotep* (Egypt); *Counsels of Wisdom* (Babylon); *The Wisdom of Jesus, Son of Sirach* (Israel).

9 For they shall be an ornament of grace unto thy head, and chains about thy neck.

The one who observes his parents' teaching has discernment (28:7). The *tôrâ* is a source of life (7:2; 13:14). It produces understanding (4:2) and kindness (31:26). In summary, the *tôrâ* of the parents is moral instruction in its broadest sense. It has the potential to influence the children for good.

The "father" and "mother" occur here in poetic variation. Both have the same level of authority. The mother holds an equal responsibility with the father in teaching her child.[8] This figure of equality occurs elsewhere in the book. Solomon urges children to respect the authority of both parents (6:20; 19:26; 23:22), to bring joy to their parents (10:1; 15:20; 23:25), and to avoid disrespect to their parents (20:20; 30:17).

9 If the son will receive this teaching, it will be "an ornament of grace" to his head and "chains" for his neck. The "ornament of grace" (*liwyat ḥen,* or "graceful wreath") and "chains" (or "necklaces") represent the attractive qualities of wise parental instruction. A child who submits to it gains these qualities. This enriches the character of the child who accepts his parents' guidance.[9]

The use of ornaments as a reward occurs elsewhere. Proverbs 4:8-9 uses almost the same symbolism. There, it is the reward that is given to the person who acquires wisdom. The teaching of the parents is as an ornament. It gives to their son a moral attractiveness of great value.

---

[8]Some have taken the "father" and "mother" symbolically. The Talmud, for instance, saw these as representing God and Israel. The father's instruction became God's written and oral revelation to Moses. The mother's teaching was the interpretation of the rabbis and scribes given to the Mosaic law. Otto Zöckler, *The Proverbs of Solomon,* in *Commentary on the Holy Scriptures,* trans. Charles Aiken (n.d.) (hereafter cited as Zöckler), p. 46, likewise spiritualizes the passage. He states that the "father" represents a teacher of wisdom. The term shows the student the nature of the relationship between the teacher and the pupil. The mother varies this thought poetically and also stands for the wisdom teacher. The literal sense here, however, makes good sense. The terms "father" and "mother" occur in the book in such a way as to show that the family is in view. For these reasons, I take 1:8-9 literally. Solomon exhorts his son to accept the teaching of his parents.

[9]W. J. Deane and S. T. Taylor-Taswell, *Proverbs,* in *The Pulpit Commentary,* ed. H. D. M. Spence and Joseph S. Exell (n.d.) (hereafter cited as *PC*), p. 7, states that the child's obedience is the jewel that adorns his character. In reality, though, it is the instruction that is the decorating feature. Through his response, the child decides whether to add the ornament to his character.

10 My son, if sinners entice thee, consent thou not.
11 If they say, Come with us, let us lay wait for blood, let us lurk privily
for the innocent without cause:

Enticement from Sinners 1:10-14

10 Solomon warns the son against the enticements of "sinners" (*ḥaṭṭaʾîm*). The form of *ḥaṭṭaʾîm* denotes men whose actions are habitual. No matter how alluring the invitation may be, the young man should avoid it. The ungodly ways of the wicked are not the ways of wisdom.

The phrase "consent thou not" is a brief but pungent warning against giving in to these evil men. The brevity of the phrase emphasizes the thought. Since the Hebrew, Vulgate, and LXX support the phrase, there is no need to emend it.[10]

11 Verses 11-14 quote the arguments given the young man by his evil friends. They invite him to join them as they ambush the innocent. There is no cause for the attack other than their greed. They plan to murder the man for his possessions. Some understand verse 11 to embrace all the ills of society, and not just murder.[11] Since the literal sense agrees with other warnings (e.g., 6:17; 12:6; 28:17), it is best to take the passage as it stands.

---

[10]Toy, p. 14-15, suggests omitting *ʾal-tobeʾ* as a gloss and taking vv. 10-11*a* as a couplet. G. R. Driver, "Abbreviations in the Massoretic Text," *Textus* I (1960) (hereafter cited as *Textus* I), pp. 128-29, proposes that the phrase is an abbreviation of *ʾal-telek bəderek ʾittam* in v. 15*a*, wrongly inserted into v. 10. Translating vv. 10*a*-11 together restores the rhythmical balance. There is no reason to reject the MT.

[11]So B. Gemser, *Sprüche Salamos* (1937) (hereafter cited as Gemser), p. 15, and J. R. Coates, *The Book of Proverbs* (1911) (hereafter cited as Coates), p. 18. Two approaches have been taken toward countering the suggestion that the passage should be softened: (1) One view takes these descriptions as the divine view of the evil man. In actuality, the innocent youth receives a much more subtle form of temptation. But under the enticing exterior of the wicked is a corrupt nature. The description here arrests the attention of the child so that he will know the true nature of the temptation that he faces. Having understood, he will turn from it. So *PC*, p. 26, "He is putting the real meaning of the tempter's suggestions into vivid descriptions. The tempter himself will take care not to expose the bloody and hideous aspect of his trade. . . . The veil is torn aside from the life of crime, and its repulsive inhumanity disclosed." (2) The second view understands the passage literally. It warns the youth against using raw power in order to gain wealth and influence. This view takes the passage as warning against the idea that "the end justifies the means." So Kidner, p. 60, who calls the offer "a quick route to *ersatz* excitement and power (the youth pictures himself a person to be reckoned with, instead of patronized and kept in his place)."

*12 Let us swallow them up alive as the grave; and whole, as those that
go down into the pit:
13 We shall find all precious substance, we shall fill our houses with
spoil:
14 Cast in thy lot among us; let us all have one purse:
15 My son, walk not thou in the way with them; refrain thy foot from
their path:
16 For their feet run to evil, and make haste to shed blood.*

The "blood" represents the death of the innocent victim.[12] The evil
friends urge the youth to join them as they wait for their victim, a man
against whom they have no cause for attack. In the last phrase, "without
cause" modifies the verb "lurk."[13]

12-14 The evil friends boast that they will swallow their victims like
the "grave" (šəʾôl) and "pit" (bôr). Neither šəʾôl nor bôr have an eschatological sense here. Both refer to the grave, v. 12. Further, these wicked
men plan to take spoil from their victims, v. 13. To this end, they urge
the youth to join them and share in the common storehouse of ill-gotten
gains. The expression "cast in thy lot" describes a future action, "you
shall cast your lot," not an imperative. The enticement portrays the
potential of sharing the booty seized by the whole group, v. 14.

Warning of the Son 1:15-19

15 Solomon closes the section by warning his son against following
these evil companions. Both the words "way" and "path" are metaphorical. They indicate a way of life that shows moral character. This way of
the friends is evil. Solomon urges his son to avoid this way of life.

16 The first reason for the warning indicates that this way is immoral.
It involves evil actions and even murder.[14] There is debate over whether

---

[12]Toy, p. 15, and Edgar Jones, *Proverbs and Ecclesiastes* (1961) (hereafter cited as
Jones), p. 60, both emend ləḏam to ləṭam, "for the perfect," on the basis of the parallelism. The change is hard to justify. "Blood" occurs often to represent the death of a
person or animal, e.g., Gen. 9:6; Isa. 34:3; Ezek. 14:19.

[13]The most natural way to understand the phrase takes ḥinnam as modifying the verb
and understanding the verse as above. It is also grammatically possible to take it as
modifying the noun "innocent," so that he is "innocent in vain," i.e., the victim's innocence will not avail to protect him.

[14]Plaut, p. 36, refers the shedding of blood to the blood of the bandits, i.e., they bring
about their own destruction. More probably, however, this refers to their wicked actions,
murdering their victims.

17 Surely in vain the net is spread in the sight of any bird.
18 And they lay wait for their own blood; they lurk privily for their own
lives.

v. 16 should be retained.[15] Vaticanus and some other lesser manuscripts
delete the verse. Paul, however, quotes it in Romans 3:15. This stamps it
as part of the inspired text.

17 The wicked resolutely forge ahead with their evil deeds. They do
this, not realizing that they bring themselves into judgment. Verse 17 develops this by using the picture of a bird flying into a net. The bird sees
the trap. Nevertheless, the warning is "in vain." The temptation of the
grain that baits the trap blinds the bird to the danger. It ignorantly takes
the bait to its own destruction.[16]

18 In like manner, the evil man ignores the warning of certain destruction. He steadfastly continues his wicked actions. He does not realize
that these actions are the basis for his own destruction. There is no need
to emend the verse.[17] In a very real sense, the evil man "lies in wait for
his own blood; he ambushes himself."

---

[15]So Skehan, p. 195. On the basis that LXX[B] deletes the verse and that Isa. 59:7 has a
close parallel to this, Toy, p. 17, omits the verse. The verse, however, logically supports
the warning of v. 15. On the basis of Paul's quotation, its genuineness is unquestionable.

[16]It is possible that v. 17 is antithetic to v. 18. In this case, the meaning is that the bird
will escape if it sees the snare. Despite the warning of judgment to come, the wicked
have not the sense of a bird. They keep moving to their destruction. Joseph Muenscher,
The Book of Proverbs (1866) (hereafter cited as Muenscher); Delitzsch; Whybray; and
AB take the verse in this sense. G. R. Driver, "Problems in the Hebrew Text of
Proverbs" (hereafter cited as Driver), *Biblica* 32:173-74, derives məzorâ from a root mzr,
"to constrict." He then explains the verse as referring to the drawing tight of the net in
the sight of a bird. If the bird sees this, he will fly away. Nothing in the context, however, indicates that vv. 17-18 use antithetic poetry. A natural way of looking at the verses
takes v. 17 as giving an illustration from nature, a common genre in this book. This introduces v. 18. Among those who accept this view are Toy, Zöckler, Greenstone, Plaut,
and Duane A. Garrett, *Proverbs, Ecclesiastes, Song of Songs*, in *The New American
Commentary*, ed. E. Ray Clendenen (1993) (hereafter cited as Garrett). Thomas, *VTS* III,
281-82, derives the verb from zarâ, "to scatter." On the basis of an Arabic cognate, he
argues that the verse has the sense of scattering seed. The net is spread in the sight of
the bird, but he sees it in vain, being attracted by the seed to his capture.

[17]Felix Perles, "A Miscellany of Lexical and Textual Notes on the Bible," *JQR* 2:126,
emends lənapšotam to lənepeš tam, "the soul of the innocent." At the same time, he suggests that lədamam be read lədam, "for blood." He feels that it is not easy to determine
what the suffixes in these words refer to. It is natural, however, to refer the suffixes to
the evil men as they bring judgment upon themselves by their actions.

*19 So are the ways of every one that is greedy of gain; which taketh
away the life of the owners thereof.
20 Wisdom crieth without; she uttereth her voice in the streets:*

19 This is the way of those who let greed undermine their moral standards. The word "ways" (*ʾarḥôt*) occurs nineteen times in the book, most
often in a figurative sense. It refers to a way of life that may be either
righteous or unrighteous.[18] Here the greed of these men leads them
along a path that will end in their destruction.

REPROOF BY WISDOM 1:20-33

In the second discourse, personified Wisdom warns of the danger of
ignoring her invitation. In a carefully crafted poem she recalls the opportunities she has given the foolish to turn to her.[19] Because they have
rejected her, she will reject them. When calamity comes, they will be
shut up to their own devices, with no hope of Wisdom's help.

20 Solomon pictures "wisdom" (*ḥokmôt*) as making a ringing cry of
invitation to passersby. The plural *ḥokmôt* is unusual. It occurs elsewhere only at 9:1, possibly at 14:1 (if emended), and 24:7. It is an intensive plural. This emphasizes the idea of wisdom in its personified role.
She cries "without" or, more literally, "in the streets." She speaks "in the

---

[18]Michael V. Fox, "Aspects of the Religion of the Book of Proverbs," *HUCA* 39:60,
emends *ʾarḥôt* to *ʾaḥarît* on the basis of the LXX. Alden, p. 26, likewise accepts this
change. Fox suggests that the verse reflects the influence of the Egyptian concept of
Maat, world order. Evil receives judgment as a natural thing. The action itself determines this rather than a divine judgment. Since the word *ʾorah* occurs regularly in
Proverbs, and since its occurrence here fits the context, there is no need for the change.

[19]Phyllis Trible, "Wisdom Builds a Poem, The Architecture of Proverbs 1:20-33," *JBL*
80:509-18, masterfully analyzes the structure of the passage. She shows that it has the
form of a chiasm.

    A.   Introduction: an appeal for listeners (vv. 20-21)
       B.   Address to the untutored, scoffers, and fools (v. 22)
          C.   Declaration of disclosure (v. 23)
             D.   Reason for the announcement (vv. 24-25)
                E.   Announcement of derisive judgment (vv. 26-27)
             D'.   Result of the announcement, with interruption (vv. 28-30)
          C'.   Declaration of retribution (v. 31)
       B'.   Address about the untutored and fools (v. 32)
    A'.   Conclusion: an appeal for a hearer (v. 33)
On the basis of this structure, Trible concludes that suggestions deleting portions of
the poem in order to gain a desired rhythm are unnecessary. Any deletion destroys the
chiasm.

*21 She crieth in the chief place of concourse, in the openings of the
gates: in the city she uttereth her words, saying,
22 How long, ye simple ones, will ye love simplicity? and the scorners
delight in their scorning, and fools hate knowledge?*

streets," literally, "in the open places," not "squares" as often suggested.
In our day a "square" is normally a parklike area. In biblical times, the
"open places" were simply open areas within the city walls.

21 Wisdom calls out in "the chief place of concourse," *bəro'š homîyôt*.
In the "openings of the gates in the city she utters her sayings." The
phrase *bəro'š homîyôt* is literally "the head of the noise," i.e., the bustle
of the city. The word *homîyôt* is from *hamâ*, "to be noisy."[20] Since the
context deals with specific places—streets, open areas, gates—it is reasonable to think of a busy section of town where people meet to talk or
bargain.

The "openings of the gates" are the entrances into the city, the places
where legal transactions and commerce took place (e.g., Deut. 16:18;
Ruth 4:11; II Kings 7:1). These were natural places for gossip (Ps.
69:12) and public declarations (Jer. 17:19-20). Wisdom speaks to the
people at this gathering place.[21] There is no need to divide the verse
with a colon.

22 Wisdom addresses three classes: "the simple" ones (*pətayim*), the
"scorners" (*lesîm*), and the "fools" (*kəsîlîm*). With these questions,
Wisdom addresses the three classes of wicked men: the *petî*, an untaught
individual; the harder *kəsîl*, who has gone deeper into sin; and the hopeless *les*.[22]

---

[20]The LXX translates *homot*, "walls." On the basis of parallelism with the "openings of
the gates," Mitchell Dahood, *Proverbs and Northwest Semitic Philology* (1963) (hereafter cited as *PNWSP*), pp. 4-5, emends the text and translates, "from the top of the
walls." He suggests the biblical scribe confused the Ugaritic *hmyt* with *homîyâ*. McKane,
p. 273, likewise adopts this position. A. R. Hulst, *Old Testament Translation Problems*
(1960) (hereafter cited as Hulst), p. 114, supports the translation "where the busiest
(streets) begin," accepting the MT without emendation.

[21]Many delete the last phrase on the ground that the verse is too long. Toy, p. 30,
deletes *ba'îr 'əmareyha* as a gloss. Oesterley, p. 11, deletes it. Length is an unreliable
basis upon which to delete the phrase. It fits nicely into the description of Wisdom's appeal to mankind.

[22]Toy, pp. 20, 24, omits 22b on the grounds that scorners are not mentioned again in
v. 32, where the other terms occur. J. A. Emerton, "A Note on the Hebrew Text of
Proverbs i.22-3," *JTS* 19:612-14, says that the verse is too long. He treats 22b-c as a separate proverb and connects 22a with 23a. This also solves the problem of the shift in

23 Turn you at my reproof: behold, I will pour out my spirit unto you, I will make known my words unto you.

23 Wisdom invites these foolish individuals to "turn at [her] reproof." This exhorts them to repentance and restoration of godly ways.[23] If they respond, Wisdom promises to "pour out" her spirit to them, and to "make known" her words to them.

The word "reproof," *tôkahat,* occurs sixteen times in Proverbs. Obeying *tôkahat* brings blessing. By heeding it, one receives the spirit of wisdom (1:23; 29:15). Others will honor him (13:18). They will consider him prudent (15:5) and wise (15:31). His willingness to accept *tôkahat* will increase his spiritual understanding (15:32). In turn, this will guide him to gain a full earthly life (6:23).

On the other hand, the rejection of *tôkahat* brings punishment and undesirable qualities of life. For these reasons, it is "stupid" to hate reproof (12:1). This rejection causes others to err (10:17). Such a man will be "broken" beyond help (29:1), eventually coming to death (15:10).

In eight verses, *tôkahat* parallels *mûsar* (3:11; 5:12; 10:17; 12:1; 13:18; 15:5, 10, 32). The distinction lies in that *tôkahat* has a narrower focus of meaning. It relates directly to reproof or correction of the individual. The word *mûsar* (cf. 1:2) can include positive instruction as well as correction.

The second half of the promise, that Wisdom will "make known [her] words," controls the statement that Wisdom will "pour out [her] spirit."

---

persons, from the second person in 22*a* to the third person in 22*b, c.* Oesterley, p. 11, connects 22*a* with 23. Emendations based on rhythmic structure are risky. They assume that we know what the original structure was. In addition, the change in person may be merely a poetic device. Dahood, *PNWSP,* pp. 5-6, solves the problem by parsing *taʾehabû* as the 3mp form, comparing it with Ugaritic parallels; thus, no change in person occurs. In any case, the verse makes good sense as it stands. It is best to accept the MT without change.

[23]Driver, *Biblica* 32:174, relocates the *hinneh* to the beginning of the verse and translates the phrase as conditional, "If you return at my reproof." He justifies this on the basis of restoring balance to the clauses. Dahood, *PNWSP,* p. 6, points to a parallel Ugaritic construction. He justifies his contention that 23*a* is a conditional clause without an introductory participle. McKane, p. 274, mentions that the imperfect can introduce a conditional clause without a conditional participle. *Gesenius' Hebrew Grammar,* ed. E. Kautzsch (1970) (hereafter cited as G.K.), 159b, d, accepts the passage this way. In any event, there is no need to change the MT. Taking the clause conditionally does not change the meaning.

24 Because I have called, and ye refused; I have stretched out my hand, and no man regarded;
25 But ye have set at nought all my counsel, and would none of my reproof:
26 I also will laugh at your calamity; I will mock when your fear cometh;
27 When your fear cometh as desolation, and your destruction cometh as a whirlwind; when distress and anguish cometh upon you.

The spirit is one of understanding. This helps the person understand truth. The verb "pour" (*naba*ᶜ) carries with it the sense of gushing forth. It is like the uncontrollable waters of a flooded river. It implies that the spirit comes without measure.[24] With this, man now understands the words of Wisdom, her teachings, or doctrines. While man may have, heard these before, it is only after he receives her spirit that he can understand them; cf. I Corinthians 2:14.

24-25 To this point, Wisdom has appealed to her audience. Now she turns to the theme for the rest of the passage, the rejection of her appeal. The call has been refused, the invitation ignored.[25] The counsel has been neglected and no one accepts Wisdom's reproof. Clearly, the sin-cursed hearts of men have been hardened against the appeal of Wisdom.

26-27 For this reason, Wisdom herself will laugh "at," or better, "in the time of," the "calamity," *ʾêd,* that falls on those who reject her. She will mock when their "fear" (*paḥad*) arises. The word *ʾêd* occurs twenty-two times, normally in poetical contexts. It denotes "calamity, destruction, distress," all of a serious nature. It may refer to a national calamity or to the final day of judgment. The word *paḥad* has a strong emotional component of terror. It is not just an intellectual awareness of calamity (cf. 1:27, 33; 3:24-25). The *gam-ʾănî* construction, "I also," lends emphasis to the statement. In the time of trouble, Wisdom will reject those who rejected her in better times.

Verse 27 expands v. 26 with *ʾêd* and *paḥad* occurring in reverse order. The terror will come as "desolation" (*kăšoʾawh,* better read with the

---

[24]Coates, p. 19, wrongly identifies Wisdom's spirit with her anger. The parallelism argues that her "spirit" is spiritual understanding.
[25]Greenstone, p. 13, calls attention to the fact that the culprit had to be given warning before his action. Otherwise, under the Jewish view of the law, there could be no punishment (cf. *Sanh,* 8b).

28 Then shall they call upon me, but I will not answer; they shall seek me early, but they shall not find me:
29 For that they hated knowledge, and did not choose the fear of the Lord:
30 They would none of my counsel: they despised all my reproof.

qərê, kašô'â),[26] and the "destruction" (or "calamity," 'ed, same word as in v. 26) will come as a whirlwind (sûpâ). Elsewhere, sûpâ represents God's judgment, e.g., Isaiah 17:13; 66:15; Hosea 8:7. "Distress" and "anguish," synonyms referring to strong emotional turmoil, will likewise overwhelm them.[27]

28-30 In the time of distress, these men will call in vain upon Wisdom. They will "seek (her) early," i.e., diligently, but will not find her. With the three verbs, *call . . . seek . . . find* (qara', šahar, maṣa'), an unusual pronominal ending emphasizes the actions of the men (cf. G.K. 60e). They call fervently, they seek earnestly, but they completely miss Wisdom, v. 28.

The reason for this failure lies in their former attitude toward wisdom.[28] They hated "knowledge" (da'at, cf. 1:4) and did not choose the "fear of the Lord" (yir'at yəhwah, cf. 1:7). The verb "choose" (bahar) indicates a carefully reasoned decision. It normally refers to theological matters. These can include the Lord's choosing of people and places or man's choice of godly things, v. 29.

In addition, they would not accept the "counsel" ('eṣâ) of Wisdom, and they rejected her "reproof" (tôkahat, cf. 1:23). The word 'eṣâ involves advice that guides someone in his actions or conduct. The word assumes that future actions will conform to the advice, and so the thoughts of "work" and "counsel" parallel one another in Scripture (cf. Ps. 106:13; Isa. 5:19; 29:15). Occasionally, the biblical authors will identify the ac-

---

[26]Virtually all commentators agree that the qərê is correct. The qərê readily explains the kətîb. Most translate "storm" (so Zöckler, Delitzsch) from the parallelism with "whirlwind" in 27b. The word, however, can be understood as "to crash," metaphorically, "to ruin."

[27]Toy, p. 25, takes 27c as a scribal addition. Manuscript evidence, however, favors its retention. Verse 27a-b chiastically expands v. 26, while 27c provides the capstone to a climactic construction in the two verses.

[28]Zöckler, p. 48, wrongly separates v. 28 from vv. 29-30. He makes these last elements antecedent to the conclusion in v. 31. Whybray, p. 20, suggests that v. 29 is an addition to the text since it alone mentions the working of God in the passage. As the analysis by Trible shows, *JBL* 80:512, however, vv. 28-30 form a unit.

*31 Therefore shall they eat of the fruit of their own way, and be filled
with their own devices.
32 For the turning away of the simple shall slay them, and the prosperity of fools shall destroy them.
33 But whoso hearkeneth unto me shall dwell safely, and shall be quiet
from fear of evil.*

tions of man with his *ʿeṣâ* (Ps. 81:12; Jer. 7:24). The word *ʿeṣâ* is neutral. The context alone decides whether the counsel is good (1:30) or
evil (21:30). There is an expressed connection between wisdom and
good counsel in Proverbs (e.g., 12:15; 19:20), v. 30.

31 Continuing the chiasmic structure, v. 31 parallels v. 23. The earlier
passage introduced the idea of judgment; v. 31 declares the results of the
judgment. These evil men will "eat of the fruit of their own way, and be
filled with their own devices [*ʿeṣâ*, or counsel]." The passage teaches the
principle of retributive punishment seen elsewhere, e.g., Job 4:8; Proverbs 12:14; 22:8; Isaiah 3:10; Hosea 8:7; Romans 2:6-10; II Corinthians
9:6; Galatians 6:7-8.

32 This "turning away" (*mašûbâ*) of the "simple" will bring about their
death. The verb *šûb* indicates a "turning back, faithlessness." If continued in, as here, it will cause self-destruction.[29] Moreover, the "prosperity" (*šalwâ*) of these fools will destroy them. The word *šalwâ* here has
the sense of "ease, carelessness, complacency."[30] Filled with the carelessness of self-confidence, these fools show no concern over divine
judgment. Yet it will certainly "destroy them" (*ʾabad*). While it is not
possible to be dogmatic here, the word *ʾabad* may refer to spiritual destruction (cf. 10:28; 11:7).

33 In contrast, one who receives wisdom will have blessing in his life.
He will "dwell safely." The word *baṭaḥ* occurs four times in the book,
also at 3:23, 29; 10:9. It is an attitude of confidence with regard to one's

---

[29]Robert Gordis, "A Note on Yad," *JBL* 52, p. 160, concludes that *šub* here means
"self-assurance." He bases this conclusion on the parallelism with *šalwâ* in 32*b*. Dahood,
PNWSP, pp. 6-7, derives *šûb* from *yašab*, "to sit," and understands the word in the sense
of "idleness." The Hebrew form, however, occurs often elsewhere, e.g., Jer. 3:6ff, Hos.
14:4. We should understand it in its normal meaning. This agrees with the sense of the
passage.
[30]The verb may mean "to prosper" (Ps. 122:6), but its more normal sense is that of
being "quiet, at ease." The Aramaic cognate *šaleh* means "to be at ease, carefree." With
this sense, the verse has better parallelism of meaning.

situation in life. This confidence flows directly from the possession of wisdom (3:21-25). In addition to this self-confidence, one who possesses wisdom will be "quiet," "at ease," or "secure," from the dread of evil ($ra^c\hat{a}$). The root ra^c may involve all kinds of bad or evil—physical, emotional, or spiritual. It has a wide range of semantic meanings. The context determines the best shade of meaning. Here, the wise man escapes this evil. Truly, the gifts of wisdom have value that far exceeds the wealth of this world!

Practical Applications from Proverbs 1

Three Kinds of Fools

1. The Simple Person (*petî,* one who is simple, or naive, not a moral fool. The word occurs only in Psalms and Proverbs.)

   a. He has potential for developing wisdom or foolishness. He is gullible, tending to believe what he hears (14:15). This may lead him into temptation (7:7-23; 9:16). He may even grow into greater foolishness (14:18). If he ignores the evil in his life, he will receive punishment (1:32; 22:3; 27:12).

   b. He is exhorted to discern prudence (8:5) and to receive wisdom (9:4). God's Word, when received, can deliver the *petî* from simplicity (1:4). He may profit from observing the judgment of other evil men (19:25; 21:11). When he forsakes his evil way, he will have life (9:4-6).

2. The Immoral Person (*kəsîl,* most often describes the fool; occurs over fifty times in Proverbs)

   a. His chief problem is spiritual. He lacks spiritual understanding (18:2). He delights himself with evil (10:23; 13:19). The Lord invites him to repent (8:5).

   b. He is marked by evil speech (10:18; 15:2; 18:6-7; 19:1; 23:9). He grieves his parents (10:1; 17:21, 25; 19:13). He lacks self-control (29:11) and repeats his folly (26:11). Because of his self-sufficiency (28:26), he lacks wisdom (17:24). He does not gain wisdom (17:16) since he will not accept rebuke (17:10). He is deceitful (14:8), arrogant and careless (14:16), and boisterous (9:13). He is wasteful (21:20). Through his conduct, he brings himself into personal harm (10:14; 19:29; 26:3).

3. The Scornful Person (*leṣ,* one who is hardened against God)

   a. Although personified Wisdom urges the scorner to accept reproof (1:22), he will not receive it (13:1). He hates one who tries to correct him (9:7-8; 15:12). For this reason, he seeks in vain for wisdom (14:6).

   b. He causes contention, strife, and dishonor (22:10). He is an abomination to others (24:9). He is proud (21:24). He inflames a city with his wickedness (29:8).

   c. He will come under God's judgment (3:34; 19:29).

There is hope for the simple fool. There is hope for the moral fool. If they do not repent, they will become scorners, hardened against God. How much better it is to receive the Wisdom of God, Jesus Christ (Col. 2:3).

1 My son, if thou wilt receive my words, and hide my commandments with thee;

PROVERBS 2
REWARDS OF WISDOM

There is little agreement on how to analyze this third discourse of the book.[1] Some suggest that much of the discourse is an addition to the original writing.[2] Despite these disagreements, the passage develops familiar and practical themes and is well worth studying. Grammatically, the passage is a single sentence. Verses 1-4 present an initial condition. A double conclusion follows, in v. 5 and in v. 9. Verses 6-8 clarify v. 5. Verses 10-22 amplify v. 9.

1 We return here to the traditional format in which the father speaks to his son. It is very natural to regard the father here as Solomon, the principal author of the book. He sets an initial condition: "if thou wilt receive . . . and hide. . . ." The father exhorts his son to receive his "words" and his "commandments." Both of these terms refer to the father's instruction, not to the Word of God. It is clear, however, that the father's instruction parallels the spiritual principles of the Bible. The promised rewards in vv. 5 and 9 indicate this.

The verb "hide" (ṣapan) has the sense of storing up something because of its value, e.g., Psalm 17:14; Obadiah 6. While ṣapan may be translated "hide," it is more than merely storing something out of sight. It is "treasuring" something, implying the worth of the father's instructions.

---

[1]For example, Gemser divides the chapter into six paragraphs: vv. 1-4, 5-8, 9-11, 12-15, 16-19, 20-22. Jones divides the chapter into four sections: vv. 1-5, 6-15, 16-19, 20-22. *PC* finds three sections in the chapter: vv. 1-9, 10-19, 20-22. Michael V. Fox, "Aspects of the Religion of the Book of Proverbs," *JBL* 113:233-43, divides it into three sections (vv. 1-11, 12-19, 20-22). Oesterley divides it into vv. 1-11 and 12-22. He further subdivides these into vv. 1-4, 5-8, 9-11, 12-15, 16-19, and 20-22. Since the passage is but one sentence, any attempt to divide it is subjective.

[2]Whybray, p. 22, states that the original stratum included only vv. 1, 9, 16-19. All else has been added as an amplification of the initial portion. He justifies this conclusion on the basis of repetitions and what he feels are natural transitions. Toy, p. 34, calls vv. 5-8 an "editorial insertion." Since no manuscript evidence supports these views, it is best to accept the MT as it stands.

2 So that thou incline thine ear unto wisdom, and apply thine heart to understanding;
3 Yea, if thou criest after knowledge, and liftest up thy voice for understanding;
4 If thou seekest her as silver, and searchest for her as for hid treasures;

2 The verse begins the development of v. 1. The youth should act vigorously to treasure up his father's instructions. How is this to be done? Verses 2-4 answer the question. The son should "incline" (*qašab*) his ear. The verb *qašab* means "to be attentive," denoting the giving of careful attention, obedience. This shows the son's need to listen closely to his father's instructions. Further, he should "apply" (*naṭâ*) his heart to understanding (cf. *bîn*, 1:2). The verb *naṭâ* occurs widely with a great variety of meanings. It often has a figurative sense in which it refers to changing of the heart. Clearly, the hearing of the son should influence his behavior as he practices the principles given by Solomon.

3 As an additional indication of the son's avid pursuit of his father's teaching, he is to cry (*qara'*) after knowledge ("discernment," *bîn*, cf. 1:2) and to lift up (*natan*) his voice for understanding (cf. *bîn*, 1:2). Practically speaking, there is little difference between "knowledge," *bînâ*, and "understanding," *təbûnâ*. About the best we can do is to relate the verb *bînâ* to discernment and the noun *təbûnâ* to understanding. The combination of the two emphasizes the need for wisdom. The verb *qara'* means "to call" while *natan* is "to give," in this context, "to devote, use." The picture is one of urgency, as the son diligently seeks for discernment and understanding.[3]

4 Picturesquely, Solomon portrays the youth as a treasure hunter, prospecting for wisdom. He should "seek" (*baqaš)* for silver. The word *baqaš* means "to seek," with a connotation of earnestness in the search. It stresses physical action more than mental questioning. He should search (*ḥapaš*) as for "hid treasure" (*ṭaman*). The word *ḥapas* occurs only four times in the *qal* theme. It is always a search conducted with diligence. The word *ṭaman* indicates something with great value. The son should exert diligence in order to gain this valuable prize.

---

[3]*The Targum of Proverbs*, trans. John F. Healey (1991) (hereafter cited as *Targum*), p. 15, vocalizes *'im* as *'em*, "mother," so that the translation would be, "If you call understanding mother." The context of vv. 1-4 rules this out.

5 Then shalt thou understand the fear of the Lord, and find the knowledge of God.
6 For the Lord giveth wisdom: out of his mouth cometh knowledge and understanding.
7 He layeth up sound wisdom for the righteous: he is a buckler to them that walk uprightly.

5 The first conclusion establishes the potential for apprehending the "fear of the Lord" (*yirʾat yəhwah,* cf. 1:7) and the "knowledge of God." The word "knowledge" (*daʿat,* cf. 1:4) refers to an experiential knowledge, acquired through developing a relationship with the Lord. As the youth walks in the ways of the Lord, he will find ample opportunity for proving God's faithfulness and seeing His power. This will indeed lead to the "knowledge" of God.[4]

6 The verse begins a parenthetical expansion of v. 5. Verses 6-8 explain the basis upon which the confident expectation of v. 5 rests. The youth will come into a deeper knowledge of the Lord because He gives this wisdom to man. He bestows "wisdom," *ḥokmâ,* cf. 1:2; "knowledge," *daʿat,* cf. 1:4; and "understanding," cf. *bîn,* 1:2. The term "mouth" is anthropomorphic, representing God's communication to man.

7 In addition, the Lord lays up (*ṣapan,* cf. v. 1) "sound wisdom" (*tûšîyâ*) for the righteous person.[5] The word *tûšîyâ* occurs just four times

---

[4]The word *ʾelohîm* occurs in the Book of Proverbs only here and at 2:17; 3:4; 25:2; 30:9. The related word *ʾelôah* occurs in 30:5. *PC,* p. 35, gives the curious view that Jehovah here refers to the "Personality of the Divine nature" while Elohim refers to "Christ's glory." Toy, p. 35, considers the use of the two names mere poetical variation. Zöckler, p. 54, on the other hand, expressly states that this is not poetical variation. In view of the fact that the name Jehovah occurs almost one hundred times, it would seem that Solomon uses Elohim these few times in a more precise sense than mere rhetorical variation would account for. The word Jehovah stresses the divine personality of the Lord, while the name Elohim brings out His divine majesty and power. In each use in Proverbs, the sense of God's majesty is appropriate.

[5]Some propose a *qərê* reading, *yiṣpon,* the *qal* imperfect, apparently feeling that the passage requires a verbal idea here. Commentators divide over the reading. Georg Beer, in the critical apparatus to Proverbs in Biblia Hebraica, ed. Rudolf Kittel, A. Alt, and O. Eissfeldt (1973) (hereafter cited as BH), proposed *waṣanip.* We can discard this as unnecessary and unsupported. Others generally follow earlier readings, the LXX and Syriac accepting the *kətîb* reading, while the *Targum* and Vulgate follow the *qərê.* KD I, 77; Zöckler, p. 54; and Thomas J. Conant, *The Book of Proverbs* (1872) (hereafter cited as Conant), p. 13; agree with the *kətîb.* Muenscher, p. 19; *PC,* p. 36; and Toy, p. 38, accept the *qərê.* The *kətîb* reading *wiṣpon* is the infinitive construct of *ṣapan.* The infinitive

8 He keepeth the paths of judgment, and preserveth the way of his saints.

in the Book of Proverbs, here and 3:21; 8:14; 18:1. Elsewhere, it parallels *ᶜezrâ,* "help" (Job 6:13), as well as *magen,* "buckler" here. In Job 5:12 the word indicates "success." Thus, there is an underlying sense of security or success in the word. The idea of "sound wisdom" or "competence" adequately conveys the significance of *tûšîyâ* here.[6]

Moreover, the Lord is a "buckler" (*magen*) to the righteous (*tom*). The word *tom,* "to be complete," here has the sense of moral uprightness or integrity, "blameless." The word *magen* describes the protection that the Lord provides. The word *magen* refers to the small round shield carried by soldiers. Elsewhere, it can refer metaphorically to God as the "shield" of His people. He acts as a shield, guarding the upright one as he walks through life.

8 To further clarify the conclusion of v. 5, Solomon notes the keeping power of God. He "keepeth" (*naṣar*) the paths of "judgment" (or "justice") as He watches over His own. The verb *naṣar* has the sense of "guarding, watching over."[7] By parallelism, the "paths of justice" best represent those paths in which God's people walk, i.e., the "paths of the just ones." This best corresponds with the "way of his saints" in 8*b*.[8]

---

[6]The word has given rise to diverse interpretations. Toy, p. 36, draws the idea of "deliverance" out of the context. KD I, 77, locates it as a *hipᶜîl* form of *yašâ,* "to stand." Delitzsch takes this in the sense of that which furthers and profits, and translates it "promotion." Muencher, pp. 18-19, takes it in the sense of "safety, help." Cyrus Gordon, "Rabbinic Exegesis in the Vulgate of Proverbs" (hereafter cited as Gordon), *JBL* 49:405-6, relates the rabbinical interpretation that equated *tûšîyâ* to the Torah. This takes the word as relating to deliverance or help. Most, however, agree that the word should be glossed in some sense relating to wisdom. *Theological Wordbook of the Old Testament,* I, ed. R. Laird Harris (1980) (hereafter cited as *TWOT*), 413, calls it "sound efficient wisdom, i.e., sound judgment, wisdom that leads to practical success."

form draws support from manuscript evidence and, in translation, fits well into the context, continuing the previous verse. Since the *kǝtîb* makes sense in this setting, and since the *qǝrê* involves an unnecessary change in the consonantal text, it is best to follow the MT.

[7]Dahood, *PNWSP,* p. 8, suggests that *linṣor* is an emphatic *lamed* with the imperfect verb. He translates, "truly guards." He supports this from north Semitic cognates. The form, however, follows standard Hebrew usage and does not need to be interpreted from a cognate language. G.K. 114i (note) rejects the view that the emphatic *lamed* is coupled with the verb.

[8]Muenscher, p. 19, suggests that the subject of v. 8 may be either God or the upright ones of v. 7. While this view is possible grammatically, it is more natural to consider the verse as following the pattern of vv. 6-7, all clarifying the apodosis of v. 5.

*9 Then shalt thou understand righteousness, and judgment, and equity;
yea, every good path.*

The Lord "preserveth" (*šamar*) the way of His "saints" (*ḥasîdaw*). The
verb *šamar* occurs widely with the sense "to guard, give attention." It
has the sense of doing something "carefully" or "diligently." Thus the
Lord faithfully watches over His "saints" (*ḥasîdîm*). The word is from
ḥesed, which occurs widely. It may indicate the reciprocal conduct of
men who stand in some relationship toward one another (Job 6:14; Prov.
19:22). It may denote the responsibility of a man in view of his relationship to God (Jer. 2:2; Hos. 6:6). It may also describe the relationship in
which God stands to His people in view of His nature (Gen. 24:27; Ps.
62:12) and His covenant with them (Deut. 7:9; II Sam. 7:14-15). In
Proverbs, *ḥesed* generally refers to the social relationship of one man
with another. Often the idea of "loyalty" expresses the meaning of *ḥesed.*
This agrees well with the nature of the book as setting forth practical
principles for living. Here, it describes one who is loyal to God.

9 The second conclusion parallels the first. Once again, it emphasizes
the potential for "understanding" (*bîn,* cf. 1:2), this time referring to ethical and moral matters. Receiving the father's words (vv. 1-4) will allow
the youth to understand "righteousness" (*ṣedeq,* cf. 1:3), "judgment" (or
"justice," *mišpaṭ,* cf. 1:3), "equity" (*mešarîm,* cf. 1:3),[9] and "every good
path" (*maʿgal*). The word *maʿgal* occurs thirteen times in the OT. It is
neutral, being connected both with good (e.g., Ps. 23:3; Prov. 2:9) and
evil modifiers (e.g., Ps. 140:5; Prov. 2:15, 18). In every case, however,
the word denotes a path of life, a metaphorical use, rather than a literal
path along which one would walk. Here, the word is metaphorical, referring to one's godly course of life.

---

[9]Driver, *Biblica* 32:174, concludes that *mešarîm* "makes no sense in the present passage" and presumably owes its occurrence to 1:3, where these same three nouns occur.
He emends the word to *ûmšammer* and translates, "(and thou art) regarding every good
path." Toy, pp. 39, 50, likewise feels that the context requires a verb. He emends *mešarîm*
to *tišmor,* "thou shalt keep (every path of good)." Oesterley, p. 16, and Whybray, p. 21,
adopt similar changes. The passage, however, does not require a verb at this point. KD I,
79, recognizes *mešarîm* as a summarizing term, the final object of *tabîn.* Greenstone,
p. 19, notes that the combination of nouns appears to be a "set formula." See, for example, Ps. 99:4; Prov. 1:3. Any emendation would destroy the pattern. Either of these last
approaches gives a reasonable understanding of the MT.

10 When wisdom entereth into thine heart, and knowledge is pleasant unto thy soul;
11 Discretion shall preserve thee, understanding shall keep thee:
12 To deliver thee from the way of the evil man, from the man that speaketh froward things;
13 Who leave the paths of uprightness, to walk in the ways of darkness;
14 Who rejoice to do evil, and delight in the frowardness of the wicked;
15 Whose ways are crooked, and they froward in their paths:

10-11 The rest of the chapter expands on the thought just stated. The initial "when," *kî*, is causal, "for" or "because." It introduces a list of significant aspects of the conclusion stated in v. 9.[10] Wisdom (*ḥokmâ*, cf. 1:2) enters into the heart, and "knowledge" (*daʿat*, cf. 1:4) becomes pleasant to the soul. Both of these phrases picture the individual's willing reception of spiritual truth, v. 10.

In addition, "discretion" (*məzimmâ*, cf. 1:4)[11] will "preserve" (*šamar*, cf. v. 8) the godly youth, and "understanding" (*bîn*, cf. 1:2) will "keep" (*naṣar*, cf. v. 8) him. Verses 12-15 and vv. 16-19 develop the threat to the young man. Evil men and women will seek to turn him aside from the godly instruction of his father. Discretion and understanding, however, will protect him, v. 11.

12-15 The first enemy of the young man is the companion who is "evil" (*raʿ*, cf. 1:33), a word often used as a moral contrast with "good." The word *raʿ* routinely indicates something bad. It includes both physical injury and moral evil. Words, thoughts, and actions are all described as *raʿ*. The evil man here is one who speaks "froward things" (*tahpukôt*). This word occurs only ten times in the OT, nine of them in Proverbs.[12] It normally denotes wicked speech, although sometimes it merely refers to general wickedness, v. 12.

These men "leave" (*ʿazab*) the paths of "uprightness" (*yošer*, cf. *mešarîm*, 1:3). The verb *ʿazab* has the sense here of "forsake, abandon,"

[10]Zöckler, p. 55; Muenscher, p. 20; and Greenstone, p. 20, suggest that the *kî* introduces a condition before the conclusion of v. 11. This view, however, breaks the organic connection between vv. 12-22 and the earlier part of the chapter.
[11]Plaut, p. 47, notes that the Talmud vocalizes *məzimmâ* as *mizzimo*, "from lewdness it (the Torah) will guard thee." The MT, however, has better parallelism with 11*b* as it stands. The manuscript evidence does not support the suggested change.
[12]Here and 2:14; 6:14; 8:13; 10:31, 32; 16:28, 30; 23:33. The word occurs also in Deut. 32:20.

16 To deliver thee from the strange woman, even from the stranger
   which flattereth with her words;
17 Which forsaketh the guide of her youth, and forgetteth the covenant
   of her God.
18 For her house inclineth unto death, and her paths unto the dead.
19 None that go unto her return again, neither take they hold of the
   paths of life.

as in apostasy. Elsewhere in Proverbs it occurs in passages that speak of the wicked who depart from godly things or qualities, e.g., reproof (10:17; 15:10), the law (4:2; 28:4), and wisdom (4:6). Here, they reject the good in order to embrace the evil. They walk in the ways of "darkness" (*ḥošek*). The word *ḥošek* often refers to literal darkness. When this has a metaphorical sense, it vividly pictures the blackness of evil, e.g., ignorance (Job 37:19; Isa. 9:2), wickedness (Isa. 5:20), or blindness (Job 12:25; Isa. 29:18). It also represents judgment (e.g., Isa. 59:9; Joel 2:2), v. 13.

In addition, these wicked men take pleasure in sinful things. They rejoice in doing "evil" (*ra^c*, cf. 1:33). Further, they delight in perversity (*tahpukôt,* cf. v. 12) of evil (*ra^c*), v. 14.

Finally, the ways of these men are "crooked" (*^ciqqašîm*), a descriptive word aptly picturing the perverted way of sin. Throughout the OT, *^caqaš* describes the twisted actions of the sinful (e.g., Deut. 32:5; Prov. 10:9; 28:6). Furthermore, these men are "froward" (*nəlôzîm*) in their actions. The root *lûz,* "to turn aside," here has the sense of deviousness. This leads to the translation "they are devious in their ways." These are the men from whom the youth receives deliverance as he follows his father's words of instruction, v. 15.

16-19 A second enemy from which the youth must gain deliverance is the "strange woman" (*^ʾiššâ zarâ*). The phrase *^ʾiššâ zarâ* parallels the idea of flattery, a concept that helps to define the meaning of the expression. The woman is not "strange" because she comes from a foreign background and has brought her heathen practices to Israel. Rather, she is "strange" because her seductive words tempt foolish men to follow ways that go contrary to the ways of God.

It is clear that Israel adopted the lower moral standards of the heathen. The word *zar* refers to someone outside a normal group. The term *zarâ* thus appropriately describes any adulterous woman who has abandoned the godly ways of wisdom. She occupies a position that is outside the normal circle of married women in Israel.[13] In referring to her as "strange" Solomon uses the word as an epithet. He refers to one who practices the standards of the heathen. She abandons the pattern set by godly women in Israel, embracing rather the ways of heathen worship.[14]

The adulteress is also described as a "stranger" (nakrîyâ), a synonym of zarâ. In the Book of Proverbs nakrîyâ generally refers to an adulteress.[15] It describes one who lives like a heathen even though she dwells among the people of God. This receives emphasis here by the further description that she has left the "covenant of her God" (2:17), the vow-staken before God at the marriage ceremony.

The appeal of this evil woman lies with her speech. She "flattereth" (ḥalaq) the unsuspecting youth. The root ḥalaq picturesquely portrays flattery. The root has the sense "to be smooth." One who "makes her words smooth" uses this technique to draw victims into her trap, v. 16.

---

[13]The participial form of zûr often refers to a foreigner (e.g., Jer. 5:19; Hos. 8:7), but it also commonly refers to Israelites (e.g., Deut. 25:5; I Kings 3:18). The root signifies someone or something that does not belong to a particular class. This sense comes through clearly in such passages as Num. 1:51; Exod. 30:9; and Lev. 22:12.

[14]Commentators have also adopted other interpretations of the "strange woman." The older Jewish view took the phrase metaphorically. This made the woman symbolic of heretical doctrine. Herman Hailperin discusses the position of Rabbi Shalomen ben Isaac in the medieval period of interpretation, *Rashi and the Christian Scholars* (1963), p. 238. John Gill, *An Exposition of the Old Testament,* IV, rpt. (1979) (hereafter cited as Gill) p. 340, understands the phrase as denoting that the faithless woman belonged to another person, not the one whom she entices into adultery. Plaut, p. 48, refers the word zarâ to the wife of another man. A. Cohen, *Proverbs* (1946) (hereafter cited as Cohen), p. 11, refers the descriptive term "strange" to a foreign woman and comments that these normally held lower moral standards than the Israelites. Whybray, p. 22, suggests that the passage is but a symbol for Israel's unfaithfulness to God. AB, p. 43, makes this idea specific by stating that the passage has in mind the offering of female devotees to Astarte or some similar cult. Although these views have elements of the truth in them, they do not adequately express the sense of the word.

[15]The MT uses nakrîyâ six times to refer to an adulteress in Proverbs (2:16; 5:20; 6:24; 7:5; 23:27; 27:13). A close variant (nakrî) occurs in 5:10. Elsewhere, including 20:16, the word denotes a foreigner, i.e., a non-Israelite (e.g., Exod. 21:8; Ezra 10:2). The point of transition to the technical sense may lie in the fact that harlots originally came from among the pagan peoples that lived in the land. Francis Brown, S. R. Driver, and C. A. Briggs, *Hebrew and English Lexicon of the Old Testament* (1974) (hereafter cited as BDB), p. 649, take this position. The view of McKane, p. 285, and Toy, p. 46, is more likely. They suggest that the term refers to the fact that the woman has gone outside the normal conventions of life.

A further indication of the character of this woman is that she has forsaken "the guide of her youth." The word "guide" (ʾallûp) refers to a "friend" or "companion," one who is with another. Here it describes the Lord, the one whom she followed in her youth.[16] She also turns from the "covenant of her God," the sacred and binding covenant into which she entered at marriage.[17] The fact that the phrase occurs again only in Jeremiah 3:4, where it clearly refers to God, supports the view that the "guide" refers to God. The parallelism of the verse also supports this view.

Verses 18-19 sternly warn against following this evil woman. Those who go after her receive the punishment of "death" (mawet).[18] The noun mawet often indicates death or dying, but it may also denote "the realm of the dead," e.g., Psalm 6:5; Isaiah 38:18. The word "death" here refers to spiritual death, more than the mere ending of physical life.[19] The use

---

[16]McKane, p. 296, refers the term to the woman's childhood teacher. Thus the passage describes her turning from her early training. Adam Clarke, *Commentary on the Holy Bible* (1840), III, 206, has a similar view. He refers the verse to the woman's childhood home and the instruction received from her parents in the home.

[17]The marriage vows had the nature of a sacred covenant in that they were entered into in the sight of God. While no specific religious ceremony of marriage occurs in the OT, Mal. 2:14-15 does speak of God as a "witness" to the husband and wife, thus implying that there was a religious aspect of marriage. According to the traditional Jewish ceremony, the bridegroom places the ring on his wife's finger and recites, "Be thou consecrated unto me by this ring according to the law of Moses and Israel," Plaut, p. 49.

[18]The verb "inclineth" is the 3fs form of šûaḥ, "to sink down." Because "house" (bayit) is masculine, various attempts have been made to reconcile the two words. Zöckler, p. 53, says that bayit "is here exceptionally treated as feminine." Toy, pp. 48, 51, suggests that the verb comes from šaḥâ, "to bow down," which he then interprets as "leads down." He also tentatively suggests an emendation to naḥat, "to descend," p. 51. Gemser, p. 18, conjectures that bayit should be emended to nǝtiba, "path." Kidner, p. 62, takes bayit in apposition to "death" and translates, "she sinks down to death [which is] her home." J. A. Emerton, "A Note on Proverbs II.18," *JTS* 30:157, suggests that the verb be repointed to the noun šaḥâ, and the verse translated "her house is a pit (leading) to death." W. Frankenberg, *Handkommentar zum Alten Testament* (1898) (hereafter cited as Frankenberg), p. 28, tentatively agrees with the LXX in deriving the verb from šaḥâ, "to bow down." The parallelism of the verse requires that "house" in some way be the subject of the phrase. This can be achieved by taking bayit as permutative of "she," defining what is meant by saying that "she sinks down to death" (cf. G.K. 131k). The phrase can then be translated, "She (that is), her house, sinks down to death."

[19]A wide range of interpretations exists for this verse. Theodor H. Gaster, *Myth, Legend and Custom in the Old Testament* (1969) (hereafter cited as Gaster), p. 802, applies the passage to the netherworld, exemplified by the legend of Tannhauser and similar stories in which mortal men are lured by a fairy mistress into a realm from which they cannot escape. McKane, pp. 287-88, asserts that 2:18 refers to the god Mot, "whose gaping throat is the gateway to Sheol." The word rǝpaʾîm denotes either the gods of the

20 That thou mayest walk in the way of good men, and keep the paths of the righteous.
21 For the upright shall dwell in the land, and the perfect shall remain in it.
22 But the wicked shall be cut off from the earth, and the transgressors shall be rooted out of it.

of the word "dead" (*rəpaʾîm*) strengthens this idea. The word *rəpaʾîm* always occurs in poetical passages. It regularly refers to the inhabitants of the afterlife. The parallelism with v. 19 defines the "house" of the woman as those who unite with her in her evil work. In becoming involved intimately with her, the young man would join this ill-fated group. The warning is thus well deserved, v. 18.

The warning climaxes with the thought that this judgment is irreversible. It leads the guilty parties to miss those paths that lead to eternal life. The statement expresses a general principle that is normally true. The grace of God allows the forgiveness of the sin of adultery, but the prevailing tendency among adulterers is to follow the path of adultery once they have begun to walk in this direction, v. 19.

20-22 The deliverance of the youth from the enticements of evil men and women has a positive counterpart. He should walk in godly ways. The introductory "that" expresses purpose: the youth accepts Solomon's teachings in order that he might company with good men and follow righteous ways, v. 20.[20]

With vv. 21-22, the passage anticipates the final judgment of God in which the wicked are cut off and the godly enjoy the blessing of God. The verses explain the statement of v. 20. The youth will enjoy the company of godly men because the "upright" (*yəšarîm*) and "perfect" will dwell in the land. The verb *yašar* literally means "to make straight." In

---

underworld or the inhabitants of Sheol taken as a group. Metaphorically, the passage refers to the expulsion of a person from society as punishment for adulterous actions. Toy, p. 48, sees the verse as an ominous warning against premature death. Plaut, p. 52, says that the main idea here is that a shortened lifespan is punishment for wickedness. The words *mawet* and *rəpaʾîm*, however, hold the potential for life beyond the grave. The noun *mawet*, for instance, occurs in Isa. 38:18; Hos. 13:14; and Ps. 49:14, where there is an implied life after death. The *rəpaʾîm*, "shades," i.e., the shadowy figures of the grave, likewise live beyond the grave, Isa. 26:19; 14:9.

[20]Toy, pp. 38-39, moves v. 20 to follow v. 9, suggesting that the verse properly expands 9b. When vv. 10-22 are understood as expanding upon the conclusion of v. 9, there is no need to restructure the order. There is already a logical flow of thought.

the *pi'el,* as it occurs here, *yašar* often means "to make [a way] straight," e.g., 9:15; 11:5. The noun form elsewhere often refers to ethical uprightness. The meaning of "perfect" (cf. *tom,* v. 7) parallels "upright." Both refer to the sense of integrity or ethical perfection, v. 21.

At the same time, the wicked inhabitants of the "earth" (or "land," same word as in v. 21) will be destroyed. In both verses, the thought is of God's blessing upon His people. For the first time in human history, He purifies the Promised Land of Palestine for Israel's enjoyment.[21] Strong verbs show the judgment of God upon the wicked. He is "cut off" (*yikkaretû*) and "rooted out" (*yissəḥû*) of the land. The verb *karat,* "to cut off," often indicates killing or a metaphorical sense of eliminating or removing. Similarly, the verb *nasaḥ,* "to tear out" or "to tear down," refers elsewhere to the removal of a people from their dwelling place.

Certainly, it is going too far to find a clear prophecy of the Millennial Kingdom in the passage. Still, it is appropriate to note that the passage will find its fulfillment at this time. God will remove the wicked from His land, and He will allow the godly to dwell there in peace, v. 22.

---

[21]Most commentators refer the "land" to Palestine. This interpretation fits in with the book as a Jewish book. T. T. Perowne, *The Proverbs* (1916) (hereafter cited as Perowne), p. 51, says that the book is addressed to all mankind; therefore, he interprets "land" as the whole earth. Since the book refers to the Mosaic law (28:4, 9) and sacrifices (7:14), it is doubtful that this view is correct.

Practical Applications from Proverbs 2

The Rewards of Wisdom
Introduction: The Bible promises that those who seek God will find
Him (Deut. 4:29; Prov. 8:17; Jer. 29:13). Proverbs 2 illustrates the re-
wards that come to those who search for godly wisdom.

1. The Search for Wisdom
   a. Acceptance of godly instruction ("receive . . . hide . . .") 1
   b. Obedience to godly teaching ("incline . . . apply . . .") 2
   c. Pursuit of godly guidance ("criest . . . liftest up . . .") 3
   d. Value of godly wisdom ("seekest . . . searchest . . .") 4
2. The Rewards of Wisdom
   a. A right relationship with God 5-8
      (1) Given by the Lord 6
      (2) Preserved for the righteous 7-8
   b. An understanding of God's ways 9-19
      (1) Delivers from evil men 10-15
      (2) Delivers from evil women 16-19
      (3) Delivers to godly company 20-22

God's Judgment on Adultery
Introduction: Six separate passages in the book describe the judgment
of God on the adulterer (2:18-19; 5:5-6, 22-23; 6:23b-33; 7:22-27;
9:18). This punishment receives the greatest emphasis in these passages
of any of the punishments that potentially await the adulterous person.
This agrees with the general emphasis of the OT, which speaks vigorously against adultery. When taken together, these comments make a
sobering warning against the sin of adultery.

1. There is first, the loss of dignity (5:9, 14; 6:33).
2. Then God promises the weakening of physical strength (5:7-12;
   31:3).
3. Next, He warns of material loss (5:10; 6:26-31).
4. There is also mental anguish (5:11-14).
5. The greatest punishment, however, is that of eternal damnation
   (2:18-19; 5:5-6, 22-23; 7:22-27; 9:18).

As mentioned in the discussion above, the grace of God is sufficient to forgive this sin. But this sin grips tightly. It is difficult to break the sensual attitudes that lead one away from God and godliness. How much better to avoid the sin, to determine that sensual attitudes will never control you. This can be yours if you focus on godly attitudes and actions in life.

1 My son, forget not my law; but let thine heart keep my commandments:
2 For length of days, and long life, and peace, shall they add to thee.

PROVERBS 3
EXHORTATIONS RELATING TO WISDOM

Chapter 3 presents the fourth discourse of the book. This primarily develops the idea of the son's obedience. Although the phrase "my son" suggests a natural division at vv. 1-10, 11-20, 21-26, vv. 11-12 belong most naturally to vv. 1-10. They continue the practice of commanding the son. Verses 27-35 conclude the chapter with a brief appendix.[1]

Need for Obedience 3:1-12

1-2 Solomon exhorts his son not to forget his "law" (*tôrâ,* cf. 1:8), his parental teachings. The command warns the son against forsaking (*šakah*) the teachings that his parents have given him. The verb *šakah* occurs widely, with about half of the occurrences in the poetical books. It occurs five times in Proverbs (here and 2:17; 4:5; 31:5, 7). Most often, *šakah* refers to one who forgets the relationship between man and God, e.g., 2:17. Here, God is not in view. The parents, God's representatives in the home, take His place. It is the son's responsibility not to turn from their teachings.

Rather than turning from his parents' teachings, the son should faithfully "keep" (*nasar,* cf. 2:8) their "commandments" (*miswâ*). The word *miswâ* occurs ten times in the book, each time in a good sense. When kept, these commandments reward the youth with peace (13:13), guidance (6:23), and life (7:2; 19:16). Clearly, a wise son will accept these parental commands (10:8), v. 1.

Verse 2 completes the exhortation of v. 1, showing that the rewards of obedience are attractive. They include "length of days, and long life, and peace." The phrase indicates that the natural outcome of obedience will be a long, full, productive life. As with many of the proverbs, this is a

---

[1]In "Wisdom's House," *CBQ* 24:468-86, Skehan tries to show that c. 1-9 has a highly organized structure. To achieve this, however, he makes wholesale adjustments to the text. He moves 3:13-24, 35, to a position following 4:1-9. His argument is arbitrary, without textual support.

3 Let not mercy and truth forsake thee: bind them about thy neck; write them upon the table of thine heart:

general rule. It does not apply in every specific instance. The phrase "long life" is literally "years of life," but "long life" captures the sense of the phrase; cf. v. 16. Similar phrases occur again in 4:10 and 9:11, also indicating physical life.

In addition, the obedient son will enjoy "peace" (*šalôm*). The word *šalôm* customarily carries with it the sense of completeness and fulfillment. It may refer to the absence of war. More often, it refers to the attitude of one who walks in harmony with God. It can, as well, refer to a situation that demonstrates this gift of peace, v. 2.[2]

The Rewards of Obedience

Proverbs places great emphasis on parent-child relationships. While the parents have the responsibility to guide their children, the child has one primary responsibility—to obey his parents. Six times the book commands the child to obey the commands of his parents (2:1; 3:1-2; 4:4; 6:20; 7:1, 2). When a child does this, God promises several specific blessings.

1. Peace 3:2

2. Fullness of life 3:2; 4:4; 7:2

3. Moral purity 6:23 (note context); 7:5 (concludes 7:2)

4. Spiritual growth 2:5 (concludes 2:1)

---

3 A second prohibition bids the son not to forsake (*ʿazab,* cf. 2:13) "mercy and truth." The word "mercy" (*ḥesed,* cf. 2:8) is broad, meaning "kindness, mercy." It has a strong component of loyalty and often has this as its primary meaning. The word occurs widely in all parts of the OT. God expects these qualities in those whom He has redeemed.

---

[2]In opposition, Toy, pp. 57, 69, relates the word primarily to the outward situations of life. He states that "the distinctive inward application of the term does not appear in OT." Others, however, agree that *šalôm* refers to the inward attitude. Alan Richardson, *A Theological Word Book of the Bible* (1950) (hereafter cited as Richardson), p. 165, states that *šalôm* can refer to well-being, "manifested in every kind of good for man." Johannes Pederson, *Israel, Its Life and Culture* (rpt. 1953) II, 313, comments: "Good is that which acts upon the soul in accordance with its nature and makes it expand, and so peace is the same as joy."

4 So shalt thou find favour and good understanding in the sight of God and man.

"Truth" (ʾ*amet*) also occurs widely. It has the root idea of certainty. Often, it indicates faithfulness as an attribute of God. When used of man, it describes truth in an absolute sense, corresponding to reality and fact. We see its use in the book by terms that contrast with it: abomination, 8:7; deception, 11:18; 12:19; going astray ("err"), 14:22; and lying, 14:25. The words ʾ*amet* and *ḥesed* are parallel in 3:3; 14:22; 16:6; and 20:28. *TWOT* I:53 aptly comments, "As we study its various contexts, it becomes manifestly clear that there is no truth in the biblical sense, i.e., valid truth, outside God. All truth comes from God and is truth because it is related to God."

With picturesque advice, Solomon exhorts his son to "bind" mercy and truth about his neck and to "write" them on the table of his heart. The figure of binding truth about the neck is familiar (cf. 6:21; 7:3; see also 1:9; 4:8-9). The figure of writing something on the "table of the heart" also occurs elsewhere (cf. 7:3; Jer. 17:1; see also Jer. 31:33).[3] By this means, the young man adorns himself with character qualities of great worth, both before God and before man.

4 The result of the young man's adherence to the teaching of his parents now appears. He will receive "favour" (*ḥen*) and "good understanding" (*śekel ṭôb*) before God and man. The imperative "find" coordinated with the verb "forsake" in v. 3 expresses a desired consequence (cf. G.K. 110f). The word *ḥen* has the sense of graciousness in Proverbs. It encompasses both gracious speech (22:11) and actions ("pleasant," 5:19; 11:16). Solomon indicates here that the young man will gain graciousness as he follows the guidance of his parents.

---

[3]AB, p. 44; Toy, p. 58; and McKane, p. 291; suggest that the phrase is an addition from 7:3. Textual evidence supporting this comes from LXX[B], where it does not occur. The argument is that a verse of three phrases does not fit into a chapter that contains verses of two phrases. The disputed phrase, however, does occur in LXX[A] and in the Syrian version of the OT. It also occurs in numerous manuscripts of lesser value. Moreover, numerous verses with three phrases appear throughout the first section of the book, e.g., 1:11, 23, 27; 4:4; 5:19; 6:3, 22; 7:22; 8:13, 29, 30, 34. We may not insist that the author slavishly follow a particular style of writing.

5 Trust in the Lord with all thine heart; and lean not unto thine own understanding.
6 In all thy ways acknowledge him, and he shall direct thy paths.

Further, he will receive *śekel tôb* as a character quality when he obeys his parent's teachings.[4] The phrase occurs only three times elsewhere (II Chron. 30:22; Ps. 111:10; Prov. 13:15; see also I Sam. 25:3), in each case indicating prudence or insight. The youth receives both of these benefits, graciousness and prudence, in the sight of God and man.[5]

5 Solomon commands his son to "trust" (*baṭaḥ,* cf. 1:33) in the Lord with all of his "heart" (*leb*). The *leb* occurs widely to describe the immaterial nature of man, including his emotions, thoughts, or will. The word occurs about one hundred times in the book, taking various senses, e.g., mental processes (7:7; 10:8), emotions (6:25; 12:25; 15:13), will (11:20; 19:3), and man's immaterial being (3:3; 12:20). The context determines the exact sense in each case. Here, the phrase "all thine heart" refers to the total inner being of the son.

Conversely, the young man should not "lean" (*šaʿan*) on his own "understanding" (*bînâ,* cf. 1:2). The verb *šaʿan* and its derivatives occur widely throughout the OT but only here in Proverbs. In the early literature (historical sections), *šaʿan* has the sense "to lean," i.e., "to rest upon." From this developed the sense of "trust." In the later literature (poetical books, prophets, Chronicles, with Ezek. 29:7 as an exception), *šaʿan* is "trust."

6 The third member of the passage enjoins the young man to "acknowledge" (*yadaʿ,* cf. 10:32) the Lord in all his ways. In this context, the word *yadaʿ* urges the son to cultivate the habit of letting the Lord guide his actions in every area. As he does this, God will direct him.

---

[4]Jones, p. 69; Toy, p. 59; and G. Currie Martin, *Proverbs, Ecclesiastes, and Song of Songs,* in *The Century Bible,* ed. Walter F. Adeney (1908) (hereafter cited as Martin), p. 39, all emend *śekel* to *šem* on the grounds that a good "reputation" fits better into the context of the verse. The textual evidence does not support the suggestion, nor is it necessary from a literary standpoint.

[5]Zöckler, p. 61, translates *śekel* as "reputation" and refers this to man's opinion. At the same time, he refers *ḥen* to God's blessing. Muenscher, pp. 25-26, refers *ḥen* to both man and God but takes *śekel,* "success," to refer to the obedient son. The translation "success" will not hold up in I Sam. 25:3; II Chron. 30:22; or Prov. 13:15. It is most natural to refer these blessings to those given the youth before other individuals, including both God and man.

7 Be not wise in thine own eyes: fear the Lord, and depart from evil.
8 It shall be health to thy navel, and marrow to thy bones.

The word "direct" (*yašar,* cf. 2:21) is better "to make straight." Elsewhere, the noun form often refers to ethical uprightness. God smooths the path of the wise man, removing obstacles that would hinder him in life. The emphasis is on the wisdom given those who seek the Lord's guidance. Wise choices let them avoid many problems that would otherwise hinder them.

7 Solomon directs yet another admonition to the son. He now warns him against pride. The phrase "wise in thine own eyes" does not occur again in this exact form. Isaiah 5:21, however, expresses virtually the same thought (cf. also Prov. 12:15; 16:2; 21:2; 26:5, 12; 28:11; 30:12). The phrase refers to one's self-evaluation, always a risky action. Rather than allowing his son to rely upon himself, Solomon urges him to "fear the Lord" (*yəraʾ ʾet-yəhwah,* cf. 1:7), i.e., to have a reverential trust in the covenant God. At the same time, the youth should depart from "evil" (*raʿ,* cf. 1:33), wicked conduct.

8 Once more, the end result of such wise conduct is highly desirable. The youth will receive "health . . . and marrow." The exact nature of these blessings is debatable; however, a metaphorical interpretation of "health . . . and marrow" as spiritual refreshment makes good sense. Commentators treat the phrase "health to thy navel" (*ripʾût . . . ləšorreka*) variously.[6] The MT, however, makes adequate sense without emendation. The "navel" is at the middle of the body and is therefore a natural symbol for the entire body of the youth. This parallels 8*b* nicely, where "bones" likewise represents the body.

"Marrow," v. 8*b*, is literally "moisture [*šiqqûy*] to your bones." The word *šiqqûy* occurs elsewhere only at Psalm 102:9 and Hosea 2:5. In both places, the meaning is "drink." Here, apparently, the thought of

---

[6]Zöckler, pp. 61-62; Toy, p. 61; Perowne, p. 53; and Hulst, *OTTP*, p. 114, all emend *ləšorreka* to something like *ləšerka* (contracted from *lišerka*). Driver, *Biblica* 32:175, argues that the meaning of *šor* is not "navel" but "health." He supports the conclusion from cognate studies. McKane, p. 293, follows Driver. Jones, p. 70, relies on the quotation of the verse in the Mishnah to argue for the accuracy of the MT.

9 Honour the Lord with thy substance, and with the firstfruits of all thine increase:

"drink," or "moisture," pictures "refreshment." This represents the physical blessings that come to the body of the obedient son.

9 Solomon now exhorts his son in a practical area. He should "honour" (*kabed*) the Lord with his "substance" (*hôn*) from the first of his "increase" (*təbûʾâ*). The command is the third in a series of four commands guiding the youth's relationship to Yahweh (cf. vv. 5, 7, 11). Recognizing the Lord as the source of all material prosperity, the son should faithfully give back to Him a portion of what he has gained each year.

The word *kabed* in the *piʿel* often denotes "honor" or "glory," both natural extensions of the root, which means "to be heavy." The verb occurs six times elsewhere in Proverbs (4:8; 8:24; 12:9; 13:18; 14:31; 27:18), with only the *nipʿal* form in 8:24 an exception to the normal meaning of "honor." The practice of tithing is early (cf. Gen. 14:20); thus, it is not strange to find it here, in a poetical section of the OT.

The youth honors the Lord by giving Him a portion of his "substance." The noun *hôn* is specially a word of poetical nature, occurring eighteen times in Proverbs, once in Canticles, and three times in Psalms. It occurs only four times elsewhere, all in Ezekiel 27. It indicates "riches," or "wealth." It parallels *təbûʾâ* here, "increase." The general sense of *təbûʾâ* is "yield," most often referring to the produce of the harvest.

What the youth gives to the Lord comes from the "firstfruits" (*reʾšît*, cf. 1:7). The word *reʾšît* generally has the sense of "first" or "best."[7] The sense of "firstfruits" comes from the sense of "first," widely seen elsewhere. This is appropriate here.

---

[7]Toy, p. 62, argues for the sense "best" since there is no other mention of the ceremonial law in Prov. 1-9. George Kufeldt, *The Book of Proverbs*, in *The Wesleyan Commentary*, ed. Charles W. Carter (1968) (hereafter cited as Kufeldt), p. 482, follows Toy. The majority of commentators follow the AV in translating "firstfruits."

10 So shall thy barns be filled with plenty, and thy presses shall burst out with new wine.
11 My son, despise not the chastening of the Lord; neither be weary of his correction·

┌───┐
A Right Relationship to God

1. Accepting divine direction 5-6
2. Adopting godly standards 7-8
3. Practicing generous giving 9-10
4. Embracing divine correction 11-12
└───┘

10 God's blessing will follow the youth's actions in honoring Him. His barns will fill with "plenty" (*sabaᶜ*), and his presses (*yeqeb*) will burst (*paraṣ*) with new wine. The passage anticipates God's blessing upon faithfulness.[8] The winepress (*yeqeb*) in biblical times was hollowed from a rock. Ordinarily an upper receptacle was used for pressing the grapes; cf. Joel 3:13. As the juice drained, it was caught in a lower *yeqeb*. Thus the sense of the verse seems more to be the "vat" than the "press." This introduces the question of how the "vat" can "burst" (*paraṣ*) with the newly pressed wine. The verb *paraṣ* also has the sense "to increase" (cf. Exod. 1:12; Job 1:10). The presses, then, "increase" with the juice as it is pressed from the grapes.

11 The final couplet in the section urges the son to recognize the value of divine chastening. He should not despise it since the chastening shows Yahweh's love. The passage is significant since Hebrews 12:5-6 quotes it.[9]

---

[8]J. Weingreen, *Introduction to the Critical Study of the Text of the Hebrew Bible* (1982) (hereafter cited as Weingreen), p. 65, argues from parallelism that the "notion of 'plenty' is too general a term to balance the mention of 'wine.'" He follows the LXX and emends to *šeber*. Mitchell Dahood, "Ugaritic and the Old Testament," *ETL* 44:40, suggests that the MT's *sabaᶜ* should be read "wheat." He notes that Ugaritic studies show that an abstract noun paralleling a concrete noun should also be translated concretely. Toy, p. 62, incorrectly states that the term is always adverbial (contra. Gen. 41:30-31; Eccles. 5:12) and accepts the emendation. The LXX apparently understood *sabaᶜ* as *šeber*, "grain." The verb *sabaᶜ*, "to be satisfied," however, is a familiar word that occurs frequently. Since a person is satisfied when he has an abundance of provision for his needs, the idea of "plenty" appropriately fits the context.
[9]Jones, p. 70, suggests that vv. 11-12 are out of place. He feels they "interrupt the development of the theme of the Benefits of Wisdom." He cites no evidence for this

12 For whom the Lord loveth he correcteth; even as a father the son in whom he delighteth.

The command again warns the son against despising (*ma²as*) the "chastening" (*mûsar,* cf. 1:2). The verb *ma²as* occurs only here and in 15:32 in the book. Elsewhere, however, it occurs widely in all parts of the OT. It has the sense "to despise" or "to reject." In the other wisdom literature, the word *ma²as* occurs frequently in the books of Job and Psalms. In every case, it has the meaning "to despise, reject, abhor." It is appropriate with this sense here.

The phrase "weary [*qûṣ*] of his correction [*tôkaḥat,* cf. 1:23]" parallels the first admonition. The verb *qûṣ* is stronger than the AV's "wearied." In the *qal,* the root occurs eight times throughout the OT. In each case, it denotes a negative emotional reaction. Here, the sense "loathe" or "despise" suits the thought.

12 Solomon now justifies his warning. Yahweh's chastisement (*yôkîaḥ*) proves His love. The root *yakaḥ* is the basis for *tôkaḥat* (see 1:23), seen often in the book. The verb *yakaḥ,* "to reprove, judge, decide," occurs ten times in the book.[10] In each case, the sense of "reprove" is appropriate. Just as a loving father corrects the son in whom he delights, so the heavenly Father corrects those whom He loves. The thought of the verse occurs earlier in Deuteronomy 8:5.

As the MT stands, Yahweh may be the subject of either "loveth" or "correcteth."[11] Parallelism, however, argues that Yahweh goes with "correcteth." We may then arrange the verse as a chiasm:
For the one He loves, the Lord corrects
As a father (corrects) the son he delights in.

---

suggestion. Jones fails to see the connection of vv. 11-12 with the three previous exhortations, all of which remind the son of his relationship with Yahweh: trust, v. 5; reverence, v. 7; and honor, v. 9.
[10]Here and at 9:7, 8 (twice); 15:12; 19:25; 24:25; 25:12; 28:23; 30:6.
[11]KD I, 90; *PC,* p. 58; McKane, pp. 214, 294; and W. A. Van der Weiden, *Le Livre des Proverbes* (1970) (hereafter cited as Van der Weiden), p. 32, connect Yahweh with "correcteth." Plaut, p. 58; Frankenburg, p. 32; and AB, p. 45, relate it to "loveth." The parallel passage in Heb. 12:6 is ambiguous, translations taking it as they do this verse. The AV and NASB, for example, make the Lord the subject of the verb "love" in both passages. The NIV and NEB, on the other hand, make "the Lord" the subject of "discipline."

13 Happy is the man that findeth wisdom, and the man that getteth understanding.

The suggestion that *yǝhweh* is a late addition to the text is weak.[12] No textual evidence supports the change. While the symmetry of the line is unbalanced, no regular pattern of symmetry anywhere in the context suggests an error here.

In 12*b*, instead of the MT's *ûkᵊᵓab*, "as a father," the LXX translates *wǝyakᵓib,* "and causes pain." Hebrews 12:6 follows the LXX. The LXX is easily explained as an interpretation of the MT. Further, the comparison of God's relationship to man with that of a father to his son is familiar in the OT, e.g., Psalm 103:13; Malachi 3:17. The MT is thus preferable here to the LXX. When the author of Hebrews follows the LXX, he correctly interprets the thought of the verse even though he does not slavishly follow the Hebrew text.

Results of Obedience 3:13-20

13 The man who makes wisdom his goal gains true blessing in life. The verse is one of several in the book that refer to the blessedness of one who walks in wisdom (cf. 8:32*b*, 34*a*, 35*b*). In addition, other verses mention specific blessings that come from seeking wisdom, e.g., 3:17; 4:8. The man who finds wisdom will be "happy" (*ᵓašrê*). The word *ᵓašrê* refers widely to man, never to God. It takes the sense "to experience blessings or praise," normally in response to some action worthy of reward. The translation "happy" is trite; "blessed" more accurately conveys the correct sense. The plural form intensifies the meaning. The occurrence here is the first of eight beatitudes in the book, all of which pronounce blessing upon different aspects of godliness.

---

[12]See, for example, Toy, p. 65. Greenstone, p. 29, argues that the word "mars the symmetry of the line." Toy, p. 66, admits that Yahweh "in v. 12 is sustained by all MSS. and Vrss." but then omits it to aid the rhythm of the verse.

14 For the merchandise of it is better than the merchandise of silver, and the gain thereof than fine gold.
15 She is more precious than rubies: and all the things thou canst desire are not to be compared unto her.

The Beatitudes of Proverbs	
1. Gaining wisdom 3:13	5. Trusting the Lord 16:20
2. Practicing obedience 8:32	6. Demonstrating integrity 20:7
3. Seeking instruction 8:34	7. Possessing reverence 28:14
4. Showing mercy 14:21	8. Accepting God's Word 29:18

The source of this blessing is "wisdom" (*ḥokmâ*, see 1:2) and "understanding" (*bîn*, cf. 1:2). The terms occur poetically, with no attempt to distinguish between them. The verb "getteth," *pûq*, occurs only four times with this sense, all in Proverbs. The parallelism of the verse establishes the meaning "to get, gain."[13]

14 Such blessing is highly desirable, comparable to the profit from silver and gold. "Merchandise" (*saḥar*) is more precisely the "gain from merchandise" rather than the merchandise itself. Realizing that the profit from wisdom may have eternal consequences, the comparison is apt. Wisdom's eternal gain is far superior to the temporal value of silver and gold.[14]

"Gold" (*ḥarûṣ*) denotes literally "that which is dug." By interpretation, it indicates "gold."[15] Here, it supplies the climax, the most precious earthly metal falling short in value in comparison with the gain from wisdom.

15 The passage continues to extol wisdom. It is better than "rubies" (*pənîyim*) and all the things that one can desire (*ḥəpaṣeyka*). The noun

[13]Cf. also 8:35; 12:2; 18:22. Driver, *Biblica* 32:176, mentions Phoenician and Ugaritic cognates with similar meanings.
[14]Toy, p. 67, draws upon the parallelism with 8:19 to suggest that we should delete the second "merchandise." Textual evidence does not support Toy's suggestion. Furthermore, the use of *ṭôb* coordinated with *min* to show comparison is common in Proverbs, e.g., 8:11, 19; 16:16, 32; 19:22.
[15]The word *ḥarûṣ* occurs six times, four of these in Proverbs (3:14; 8:10, 19; 16:16). In each case, the context virtually demands "gold" as the meaning. In addition, the Akkadian cognate means "gold."

16 Length of days is in her right hand; and in her left hand riches and honour.
17 Her ways are ways of pleasantness, and all her paths are peace.
18 She is a tree of life to them that lay hold upon her: and happy is every one that retaineth her.

pənîyim often refers to a thing of value, e.g., 8:11; 20:15; 31:10.[16] Lamentations 4:7 indicates that *pənînîm* are reddish in color. No compelling argument decides between "rubies" or "corals." The easiest gloss is "jewels." This leaves open the question of whether a specific stone of value is intended.

There is some disagreement about the suffix on *ḥapaṣeyka,* "thou canst desire."[17] The MT, however, fits nicely into the context. There is no strong argument to force a change. Certainly, wisdom offers more benefits than does anything else one can desire.

16-18 Solomon now begins to enumerate some of the benefits that come from wisdom. She gives long life, a full lifespan to the youth; cf. v. 2.[18] Since he walks in the ways of wisdom, he may confidently expect to live out the full number of his days. He need not have his life terminated prematurely by divine judgment.

Wisdom further confers "riches [*ᶜošer*] and honour [*kabôd,* cf. v. 9]" upon the one who receives her. Throughout the book, *ᶜošer* refers to material wealth rather than the immaterial wealth of peace and contentment. It is reasonable to take *ᶜošer* here in a comparative sense, i.e., more wealth than would otherwise have been gained. The righteous do not make wealth an end in itself (cf. 22:1; 23:4; 28:20; 30:8-9). Still, God promises material blessings to those who are faithful to Him, e.g., 10:22; 22:4. Experience proves that not all of the righteous are rich.

---

[16]Kidner, p. 65, and the NIV take *pənîyim* as "rubies." Alden, p. 41; McKane, p. 214; and the NASB render it as "jewels." Conant, p. 18; Frankenberg, p. 32; Zöckler, p. 62; Muencher, p. 32; and William French and George Skinner, *A New Translation of the Book of Proverbs* (1831) (hereafter cited as French and Skinner), p. 8, understand it as "pearls." Toy, p. 68; Van der Wieden, p. 34; KD I, 92; Coates, p. 26; Gemser, p. 22; and Martin, p. 41, translate it as "corals."

[17]Driver, *Textus* I, 117, understands *ḥapaṣ* as an abbreviation that was misread by a scribe as *ḥapaṣeyka* instead of *ḥapaṣim.* Toy, p. 72, cites evidence from ancient versions and omits the suffix. He reads *ḥapaṣim,* "no treasures." The argument is weak.

[18]The phrase is literally "length of days," an idiomatic portrayal of a long lifespan. In 4:10, the promise is more direct, *šənôt ḥayyîm,* "years of life"; cf. 9:11.

Thus "riches" here indicate an abundance that would not normally come to a person.

"Honour" (kabôd) also is literal. The noun kabôd denotes the general esteem one receives from others as he exercises his responsibilities in society. A wise man will naturally receive respect from others as they interact with him.[19]

Some draw a contrast between the use of the "right hand" and "left hand" to dispense these gifts.[20] The right hand supposedly confers the greater gift while the left hand dispenses lesser favors. It is difficult to support the interpretation. Ecclesiastes 10:2 suggests that the right hand is the position of greater blessing. But Judges 7:20; Ezekiel 16:46; and Daniel 12:7 strongly support the notion that the two hands have equal importance. The usage here is simple poetic variation, v. 16.

The ways of wisdom are "pleasant" (no'am). This root has a broad range of meanings, e.g., "sweet," II Samuel 23:1; "pleasant" (or "charming"), Song 1:16; and "beauty" (or "favor"), Psalm 90:17. The AV most often glosses no'am as "pleasant." One aspect of these pleasant paths is "peace" (šalôm, cf. v. 2), v. 17.

Wisdom is a "tree of life" ('eṣ ḥayyîm) to those who possess her. This joins the fullness of physical life with eternal life. The expression "tree of life" occurs in the book at 11:30; 13:12; and 15:4. It comes from Genesis 2:9 and 3:22. In the NT, the phrase occurs again in Revelation 2:7 and 22:2, 14, 19 (from the Greek). From its first mention in Genesis and its last mention in Revelation, it is associated with eternal life. It is therefore natural to so associate it here in the Book of Proverbs.

---

[19]Cohen, p. 17, states that the word kabôd always "signifies the splendour of luxury" when combined with 'ošer. He cites Exod. 28:2, 40 and Isa. 35:2 in support of this position. These references illustrate only the basic meaning of luxuriousness. Neither involves the particular combination of words that Cohen refers to. The grouping of kabôd and 'ošer occurs often in the OT, particularly in Chronicles. Only three times does this word clearly refer to the splendor of wealth (Esther 1:4; 5:11; Eccles. 6:2). On other occasions, the context allows the idea of honor to come through, e.g., I Chron. 29:12, 28; II Chron. 18:1; 32:27. In I Kings 3:13, the gam . . . gam construction requires that Solomon receive "both riches and honour." The parallelism in Prov. 8:18 likewise requires the idea of honor.

[20]Among others, Plaut, p. 59; Kufeldt, p. 484; KD I, 93; and Frankenberg, p. 32, take this position. On the other hand, PC, p. 60, while agreeing that the right hand holds the greater gift, comments that the use of two hands signifies "the abundance of Wisdom's gifts."

19 The Lord by wisdom hath founded the earth; by understanding hath
he established the heavens.
20 By his knowledge the depths are broken up, and the clouds drop
down the dew.

Eternal life, however, has its roots in this present life. The "tree of
life" acts as a source of renewal to the godly individual now. "Life" is a
plural of intensity. The word conveys the thought of a present life in all
of its fullness and richness. This blessed existence becomes the entrance
to eternal life, with its accompanying intensification of blessing.

These results of wisdom make it clear that the pursuit of wisdom is
highly desirable. The wise youth will strengthen his ties to the Lord
since this relationship is the source of his spiritual blessing. Not only
will he be rewarded with a general blessedness for his wise actions, but
he will also have the specific blessings of long life, riches and honor,
peace, and eternal life. Such a worthy reward amply justifies a walk of
wisdom in this life.

19-20 To illustrate the importance of walking in wisdom, Solomon
shows that even God Himself acts in wisdom. Verse 19 states the general principle that Yahweh established the Creation by His wisdom.
Verse 20 follows with an example to illustrate Yahweh's wisdom, showing how He supplies the earth with water both from beneath (springs,
rivers, lakes) and from above (rain, snow, hail, dew).[21]

Verses 19-20 illustrate the importance of wisdom. It is a divine attribute. God Himself acts in wisdom to supply the needs of His creation.
Since the word parallels "understanding," we should not take wisdom as
anticipating the hypostatized wisdom that occurs in chapter 8.[22]

---

[21]Perowne, p. 55; AB, p. 48; and Plaut, p. 61, refer v. 20 to the Flood (Gen. 7:11).
French and Skinner, p. 9; Greenstone, p. 32; Zöckler, p. 64; and Muenscher, pp. 34-35,
refer the verse to Creation. Even with these interpretations, however, the last phrase of
the verse is generally related to the ongoing supply of rainwater to the earth. The parallelism is synonymous. Both phrases relate to the provision of Yahweh for giving water to
mankind. There is no scientific error here as suggested by A. D. Power, *The Proverbs of
Solomon* (1949) (hereafter cited as Power), p. 100. In the language of appearance, "dew"
does drip down from the heavens (Job 38:28; Ps. 133:3). KD I, 95, takes the word poetically. It represents all the waters that come down from heaven.

[22]*PC*, p. 62, states that "wisdom is here something more than an attribute of Jehovah."
The authors consider it "as an anticipation of that which is more fully developed in
chapter viii." Jones, p. 72, likewise suggests that the concept of Wisdom here goes "far

21 My son, let not them depart from thine eyes: keep sound wisdom and discretion:
22 So shall they be life unto thy soul, and grace to thy neck.

Assurance of Protection 3:21-26

21 The lack of a clear antecedent to "them" brings a puzzling element to the verse. One possible explanation refers this to "wisdom . . . understanding" in v. 13. Verse 21 picks up the thought developed in vv. 13-18. Verses 19-20 have broken the thought with an illustration showing the importance of wisdom. Solomon now exhorts the youth not to "depart" (*lûz*, cf. 2:15) from these elements or "sound wisdom" (*tûšîyâ*, cf. 2:7) and discretion" (*məzimmâ*, cf. 1:4) that offer such valuable benefits.[23] The parallel phrase in 21*b* reinforces this thought.

The exhortation to practice wise habits of living is the first of four injunctions in this area (cf. also 4:4*c*, 6*a*; 7:2*a*). The command shows that the day-by-day practice of wisdom is not optional. The thought that the wisdom and understanding mentioned in v. 13 should never "depart from thine eyes" conveys a strict requirement for consistency of life.

22 The practice of wisdom has wholesome benefits for the individual. It brings fullness of life to the soul and grace to the individual. "Neck" poetically stands for the whole outward appearance. There is a deliberate use of "soul" and "neck." The union of these terms brings out the effect of wisdom upon the whole man. It affects him both inwardly and outwardly.

The book pictures wisdom as an adornment here, a becoming headdress (cf. 4:9). The idea is that of an attractiveness that the youth gains

---

beyond any poetic personification." Zöckler, p. 63, states that God works "not merely with the manifestation of wisdom as an attribute of His, but by means of the personal, essential wisdom, as an independent, creative power indwelling in Him from eternity. . . . In the same hypostatic sense, therefore, are also the interchangeable ideas of 'understanding'. . . and 'knowledge'. . . to be understood." Most likely, however, we should simply accept wisdom here as an attribute of Yahweh.

[23]The greater number of commentators find the antecedent "sound wisdom and discretion" in v. 21*b*. So *PC*, p. 63; Zöckler, p. 64; Plaut, p. 61; French and Skinner, p. 9; Coates, p. 27. The attractiveness of this has led Toy to emend the verse by interchanging the phrases, although he admits there is no textual support for this, pp. 73-74. McKane, p. 215, likewise follows this approach, along with the RSV and the NIV. KD I, 96, takes a different approach. Delitzsch there finds the antecedent in vv. 19-20, understanding "wisdom . . . understanding . . . knowledge" as underlying the pronoun "them." Kufeldt, p. 484, basically follows this approach.

23 Then shalt thou walk in thy way safely, and thy foot shall not stumble.
24 When thou liest down, thou shalt not be afraid: yea, thou shalt lie
down, and thy sleep shall be sweet.
25 Be not afraid of sudden fear, neither of the desolation of the wicked,
when it cometh.
26 For the Lord shall be thy confidence, and shall keep thy foot from
being taken.

by wisdom. The association with wisdom so molds his character that he attracts others to him.

23-26 Solomon now begins to enumerate the ways in which the youth may rest secure in the protective care of Yahweh. He will walk in life "safely" (*betaḥ*, "securely," see 1:33). The godly person may thus face the challenges of life with confidence. He has a personal assurance that he will not "stumble" over obstacles (see also 3:26*b*; 4:12). He will have sure footing and will not become caught in traps along the way, v. 23. This security extends to the hours of rest, when the youth lies down upon his bed to relax, v. 24.[24]

There is no need to fear sudden alarms.[25] Nor is there any reason to fear when destruction overtakes the wicked.[26] Once again, the injunction develops the thought of security; cf. v. 23. The youth may rest in the confidence that these terrors will not engulf him, v. 25.

---

[24]There is no need to follow the LXX in reading *tešeb*, "sit," for the MT *tiškab*, "liest down." Toy, p. 75; Gemser, p. 22; and Martin, p. 42, suggest this but the argument is weak.

[25]Weingreen, p. 63, suggests that *pitʾom*, "sudden," should be vocalized *paṭʾaîm*, "the foolish," in order to achieve parallelism with the second half of the verse. While it is true that the *petî*, "fool," is often in view in the book, there is no need to introduce him at this point. Satisfactory parallelism already exists between the different calamities that the youth need not fear.

[26]Jones, p. 73, finds a parallel to the verse in the Egyptian wisdom book *The Instruction of Amen-em-opet* by joining 25*a* and 26*a*. This gives
"Do not be afraid of sudden panic . . .
For the Lord will be your confidence"
similar to
"Be sincere in the present of the common people,
For one is safe in the hand of the god"
in the Egyptian writing. He thus considers vv. 25-26 as an "expansion and adaptation of the Egyptian couplet." The suggestion is worthless. The similarity between the two statements is contrived and tenuous. The mere similarity of a few words does not justify the conclusion that one statement comes from the other.

27 Withhold not good from them to whom it is due, when it is in the power of thine hand to do it.
28 Say not unto thy neighbour, Go, and come again, and to morrow I will give; when thou hast it by thee.

Yahweh Himself is responsible for the security of the youth.[27] This promise lets us make a direct connection between Yahweh and wisdom. To walk in wisdom is to walk in the ways of Yahweh, and to walk in the ways of Yahweh is to walk in wisdom, v. 26.

Warnings Against Wickedness 3:27-35

The final part of the chapter contains two distinct sections. Verses 27-30 express a series of warnings relating to one's neighbor, and vv. 31-35 warn against involvement with the wicked. This is the first portion of the book to group isolated proverbs.[28] Since, however, the same author is responsible for other sections of grouped proverbs, we may permit him to vary his style here.

27-28 Although the verse is awkward to translate, the meaning is clear. The phrase "to whom it is due" denotes the one who has control of the good, i.e., control in the sense that the good is naturally due him.[29] The admonition gives no details of this control. We may logically speculate that it is a control that stems from a friendly relationship between the two parties. Since v. 28 focuses on neighbors, it is reasonable to assume a neighborly relationship here. When you are able to help your neighbor, do it without delay.

---

[27]Plaut, p. 62, understands *kesel* as "foolishness." Thus, the Lord will be with the youth, even in those moments when he foolishly fails to walk in wisdom. The context of the passage, however, argues for the meaning "confidence" rather than "foolishness." There is no thought here of divine protection in times of waywardness.

[28]Martin, pp. 42-43, wants to attribute vv. 27-35 to another author or to the displacement of the passage from another section of the book. He offers no evidence to support his view.

[29]After discussing uses of *baʿal* in the OT, Toy, pp. 77, 79, concludes that the word here must be either omitted or changed. He suggests *rʿyk* as a possible source for *mibʿalayw* and translates, "withhold not good from thy neighbour." Plaut, p. 63, accepts the MT but limits the meaning to the poor who are owed assistance by others. Mitchell Dahood, "Qoheleth and Northwest Semitic Philology," *Biblica* 43:362, suggests that *baʿal* is a variant of *paʿal,* leading to the thought that we should not withhold good, i.e., their salary "from those working for it." James Barr, *Comparative Philology and the Text of the Old Testament* (1968) (hereafter cited as *CPTOT*), pp. 100-101, gives some linguistic considerations that argue against Dahood's view. KD I, 99, defends the MT, taking *baʿal* as an intensive plural with a singular meaning.

29 Devise not evil against thy neighbour, seeing he dwelleth securely by thee.
30 Strive not with a man without cause, if he have done thee no harm.

The "hand" often represents power, e.g., Psalm 17:7; 118:15-16. One who has this power should use it promptly, v. 27.[30] Verse 28 repeats the thought of v. 27 even more forcefully by forbidding delay when providing assistance to one's neighbor. If given the opportunity to help, you should not put it off by telling your neighbor, "to morrow I will give," a transparent attempt at delay, v. 28.[31]

29-30 No evil should be planned against a neighbor. The close association between your dwellings should lead to a mutual trust between you. The word "devise" (*haraš*) is picturesque. The root *haraš* means "to plow, engrave, devise." The basic idea is that of cutting through some material (dirt or metal) or, in the case of thinking, through the mental fog that must be cleared away. When the word concerns thinking, it normally refers to the devising of evil plans, v. 29.

Further, you should not "strive" with another who has not provoked you. The word "strive" (*qərê, tarîb*) most often refers to a physical conflict, combat between two men or groups. By extension, the verb *rîb* may refer to a verbal conflict, or quarreling. It may refer as well to a legal conflict. It often refers to God's judicial chidings of Israel for breaking the covenant. Most likely, in view of the setting of this verse, the thought here is of quarreling, verbal reproof of your neighbor when he is innocent of wrongdoing, v. 30.[32]

---

[30]The *qərê* reads *yadka* for *yadyka,* "thine hand." This rejects the dual for the singular. Grammatically, the change makes no difference in the meaning. Conant, p. 20, and Toy, p. 79, both accept the *qərê.* Zöckler, p. 60, notes that "there is no grammatical reason whatever for the change." KD I, 99, likewise rejects it.

[31]The word *lərecəyka* is irregular. Mitchell Dahood, "The Archaic Genitive Ending in Proverbs 31, 6," *Biblica* 56:241, repoints the word to *lərecika* and explains it as an archaic genitive ending. The word *reac,* however, occurs in irregular forms elsewhere, e.g., II Sam. 12:11, and the *yod* is probably just a remnant of an original *he.*

[32]McKane, p. 300, refers the verse to needless litigation. We have no evidence that this was a problem in biblical days. For this reason, it does not seem to call for biblical guidance. The injunction against needless quarreling would include the prohibition of senseless litigation.

31 Envy thou not the oppressor, and choose none of his ways.
*32 For the froward is abomination to the Lord: but his secret is with the
  righteous.*

31-32 These verses begin a series of warnings against the wicked.
We should not envy the "oppressor" (*ʾîš ḥamas*) nor choose to pattern
our ways after his manner of life. The word *ḥamas* regularly indicates
violence throughout the OT, normally sinful violence rather than the
violence of a natural calamity, e.g., Genesis 49:5; II Samuel 22:49;
Habakkuk 1:2. It may also be translated "wrong," e.g., Genesis 16:5;
I Chronicles 12:17; Job 19:7; Psalm 35:11 ("false"). Violent men are
often powerful men, successful to a degree. Thus the necessary warning
follows: "Choose none of his ways," v. 31.[33]

The reason for the warning of v. 31 follows immediately. The
"froward" (*lûz,* cf. 2:15) man is an abomination to the Lord. Each time
the *nipʿal* form occurs, the idea of deviousness or crookedness is appropriate. The "devious man" is thus an "abomination to the Lord," *tôʿᵊbat
yᵊhwah.* The word *tôʿᵊbat* refers to anything that is morally repulsive.
The word describes various abominations more than twenty times in
Proverbs. The phrase *tôʿᵊbat yᵊhwah* relates man's wicked conduct to
the Lord. The phrase occurs eleven times in the book, all of them describing the Lord's attitude toward man's evil conduct.

Abominations to God	
1. Devious actions, 3:32; 11:20	4. Evil actions, 15:9; 17:15
2. Stealing ("false balances"), 11:1; 20:10, 23	5. Evil thoughts, 15:26
	6. Lying, 12:22
3. False religion, 15:8	7. Pride, 16:5

In contrast, God's "secret is with the righteous." We translate this obscure phrase "but with the upright is His counsel." This understands
"counsel" (*sôd*) as having an element of confidentiality that distinguishes *sôd* from the more general *ʿeṣâ;* cf. 1:30. There is thus a stark
contrast between the wicked and the upright. The one is morally repul-

---

[33]The LXX suggests *tithar,* "be vexed at," rather than *tibhar,* "choose." McKane,
p. 300, adopts the reading as better suiting the parallelism. The textual evidence for the
change is weak, and the MT gives satisfactory parallelism.

33 The curse of the Lord is in the house of the wicked: but he blesseth
   the habitation of the just.
34 Surely he scorneth the scorners: but he giveth grace unto the lowly.
35 The wise shall inherit glory: but shame shall be the promotion of
   fools.

sive to the Lord while He takes the other into His confidence, revealing
His will to him by His Word and His Spirit, v. 32.

33-35 The passage recalls further contrasts between the wicked and
the righteous. God directs His curse (*mə'erat*) toward the house of the
wicked but blesses the dwelling of the righteous. The word *mə'erat* denotes the placing of obstacles, a "curse" in the sense of hindering the
way. God brings this upon the "house" of the wicked man, affecting not
only the wicked one himself but others of his family as well.

At the same time, God's blessing is upon the dwelling of the righteous.
The "blessing" is best understood here as a contrast to the curse. With
the one, God places obstacles in the path of the wicked. With the other,
He removes obstacles, giving every opportunity for smooth progress
along the path of life. This comes upon the "habitation" (*naweh*) of the
just. The basic idea of *naweh* is "pasture, sheepfold." It poetically represents the peaceful dwelling of the righteous (cf. Job 5:24), the place of
the shepherd's care (II Sam. 7:8), or a place of safety (Isa. 32:18). The
dwelling place is thus itself evidence of God's blessing upon the
righteous, v. 33.

God "scorneth the scorners." The *leṣ* (cf. 1:22) is one who has hardened himself against God. God responds to this rejection by rejecting
the scorner.[34] The verse underlies James 4:6 and I Peter 5:5. It gives still
one more significant contrast between the godly and the wicked. The
same God who turns from the scorner gives "grace unto the lowly," v. 34.

In the final contrast, we find that the wise (*ḥakamîm,* cf. 1:2) will inherit glory (*kabôd,* cf. v. 9) while fools (*kəsîl,* cf. 1:22) will receive only
"shame" (*qalôn*).[35] The word *qalôn* occurs seventeen times, eight of

---

[34]Beer, in BH, suggests that *'im⁻lalleṣîm,* "surely . . . the scorners," should be read
ʿim⁻leṣîm, "with the scorners." This follows the pattern set in Ps. 18:25-26. Driver,
Biblica 32:176, defends the MT. The text makes good sense as it stands.
[35]While the sense of the verse is clear, there is little agreement on how to reach it. The
problem revolves around the singular verb *merîm.* The AV takes *qalôn* as the subject and
translates, "shame shall be the promotion of fools." There would be better parallelism,

them in Proverbs.[36] In most cases, the term is general, denoting some form of public degradation, the loss of social esteem. It can refer to one whose nakedness has been openly displayed (Jer. 13:26; Nah. 3:5) or who is openly drunken (Hab. 2:16). It may refer to a slave (Isa. 22:18) or to idolatry (Hos. 4:7). It may also denote one who lacks a good reputation (Prov. 18:3). This is the portion of one who rejects godly ways.

however, if *merîm* could be parsed as a plural form. Accordingly, Thomas, *VTS* III, 282-83, emends to *mərîmîm*. G. R. Driver, "Notes on Some Passages in the Book of Proverbs," *JTS* 38:403, transposes *ukəsîlîm merîm* to *umiryam kəsîlîm*, "the desire of fools is shame(ful)." Later, *Biblica* 32:177, he suggests an emendation to *maddam*, "their garment." Joseph Reider, "Etymological Studies in Biblical Hebrew," *VT* 2:124, parses *merîm* as the plural participle of *mîr*, "to procure." B. Halper, "The Notions of Buying and Selling in Semitic Languages," *ZAW* 31:265, parses the verb as the *qal* plural participle of *mûr*, "to acquire," a form not occurring in Hebrew but supported from cognate languages. Others make still additional suggestions. Despite all the furor over the verb, the MT makes good sense as it stands. The form *merîm* occurs elsewhere at Exod. 35:24; Ps. 3:4; and, notably, at Prov. 14:29. We cannot arbitrarily derive the word from *mîr* or *mûr* since the regular use requires the source *rûm*. If we understand *kəsîlîm* distributively, the singular verb fits the verse. Likewise, we may understand the subject as an abstract plural. This would justify a singular verb.
[36]See 3:35; 6:33; 9:7; 11:2; 12:16; 13:18; 18:3; 22:10.

1 Hear, ye children, the instruction of a father, and attend to know understanding.
2 For I give you good doctrine, forsake ye not my law.
3 For I was my father's son, tender and only beloved in the sight of my mother.

PROVERBS 4
THE VALUE OF WISDOM

1-2 The new section begins with a call to the "children" (literally, "sons") to hear the "instruction [*mûsar,* cf. 1:2] of a father." The exhortation differs from previous ones, e.g., 1:8; 2:1; 3:1, in that the object, "sons," is plural. When coupled with v. 3, it is clear that Solomon speaks here of the instruction given him by his own father, David. Solomon's words, then, are not merely his own creative ideas. They reflect the wisdom of past generations which came to him. This coupling of three generations parallels the similar coupling in II Timothy 1:5.

Because these teachings reflect the time-tested wisdom of the fathers, they are good "doctrine" (*leqaḥ,* cf. 1:5). The sons should not "forsake" (*ʿazab,* cf. 2:13) this "law" (*tôrâ,* cf. 1:8). "Law" has a broad sense here, referring to the father's teachings to his son.

3 The AV translates "for," *kî,* as causal. It suits the context better if we give it a temporal sense: "when I was my father's son," i.e., still dwelling in his house. This gives the time frame for the teaching of v. 4. At this time, he was "tender [*rak*] and only *beloved* [*yaḥîd*]" in his mother's sight. The two terms reinforce one another in showing the deep love of Solomon's mother for her son. The word *rak* occurs sixteen times in the OT. It normally denotes something "soft, weak, or tender." The term *yaḥîd* occurs twelve times. It can refer to an only child (Judg. 11:34; Jer. 6:26). Sometimes, however, it lays stress on the preciousness of a unique thing (Ps. 22:20; 35:17). Since it parallels *rak* here, the emphasis lies on the nature of the relationship rather than on his being numerically an only son. Undoubtedly, he was an "only one" in the sense of being loved as though he were an only child.

*4 He taught me also, and said unto me, Let thine heart retain my
words: keep my commandments, and live.
5 Get wisdom, get understanding: forget it not; neither decline from
the words of my mouth.
6 Forsake her not, and she shall preserve thee: love her, and she shall
keep thee.*

4-6 David had urged Solomon: "Let thine heart [*leb*, cf. 3:5] retain
[*yitmak*] my words." In context, David undoubtedly had the will in view.
Solomon was to seize wholeheartedly upon David's instructions. The
verb *tamak*, "retain," further emphasizes this attitude. This word may
occur in contexts of spiritual or moral truths. Solomon should hold fast
these spiritual instructions from his father.

The second exhortation parallels the first: "keep [*šamar*, cf. 2:8] my
commandments [*miṣwâ*, cf. 3:1], and live [*hayâ*]." The word *hayâ* may
indicate earthly life or eternal life, e.g., 2:19; 13:14; 15:24. The context
must guide as to which sense is in view. There is no reason to see more
than earthly life here. The promise is for fullness of life, abundant life.
The consistent practice of wisdom gains this kind of life, v. 4.

In view of this, David had exhorted his son to acquire wisdom (*hokmâ*,
cf. 1:2) and understanding (*bîn*, cf. 1:2). He had warned him not to "forget" (*šakah*, cf. 3:1)[1] or "decline" (*natâ*) from his words. The verb *natâ*
has a wide range of meanings, one of which is to "turn away"; cf. 2:2.
In view of the importance of David's words, it is appropriate that he
warn his son against turning from them, v. 5.[2]

Verse 6a refers to the "wisdom" and "understanding" mentioned in
5a.[3] These are synonymous terms that provide a single antecedent to v. 6.

---

[1]Dahood, *PNWSP*, pp. 11-12, traces the source of *tiškah* to *šakah* II, "to wilt, be
weary," on the basis of a Ugaritic cognate. It is unlikely, however, that the well-known
šakah would take a specialized meaning here since its normal sense fits nicely into the
context.

[2]While the sense of vv. 4-5 is clear, attempts have been made to suggest textual
changes to improve the thought. Skehan, *CBQ* 9:193-94, states that *wêhayeh* in 4:4 is a
gloss picked up from 7:2. He further suggests that 4:5a is not original since the words
duplicate portions of 4:7. Toy, p. 87, omits 5b in order to make 5a the antecedent of v. 6.
The RSV reverses 5a and 5b to gain the same purpose. Despite this confusion, the MT
is clear and defensible as it stands. There is no need to change the text.

[3]The NEB reverses vv. 6-7 in order to find the antecedent for "her" in v. 7. Gemser,
p. 25, does the same, and Beer, BH, suggests this. There is no need for change since the
MT gives a clear sense.

7 Wisdom is the principal thing; therefore get wisdom: and with all thy getting get understanding.
8 Exalt her, and she shall promote thee: she shall bring thee to honour, when thou dost embrace her.
9 She shall give to thine head an ornament of grace: a crown of glory shall she deliver to thee.

Solomon should not "forsake" (ʿ*azab,* cf. 2:13) this wisdom. She will "preserve" (*šamar,* cf. 2:8) and "keep" (*naṣar,* cf. 2:8) him as she rewards his faithfulness, v. 6.

7-9 Literally, v. 7 says, "The beginning of wisdom is: Acquire wisdom."[4]

The meaning and translation of the verse depend upon the sense given the word *reʾšît* (cf. 1:7). This can mean "beginning" or "principal," depending on the context. Since the construction here is virtually the same as that found in 1:7 and 9:10, it is likely that *reʾšît* means "beginning" rather than "principal thing" as in the AV. Solomon teaches that the very effort of acquiring wisdom is wisdom. In other words, wisdom begins with the desire for wisdom.

The second half of the verse reinforces the thought: "with all thy getting, get understanding." The noun "getting" (from *qanâ*) refers to the purchased property of an individual. The verb *qanâ* regularly indicates the acquisition of something. The idea of the verse is that we should use all of our possessions for the gain of understanding (cf. *bîn,* 1:2), v. 7.

When we place this premium upon the quest for wisdom, she reciprocates by blessing us. When we "exalt" (*salal*) her, she rewards us. The verb *salal* may mean either "to lift up" (thus "to exalt") or "to plait" (thus "to embrace"). Either word fits the context.[5] To my way of thinking, there is a natural parallel between the first and last parts of 8*a*. We

---

[4]AB, p. 51; Charles T. Fritsch, *Proverbs,* in *The Interpreter's Bible* IV, ed. Arthur Buttrick (1955) (hereafter cited as IB), 409; McKane, p. 305; and Martin, p. 45, all suggest the possibility that the verse is an addition. They feel it intrudes into the text. Toy, p. 88, more forcefully states that "the text is corrupt, and the verse should probably be omitted." Contextually, however, the verse makes a smooth introduction to v. 8. The MT should be retained.

[5]Martin, p. 45, and AB, p. 49, choose "embrace." Garrett, p. 87, says "the notion of embracing is certainly present." Van der Wieden, p. 44, translates, "*Etreins-la,* 'embrace.'" The majority of commentators accept "exalt."

10 Hear, O my son, and receive my sayings; and the years of thy life shall be many.

11 I have taught thee in the way of wisdom; I have led thee in right paths.

12 When thou goest, thy steps shall not be straitened; and when thou runnest, thou shalt not stumble.

13 Take fast hold of instruction; let her not go: keep her; for she is thy life.

14 Enter not into the path of the wicked, and go not in the way of evil men.

15 Avoid it, pass not by it, turn from it, and pass away.

16 For they sleep not, except they have done mischief; and their sleep is taken away, unless they cause some to fall.

17 For they eat the bread of wickedness, and drink the wine of violence.

exalt her and, in turn, she exalts us. In addition to the promotion and honor bestowed by wisdom, she rewards the individual with ornaments (*liwyat⁻hen,* cf. 1:8-9). The nature of the ornament is left undeveloped since there are many ways in which wisdom can convey attractiveness, v. 9.

10 The second paragraph of the chapter begins by promising to reward the son's obedience. If he will keep the words of his father, he will gain all the years God desires him to have. The "many" years are a full life rather than a long life; cf. 3:16.

11-13 Solomon has led his son in "right paths" (*bəmaʿgəlê⁻yošer*). The word *maʿgal,* cf. 2:9, is metaphoric, referring to ways of life. The son has been "taught" in wise ways, v. 11. When he follows these teachings, he will not be hampered. Nothing will cause him to stumble, v. 12. He therefore should "take fast hold," grasping the instructions, not letting them slip from his mind and practice. They are the essentials of a full life, v. 13.

14-17 This is the third of three passages (also 1:10-14; 2:12-15) that describe the evil nature of the men whom the youth should avoid. From the emphasis here, it is clear that these men have a criminal bent to them. Because this perverted streak of evil governs their actions, Solomon charges the child to avoid close contact with them. He should avoid them so that he can avoid their evil ways.

Two possibilities exist as to the nature of these men. These answer the objections that a good man will not succumb to such blatant temptations

*18 But the path of the just is as the shining light, that shineth more and
more unto the perfect day.*
*19 The way of the wicked is as darkness: they know not at what they
stumble.*

as the offer to join a murderous ambush (1:11) or the offer to join with
one whose character is such that it would prevent him from sleeping at
night unless he had done some evil (4:16).

One possible description sees these verses as the divine view of evil
men. In reality, the innocent youth receives a much more subtle temptation. But under the smooth and enticing exterior of the wicked is a corrupt and perverted nature. The description arrests the attention of the
youth so that he will understand the true nature of the temptation that he
faces. Having understood, he will turn away from the enticement to do
evil.

The second view takes the passage more literally. The father warns his
son against substituting an immoral route in which he uses raw power in
order to gain material wealth and influence. In summary, this view considers the passage a warning against the position that "the end justifies
the means."

The youth, then, should turn from this way. These wicked men have
become so perverted that they do not sleep without first performing
some evil action against someone else. Their lives draw strength from
perversity. Wickedness has such a grip upon them that they must do evil
in order to find contentment, vv. 14-16.[6] Evil is as bread and wine to
them, nourishment to their souls. The verse vividly pictures the power of
sin in this present life (cf. 5:22), v. 17.

18-19 In the midst of a passage describing the criminal nature of the
wicked, the author places a single verse to show the blessedness of the
righteous as he turns from evil. Set against the darker background of
vv. 14-17, 19, the blessed condition of the righteous shines brightly.[7] His
path is like the light of the sun, first only a glimmer as it breaks into the

---

[6]The MT *yakšiwlû,* "they stumble," is not appropriate to the context. The *qərê yakšîlû,*
followed by the AV, "they cause *some* to fall," is the proper reading.

[7]Toy, p. 93; Skehan, *CBQ,* 9:194; KD I, 111; Oesterley, p. 32; Martin, p. 46; and
Greenstone, p. 42, all suggest that vv. 18 and 19 should be transposed to allow v. 19 to
connect naturally with v. 17. As with most suggestions of this kind, no textual evidence
supports the transposition. Verse 18 fits into the passage well in its present location.

20 My son, attend to my words; incline thine ear unto my sayings.
21 Let them not depart from thine eyes; keep them in the midst of thine
   heart.
22 For they are life unto those that find them, and health to all their
   flesh.

night sky, then growing stronger and stronger until it blazes forth with
its full noontime glory. The passage is important because of its unique-
ness. In KD I, 113, Delitzsch notes that this is the only passage in the
OT that pictures the gradual growth of the godly individual in the ways
of God. In the NT, only Mark 4:28 gives a similar picture of gradual development.

The "light" of v. 18 contrasts sharply with the darkness of v. 19. The
picture relates more naturally to the growing knowledge of divine truth
than to anything else. This knowledge, for the godly man, continues to
grow in its extent throughout life. It reaches its peak at that day when
we come into the presence of God, v. 18.

The ignorance of the wicked is "darkness" (*ka'ăpelâ*). The word *'apal*
regularly has a metaphorical use. It picturesquely indicates "gloom"
(Amos 5:20; Zeph. 1:15). When it takes its root meaning of darkness, it
indicates a deep darkness, as in the darkness of the ninth plague (Exod.
10:22) or the darkness of a blind man (Deut. 28:29).[8] Here, then, the life
of the wicked individual is as the height of darkness. He gropes along
his way but does not see the pitfalls ahead until it is too late. He will
"stumble" into the judgment of God, v. 19.

20-22 These verses call the son to obedience. Through the poetic
mention of various parts of the body, the author exhorts the son to devote himself to the practice of the teachings that he has received.
Initially, he should listen closely to his father's teachings, v. 20. Then,
having heard them, he should not allow them to "depart" (*lûz*, cf. 2:15)
from him through carelessness or indifference. As elsewhere, the "heart"
(*leb*, cf. 3:5) here denotes the will, v. 21. Such obedience will bring a
fullness of life to the obedient son; cf. 3:22; 4:13. Moreover, it will be

---

[8]Jones, p. 78, carries the interpretation of "darkness" to an extreme. He comments that
"there is always a dimension of the supernatural if not demonic in this word." While it is
true that the word may have a figurative sense to it (e.g., Isa. 8:22; 59:9), the metaphor
does not necessarily involve the demonic world. It regularly embraces the judgment that
men bring upon themselves through their sin (e.g., Joel 2:2; Zeph. 1:15).

23 Keep thy heart with all diligence; for out of it are the issues of life.
24 Put away from thee a froward mouth, and perverse lips put far from thee.
25 Let thine eyes look right on, and let thine eyelids look straight before thee.
26 Ponder the path of thy feet, and let all thy ways be established.
27 Turn not to the right hand nor to the left: remove thy foot from evil.

"health" (*marpe³*) to him. The word *marpe³* regularly indicates "healing" elsewhere in the book (e.g., 13:17; 16:24). Perhaps there is a hint here that the healing powers of spiritual wisdom overcome the ravages of sin, v. 22.

23-27 Verse 23 literally reads, "Above all guarding [*šamar*, cf. 2:8], guard [*naṣar*, cf. 2:8] your heart [*leb*, cf. 3:5]." As it often does, the *leb* indicates the mind. The concern for the keeping of one's own mind should transcend any other self-protecting act. This is so because the mind is the source of every thought, every word, and every action of man.[9] It is therefore appropriate to saturate one's own mind with the spiritual wisdom so abundantly given in God's Word, v. 23.

Verses 24-25 are first negative, then positive. The son must not react negatively to his father's teachings. The "froward" (or "perverse," *ciqqašût, caqaš*, cf. 2:15) mouth and the "perverse" (or "devious," *lûz*, cf. 2:15) lips should be put far away. By implication, the youth should readily accept the teachings of wisdom, v. 24.

Positively, the young man should look straight at the path along which he must travel. Again, by implication, he should not cast envious looks at the ways of evil men. Both "eyes" and "eyelids" (*capcappeyka*) poetically refer to one's gaze. The word "eyelids" comes from the verb *cûp*, "to fly." It refers to eyelids because of their fluttering motion, v. 25.

He should think well upon the path that he takes in order that his ways should be established, v. 26.[10] His path through life, then, must be one of

---

[9]Toy, pp. 97-98, takes the "guarding" of 23*a* as the antecedent to the pronoun "it." Thus, the act of "guarding" (= obedience) becomes the source of one's life. This is a possible interpretation if *tôṣ³ôt hayyîm*, "issues of life," is understood as life itself. This, however, neglects *tôṣ³ôt*, "outgoing." It is more likely that the "outgoings of life" refer to those things that find their source in the mind.

[10]The word "ponder" (*palles*) is variously taken as "to make level, prepare" (NIV; Kufeldt, p. 486; Toy, p. 99; Greenstone, p. 44; Frankenberg, p. 40) or "to weigh, consider" (NASB; Kidner, p. 68; McKane, p. 311; AB, p. 51; Aitken, p. 56). The Akkadian

complete adherence to the teachings of his father. He should not turn aside from these standards. He thus will keep himself from engaging in wicked actions, v. 27.

The Dedication of the Body to God 20-27

1. Ears 20—thus, we should listen only to godly words
2. Eyes 21*a*, 25—thus, we should look at that which builds us up
3. Heart 21*b*, 23—thus, we should set our affections on godly things
4. Mouth 24—thus, we should speak of godly matters
5. Feet 26-27—thus, we should walk in places that please the Lord

When we dedicate these to God, He gives "life," an abundant life, to our "flesh," v. 22.

---

cognate *palasu,* "to look upon, behold," argues for the meaning "to observe, consider." This sense is intelligible in each of the other two appearances of the verb in Prov. 5:6, 21.

Practical Applications from Proverbs 4

1. The need for children to obey their parents 1-2, 3-4, 10-13, 20-22
2. The need for a right relationship to wisdom: Embracing of Wisdom, Importance of Wisdom 7; Rewards of Wisdom 8-9
3. The importance of friends: Avoid the path of the wicked 14-17, 19; follow the path of the just 18
4. The importance of right thinking 23

1 My son, attend unto my wisdom, and bow thine ear to my understanding:
2 That thou mayest regard discretion, and that thy lips may keep knowledge.

PROVERBS 5
FIRST WARNING AGAINST ADULTERY

1-2 These verses introduce the chapter by once again urging the young man to follow his father's teaching.[1] The three exhortations addressed to "my son" (vv. 1, 7, 20) naturally mark the divisions of the chapter. Together, these three exhortations make up the first extended treatment of adultery in the book. Although the father advises his son, v. 18 makes it clear that the son is already married.[2]

The opening verses warn the son against adultery.[3] The father speaks to his son, urging him to follow the wise guidance that he is about to receive, v. 1. This will enable him to practice discreet and knowledgeable conduct despite the seductive nature of the adulteress's temptations.[4] We

---

[1]Kufeldt, p. 490, notes that this is the only place in the book where the pronoun "my" is used with either "wisdom" or "understanding." On this basis, he suggests that Solomon speaks out of his personal experience. While this cannot be proved, Solomon's lifestyle certainly included promiscuity and may well have served as the basis for his teachings.

[2]Kenneth T. Aitken, *Proverbs,* in *The Daily Study Bible,* ed. John C. L. Gibson (1986) (hereafter cited as Aitken), p. 65, makes vv. 1-14 refer to an unmarried man and vv. 15-23 to married men. The distinction is artificial. It is best to allow v. 18 to establish the context for the entire chapter.

[3]Norman C. Habel, "The Symbolism Wisdom in Proverbs 1-9," *Interpretation* 26:143, takes the section as a warning against cultic prostitution. McKane, p. 312, applies the passage to dealing with "sexual intercourse with prostitutes." Kathleen A. Farmer, *Who Knows What Is Good? A Commentary on the Books of Proverbs and Ecclesiastes,* in *International Theological Commentary,* ed. Fredrick Carlson Holmgren and George A. F. Knight (1991) (hereafter cited as Farmer), p. 41, understands the woman as a metaphor "for the lure of foreign ways." Verses 15-19, especially vv. 18-19, show that adultery is more in the mind of the author than mere prostitution or ritual cult worship. The many warnings against this sin in the OT and the context of a warning to the young man forcefully argue that the passage is literal.

[4]Oesterley, p. 34, is typical of many who conclude that the text is corrupt. They object that the idea of "lips" keeping knowledge is nonsensical and that some change is necessary. AB, pp. 53-54, suggests that there is a missing couplet following v. 2. From the similarity of words in 6:24 and 7:5, he supplies, "May preserve you from the adulteress, from the 'strange woman' with her smooth talk." There is no textual evidence to support this rather wild suggestion. The verse, however, makes good sense as explained above.

*3 For the lips of a strange woman drop as an honeycomb, and her
mouth is smoother than oil:*
4 But her end is bitter as wormwood, sharp as a twoedged sword.
5 Her feet go down to death; her steps take hold on hell.
*6 Lest thou shouldest ponder the path of life, her ways are moveable,
that thou canst not know them.*

understand the phrase "that thy lips may keep knowledge" to contrast
with v. 3. While the lips of the harlot are deceitful, speaking words that
lead one astray, the lips of the godly youth should speak only that which
springs from a wise and prudent heart, v. 2.[5]

3-6 On the surface, the words of the adulteress (cf. *zar,* 2:16) are ap-
pealing, honey-coated, and smoother than oil (cf. the example in 7:14-
21), v. 3. In reality, though, the promised pleasures leave a bitter taste in
the mouth of the youth and turn into a two-edged sword that wounds no
matter which way it strikes. The term "wormwood" represents the suffering that comes from man's wickedness or from divine punishment.[6]
Here, the woman produces bitter suffering in the young man's life. This
comes from yielding to her flattering speech.[7] Literally, the phrase "two-
edged sword" is a "sword of mouths," i.e., a sword that cuts no matter
how it is swung. The common translation is "double-edged sword." The
plural word, however, also includes the cutting potential of the point.
The sword thus has three ways of cutting. The plural brings this out, v. 4.
The adulteress herself ends her life with spiritual death. Her ways lead
to the spiritual judgment of eternal death, v. 5. We should translate v. 6
with a feminine subject rather than mixing the 2ms and the 3fs: "She

---

[5]Mitchell Dahood, "Honey That Drips: Notes on Proverbs 5,2-3," *Biblica* 54:65-66, derives "keep" (*yinṣorû*) from an unknown Hebrew verb *ṣry/w,* "to flow, ooze," on the basis
of cognate words. He translates, "and your lips ooze knowledge." It is unlikely that we
should replace the familiar verb *naṣar* with a word that does not otherwise occur. The
verb *naṣar* occurs elsewhere in the book to refer to the guarding of some ethical truth,
e.g., 2:8; 3:1.

[6]Wormwood (*laʿănâ*) is an aromatic plant (*Artemisia absinthium*) that grows two to
three feet high. It often grows in wilderness areas of desert regions. Small, roundish,
white blossoms droop from its branched stalks. The plant has a bitter taste. Its juice is
sometimes applied to clothing to repel insects. The word *laʿănâ* occurs seven other
times. It metaphorically indicates divine judgment (Jer. 9:15; 23:15; Lam. 3:15, 19) or
the suffering that comes from human wickedness (Deut. 29:18; Amos 5:7; 6:12).

[7]Among others, Jones, p. 81, takes the phrase "her end" to refer to the adulteress's own
end, what happens to her. This is possible; however, the description given above, the effect she has upon the man, is more in keeping with the general context of vv. 9-11.

7 Hear me now therefore, O ye children, and depart not from the words of my mouth.
8 Remove thy way far from her, and come not nigh the door of her house:
9 Lest thou give thine honour unto others, and thy years unto the cruel:
10 Lest strangers be filled with thy wealth; and thy labours be in the house of a stranger;
11 And thou mourn at the last, when thy flesh and thy body are consumed,
12 And say, How have I hated instruction, and my heart despised reproof;
13 And have not obeyed the voice of my teachers, nor inclined mine ear to them that instructed me!
14 I was almost in all evil in the midst of the congregation and assembly.

does not consider the way of life; her ways are unstable; she does not know *it.*" The verbs focus on the actions of the adulteress. She does not consider the path that leads to eternal life; rather, she staggers, as though drunken, along her evil path through life. She does not realize its inevitable end. As she moves along the path of life toward her eventual judgment, she is ignorant that her ways lead to this end. She staggers from one sensual thrill to another, unconcerned and uncaring about her ultimate fate.[8] "She" does not distinguish the error of her evil way, v. 6.[9]

7-14 The passage now develops the nature of the punishment that will come upon those who ignore the warnings against adultery. Initially, Solomon exhorts his "children" (lit., "sons") to flee from the adulterous woman.[10] The advice rests upon the fact that temptation comes from the

---

[8]The word "lest" (*pen*) does not normally precede the principal clause of a verse. Toy, p. 107, calls it "unintelligible" and suggests an emendation. Frankenberg, p. 41, omits the line. To explain this unusual construction, KD I, 121, takes the word as an emphatic negative. Prov. 9:13 also mentions the ignorance of the woman. Hulst, *OTTP*, p. 115, defends the usual meaning of "lest," taking the verb as a 2ms and translating generally with the AV.

[9]D. Winton Thomas, "A Note on לא תדע in Proverbs v 6," *JTS* 37:59-60, suggests that *teda*ᶜ is from *yada*ᶜ II, "to become still, quiet, at rest." He supports this from cognate studies. There is no need to adopt the suggestion. The verb *yada*ᶜ occurs widely with the sense of "knowing." This meaning fits the context here.

[10]Dahood, *PNWSP*, p. 12, explains the plural "children" (*banîm*) as a singular noun with an enclitic *mem*. Toy, p. 111, emends to the singular as in 5:1, 20, and in the LXX and makes the verbs singular. The difficulty in emending *banîm* is that the verb "depart" (*tasûrû*) in 7*b* is plural. It is true that verbs and pronouns in vv. 8-13 are singular, but this does not require a change in v. 7. It seems likely that the author set down his thoughts on the subject of adultery, applying them first to all of his sons and then focusing on his first-born.

mere presence of such a woman. For this reason, she should be avoided; one should not even come near her house. To do otherwise provides for the flesh and opens the door to a willful violation of God's standard. Cohen illustrates the principle of the verse by quoting the proverb "Do not play with fire lest you be burnt," vv. 7-8.

In the first place, the man who involves himself with adultery may suffer irreparable harm to his reputation among others. The writer cautions the young man against losing his "honour" (hôd) before others.[11] This is the only use of hôd in the book. It occurs throughout the OT, primarily in the poetic and prophetic sections. Consistently, when used of God, hôd indicates His majesty and glory (e.g., Ps. 8:1; Hab. 3:3). When used of man, it denotes his splendor, honor, or dignity (e.g., Num. 27:20; Ps. 21:5). The young man, then, loses his dignity, his reputation, by means of his involvement with the evil woman.

Moreover the youth may lose his "years" (šanâ) to the "cruel." The normal sense of years fits nicely into the context.[12] The parallelism with 9a suggests that he will lose the strength of his years. He will lose his youthful health and energy as the direct result of his adultery. The "cruel" will take the physical strength of the youth from him. The term "cruel" is indefinite. This has led to many suggestions about its meaning.[13] The fact that the word parallels "others" suggests that a group of individuals have banded together to persecute the youth physically and

---

[11]There is disagreement over the meaning of hôd. Jones, p. 82, suggests that the word means "substance," covering both physical strength and wealth. Toy, p. 108, relies on the parallelism with v. 10 and concludes that hôd must mean "wealth." KD I, 123-24, suggests that it refers to the "freshness of the bloom of youth." Power, p. 102, and Allen Ross, *Proverbs*, in *The Expositor's Bible Commentary* (1991) (hereafter cited as *EBC*), V, 928, refer it to "vigour." Oesterley, p. 36, emends the word on the basis of the LXX to read "thy life." Other suggestions also exist. None of these, however, follow the normal use of the word elsewhere.

[12]D. Winton Thomas, "The Root שנה = سني in Hebrew II," *ZAW* 55:174-75, concludes on the basis of an Arabic cognate that šanâ should be glossed "dignity." While this has the attraction of paralleling hôd, it is highly unlikely that such a widely used word as šanâ would require this specialized meaning here. The sense given above, "strength of years," suits the context.

[13]Zöckler, p. 78, relates the word to the husband of the faithless wife, one who punishes his wife's love with unrestrained fury. Power, p. 102, translates, "aliens," apparently following the Targum, which reads "strangers." Kidner, p. 70, suggests that it implies a blackmailer. Moses Stuart, *Commentary on the Book of Proverbs* (1860) (hereafter cited as Stuart), p. 191, says that the term refers to the slavery into which the young man is sold as punishment for his adultery. The interpretation given above has the support of the immediate context.

materially. The group possibly includes the adulteress and her accomplices who cruelly oppress their victim, v. 9.

There is another category of punishment. The guilty man may suffer materialistic oppression, losing much of his personal wealth. Nothing is said about the means whereby this punishment takes place. God, however, is the ultimate source of power behind each of the punishments that fall upon the adulterer. The means for bringing about this penalty lie well within the routine exercise of His omnipotence.

The word *koaḥ*, "wealth," normally means "strength," and some take it in this sense here.[14] In context, however, the word indicates the means whereby the man produces his material possessions. The word poetically indicates the possessions themselves. The parallel phrase in 10*b* strengthens the idea that the adulterous man will find himself impoverished as the result of his actions. Apparently, the adulteress and her circle of friends draw upon his material goods until he comes to ruin, v. 10.[15]

The young man will lament (*naham*) the loss of his bodily strength. The root "lament" (*naham*) occurs nine times in the OT, five as a verb and four as a noun. Five times it pictures the roar of a lion (Prov. 19:12; 20:2; 28:15; Isa. 5:29) and once the roar of the sea (Isa. 5:30). Three times it refers to the judgment of a man (Ps. 38:9; Prov. 5:11; Ezek. 24:23). The translation "groan" is acceptable at 5:11. The indefinite nature of vv. 11-12 does not let us be dogmatic about the exact significance of this loss. At the least, it is the total exhaustion of the man's physical powers as the oppression from the "cruel" (v. 9) brings him to the limit of his self-reliance. At the other extreme, it refers to the broken physical condition of someone inflicted with a disease like AIDS or venereal disease. This is a common outcome from an illicit sexual relationship involving a promiscuous woman, v. 11.[16]

---

[14]Among others, Plaut, p. 76; Cohen, p. 27; and French and Skinner, p. 14, understand *koaḥ* to refer to "strength."

[15]Whybray, p. 36, states that the woman's husband takes action against the adulterer that impoverishes him. This interpretation goes counter to the text, which states that "strangers" benefit from his downfall.

[16]Toy, p. 109, says that the man comes to a state in which he is "consumed" and then, curiously, states that this relates "to the loss of social position and power." The view does not agree with the text.

15 Drink waters out of thine own cistern, and running waters out of thine own well.
16 Let thy fountains be dispersed abroad, and rivers of waters in the streets.
17 Let them be only thine own, and not strangers' with thee.
18 Let thy fountain be blessed: and rejoice with the wife of thy youth.
19 Let her be as the loving hind and pleasant roe; let her breasts satisfy thee at all times; and be thou ravished always with her love.

The guilty man has mental anguish and conviction over the nature and extent of his sin. In addition to his groan over the decay of his body, his conscience also condemns him over the failure to follow his earlier training. The word "how" (*'êk*) often introduces a lament, e.g., Jeremiah 9:19; Obadiah 6. It does this here as the son realizes that his own actions have brought him into this state. He bitterly engages in self-recrimination over his indifference to the teaching that he has spurned, vv. 12-13.

The son mentions the extent of the results that have come from his adultery. He characterizes these as "all evil" (or "utter ruin," *ra‘*, cf. 1:33). This indicates the magnitude of his judgment. Elsewhere, in 6:33, the punishment of the adulterous man involves "wounds and disgrace," apparently a public scourging with its accompanying shame. This, potentially, was the lot of the adulterer in this situation, and he acknowledges it with the statement, v. 14.[17]

15-19 This passage uses a rare allegory as Solomon picturesquely teaches the need for faithfulness to one's wife. The passage strongly implies that the wife can satisfy her husband's emotional needs so that there is no need for adulterous activity. Although the instruction is brief, it still communicates God's standard of faithfulness for the husband. The sexual union, the highest expression of the unity that marks the couple's love relationship, must not be taken lightly. The husband must not look upon this as a means only for gratifying his physical lusts.

---

[17]Others take the word *ra‘* to refer to the evil conduct of the adulterer as he acknowledges the unrestrained wickedness that he has openly exhibited before others. *PC*, p. 111, and Perowne, p. 63, both understand the word this way. The context, however, argues strongly that the phrase should include one more of the consequences of the man's actions, i.e., some reference to his public chastisement. Plaut, p. 80, relates this to the Mishnaic penalty (Sota VI 1) of scourging.

The love relationship draws the husband and wife together. In view of this, Solomon poetically exhorts the husband to remain faithful to his wife. The husband should find satisfaction in drinking from his own source of water. "Water," of course, has the same sense here as in 9:17, both referring to sensual pleasures, v. 15.[18] The "fountains" and "waters" of v. 16 poetically picture children. Numbers 24:7 and Hosea 13:15 use the same image to represent children. These stream forth to be joined with the flowing waters of other marriage unions, thus forming new rivers that repeat the propagation cycle, v. 16.[19] In order to maintain this ideal, the man and his wife must practice sexual purity. The children should be his alone, not those fathered by unknown individuals. The repeated 2ms pronoun emphasizes this thought, v. 17.

In language that suggests the Song of Solomon, the text now urges the husband to find delight and satisfaction in his wife. Underlying the entire passage is the truth that sexual pleasure is a gift from God for man's enjoyment and overall good. Through this action, the woman satisfies the God-instilled sex drive within her husband. Clearly, the Scriptures do not associate evil with this aspect of marriage. The act of copulation normally and wholesomely expresses love when carried out within the bonds of marriage, v. 18.[20]

The wife is as "a loving hind (*'ayyelet*) and pleasant doe (*ya'alat*)." The word *'ayyalâ* occurs eleven times elsewhere, all in poetic contexts. It refers to the "hind," the female deer. The *ya'alâ* is the "doe," a female goat, an animal that moves gracefully over the wild terrain of Palestine.

---

[18]The passage refers to sensual pleasures, not to children. So, among others, Kufeldt, p. 491; Perowne, p. 63; Toy, p. 112; and Aitken, p. 65. Song 4:12 uses the same image.

[19]If the passage is referred to sensual pleasures, v. 16 is often taken as a question rather than a statement (see G.K. 150a). The NASB and NIV, along with Toy, p. 113; McKane, p. 218; Zöckler, p. 79; Plaut, p. 77; and Paul A. Kruger, "Promiscuity or Marriage Fidelity? A Note on Prov. 5:15-18," *JNSL* 13:61-68, interpret the verse in this manner. A variation of this view supplies a negative particle and translates, "let not thy springs. . . ." Oesterley, p. 37, and Power, p. 102, follow this approach. The positive exhortation of vv. 18-19, however, favors the translation of the AV and the interpretation that the passage encourages fidelity within the marriage union.

[20]Toy, p. 118, suggests *bə'ešet,* "with the wife," instead of *me'ešet,* "from the wife," since *me'ešet* occurs elsewhere only at II Chron. 20:27 and Eccles. 2:10. Dahood, *PNWSP*, p. 12, argues for the MT on the basis of Ugaritic. Van der Weiden, p. 60, similarly supports the MT. In my judgment, the *min*-preposition fits nicely here. It signifies the source from which the husband is to draw his pleasure.

20 And why wilt thou, my son, be ravished with a strange woman, and embrace the bosom of a stranger?
21 For the ways of man are before the eyes of the Lord, and he pondereth all his goings.

These emblems come from animals that show affection for their young. While we might not think of the terms "hind" and "goat" as complimentary, this is a cultural matter. To the Jewish mind, this was a natural reference. See Song of Solomon 2:9, 17; 4:1, 2; 6:5. The wife centers her affections upon her husband. He therefore should be satisfied with her physical charms.[21] Her love alone should "ravish" (*šagâ*) him. The word *šagâ* means "to go astray, err," and by extension "to be intoxicated." The idea here is that the youth is intoxicated with the love of his wife.[22]

20-21 Since God is holy, He must punish those who violate His commandments. The man who is unfaithful to his wife invites the chastening of God. Solomon warns the young man about the dangers of adultery since the Lord Himself will judge one who involves himself with this. In view of this judgment, Solomon rhetorically asks why anyone would give in to the enticements of this woman, v. 20.

Should the youthful husband give in to unfaithfulness, the omnipresent Lord will see his actions.[23] Moreover, the Lord will not only note his sin but He will also reflect (see *palles,* 4:26) upon the nature of the actions. Undoubtedly, the Lord ponders such things as the amount of spiritual

---

[21]Greenstone, p. 52; AB, p. 58; Gemser, p. 28; and Frankenberg, p. 44, suggest emending *daddeyha* to *doddeyha,* "her love," on the grounds that it better parallels 19*b* and agrees with 7:18. But *daddeyha* is also erotic and parallels 19*b* satisfactorily. There is no need for the change, which has only weak textual support in the LXX.

[22]Driver, *Words and Meanings,* ed. Peter Ackroyd and Barnabas Lindards (1968), p. 51, suggests the meaning "to be wrapped up, addicted to" for *šagâ,* basing the idea on Arabic parallels. Thus, the youth should be "wrapped up" in the love of his wife, v. 19. Why should he be "wrapped up in a strange woman," v. 20? He is "wrapped up in the abundance of his folly," v. 23. McKane, pp. 218, 319, follows Driver. The suggestion fails to account for the appearance of *šagâ* in 19:27; 20:1, where the meaning "to be wrapped up" is not satisfactory. The *hipᶜîl* form in 28:10 can be translated either way.

[23]McKane, p. 313, doubts that the Yahwistic motif is original to the passage. He states that there is no trace elsewhere in the chapter of Yahweh's interaction in the affairs of men. He therefore feels that these verses are a reinterpretive expansion of the chapter. Solomon's writings, however, refer elsewhere to the omniscience of God. The identical phrase occurs in 15:3; 22:12, showing that God knows what happens throughout the earth. In view of this repetitive use of *ᶜênê yahwah,* I reject McKane's suggestion. Verses 21-23 furnish a natural conclusion to the warning of vv. 1-20.

22 His own iniquities shall take the wicked himself, and he shall be holden with the cords of his sins.
23 He shall die without instruction; and in the greatness of his folly he shall go astray.

light that has been spurned and the spiritual maturity of the guilty party. Taking these matters into account, the verse implies that God judges the offending one, v. 21.[24]

22-23 These verses highlight still another result of adultery. A man who enters into a relationship with the unfaithful wife of another man will find that the relationship soon becomes habitual. Once the man whets his sensual appetites, the increased desire becomes an immoral straightjacket that binds him in its power. The man's own sins bind him fast, v. 22.[25] He continues blindly in his actions, blissfully ignoring God's commandments. This leads him "astray" (*šagâ*, cf. 5:19) from the path that potentially could give him spiritual life, v. 23.[26]

---

[24]While the discussion focuses on the man, the principle holds true for the woman as well. The word *ʾîš* readily refers generically to mankind, e.g., Job 34:21; Ps. 1:1; Isa. 5:3.

[25]On the basis of very weak textual support, Toy, p. 118, omits "the wicked," *ʾet̄ harašaʿ*, and emends *yilkədunô*, "shall take . . . himself," to *yilkədun*, "shall catch him." McKane, p. 218, follows his line of reasoning. The evidence for the MT is far stronger, and it makes good sense as it stands.

[26]Many commentators feel that the verb must have a stronger sense. Toy, p. 119, suggests that some other verb such as *gawaʿ*, "to perish," should be substituted. KD I, 132, translates *šaga*, "staggers to ruin." Power, p. 102, translates the verb as "perish," its figurative sense. IB 4, 816, emends the verb to *yighwaʿ*, "is lost." These suggestions seek to strengthen the warning. The translation "go astray," however, adequately conveys the meaning of the word.

Practical Applications from Proverbs 5

1. Obedience to parents 1-2, 7
2. Warning against adultery 3-6, 8-14, 20-23
   a. Nature of her speech 3
   b. Prospect of her judgment 4-6
   c. Results of adultery 9-14, 20-23
      (1) Damage to reputation (9*a*, 14),
          personal health (9*b*, 11),
          loss of material possessions (10),
          reaction of conscience (12-13)
      (2) Divine judgment 20-21
      (3) Sin's power 22-23
3. Faithfulness to wife 15-19

1 My son, if thou be surety for thy friend, if thou hast stricken thy hand
with a stranger,
2 Thou art snared with the words of thy mouth, thou art taken with the
words of thy mouth.
3 Do this now, my son, and deliver thyself, when thou art come into the
hand of thy friend; go, humble thyself, and make sure thy friend.
4 Give not sleep to thine eyes, nor slumber to thine eyelids.
5 Deliver thyself as a roe from the hand of the hunter, and as a bird
from the hand of the fowler.

PROVERBS 6
MISCELLANEOUS WARNINGS

Due to the stylistic differences between the first and second halves,
many assume that the material in this chapter has been collected and edited.[1] The first part consists of four short sections that take up topics not
seen extensively in the prologue: surety, vv. 1-5; the sluggard, vv. 6-11;
the evil man, vv. 12-15; and sins that displease the Lord, vv. 16-19. With
regard to the stylistic differences, other wisdom literature from the ancient Near East also covers a variety of topics with no unifying theme,
e.g., *Counsels of Wisdom, Instruction of Amen-em-opet*. Further, the repetition of topics, as in 6:1 (cf. 11:15; 17:18; 20:16 [27:13]; 22:26) and
6:20-35 (cf. 5:1-23; 7:1-27), is also a stylistic feature of wisdom literature.

1-5 The first section gives specialized advice for the area of personal
finances. It is common for close associates to enter into surety bond
arrangements. The advice given here is therefore practical. It pertains to
an experience that many people face.

The advice relates to a situation that developed after Israel settled into
the land. Initially, the Mosaic law charged the people to offer financial aid
to those in need, e.g., Exodus 22:25; Leviticus 25:35-37. No interest was
necessary when one Israelite borrowed from another. With the passage of

---

[1]Toy, p. 119, states of vv. 1-19: "It is not likely that they were here inserted by the author of this Division; they were probably misplaced by an editor or scribe, and at an
early period, since they occur here in all the Ancient versions." AB, p. 58, says that the
material in vv. 1-19 is "generally recognized as intrusive here." Greenstone, p. 54, comments: "Because of the detached character of the first division, 1-19, it is regarded as
out of place here, inserted from some other part of the book." All of the ancient versions
include vv. 1-19 in their present locations. There is thus no reason to conclude that an
editor is responsible for the arrangement.

time, a business community developed as well as an agrarian society. Personal needs no longer determined financial requirements. Now, the obligations of business brought the need for borrowing. Since these loans had an element of risk, the lenders began the practice of seeking surety to guarantee repayment. This section gives advice to guide a person's response when approached by someone else about becoming surety for a loan.

The passage assumes that the young man has already burdened himself with a surety agreement. He has been "snared" by his rash pledge to give security for another's loan, vv. 1-2. He must therefore set about to undo the financial agreement with all of the vigor that he can muster, vv. 3-5.

The "friend" (*rea^c*) and "stranger" (*zar,* cf. 2:16) are the same person. The word *rea^c* simply refers to a friend. The context must show whether this is casual or close. The word *rea^c* itself is inconclusive. The youth has "stricken" (*taqa^c*) his hand with this one. This is an idiomatic expression akin to our modern handshake (Job 17:3; Prov. 22:26). This guarantees the son's means as surety for the loan. The word *rea^c* occurs broadly throughout the OT. It denotes a friend, neighbor, or companion of some kind. It may indicate either a close or a casual relationship, but here, used in parallel with *zar,* the relationship is more casual. The *zar* is a "stranger" in the sense of being outside of one's accustomed circle of movement. He may or may not be a foreigner. He is one who does not have a formal association with the individual.

From the situation described here, it is clear that the *rea^c* and the *zar* are the same person, the debtor rather than the creditor.[2] In order to release himself from the financial obligation, the youth must return to the

---

[2]McKane, pp. 321-22, argues that the "friend" is the creditor. He reasons from v. 3*b* that the youth is in the power of the friend. At the same time, the "stranger" is the debtor whose default on the loan places the youth in such an awkward position. The parallelism of the verse, however, involves the juxtaposition of the words and also the identical use of the *lamed* preposition. This favors the identification of the two people. Further, the additional reference in v. 3 favors the identification of these two with the debtor, rather than the creditor. It would do little good to plead with a creditor for release from the obligation. Robert L. Giese Jr., "Strength Through Wisdom and the Bee in LXX-Prov 6,8^{a-c}," *Biblica* 73:405, argues that the *zar* and *rea^c* must be different. He states that *rea^c* "is never used of a fellow citizen who is not known in some way." This misses the point. The *rea^c* here is not a close friend; thus he is a *zar.* Compare 14:20; 18:24 (see notes); and 19:4, 6 for examples of the *rea^c* being a casual friend.

debtor and seek his freedom from the bargain. The debtor can do this either by paying the debt for which the young man is security or by securing his debt through another means.

Verse 2 concludes v. 1.[3] If the youth has become surety for a *zar,* his words have "snared" (*yaqoš*) him. The verb *yaqoš* often has the metaphorical sense of trapping a person, e.g., 20:25; 22:24-25; 29:6. Thus the statement of surety binds the youth, keeping him from gaining financial freedom, vv. 1-2.

The youth should vigorously seek his release. He "humbles" (*rapas*) himself. The word *rapas* has the root meaning "to trample"; cf. Psalm 68:30 and Ezekiel 34:18. Used in the *hitpaˤel* theme with a reflexive sense, it conveys the idea that the youth should "trample himself," i.e. humble himself. This picturesquely shows his self-humiliation as he pleads with the debtor to release him from his bond.[4]

The youth should "make sure" (*rahab*) his friend. The verb *rahab* has the root meaning "to act stormily." Thus, he should earnestly petition the debtor as he tries to gain release from his financial obligations. He does not merely request the debtor to free him. He assails him with the fervor of his plea as he presses home his need for release from the surety agreement. This approach alone will "deliver" him, v. 3.[5]

He must not sleep or even doze. This idiomatic expression indicates that he should not rest as he pursues his goal, v. 4. Like a "roe" (or "gazelle") caught in the hand of the hunter, or the bird in the fowler's control, he should struggle to free himself, v. 5.[6]

---

[3]Many others extend the introduction through v. 2. This makes v. 2 part of the "if" clause. The thought is "if thou art snared . . . if thou are taken. . . ." Verse 3 then is the conclusion. So, among others, Muenscher, p. 59; Greenstone, p. 56; *EBC,* p. 931; Zöckler, p. 83; and Plaut, p. 83. Either approach gives good sense. It is a question of how far the control of "if," *ʾim,* in v. 1 extends.

[4]Others understand *rapas* in the sense of "bestir thyself, make haste." So Martin, p. 52; Whybray, p. 39; and Toy, p. 121. G. R. Driver, "Some Hebrew Verbs, Nouns, and Pronouns," *JTS* 30:374-75, relates *rapas* to the Akkadian *rapasû,* "to tread," thence, "to tread oneself, to crush," and the metaphorical sense "to weary oneself." The Aramaic cognate means "to tread down." The only other occurrence of *rapas* in the *hitpaˤel,* "submit himself," Ps. 68:30, can be understood as a picture of one humbling himself.

[5]With no textual support, Toy, p. 120, deletes *wəhinnaṣel,* "deliver thyself," as an insertion picked up from v. 5. The change is unnecessary.

[6]The phrase "of the hunter" is supplied, the Hebrew only giving *mîyad,* "from the hand." The LXX emended this to *maṣod* (Greek βροχων, "net"). AB, p. 56, suggests *mîyad ṣayyād,* "from a hunter's hand," with the second word having fallen out due to the

The entire subject of suretyship presents a problem. The passage clearly forbids this. Yet, just as clearly, other portions of the Bible refer to it as a practice among God's people, e.g., 20:16; 27:13. In some cases, it is seen as a godly action.[7] Moreover, even Proverbs imposes an obligation to assist the poor and friends (14:21, 31; 29:7). Thus, the propriety of acting as surety for another person's financial obligation raises questions.

One possibility for resolving the dilemma focuses on the word *zar,* "stranger"; cf. v. 1. This word basically denotes one who is not a member of a group, one who is an outsider to the circle of close relationships within that group. The warning thus would be that the youth should not enter into a surety relationship with one whom he knows only slightly. The passage then would allow the young man to assist a close friend who was poverty-stricken. At the same time, it provides the youth with sound financial advice in connection with casual relationships.

A second way to resolve the issue distinguishes between loans made to relieve poverty and loans made for business purposes. The first satisfies a Christian obligation, but the second incurs an unnecessary element of risk. The wise child could morally offer his support to a person who was destitute. At the same time, he could refuse support to an individual who simply sought a means of financial gain.

---

same ending. Toy, p. 130, substitutes *pah,* "snare," for *yad,* "hand." Plaut, p. 84, reads *mîyod* but translates it according to late rabbinical usage, "at once." McKane, p. 323, emends to *ṣayyad,* "hunter." From the verse, *mîyad* in 5*a* parallels *mîyad* in 5*b*. Where the meaning is clear, it is not unusual to supply words. Thus, "of the hunter" or some such phrase is appropriate.

[7]References to suretyship outside of Proverbs include Gen. 43:9; 44:32-33 (Judah's guarantee of Benjamin's safety); Neh. 5:5 (children of the resettled Jerusalemites who had been delivered over to slavery in payment for their fathers' debts); Job 17:3 and Isa. 38:14 ("undertake," i.e., become surety); Ps. 119:122 (God's position as surety for His people); Philem. 19 (Paul's guarantee of Philemon's debts); and Heb. 7:22 (Christ's guarantee of the new covenant).

6 *Go to the ant, thou sluggard; consider her ways, and be wise:*
7 *Which having no guide, overseer, or ruler,*
8 *Provideth her meat in the summer, and gathereth her food in the harvest.*
9 *How long wilt thou sleep, O sluggard? when wilt thou arise out of thy sleep?*
10 *Yet a little sleep, a little slumber, a little folding of the hands to sleep:*
11 *So shall thy poverty come as one that travelleth, and thy want as an armed man.*

6-11 The second part of the chapter focuses on the sluggard. The author uses the ant as an example of industriousness.[8] The sluggard (ʿaṣel) should learn from this small creature rather than persisting in his laziness and coming to eventual ruin. The ʿaṣel is almost completely a man of Proverbs. In all of its forms, the word occurs eighteen times. All but two of these are in Proverbs. In Judges 18:9, the *nipʿal* form has the sense of being sluggish, i.e., hesitating. The noun also occurs in Ecclesiastes 10:18. Over and over, the word carries with it the sense of not working (13:4; 21:25; 24:30) or of sleeping (6:9; 19:24; 26:14). Here, the ant sets an example for the nonworking sluggard, v. 6.

This insect gets along without a structured supervisory group. The terms "guide" (or "leader"), "overseer" (or "foreman"), and "ruler" occur loosely with no great distinction between them, v. 7.[9] Yet, this small insect gathers its food during the warm weather when it is able to work, v. 8.

How long will the sluggard continue in his sleep? The questions call the sluggard's attention to his laziness, v. 9. Solomon graphically warns

---

[8]The ant set an example in other Near Eastern cultures as well. Compare W. F. Albright, "An Archaic Hebrew Proverb in an Amarna Letter from Central Palestine," *BASOR* 89:29, in which he quotes from the Amarna tablets. These were found at Tell el Amarna, two hundred miles south of Cairo. Tablet no. 252 says, "If ants are smitten, they do not accept (the smiting) quietly, but they bite the hand of the man who smites them."

[9]KD I, 140, relates these offices "to the highest judiciary, police, and executive powers." *PC*, pp. 125-26, relates them to judicial leaders, general leaders, and rulers. The OT does not make a clear distinction between the words. The "guide," *qaṣîn,* denotes both civil (Mic. 3:1) and military (Josh. 10:24) leaders. The "overseer," *šoṭer,* is a lesser official (Deut. 20:5, 8, 9) or a foreman of a group of workers (Exod. 5:10, 14, 15, 19). The "ruler," *mošel,* is a ruler (Gen. 45:8). Most probably, here, the terms simply show randomly the lack of leadership over the ant as it works.

12 A naughty person, a wicked man, walketh with a froward mouth.
13 He winketh with his eyes, he speaketh with his feet, he teacheth with
  his fingers;
14 Frowardness is in his heart, he deviseth mischief continually; he
  soweth discord.
15 Therefore shall his calamity come suddenly; suddenly shall he be
  broken without remedy.

him.[10] A little more sleep, a little more delay before beginning work, v.
10, and poverty will surely come upon him. "One that travelleth
[*məhallek*]" is "one who walks." The *pi⁽ᶜ⁾el* theme intensifies the thought.
Poverty will vigorously march its way into his life.[11]

In the same way, want will come "as an armed man" (*magen*, cf. 2:7).
Since *magen* refers to the small rounded shield sometimes carried by
soldiers into battle, this refers to "a shielded man." His "want" shields
itself against futile efforts to bring prosperity into his life, v. 11.[12]

12-15 The third part of the chapter describes some characteristics of a
wicked man. This is poetic, with different parts of the body pictured as
they contribute to the evil of this person. Verse 15 climaxes the description, showing that all of his wickedness will come to naught when the
judgment of God falls on him.

He is "naughty" (*bəlîyaᶜal*) and "wicked" (*ʾawen*). The word *bəlîyaᶜal*
likely comes from *bəlî*, "no," and *yaᶜal*, "worth" (or "use"), thus "without worth or use, worthless."[13] The word occurs again at 16:27 and
19:28. In each case, the meaning of "worthless man" adequately expresses the sense.

---

[10]Among others, Alden, Coates, French and Skinner, and Plaut interpret the verse as
though the statement "a little sleep . . . ," were the response of the sluggard as he pleads
for just a little bit more sleep. The passage, however, is repeated in 24:33-34 and the
context there does not allow this to be a response. It is a statement about what will result
from this man's laziness.

[11]To emphasize the thought, Greenstone, p. 59, and Plaut, p. 87, translate "like a run-
ner." Both Power, p. 103, and Zöckler, p. 84, understand the term to refer to a "highwayman," one who is out on the road. McKane, p. 324, understands the meaning as
"vagrant." These all interpret the phrase "one that travelleth."

[12]W. F. Albright, "Canaanite-Phoenician Sources of Hebrew Wisdom," *VTS* III, 10,
suggests that *magen* is "meaningless here." He thus repoints it to *môgēn* or *maggān*,
"beggar." McKane, pp. 324-25, and AB, p. 59, follow Albright. None of these suggestions add materially to the MT, which makes suitable sense. The word *magen* is not rare,
occurring about sixty times. It is best to understand it in the traditional sense.

[13]Another possibility finds its source in *balaᶜ*, either "to swallow" (so D. Winton
Thomas, "בְּלִיַּעַל in the Old Testament," *Biblical and Patristic Studies*, ed. J. N.

The word *ʾawen* is not in the Pentateuch but occurs widely elsewhere. It occurs ten times in Proverbs. Twice, it is connected with speech (17:4; 19:28) and once with adultery (30:20). Elsewhere, it refers to evil in general. This man has a "froward" (*ʿiqqeš,* cf. 2:15) mouth, i.e., one with perverted speech. The reference may encompass all of the common sins of speech, v. 12.

Further, he "winketh with his eyes . . . speaketh with his feet . . . teacheth with his fingers." To wink with the eye is a common method of signaling, often indicating some form of deviousness. At the same time, he "speaketh" ("signals" or "scrapes") with his feet. This is also an attempt to communicate, perhaps through the direction in which his feet point. Finally, this wicked man "teacheth" ("points") with his fingers. This again refers to speechless communication. Thus understood, the verse expands the final thought of v. 12, giving additional ways in which the wicked man communicates his evil plans, v. 13.[14]

In addition, the evil man has a "froward" (*tahpukôt,* cf. 2:12) heart. This denotes his general wickedness. It leads him to devise "mischief" (or "evil," *raʿ,* cf. 1:33). Further, he fosters "discord" (*madôn*). The word *madôn* occurs primarily in poetical contexts, with nine of its twelve appearances being in Proverbs. It is a general term for "strife, contention." The plural word emphasizes the intensity of the problems caused by the evil man, v. 14. For these reasons, he comes into sudden judgment. There is no significant difference between "calamity" (*ʾed,* cf. 1:26) and "broken" (*šabar*). The word *šabar* is strong. It often indicates complete destruction (of idols, of kingdoms, etc.). The repetition of the sudden nature of this judgment underscores the unexpectedness of it (cf. 29:1). This will be without "remedy" (or "health," i.e. incurable, *marpeʾ,* cf. 4:22), v. 15.

Birdsall and R. W. Thomson [1963], p. 18), or "to afflict" (so Alfred Guillaume, "A Note on the √בלע," *JTS* 13:321), or "to confuse" (so G. R. Driver, "Hebrew Notes," *ZAW* 52:52-53). Other derivations have also been suggested.

[14]The passage has been taken to refer to the practice of magic in Israel. See Gaster, pp. 802-3; McKane, p. 325; and Glendon E. Bryce, "Omen-Wisdom in Ancient Israel," *JBL* 94:31-33. The evidence for this is not conclusive. The context here emphasizes more the evil nature and actions of the individual, all of which will come into God's judgment.

16 These six things doth the Lord hate: yea, seven are an abomination unto him:
17 A proud look, a lying tongue, and hands that shed innocent blood,
18 An heart that deviseth wicked imaginations, feet that be swift in running to mischief,
19 A false witness that speaketh lies, and he that soweth discord among brethren.

16-19 The next part of the chapter poetically describes sins that God hates. The formula "six . . . seven . . ." follows a standard Semitic form in which the second numerical value is the significant one.[15] The seven listed sins are not an exhaustive list of evil actions that displease God. The list is representative and poetic. It conveys the lesson that sin is an "abomination" (*tôˁabat,* reading the *qərê*) to the Lord. The *tôˁabat,* see 3:32, is normally anything that is morally repulsive. The word occurs in Proverbs more than twenty times, describing various abominations, v. 16.

The first of the seven sins is "a proud look," literally, "haughty eyes." The eyes serve as the mirror of the soul, reflecting a superior attitude. Then comes the "lying [*šaqer*] tongue." The word *šeqer* occurs primarily in poetical passages and prophecy. It denotes that which has no basis in fact. It often describes deceitful speech but also indicates deceptive character or actions. Thirdly, the murderer is singled out for his attack upon the innocent victim, v. 17.

The passage condemns the "heart that deviseth wicked imaginations" (*maḥšəbôt*). The word *maḥšəbôt* is neutral with the context showing whether the thoughts are good or bad. Here *maḥšəbôt* refers to the schemes of a wicked person who plots to take advantage of others. "Feet that be swift in running to mischief" are those that are all too ready to become involved with wickedness. "Mischief" here is not the childish shenanigan of an immature person. It is rather the sinful way of one who knows what he does, v. 18.

The sixth sin of the list is the "false witness that speaketh lies." The reference to a "false witness" probably suggests a legal application, that this person perjures himself with his words. The final member of this

---

[15]Compare the extended discussion by Wolfgang M. W. Roth, *Numerical Sayings in the Old Testament,* in *VTS* XIII, 300-311. Similar patterns occur in Job 5:19; Prov. 30:11-31; Eccles. 11:2; Amos 1:3, 6, 9, 11, 13; 2:1, 4, 6.

catalog of sins is the man who sows "discord [*madôn,* cf. v. 14] among brethren," stirring them up over issues as he misrepresents the truth to them, v. 19.

Sins That God Hates

God calls these sins an "abomination." This word occurs more than one hundred times in the OT. It refers to things that are morally repulsive. The OT uses it to refer to idolatry, I Kings 21:26; homosexuality, Leviticus 18:22; human sacrifice, Deuteronomy 12:31; and occult practices, Deuteronomy 18:9-12. Here God lists seven sins to show us that He wants His people to be morally pure, to avoid sin in all of its forms.

1. Pride—Psalm 101:5*b*; Isaiah 2:11 (2:17); I Peter 5:5

2. Lying—Proverbs 12:22; John 8:44; Revelation 21:8

3. Murder—Isaiah 1:15*b*; strengthened to include the inner attitude, Matthew 5:21-22

4. Evil plans—Genesis 6:5; Proverbs 24:8; Jeremiah 4:14

5. Involvement with wickedness—Proverbs 1:15-16*a*; Isaiah 59:7

6. Perjury—Proverbs 12:17; 19:5 (19:9); 25:18

7. Griping—Proverbs 6:14*b*; 16:28; II Timothy 2:23

The author returns to the theme of the adulterous woman (vv. 20-35), warning the youth to avoid her. Initially (vv. 20-24), he exhorts the young man to walk according to the instructions of his parents. In the rest of the passage, Solomon gives several pragmatic reasons for avoiding the temptations of the adulterous woman. By example, the passage shows that the parents have a deep concern about the direction of life taken by their child. They therefore counsel him wisely to avoid the temptation to commit adultery.

20 My son, keep thy father's commandment, and forsake not the law of thy mother:
21 Bind them continually upon thine heart, and tie them about thy neck.
22 When thou goest, it shall lead thee; when thou sleepest, it shall keep thee; and when thou awakest, it shall talk with thee.
23 For the commandment is a lamp; and the law is light; and reproofs of instruction are the way of life:
24 To keep thee from the evil woman, from the flattery of the tongue of a strange woman.

20-24 The opening paragraph stresses the practical value of conduct that avoids adultery. To communicate this lesson, Solomon personifies the instruction of the parents. This is an aspect of wisdom although the word itself does not occur in the passage. Wisdom acts as a guide, restraining the young man from becoming involved with the evil woman. Proverbs 7:1-5 demonstrates a similar approach in advising the youth.

The opening words are broader than the limited topic of adultery. The author urges the youth to pay close attention to the guidance of his parents. He is to "bind," "tie," and "write" these instructions upon himself. These words remind us of the Jewish practice of wearing a phylactery about the forehead or wrist. The practice probably grew out of the misinterpretation of Deuteronomy 6:8 or 11:18. In neither Deuteronomy nor Proverbs, however, do the authors intend a literal application. The expression states poetically that the youth should keep his parent's guidance in mind. Linking this teaching to the body and heart suggests that the child's continued obedience to the instructions of his parents provides moral character development, vv. 20-21.

There is widespread disagreement about the subject of 6:22.[16] Verses 20-21 introduce a plural subject, but v. 22 changes abruptly to a singular: "it will guide . . . it will watch over you." A logical way to resolve the problem takes the parental directions as synonymous with true wisdom. As personified, it serves as the ongoing companion of the son. No

---

[16]Although the verbs are singular, the NASB and NIV make the subject plural, "they." Toy, p. 134, transposes vv. 22 and 23. He omits 22c to make the verse symmetrical and takes the verbs in 22a, b as singular. He translates them as "she" in keeping with the 3fs verb. Patrick W. Skehan, "Proverbs 5:15-19 and 6:20-24," *CBQ* 8:294, transfers 6:22 to follow 5:19, rearranging the clauses to b-c-a. AB, p. 61, without rearrangement, also transfers the verse to follow 5:19. None of these changes have textual support.

matter if he is walking, sleeping, or fully awake and reflecting on the issues of life, wisdom will be with him to keep him from falling prey to
sin's temptations. It thus directs him into "the way of life" (v. 23).
Obedience produces growth. It helps the young man develop himself to
the fullest extent.

The function of this wisdom from the parents is not merely theoretical.
It has a practical value as well. This can, if observed, bring about valuable
results in the child's life. Verse 22 expresses these poetically. The wisdom
provides guidance to the youth in his day-to-day activities, v. 22.

Verse 23 further develops these thoughts. The parent's guidance is a
lamp to help the youth find his way through a sin-darkened world. The
words "commandment" and "teaching" parallel "lamp" and "light." This
parallelism implies a correspondence between them. It is logical that
each pair includes two roughly equivalent terms.[17] The author's concern
here is to show that parental guidance lightens the young man's path
through life.

In contrast with the positive light of the parent's guidance, the phrase
"reproofs [tôkaḥat, cf. 1:23] of instruction" (or "reproofs for discipline") sets forth the negative aspect of this guidance. The genitive relationship between "reproofs" and "discipline" expresses purpose,
correction for the sake of discipline in the child's life.[18] The phrase indicates that the reproving words of the parents give moral guidance to the
young man. This helps him develop a successful way of life, v. 23.[19]

---

[17]Jones, p. 89, follows the ancient Jewish position in interpreting the words "commandment" and "teaching." He regards the first as the oral law and the second as the
written law. He does not justify the interpretation. Among others, Oesterley, p. 45, and
Cohen, p. 35, accept the words "law" (or "teaching") and "light" as broad, generic
terms. The corresponding words "commandment" and "lamp" are restricted, specific
terms that flow out of the broader terms. It is difficult to accept this view, however,
since the usage of the same words elsewhere argues against it. These words occur elsewhere with no clear distinction between them. The terms "light" and "lamp" are parallel
in Ps. 119:105; Job 18:6; 29:3; and Prov. 13:9. The word "commandment" occurs as a
synonym for "law" in Deut. 8:1, 2, 6 and Ps. 19:8. Josh. 22:5 parallels the two words.
For these reasons it is best to take the words as equivalent, representing only poetic variation. There is no particular distinction in their meanings.
[18]Oesterley, p. 46, reads the verse with the LXX, Syriac, and Targum. He would translate the phrase "reproof and instruction." This has only weak textual support. It is best to
accept the MT.
[19]Kufeldt, p. 496, follows W. F. Albright, "The Oracles of Balaam," JBL 63:219, in understanding derek, "way," as "dominion." He translates derek ḥayyîm, "way of life," as the

25 Lust not after her beauty in thine heart; neither let her take thee with her eyelids.
26 For by means of a whorish woman a man is brought to a piece of bread: and the adulteress will hunt for the precious life.

Verse 24 climaxes the warning. Both the positive illumination of vv. 20-23*a* and the negative reproofs of the parents in v. 23*b* should turn the young man away from the adulteress. She is "evil" (*ra*ᶜ, cf. 1:33), appropriate language for one who lures men to unfaithful actions.[20] Paralleled with this expression is the thought that she uses "flattery" (literally, her tongue is "smooth," *ḥalaq*, cf. 2:16). She uses "smooth" words as she entices men into sin, v. 24.

25-26 The first warning focuses on the attractive force of her beauty and on the result that comes to one who yields to this woman. The man should not "lust" (*ḥamad*) after her physical appearance. The verb *ḥamad* means "to desire, take pleasure in" but also "to covet, lust." The context determines the exact sense. The translation "lust" unnecessarily strengthens the word and, thereby, weakens the warning. The verse urges the son to avoid more than lust. It exhorts him to avoid even the earliest hint of desire.

This woman's "beauty" stimulates the young man's lustful cravings. Her painted eyelids enhance her attraction to men. Solomon cautions the young man not to yield to this device.[21] Despite the fact that her eyes entice the youth to respond, her appearance is without substance or endurance; cf. 31:30. This is so because the youthful outward appearance is temporary. It passes away. It further masks the inner loathsomeness of a perverted soul. The young man should not respond to the woman's appearance.

"control (or restraint) of life." While it is true that "the reproofs of instruction" provide a restraint upon our way of living, the unusual translation is not necessary here. The "reproofs" that come from the instruction of the parents do become a "way of life," a manner of living.

[20]The LXX reads "neighbor's wife." This involves a change in the pointing of *ra*ᶜ to *rea*ᶜ. Toy, p. 135; Oesterley, p. 46; Farmer, p. 46; AB, p. 61; and Jones, p. 89, all adopt the reading. R. N. Whybray, *Wisdom in Proverbs* (1965), (hereafter cited as *WIP*), p. 49, reads *ʾiššā zārā* for *ʾešet ra*ᶜ, after the analogy of 2:16 and 5:20. Since the MT makes good sense, there is no need to change it.

[21]Second Kings 9:30; Jer. 4:30; and Ezekiel 23:40 also refer to painting the eyes. The woman applied an ointment of antimony to her eyelids to darken them, thus increasing her attractiveness.

There is a hint here of still another attempt to entice the man. The adulteress stimulates him by her seductive actions. She catches him "with her eyelids" as she engages him with coquettish actions to draw him to herself, v. 25.[22] The man is "brought to a piece of bread" as the result of his yielding to the adulterous woman. He has become her victim in her "hunt for the precious life."[23] In general, two views explain the relationship between the "whorish woman" and the "adulteress." Some feel that the verse is antithetic. While the harlot seeks only material gain from the man, the adulteress will bring him to the loss of his life, probably at the hands of her husband. In other words, adultery carries with it a potentially greater punishment than mere prostitution.

Another view holds that the harlot and the adulteress are poetically the same person, the married woman who enters into an illicit relationship with a man other than her own husband. She has the potential to bring the man into both poverty and the loss of his life. This view is more consistent with the overall teaching of the book against adultery.

The final end of all wrongdoers consists of more than the mere temporal punishments that occur in this life. God uses these to warn sinners to turn from their chosen path. In the end, however, the unrepentant sinner experiences spiritual death. In the book, six different passages mention this possibility for the adulterer (2:18-19; 5:5-6, 22-23; 6:23b-33; 7:22-27; 9:18). When taken together, these comments are a sobering warning against adultery, v. 26.

---

[22]Joseph Reider, "Miscellanea Hebraica," *JJS* 3:79, proposes *laqaḥ* as "to seize forcibly, to overpower." The youth is warned not to allow the woman to "overpower" him with her sensual actions. The verb *laqaḥ*, "to take," is often associated with the taking of a woman in marriage, e.g., Gen. 12:19; 24:4. Thus the semantic field of the word already includes the physical area of sexual involvement. It is not necessary to expand the meaning of the word here.

[23]Driver, "Problems and Solutions," *VT* 4:243-44, sees the meaning "abundance" in *nepeš* (on the basis of Isa. 63:10). Further, he reads a form of *baᶜad*, "price," for *bəᶜad*, "by means of," and translates, "the price of a harlot." Driver thus understands the verse as saying that the services of a harlot can be obtained cheaply while a married woman gives herself to another only in exchange for a life of luxury. Thomas, *VTS* III, 283-84, accepts Driver's emendation of *baᶜad* but prefers to take *nepeš yəqarâ* as a construct relationship, "a person of weight." The end result parallels Driver's interpretation: the married woman seeks "a man of means." These views ignore the context, which requires some aspect of judgment.

27 Can a man take fire in his bosom, and his clothes not be burned?
28 Can one go upon hot coals, and his feet not be burned?
29 So he that goeth in to his neighbour's wife; whosoever toucheth her
shall not be innocent.

27-29 The passage asks two rhetorical questions, both of which require a negative answer, and makes a logical application of the two questions. This is one of two passages (see also 23:27-28) that develop the idea of punishment for the adulterer in a general way. Though there is no punishment specified here, the idea of certain punishment is clear. By this means, Solomon implies that the guilty man has the potential of any of the punishments that receive emphasis elsewhere. God applies the punishment so as to most effectively chasten the guilty man. At the same time, the warning of punishment encourages the man to repent.

In vv. 27-28, the two rhetorical questions develop the principle that a man reaps what he has earlier sowed. One who takes fire to himself will burn his clothes. One who walks on burning coals will sear his feet. In the same way, a man who enters into an adulterous relationship with his neighbor's wife will bring punishment upon himself. The one naturally grows out of the other.

The basic idea of "bosom" (*ḥêq*) is that of a depression formed by the fold of a garment, either at the breast or lap, thereby forming a pocket. Can a man fill this with burning coals and not burn his clothing? Clearly, such a thing is impossible, v. 27. In the same way, can one walk upon hot coals without burning his feet?[24] Again, the answer is no, v. 28. Just as the one carrying coals in his lap will burn his clothes, and one walking upon coals will burn his feet, so the one going in to his neighbor's wife will receive punishment. The phrase "shall not be innocent" (*loʾ yinnaqeh*) is better "shall not go free." This judicial term indicates guilt and subsequent punishment. The word "toucheth" here is euphemistic, denoting the act of adultery, v. 29.

---

[24]Alden, p. 60, considers "feet" as euphemistic for the male sex organ. Giving in to this sin brings certain "burning" to one's manhood. James L. Crenshaw, "Impossible Questions, Sayings, and Tasks," *Semeia* 17:23, likewise sees the "coals of fire" and "feet" as having erotic overtones. It is true that the "feet" sometimes euphemistically denote the genitalia, e.g., Gen. 49:10; Deut. 28:57; Ezek. 16:25. Since v. 28 clearly parallels v. 27, however, it is best simply to take both questions as rhetorical, preparing the way for the application of v. 29.

30 Men do not despise a thief, if he steal to satisfy his soul when he is
hungry;
31 But if he be found, he shall restore sevenfold; he shall give all the
substance of his house.
32 But whoso committeth adultery with a woman lacketh understanding:
he that doeth it destroyeth his own soul.
33 A wound and dishonour shall he get; and his reproach shall not be
wiped away.
34 For jealousy is the rage of a man: therefore he will not spare in the
day of vengeance.
35 He will not regard any ransom; neither will he rest content, though
thou givest many gifts.

30-31 Another illustration prepares the way for the final application of
the passage in vv. 32-35. To show the need of punishment for adultery,
Solomon contrasts it with the sin of theft when extenuating circumstances lessen the punishment. The poverty-stricken man who steals
only to satisfy his need for food does not receive the scornful rejection
of mankind, v. 30.[25] Despite the fact that circumstances explain his theft,
when he is caught he will be required to restore "sevenfold." Society expects him to make a full restitution for his sin, v. 31.[26]

32-35 The application of vv. 30-31 now comes. One who can somewhat justify his sin receives severe punishment. How much more shall
justice be required of the adulterer, a man who sins with no more reason
than the desire to satisfy his own lust? Such a man lacks spiritual understanding, and by his actions he brings spiritual destruction upon himself.

Initially, the father warns his son: a man who commits adultery
thereby embarks upon a foolish way of life. He shows that he lacks
good sense (*ḥasar-leb,* "lacks heart"). This is idiomatic for the want of

---

[25]The verse can also be taken as a question: "Do we not despise a thief when he
steals . . . ?" This avoids the obvious problem of seeming to justify theft under certain
conditions. McKane, p. 330; Frankenberg, p. 49; Crenshaw, p. 26; and the RSV and
NEB take it this way. Still, the interrogative particle *hə* is not present in the text, and the
text makes sense if it is understood as above. In general, men have compassion toward
a thief who steals only when he is in desperate straits.

[26]The law never required sevenfold compensation for theft. Exod. 22:1 requires only a
fivefold restitution, the most required for any offense. Other thefts required a twofold or
fourfold repayment. Probably the figure of "sevenfold" repayment should be understood
in the sense of a "full," or "complete," repayment, even to the extent of giving "all the
substance of his house."

understanding.[27] His actions result in self-destruction.[28] While the phrase may refer to the destruction of his reputation, it is also possible that a spiritual destruction is in view, v. 32.

The young man will receive "a wound and dishonour," a phrase that parallels "reproach" in the second half of the verse. The legal penalty for adultery was death (Deut. 22:22-24), but there is no evidence that Israel carried out this punishment. It seems rather that the guilty party (or parties) received a public scourging with an accompanying loss of reputation. Most likely, the offended husband avenged the wrong by beating the guilty party with a rod or with his own hands, heaping humiliation upon him, v. 33.

The woman's husband becomes enraged with jealousy.[29] He will not rest until he takes vengeance on the one who has been involved with his unfaithful wife, v. 34.[30] No gift, no matter how large, will placate the husband's anger. Only judgment upon the guilty man will satisfy him, v. 35.

---

[27]The context of *ḥesarˉleb,* "lacketh understanding," often implies a lack of spiritual understanding. See also 7:7; 9:4, 16; 10:13, 21; 11:12; 12:11; 15:21; 17:18; 24:30.

[28]Dahood, *PNWSP,* pp. 13-14, notes that the second punishment stated in the verse exceeds the first in severity. He therefore feels that the second statement of wrongdoing must also exceed the first in its description of the sin. To this end, he translates *ʿaśâ* by a secondary meaning, "to press" or "to squeeze." He renders, "a destroyer of his own soul is he who violates her." Ugaritic parallels support Dahood but the argument is still unconvincing. His own translation does not measurably strengthen the second clause over the first clause. The translation of the AV adequately states the sense.

[29]Driver, *Biblica* 32:177, concludes that "rage," *ḥəmat,* is not "satisfactory" here. He emends it to *taḥem,* transposing the consonants, and translates, "jealousy enflames a man." The change adds nothing to the interpretation. The MT is intelligible and readily understood. "Jealousy is the rage of a man" in the sense that it is the source of his rage.

[30]Hendrik G. L. Peels, "Passion or Justice? The Interpretation of *beyôm nāqām* in Proverbs VI 34," *VT* 44:270-74, argues that *naqam* refers to a legal punishment of the adulterer. He notes that private revenge would have been a crime. His view is certainly possible although we have no details of how such legal punishment would have been carried out.

Practical Applications from Proverbs 6

1. Surety 1-5
2. Work and laziness 6-11 (see Subject Study)
3. Characteristics of the wicked 12-15
4. Sins that God hates 16-19
5. Warning against adultery 20-35

1 My son, keep my words, and lay up my commandments with thee.
2 Keep my commandments, and live; and my law as the apple of thine eye.
3 Bind them upon thy fingers, write them upon the table of thine heart.
4 Say unto wisdom, Thou art my sister; and call understanding thy kinswoman:
5 That they may keep thee from the strange woman, from the stranger which flattereth with her words.

PROVERBS 7
WARNING AGAINST ADULTERY

1-5 These verses follow very closely the previous warning of 6:20-24. The repetition emphasizes the practical value of avoiding the adulteress. Once more, Solomon personifies wisdom as he shows how the pursuit of wisdom will keep the son from becoming physically involved with the immoral woman.

Initially, Solomon exhorts his son to "keep" (or "guard," *šamar,* cf. 2:8) his words, and to "lay up" (or "treasure," *ṣapan,* cf. 2:1) his commandments, v. 1. The son should "keep" (*šamar*) his father's commandments in order to experience a full life. Further, he should consider the "law" (or "teaching," *torâ,* cf. 1:8) as "the apple of *his* eye" (*kə²îšôn ʿêneyka*). The phrase, *kə²îšôn ʿêneyka* could be translated "little man of the eyes." This draws upon the reflection seen in the pupil of the eye. The phrase denotes the dark areas of the eyes. The phrase *kə²îšôn ʿêneyka* and close variants occur three times: here, Deuteronomy 32:10, and Psalm 17:8. In each case, it represents something that is precious.[1]

These instructions warn the child against involvement with the adulteress. Verse 4 develops the thought that the father's instructions are tantamount to "wisdom" and "understanding," v. 2. The son should "bind" these instructions upon his fingers and "write" them on the table (or tablet) of his "heart" (*leb,* cf. 3:5).[2] Here, the *leb* represents the mind of

---

[1]Oesterley, p. 50, thinks that the term "apple of his eye" refers to the belief "that the soul resided in the pupil of the eye." Rather than adopting pagan beliefs, however, it is more likely that the biblical authors spoke poetically, picturesquely describing that which was precious in nature.

[2]Some think that the verse refers to the Jewish practice of wearing the phylactery on the wrist; cf. Deut. 6:8; 11:18. Greenstone, p. 69, mentions that the strap was wound around the middle finger. While the allusion to this may underlie the phrasing of the verse, there is no direct reference to a phylactery here.

the young man. He should thoroughly absorb those principles that his parents have taught him, v. 3.

The father personifies wisdom and understanding. He tells the son to consider wisdom as his "sister" and understanding as his "kinsman." Both terms refer to a close familial relationship. The son should thus become intimately associated with wisdom and understanding, both terms describing the father's teaching, v. 4.

The result of following this guidance will be moral purity. The son will not become involved with the "strange woman" (*ʾiššâ zarâ,* cf. 2:16), the "stranger" (*nakrîyâ,* cf. 2:16) who attempts to entice him with her flattery. The verse is virtually identical with 2:16 and parallels 6:24 in thought, v. 5.

6-23 The bulk of the chapter tells of a young man's fall into the snare set for him by an immoral woman. The detailed description of the passage comes from Solomon's role as an eyewitness. He observes the couple when they think they are alone and have no reason to temper their language to meet social expectations. So taken, the passage logically follows vv. 1-5 and precedes vv. 24-27.[3] From the nature of the narrative, it is likely that Solomon had observed the woman on several occasions. While he relates the incident as though it involves one particular youth, he adds details that have come from other occasions, e.g., vv. 7, 9, 12.

The narrative begins with the statement that this is an eyewitness account by the author.[4] The "window" (*ḥallôn,* "to pierce") was an opening in the wall to provide ventilation and light. The "casemate" (or "lattice,"

---

[3]Whybray, *WIP,* p. 50 (also "Some Literary Problems in Proverbs I-IX," *VT* 16:483-86) states that vv. 6-23 are an addition to an original narrative consisting of vv. 1-5, 24-27. His argument is tenuous. He relies on the use of "harlot" (*zonâ*) in v. 10 (not used in vv. 1-5, 24-27) and on the differences in style between the two passages. The stylistic differences stem from the nature of the material, an eyewitness account rather than an exhortation. The use of *zonâ* rather than *zarâ* logically follows from the fact that he describes the "attire" of the woman rather than the woman herself. It would be meaningless to speak of the "attire of a *zarâ*" since no distinctive attire marked the *zarâ.*

[4]The LXX makes the verbs in vv. 6-7 feminine and refers them to the woman. Albright, *VTS* III, 10, connects the woman with an Aphrodite cult. Farmer, p. 49, makes the woman a symbol of "cultic apostasy." Mitchell Dahood, "Canaanite-Phoenician Influence in the Qoheleth," *Biblica* 33:214, describes extrabiblical references using the motif of a woman looking out a window. Judges 5:28; II Sam. 6:16 (I Chron. 15:29); II Kings 9:30; and Song of Sol. 2:9 also mention this. It is rash to connect this with a cult. From the context, v. 6 merely sets the stage for what Solomon says as he warns his son to avoid the adulteress.

6 For at the window of my house I looked through my casement,
7 And beheld among the simple ones, I discerned among the youths, a
  young man void of understanding,
8 Passing through the street near her corner; and he went the way to
  her house,
9 In the twilight, in the evening, in the black and dark night:

ʾešnab) was probably a lath framework covering an opening. This allowed ventilation and light but shut out the direct rays of the sun, v. 6.
Looking through the opening, he saw a group of "simple ones" (cf. *petî,*
1:22). He discerned, no doubt through their later actions, one of the
group who lacked "understanding" (*ḥasar-leb,* cf. 6:32). The word
"youths" is used here in its most general sense to refer to a group of
young men, v. 7.[5]

The young man passes over the street near "her corner," an obscure
expression that may be taken in two ways. Some explain "her corner" as
the corner near her house.[6] Others see it as the corner to which she ha-
bitually came to lead others into immorality. Either view adequately explains the expression. Perhaps the first explanation better suits the
context since nothing here suggests that the woman is a professional
harlot, v. 8.

All of this takes place at night, poetically described with several synonyms. These range from "twilight," early evening, to the "black and dark
night," the deepest darkness of the night. This is not saying that the
youth paced back and forth through the whole period (it is improbable
that Solomon stood at his lattice watching for several hours). Rather, the
idea is simply that these incidents involving the woman took place in
the nighttime, at different hours of the night, v. 9.[7]

---

[5]AB, p. 63, emends "youths," *banîm,* to *bênêhem,* "among them." Toy, p. 147, omits the
phrase "among the simples ones, I discerned," *bappətaʾyim ʾabînâ.* This avoids the repetition ("simple" = "void of understanding"). Neither change has support and nothing requires the change.

[6]KD I, 159, holds that the young man was going back and forth, near her corner, until
she arrived. This suggests that the meeting was prearranged or, at the least, not the first
liaison between the two. This does not fit the context of the chapter.

[7]Dahood, *PNWSP,* p. 15, explains *bəʾîšôn* as from *yašan,* "to sleep." He translates, "the
quietness of the night." This solves no problems in the verse. Further, the guttural *alep*
makes no sense in the form with this derivation.

*10 And, behold, there met him a woman with the attire of an harlot, and
subtil of heart.*
11 (She is loud and stubborn; her feet abide not in her house:

The evil woman meets the youth. She is clothed with the "attire [*šît*] of
an harlot." This probably involved a distinctive style or article of dress
rather than seductive apparel since clothing in OT times was generally
loose fitting. Only two other passages refer to the dress of a harlot.
Genesis 38:14 mentions a "veil" (or "shawl"), and Ezekiel 16:16 refers
to "garments" in connection with the harlotry of Judah. The word *šît* occurs again only at Psalm 73:6. There the adjective *hamas* modifies it and
the phrase denotes a "garment of violence." Logically, the word relates
to the verb *šît*, "to put, set, lay." Possibly the garment acquired its name
from the action of putting it on. In any case, the word does not give any
information about the nature of the garment.[8] The attire attracts the
young man's attention as the adulteress comes to meet him.

The woman further is "subtil of heart" (*naṣurat leb*). The word *naṣurat*
comes from *naṣar* ("to guard, keep," cf. 2:8).[9] Someone who is "guarded
of heart" conceals her inner plans. Thus, she is "wily" or "cunning of
heart," v. 10. She is "loud [cf. *hamâ*, 1:21] and stubborn [*soraret*]." The
word *homîyâ*, from *hamâ*, denotes a boisterous nature. The word *soraret*,
from *sarar*, indicates the "rebellious" nature of the woman as she reacts
against both social customs and her vows of marriage, v. 11.[10] At one
time she is "without" (better, "in the street"); at another time, she is "in
the streets" (or "squares," *barhobôt*, "open places"). She carries out her
seductive actions "at every corner," wandering here and there through-

---

[8]Power, p. 104, suggests that the article involved a headdress or veil. From *šît* he infers
that "design, order or ornament" characterize the garment. His suggestion that it is a
garment worn on the head probably comes from Gen. 38:14.

[9]G. R. Driver, "Hebrew Notes," *VT* 1:250, relates the word to the Akkadian *naṣrat* and
translates, "wily." Ross, *EBC* V, 940, and Toy, p. 149, interpret the phrase as "wily of
heart." While the form is irregular, the root *naṣar* is readily connected. Oesterley, p. 51,
and AB, p. 63, emend to *naṣōrat lōt*, "heavily veiled." There is no support for this.

[10]G. R. Driver, "Problems in 'Proverbs,'" *ZAW* 50:141-42, explains *soraret* with reference to the Akkadian *sararu*, "to be unstable." He translates, "fickle." This is possible;
however, the Akkadian *sararu* may also mean "to resist"; thus, the meaning "stubborn" is
appropriate. Elsewhere in the OT, the sense of "stubborn" or "rebellion" dominates.
Greenstone, p. 71, suggests a change to either *sobabet* or *sharet* to obtain the meaning of
"gadabout," which parallels the second half of the verse. The suggestion lacks textual
support and is without merit.

12 Now is she without, now in the streets, and lieth in wait at every corner.)
13 So she caught him, and kissed him, and with an impudent face said unto him,
14 I have peace offerings with me; this day have I payed my vows.
15 Therefore came I forth to meet thee, diligently to seek thy face, and I have found thee.
16 I have decked my bed with coverings of tapestry, with carved works, with fine linen of Egypt.

out the city to find her victims. Solomon, of course, recalls other times when he has seen the woman, v. 12.[11]

She boldly arouses the young man with her kisses. Her face is "impudent" (*ʿazaz,* "to be strong"; here this has the sense of "brazen") as she speaks to him. It refers to her boldness in approaching the man, v. 13. She begins her conquest by referring to her religious vows. She has offered her peace offering at the temple in payment of her vows (*šillamtî*)[12] and thus has the sacrificial meal that must be eaten (Lev. 7:15-17; 22:29-30), v. 14. She has accordingly come to seek him to be her guest. This is not merely an evening of sex. She plans for hedonistic pleasures. She invites the youth to join her, v. 15.

Her bed has been covered over with "coverings of tapestry" (*marbaddîm*). The word *marbaddîm* occurs only here and at 31:22. The context in both places suggests something more than mere coverings. Perhaps "decorated spreads" is appropriate. The phrase "with carved *works* [*ḥaṭubôt*], with fine linen of Egypt" is better "with embroidered fabric from the yarn of Egypt." It refers to colored Egyptian fabrics

---

[11]Toy, p. 149, calls the paragraph a "vivid description of the city manners of the late time (probably third cent. B.C.)." He forgets, though, that harlotry has been with us since early times; cf. Gen. 38:12-26.

[12]Karel Van Der Toorn, "Female Prostitution in Payment of Vows in Ancient Israel," *JBL* 108:197-99, translates *šillamtî* as "I must fulfill." The argument is that the woman prostitutes herself to gain money to pay a vow she has made. Garrett, pp. 103-4, thinks that the woman lies to the man. She tells him that her prostitution is to gain money to fulfill her religious vow. He agrees with Van Der Toorn. The word *šillamtî,* however, is a perfect tense verb and would normally represent a completed action. There is no clear evidence that women prostituted themselves to enable payment of vows. Deuteronomy 23:17-18 specifically prohibited this.

17 I have perfumed my bed with myrrh, aloes, and cinnamon.
18 Come, let us take our fill of love until the morning: let us solace our-
selves with loves.
19 For the goodman is not at home, he is gone a long journey:

woven to form an elaborate (and expensive) bed covering. She has also covered the bed with "fine linen" (ʾeṭûn), v. 16.[13]

She has also "perfumed" (or "sprinkled," naptî) her bed with spices, enhancing the sensual atmosphere. The verb naptî is from nûp, used only here in the qal and in Psalm 68:9 in the hipʿîl, where the idea of "sprinkling" is appropriate. The related word nûp, "to move to and fro, wave," occurs numerous times, especially in connection with the sacrifices.

"Myrrh" is an Arabian spice, exuded from the bark of the balsam tree. The tree produces a gummy, translucent, reddish yellow resin from which the spice comes. "Aloes," *Aquilaria agallocha,* come from trees grown in India and China. The heart of the tree and the roots yield a fragrant resin from which the spice comes. "Cinnamon" comes from the bark of the *Cinnamomum zeylanicum,* a broad-leaved plant growing in Africa, Ceylon, and Java, v. 17.

Having stimulated the youth's imagination by describing what awaits, the woman now urges him to join her for a night of sensual pleasures. The parallel words "love" (dodîm) and "loves" (baʾăhabîm) are synonyms, with no major difference of meaning, v. 18.[14]

To further encourage the youth, the woman tells him that "the good-man" (haʾîš, better, "the man"), her husband, is gone on a long business trip, v. 19. He has a "bag of money" with him, an unspecified amount but clearly enough to support him while he is gone. Thus, there is no

---

[13]The feminine plural construct noun ḥăṭubôt occurs only here. It is in apposition to marbaddîm in 16a. The word ʾeṭûn also occurs only here. Kitchen, *TB* 28:107, suggests a derivation from Egyptian ʾidmy, "linen." Thomas O. Lambdin, "Egyptian Loan Words in the Old Testament," *JAOS* 73:147, also derives it from the Egyptian root, which he thinks passed over into Phoenician, then into Greek, and finally into Hebrew, a circuitous and highly speculative route. Other suggested meanings include "thread" or "yarn."

[14]Toy, p. 155, mistakenly comments that the plurals of these words "are used always of sensual love." The plural dodîm occurs again in Song of Sol. 5:1; Ezek. 16:8; 23:17 without a special emphasis on sensual love. The plural of ʾahab occurs in Hos. 8:9 without stressing sensual love. The idea of sensuality occurs here naturally in the context.

20 He hath taken a bag of money with him, and will come home at the day appointed.
21 With her much fair speech she caused him to yield, with the flattering of her lips she forced him.

fear that he will return before the "day appointed" (*keseʾ*). The meaning of *keseʾ* is uncertain. The variant *keseh* occurs in Psalm 81:3, in contrast with *ḥodes,* "new moon." The context here suggests a lengthy period of time from the new moon. "Full moon" is an appropriate conjecture. From v. 9, the time is now close to new moon, when it is dark at night. Thus, the husband is not expected for about two weeks, v. 20. The woman breaks down the resistance of the young man with her comments. Her flattery and persuasive speech (*laqaḥ,* cf. 1:5) cause him to yield to her suggestion of a night of sensual pleasures.[15] See the discussion at the end of this chapter of speech as one of the appeals of the adulteress, v. 21. The unsuspecting youth follows the adulteress to his judgment. He goes as "an ox goeth to the slaughter or as a fool to the correction of the stocks." Literally, *ûkəʿekes ʾel-mûsar ʾəwîl* is "and as fetters to the discipline of a fool." Supplying the subject, the phrase reads "and as *one in* shackles to the discipline of a fool."[16] Thinking only of gratifying his sexual appetite, the youth allows this sin to lead him to divine judgment.[17]

---

[15]Oesterley, p. 53, translates *liqhah* as "learning," emphasizing the root meaning of the word. It makes better sense, however, to lay stress on the action of the adulteress in "teaching," rather than on her qualifications for enticing the youth into her snare. Thomas, *VTS* III, 284, suggests the woman's "taking ways," a term that includes her gestures as well as verbal persuasion. The word "persuasion" includes this same significance, and many translations, e.g., NASB, NIV, use the word.

[16]Interpretations of the verse range over a wide area. The MT reads: "as a fetter to the discipline of a fool" (so Zöckler, p. 92; Cohen, pp. 42-43). Zöckler, however, understands the "fetter" as referring to the adulteress's power over the man. Cohen sees it as a reference to the "fettered criminal," who is led to his punishment. Others rearrange the word order so as to have a personal subject, "as a fool to the restraint of fetters" (so AV, PC, pp. 156-57; KD I, 169). Still others emend *ʿekes* to find variously a verb, "skips" (Driver, *VT* 1:241), or nouns, "dog" (James Moffatt, *A New Translation of the Bible*), "calf" (Toy, p. 155), *"agnus"* (a lamb, Vulgate), "stag" (*Confraternity Bible*), or something else. No convincing evidence forces the emending of the text, particularly since no agreement has been reached over one suggestion. The parallel form of the two phrases argues for a personal subject in the second clause. With the supply of two words, "one in," we gain parallelism without emending the text.

[17]Prov. 6:32; 7:22-23; and 22:14 all refer to the divine punishment of the adulterer. The NT develops the spiritual ramifications of this in I Cor. 6:9-10; Gal. 5:19-21; Eph. 5:5.

*22 He goeth after her straightway, as an ox goeth to the slaughter, or as
   a fool to the correction of the stocks;*
*23 Till a dart strike through his liver; as a bird hasteth to the snare, and
   knoweth not that it is for his life.*
*24 Hearken unto me now therefore, O ye children, and attend to the
   words of my mouth.*
25 Let not thine heart decline to her ways, go not astray in her paths.
*26 For she hath cast down many wounded: yea, many strong men have
   been slain by her.*
27 Her house is the way to hell, going down to the chambers of death.

Metaphorically, the judgment is seen as an arrow, piercing the liver
(*kabed,* cf. 3:9) of the youth. The word *kabed* is literally "heavy" and, by
extension, "glory, honor." The traditional etymology holds that the
"liver" is the heavy organ, either heavy by weight or heavy with blood.
Metaphorically, *kabed* represents the emotional center (cf. Lam. 2:11). It
is equivalent to our "heart." Here, however, the idea is more a word picture of the judgment that will fall upon the youth as the consequence of
his sin, v. 22.[18]

The passage concludes with a final picture of judgment. Just as the
bird flies hastily into a snare, so the young man goes after the woman
without knowing the end of his actions. He does not know that his actions will cost his "life" (*nepeš*). The word *nepeš* has a broad range of
meaning. It may refer to inner desires, to the immaterial nature of man,
or to the person himself. The context here does not allow a dogmatic
reference to the eternal soul (although vv. 30-31 do stress this idea). It is
enough here to see that adulterous conduct robs a man of his "life," vitality with its normal desires and cravings. This may happen as the result
of a guilty conscience or, ultimately, from the termination of life, v. 23.

24-27 The father now draws the conclusion to his teaching. He exhorts his sons to listen to him, v. 24.[19] He charges his son not to allow

---

[18]Commentators have difficulty with 23*a* in the setting. McKane, p. 341, rearranges
the verse to have 23*a* follow 23*b*. KD I, 170; and Toy, pp. 156-57, rearrange the verse to
b-c-a. These attempt to have the arrow pierce the heart of an animal or bird. The MT is
defensible, however, by taking 23*a* as the logical conclusion of v. 22. The youth follows
the woman, just as an ox goes to slaughter or a bound criminal to his punishment, until
an arrow pierces him through. The *a:b::b:a* construction is common in Scripture.

[19]The alternation between "son" and "sons" ("children," AV, so 4:1; 5:7; 7:24; 8:32) is
merely poetic variation. This does not refer to a teacher and his students (so Plaut, p. 66;
Greenstone, p. 77). AB, p. 64, locates *banîm* as a singular with an enclitic *mem* being misunderstood for the plural ending. While this is possible, the frequency with which the word

his "heart" (*leb,* cf. 3:5), i.e., his emotions, to be caught up in the way of life of the adulteress. The warning is broad and should be applied broadly. The youth should not only avoid the woman physically but should as well avoid her mentally, not thinking about her. When the mind feeds the person, it breaks down the will. The only safe practice, then, is to channel the mind into godly thinking patterns, v. 25.

> When the mind and the will come into prolonged conflict, the mind will always win.

There are spiritual consequences to the involvement with this evil woman. She has conquered many others by her way of life. Her house is the entrance to many different paths, all of which lead to "hell" (*šə'ôl*). The thought is that adultery can lead to many distinct changes in one's lifestyle. No matter what the change, its logical end is judgment.

The noun *šə'ôl* here is more than merely a synonym for the grave. Adultery does not have to bring physical death.[20] Nothing inherent in an illicit sexual relationship demands that the parties involved should die physically. But spiritual death meets the requirements of the verse. The use of *šə'ôl* argues for the interpretation of spiritual death. The word occurs nine times in Proverbs. In five places (1:12; 7:27; 9:18; 23:14; 30:16), the word could indicate either the grave or hades, the abode of the dead. In the remaining four places, however, the apparent sense is to the abode of the dead. In 5:5-6 and 15:24, the word parallels the "path of life," an evident contrast between the blessed existence of the godly and the unblessed subsistence of the wicked. In 15:11 and 27:20, a parallel occurs between *šə'ôl* and *'əbaddôn,* once again implying a future existence of the dead.

---

occurs in the book (seven times, including 7:7; 13:22; 17:6, where the context requires a plural) argues against this view.

[20] The reference to Sheol has been variously taken. Toy, p. 158, directly states that this is "premature physical death . . . not punishment after death." McKane, p. 341, cf. pp. 269-70, asserts that the comment comes from Canaanite mythology in which the god Mot (death) is characterized by "the gaping throat." This forms the entryway by which the living pass into the realm of the dead. References to individuals going down to Sheol reflect this pagan mythology. *PC,* p. 157, allegorizes the passage into a reference to the fate of those who are ensnared by heretical teaching. The overall use of Sheol, discussed above, strongly argues against these views.

Other writings from the Davidic-Solomonic period indicate that the authors held a view of life after death. In Psalms 16:10-11 and 49:14-15, *šəʾôl* clearly refers to the abode of the dead. Such references as Psalm 73:24 and Ecclesiastes 12:7 reveal that the belief of life after death existed in Israel at this time. In view of this development of life and death, it is likely that the book here refers to something more than spiritual death. Death here should be taken in its full potential of eternal separation from God, divine punishment, and not merely the cessation of life. While God can forgive adultery, one who begins the practice will likely become bound by its emotional chains. For this one, the end of adultery is "hell," vv. 26-27.

Practical Applications from Proverbs 7

The Fourfold Appeal of an Adulteress
1. Beauty, 6:25*a*

A physical attraction draws people together. They overlook the minor arguments that regularly characterize their association, and they allow the physical relationship to dominate their activities. Any marriage that develops out of this kind of association faces bleak prospects for success. The emotional pressures that drive the couple apart are stronger than the physical attraction that draws them together.

2. Dress, 7:10

Note that this attraction rests upon an external quality. The woman's dress covers the unattractive qualities of her inward character. Because the attire hides the truth behind an attractive façade, a woman's appearance is not a good basis upon which to build a relationship.

3. Speech

Surprisingly, this aspect of the adulteress's appeal receives the major emphasis in the book (2:16; 5:3-4; 6:24; 7:13-21; 9:13-17; 22:14). For all of its appeal, though, speech is still an external quality of the adulteress. As such, it is an untrustworthy guide. Her speech is deceptive. She promises pleasure but instead brings the man into the grip of sin's power and ultimate judgment. One must measure the persuasiveness of temptation's appeal against the objective standard of God's Word in order to see the temptation in its real light.

4. Sensual actions, 6:25*b*; 7:13, 18

This is a powerful attraction. The primary means to overcome this requires that the young man set his priorities before he faces temptation. The choice is straightforward—God or self? By making God and spirituality the focus of one's life, well in advance of the time when temptation comes along, a young man can acquire the spiritual strength to reject a sensual appeal.

1 Doth not wisdom cry? and understanding put forth her voice?
2 She standeth in the top of high places, by the way in the places of the paths.
3 She crieth at the gates, at the entry of the city, at the coming in at the doors.
4 Unto you, O men, I call; and my voice is to the sons of man.
5 O ye simple, understand wisdom: and, ye fools, be ye of an understanding heart.

PROVERBS 8

1-5 Solomon now comes to the high point in his discussion of wisdom. The chapter draws a stark contrast with the "strange woman" of c. 7. The fruit of that woman was death (7:26-27). The fruit of wisdom is eternal life (8:35). The vivid difference exalts the value of godly wisdom.

The author asks rhetorically if wisdom calls out to men. Clearly, the answer is yes! Wisdom does call out to mankind as she invites men to receive her, v. [1]. To this end, she meets them in the various walks of life. The "top of the high places" refers to the high places of the city.[1] She likewise appears "by the way in the places of the paths" (better "where the paths meet, she stations herself"). This is at the crossroads of the city, v. 2. Finally, she cries out at the city's gates, the centers for business and political matters, v. 3.[2] St. Gregory's comments are appropriate: "It is one thing to be ignorant; another to have refused to learn. For not to know is only ignorance; to refuse to learn is pride. And they are the less able to plead ignorance in excuse, the more that knowledge is set before them, even against their will. We might, perhaps, be able to pass along the way of this present life in ignorance of this Wisdom, if she herself had not stood in the corners of the way."[3]

---

[1]AB, p. 66, emends ʿalê darek, "by the way," to ʿōlāh baddérek, "ascending the road." The suggestion lacks textual support and adds nothing to the understanding of the verse.

[2]Dahood, *ETL* 44:43, parses qrt as a verb, *qarat*, "call," rather than *qaret*, "city," as in the MT. He argues on the basis of Ugaritic and parallelism. The suggestion adds nothing to the interpretation of the passage and has no textual support. On the other hand, Dahood correctly argues for understanding *taronnâ* as an energetic singular form of *ranan*. This contradicts G. R. Driver, "Studies in the Vocabulary of the Old Testament," *JTS* 31:280-81, who argues that we should read *tirneh* rather than the MT.

[3]*Moralities*, xxv.29, quoted by *PC*, p. 161.

6 Hear; for I will speak of excellent things; and the opening of my lips shall be right things.
7 For my mouth shall speak truth; and wickedness is an abomination to my lips.
8 All the words of my mouth are in righteousness; there is nothing froward or perverse in them.
9 They are all plain to him that understandeth, and right to them that find knowledge.
10 Receive my instruction, and not silver; and knowledge rather than choice gold.
11 For wisdom is better than rubies; and all the things that may be desired are not to be compared to it.

Wisdom calls to "men" and to "the sons of man." The terms embrace both those of high degree and those of low degree, v. 4. She urges the "simple" (cf. *petî*, 1:22) to have "prudence" (*ᶜormâ*, cf. 1:4). Likewise, the "fool" (cf. *kəsîl*, 1:22) should strive for "understanding" (cf. *bîn*, 1:2).[4] These objects of wisdom's call show that simple or obstinate men do not need to remain in that condition. Wisdom invites them to change or, in a sense, to repent, v. 5.

6-11 Following the introduction, a lengthy discourse sets forth the nature of wisdom. In 8:6-9 a series of synonymous clauses set forth the essential nature of wisdom's call as trustworthy. Successively, Solomon describes her speech as "excellent" (*nəgîdîm*) and "right" (*mêšarîm*, cf. *yašar*, 3:6). The adjective *nəgîdîm* comes from *nagîd*, "ruler" or "captain." It refers to one who is a leader. Wisdom thus speaks of "excellent" (or "noble") things that surpass other things in value, v. 6.[5] She speaks "truth" (*ʾəmet*, 3:3), not "wickedness" (*rešaᶜ*). The word *ʾəmet* occurs widely to refer to that which is reliable or dependable. The word has a distinct component of faithfulness associated with it. The word *rešaᶜ*

---

[4]Zöckler, p. 95, accepts the LXX reading *hakînû leb*, "direct your heart, i.e., exert your understanding," rather than the MT *habînû leb*, "an understanding heart." The proposed *hakînû*, however, destroys the parallelism of the verse. The MT repeats the verb but is nonetheless clear in meaning. Repetition of words is not unknown elsewhere and is shaky ground upon which to change the MT.

[5]Among others, Toy, p. 166; McKane, p. 345; Zöckler, p. 97; and Irwin, p. 106, suggest emending *nəgîdîm* to *nəkohîm*, as in v. 9. The sense of "straightforward"or "plain" supposedly parallels *mêšarîm* to a better degree than that yielded by the MT. This radical suggestion involves switching two palatals and substituting the guttural *ḥ* for the dental *d*. This is highly unlikely. While *nəgîdîm* does not occur elsewhere with the sense of an abstract noun, it is a reasonable interpretation here. That a word occurs only once does not justify the emendation.

often occurs as an antonym of "righteous" (*ṣedeq*, cf. 1:3). It is sometimes a legal term but more often a general reference to evil thoughts,
actions, or words. Further, the "mouth" (*ḥikî*) of wisdom will "speak
[*hagâ*] truth." The noun *ḥek* regularly indicates the "mouth," the organ of
speech. The verb *hagâ*, "to mutter, meditate, devise," signifies inward
meditation as well as an utterance going forth from the mouth. The verb
occurs primarily in poetical contexts to indicate a repetitive sound or
thought.[6] The thought of an utterance occurs only in poetical contexts.
Since the idea of meditation is not appropriate here, the translation
"speak truth" best expresses the sense. The negative aspect is set in antithetic parallelism, "wickedness is an abomination to my lips," v. 7.[7]

Her words are "in righteousness" (*ṣedeq*, cf. 1:3), not "froward"
(*niptal*) or "perverse" (*ʿiqqeš*, cf. 2:15). Verse 8 follows the antithetic
pattern set by v. 7 and adds the negative thought that nothing about wisdom's speech is "crooked or perverse." The descriptive term *niptal*
comes from *patal*, "to twist." From this, we get the idea of "distorted." It
occurs only here and Job 5:13 with this sense. Clearly, wisdom's voice
is trustworthy, v. 8.

Finally, her words are "plain" (*nəkoḥîm*) and, once again, "right"
(*yəšarîm*, cf. 2:21). The word *nəkoḥîm* describes that which is "straight"
or "right." It most often refers to the ethics of life, both personal and national. The word *yəšarîm* often denotes the ethical uprightness of a man,
his blamelessness. Verse 9 adds a significant thought. The trustworthiness of wisdom's call is clear only to those with understanding and
knowledgeable hearts. This expresses the principle that the NT develops
further (John 7:17; I Cor. 2:14). The Holy Spirit bears witness to godly
hearts regarding the truth of right doctrine.

It is worth noting that this does not say that the teachings of wisdom
are easily understood. The passage states only that understanding hearts
will respond, acknowledging the truth. The godly individual still must

---

[6]Power, pp. 18, 106, translates, "my mouth shall study truth." It is difficult to grasp the
concept of a "mouth" studying truth. The word better expresses the act of declaring
truth.

[7]Toy, pp. 162, 166; Oesterley, p. 57; and Martin, p. 62, follow the LXX and emend to
something like "false lips are an abomination to me." The change requires the addition
of *lî* to the phrase. Once again, the change adds nothing to the interpretation. It is best to
follow the MT.

12 I wisdom dwell with prudence, and find out knowledge of witty inventions.

be diligent in his studies (II Tim. 2:15). But with diligence, there is the promise of being able to distinguish truth from error, v. 9.

In vv. 10-11, wisdom once more appeals to mankind. This time, however, her appeal stresses the value of wisdom when one receives it. It has more value than fine silver or gold, v. 10; and it is better than fine jewelry (*pənînîm*, cf. 3:15), v. 11.[8] This is not a material comparison. Wisdom's value is far above that which might accrue from the sale of silver or gold. Material things cannot buy happiness, peace, spiritual blessedness, or confidence for the eternal future of the soul. Therefore, wisdom has more value than that of material objects. The passage does not forbid silver, gold, jewels, or other objects of value. The teaching here focuses on the greater value of wisdom. This leads to the logical conclusion that one should seek for wisdom rather than wealth.

12-21 Solomon now turns to the rewards given to those who follow wisdom. Descriptive words in v. 12 support the conclusion that wisdom is discerning. In the first place, she dwells with "prudence" (*ʿormâ*, cf. 1:4), that godly shrewdness that recognizes right things.[9] The thought of dwelling with prudence implies that wisdom associates herself readily with prudence. They are as two sisters living together in harmony.

Wisdom also finds out "knowledge of witty inventions" (*daʿat məzimmôt*, cf. 1:4). The interpretation here hinges on whether *daʿat* is absolute or construct. The word occurs forty times in the Book of Proverbs. In thirty-four cases, it is clear that *daʿat* is absolute. Twice, at 3:20 and 22:17, it occurs with a pronominal suffix. In two other places, 9:10 and 30:3, the word is in construct as a name for God. The weight of evidence, from the pattern of use elsewhere, argues for taking it here in an absolute sense. In this case, the translation must be "knowledge *and* discretion," supplying the copulative. The parallel phrase in 1:4 is similar, v. 12.

---

[8]Toy, pp. 163-64, with his penchant for following the LXX, omits the personal pronoun "my" in v. 10. He argues that this furnishes better parallelism with "knowledge" in 10*b*. But the context forcefully argues that this is not "instruction" in general but the instruction that comes from wisdom. As in the MT, we should retain the suffix.

[9]Toy, p. 171, calls "dwell," *šakantî*, "an improbable expression" and emends it to *hiskantî*, "understand," or *qanîtî*, "possess," which he follows in his translation. The suggestion has weak textual support. The MT is understandable.

13 The fear of the Lord is to hate evil: pride, and arrogancy, and the evil way, and the froward mouth, do I hate.

Solomon now expresses the thought that wisdom is pure. She hates evil, in particular singling out "pride, and arrogancy, and the evil way, and the froward mouth." Note the antithesis between godliness and wickedness; the two cannot exist together in harmony. The first half of v. 13 states the general principle that godliness ("fear of the Lord," cf. 1:7) hates evil. The second half parallels this with the statement that wisdom also hates evil, illustrated with the three specific examples of wickedness.[10]

The examples occur with a logical pattern. The initial group, "pride [*ge'â*] and arrogance [*ga'ôn*]," refers to the sin of self-exaltation. The word "pride" (*ge'â*) occurs only here, although related words occur widely elsewhere. The verb *ge'â* signifies "to grow up, be high." It is used of the exaltation of God (Exod. 15:1, 21) as well as of the natural growth of a plant (Job 8:11) and the rising of a river (Ezek. 47:5). A natural extension of the thought gave the word its meaning of majesty and exaltation (Ps. 68:35) or of pride (Prov. 29:23). The prophets and poetical books especially use the word in this sense.

"Arrogancy" (*ga'ôn*) is the masculine form of *ge'â*. The combination of masculine and feminine forms indicates totality, every indication of pride. Wisdom hates every manifestation of this wicked emotion, v. 13. The "evil way" (*ra'*, cf. 1:33) denotes the evil way of life, the conduct of an individual. The "froward [*tahpukôt*, i.e., perverted, cf. 2:12] mouth" describes the speech of the wicked person. Wisdom hates all of these.

These three examples together embrace sins of the mind (cf. II Cor. 10:3-5), sins of conduct (cf. Rom. 6:8-13), and sins of speech (cf. Matt. 12:36), the three areas in which man goes astray from God.

---

[10]Skehan, *CBQ* 9:197, attempts to organize the chapter into seven stanzas of five lines each. He describes 8:13*a* as a "jarring element" and rejects it as a gloss. Among others, Toy, p. 164, and Power, p. 106, likewise feel that the verse disturbs the rhythm of the passage. This idea is subjective and has no textual support. It can just as readily be argued that v. 13 is a new paragraph in the chapter, with 13*b* and *c* developing the positive statement of 13*a*. The logical development of the verse indicates that it belongs where it is.

*14 Counsel is mine, and sound wisdom: I am understanding; I have
    strength.*
15 By me kings reign, and princes decree justice.
16 By me princes rule, and nobles, even all the judges of the earth.

In 8:14-16, the passage presents wisdom as the basis upon which all successful government rests. Initially, the author expands the scope of wisdom to include "counsel" (*ʿeṣâ*, cf. 1:30), "sound wisdom" (*tûšîyâ*, cf. 2:7),
"understanding" (cf. *bîn*, 1:2), and "strength" (*gəbûrâ*). The word *gəbûrâ*
occurs widely as a reference to the power of royalty and, by extension, to
the power of God. This is the only time the word occurs in Proverbs.
Wisdom displays all of these attributes as she guides the affairs of man.

There is a logical progression within the verse. The first three terms—
"counsel," "sound wisdom," and "understanding"—are synonymous.
They describe the range over which wisdom manifests itself. The word
"strength" (or "power"), however, shows the character of wisdom's action as she displays these aspects. An individual, therefore, who follows
the ways of wisdom has the assurance of success, v. 14.

This, then, is the basis for continuing competence in government.
Kings and other governmental officials who are wise will achieve a degree of success. The qualifying phrases "rulers decree justice," v. 15,
and "all the judges of the earth" (or "all who judge rightly," v. 16), show
that the verse has in mind officials who rule in a godly manner.[11] Evil
rulers may succeed in their duties for a time, especially as God uses
them to accomplish His will (21:1). Ultimately, however, God will judge
their wickedness. Only godly government can continue to enjoy God's
favor, vv. 15-16.

Wisdom presents herself in 8:17-21 as the basis for success: "I love
those who love me," v. 17.[12] The love for wisdom shows itself by a diligent search (*mašaḥəray*) on the part of those who wish to know her. The

---

[11]The textual problem in v. 16 does not affect the conclusion. Many follow the variant
reading "earth," *ʾereṣ*, instead of the MT reading, "rightly," *ṣedeq*. The argument is that
the MT repeats the last word of v. 15. Among these with this position are the AV; KD I,
180; *PC*, p. 163; and Oesterley, p. 59. McKane, p. 348, and Dahood, *PNWSP*, p. 15, follow the MT but both understand *ṣedeq* as "legitimate." The Syriac, Targum, and many
Hebrew manuscripts support the MT. In addition, the MT has the advantage of paralleling v. 15.

[12]The *kətîb* reading is "love her" and the *qərê* is "love me." Virtually all commentators
and versions follow the *qərê* reading. This best agrees with the preceding verses.

17 I love them that love me; and those that seek me early shall find me.
18 Riches and honour are with me; yea, durable riches and righteous-
ness.
19 My fruit is better than gold, yea, than fine gold; and my revenue than
choice silver.
20 I lead in the way of righteousness, in the midst of the paths of judg-
ment:

participle is from *šaḥar,* "dawn." This refers to one who rises early to begin his search, i.e., a diligent search. Wisdom gives blessings to these as she responds to their attitude of love (cf. v. 21).

Blessings belong to wisdom to give to whom she will. She has both material resources and personal honor, v. 18.[13] That which she gives to others has more value than "fine gold" and "choice silver." This is the purest gold and silver that earth can yield, v. 19. She will "lead" (*ʾahallek,* better, "walk," cf. 6:11) in the "way of righteousness." "Judgment" (*mišpaṭ,* cf. 1:3) is better translated "justice." The word *mišpaṭ* has broad meaning in the legal and ethical realm. It normally refers to action that brings about right ends. This often involves governmental action. "Justice" here parallels "righteousness." This way requires her to requite the pure love of those who have sought her, v. 20. She does this by showering material blessings upon them; cf. 3:16*b.*[14]

The discussion assumes that the search for wisdom comes from a sincere heart. That one could search for wisdom only so as to gain her wealth is foreign to the author's thought. Such a search is unwise and, therefore, would not gain blessings from wisdom.

---

[13]Different commentators dispute the meaning of "righteousness" (*ṣədaqâ*) in v. 18. Toy, p. 169, and Jones, p. 99, are among those who translate "prosperity" and refer it to material blessings of some sort. Plaut, p. 118, and McKane, p. 350, retain the more normal thought of "righteousness." In view of the parallelism with "honour," as well as the emphasis of v. 20 that wisdom walks in the way of *ṣədaqâ,* this last position best suits the context. Note that the passage does not say that wisdom confers righteousness upon the one who loves her. Rather, wisdom herself possesses righteousness. This personal characteristic moves her to bestow personal blessings on those who diligently seek her.

[14]*PC,* p. 164, takes this as the heavenly reward that will one day come to those who have lived a godly life. "Wealth" is thus here a metaphor, used in much the same way as the "treasures" of Matt. 6:20. This is a possible interpretation, but it is more natural to relate the reward to this life rather than to the life to come. Individuals seek wisdom in this life, and they find wisdom in this life. It is logical that they should receive rewards in this life, consistent with the limitations discussed above.

21 That I may cause those that love me to inherit substance; and I will fill their treasures.

Further, the thought of material blessings must assume that these blessings flow within the context of 30:8-9. A wise person seeks only material prosperity for the basic needs of life. In all of his needs, he remains in complete dependence upon the Lord. Wisdom fills the "treasures" (*ʾôṣor*, in this context, "treasuries") of those who follow her. In the OT, *ʾôṣor* refers to personal, royal, temple treasures and to heavenly treasure. Nothing in the passage implies that a godly person will also be a rich person. Rather, he will gain all that wisdom wants him to have. This, indeed, is material success, v. 21.

22-31 The importance of wisdom is unmistakable in the book. Over and over again, the author urges the youth to seek this goal. By repeating these commands, the writer communicates the primacy and desirability of wisdom. These commands to seek wisdom come to the child from two distinct sources. The first, and more prominent source, is the command that comes from his parents (2:1-2; 3:21; 4:4-13; 5:1; 7:1-4; 23:22-23). By means of a poetical device, a second source also bids the youth to seek wisdom. This source comes only in c. 8, where wisdom, as a hypostatized being, urges children to receive her (8:1-5, 10-11, 22-32).

The personification of wisdom reaches new heights here. We may justly term the portrayal of wisdom here as a hypostasis, the representation of wisdom as a being with an independent existence. This is more than merely attributing human characteristics to wisdom. This represents wisdom as a character with real existence. In this sense, it is appropriate to identify wisdom in Proverbs 8 with Jesus Christ, that one "in whom are hidden all the treasures of wisdom and knowledge" (Col. 2:3).

Commentators debate the hypostasis of wisdom in c. 8.[15] From its description in the chapter, however, it certainly meets every test that such a poetic characterization must satisfy. Wisdom existed before Creation

---

[15]Among those who specifically reject the hypostasis of wisdom are Kidner, pp. 78-79; Toy, p. 171; Roland E. Murphy, "The Kerygma of the Book of Proverbs," *Interpretation* 20:5; and J. Coert Rylaarsdam, *The Proverbs, Ecclesiastes, The Song of Solomon*, in *The Layman's Bible Commentary*, ed. Balmer H. Kelly (1968) (hereafter cited as Rylaarsdam), p. 45. On the other hand, a number of equally eminent men accept the concept of hypostatized wisdom in the chapter. Among these are Zöckler, pp. 101, 103; Whybray, *WIP*, pp. 12-13; and Walther Eichrodt, *Theology of the Old Testament*, trans. J. A. Baker (1967), II, 86-87.

*22 The Lord possessed me in the beginning of his way, before his works
of old.*

(8:22-30), even participating together with the Father in the act of
Creation (8:30). Wisdom was the object of God's delight (8:30). At the
same time, wisdom rejoiced in mankind (8:31). It gives blessing (8:32)
and life (8:35) to those who find it. On the other hand, those who do not
follow the ways of wisdom come to death (8:36).

Several important words lie at the heart of the debate. There are contrasting interpretations, depending on how the terms are understood.
One of the most debated words, *qanâ* (cf. 4:7), occurs in v. 22. The root
qanâ occurs over seventy times as a verb and more than one hundred
times as a noun or participle. The meanings of these words rest upon the
decision as to whether there are one or two roots of *qanâ*.[16] The internal
and external evidence both support the conclusion that only a single root
exists.

Virtually all of the verbs refer to property acquired in some way.
Commentators often cite several verses that support the meaning "create." A survey of these reveals that the meaning of "possess," or "acquire," normally satisfies the context.[17] Only in Genesis 4:1 and Psalm
139:13 does the context require something like "create." Both of these
involve a birth context; therefore, the meaning "begat" fits better than
"create." Since the word "begat" logically relates to "acquire" through
the idea of "acquiring a child," the evidence supports "possess," or "acquire."

With the noun and participial forms, much the same story occurs. A
possible exception occurs in Psalm 104:24. Even here, the word can
have the meaning of "possessions." The internal evidence here, then,
favors something connected with "possession," or "acquisition."

The external evidence likewise supports the existence of a single root.
There is no cognate language with a root *qnw/qny* that indicates "to cre-

[16]Ludwig Koehler, *Lexicon in Veteris Testamenti Libros* (1953), II, 843, asserts that two
separate roots exist: *qnh* I, "erwerben" (to acquire), and *qnh* II, "erschaffen" (to create)
or "hervorbringen" (to acquire). This position rests upon the Ugaritic *qny*, a word that is
discussed in note 18. BDB, pp. 888-89, lists only one root that relates to this discussion.
It has the meaning "to get, acquire."
[17]Verses offered in support of the meaning "create" include Gen. 4:1; 14:19, 22; Exod.
15:16; Deut. 32:6; Ps. 74:2; 78:54; 139:13; Isa. 11:11.

*23 I was set up from everlasting, from the beginning, or ever the earth
was.
24 When there were no depths, I was brought forth; when there were no
fountains abounding with water.
25 Before the mountains were settled, before the hills was I brought
forth:*

ate." In every case, the cognate words support the meaning "to purchase," or "to acquire." These meanings easily relate to the sense "possess."[18]

The context of v. 22 requires a meaning that relates to the bringing of
wisdom into existence. Verses 23, 24, and 25 all speak of the establish-
ment of wisdom in its independent existence. Thus a birth context influences our choice of words at this point. In view of this point of
association with other birth contexts in which the word *qanâ* occurs, the
translation "the Lord begat me . . ." is appropriate.

The phrase "beginning of his way" is open to several mutually exclu-
sive interpretations. Perhaps the most frequent way of understanding the
phrase gives it a temporal sense: "the beginning of his way," i.e., the
first of God's works in Creation.[19] Another possibility takes the phrase
as referring to an attribute possessed by God "at the beginning of His
works." This sees the phrase as mentioning the eternal attribute of God's
wisdom.[20] Still another possibility looks upon it as singling out the relative importance of God's creative works. Wisdom, "the beginning,"
stands as the foremost in importance.[21] Some think that the phrase refers

---

[18]Although some have translated the Ugaritic *qny* by "create," the sense is that of birth,
not that of bringing something into existence through the working of the hands. The
Ugaritic word *qny* occurs about nine times. Of these, the phrase *qnyt ilm,* "Creatress of
the gods," gives the strongest support for the interpretation "to create." Again, Asherah
is the "Creatress" only in the sense that she "begets" the gods. Additional evidence from
cognate languages does not support the translation "to create." See G. Levi Della Vida,
"El ʿelyon in Genesis 14:18-20," *JBL* 63:1, and William Irwin, "Where Shall Wisdom
Be Found?" *JBL* 80:142.

[19]Among those holding this position are Garrett, p. 108; Oesterley, p. 61; and Kidner,
p. 80.

[20]Rylaarsdam, p. 45, views the phrase this way. His argument is weak in that he bases
his conclusion on the fact that "the poet has difficulty in finding the right words to say
what he wants to say; namely that God has always possessed this attribute and never acts
without it."

[21]Irwin, *JBL* 80:140, argues that the context calls for something that preceded
Creation, i.e., something that was first in importance.

to wisdom as the "beginning," the first begotten of God's works.[22] Finally, some look upon the phrase as a description of the initial self-revelation of God.[23] The phrase re'šît darkô parallels the word "before," qedem, in the last half of the verse. For this reason, we must determine the meaning of qedem before drawing a conclusion to the discussion.

The word qedem has a temporal sense. It may modify a noun (e.g., Deut. 33:15; Lam. 1:7), act as the object of a preposition (e.g., Neh. 12:46; Isa. 45:21), or modify a verb (Ps. 74:2; 119:152). From this, we may draw some conclusions. In the first place, the word qedem never acts as a comparative term, allowing the contrast of two things, except in a temporal sense. When used with the meaning "before," the word always has a temporal sense. This rules out the possibility that the last part of the verse refers to the creation of wisdom as the act that is first in importance when compared with other creative works of God.

In view of the use of qedem here, it is natural to give it the same use as in the corresponding verses in the Psalms, where the word also occurs without any modifier or governing words. In this case, "before his works of old," qedem mip‘alyw me'az, parallels "the beginning of his way," re'šît darkô. Both phrases modify the action of the verb. The translation of the verse should accordingly be "The Lord begat me, the beginning of His way, before His works of old."

The assignment of a temporal sense to v. 22 agrees with the context. In every verse from 8:22 to 8:30, the author states in some way that wisdom preceded Creation. Verses 22-26 refer to the begetting of wisdom, while vv. 27-30 note that wisdom was present with Yahweh during His creative work.

The actual interpretation of the verse now falls back on the translation of qanâ. If we accept the meaning "begat," the verse then refers to wisdom as the first begotten of God. Proverbs 8:22 therefore becomes the underlying basis for such NT teaching as the equivalency of Christ and wisdom (Luke 11:49; Col. 2:3; I Cor. 1:24, 30) and the exalted

---

[22]C. F. Burney, "Christ As the ΑΡΧΗ of Creation," JTS 27:167, holds this position. He considers the phrase as an accusative in apposition to the suffix on the verb. He proceeds from this conclusion to see a distinct reference to Christ in the verse (cf. Col. 1:15).

[23]KD I, 184, and PC, p. 165, take this position.

position of Christ as the first begotten of the Father (John 1:1-18; Rom. 8:29; Col. 1:15; Heb. 12:23; Rev. 3:14).

Note that the "begetting" of wisdom does not refer to a creative act of God the Father by which the Son comes into existence. The Bible does not teach this (Mic. 5:2; John 1:1-2; Col. 1:17; Rev. 1:8, 17). The "begetting" of Jesus not only shows His eternal pre-existence before Creation but also His eternal generation from the Father, v. 22.

The following verses continue to stress the temporal sense. Wisdom was "set up" *(nissaktî)* from eternity past. The verb *nasak* comes from *nasak* II, "to weave," as in Isaiah 25:7; 30:1, rather than *nasak* III, "to install," as in Psalm 2:6. The birth context favors the meaning "to weave," indicating God's handiwork of fashioning the fetus in the womb, v. 23.[24]

Wisdom preceded the waters of the earth, v. 24.[25] She existed when the mountains and hills came into existence, v. 25. Even before the land itself was created, wisdom was there. The phrase "highest part [*ro²š*] of the dust of the world" is better "first dust of the world." The sense of *ro²š* is "first, beginning." The teaching here is that wisdom preceded the creation of the first speck of dust, v. 26.[26] Wisdom was present at the formation of the universe. When God brought the heavens into existence,

---

[24]Mitchell Dahood, "Proverbs 8,22-31," *CBQ* 30:515-16, understands "old," *ʿolam* as "the Eternal," a divine name, on the basis of Ugaritic. This requires the parallel "ever," *miqqadmê,* also to be an appelative; hence, Dahood reads *miqqadmî,* "the Primeval." He further repoints the familiar *²ereṣ,* "earth," as *²aruṣ,* from *rûṣ,* "to run," in the sense "to flow." His exercise is largely subjective and adds nothing significant to the verse.

[25]The *nipʿal* participle "abounding," *nikbadê,* occurs only here in construct with a physical object. Elsewhere it is associated with "honor" and "glory." This has led to the supposition that the form is incorrect. Beer, BH, following the LXX, suggests *nibkê.* Albright, *VTS* III, 8, and George M. Landes, "The Fountain at Jazer," *BASOR* 144:33, also correct what they perceive as a corrupted text. It is, however, unwarranted to assume that *kabod* cannot modify something tangible. The cognate *kabatû* occurs several times in *Atrachasis,* the Babylonian Flood epic, describing "intense" noise or "heavy" work. It is entirely possible that the MT's "heavy," i.e., "abounding," waters is correct. For the general sense of the word, see the discussion at 3:9.

[26]Toy, p. 182, omits *wǝḥûṣôt* as incompatible with *²ereṣ.* D. Winton Thomas, "Notes on Some Passages in the Book of Proverbs," *VT* 15:272, tentatively suggests a Hebrew root *ḥûṣ,* a place that collects water. Beer, BH, proposes *ḥaṣîr* and reads "grass." None of the suggestions add materially to the interpretation of the verse. KD I, 186, argues that *²eret* refers to developed land while *ḥûṣ* denotes the undeveloped fields. Dahood, *CBQ* 30:516, accepts Delitzsch's argument, adding support from the Phoenician cognate for *²ereṣ.*

*26 While as yet he had not made the earth, nor the fields, nor the high-
est part of the dust of the world.*
*27 When he prepared the heavens, I was there: when he set a compass
upon the face of the depth:*
*28 When he established the clouds above: when he strengthened the
fountains of the deep:*
*29 When he gave to the sea his decree, that the waters should not pass
his commandment: when he appointed the foundations of the earth:*
*30 Then I was by him, as one brought up with him: and I was daily his
delight, rejoicing always before him;*

wisdom was there. When He bounded the oceans with their circular face
(cf. Job 26:10; Isa. 40:22), wisdom was there, v. 27. When God established the clouds in the heavens, wisdom was there. When He brought
into being the springs beneath the sea, wisdom was there, v. 28.[27]

When God decreed the boundary for the oceans, so that the waters
would not overflow the earth, wisdom was there. When He decreed the
foundations of the earth, wisdom was there, v. 29.[28] In all of the creative
work of God, wisdom was with Him as "one brought up with him"
('amôn). The noun 'amôn occurs only here and at Jeremiah 52:15, where
it refers to craftsmen. A related form occurs at Song of Solomon 7:1. It
refers to a "master workman," the designer of Creation.[29] The phrase
"daily *his* delight" is better "I was daily delighted." The context argues
that this is the delight experienced by wisdom as she rejoiced before

---

[27]Toy, p. 182, repoints "strengthened," ʿəzôz, to ʿazzô and interprets as God's fixing or
restraining of the oceans. It is routine to use the infinitive construct with the *beth* preposition to show time. There is, therefore, no need to change the MT. The subject of the
action is obvious from the context.

[28]AB, p. 68, follows the LXX and emends "appointed," bəhûqô, to bəhazzəqô, "when he
laid (the strong foundations of the earth)." Driver, *Biblica*, 32:178, supports the MT by
relating it to Akkadian "to mingle." He suggests that God gathered together the elements
as He formed the earth. The traditional sense of *hôq*, "to cut, inscribe," may refer to an
unchangeable decree of God, e.g., Exod. 15:26; 18:16; I Kings 8:61; Ps. 50:16. This
leads to the view expressed above, that God decreed the foundations of the earth.

[29]The Hebrew 'amôn has a myriad of interpretations, each with logical arguments in
support. The gloss "master craftsman" has probably the majority of support from modern authors. Although I disagree with his conclusion, R. B. Y. Scott has an excellent discussion in "Wisdom in Creation: the 'Amon of Proverbs VIII 30," *VT* 10:213-23. He
vocalizes 'amôn as 'omen, "binding," and considers wisdom as the link binding the
"Creator to his creation."

31 Rejoicing in the habitable part of his earth; and my delights were with the sons of men.
32 Now therefore hearken unto me, O ye children: for blessed are they that keep my ways.
33 Hear instruction, and be wise, and refuse it not.
34 Blessed is the man that heareth me, watching daily at my gates, waiting at the posts of my doors.
35 For whoso findeth me findeth life, and shall obtain favour of the Lord.
36 But he that sinneth against me wrongeth his own soul: all they that hate me love death.

God, v. 30.[30] Thus, she rejoiced in "the habitable parts of his earth" (better, "the world, His earth") and in its inhabitants, v. 31.[31]

32-36 Several passages in the book refer generally to the blessedness of the one who walks in wisdom, without specifically developing the nature or scope of this blessed condition. This promise occurs three times in the final paragraph of the chapter, in 32b, 34a, and 35b. Wisdom thus has great value to it (3:13-15; 8:10-11), even though the exact nature of this value is not defined.

Wisdom exhorts the sons to heed her instruction. She promises blessing to those who keep her ways, v. 32. She urges the youths to follow her instruction rather than neglecting it, v. 33. She describes the man who avidly awaits her instruction, remaining outside her house so that he can catch the first glimpse of her as she comes out to give further instruction. The word "watching" (šaqad) has the connotation of alertness, as of the leopard who watches for the chance to seize its prey (Jer. 5:6) or the mourner who is alert when he would prefer to sleep (Ps. 102:7).

---

[30]Theodor H. Gaster, "Short Notes," *VT* 4:77-78, links məśaheqet, "rejoicing," to "jesting," as though the ʾamôn were a court jester who served his lord as a counselor. McKane, p. 356, likewise relates the verb to jesting. The view seems too light to me, interpreting the ʾamôn in the context of an Akkadian or Babylonian king. It is more appropriate to think of the delight felt by wisdom as she begins the creative work that will culminate in a people voluntarily serving the God they have come to love.

[31]With weak justification, Toy, pp. 173, 179, deletes 31b. Dahood, *CBQ* 30:520, derives "his earth," ʾarṣô, from rṣy/w, "to be pleased with." He translates, "I enjoyed myself rejoicing in the world." The form would be exceptional, however. It does not seem likely that such a common word should have an uncommon meaning.

The word parallels *šamar*, "to guard," (cf. 2:8) here and in Ezra 8:29 and Psalm 127:1, v. 34.[32]

If we accept the idea of a hypostasis, vv. 35-36 present an incipient gospel. The person who finds wisdom finds "life" (*hayâ*, cf. 4:4). While it is true that *hayâ* normally indicates simply a fullness of earthly life, it goes beyond this here. The antithetic parallelism with v. 36 draws a sharp contrast between eternal life and eternal death. Thus, *hayâ* stresses the possibility of eternal life for those who gain "wisdom" (cf. 2:18-19; 12:28; 15:24), v. 35. The word *hot°î* (cf. 1:10), "he that sinneth," must be taken in the sense "he who misses," the root idea of *hata°*. The contrasting parallelism with v. 35 demands this. Thus, the person who fails to find wisdom "wrongeth his own soul" (better, "treats himself violently"). The hatred of wisdom leads to eternal death, v. 36.

---

[32]Various attempts have been made to rearrange the order of vv. 32-34 to gain better parallelism. Whybray, *VT* 16:493-96, concludes that 32*a*, 35*b*, and 36*b* are editorial insertions. After deleting them and rearranging the passage, he ends with 34*a*, 32*b*, 34*b*, *c*, 35*a*, 36*a*. Toy, p. 179, suggests reading 32*a*, 33*a* (emended to eliminate the triplet), 32*b*, and 34*a*, 34*b*-36. Gemser, p. 38, deletes 33*a* (with the LXX) and transposes 32*b* after 34*c*. He inserts *tôkahatî* into 33*b*, following the *°al*. The LXX also rearranged the passage. None of these changes are necessary. The passage stands quite well as it is. Verses 32 and 33 are synthetic poetry, while verses 34-36 develop the idea of the blessing that wisdom bestows.

Practical Applications from Proverbs 8

More than most chapters, a detailed outline of this, the "wisdom chapter," is helpful. While the subject matter is complex, the structure of the chapter is clear and helpful for teaching purposes.

I. The Cry of Wisdom 1-5
   A. The Place of Her Cry 1-3
   B. The Objects of Her Cry 4-5
II. The Morality of Wisdom 6-11
   A. The Truth of Wisdom 6-7
   B. The Righteousness of Wisdom 8-9
   C. The Choice of Wisdom 10-11
III. The Rewards of Wisdom 12-21
   A. The Associations of Wisdom 12-13
   B. The Administration of Wisdom 14-21
       1. Her Nature 14
       2. Her Rule 15-16
       3. Her Fruit 17-19
       4. Her Reward 20-21
IV. The Creation by Wisdom 22-31
   A. The Pre-existence of Wisdom 22-26
   B. The Place of Wisdom 27-31
V. The Appeal of Wisdom 32-36
   A. The Ground of Blessedness 32-34
   B. The Ground of Eternal Life 35-36

1 Wisdom hath builded her house, she hath hewn out her seven pillars:
2 She hath killed her beasts; she hath mingled her wine; she hath also furnished her table.
3 She hath sent forth her maidens: she crieth upon the highest places of the city,
4 Whoso is simple, let him turn in hither: as for him that wanteth understanding, she saith to him,
5 Come, eat of my bread, and drink of the wine which I have mingled.
6 Forsake the foolish, and live; and go in the way of understanding.

PROVERBS 9

This final chapter of the introductory part of the book contrasts wisdom and folly. Both invite the "simple" to a banquet, but the differences in the invitations and banquets are stark. Wisdom's invitation is open and public; folly's invitation is private and secretive. Wisdom offers meat and wine; folly prepares bread and water. Wisdom herself prepares her banquet; folly offers water stolen from someone else. Wisdom's banquet leads to life; folly's banquet leads to death.

The chapter divides naturally into three stanzas of six verses each. Some relocate vv. 7-12 as a later addition interfering with the contrast between wisdom (vv. 1-6) and folly (vv. 13-18).[1] The chapter, however, shows a logical development of the theme. Verses 1-6 describe wisdom's call. Verses 7-12 contrast the wise man with the scorner. Verses 13-18 describe folly's call. Verses 7-12 make a logical transition by contrasting those who respond to each of the invitations.

1-6 Two questions confront us as we approach the chapter. What is wisdom's "house"? What are the "seven pillars" of the house? We cannot be dogmatic with either answer since the text does not give an answer. The context, however, favors the view that wisdom's house is not a literal house at all. Rather, it is wisdom herself, to whom she invites others to come. It follows then that the pillars are likewise not literal

---

[1]For example, Martin, p. 67, states that the passage is "supposed by some to be an address of Wisdom, but which is much more probably a set of aphorisms drawn from some other source and put in this place by some later editor." McKane, p. 359, holds that "Verses 7-12 disturb both the balance and continuity of the chapter and it is probable that v. 13 originally resumed v. 6." Toy, p. 183, states that the passage is "inserted by scribal error." The textual evidence, however, supports the MT. Considering the logic and structure of the chapter, together with the textual support, there is no need to relocate the passage.

pillars.[2] They represent the nature of the house as a well-supported building. The number seven occurs widely in ancient cultures in a symbolic sense, representing completeness. It further is often associated with God, e.g., the length of feasts, Exodus 34:18 and Leviticus 23:34; number of sacrifices, Numbers 28:11, 19; sprinkling of blood, Leviticus 16:14, 19; praising God, Psalm 119:164, and numerous NT uses of a similar nature. While the number seven has a literal use in many places, it also has a symbolic sense much of the time. The number seven is appropriate here. It indicates the thoroughness with which wisdom's "house" is built, together with its sacred nature.

As in 1:20, 14:1 (possibly), and 24:7, *hokmôt* is a plural of intensification here. This lays stress upon the personified wisdom who invites mankind to partake of her "feast." She has "hewn out" (*hasabâ*) her seven pillars. The word *hasab* denotes the work of the stone mason. Here, wisdom carves the pillars from stone as she both adorns and strengthens her house, v. 1.[3]

---

[2]The variety of interpretations of the "seven pillars" is almost laughable. The Talmud, in *Sanhedrin* 38a, refers to the seven days of Creation. In *Shabbat* 116a, the phrase refers to the seven books of the Pentateuch. The rabbis divided Numbers into three books, 1:1–10:34; 10:35-36; 11:1–36:13. Inverted *nuns* set off 10:35-36, but there is no clear explanation for this. Plaut, p. 116, refers to a Jewish interpretation that divided the Pentateuch into four books and Genesis into three books—1:1a, 1:1b, and 1:1c–50:26. He also mentions the view of Ibn Ezra, taking it as "the seven liberal arts" and that of Böstrom, who understood it to be the seven ancient planets known to man. Among others, Cohen, p. 52; Jones, p. 104; and KD I, 196, relate the pillars to a Near Eastern house built around an inner court, with pillars at each of the four corners and in the middle of three of the sides, the fourth side being reserved for the opening. Hippolytus refers to the "all-holy Spirit" but mentions others who equate it with "the seven divine orders which sustain the creation by His holy and inspired teaching; to wit, the prophets, the apostles, the martyrs, the hierarchs, the hermits, the saints, and the righteous" (*The Ante-Nicene Fathers*, ed. Alexander Roberts and James Donaldson [1886], I, 175). Gosta W. Ahlstron, "The House of Wisdom," *Svensk Exegetisk Arsbok* 44:75, connects it with a house in which the six pillars are on opposing sides while the seventh supports the ridgepole. Skehan, *CBQ* 9:190-98, gives a not very convincing picture of a seven-sectioned Proverbs 2-7, each section containing twenty-two verses. All that these suggestions accomplish is to show the danger of allegorical interpretation, in which the interpreter becomes the authority. Jonas C. Greenfield, "The Seven Pillars of Wisdom (Prov. 9:1)—a Mistranslation," *JQR* 76:13-20, emends the phrase to read "The Seven have set its foundations." He relates the number to the seven sages of Babylonian literature, who guided the foundation of cities and gave wisdom to kings. There is no textual support for the change.
[3]AB, p. 74, emends "hewn out," *hasabâ*, to *hissîbâ*, "to set up, erect." In this, he follows the LXX, ὑπηρεισεν and considers the change a more suitable parallel to "built" in 1a.

In preparation for the feast, wisdom has "killed her beasts" (or "slaughtered her meat") and "mingled her wine," mixing it with either spices or water; cf. Proverbs 23:30 and Isaiah 5:22. Limited scriptural evidence supports the idea of spices rather than water. Isaiah 1:22 and Psalm 102:9 both portray the mixing of wine with water as associated with judgment and grief, while Song of Solomon 8:2 presents spiced wine as desirable.[4] Further, wisdom has set her table (*šulḥan,* originally a piece of leather rolled out on the ground for use as a table, but later the table itself) with an implied array of dainties for eating.

The feast elsewhere is an emblem of fellowship between man and God. Isaiah 25:6 and 55:2 look forward to this. Jesus used the idea of a wedding feast in the parable of the Marriage Supper (Matt. 22:4; Luke 14:16). The saints will enjoy the Marriage Supper of the Lamb as they enter into the Millennial Kingdom (Rev. 19:9), v. 2.

Wisdom sends her maidens throughout the city to invite others to her feast. The invitation resounds from the heights of the city, a true public invitation to others, v. 3.[5] She invites the "simple," or "naive," one (*petî,* cf. 1:22) to turn in to her house. One who lacks understanding (*ḥasar-leb,* literally, "lacks heart," cf. 6:32) may also come. The phrase "she saith to him" makes the transition to the next verse in which she gives some details of the feast, v. 4.

She invites her guests to eat of her "bread" (*laḥem*) and to drink from her "wine" (*yayin*). The noun *laḥem* often refers generally to "food," e.g., Psalm 136:25; 146:7. The noun *yayin* is the familiar drink made from grapes. With both "bread" and "wine," the *beth* preposition has a rare partitive use (G.K. 119m). The implied thought is that there is plenty of food and wine. The guests may eat and drink from this abundant supply, v. 5. Verse 6 explains what it means to partake of wisdom's banquet. One must turn from "foolish" friends and go along the path of

---

The act of hewing out a pillar, however, is certainly as parallel a thought as is "setting up" or "establishing." There is no need for the change.

[4]In later years, wine mixed with water became normal, II Macc. 15:39. Robert H. Stein, "Wine Drinking in New Testament Times," *Christianity Today,* June 20, 1975, pp. 9-11, is the classic article discussing the mixing of wine with water.

[5]AB, p. 77, understands this as wisdom speaking. Most commentators, however, state that the maidens speak on wisdom's behalf. It is reasonable to relate this to wisdom's speech, a speech that her servants declare. This is consistent with the usual method of God in which He works through His servants as they proclaim His Word to the world.

7 He that reproveth a scorner getteth to himself shame: and he that rebuketh a wicked man getteth himself a blot.

8 Reprove not a scorner, lest he hate thee: rebuke a wise man, and he will love thee.

9 Give instruction to a wise man, and he will be yet wiser: teach a just man, and he will increase in learning.

10 The fear of the Lord is the beginning of wisdom: and the knowledge of the holy is understanding.

11 For by me thy days shall be multiplied, and the years of thy life shall be increased.

12 If thou be wise, thou shalt be wise for thyself: but if thou scornest, thou alone shalt bear it.

"understanding."[6] This gives "life," here used in the same sense as in 8:35, eternal life as opposed to the death that v. 18 pictures, v. 6.

7-12 Wisdom justifies her appeal to the "simple." The "scorner" (*lēṣ,* cf. 1:22) and the "wicked man" (*rašaʿ,* cf. 8:7) are too far gone. One who reproves them gets only "shame" (*qalôn,* or "dishonor," cf. 3:35) and "a blot" (*mûm*). The word *mûm* is rare with the sense of "insult" or "shame,"occurring elsewhere only at Deuteronomy 32:5 and Job 11:15. The parallel with *qalôn,* however, leaves no doubt to the meaning, v. 7.[7] If you reprove a "scorner," he will hate you. The lesson is clear. Why cast your "pearls before swine," who will scorn, insult, and hate you for your reproofs, v. 8a?

In contrast, if you reprove a wise man, he will "love" (*ʾahab,* best taken in the sense of appreciation) you for your faithful actions. "Love," *ʾahab,* occurs widely to express a positive emotional attachment or desire. The scope of the word is broad, including lust, preferment, friendship, as well as what we customarily think of as love. For this reason, the context must determine the exact meaning in each passage, v. 8b. Give "instruction" (the parallel requires something of this sort to be supplied) to the wise man and he will increase in wisdom. Teach the

---

[6]This is the easiest way in which to take the MT. Others have understood the plural "foolish," *pǝtaʾyim,* as an abstract plural and interpreted the phrase as forsaking "foolishness." Toy, p. 187, emends the word to *petî* to arrive at the same conclusion. AB, p. 74, emends to *pǝtîkem* and translates, "ignorance," again the same general conclusion. The emendations add nothing to the verse.

[7]H. Neil Richardson, "Some Notes on לִיץ and Its Derivatives,"*VT* 5:172, translates, *mûmô* as "faulty." McKane, p. 224, suggests "blemish." NET, p. 18, translates, "gets hurt." The context of "shame" in 7a argues for something more directly parallel, such as "insult" or "abuse," rather than a physical result.

13 A foolish woman is clamorous: she is simple, and knoweth nothing.
*14 For she sitteth at the door of her house, on a seat in the high places of
    the city,*
15 To call passengers who go right on their ways:
*16 Whoso is simple, let him turn in hither: and as for him that wanteth
    understanding, she saith to him,*
17 Stolen waters are sweet, and bread eaten in secret is pleasant.
*18 But he knoweth not that the dead are there; and that her guests are
    in the depths of hell.*

"righteous" (*ṣaddîq,* cf. 1:3) and he will grow in learning. Note that
"wise" and "righteous" are parallel, indicating that wisdom requires
righteousness, v. 9.

Verses 10-11 provide a natural conclusion to the thought of becoming
wise. The first step toward true wisdom requires that one "fear the
Lord" (*yirʾat yǝhwah,* cf. 1:7). The "knowledge" (*daʿat,* experiential
knowledge, cf. 1:4) of "the holy" (*qǝdošîm*) leads to understanding. The
word *qǝdošîm,* from *qadôš,* must refer to God, the Holy One. The parallelism argues that the word is a plural of majesty and refers to "the Holy
One." To develop the parallelism more fully, a supplied word should
parallel "beginning." Thus, the "knowledge of the Holy One is *the way*
to understanding," v. 10.

Wisdom gives long life to those who embrace her. The emphasis here
is on the fulness of human life. The wise person has God's blessing
upon his life. He lives out all of the days God wills for him. Elsewhere,
the Scriptures speak of premature death (e.g., I Cor. 11:30; Heb. 10:26-
29) for those who profess faith in Christ but live far off from Him, v. 11.

To close her admonition, wisdom returns to the contrast between the
wise and the foolish man. We may not give wisdom and folly away.
Each man must make his own decision in this area. Thus, a wise man is
wise for himself alone, and, likewise, a scorner alone bears the responsibility for his scorning, v. 12.

13-18 Wisdom now draws the contrast with the banquet offered by the
foolish woman. As the passage develops, she is seen to be an adulteress.
This is an appropriate figure with which to personify folly since adultery fittingly represents the fullest degree of folly.[8]

---

[8]Perowne, p. 85, and Greenstone, p. 95, reject the idea that the passage personifies
folly. They assert that the passage deals specifically with adultery, not generally with

The woman whose very nature is folly is "clamorous" (or "boisterous," cf. *hamâ*, 1:21).[9] She is "foolish" (cf. *petî*, 1:22). The word is an intensive plural. It emphasizes the woman's folly. She consequently "knoweth nothing," a phrase that has become a battleground for interpretation.[10] From the context, which draws a contrast between wisdom and folly, it is reasonable to apply the phrase to folly's inability to discern right from wrong, v. 13.

Folly's invitation is private, a sharp contrast with that of wisdom. Wisdom's invitation is public, uttered openly on the high places of the city (v. 3). Folly calls privately from in front of her house. She is seated in a chair there, with her house located on the "high places of the city," where she has access to people as they pass by, v. 14.[11] In this way, she distracts people from their otherwise productive activities, v. 15.

The adulteress invites the "simple" (*petî*, cf. 1:22) youth to enjoy her offerings. The form of her invitation parallels that of wisdom's invitation (cf. v. 4). This is natural since Satan often counterfeits God's truth. The difference lies in what she offers, sensual pleasures rather than spiritual understanding. The adulteress appeals to the carnal nature of the youth with an attraction that involves only temporal pleasures.

---

folly. The correspondence with vv. 1-6 argues strongly, however, that this is a deliberate literary form. It purposely contrasts wisdom and folly. Both occupy a house, both prepare a meal for those who respond to their invitation, both appeal to the "simple," and both lead their followers to an end.

[9]Driver, *Biblica*, 32:179, changes the accenting to a 2-2-2 form, instead of the 3-3 form found in the MT. He understands *homîyâ* as a verb rather than a predicate. This is contrary to the similar use in 7:11. Moreover, it adds nothing significant to the meaning.

[10]Oesterley, p. 71; Zöckler, p. 108; and Kidner, p. 84, among others, follow the LXX and emend *mâ* to *kalimma*. The MT makes sense if we take *mâ* as an indefinite pronoun (so G.K. 137c) and translate, "she knows nothing whatever." D. Winton Thomas, "Note on בַּל־יָדְעָה in Proverbs 9¹³," *JTS* 4:23, parallels *yadaʿâ* with an Arabic word, "to become still, quiet, at rest." He therefore translates, "she wanders to and fro," i.e., she is restless. It is not likely that such a well-known Hebrew root would have such an unusual sense.

[11]The word *kisseʾ* normally denotes a "throne." Henry III, 841, accepts the idea of a throne. He feels this shows the woman's authority. Zöckler, pp. 106, 108, translates, "enthroned in the high places of the city." He considers the throne metaphorical. Second Kings 4:10 and 25:28 show that *kisseʾ* can designate an ordinary chair or the chair of a special person. Here, *kisseʾ* describes the chair of the adulteress as she sits outside in order to invite others to enter. Whybray, p. 56, suggests that this woman, sitting at the door, indicates her position in a Babylonian sexual cult of the love goddess. The position is, however, highly arbitrary with no supporting evidence.

The "stolen waters" here have the same symbolism as in 5:15, where "water" also stands as a symbol of sensual pleasures. The waters are "stolen" in that the woman's husband is the only one who has the right to enjoy these. "Bread" occurs elsewhere in Proverbs 4:17; 20:17 with a symbolic meaning, indicating the fruits of evil labors (see also 30:20). So here, the "bread" is that which does not belong to the "simple" youth, the sensual offerings of the woman, vv. 15-17.

The youth who responds to folly's invitation enters a spiritual trap from which he may not escape. Others who have responded before him now are "in the depths of hell" (šəʾôl, cf. 7:27). As with other passages referring to Sheol with this same context of adultery (2:18-19; 7:27), the thought is of spiritual death, eternal judgment, v. 18.

Practical Applications from Proverbs 9

The Banquet Invitation
I. The Invitation from Wisdom—open and public
  A. Her menu 2, 5
  B. Her invitation 3-5
  C. Her goal 6
II. The Invitation from Folly—private and secretive
  A. Her menu 17
  B. Her invitation 14
  C. Her goal 18

Everyone responds to one of these two invitations. Folly's invitation is "sweet" and "pleasant" now, v. 17, but the end is eternity in hell. Wisdom's invitation may not have the immediate attraction, but the end is a full life, v. 11, and eternity in heaven (note the symbolism of a feast elsewhere in the Bible). To which invitation will you respond?

FIRST COLLECTION OF SOLOMONIC PROVERBS
PROVERBS
10:1–24:24

1 The proverbs of Solomon. A wise son maketh a glad father: but a foolish son is the heaviness of his mother.

PROVERBS 10

We come now to the main body of the text of Proverbs, continuing through 24:34.[1] This block of material consists of 447 proverbs, most of them isolated aphorisms but some (e.g., 10:18-20; 15:8-9; 16:12-15) grouped together by subject. The majority of these proverbs are antithetic, contrasting the two halves. Other forms of poetry also occur.

1 After a brief subtitle, identifying himself once more as the author, Solomon states the first of the isolated maxims. Appropriately, the proverb focuses on wisdom. This makes a transition from the introductory chapters to the body of the book. A "wise" (*ḥakam,* cf. 1:2) son brings "joy" (*śamaḥ*) to his parents. The verb *śamaḥ* is a spontaneous attitude of inward rejoicing. It is often strong enough to find some outward expression by means of a tangible action. A "foolish" (*kəsîl,* cf. 1:22) son causes "grief" (*tûgâ*). The word *tûgâ* is mental affliction, distinguished from the pain and humility that may also accompany the attitude. The "father" and "mother" occur here in poetic variation. There is no attempt to contrast the joy of a father with the grief of a mother as the outcome of a child's actions.[2]

The book stresses the blessings that come to parents of an obedient child (10:1; 15:20; 23:15-16, 24-25; 27:11; 29:3, 17). There is a remarkable unity of thought in these passages. Over and over, the joy (*śamaḥ*) of the parents stands out as the great benefit that comes from the wise behavior of a child. They receive deep satisfaction as they consider the actions of their child. Only 29:17 does not stress this directly. There, Solomon emphasizes the comfort received by the parents from their child.

---

[1] I refer again to Kitchen's analysis in *Tyndale Bulletin* 28:69-114. The article shows that the structure of Proverbs parallels that found in other ancient wisdom literature from the Solomonic period.

[2] Cohen, p. 56, goes too far when he suggests that the verse implies that the mother has a greater capacity for grief than does the father. Proverbs 17:21 reverses the picture, with the father there expressing grief over his son's conduct. The interchange of "father" and "mother" is poetic variation only. It is not meant to teach a differing response of the parents to their child's behavior.

2 Treasures of wickedness profit nothing: but righteousness delivereth from death.
3 The Lord will not suffer the soul of the righteous to famish: but he casteth away the substance of the wicked.
4 He becometh poor that dealeth with a slack hand: but the hand of the diligent maketh rich.
5 He that gathereth in summer is a wise son: but he that sleepeth in harvest is a son that causeth shame.

2 The verse draws a distinct contrast between "wickedness" (*rešaᶜ*, cf. 8:7) and "righteousness" (*ṣedaqâ*, cf. 1:3). Wealth gathered by evil means brings no lasting profit, while righteous actions bring deliverance from death. The seeming contradiction with v. 15, in which the proverb says that wealth has profit, makes it likely that Solomon has in mind eternal matters. Wealth profits nothing in this area; righteousness profits everything.

3 The proverb here is generally true. The Lord does not normally let frustration come to His children in their desires. He does, however, oppose the desires of the wicked to succeed. The word "soul" (*nepeš,* cf. 7:23) has a broad variety of meanings in the OT. Here, the thought seems to be of inner desires and cravings. God places these in the hearts of the godly. As they agree with Him, they cooperate with Him to carry out His will. He blesses them as they seek to gain these desires because these desires are His desires as well. At the same time, He often frustrates the efforts of wicked men to reach their wicked goals.[3]

4-5 Two verses now follow that focus on the theme of work. These are one of only two passages in Proverbs (cf. 20:11) that directly apply to the child's responsibilities in this area.[4] Here, Solomon observes that the lazy person will become poor (*ra²š*).[5] The *ra²š* is a person who is destitute. In contrast, a diligent person will increase his wealth. In like manner, a wise child will anticipate his future needs while a shameful child

---

[3]S. R. Driver, "Witchcraft in the Old Testament," *JRAS* (1943), pp. 9-12 (see also *Biblica* 32:179), suggests a meaning of "windy" for *hawwat* when used in connection with speech. The parallelism here, however, supports the normal meaning of "craving" (rather than "substance," AV) with a distinct sense of evil associated with it (cf. also 11:6).
[4]Numerous other passages develop the broader aspects of work; cf. 6:6-11; 10:26; 12:11, 24, 27; 13:4, 23; 15:19; 16:26; 18:9; 19:15, 24; 20:4, 13; 21:5, 25, 26; 22:13; 24:30-34; 26:13-16; 27:18, 23-27; 28:19; 31:13-19, 27. See the subject study on work.
[5]The word *ra²š*, "poor," is from *rus,* "to be poor." The *aleph* is an orthographic insertion denoting the long vowel sound (see G.K. 23g). This occurs again in 13:23.

6 Blessings are upon the head of the just: but violence covereth the mouth of the wicked.

will lazily ignore them. There is both practical and spiritual justification for these observations. Practically, the hard-working individual who plans for the future provides for himself and assures that he will reach his full potential for income. Conversely, the lazy son who lives only for the present follows a path of life that will likely bring shame to himself and his family, v. 4.

The word "sleepeth" (*radam*) implies a deep sleep. Thus, the verse speaks of one who is indolent, not diligent in his work. The man who is inefficient in his work and the man who is lazy from time to time are not in view in the verse. All of us are guilty of these from time to time. It is the indolent person who becomes poor.

There is a spiritual application also. A child who labors diligently in his work responsibilities prepares himself to labor diligently in spiritual opportunities. And, likewise, a child whose labor reflects a lazy character does not prepare himself for substantial spiritual responsibilities. The response of the child to work influences his ability to serve the Lord in later years, v. 5.

6 There is no question about the meaning of 6*a*. God blesses the "just" (*sadîq*, the "righteous" man, cf. 1:3). While the verse does not mention God directly, in view of v. 3 it is likely that He is the source of the blessings.

The understanding of 6*b*, "violence covereth the mouth of the wicked," turns on the view taken of "covereth" (*kasâ*, "to cover, conceal, hide").[6] The word occurs broadly throughout the OT with the above meanings. Specifically, it occurs seven times in Proverbs (10:6, 11, 12, 18; 11:13; 17:9; 28:13). All of these have a similar sense of covering up or concealing something. It is appropriate here, then, to translate "the mouth

---

[6]Alfred Guillaume, "Magical Terms in the Old Testament," *JRAS* (1942), pp. 117-18, 129, takes *kasâ* as "to utter a spell" and finds in this a reference to some magical incantation. Toy, p. 203, tentatively suggests that the original line has been lost and 11*b* substituted. AB, pp. 81, 83, takes *kasâ* with the sense "to uncover" (so Dahood, *PNWSP*, p. 19) and translates, "the mouth of the wicked uncovers violence." He also comments that the original line has been lost and 11*b* supplied in its place. The AV translation, "violence covereth the mouth of the wicked," focuses on the hardened look on the face of many sinners. The view discussed above gives a better parallelism.

*7 The memory of the just is blessed: but the name of the wicked shall
rot.
8 The wise in heart will receive commandments: but a prating fool
shall fall.
9 He that walketh uprightly walketh surely: but he that perverteth his
ways shall be known.*

of the wicked conceals wrong [*hamas,* cf. 3:31]." With this, we have an
antithetic parallelism. God openly displays His blessing upon the right;
in contrast, the wicked covers up wrongdoing.[7]

7 Once more, the thought of the proverb relates to the eternal realm.
The memory of the righteous is always blessed, from an eternal perspective. And the name of the wicked will likewise always "rot" (*yirqab*),
again from an eternal perspective. The root *raqeb* occurs three times in
Proverbs (see also 12:4; 14:30). In each case, the word poetically indicates that which fades away or causes something to deteriorate.

There is a sense is which the proverb is also true in this life. It states a
generalization, a truth that is usually true. The memory of the righteous
is normally a blessed memory to those who knew the righteous one.
And the name of the wicked will often decay with the passage of time.

8 The wise person receives "commandments." This word apparently
refers to the commandments that come to him from his father, although
it can refer generally to directions from his superiors. In contrast, the
"prating fool" will "fall." The "prating fool" is more literally "a fool of
lips," i.e., one who talks without carefully reasoned thought. This one
will "fall" (*labat*). The verb *labat* occurs only in 10:8, 10 and in Hosea
4:14, all in the *nip^al* theme. The Arabic cognate means "to throw
[someone] down." The context in each biblical reference requires something more than "stumbling." The idea is that of being "thrown down."

9 The word "uprightly" (*tom,* cf. 2:7) denotes moral uprightness or integrity. One who is morally upright can walk with security (*betah,* cf.
1:33). This confident self-assurance comes from the fact that wisdom
guides his actions. In contrast, the one who "perverteth his ways" must

---

[7]Kidner, p. 85, reverses the subject and object. He understands that the man's evil covers his face, openly seen by all. There is only weak textual support for this view.

10 He that winketh with the eye causeth sorrow: but a prating fool shall fall.
11 The mouth of a righteous man is a well of life: but violence covereth the mouth of the wicked.
12 Hatred stirreth up strifes: but love covereth all sins.

cover things up that he does not want known. His effort is of no avail. He will be "known," found out by others.[8]

10 One who "winketh with the eye" is one who deceives, saying one thing while signaling with the eye that he means something else. Compare 6:13. This one brings "sorrow" (ʿeṣeb). The word ʿeṣeb occurs throughout the OT to indicate both physical and emotional pain. In synonymous parallelism with 10a, 10b repeats the thought of 8b. The one who speaks without thinking will "fall" (labaṭ, cf. v. 8), be thrown down.[9]

11 The "mouth," i.e., the speech of the righteous, is a "well of life," better rendered as "fountain of life." The picture is of a vibrant, bubbling fountain rather than of a quiescent well of water. The thought is well expressed by Delitzsch. The speech of the righteous "is morally strengthening, intellectually elevating, and inwardly quickening in its effect on the hearers." The interpretation of 11b is identical to that of 6b (see notes).

12 This is one of only two proverbs to contrast "hatred" and "love" (cf. also 15:17). Hatred fosters strife. Rather than the numerical plural, the plural here is intensive. This brings out the nature of the strife that may be engendered because of hatred. In contrast, love covers all kinds of "sins" (pašaʿim). The word pešaʿ has the sense of "transgressions" with a fundamental idea of rebellion. The use of pešaʿ heightens the extent of the gracious action of love. This sin involves rebellion against the

---

[8]Several authors emend in order to create better parallelism. Toy, pp. 204, 207, suggests yeroaʿ, "to suffer." AB, p. 84, and Gemser, p. 42, also propose this. D. Winton Thomas, "The Root ידע in Hebrew," *JTS* 35:303-4, basing his suggestion on an Arabic cognate, advocates yadaʿ, "be made submissive." These suggestions are not persuasive.

[9]Several authors follow the LXX in order to achieve an antithetic parallelism. Among others, Alden, pp. 85-86; Toy, p. 207; and Martin, pp. 72-73, basically follow the LXX, "he who reproves makes peace." It is, however, a radical change from the Hebrew. The *Targum*, p. 28, further supports the Hebrew. Since the MT makes sense, there is no need to emend it to follow the LXX. Bryce, *JBL* 94:25-27, takes the closing of the eyes as an evil omen, relating it to 6:13 and 16:30. This is so totally out of character with the Scriptures that the suggestion cannot be taken seriously.

13 In the lips of him that hath understanding wisdom is found: but a rod is for the back of him that is void of understanding.
14 Wise men lay up knowledge: but the mouth of the foolish is near destruction.
15 The rich man's wealth is his strong city: the destruction of the poor is their poverty.
16 The labour of the righteous tendeth to life: the fruit of the wicked to sin.

normal relationship that should exist between two people. Yet love "covers" (*kasâ,* cf. v. 6) this evil. James 5:20 and I Peter 4:8 quote the phrase and apply it practically.

13-14 The common theme of speech binds these two verses together. The speech of one who has "understanding" (*bîn,* cf. 1:2) demonstrates wisdom. The end of one who is "void of understanding" (*ḥasar-leb,* cf. 6:32) is a rod on his back, cf. 26:3, v. 13. The contrast is clear. We find wisdom with the man of understanding; with the man who lacks understanding, we find punishment, v. 13.

Wise men weigh their words carefully. They store up knowledge in anticipation of the time when they will need it. The fool, however, speaks without thought as he gossips, lies, criticizes, and curses. Eventually, his words bring "destruction" (*məḥittâ*) to him. The noun *məḥittâ* is a strong word. It may refer to actual physical destruction or to emotional destruction or dismay. This is the sense in which it occurs here, the dismay likely as others reproach him for his speech, cf. 18:7, v. 14.

15 The verse makes a practical observation on life, not a statement as to what ought to be. A wealthy man finds that his riches are a source of strength amid the changing circumstances of life. Proverbs 18:11*a* repeats the phrase. On the other hand, even small setbacks may readily overwhelm a poor man. Compare 14:20.

16 Once again, an eternal perspective is in view. The word "labor," *paʿal,* when applied to man, most often denotes a moral action. This shows the faith of the righteous that produces eternal life; cf. 12:28; 15:24. "Fruit" (*təbûʾat,* cf. 3:9) normally refers to the produce of the ground. When used of man, it poetically indicates the "result" of his action. In the case of the wicked, the "fruit" is sin.[10]

---

[10]Toy, p. 211, and Martin, p. 74, emend *ləḥattaʾt* to *limḥitta,* a drastic change involving the consonants. AB, p. 82, emends to *ləmāwet.* The only justification for these suggestions

*17 He is in the way of life that keepeth instruction: but he that refuseth
reproof erreth.
18 He that hideth hatred with lying lips, and he that uttereth a slander,
is a fool.
19 In the multitude of words there wanteth not sin: but he that refraineth
his lips is wise.
20 The tongue of the just is as choice silver: the heart of the wicked is
little worth.
21 The lips of the righteous feed many: but fools die for want of wisdom.*

17 There is no need to supply "in" here. The one who keeps "instruction" (*mûsar,* cf. 1:2) is a "path of life" (*ḥayyîm,* cf. 4:4). The one who
carefully heeds the teaching he has received will himself become a
guide to turn others to the way of life. The one, however, who spurns
"reproof" (*tôkaḥat,* cf. 1:23) "erreth" (*mataʿeh*). The verb *taʿâ* is "to
err." It refers to either mental or moral errors. The *hipʿil* has its normal
causative sense; thus *mataʿeh* is "causes to err." Because he turns from
the reproofs that would bring correction, he has a destructive influence
upon others.

18-21 The four proverbs focus on the general theme of speech. This
theme occurs again and again in the book because of its close association with the nature of one's walk. Initially, we find that the one who
"hideth" (*mǝkasseh,* cf. v. 6) his hatred has "lying lips," i.e., is deceitful.[11] But one who openly utters his slander is a "fool" (*kǝsîl,* cf. 1:22),
v. 18.

Verse 19 parallels v. 14. The man who speaks much will inevitably
speak without thinking. He cannot avoid "sin" (*pešaʿ,* cf. v. 12). The
one, however, who chooses his words purposefully, disciplining himself
to speak carefully, shows himself "wise" (*śakal,* cf. 1:3), v. 19. "Choice
silver" is purified silver, metal that has been cleansed from its impurities and thus has the highest value. The speech of the righteous has this

---

is the desire to achieve better parallelism. The MT should be retained. D. Winton
Thomas, "The Meaning of נְאֵסָה in Proverbs X. 16," *JTS* 15:295-96, interprets "life,"
ḥayyîm, as "maintenance." This is parallel with *lǝhaṭṭat,* which he interprets as "penury"
on the basis of an Ethiopian cognate. This view unnecessarily restricts the verse to a
comment on money.
[11]The LXX has δικαια,"righteous," for *šaqer,* "lying." Martin, p. 74; J. M. Powis Smith
(The Complete Bible); and James Moffatt (A New Translation of the Bible) follow this.
The Hebrew is clear as it is, however, and does not need emending here. AB, p. 84,
wrongly takes *kasâ* as it does in vv. 6, 11, "to reveal." See the discussion of v. 6.

22 The blessing of the Lord, it maketh rich, and he addeth no sorrow with it.
23 It is as sport to a fool to do mischief: but a man of understanding hath wisdom.

same quality. The "heart" (*leb,* cf. 3:5) occurs appropriately here as the source of one's speech; cf. Matthew 12:35. The wicked man's heart is full of impurities. Therefore, it has little value to it, v. 20.

The righteous man's speech "feed[s]" (*ra'â*) many. The word *ra'â* occurs widely in connection with shepherding. In this sense, it involves more than mere feeding. It is not too much to say that "the speech of the righteous pastures many," guiding, instructing, caring, and guarding, as it communicates to others.[12] In contrast, the "fool" (*'awîl,* cf. 1:7) perishes because he lacks spiritual understanding (*hasar-leb,* cf. 6:32), v. 21.

22 It is God's blessing upon an individual that makes him prosperous, acquiring more material possessions than he could otherwise have been expected to gain. The word "rich" (cf. *'ošer,* 3:16) denotes material wealth. With this blessing, He adds no "sorrow" (*'eşeb,* cf. v. 10).[13] God's blessings are free of such pain.

23 A man's character determines what he delights in. The foolish man (*kəsîl,* cf. 1:22) delights to do "mischief" (better, "wickedness," cf. *məzimmâ,* 1:4). Here, this refers specifically to the evil plans of the ungodly. In contrast, the man of understanding delights in wisdom; cf. Philippians 4:8.[14]

---

[12]Thomas, *JTS* 15:55, notes the fact that *yada'* is found for *yir'û* in a few Hebrew manuscripts. He draws upon an Arabic cognate to obtain the meaning "to make calm" and translates, "the lips of the righteous bring tranquility to many." The textual evidence for this is slight. The MT makes adequate sense.

[13]KD I, 223; Zöckler, p. 115; and Plaut, p. 132, translate *'eşeb* as "labor" and understand it as the subject, "labor adds nothing to it." This makes the proverb say that man's works cannot add to God's blessing. This view is contrary to the overall teaching of the book, which states that God blesses man's hard work; cf. 10:4; 14:23.

[14]Toy, pp. 213, 215, feels that "wisdom," *hokmâ,* stands in antithetic parallelism to the phrase "to do mischief," *'aśôt zimmâ.* He therefore emends *hokmâ* to *to'ebâ,* "abomination," and translates, "It is as sport to a fool to do wrong but it is abomination to a man of sense." To gain the same parallelism, Frankenberg, p. 69, suggests *hamâ,* "anger." These suggestions overlook the fact that righteousness is a characteristic of wisdom. While the fool delights in his evil plans, the man of understanding delights in godly wisdom.

24 The fear of the wicked, it shall come upon him: but the desire of the righteous shall be granted.
25 As the whirlwind passeth, so is the wicked no more: but the righteous is an everlasting foundation.
26 As vinegar to the teeth, and as smoke to the eyes, so is the sluggard to them that send him.

24 The "fear" (*məgôrat*) of the wicked will come to him; the "desire" (*taʾăwat*) of the righteous will likewise come to him. The word *məgôrat* has the connotation of one who fears some powerful one or thing. It is used elsewhere of man's fear of judgment by God (Ps. 34:4; Isa. 66:4). There is a strong sense of "dread" in this word. The noun *taʾăwat* is neutral in the OT, with the context determining whether the desire is good or bad. Here, the thought is good. The eternal desire of the righteous is given on the basis of faith in Christ. In addition, the righteous have the temporal blessing of God upon their lives.[15]

25 The righteous have a secure foundation that will not fail them in trouble. The wicked, however, will be overcome by the "whirlwind" (cf. 1:27). The second half needs a verb. The AV supplies "is," a true thought, but the parallelism supports "has" better. The wicked is overcome by the storms of life, but the righteous has a foundation that lets him withstand difficulties.

26 Solomon uses emblematic poetry to describe the irritation that a lazy person causes his employer. The "sluggard" (*ʿaṣel*, cf. 6:6) occurs sixteen times in Proverbs and elsewhere only in Ecclesiastes 10:18, also written by Solomon. The lazy person is like vinegar, which causes an unpleasant tingling sensation to the teeth, and like smoke, which brings tears and stinging to the eyes.

---

[15]Israel Eitan, *A Contribution to Biblical Lexicography* (1966) (hereafter cited as Eitan), pp. 50-51, derives *yitten* from *yatan*, "to be strong, permanent." He translates, "the repose of the righteous will last forever." This does not parallel 24*a* well. Toy, p. 216, makes the verb passive, suggesting it be pointed either as a *hopʿal* or *nipʿal*. It is just as reasonable to take the imperfect verb as describing a future act, "will be granted." See G.K. 107i and Bruce Waltke and M. O'Connor, *An Introduction to Biblical Hebrew Syntax* (1990) (hereafter cited as Waltke and O'Connor), 31.6.2b. Conant, p. 60, and McKane, p. 426, treat the indefinite subject as God, thus "the desire of the righteous, He will grant." The NET so translates, supplying "the Lord" as the subject. This is also a possible view.

27 The fear of the Lord prolongeth days: but the years of the wicked shall be shortened.
28 The hope of the righteous shall be gladness: but the expectation of the wicked shall perish.
29 The way of the Lord is strength to the upright: but destruction shall be to the workers of iniquity.
30 The righteous shall never be removed: but the wicked shall not inhabit the earth.

27 The "fear of the Lord" (*yirʾat yahwah,* cf. 1:7) gives the individual the fullness of life that God intends for him. The idea of prolonging life should be taken in this sense rather than referring to a longer than average life span. In contrast, the wicked have their life span shortened. Both the debilitating effects of their lifestyle and the judicial actions of God shorten the life of the wicked.

28 The "hope" (*tôhelet*) of the righteous man is a source of "gladness" (*śimḥâ,* cf. v. 1).[16] The noun *tôhelet* is a "confident expectation." It may be associated with one's faith or trust in God, e.g., Psalm 39:7. In sharp distinction, the "expectation" (*tiqwat*) of the wicked will come to nothing; cf. Proverbs 11:7. The noun *tiqwat* refers to "hope," e.g., Job 7:6; 8:13; Psalm 62:5; Proverbs 11:7. It is a neutral word that relies on context to determine the nature of the hope.

29-30 These two verses center on the contrasting destinies of the righteous and wicked. While the AV often translates *maⁿôz* as "strength," it is more precisely a "place of safety," a "stronghold," or a "fortress." It often describes God as the "fortress" in whom His people may find security, e.g., Psalm 27:1; 31:4; Jeremiah 16:19; Nahum 1:7. Those who walk according to the "way of the Lord" find it to be a "stronghold."[17] Those, however, who walk in iniquity find that it ends in destruction (*mahittâ,* cf. v. 14), v. 29.

---

[16]Driver, *Biblica* 32:179, argues that *śimḥâ* is impossible. He repoints the word to a verb. On the basis of cognates, he translates, "(the hope of the righteous) springs up," i.e., it wells up within him. AB, p. 82, reads *simaḥâ* for *śimḥâ* and translates, "the expectation of good men flourishes." Neither of these emendations is required to make sense of the verse.

[17]McKane, p. 427, emends *lattom derek* to *latam derek* in order to take *derek* with *tam* rather than *yahwah.* He translates, "Yahweh is a fortress to *the man whose conduct is blameless.*" The change is necessary in order to make Yahweh the fortress, rather than the "way of Yahweh." But the emendation is not necessary since the sense of the verse is clear.

31 The mouth of the just bringeth forth wisdom: but the froward tongue shall be cut out.
32 The lips of the righteous know what is acceptable: but the mouth of the wicked speaketh frowardness.

As a result of walking in the "way of the Lord," the righteous will never be "removed" (*môṭ*). The verb *môṭ* means "to shake, slip." It may poetically indicate insecurity; cf. 12:3; 24:11. The negative of *môṭ* here denotes great security, achieved only by the righteous. The wicked will not "inhabit the earth." The phrase is better "dwell in the land." It is an eschatological reference to the judgment of wicked men, v. 30.

31-32 The final passage of the chapter takes up the theme of speech once more (cf. vv. 11, 13-14, 18-21). The speech of the righteous "bringeth forth" (*nûb*), i.e., produces, wisdom.[18] The verb *nûb*, "to bear fruit," occurs only three times in the *qal*, all in poetic material and all picturing an increase. "Froward" (*tahpukôt*, cf. 2:12) speech, however, is "cut out" (*karat*, cf. 2:22). This refers to God's judgment, which cuts off the wicked from their insidious influence upon others, v. 31.

The lips of the righteous person "know" (*yedəʿûn*) what is acceptable, while the wicked continue to speak "frowardness" (*tahpukôt*, perhaps better rendered here "perversity"). The verb *yedəʿûn*, from *yadaʿ*, a verb, occurs almost one thousand times. It has the standard meaning "to know," especially referring to experiential knowledge but also to the knowledge that rests upon observation and thinking. It occurs properly here to describe words that rest upon both experience and reflection.[19]

---

[18]Dahood, *PNWSP*, pp. 20-21, argues from Ugaritic that *yanûb* should be glossed "flow." This makes 31*b* a better parallel in "cutting off" the flow of wicked speech. AB, p. 84, follows Dahood. Toy, p. 219, feels that *yanûb* is doubtful, but he is not dogmatic in suggesting a change. These are efforts to force a Hebrew idiom into an English mold and should be rejected.

[19]Gemser, p. 43, follows the LXX and emends *yedəʿûn* to *yabbiʿûn*. Toy, p. 219, suggests a change to *yibbiʿûn*. He also rearranges 31-32 to 31*a*, 32*b*, 32*a*, and 31*b* as a more suitable arrangement. Thomas, *VTS* III, 285, rejects this in favor of the emendation *yidəʿûn*, from *daʿâ*, "to seek." He translates, "the lips of the righteous seek goodwill," and explains that they "seek by words uttered to spread goodwill." Dahood, *PNWSP*, pp. 20-21, sees *yedəʿûn* as a by-form of *yezəʿûn*, "to flow." He translates, "the lips of the just exude goodwill." These attempts to clarify the verse are unnecessary.

Practical Applications from Proverbs 10

1. Parent-child relationships 1, 8

2. Contrast between righteousness and wickedness 2, 3, 6, 7, 9, 16, 24, 25, 27, 28, 29, 30

3. Contrast between diligence and laziness 4, 5, 26 (discusses the lazy man only)

4. Contrast between hatred and love 12

5. Contrast between wise and foolish speech 10, 11, 13, 14, 18, 19, 20, 21, 31, 32

6. Contrast between wealthy and poor 15

7. Contrast between obedient and disobedient 17

8. Contrast between wise and foolish 23

9. Blessing of God 22

1 A false balance is abomination to the Lord: but a just weight is his delight.

PROVERBS 11

Chapter 11 continues the sequence of randomly grouped proverbs. As is normal in the section, most of the proverbs stand alone. Occasionally, some of the maxims dealing with a common theme occur together, e.g., vv. 5-8, 24-26. There is no clear reason for the chapter divisions, excepting that they contain roughly the same amount of material. Even here, however, there is enough variation that this cannot be the sole reason behind the divisions, e.g., c. 13 and c. 14.

1 Israel used the balance scale for their commercial dealings. In some cases, the object was measured against a known "weight" (*ʾeben*). The word *ʾeben,* literally "stone," occurs in this sense here, in 16:11, and in 20:10, 23. It also has this sense in Leviticus 19:36; Deuteronomy 25:13, 15; II Samuel 14:26; and Micah 6:11. There must have been a standard weight in Israel but we do not know what it was. Later, metal weights were used. Archaeologists have found both stone and metal weights in Palestine and in neighboring countries.

There was the temptation to cheat, either by using a mismarked weight or by making the balance with arms of an unequal length.[1] For this reason, the Lord regularly warns against the practice (Lev. 19:35; Amos 8:5; Mic. 6:10-11). At the same time, He exhorts His people to be honest in this area (Lev. 19:36; Deut. 25:15; Ezek. 45:10-11). The national standard must have been kept in the tabernacle or temple ("shekel of the sanctuary," Exod. 30:13, 24; Lev. 27:25; Num. 7:13, 19, and numerous other references). The Levites bore the responsibility of caring for this, I Chronicles 23:29 ("all manner of measure and size").

The present passage shows God's concern for honesty in Israel's commerce. The word "abomination" (*tôʿăbat,* cf. 3:32) is strong, frequently

---

[1]*The Babylonian Talmud* says, "The wholesaler has to clean his measures once within thirty days (because the stuff sticks to them and impairs accurate measuring). A retailer, however, has to do so once within twelve months. . . . The storekeeper must do the same with his measures twice a week, and the weights once a week (as he takes hold of them with wet hands, and consequently they become heavier, and when he buys something, in weighing the stuff he deceives the seller). The scales, however, he must clean before each weighing thereon." *The Babylonian Talmud,* "Baba Bathra" ("Mishna XI"), ed. and trans. Michael L. Rodkinson (1903), 5:192.

2 When pride cometh, then cometh shame: but with the lowly is wisdom.
3 The integrity of the upright shall guide them: but the perverseness of transgressors shall destroy them.
4 Riches profit not in the day of wrath: but righteousness delivereth from death.
5 The righteousness of the perfect shall direct his way: but the wicked shall fall by his own wickedness.
6 The righteousness of the upright shall deliver them: but transgressors shall be taken in their own naughtiness.

referring to idolatry or to God's attitude toward idolatry. The passage heightens the contrast here by the use of "delight" (*raṣôn*). The word *raṣôn* often describes God's pleasure or the favor bestowed by Him. It most often occurs in connection with the ritual of sacrifice but also broadly in other areas as well.

2 The proud man overestimates himself and brings himself into public "shame" (or "dishonor," *qalôn*, cf. 3:35). The "lowly" (*ṣənûʿîm*) on the other hand develops "wisdom" (*ḥokmâ*, cf. 1:2). The adjective *ṣənûʿîm* occurs only here. The verb *ṣanaʿ*, in the *hipʿîl*, occurs in Micah 6:8. In both places, the context requires something like "humble" or "modest." This contrasts with the proud man of 2*a*.

3 The "integrity" (cf. *tom,* 2:7) of the "upright" (*yəšarîm,* cf. 2:21) guides him in right paths of life. The term *yəšarîm* often denotes the ethical uprightness of a man, his blamelessness; cf. v. 5. He will avoid sinful attitudes and actions that would lead him away from righteousness. In 3*b*, "perverseness" comes from *salap,* "to twist, distort," and thus "crookedness, falsity, deceit." "Transgressors" is from *bagad,* "to act treacherously, unfaithfully." The word often describes one who does not keep his word. The phrase contrasts with 3*a*. The "perverseness" of the treacherous person causes him to be destroyed (*šadad*). The word *šadad* is strong, denoting "ruin, destruction." It often has the connotation of violence. Here, the AV correctly reads the *qərê yəšoddem,* "shall destroy them," rather than the *kətîb wəšoddem,* "and their destruction."

4-6 These maxims focus on righteousness. One's "riches" (*hôn,* cf. 3:9) will not help him in the "day of wrath." This phrase occurs four other times (Job 21:30; Ezek. 7:19; Zeph. 1:15, 18), all referring to the day of God's judgment of the heathen. The word "wrath," *ʿebrâ,* is from *ʿabar.* It is literally "an overflowing." This portrays the moment when

God's anger bursts through the bounds of His longsuffering and mercy that have held it back. It sweeps across His enemies, taking them away in their wickedness.[2]

In contrast, "righteousness" (cf. *ṣedeq,* 1:3) delivers from "death" (*mawet,* cf. 2:18). Here, the contrast of "death" with "wrath" indicates that this refers to the realm of the wicked dead. This sense also occurs in 7:27 and Psalm 49:14, v. 4.

The righteous actions of the "perfect" (cf. *tom,* 2:7), here better rendered "blameless," will "direct his way." The verb "direct" (*təyaššer,* cf. 2:21) in the *piʿel* describes the making straight of a way. It has an ethical sense. The thought is that righteousness helps the godly person to avoid those things that could become stumbling blocks along his path in life. The wicked (*rašaʿ,* cf. 8:7) person, however, has no such hope. His evil actions will surely cause him to stumble into judgment, v. 5.

The righteous actions of the "upright" (*yəšarîm,* cf. v. 3) "deliver" (*taṣṣîlem*) him from the potential traps of life. The verb *naṣal* may refer to physical deliverance or to spiritual deliverance from sin, e.g., Psalm 39:8; 79:9. "Transgressors" (*bogdim,* cf. v. 3), however, will be caught by their "naughtiness" (*hawwat*). The word *hawwat* is either "destruction" or "strong desire, craving or covetousness," depending on the context.[3] The flow of thought here favors the latter meaning, that the covetousness of the wicked brings judgment to him, v. 6.[4]

---

[2]Among others, Whybray, p. 67; Oesterley, p. 82; and Martin, p. 77, deny that this is the day of final judgment. They relate it to an individual judgment that comes to a man during his life. The use of the phrase elsewhere, however, argues for an eschatological meaning.

[3]Guillaume, *JRAS* (1942), p. 114, sees the word as reflecting the sorcerer's curse. The wicked, then, is destroyed by his own cursing. Driver, *JRAS* (1943), pp. 11-12, rightly rejects Guillaume's argument and then advances a meaning of "windy words." The wicked here, then, is caught by his own blustering speech. Driver's argument is not persuasive.

[4]Toy, p. 225, suggests that the text should read *bahawwatam* so as to clarify the subject of the "desire." The versions are interpretive and support this. Driver, *Textus* I (1960), 117, sees the omission of the pronominal suffix as an abbreviation. The sense of the MT is clear and, in view of the poetical nature of the passage, it should not be emended. Driver's view is possible although it is not possible to prove the presence of an abbreviation.

7 When a wicked man dieth, his expectation shall perish: and the hope of unjust men perisheth.
8 The righteous is delivered out of trouble, and the wicked cometh in his stead.
9 An hypocrite with his mouth destroyeth his neighbour: but through knowledge shall the just be delivered.

7 The "expectation" (*tiqwâ,* cf. 10:28) undoubtedly includes all of his aspirations and dreams for possessions, reputation, and long life. The death of a wicked man brings these hopes to nothing. In like manner, the "hope" (*tôhelet,* cf. 10:28) of the "unjust *men*" comes to nothing. The word "unjust" comes from the plural of *'ôn,* "strength," from *'awen.* The plural is intensive; thus, the phrase refers to men who trust in their great strength, their extensive resources.[5] This too will perish!

8 The righteous man avoids many troubles. He is "delivered" (*nehạlaṣ*). In the *nip'al, hạlaṣ* is "to rescue." It has this sense only in poetical parts of the OT. The passive sense implies that God watches over His own to care for them. The wicked, however, have no one to care for them. They rush on blindly to take the place of trouble vacated by the righteous.

9 Solomon notes the potential for harm that lies with the tongue. The "hypocrite" (*hạnep*) destroys his neighbors by his gossip and lies. The noun *hạnep,* "pollute," is better "profane" or "godless" rather than "hypocrite."[6] The "just," however, have "knowledge" (*da'at,* cf. 1:4) that allows them to see through evil intentions, and they therefore escape.

---

[5]*PC,* p. 215, derives the word from *'wn* I, "emptiness," and relates it to "men of vanity," although it allows for the rendering of the AV. Toy, pp. 222-23, notes that *'wn* II never occurs elsewhere in an ethical sense. He suggests that an emendation is necessary but does not propose one. Reider, *VT* 2:124, describes the MT as "incoherent and far from satisfactory." He emends to *'ạmunîm,* "faithful," and translates *'bd* based on an Arabic cognate "to last." With this tortuous reasoning, he obtains "the hope of the faithful is everlasting." Greenstone, p. 114, follows Rashi and refers *'on* to the children, i.e., at the death of the powerful one, the hope of his children, that they will follow him, perishes. Other suggestions also exist but this sampling is enough to show the nature of the problem. It is likely that *'on* is "strength," not necessarily an ethical strength but simply the strength possessed by the powerful and resourceful man.

[6]Dahood, *PNWSP,* p. 22, relates *peh,* "mouth," to Ugaritic "to see, watch." He adopts the suggestion of Delitzsch that *yašḥit* is a denominative verb from *šaḥat,* "pit," and translates, "By watching the godless man, his friend falls into the pit." This raises the question of what hazard the "pit" describes. It certainly makes the verse no clearer. There is no need to linguistically emend the well-known *peh* on the basis of a cognate variant.

*10 When it goeth well with the righteous, the city rejoiceth: and when
the wicked perish, there is shouting.
11 By the blessing of the upright the city is exalted: but it is overthrown
by the mouth of the wicked.
12 He that is void of wisdom despiseth his neighbour: but a man of understanding holdeth his peace.*

10-11 These two statements relate the relationship between cities and
righteous or evil people. Though cities may not always appreciate the
righteous, they still rejoice in the favor that falls on the city as God
blesses His own. By the same token, cities shout with joy when the
wicked "perish," leaving the cities without their wicked influence, v. 10.

When God's blessing comes upon the righteous, the city is "exalted"
(*tarûm*). The verb *rûm* is "to be high, rise up" and, by extension, "to be
exalted." If, however, wicked men are allowed unrestrained speech,
chaos and confusion result in its ultimate destruction, v. 11.

12 The one who "despiseth" (*bûz,* cf. 1:7) his neighbor demonstrates
that he lacks good sense (*ḥasarˉleb,* cf. 6:32). When you look down on
someone else, you judge him by your standards, often comparing their
standards to your own, a risky act unless you are infallible. One who
truly has "understanding" (cf. *bîn,* 1:2) will keep his peace. A neighbor
who is worthy of scorn will show that by himself. Your comments are
unnecessary and, in fact, destructive to your own testimony.

The Value of Counsel

I. The Offenses Listed

    A. The Practice of Sinful Adultery, 6:32; 7:7; 9:16

    B. The Evidence of Arrogant Pride, 11:12

    C. The Choice of Wrong Friends, 12:11

    D. The Foolishness of Wicked Behavior, 15:21

    E. The Acceptance of Risky Business, 17:18

    F. The Lack of Diligent Effort, 24:30

    G. The Want of Godly Wisdom, 10:13, 21

II. The Invitation Given, 9:4

---

13 A talebearer revealeth secrets: but he that is of a faithful spirit con-
cealeth the matter.
14 Where no counsel is, the people fall: but in the multitude of counsel-
lors there is safety.
15 He that is surety for a stranger shall smart for it: and he that hateth
suretiship is sure.

13 The word "talebearer" (*rakîl*) is too soft. The noun occurs six times
(Lev. 19:16; Jer. 6:28; 9:4; Ezek. 22:9; and Prov. 11:13; 20:19), all referring to a "slanderer." He will tell openly even those things that have
been confidentially revealed to him ("secrets," *sôd,* cf. 3:32). In 13*b*,
"faithful" comes from *ʾaman,* "to confirm, support." In the *nipʿal,* as
here, it means "to be confirmed" and thus "to be established, faithful."
"Matter" comes from *dabar.* This is the most general word in Hebrew
for "speech." It occurs widely in all parts of the OT with a broad variety
of meanings, most of which relate generally to communication. The
"faithful" man conceals (*kasâ,* cf. 10:6) the "matter" by refusing to
bring it out into the open.

14 When people decide their own way, they often fail. They need
"counsel" or "guidance" (*taḥbulôt,* cf. 1:5). "Safety" comes from *yašaʿ,*
normally "deliverance, salvation" but also used of "success, prosperity."
The first meaning fits better here. When several wise counselors can
pool their experience and wisdom, there is "deliverance," a solution to
the problem.

15 One who becomes surety for a "stranger" (*zar,* cf. 2:16) will suffer
as the result. The phrase "shall smart for it" is intensive, with both the
noun *raʿ* (cf. 1:33) and the verb *yeroaʿ* coming from *raʿaʿ;* cf. 1:33. The
verb *raʿaʿ* consistently means "to be bad, evil." Here, the coordination
with *raʿ* gives the sense "will surely suffer."[7] A person, however, who
"hateth" (*śanaʾ*) "suretiship" (*toqʿîm,* cf. 6:1) is "sure" (*bôṭeaḥ,* cf. 1:33).
The verb *śanaʾ* covers a broad range of negative emotions ranging from
mild dislike to extreme detesting. The context must determine the

---

[7]The construction is unusual and has engendered several creative explanations.
Gemser, p. 44, and McKane, p. 429, repoint *raʿ* to *roaʿ* and take it as the infinitive absolute. G. R. Driver, "Once Again Abbreviations," *Textus* IV (1964) (hereafter cited as
Textus IV), p. 82, understands it as a misread abbreviation for the infinitive absolute
raʿoaʿ. Alfred Guillaume, "A Note on the Roots רוע, ירע, and רעע in Hebrew," *JTS*
15:294, repoints to *reaʿ.* Taking *yeroaʿ* from *rîaʿ,* he translates, "lives in constant dread."
Without changing the MT, however, one can make sense of this unusual construction.

16 A gracious woman retaineth honour: and strong men retain riches.
17 The merciful man doeth good to his own soul: but he that is cruel troubleth his own flesh.
18 The wicked worketh a deceitful work: but to him that soweth righteousness shall be a sure reward.

strength of feeling involved. Here, the idea is that of "aversion." The word *toqᶜîm*, "to strike hands," is similar to our handshake. In biblical times, this signified an agreement over some business arrangement. By avoiding becoming surety for another, he is "secure," not in danger of falling into ruin. Compare the discussion at 6:1-5.

16 The gracious woman demonstrates godly qualities in her actions. For this reason, she "retains" (*tamak*, cf. 4:4) honor (*kabôd*, cf. 3:9). The verb *tamak* is broad in meaning, "to lay hold of, attain, support." Here, the idea is that she gains honor. "Strong men" (*ᶜarîṣîm*) is better "mighty, awe-inspiring, violent, ruthless" men.[8] They gain riches. The point of the proverb lies in the contrast between the reward that comes to godly character and the reward that is gained by raw strength. The one is eternal and of great worth; the other is temporal and of little value.

17 The "merciful" (or "loyal," *hesed*, cf. 2:8) person who helps his fellow man actually benefits himself. What is good for the community is good for the individual. The "cruel" man (*ᵓakzar*) is "cruel, merciless, fierce." The word *ᵓakzar* indicates strong behavior toward others. This person hurts himself, "his own flesh."

18 The "wicked" (*rašaᶜ*, cf. 8:7) "works a deceitful work [*paᶜal*, cf. 10:16]." This is a brief commentary on the evil man's labors. Since he works only for himself, not giving any heed to his responsibilities to

---

[8]Oesterley, pp. 85-86, and Zöckler, p. 121, follow the LXX in supplying lines that have supposedly dropped out of the MT. Oesterley translates the proverb as follows:

A gracious woman raiseth up honour to (her) husband,
But a woman who hateth righteousness is a throne of dishonour.
They that are slothful become lacking in wealth,
But manly men rest secure in their riches.

In and of itself, this reading communicates correct principles. Nonetheless, it requires an unnecessary change in the MT. Apparently, the LXX translator misunderstood the sense of the Hebrew, thinking that 10b wrongly taught that violent men would be rewarded for their evil actions. Driver, *Biblica*, 32:180, translates, "strong men," *ᶜarîṣîm* as "vigorous" and takes it in a good sense. The consistent use elsewhere, however, opposes this view.

*19 As righteousness tendeth to life: so he that pursueth evil pursueth it
to his own death.
20 They that are of a froward heart are abomination to the Lord: but
such as are upright in their way are his delight.
21 Though hand join in hand, the wicked shall not be unpunished: but
the seed of the righteous shall be delivered.*

God, his words are "deceitful" (*šeqer,* cf. 6:17). He gains that which has
no eternal value to it. In contrast, the righteous person gains a "sure
[*ʾamet,* cf. 3:3] reward," one that will never vanish or disappoint him.

19 Righteousness is associated with "life" (*ḥayyîm,* cf. 4:4). So one
who pursues evil associates himself with "death" (cf. *mawet,* 2:18).[9]
This is the first of four times that the words "life" and "death" occur in
parallel in the book (cf. 12:28; 13:14; 14:27; see also 18:21). In each
case, the idea of spiritual life and spiritual death is prominent.

20 There is a clear contrast between the evil and the righteous in their
relationships to the Lord. Those whose hearts are "froward" (or "perverse," *ʿiqqeš,* cf. 2:15) are an "abomination" (*tôʿabat,* cf. 3:32) to the
Lord. Those, however, who are "upright" (or "blameless," cf. *tom,* 2:7)
are His "delight" (*raṣôn,* cf. v. 1).

21 The phrase "*though* hand *join* in hand" probably does not refer to
the determined opposition of the wicked to God. It more likely is a
strong statement of certainty, "surely," perhaps drawing upon the action
of "striking hands" when entering into an agreement. The phrase presents the certainty of divine judgment upon the wicked. He will not "be
unpunished" (*loʾyinnaqeh,* cf. 6:29). Chastisement catches "the
wicked." The "seed of the righteous," the offspring of the righteous, will
be "delivered" (*nimlaṭ*). The *nipʿal* of *malaṭ,* "to deliver, escape," in the
poetical books, often stresses the role of the Lord in delivering His people from trials. So, here, He sustains His own.

---

[9]The introductory *ken,* "as," is unusual. AB, p. 86, emends to *mēbīn* and translates,
"He who discerns what is right. . . ." Kidner, pp. 92-93, follows the LXX and reads *ben,*
translating "a son of righteousness. . . ." Toy, p. 236, tentatively emends to *roʿeh,* "he
who associates with righteousness. . . ." Zöckler, p. 122, derives the word from *kûn,* "to
be firm," and translates, "he who is steadfast in righteousness." The simplest way to understand it is as an adjective *ken,* "right, correct, true." The phrase then reads "true righteousness is for life."

22 As a jewel of gold in a swine's snout, so is a fair woman which is without discretion.
23 The desire of the righteous is only good: but the expectation of the wicked is wrath.
24 There is that scattereth, and yet increaseth; and there is that withholdeth more than is meet, but it tendeth to poverty.
25 The liberal soul shall be made fat: and he that watereth shall be watered also himself.
26 He that withholdeth corn, the people shall curse him: but blessing shall be upon the head of him that selleth it.

22 The emblem is blunt and to the point. A *nezem* is a "ring" of all kinds, an earring, finger ring or, as here, a nose ring. A golden *nezem* in the snout of a pig would be highly inappropriate. So beauty is inappropriate to a woman who lacks "discretion" (*ṭaʿam*). The primary meaning of *ṭaʿam* is "taste," with the derived secondary meaning of "discernment." Seven times (I Sam. 21:13; 25:33; Job 12:20; Ps. 34, title; Prov. 26:16; 31:18; Jon. 3:7) the intellect is in view. But three times (here and Ps. 34:8; 119:66) it indicates moral or spiritual discrimination.[10] Ornamentation on an unclean beast is the same as beauty in a woman with a depraved character.

23 The "desire" (cf. *taʾăwat,* 10:24) of a righteous person is good. It has wholesome and beneficial consequences. A wicked man, however, has an "expectation" (*tiqwat,* cf. 10:28) that can bring only divine wrath (*ʿebrâ,* see v. 4) upon him in judgment.[11]

24-26 Verses 24-26 form an almost perfect chiasmus, with an a:b:c::c¹:b¹:a¹ structure. The following development shows the structure.

---

[10]Oesterley, p. 87, suggests that the word be rendered "modesty" here. Nowhere else, however, does this sense occur.

[11]The verse can be interpreted either as describing the results of godly and ungodly desires (as above) or as describing the nature of godly and ungodly desires. In the second case, the righteous man has "good" desires, conformable to the will of God for him; the wicked man has "proud" desires, centered upon himself. As far as I can tell, Delitzsch I, 245, stands alone in adopting this position. Jones, p. 119, follows weak textual support and emends *ʿebrâ* to *ʾabadâ,* "perishes." This is a totally unnecessary change. McKane, p. 440, understands 23*b* to say that the expectation of the wicked brings forth rage. His frustration at unfilled hopes causes him to grow angry. I have chosen the above interpretation as being in line with the more natural sense of *ʿebrâ;* cf. v. 4 above.

24*a* There is that scattereth, and yet increaseth;

24*b* And there is that withholdeth more than is meet, but it tendeth to poverty.

25*a* The liberal soul shall be made fat:

25*b* And he that watereth shall be watered also himself.

26*a* He that withholdeth corn, the people shall curse him:

26*b* But blessing *shall be* upon the head of him that selleth *it*.

These three proverbs contrast generosity and greed. The verb "scattereth" comes from *pazar*, "to scatter, spread." The word occurs only ten times, seven of these in the *pi*^c*el*. The normal reference is to the scattering of Israel or of Israel's enemies. Psalm 112:9, however, parallels the thought of our verse here, speaking of charitable giving to the poor. One who "scatters" his wealth in charity will be increased. The verse implies God's blessing upon benevolence (cf. 19:17; 22:9; 28:27).

The greedy man, however, who refrains from benevolence will himself come to poverty. The implied thought is that he will lack God's blessing upon his life (cf. 21:13). The phrase "withholdeth more than is meet" is better "one who withholds what is due," speaking in the sense of a moral obligation, v. 24.

Solomon repeats the thought of 24*a*. The "liberal [*bərakâ*] soul" is better a "generous man." The word *bərakâ*, from *barak*, normally refers to "blessing." Here this refers to the blessing brought to others by generosity. The generous soul will be made "fat." Fatness in the OT is often an emblem of prosperity; cf. Genesis 27:28; 45:18; Deuteronomy 32:14. Thus, again, there is the implied blessing of God upon the charitable person. Verse 25*b* repeats this thought, using the emblem of watering to make the point, v. 25.[12]

"Corn" (*bar*) is from *barar*, "to cleanse." This is threshed grain, separated from the impure chaff. The one who fails to sell his "corn" drives up the price at the expense of the people. This causes them to "curse"

---

[12]The form of "watered," *yôre*^ɔ, is unusual. The Syriac, followed by BH, derives the form from ^ɔ*rr*, "to curse," and makes the phrase antithetic, "he who curses will be cursed," an unlikely solution. William L. Holladay, *A Consise Hebrew and Aramaic Lexicon of the Old Testament* (1971), p. 334, suggests parsing as a *nip*^c*al yeraweh*. BDB, p. 924, locates it as *hop*^c*al* from *rawa*^ɔ, "to be saturated." Dahood, *PNWSP*, p. 24, derives it from *yr*^ɔ, "to be fat."

27 He that diligently seeketh good procureth favour: but he that seeketh mischief, it shall come unto him.
28 He that trusteth in his riches shall fall: but the righteous shall flourish as a branch.
29 He that troubleth his own house shall inherit the wind: and the fool shall be servant to the wise of heart.

(*naqab*) the man. The verb *naqab* is the act of speaking a curse, expressing the desire for some lowered form of existence to come upon the object. The one who is willing to sell at the going price relieves the needs of the people. He therefore receives "blessing" (*bərakâ,* cf. v. 25) from them, v. 26.

27 One who "diligently seeketh" (*šaḥar,* cf. 8:17) that which is good "procureth" (better "seeks," cf. *baqaš,* 2:4) divine "favour" (*raṣôn,* cf. v. 1) for himself.[13] The second "seeketh" is from *daraš,* "to seek." This often stresses the intellectual aspect of a search. One who seeks "mischief" (or "evil," cf. *raᶜ,* 1:33) will find it coming upon him in greater measure than he anticipated.

28 Wealth is an uncertain staff upon which to lean. One who trusts in riches will assuredly "fall" into ruin.[14] But one who is righteous, trusting in the living God, will flourish like a "branch" (*ᶜaleh).* The word *ᶜaleh* is a collective noun denoting "leaves." The biblical authors in the OT use the green tree elsewhere as a picture of health and divine blessing, e.g., Psalm 1:3; Jeremiah 17:8.

29 "Troubleth" is from *ᶜakar,* "to trouble, disturb." The man who troubles his household by his actions will "inherit wind," idiomatic for

---

[13]Among others, Delitzsch I, 247, and McKane, p. 434, take *raṣôn* as referring to the goodwill of others. The word *raṣôn,* however, normally refers to divine favor or acceptance. The word occurs fifty-six times, with thirty-one of these referring to God's favor or acceptance and three to God's will. The meaning of self-will or the will of a king occurs most frequently in the late writings of Esther, Nehemiah, and Daniel. On the basis of this distribution of meanings, I prefer to relate this passage to divine favor. In a different vein, G. R. Driver, "Review of the Assyrian Dictionary," *JSS* 12:108, relates *baqaš* to the Akkadian *baqāšu,* "to be large," and translates, "the upright amply esteem, i.e., make much of . . . his life." The meaning of *baqaš* is well attested in Hebrew, making this suggestion unlikely.

[14]AB, p. 87, and Aitken (RSV), p. 187, translate an emended version, substituting *yibbol,* from *nabel,* "to wither." This gives better parallelism with the second half of the verse but is unnecessary. It is not unusual for a single verse to draw upon differing figures, e.g., v. 29.

30 The fruit of the righteous is a tree of life; and he that winneth souls is wise.
31 Behold, the righteous shall be recompensed in the earth: much more the wicked and the sinner.

possessing nothing.[15] His harsh treatment of his servants alienates them so that they fail to serve him faithfully. Little by little, his property loses value until he finally has nothing. This man is a "fool" (*ʾəwîl,* cf. 1:7), and he will end his days as a servant to those who are "wise" (cf. *ḥokmâ,* 1:2).

30 The "fruit," i.e., the righteous man's activity, is a "tree of life" (*ʿeṣ ḥayyîm,* cf. 3:18). The idiom refers to introducing others to the fulness of life that those who walk with God enjoy. For this reason, the one "who winneth souls" (*loqeaḥ nəpašôt*) is wise. The interpretation turns on what is done with *loqeaḥ nəpašôt,* literally, "he who taketh souls." The simplest view is also the historical one, to understand the phrase as winning others to your own philosophy of life, thereby introducing them to the fulness of life.[16]

31 The final verse of the chapter underlies I Peter 4:18, which follows the LXX translation. The LXX glosses *baʾareṣ,* "in the land," with μολις, "scarcely," leaving us to find the logical connection. Several pro-

---

[15]McKane, p. 430, limits *ʿôker* to financial mismanagement, which destroys the family's wealth. This is possible but too restrictive. I prefer a broader view of *ʿôker,* which may include misuse of the family's resources.

[16]McKane, p. 432, understands *loqeaḥ nəpašôt* in an antithetical manner. Here, the thought is of the fruit of one who takes lives, i.e., murders. He emends *ḥakam* to *ḥamas* so that it produces violence. The phrase is so understood in Ps. 31:13; Ezek. 33:6; Jon. 4:3; and elsewhere. Several others follow this same approach. Toy, p. 239, translates, "the wicked harms himself." Garrett, p. 129, translates, "violence takes away lives." AB, p. 87, translates, "crime takes lives away." The emendation, however, is not necessary since sense can be made of the MT. The ideas of taking a life and of winning someone to your point of view are parallel, and so the phrase occurs naturally. On the basis of Ugaritic, Dahood, *PNWSP,* p. 25, understands *nəpašôt* as a plural of excellence, referring to immortality rather than souls. Thus, the wise man "attains eternal life." William H. Irwin, "The Metaphor in Prov 11,30," *Biblica* 65:97-100, defends the MT. He takes *loqeaḥ* in the sense of gathering fruit, a sense it has elsewhere, e.g., Gen. 3:6, 22. The wise man gathers life, a future reward, or lives, teaching them of wisdom. Robert G. Bratcher, "A Translator's Note on Proverbs 11.30," *BT* 34:337-38, reports that the Brazilian OT Translation Committee has translated 30*b* as "whoever increases the number of friends is wise." These last views attempt to maintain the MT and are possible views. I prefer the view discussed above.

posals have been made, none of which is completely persuasive.[17] It is enough that the general sense of the verse is clear. If the righteous receive judgment, how much more will God also judge the wicked?

---

[17]In a thorough discussion, James Barr, בְּאֶרֶץ ~ ΜΟΛΙΣ Prov. XI. 31, I Pet. IV. 18," *JSS* 20:149-64, argues for a translation of the MT, which probably was misread by the translator. Dahood, *PNWSP*, pp. 25-26, understands *baʾareṣ* in an eschatological sense, teaching that God will bestow differing degrees of punishment upon men in Sheol. This is an extreme view. Driver, *Biblica* 32:180, understands the LXX as based upon the Samaritan *ʾəraṣ,* "coerced, compelled," thus confirming the consonants of the MT. KD I, 250, considers the LXX a "free translation" of the MT. Since the LXX is often interpretive, this is the likely explanation.

Practical Applications from Proverbs 11

1. Business practices 1, 15
2. Character traits (pride, greed, righteousness) 2, 12, 28, 30
3. Contrast between righteousness and wickedness 3, 5, 6, 8, 10, 11, 17, 18, 19, 20, 21, 23, 27, 31
4. Eternal life 4, 7
5. Contrast between good and bad speech 9, 13
6. Contrast between benevolence and greed 24, 25, 26
7. Reliance on counsel 14
8. Women 16, 22
9. Foolish behavior 29

1 Whoso loveth instruction loveth knowledge: but he that hateth reproof is brutish.

2 A good man obtaineth favour of the Lord: but a man of wicked devices will he condemn.

PROVERBS 12

1 The book commends those who love "instruction" (better, "discipline," *mûsar,* cf. 1:2) as also loving "knowledge" (*daᶜat,* cf. 1:4). The connection between *mûsar* and *daᶜat* implies that it is the willingness to receive correction that helps us to gain knowledge. That it is receiving correction, rather than instruction, follows from the parallel phrase "he who hates reproof is brutish." The person who accepts reproofs as they occur in life will learn from the experiences. His character will grow stronger as he learns not to repeat those actions that bring him into difficulty.

One who "hates" (*sanaᵓ,* cf. 11:15) "reproof" (*tôkaḥat,* cf. 1:23) is "brutish" or, perhaps better, "stupid" (*baᶜar*). The term *baᶜar* occurs widely throughout the OT. It denotes one who has a low moral condition that causes him to live carelessly. In this case, the individual stupidly rejects the advice of others and continues to live his own self-centered life.

The Value of Counsel

Three verses in the chapter deal with the influence of counsel on a person. Your reaction to this advice is important.

1. Growth or stupidity in nature 1
2. Acceptance or rejection by others 8
3. Foolish or wise behavior 15

---

2 A good person obtains "favor" (*raṣôn,* cf. 11:1) from the Lord. This generally states divine blessing without limiting it to any one area of life. At the same time, the Lord will condemn a man of "wicked devices" (or "evil plans," *məzimmôt,* cf. 1:4). The thought again suggests punishment without limiting the area in which it comes.

3 A man shall not be established by wickedness: but the root of the righteous shall not be moved.
4 A virtuous woman is a crown to her husband: but she that maketh ashamed is as rottenness in his bones.
5 The thoughts of the righteous are right: but the counsels of the wicked are deceit.

3 The verb "establish" comes from *kûn,* "to establish, prepare, make firm." This often refers to a sense of confidence or well-being that comes from a right relationship to God. In 3*b*, "root," *šoreš,* can refer to a literal root of a plant. More often, it occurs poetically to represent the foundation of a thing. The verb "moved" is from *môṭ* (cf. 10:30), "to totter, shake, slip," often indicating insecurity and uncertainty in life. Wickedness cannot "establish" a person. In contrast, the "root" of the righteous, implying their sure support in life, will never be "moved."

4 For the first time, the book describes the great potential that the wife has in the home. The phrase "virtuous [*ḥayil*] woman" occurs three times to describe a "worthy woman," Ruth 3:11; Proverbs 12:4; 31:10; cf. also 31:29. In each case, the word stresses the character of the woman. She is her husband's crown.[1] In other words, she serves as his glory, bringing him to the fullness of his honor. Conversely, the wife who openly shames her husband in any way is as a cancerous disease, slowly but inevitably destroying him.

5 The word "plans" (*maḥšabôt,* cf. 6:18) is a neutral word that relies on context to determine whether good or evil thoughts are in view. Here, the "thoughts" of the righteous man are "right" (or "just," *mišpaṭ,* cf. 1:3). The descriptive term "deceit" is from *mirmâ,* "deceit, "treachery." It most often refers to false speech. While the righteous man has just plans, the "counsels" (*taḥbulôt,* cf. 1:5) of the wicked are deceitful.

---

[1]Toy, p. 243, relates *ḥayil* to the economic ability of the wife, although he recognizes the broader connotation of the word. Through her domestic prosperity, she aids the development of her husband's increased influence. While this may be a part of her role as a wife, the word *ḥayil* does not have a component of meaning that limits it to the economic realm. It occurs broadly, denoting "strength" and "power" (used both of man and God), the "valor" of a warrior, and the "ability" of a man. All of these traits may be included within the meaning of "worthy" when applied to a woman.

6 *The words of the wicked are to lie in wait for blood: but the mouth of the upright shall deliver them.*
7 *The wicked are overthrown, and are not: but the house of the righteous shall stand.*

6 Solomon adopts a military term to describe wicked speech. The phrase "lie in wait" comes from ʾarab. The OT uses ʾarab over twenty times to refer to setting an ambush for the enemy, e.g., Judges 9:32, 43; 16:12. The speech of the wicked man "lies in wait" for blood, setting a trap so as to take others unawares. In contrast, the speech of the righteous "shall deliver them" (cf. naṣal, 11:6). The verb naṣal often has spiritual significance, as in prayers for deliverance from evil. It may as well refer to physical deliverance from danger. The pronoun "them" could refer to the righteous who are delivered from evil by their forthright speech. It could also refer to the innocent victims of the wicked who are guided away from his evil verbal trap. Most probably the latter idea is in view.[2]

7 Once more Solomon contrasts the wicked and righteous men. The verb "overthrown" is from hapak, "to overthrow, throw down, turn over." This often refers to God's judgment upon the wicked although other uses also occur.[3] The verb "stand" comes from ʿamad, "to stand." This regularly denotes the physical act of standing. It also occurs figuratively of those who "stand" before the Lord in prayer or service. We see now the contrast between the wicked and the righteous. The wicked are "overthrown." The phrase implies that some calamity, most probably the chastisement of God, falls upon them. They *"are* not," clearly indicating the complete and final judgment of God. The righteous, however, do not come under this judgment. Their "house," their families, avoids this judgment and continues to "stand."

---

[2]Gemser, p. 46, emends *dam* to *tam,* "den Redlichen," honest. Thus, the wicked man's speech lies in wait for the "blameless," a correct thought but requiring an unnecessary change in the MT. Toy, p. 244, omits the pronoun "them" to avoid its indefinite nature. This is again an unnecessary change.

[3]Kidner, p. 96, proposes to read "Overthrow the wicked, and they are not." This would give *hapak* the transitive sense, which it often takes. It would also require that *hapak* be repointed to the imperative *hapok.* Since the verb is often intransitive, there is no need for the change.

8 A man shall be commended according to his wisdom: but he that is of a perverse heart shall be despised.

9 He that is despised, and hath a servant, is better than he that honoureth himself, and lacketh bread.

10 A righteous man regardeth the life of his beast: but the tender mercies of the wicked are cruel.

8 A man of "wisdom" (*śakal*, cf. 1:3) will act properly and with unusual discernment. This will cause him to receive the praise of others. The descriptive term "perverse" comes from *ʿawâ*, "one who is bent, twisted, or distorted." A "perverse heart," then, is a "twisted mind." In contrast with the wise man, one who has a "perverse heart" will act improperly. This will cause him to "be despised" (or "be put to shame," *bûz*, cf. 1:7).

9 There are men who have little social position, yet are economically well off.[4] And there are others who make a great public show, yet are in dire straits financially. The first is better off than the second! The word "despised" (cf. *qalôn*, 3:35) here refers to one who is lightly esteemed by others, without great reputation.

10 The verse sums up the teaching of Scripture (e.g., Exod. 23:4, 19; Deut. 22:6; 25:4) into a terse maxim. The verb "regardeth" comes from *yôdeaʿ*, normally translated "know" (cf. 10:32), but here poetically taking the sense of "caring." The noun "beast" (*bɘhemâ*) can be any four-footed animal although it most frequently denotes a domestic animal.[5] A righteous man "regardeth" his "beast." Thus, while God has given dominion over animals to man, He expects that there will be kindness shown to them even while using them for service or for food. The verse does not forbid the killing of animals for food or other uses since this

---

[4]AB, p. 89, emends to *ʿɘbodâ*, "work," and translates, "who has employment." Kidner, p. 96, and Perowne, p. 97, follow the LXX and read *ʿobed lô*, "is a servant to himself," i.e., works for himself. These suggestions do not materially add to the understanding of the verse. Following Ugaritic, Dahood, *PNWSP*, p. 26, understands "servant," *ʿebed*, as referring to the serving of food. Thus, "Better a man of no rank who has a helping than he who assumes honor, yet has nothing at all." It is unlikely that such a common word as *ʿebed* should have such a restricted sense here.

[5]Literally, the phrase says that the righteous man cares for "the life [*nepeš*, cf. 7:23] of his beast." Dahood, *PNWSP*, pp. 26-27, glosses *nepeš* with "appetite" on the basis of Ugaritic parallels. While this is certainly included within the general care of the righteous man, it is too restrictive to limit the thought only to the feeding of an animal.

*11 He that tilleth his land shall be satisfied with bread: but he that fol-
loweth vain persons is void of understanding.*
*12 The wicked desireth the net of evil men: but the root of the righteous
yieldeth fruit.*

would violate the principle earlier established by God; cf. Genesis 9:3;
Deuteronomy 12:15.

The phrase "tender mercies" (or "compassions") glosses *raham,* "tender mercy, compassion." This often refers to God's love for man, but it
may also, as here, refer to a deep-seated emotional feeling on the part of
man toward others with special needs. The word "cruel" is from *ʾakzarî,*
"cruel, fierce, merciless." The word *ʾakzarî* occurs eight times, half of
them in Proverbs and the others in Isaiah and Jeremiah, all in poetical
sections. The emotions of the wicked are "cruel." This general statement
compares the treatment of animals by the righteous and by the wicked.
The one cares for them; the other treats them with no more concern than
is necessary. In comparison with the care shown by the righteous, the
"compassions" of the wicked are as cruelty.

11 The thought returns to the familiar theme of work. The verb "followeth," or "pursues," is from *radap,* "to follow after, pursue." This is a
neutral word used of going after both good and bad. The one who diligently tends his crops will reap a bountiful harvest. One, however, who
follows "vain persons" lacks good sense (*hasar‑leb,* cf. 6:32). The word
"persons" is supplied and does not fit the context as well as *"things."*

12 The verb "desireth" comes from *hamad* (cf. 6:25), "to desire, take
pleasure in" but also "to covet, lust." The context determines the exact
sense. The wicked desires the "net" of other wicked men. Here, the net
represents the contents of the net, the spoil or booty. One wicked man
lusts after the illicit gain of another wicked man.[6] Verse 12b literally
says, "but the root of the righteous he will give." The idea is that God
Himself gives the righteous a "root," i.e., a stable foundation upon
which to build a life. This takes *natan,* cf. 2:3, in its normal transitive

---

[6]Beer, in BH, emends 12a to *yiššamed yǝsod raʿim,* "the counsel *of the wicked* will be
blotted out." AB, p. 90, emends to *tiššamēd mǝudat raʿim,* "the stronghold of the wicked
will be blotted out." While the MT is awkward, the use of "net" to represent the contents
of the net by metonymy is a routine poetical device. No change of the MT is necessary.

*13 The wicked is snared by the transgression of his lips: but the just
shall come out of trouble.*
*14 A man shall be satisfied with good by the fruit of his mouth: and the
recompence of a man's hands shall be rendered unto him.*

sense.[7] Verse 12b contrasts with 12a. While the wicked seek additional
material gain, the righteous have a stable foundation that never fails.

13-14 These two proverbs share the common theme of speech.
Wicked speech is an evil snare to those who utter it.[8] The wicked man
slanders, lies, uses profanity, calls names, and gossips. Eventually, his
words come back to hurt him. The just man, however, abides by the
guidance of God's Word. He therefore will be able to escape the dangers
that could come from evil speech, v. 13.

"Fruit" comes from *pərî*, normally the fruit of a tree or of one's body.
It can also indicate results and consequences of one's speech or actions.
With the exception of 27:18, *pərî* always has a figurative sense in
Proverbs. The adjective "good" comes from *ṭôb*, a broad word indicating
a wide span of goodness. The noun "recompence" is from *gəmûl*,
"deeds, recompense, benefit." It is used of both good and bad actions,
with the context determining the nature. A man will receive great personal satisfaction as he sees the fruit born in others as the "fruit" of his
conversation with them. He will be satisfied with "good."[9] In like manner, the works of his hands will also return to him, bringing him satisfaction.

---

[7]McKane, p. 450, vocalizes "yieldeth," *yitten,* as *yitan,* "to be permanent," and translates, "the root of the righteous abides." AB, p. 90, emends to *ʾetan,* from *yatan,* and
translates, "the roots of the just are enduring." Eitan, p. 51, similarly derives *yitten* from
yatan, "the root of the righteous will last forever." All of these suggestions attempt to explain the lack of an object for *natan,* normally a transitive verb. This is not a problem,
however, if we take God as the subject of *yitten* and make *šoreš* the object.

[8]Among others, Toy, p. 252; Gemser, p. 46; and Frankenberg, p. 79, emend *môqeš,*
"snared," to *nôqaš.* This follows the LXX and turns the verb into a noun. This gives
something like "the sinner falls into a snare," a right sense but an unnecessary change.
The book regularly warns against paying heed to wicked words, e.g., 11:9; 15:2; 18:7.

[9]Martin, p. 84; Oesterley, p. 94; and Toy, p. 251, omit *ṭôb,* "good," as a scribal interpretation. This change is subjective, made to obtain better balance in the phrases. There is
no real argument against the MT. It certainly states a correct principle.

*15 The way of a fool is right in his own eyes: but he that hearkeneth
unto counsel is wise.
16 A fool's wrath is presently known: but a prudent man covereth shame.
17 He that speaketh truth sheweth forth righteousness: but a false witness deceit.
18 There is that speaketh like the piercings of a sword: but the tongue of
the wise is health.
19 The lip of truth shall be established for ever: but a lying tongue is but
for a moment.*

15 Solomon now makes a pungent observation. The "fool" (*ʾəwîl,* cf.
1:7) is fully satisfied with his own way of life. He sees no need to consult with others; he is the master of his fate. The "wise" (cf. *ḥokmâ,*
1:2), however, recognizes the value of counsel. He weighs advice carefully before deciding upon his way; cf. 11:14; 15:22.

16 "Wrath" (better, "vexation) is from *kaʿas,* a word that occurs in
Proverbs only here and at 17:25; 21:19; and 27:3. It occurs widely elsewhere indicating the angry and excited response of a person to some offense received from someone else. The word "presently," literally, "in
that day," is idiomatic for "at once." The fool's "wrath" is made known
"in that day."[10] He shows it immediately. The "prudent" (*ʿarûm,* cf. 1:4)
man, however, covers that which would "shame" (or "dishonor," *qalôn,*
cf. 3:35) him.

17-19 These three proverbs focus on the theme of speech. One who
speaks "truth" (cf. *ʾaman,* 11:13) speaks "righteousness" (*ṣedeq,* cf. 1:3),
while one who perjures himself speaks "deceit" (*mirmâ,* cf. v. 5).[11] The
maxim has an obvious forensic sense, as though describing a courtroom
scene, cf. 14:5, v. 17.

In v. 18, the word "speaketh" is from *baṭâ,* "to speak rashly, inconsid-
erately." The word occurs only here, in Psalm 106:33, and twice in
Leviticus 5:4. A related noun also occurs in Numbers 30:6, 8. One who
speaks without thinking is "like the piercings of a sword," cutting the

[10]AB, p. 90, emends *yiwwadaʿ,* "known," to *yōdīəʿ* [*sic*], following the versions. This
gives an active sense, "the fool shows his vexation," rather than the passive sense of the
MT. The change is not significant and not necessary.
[11]AB, p. 90, emends *ṣedeq* to *ṣidqô* and translates, "One who brings out the facts makes
evident his innocence," a statement that may or may not be true. In any case, the change
is unsupported and unwarranted.

20 Deceit is in the heart of them that imagine evil: but to the counsellors of peace is joy.
21 There shall no evil happen to the just: but the wicked shall be filled with mischief.
22 Lying lips are abomination to the Lord: but they that deal truly are his delight.
23 A prudent man concealeth knowledge: but the heart of fools proclaimeth foolishness.

subjects of his talk. The wise man, however, weighs his words carefully. He speaks words of encouragement and confidence, which bring healing to the hearers, v. 18.

The one who speaks truth (*ʾəmet,* cf. 3:3) will "be established for ever" since truth will never fail. In sharp contrast, the one who speaks falsehood (*šaqer,* cf. 6:17) will endure only for a "moment." This last is picturesque in Hebrew, literally, "as long as I wink with the eye," a brief period of time, v. 19.

20 The word "counsellors" is from *yaʿaṣ,* "to counsel, devise, plan." The word occurs in a neutral sense, referring to both good and evil plans, with the context determining the exact sense. Those who "imagine [or "devise," *haraš,* cf. 3:29] evil" (*raʿ,* cf. 1:33) have hearts filled with "deceit" (*mirmâ,* cf. v. 5). In contrast with this, those who bring peace through their counsel will have hearts filled with joy.[12]

21 No "trouble" (*ʾawen,* cf. 6:12) will come upon the just (*ṣedeq,* cf. 1:3), a general statement implying God's care of the righteous. But the "wicked" (cf. *rešaʿ,* 8:7) will encounter "mischief" (or "trouble," *raʿ,* cf. 1:33) on his journey through life. This is also a general principle that is often true of man.

22 God considers the person who lies to be an "abomination" (*tôʿəbat,* cf. 3:32) since his speech is untrustworthy and at odds with the ways of righteousness. The person who speaks truthfully, however, is God's "delight" (cf. *raṣôn,* 11:1) since this speech is in full accord with the divine desires and standards for man.

23 A "prudent" (*ʿarûm,* cf. 1:4) man conceals his knowledge. He realizes there is potential harm in gaining a reputation of being a "know-it-

---

[12]Toy, p. 256, proposes to replace "joy," *śimḥâ,* with "just," *mišpaṭ,* a suggestion totally without merit.

24 The hand of the diligent shall bear rule: but the slothful shall be under tribute.
25 Heaviness in the heart of man maketh it stoop: but a good word maketh it glad.
26 The righteous is more excellent than his neighbour: but the way of the wicked seduceth them.

all." Further, his knowledge will be more effective if he saves it for the appropriate occasions. "Fools" (kəsîlîm, cf. 1:22), however, openly proclaim their foolishness as they speak freely upon things about which they are ignorant.

24 "Rule" is from mašal, a word that refers to various kinds of leadership roles. "Slothful" comes from rəmîyâ, "slack, negligent, idle, sloth," while "tribute" is from mas, "tribute, forced labor." The man who is "diligent" (ḥaraṣ) will one day "bear rule" (or "have dominion"). The word ḥaraṣ has as its root sense the idea "to cut" or "to sharpen." The sense of "diligent" comes from the picture of "sharp work," work that is well honed. The verse refers to the greater influence gained by a diligent man. The "slothful" man, on the other hand, will "be under tribute." The idea is that he will serve unwillingly under others as the natural consequence of his laziness in work.

25 "Heaviness" is from dəʾagâ, "care, anxiety" while the verb "stoop" comes from šaḥâ, "to bow down, prostrate," and thus, by extension, "to be depressed." The word occurs only here with this meaning.[13] "Heaviness" in a man's mind gives rise to depression. In contrast, a good word makes the heart "glad" (śamaḥ, cf. 10:1).

26 The AV apparently takes the verb "more excellent" from yatar, "to remain over." If we think of something left over as a remnant, it is possible to take the thought of a small portion that is "more excellent" than the other part. Others take it as the hipʿîl of tûr, "to search, explore,"

---

[13]The form yašḥennâ is difficult, not only because of the relative rarity of the verb, but also because dəʾagâ is masculine and leb feminine. This has caused several suggested emendations. Beer in BH, proposes tašhennû or tašhenhû. Driver, JTS 31:280, repoints to yəšîhennâ, from šuaḥ, "to melt," and translates, "anxiety in the heart of a man causes it to melt." Dahood, PNWSP, p. 27, relates the form to Ugaritic and translates, "causes fever." The MT makes generally good sense.

27 The slothful man roasteth not that which he took in hunting: but the substance of a diligent man is precious.

which again requires interpretation. The uncertainty has led to many emendations.[14]

Whatever interpretation we accept is subjective to a degree. I accept the MT since it at least has the weight of tradition behind it. I take the verb as the *hip⁽îl* from *tûr*: the righteous man "searches out" his neighbor, i.e., investigates him carefully before confiding in him. The verb "seduceth" is from *ta⁽â*, "to err"; cf. 10:17. The *hip⁽îl* of this is causative and thus "to cause to go astray." The word may refer to mental or moral error. In contrast with the righteous man, the wicked man's practice seduces others. While the righteous avoids trouble by his caution, the wicked rushes headlong into error.

27 The verb "roasteth," *yaḥərok,* occurs only here, and the grammar of the second half is difficult.[15] The bulk of the evidence supports the meaning "roast" for *ḥarak*. The "slothful" (*rəmîyâ,* cf. v. 24) man does not cook the game that he has taken in hunting, permitting it to spoil. The proverb heightens the image of slothfulness so as to make the point more vivid.

---

[14]The *Targum* takes it in the sense of "better." The NASB translates, "the righteous is a guide to his neighbor." *TWOT*, p. 967, gives the meaning "careful examination." The NIV apparently follows this, translating, "a righteous man is cautious in friendship." AB, p. 91, emends *mērē⁽ēhū,* "than his neighbor," to *mērā⁽ātō* and translates, "the good man survives his misfortune." J. A. Emerton, "A Note on Proverbs xii.26," *ZAW* 76:192-93, repoints the phrase to *yuttar mera⁽â,* taking the verb from *natar,* "to set free," and translating, "The righteous is delivered from harm." KD I, 266, follows the eighteenth-century commentary by Doderlein and repoints the phrase to *yater mir⁽ehû,* "the righteous looketh after his pastures." Toy, p. 260, tentatively suggests *yasur mera⁽â,* "the righteous departs from evil," but also notes that this does not contrast with 26*b*. Many other suggestions have also been made, all in the attempt to explain an uncertain verse.

[15]The question is whether we should understand *ḥarak* after the Aramaic and Ugaritic cognates, "to singe," or after an Arabic cognate, "to set in motion," i.e. "pursue." Mitchell Dahood, "The Hapax *ḥārak* in Proverbs 12,27," *Biblica* 63:61, understands *ḥarak* as "roasts" on the basis of a fourteenth-century B.C. Ugaritic text. The Aramaic *ḥərak* means "to roast, singe," but the Arabic cognate signifies "to start in motion, move," which some have interpreted as "to hunt." Eitan, p. 27, emends to *ḥarap* and translates, "the sluggard *gathereth* not (even) his provision." No matter which view is taken, the end result is the same. The slothful man fails to profit because of his failure either to hunt or to roast that which he has taken.

28 In the way of righteousness is life; and in the pathway thereof there is no death.

In contrast, "the precious [*yaqar*] possession of a man is diligence." The word *yaqar* is "to be rare" and, by extension, "to be precious." There is no good reason to reverse the order of *yaqar ḥarûṣ* and translate "the substance of a diligent man is precious" as in the AV.[16] The adjective *yaqar* modifies *hôn,* referring to the man's "precious possession." The attribute of diligence is indeed precious, one that contrasts with the slothfulness of one who wastes the prey that he has gained from hunting.

28 The word "way" comes from *ʾoraḥ,* "way, path," used most often in poetical contexts to picture the way leading to life or death. There is virtually total agreement with 28*a*: "In the way of righteousness *is* life." At the same time, there is virtually no agreement with 28*b*. The problem lies in the negative *ʾal,* generally used with a jussive verb. Since there is no verb in the clause, this has caused numerous emendations and creative interpretations.[17] But *ʾal* occurs as a negative without the verb in other contexts, e.g., II Samuel 1:21; Job 24:25. G.K. 152g recognizes the ability of *ʾal* to form a compound word and singles out Proverbs 12:28 as an example. Thus, it is appropriate here to accept the traditional view, "in its path there is no death," i.e., immortality. In this view, the verse is one of the clearer ones of the book to touch on the matter of spiritual life after physical death.

---

[16] Driver, *Biblica* 32:180, reverses the two words, although he takes *yaqar* as "heavy" in the sense of "much." Kidner, p. 99; Oesterley, p. 98; Alden, p. 104; and the AV follow this with minor variations. To gain parallelism, Eitan, pp. 27-28, vocalizes *yaqar* as *yaqur,* from the verb *qûr,* "to dig," and translates, "the diligent [man] diggeth out a delightful treasure." Toy, p. 259, understands *ḥarûṣ* as "gold" rather than diligence. Reversing *yaqar ḥarûṣ,* he translates, "the diligent man possesses wealth." AB, p. 91, translates, "the keen one gets plenty of it." This gains a contrast with 27*a* but is only loosely related to the Hebrew.

[17] The most common solution is to repoint *ʾal* to the preposition *ʾel* and to emend "pathway," *nətîbâ,* to some other word. Gemser, p. 47, and Hulst, *OTTP,* p. 121, suggest *məšubâ,* "backsliding, sin," which lies behind the RSV's "the way of error leads to death." Whybray, p. 75, calls the phrase "obscure" and proposes a similar change. Beer, BH, proposes *tôʿebâ,* "abomination." McKane, p. 451, adopts *petî bāʾ ʾel māwet,* "the way of folly leads to death." AB, p. 91, takes a different approach by understanding the pronoun *nətîbātō* for *nətîbāh.* AB translates, "the treading of its path. . . ." Kidner, p. 100, repoints to *ʾel* and translates, "*there is* a way *which is* a path to death." Mitchell Dahood, "Immortality in Proverbs 12,28," *Biblica* 41:176-81, supports from Ugaritic the possibility of taking *ʾal* as a negative. In *ETL* 44:52, Dahood reaffirms his translation, although he understands *nətîbâ* as the masculine form *natîb* with the 3fs suffix, "her way."

Practical Applications from Proverbs 12

1. Contrast between accepting or rejecting instruction 1, 8, 15
2. Contrast between good and bad behavior 2, 3, 5, 7, 10, 12, 16, 20, 21, 24, 28
3. Contrast between good and bad wives 4
4. Contrast between humility and pride 9
5. Contrast between work and laziness 11, 24, 27
6. Contrast between good and bad speech 6, 13, 17, 18, 19, 22, 23, 25
7. Reward of the good 14

1 A wise son heareth his father's instruction: but a scorner heareth not rebuke.
2 A man shall eat good by the fruit of his mouth: but the soul of the transgressors shall eat violence.
3 He that keepeth his mouth keepeth his life: but he that openeth wide his lips shall have destruction.

PROVERBS 13

1 Solomon contrasts the wise and foolish sons by showing their differing responses to the discipline of their parents. The word "rebuke" (*ga'ar*) indicates a firm reproof, either from man (Prov. 13:1, 8; 17:10; Eccles. 7:5; Isa. 30:17) or from God (II Sam. 22:16; Job 26:11; Ps. 18:15; 76:6; 80:16; 104:7; Isa. 50:2; 51:20; 66:15). The father's "instruction" (*mûsar*, cf. 1:2) parallels the word "rebuke" and thus conveys the thought of discipline or correction. The wise son accepts parental reproof, while the "fool" (*lēṣ*, cf. 1:22) rejects it. The first clause is a noun clause and requires the supply of a verb. There is a wide diversity of opinions as to how to understand the verse.[1] In general, these views agree that the wise son "accepts" the correction and training of his father.

2-3 These two proverbs deal with the subject of speech. The first expresses the simple idea that a person's good speech brings good things that he may enjoy. The "fruit of . . ." is a broadly used idiom that denotes results or consequences (cf. *parî*, 12:14); see 1:31; 10:16; 11:30; 12:14; 18:20; 31:16, 31. Here, then, the results of good speech are good. Wicked persons, however, have an insatiable appetite for those things that result in "violence" (*hamas*, cf. 3:31).

The interpretation of 2*b* turns on the view that is taken of *nepeš* (cf. 7:23). The AV understands it of the person himself and supplies the verb "shall eat." This indicates that he will receive undesirable results from

---

[1]Oesterley, p. 98, emends "father" (*'ab*) to the verb *'ahab*, "to love," and translates, "a wise son loveth instruction." Driver, "Hebrew Notes on Prophets and Proverbs," *JTS* 41:174, emends *mûsar* to *mayussar* and translates, "a wise son (is one) chastened of (= by) a father." Neither of these suggestions has textual support in their favor. KD I, 270, understands the phrase as "a wise son *is* his father's correction," i.e., he is the product of his father's instruction. Gemser, p. 48, understands *mûsar* in a passive sense. Thus, the son "is instructed by his father." The parallelism favors the view discussed above, that the son favorably hears his father's instruction.

4 The soul of the sluggard desireth, and hath nothing: but the soul of the diligent shall be made fat.
5 A righteous man hateth lying: but a wicked man is loathsome, and cometh to shame.
6 Righteousness keepeth him that is upright in the way: but wickedness overthroweth the sinner.

his wicked actions. Others refer *nepeš* to desires or cravings and supply the verb "is" (so NASB) to indicate that the wicked man craves evil things. The end result, "violence," fits equally well into either interpretation. Similarly, both views are parallel to *2a*. In reading the proverb, it is natural to allow the verb "eat" to govern both clauses. I would explain it with the AV, v. 2.

As a practical matter, a person should guard his speech. One who speaks carefully avoids speech that may bring harm upon him. The one who speaks without thinking will bring himself to "destruction" (*məhittâ*, cf. 10:14), some unspecified "ruin." The concept of guarded speech is a familiar theme throughout the book (cf. 10:14, 19; 12:18; 18:13; 21:23; 29:20), v. 3.

4 The "sluggard" (*ᶜaṣel*, cf. 6:6) "desires . . . and nothing." There is no object specified; hence, we may apply the proverb in any area. The lazy person wants good things, but he is not willing to work to gain them. He has nothing! In contrast, the "diligent" (cf. *ḥaraṣ,* 12:24) person is "fat." The word "be made fat," *dašan,* has the sense of "prosper," derived from the literal meaning of "fat." The fat parts of a sacrifice were regarded as the choicest parts, reserved for offering to God. It is a natural step from "the choicest, the best" to "the prosperous." The "diligent" person prospers as the reward of his work.

5-6 These two statements contrast righteous and wicked individuals. The righteous person "hates" (*śanaʾ,* cf. 11:15) false words (*dəbar-šeqer*). The phrase *dəbar-šeqer* refers to perjury (Exod. 23:7) and deceit or lying (Exod. 5:9; Ps. 119:29; Jer. 7:4). It is best here to limit it to lying rather than including such evil speech as gossip, profanity, or name calling. The verb *śanaʾ* has a forceful sense here, i.e., the righteous man "detests" such speech.

The wicked person, however, is "loathsome" (*baʾaš*) and "cometh to shame" (*ḥaper*). Both of these *hipᶜîl* verbs have a causative sense. The

7 There is that maketh himself rich, yet hath nothing: there is that maketh himself poor, yet hath great riches.
8 The ransom of a man's life are his riches: but the poor heareth not rebuke.

verb *baʾaš* is picturesque. Elsewhere, it refers to the rotting of fish and frogs, Exodus 7:21; 8:14; Isaiah 50:2; to the decay of manna, Exodus 16:20; and to the putrefying of flies, Ecclesiastes 10:1. Poetically, it describes relationships that have deteriorated. The verb *ḥaper* regularly refers to "shame." In contrast to the righteous man who hates deception, the wicked person creates a stench and brings others to shame by his actions, v. 5.

Righteousness preserves the walk of integrity (cf. *tom*, 2:7) but wickedness (cf. *rešaʿ*, 8:7) "overthroweth" (or "perverts," cf. *salap*, 11:3) the sinner.[2] Righteousness thus breeds more righteousness, while wickedness twists and distorts the character of the evil man, v. 6.

7-8 The next two proverbs contrast riches and poverty. The first suggests that wealth is not very valuable. A rich man may well be bereft of eternal riches, while the poor man may well possess them. It is equally possible to take the proverb as warning against pretense. One may pose as a wealthy person when he in fact has nothing. Another may pose as poverty-stricken while he actually possesses great riches. Still another way of taking the adage applies it to making one's way in life. Though one begins with nothing, he is able to make himself rich. Though another begins with great wealth, through foolishness he squanders it so that he becomes poor. I prefer the first of these views, v. 7.

> The NT develops these thoughts: the poor rich man; cf. Luke 6:24, 25*a*; 12:16-21; 18:24*b*-25; I Timothy 6:9-10; James 5:1-3; Revelation 3:17-18; and the rich poor man; cf. Matthew 6:19-21; Luke 12:22-34; I Timothy 6:8; Hebrews 13:5; James 2:5; Revelation 2:9*a*.

---

[2]Eitan, pp. 38-42, draws upon an Arabic cognate to argue that *ḥaṭṭaʾt* has the meaning of "step," or "walk," and is thus parallel to *derek* in 6a. He translates 6b "wickedness perverteth the walk." The word *ḥaṭṭaʾt*, however, occurs widely with the meaning of

9 *The light of the righteous rejoiceth: but the lamp of the wicked shall
be put out.*
10 *Only by pride cometh contention: but with the well advised is wisdom.*

Wealth has its dangers. A wealthy man may pay to ease some difficulty, e.g., a bribe, ransom for a kidnapping, theft of his goods. A poor
man, however, hears no "rebuke" (cf. *ga^{c}ar,* v. 1), i.e., no one threatens
him since he has nothing to give. The *Pulpit Commentary* aptly quotes
the proverb "A hundred men cannot rob one pauper" (p. 252), v. 8.

9 Light may symbolize the life of an individual (e.g., Job 18:5-6;
21:17). Here, blessing rests upon the righteous while judgment awaits
the wicked. The word "rejoiceth" (cf. *śamah,* 10:1) has occasioned controversy, since a light does not "rejoice."[3] The word, however, gives a
metaphorical picture of blessing and is elsewhere associated with light
(Esther 8:16; Ps. 97:11; Prov. 15:30). For the discussion of the parallel
words "light" and "lamp," cf. 6:23, n. 17.

The most natural way of understanding the verse relates it to divine
blessing and punishment. God rewards the righteous with a vibrant,
bright, blessed life. The wicked, however, will be cut off with His
judgment.

10 The word "pride" comes from *zûd,* "to boil" and, by extension, "to
act proudly." The idea of "presumption" is a major part of the meaning
since one's pride leads him to presumptive actions. The word *zûd* is better translated "presumption" since the actions of a proud person are

---

"sinner." No significant change forces this change in meaning. Similarly, Zöckler, p.
134, tries to introduce a more vigorous meaning of "to plunge" (cf. "overthrow," AV) for
sallep. The verb *salap,* however, more naturally indicates the perversion that wickedness
brings about in the sinner.

[3]Eitan, p. 5, relates *śamah* to an Arabic cognate, "to be high," and translates, "the light
of the righteous shall *rise* (or *be high*)." While this conveys the correct sense of the
verse, it takes an unnecessary liberty with the well-established verb *śamah,* "to rejoice."
Several authors (e.g., Oesterley, Jones, Greenstone) emend *yiśmah* to *yizrah,* "to shine."
This expresses a correct sense but is an unnecessary change in the MT. Frankenberg,
p. 82, reads *yiśmah* as a *pi^{c}el,* a transitive verb, and translates, "Licht erfreuet die
Gerechten," "light gladdens the righteous." The parallelism is against this. No change to
the text is necessary to understand the verse. As Zöckler points out, "The verb is here
intransitive: 'is joyous, i.e., burns brightly, with vigorous blaze.' " Driver, *Biblica* 32:180
supports the MT by relating *yiśmah* to Ugaritic.

11 Wealth gotten by vanity shall be diminished: but he that gathereth by labour shall increase.
12 Hope deferred maketh the heart sick: but when the desire cometh, it is a tree of life.

what generally cause strife. "Only" belongs with "contention" rather than "pride," i.e., a person's arrogant actions can lead only to strife (cf. G.K. 153).[4]

In contrast, those who seek counsel (cf. *ya⁽aṣ*, 12:20) are wise.[5] Rather than presumptively barging ahead with their own opinions, they cautiously seek advice from others. This leads them to wise decisions and actions.

11 The phrase "by vanity" (*hebel*) is puzzling. There are various ways of understanding it: use of speculative methods, e.g., gambling, speculative investment (so Cohen, Perowne); to the hurried accumulation of wealth (so Martin, Oesterley); or to the use of immoral methods, e.g., fraud or extortion (so Jones, NASB, NIV). The word *hebel* occurs primarily in the poetical sections of the OT. The word has various senses: referring to (1) idolatry; (2) the lack of accomplishment; (3) the insubstantial character of life. Here, it is appropriate to understand the last of these senses, wealth gotten through insubstantial means. This is a broad enough idea to encompass fraudulent actions or speculative methods.[6] The better way focuses on wealth gathered by one's own "labor" (*⁽al yad*, literally, "by the hand"). The phrase is idiomatic for "gradually." The gradual, yet persistent, accumulation of wealth brings success.

12 The word "sick" comes from *ḥalâ*, "to be sick." The word elsewhere refers to both physical illness or hurt and to mental anguish. An

---

[4]McKane, p. 454, following BH and Gemser, p. 48, reads *req* for *raq* and translates, "an empty-head produces strife by his arrogance." This introduces an unnecessary change. Eitan, pp. 50-53, rejects *natan* as the source of *yitten* and derives it instead from *ytn*, "to exist permanently." He translates, "Only through insolence (or presumptuousness) does contention last." The form *yitten*, from *natan*, occurs widely. Since it fits nicely here, there is no need to derive it from a root that is relatively rare.

[5]Several authors (e.g., Toy, Greenstone, Oesterley, Jones) transpose letters to obtain *ṣǝnu⁽îm*, "humble, lowly." This makes a nice parallel with 10*a*, "with the lowly is wisdom," but is nonetheless an unjustified change. There is no textual support for the emendation.

[6]AB, p. 94, and Toy, p. 271, follow the LXX and emend *mehebel* to *mǝbōhāl* and translate, "in haste." The LXX, however, interprets *hebel* and thus does not provide a solid basis for the emendation. The MT can be satisfactorily treated.

13 Whoso despiseth the word shall be destroyed: but he that feareth the commandment shall be rewarded.
14 The law of the wise is a fountain of life, to depart from the snares of death.

expectation that lasts for a protracted period of time makes the heart "sick." The idea is that the man becomes discouraged, despairing that his hope will ever be realized. On the other hand, the fulfilled desire is "a tree of life" (*ʿeṣ ḥayîm,* cf. 3:18), life with all of its fullness and richness.

13 The word "destroyed" (*ḥabal,* cf. 1:5) is too strong. The root *ḥabal* has several different meanings but the sense of destruction does not occur in the *nipʿal*. It is better to understand *ḥabal* in its normal sense, "to bind," and to translate, "whoever despises the word will be bound by it." The "word" is not defined; however, the only "word" that has the power to control men is the Word of God.[7] This aptly parallels the last half of the verse. The one who "feareth (*yareʾ*) the commandment shall be rewarded (*yəšullam*)."[8] The word *yareʾ* occurs widely, referring variously to fear, reverence, awe, piety, and so forth. Here, it indicates a reverence for the Word. The word *šalem,* cf. 3:2, here has its normal sense of "be at peace." It is appropriate to apply it here to commands from God. This is the reward God gives those who hold His Word in reverence.

14 The "law" (or "instruction," *tôrâ,* cf. 1:8) of the wise person is a "fountain of life." This same figure occurs in 10:11; 14:27; and 16:22. A person who receives such instruction finds that it produces a full, vibrant life. In turn, this gives discernment that allows one to avoid the "snares of death," i.e., those paths of life that lead one to premature judgment.

---

[7]McKane, p. 454, argues that this refers to the words of the wisdom teacher. In a Jewish context, this would have been drawn from the OT. It is better, then, to apply the verse directly to God's Word.

[8]Several authors read *yəhabel* for *yəhabel lô.* Toy, Gemser, and BH delete *lô* (Gemser calls it a dittography) and read *yišlam* for *yəšullam.* This leads to a more direct contrast in the two phrases: "He who despises the word will perish but he who fears the command will be safe." This has partial support from the LXX but the support is not strong. The change to the MT is unnecessary since the text already makes good sense.

15 Good understanding giveth favour: but the way of transgressors is hard.
16 Every prudent man dealeth with knowledge: but a fool layeth open his folly.

Sources of Life

The phrase *məqôr hayyîm,* "fountain of life," occurs four times in Proverbs. While the translators expressed this in different ways, the meaning is the same. We may drink from the waters that produce abundant life.

1. Producing Life for Ourselves
   a. Fear of the Lord 14:27
   b. Understanding of the Wise 16:22

2. Producing Life for Others
   a. Speech of the Righteous 10:11
   b. Instruction of the Wise 13:14

---

15 "Favour" (*ḥen,* cf. 3:4) occurs widely in Proverbs. It regularly denotes "favor" or "grace." The initial phrase is clear. A man who has good "understanding" (cf. *śakal,* 1:3) receives "favour." The statement is broad and could include favor from both man and God. In contrast, the "way of transgressors [*bogədîm,* cf. 11:3] is hard [*ʾêtan*]." The final word of the verse (*ʾêtan*) has led to numerous conjectures.[9] The translation "hard" is interpretive, not supported elsewhere. The word *ʾêtan* normally means "permanent, enduring" and so, when used of streams, "ever flowing." It is appropriate here to translate, "the way of the treacherous is constant," a generally true statement of the wicked.

16 The proverb is similar to 12:23, comparing prudent and foolish individuals. Every "prudent" (*ʿarûm,* cf. 1:4) person acts with "knowledge"

---

[9]KD I, 280, says, "the fundamental idea of . . . continuing passes over into the idea of the firm, the hard. . . ." He translates, "the way of the malicious is uncultivated," which does not seem to be especially apt. Driver, *Biblica* 32:181 emends to *ʾî-ʾêtan* and translates, "not lasting." While this is true, it requires the addition of *ʾî,* used only once elsewhere. Several authors (e.g., Jones, Whybray, RSV, Confraternity) follow the LXX and emend to *ʾêdam,* "their ruin." The idea makes sense but, since we may explain the MT, the change is not required.

17 A wicked messenger falleth into mischief: but a faithful ambassador is health.
18 Poverty and shame shall be to him that refuseth instruction: but he that regardeth reproof shall be honoured.

(da^cat, cf. 1:4) in what he does. The "fool" ($k\partial s\hat{\imath}l$, cf. 1:22), however, openly displays his foolishness ($^{\partial}aw\hat{\imath}l$, cf. 1:7) by his actions.[10]

17 The maxim contrasts wicked and faithful servants. The wicked ($ra\check{s}a^c$, cf. 8:7) falls into "mischief" (better, "adversity," ra^c, cf. 1:33).[11] In opposition to this, the "faithful" (cf. $^{\partial}aman$, 11:13) envoy is "health" ($marpe^{\partial}$, cf. 4:22). We must supply something to develop this last thought, e.g., the faithful messenger *brings* healing through his work.

18 One who neglects "instruction" ($m\hat{u}sar$, cf. 1:2) will receive "poverty and shame." We must regard $m\hat{u}sar$ here as "correction" or "instruction leading to correction." The parallelism here with "reproof" ($t\hat{o}ka\d{h}at$, cf. 1:23) requires this. The idea is that this person rejects attempts at reorienting his conduct. The result of this is that he sinks further into the natural consequences of his actions.[12] On the other hand, one who receives correction will be "honored" ($kabed$, cf. 3:9), given an enhanced reputation by others.

---

[10]Eitan, pp. 57-58, argues that "dealeth," $^c a\acute{s}\hat{a}$, should be glossed "to cover, envelop." He tries to show that the wise man conceals his wisdom while the fool openly displays it. Since the only way to conceal wisdom is to act as a fool (or, more charitably, a dunce), this does not seem to be a viable option. This is particularly true in view of the fact that $^c a\acute{s}\hat{a}$, occurs widely with the meaning "to do, work," naturally embracing the thought "to act."

[11]Without strong textual support, several authors (e.g., Martin, McKane, Toy) suggest reading the $hip^c\hat{\imath}l$ $yapp\hat{\imath}l$ for $yippol$, "falleth," and translate, "an incompetent messenger brings into evil." The object of his work is variously taken as those who send the messenger or those whom he leads astray.

[12]McKane, p. 456, follows Toy, p. 275, and inserts $l\partial$ before $p\hat{o}rea^c$, "refuseth," in order to smooth out the reading. The change adds nothing to the interpretation. Toy, Cohen, and Oesterley all relate the verse to success or failure in business. A man who refuses to listen to the counsel of others who have a broad experience in business affairs will likely end up with his business ruined. In contrast, the man who accepts such advice will enjoy the honor that comes from success in business. This view is highly arbitrary and limits the application only to a few individuals. It also goes contrary to the normal use of "reproof," $t\hat{o}ka\d{h}at$, which never is limited to the business world elsewhere in the book.

19 The desire accomplished is sweet to the soul: but it is abomination to
fools to depart from evil.
20 He that walketh with wise men shall be wise: but a companion of
fools shall be destroyed.
21 Evil pursueth sinners: but to the righteous good shall be repayed.

19 The opening phrase lays the foundation for the conclusion of the
thought. It is sweet to satisfy one's desires (*taʾǝwâ*, cf. 10:24).[13] The
word *taʾǝwâ* can refer to either wholesome desires or wicked desires. In
either case, it is gratifying to accomplish one's hopes. Since the poetry
here is antithetic, 19*a* best refers to wholesome desires. Verse 19*b*, then,
notes that it is almost impossible for an evil man to leave his wickedness. Sin's hold grips him, and he avidly seeks to fulfill his evil desires.[14]

20 The first clause is better read with the *qǝrê holek . . . yeḥkam*. This
gives the sense of the AV, "he who walks with wise men will become
wise!" Verse 20*b* gives the result of failing to do this: "he who compa-
nies with fools will suffer harm." "Destroyed" (*yerôaʿ*), as in the AV, is
too strong. The word *yerôaʿ*, from *raʿaʿ*, "to be evil," cf. 11:15, is thus
"to suffer hurt." The text indicates only that this man's associations will
harm him in some way.[15]

21 The proverb repeats a familiar theme in the book, that the wicked
receive punishment while the righteous reap a bountiful reward. The
word "evil" (*raʿâ*, also from *raʿaʿ*) should be translated "adversity." The
idea is a broad one. The wicked generally receive a harvest of

---

[13]Zöckler, p. 136, takes the puzzling view that *nihyâ* (*nipʿal* participle from *hayâ*, thus,
"desire that is done," i.e., accomplished) indicates "a desire that is just originated," not
yet fulfilled. The *nipʿal* would rather suggest a reflexive thought, that one has satisfied
the desire for himself.

[14]Various commentators (e.g., Whybray, Jones) take the two halves as mismatched,
having nothing to do with one another. This has led to conjectured readings to resolve
the supposed difficulty. AB, p. 95, proposes to read *tōḥelet*, "expectation," for *tôʿabat*,
and to translate, "the (unfulfilled) expectation of fools is to avoid disaster" (taking *raʿ* as
"disaster"). BH suggests *wǝtôḥelet kǝsîlîm mûsar raʿ*, "but the expectation of fools is disagreeable correction." This is a violent change to the MT. These approaches fail to connect the two phrases properly.

[15]Thomas, *JTS* 15:55-56, relies upon the LXX to emend to *yiwwadeaʿ*, from *yadaʿ*, "to
be quiet." He translates, ". . . shall be subdued." Guillaume, *JTS*, 15:294, relies on an
Arabic cognate to derive *yerôaʿ* from *rwʿ* with a secondary meaning "to deceive." He
translates, ". . . will be left a fool." Neither of these approaches is convincing.

22 A good man leaveth an inheritance to his children's children: and the wealth of the sinner is laid up for the just.
23 Much food is in the tillage of the poor: but there is that is destroyed for want of judgment.

adversity in this life. In contrast, the righteous will be "repayed" with good things.[16] Once again, the statement is general, picturing the fact that the righteous normally receive good in this life.

22 The "good man," in this context clearly a morally good person, experiences the joy of leaving an inheritance to his grandchildren. This implies a prosperous life, a long life, and posterity, all blessings generally enjoyed by the righteous. Conversely, the "sinner" holds his wealth in store for the righteous. The implied thought is that he will lose his material possessions through wicked conduct. Righteous individuals will benefit from his foolishness. The proverb is a general statement of what happens in life.

23 The Hebrew of the verse is open to a variety of interpretations.[17] It is reasonable to understand it as a commentary on the age-old problem of the poor (*ra'šîm,* cf. 10:4), how to keep that which belongs to them.[18] The word *rûš* describes a destitute condition. The poor man has the potential of an abundant harvest in his "tillage" (or "fallow ground").

---

[16]There is a minor grammatical problem in 21*b.* Literally, the phrase reads, "and the righteous he will reward good." The double accusative and the indefinite subject have led some to emend the verb. It is entirely possible, however, to translate as a passive, "the righteous will be rewarded with good." Toy, p. 279, and Gemser, p. 49, variously emend "repayed," *yəšallem,* to some form of *šagâ,* and translate, "good overtakes the righteous." AB, p. 94, without comment, also translates this way. This approach solves the grammatical problem arbitrarily by making "good" the subject and accepting the emendation. Since this is essentially what the MT says, there is no advantage gained by emending the text. Dahood, *ETL* 44:53, takes a different approach by making *tôb* a name for God, "the Good One." This logically leads to the parallel thought that *ra'â* is "the Evil One." While the argument draws support from Ugaritic parallels, there is no clear usage of this kind in the OT.

[17]Kufeldt, p. 524, and AB, p. 94, accept the emendation *rîb 'okel* for *rab 'okel,* "much food," and translate, "litigation devours the poor." While this sense is possible, the change is unnecessary since the MT is explicable. Driver, *JTS* 31:278, understands *ra'aš* as "rich," basing his interpretation on an Arabic and a possible Akkadian cognate. McKane, p. 463, apparently derives *ra'šîm* from *ro'š,* "chief," and understands it as "notable" or "grandee." The verse then is a warning that the wealth of the wicked rich will be snatched from them. While this is possible, I prefer the more traditional view above.

[18]The word *ra'šîm,* "poor," is from *rûš,* "to be poor." The *aleph* is an orthographic insertion denoting the long vowel sound (see G.K. 23g). The same form occurs in 10:4.

*24 He that spareth his rod hateth his son: but he that loveth him chas-
teneth him betimes.*
*25 The righteous eateth to the satisfying of his soul: but the belly of the
wicked shall want.*

Despite this, it is swept away from him by "want of judgment" (better,
by "injustice"). Thus, the rich, through oppression of the poor, increase
their own wealth.

24 Parents should use corporal punishment in training their children.[19]
Solomon here points out that a parent who fails to use corporal punishment actually "hates" (cf. *śana᾽*, 11:15) his child. Conversely, the discipline of a child provides evidence that the parents "love" (*᾽ahab,* cf. 9:8)
their child. The rod of correction demonstrates the love held by the parents for their child.

25 The chapter ends by stressing the theme of prosperity for the righteous and poverty for the wicked. This general statement contrasts the
condition of the two. The righteous man eats with the result that he is
satisfied. The word "soul" (*nepeš,* cf. 7:23) has the sense here of inward
desires, more than mere appetite. He achieves a sense of deep contentment with the achievements of his life. On the other hand, the wicked
experiences continual frustration. The word "belly" (*beṭen*) occurs eight
times in the book.[20] Only in 31:2 does it take the meaning of "womb,"
referring directly to the physical body. Elsewhere, however, it always
refers to the innermost depths of one's own being. Thus, the verse expresses the lack of satisfaction in life experienced by the wicked.

---

[19]The phrase "chasteneth him betimes" is awkward. The word "betimes" (cf. *šaḥar,*
8:17) gives a metaphorical picture of seeking the child early, i.e., diligently. The loving
parent "seeks his son early with discipline," i.e., carefully trains him throughout his
whole life.
[20]Prov. 13:25; 18:8, 20; 20:27, 30; 22:18; 26:22; 31:2.

Practical Applications from Proverbs 13

1. Parent-child relationships 1, 24
2. Contrast between good and bad speech 2, 3, 5
3. Contrast between diligence and laziness 4, 11
4. Contrast between righteousness and wickedness 6, 9, 17, 21, 22, 25
5. Contrast between wealth and poverty 7, 8, 23
6. Contrast between pride and humility 10
7. Contrast between delayed and fulfilled desires 12
8. Contrast between obedience and disobedience 13, 14, 15, 18
9. Contrast between wisdom and folly 16
10. Contrast between wholesome and evil desires 19
11. Contrast between wise and foolish friends 20

*1 Every wise woman buildeth her house: but the foolish plucketh it
down with her hands.
2 He that walketh in his uprightness feareth the Lord: but he that is
perverse in his ways despiseth him.*

PROVERBS 14

1 The wife has the ability to bring happiness and fulfillment to a home
as she "builds" it. The contrasting comment about folly in the second
half of the verse makes it likely that Solomon has the stability of the
home in mind. The wise woman builds the harmony and order of the
home. She contributes cohesiveness to firmly bind the members of the
household together. The foolish one tears her home apart.[1]

2 A person's relationship with God will determine his conduct in life.
One who walks in "uprightness" (cf. *yašar*, 2:21) shows that he has a
wholesome reverence for God (*yəreʾ yəhwah,* cf. 1:7). On the other hand,
a person who is "perverse" (cf. *lûz*, 2:15) shows that he "despises" (cf.
bûz, 1:7) God. The pronoun "him" refers to God, although grammatically it could denote either the godly person or God.

The theme of the two ways is familiar in the book, e.g., 10:9; 11:3;
14:14. In fact, more individual verses deal with this theme than with any

---

[1]There is little doubt as to the meaning of the verse; but there is considerable doubt
over the form of "wisdom," *ḥakmôt,* and whether it should be treated as an abstract
noun. Most commentators follow the pattern of 1:20; 9:1; and 24:7, where the form is
pointed *ḥokmôt.* The word is understood as an intensive plural, describing the wisdom of
a woman as she guides the development of her home. This parallels 1*b*, in which "folly"
tears down the house. There are difficulties with this view. The construction of the verse
argues against it. Why should an abstract noun be used with "women" (*našîm*)? The plural construct *ḥakmôt* can readily be translated "the wisdom of women," with *ḥakmôt* understood as an intensive plural. But what does it add to take *ḥakmôt* as *ḥokmôt?* Further,
if it is understood as an abstract, on the basis of 1*b*, this is still not parallel since 1*b* adds
the phrase *bəyadêha,* "with her hands." For these reasons, I accept the MT as it stands,
without repointing it. KD I, 288, and Zöckler, p. 139, are among those who repoint the
word. More radical suggestions involve the omission of *našîm* and *bəyadêyha* on the
grounds that these are scribal insertions based on a misunderstanding of the text.
Oesterley, p. 106; Toy, pp. 280-81; and McKane, p. 472, are among those who accept
variations of this view. Dahood, *PNWSP,* p. 30, understands *nšym* as a superlative on the
basis of Ugaritic parallels, "the Wisest of Women built her house." Cohen, p. 86, and
Toy, p. 280, both interpret the verse in an economic sense, as though "building" refers to
an increase in prosperity in the home. While the wife may contribute to the household's
economy, I would apply the verse to the family's total harmony. The verse thus gives a
picture of the wife's capacity to influence the home for good or bad.

3 In the mouth of the foolish is a rod of pride: but the lips of the wise shall preserve them.
4 Where no oxen are, the crib is clean: but much increase is by the strength of the ox.

other topic. That this is so is not surprising. The book deals with life. Its theology is not theoretical; it is intensely practical. It is natural that the contrasting ways of righteousness and wickedness should be set in opposition to one another. In this way, Solomon compares the contrasting natures of these ways and sets forth the contrasting results of these ways of life.

3 The speech of the foolish is a "rod of pride." The word "rod," *hoter,* a "branch" or "shoot" of a tree, occurs again only in Isaiah 11:1. The phrase vividly portrays the haughty spirit that grows out of the words of a foolish person.[2] Such speech would clearly bring the person into difficulty. In sharp contrast, the speech of the wise person "shall preserve him," keeping him from the personal trials and consequences of boastful, rash, or intemperate speech.

4 The interpretation rests on the understanding of the word "clean" (*bar,* cf. 11:26). This is translated either "pure, clean" (and, by extension, "empty") or "grain, corn." Both ideas occur about the same number of times. The word *bar,* "pure," however, overwhelmingly refers to moral purity, and that is not the case in this verse. It is best, then, to translate: "where *there are* no oxen *there is* a crib of corn, but a great yield *is* by the strength of the ox."[3]

The verse now is a practical observation on the economics of farm life. If you have no oxen, you may have a crib full of grain (corn). But when you have strong oxen available to work the fields, you will have your barns filled with the increase from their labors.

---

[2]Kufeldt, Garrett, McKane, and Whybray, along with the RSV, NIV, and NASB, accept the emendation of "pride," *ga'awâ,* to "back," *gēwō.* The phrase would then read, "a rod for the back," i.e., the fool brings severe punishment upon himself through his speech. The change, however, has no textual support nor is it necessary to make sense of the passage.

[3]Toy, p. 286, and Greenstone, p. 148, among others, emend *'ebûs,* "crib," to *'epes,* "no," and translate, "when there are no oxen, there is no corn." The change is unsupported and is unnecessary when we take *bar* as discussed above.

5 *A faithful witness will not lie: but a false witness will utter lies.*
6 *A scorner seeketh wisdom, and findeth it not: but knowledge is easy unto him that understandeth.*
7 *Go from the presence of a foolish man, when thou perceivest not in him the lips of knowledge.*
8 *The wisdom of the prudent is to understand his way: but the folly of fools is deceit.*
9 *Fools make a mock at sin: but among the righteous there is favour.*

5 We have here a second contrast between the two ways possible to mankind. The faithful man is reliable in his speech; he will not lie. In contrast, the "false witness" literally "breathes [*yapîaḥ*] lies." The verb *pûaḥ* means "to breathe, blow." By extension, it also refers to speaking. The picture is of one whose very breath is untrustworthy.

6 Once again, there is a contrast between the "scorner" (*leṣ*, cf. 1:22) and the man of "understanding" (cf. *bîn*, 1:2). The *leṣ* has rejected truth (13:1). He therefore is unable to attain wisdom even though he may seek it in his own way. The man who has understanding, however, grasps truth easily, with no great difficulty.

The only real question here lies with the nature of "wisdom" (*ḥokmâ*, cf. 1:2). Should we limit this to religious and moral issues, or is the scope a broad one?[4] Consistently, throughout the OT, *ḥokmâ* deals with the practical application of knowledge, with no particular emphasis on spiritual matters. Since all forms of wisdom come from God, we should not limit it here to the spiritual realm. One who scorns correction, in any area, will never gain wisdom in that field.

7-9 These three proverbs deal with the "fool." We best capture the contrast between the halves of v. 7 by translating the *waw* as "or" rather than "when." Unless one leaves the close company of a "foolish man" (*kəsîl*, cf. 1:22), he will not "perceive"(cf. *yadaʿ*, 10:32), experientially know, the words of truth. The proverb points out the importance of friends; cf. 27:17. The problem lies in the source of learning. If one learns from a *kəsîl*, his experiential knowledge will develop from one who holds a wrong perspective on life. He therefore needs to leave the

---

[4]W. H. Phillott, *The Proverbs*, in *Commentary on the Old Testament*, II (1880) (hereafter cited as SPCK), states that this is "divine wisdom" and compares it with "those who apply themselves to the study of God's Word." Muencher, p. 147, speaks of the *leṣ* as one "who pretends to be a candid inquirer to the subject of divine revelation." As briefly discussed above and at 1:2, this view restricts wisdom too much.

company of this one for wiser companions. This will allow him to develop a right philosophy of life, v. 7.[5]

The "prudent" (*ᶜarûm*, cf. 1:4) man manifests his wisdom by carefully discerning "his way," his manner of life. In contrast, "fools" (*kəsîlîm*, cf. 1:22) demonstrate their "folly" (cf. *ʾəwîl*, 1:7) by "deceit" (*mirmâ*, cf. 12:5) as they devise ways of snaring others. A different spirit moves these two, and their paths in life diverge radically. The godly man carefully considers his way so that the end result is righteousness. The foolish man constantly strives for personal advantage and, to that end, constantly seeks to deceive others for what he perceives as an advantage, v. 8.[6]

The third member of this triplet of verses dealing with the fool is by far the most controversial. Do "fools mock sin" or does "sin mock fools"? Both translations (and interpretations) are grammatically possible. Commentators take both approaches to the verse.

The "fool" here is the *ʾəwîlîm* (cf. 1:7), a plural word basically used as a synonym for *kəsîlîm*. The verb "mock," however, is the singular *yalîṣ*, related to the familiar *leṣ*, "scorner." Most naturally, then, we would expect a singular subject. We have this in the word "sin," *ʾašam*. The word *ʾašam* may refer to the "guilt" of a sinner, to the punishment for sin, or to the trespass offering that was required for the sin. The primary component of meaning in *ʾašam* is "guilt." So we have here the possibility

---

[5]The verse lacks the nice parallelism of most of the aphorisms of the book. Toy, p. 286, assumes that the verb is third person rather than second. He radically emends and translates, "for his lips do not utter knowledge." Gordon, however, *JBL* 49:396, notes that both the *Targum* and Vulgate are second person here. AB, p. 96, suggests *tabbēəᶜ*, "lavish," for the MT *yadaᶜta*, "thou knowest." Frankenberg, p. 86, calls 7*b* "komplizierte und sonderbare," "complicated and extraordinary," and gives up trying to express the phrase cogently. These frustrations come from trying to force the proverb into a mold with both phrases perfectly balanced. While this is as a whole true, there are numerous exceptions of synthetic parallelism in which the second part completes the first. That is the case here.

[6]Farmer, p. 77; Plaut, p. 160; and Alden, p. 111, among others, limit *mirmâ* here to self-deceit. It is true that the fool is self-deceived in his actions; however, *mirmâ* refers to the deception of others. The word occurs almost forty times in the OT, regularly referring to the deception of others. Another approach to the verse involves emending *mirmâ* on the basis of the LXX's εν πλανη. Toy, p. 286, suggests *matᶜâ*, "leads astray." Thomas, *VTS* III, 285-86, rejects this but vocalizes *mirmâ* as *mərammâ*, "to mislead." While this makes sense, the basic meaning of *mirmâ* also is explicable; hence, there is no need to repoint the word.

10 The heart knoweth his own bitterness; and a stranger doth not inter-
meddle with his joy.

that guilt mocks the foolish practitioner of sin. And we have the equal
possibility that the guilt offering mocks its offerer. On the one hand, we
have the guilt that comes after sin, with its constant accusing voice jeer-
ing at the guilty party. On the other hand is the futility of a ritualistic
guilt offering, as if God were mollified by someone going through the
motions of sacrifice (I Sam. 15:22; Hos. 6:6).

I choose the first of these views, that guilt mocks the sinner. Proverbs
places little stress upon worship. We would not expect to find a warning
against ritualism here. But the practical observation that guilt mocks the
sinner is very appropriate to the tone of the book.[7]

The last half of the verse is clearer but still subject to some confusion.
In contrast to the mockery that follows the fool, "among the righteous
there is favor [raṣôn, cf. 11:1]." This is the favor bestowed by God upon
those who obey Him. The most natural way of understanding this is in
contrast to yalîṣ, i.e., of the contentment and quiescent conscience that
the righteous enjoy, v. 9.[8]

10 This observes the impossibility of sharing one's innermost emotional feelings. The "heart" (*leb,* cf. 3:5) here represents the emotional
nature of man. This alone knows the bitterness of the soul. Even when

---

[7]KD I, 294-95, peculiarly reads the *hipˤîl helîṣ* and takes this and *ʾašam* in a construct
relationship, "the guilt-offering of fools." This gives a correct sense but is grammatically
wrong. AB, p. 96, divides the words differently from the MT, obtaining *ʾawîl melîṣ,* giving a singular subject "fool." Coates, p. 62, suggests reading the verb as in I Sam. 18:27
(*malaʾ*) and translating, "a fool shall pay full compensation." Martin, p. 92, simply says,
"There is probably some original corruption of the text that it is not now possible to discover." These are speculative approaches to the verse, not founded upon textual evidence.

[8]Gemser, p. 50, follows the LXX. He inserts *battê* as an accusative of place, emends
yalîṣ to *yalîn* (following Frankenberg), and reads *batê* for *bên* and translates, "Guilt tar-
ries in the tent of the fool, but in the house of the righteous is pleasure." This has textual
support but involves such radical change in the MT as to be unacceptable. Driver,
Biblica 32:181 suggests reading *ûban* or *ûbanû* for *ûbên,* and translates, "and upright
men discern what is acceptable." McKane, p. 476, says, "This can hardly be accepted as
a satisfactory elucidation of the verse." He has, however, no better suggestion and so accepts *ûbanû* and translates similarly. Others limit the meaning of *raṣôn* to the goodwill
that prevails among men of righteous character (so Toy, p. 286). This limitation goes
contrary to the normal usage of the word.

11 The house of the wicked shall be overthrown: but the tabernacle of the upright shall flourish.
12 There is a way which seemeth right unto a man, but the end thereof are the ways of death.

shared with others, they cannot know the depths of feelings that you alone experience. The same principle is true with joy. No "stranger" (*zar*, cf. 2:16) "intermeddleth [ʿ*arab*, cf. 12:6] with his joy." The "stranger" is so named because he is outside the experience of the joy being felt. The word ʿ*arab*, "to associate with, share," is best rendered here "share." Thus, the phrase reads, "no stranger shares in his joy." This again brings out the idea that no one can fully empathize with the feelings of another. Paul brings out this same idea in his argument in I Corinthians 2:11-13.

11 There is a contrast between the destinies of the righteous and the wicked. The "house," *bêt,* of the wicked is a permanent dwelling place. Early houses had thick walls of wood, stone, and mortar. The doorposts and lintel were made of thick wooden beams. Pillars supported the roof in larger houses. Archaeological remains of some of these date back to the third millennium B.C. Despite the anticipated permanence of the house, it would be "overthrown" (*šamad*). The verb *šamad* is strong, meaning "to destroy, annihilate." It often occurs in connection with divine judgment. Poetically, the "house" here represents the wicked and his way in life.

The contrast is stark. The "tabernacle" (ʾ*ohel,* also "tent") of the righteous is a temporary dwelling. It is portable and less able to withstand the elements. Despite this, it will "flourish [*parah*]," having the favor of God upon it. The word *parah* is "to make fruitful," thus "to flourish." Once again, the figure represents the righteous and his way of life. The proverb is similar to 12:7.

12 This is one of the most widely quoted proverbs in the book. Proverbs 16:25 repeats it exactly. The particle *yeš* draws attention to the false way: "there is indeed a way . . . " The natural man sees this and follows it. He thinks that he betters himself through his pursuits. But the "end" (ʾ*aḥarît*) of this way is "death" (*mawet*, cf. 2:18). The only real question here is the nature of ʾ*aḥarît*. Does this refer to death, or does it refer to the immortal state? The verse is ambiguous, so there is no certain conclusion. It is, however, true that ʾ*aḥarît* elsewhere in Proverbs in-

13 Even in laughter the heart is sorrowful; and the end of that mirth is heaviness.
14 The backslider in heart shall be filled with his own ways: and a good man shall be satisfied from himself.

cludes the eternal realm. In 23:18, we find ʾaḥărît parallel to tiqwâ, "expectation," which shall not be cut off. Proverbs 24:14 repeats the thought with "reward," ʾaḥărît, parallel to tiqwâ again. In stark contrast, the evil man has no "reward" (ʾaḥărît) in 24:20. Thus, ʾaḥărît may embrace the thought of the eternal state. The plural "ways" here refers to the many ways of life that a man may travel. The "ways" of the natural man inevitably lead him to condemnation.[9]

13 Solomon now makes another practical observation on life. "Life is strife"; thus, man outwardly can live normally while inwardly he grieves over some personal burden. Further, the ultimate end of all joy is "heaviness," either the dominating grief of the next personal difficulty or the sorrow of death. Ultimately, of course, the sorrow of death will win the victory over temporal joy.[10]

14 The "backslider in heart" is satisfied with his own ways. Is this the satisfaction that he feels with himself as he lives for the moment and is content with this? Or is this the recompense that he will receive as the result of his wicked life? The verb "satisfied" (cf. śabaʿ, 3:10) customarily refers to personal satisfaction. There is a component of "fullness" here; one is satisfied because one is full, having his needs supplied. It is likely, then, that the backslider is satisfied with himself, caught up with the excitement of the moment and having no thought for the future.

---

[9]KD I, 298, applies ʾaḥărît to physical death, with every path of the wicked man leading him toward the end of his life. McKane, pp. 467-68, and Toy, p. 289, likewise limit the thought to mortal death.

[10]The Hebrew of 13b, wəʾaḥerîtah śimḥâ tûgâ, literally reads "and the end of it, joy, *is* grief." The permutation of a noun and a preceding pronominal suffix is not frequent, but it is not rare either. For that reason I reject the suggestion that the phrase be read wəʾaḥărît haśśimḥâ tûgâ. The word śimḥâ occurs ninety-three times, but only three of these have the article. The word more often expresses an indefinite thing, and it should be so taken here. G.K. 131n (note); McKane, p. 471; and Gemser, p. 50, all adopt this reading. There is no change in the interpretation, only an attempt to smooth out the Hebrew. This, however, is not necessary.

15 The simple believeth every word: but the prudent man looketh well to his going.
16 A wise man feareth, and departeth from evil: but the fool rageth, and is confident.
17 He that is soon angry dealeth foolishly: and a man of wicked devices is hated.

Verse 14*b* literally reads "and from himself a good man." The lack of focus has led to various emendations.[11] It is reasonable, however, that we should supply the verb from the first phrase, i.e., "the good man *is satisfied* from himself." In this case, the idea is that the good man experiences great personal satisfaction from the knowledge that his ways are right before a holy God.

15 The "simple" (*petî,* cf. 1:22) believes what he is told, not taking the time to weigh the wisdom of the words. For this reason, he is easily led astray. In contrast, the "prudent" (*ʿarûm,* cf. 1:4) pays attention to his "going" (*ʾašûr*). While *ʾašûr* literally means "step" or "feet," it always refers poetically to one's mode of life. We see here, then, that the "simple" is careless and rash while the "prudent" is careful and reserved. The verse makes an astute observation of people in this life.

16 The verse continues the contrast of the "wise" and the "fool." The wise man "feareth" (*yareʾ,* cf. 13:13) evil. His reverential trust in God leads him to turn from wickedness. The "fool" (*kəsîl,* cf. 1:22), on the other hand, "rages and is confident" (better, "is arrogant and secure"). The implication is that the fool rushes on in his headstrong evil way, supremely confident that his way is right.

17 The phrase "soon angry," *qəṣar ʾappayim,* is picturesque in Hebrew. Literally, this is "short of nostrils." The image is of someone whose emotions have caused him to breathe rapidly. He is "short of breath," the "nostrils" poetically standing for "breath." The patient man, by contrast, is "long of nostrils," 14:29. One who gives way to the emotion of anger does so foolishly.

---

[11]Jones, p. 135, follows the LXX απο δε των διανοηματων αυτου "but a good man from his thoughts." KD I, 300, suggests emending *ûmeʿalayw* to *umimmaʿᵃlalayw,* "from his deeds," parallel to *midrakayw,* "from his own ways," in 14*a*. McKane, p. 474, suggests either the same change or *mimmaʿᵃgalaw,* "tracks," more precisely parallel to "ways." The MT is explicable, however, and should therefore be left alone.

18 The simple inherit folly: but the prudent are crowned with knowledge.

19 The evil bow before the good; and the wicked at the gates of the righteous.

At the same time, a person of "devices" (*məzimmôt,* cf. 1:4) is hated (cf. *śana*ʾ, 11:15). The context demands that the man of "devices" is one of "wicked devices." The contrast, then, with 17*a* lies in the differences between the two men. The first is angry, an impetuous, rash emotion that suddenly seizes control. The second makes evil plans, carefully calculating his course of action. The first is foolish; the second will be hated by those whom he acts against.[12]

18 Once again, Solomon contrasts the results of the two ways of life. The "simple" (*pəta*ʾ*yim,* cf. 1:22) receive folly as their inheritance. In contrast, the "prudent" (ʿ*ərûmîm,* cf. 1:4) are crowned with "knowledge" (*da*ʿ*at,* cf. 1:4). The principle of Galatians 6:7-8 remains true. One sows folly, and he reaps the harvest of folly; the other sows a life of prudent behavior, and he is adorned with knowledge.[13]

19 While there may be exceptions, the proverb sets forth a true general principle. Wicked men (*ra*ʿ, cf. 1:33) bow down before good men (cf. *ṭôb,* 12:14). The unspoken assumption here is that good men have the blessing of God upon their lives and so are exalted to positions of leadership and dominance over the wicked. There is as well an eschatological sense to the verse, looking forward to the end times when the righteous will rule with Christ over this world.

---

[12]Some look for the contrast between the two ways of men. They take ʾ*iš məzimmôt* as a "man of good plans." To complete the contrast, they emend *yiśśane*ʾ, "is hated," variously. Thomas, *VTS* III, 286, repoints the verb to *yiśne*ʾ, from *śana*ʾ, and translates, "to become high, exalted in rank." This is the most conservative attempt at changing the MT, but it is still unnecessary. It is also debatable if *śana*ʾ, "to exalt," exists in Hebrew. The word *məzimmôt* does not necessarily refer to a good man, e.g., 12:2; 24:8. It is a neutral word that takes its meaning from the context. Other suggested changes freely change the MT. On the basis of the LXX, BH (so also Gemser, p. 50; Jones, p. 136) suggests *yiš*ʾ*ənan,* "to remain composed, calm." Toy, p. 294, also follows the LXX but suggests *yiśśa,* "to endure."

[13]Driver, *Biblica* 32:181, rejects "inherit" (*naḥəlû*). He feels that the parallelism calls for something like "be adorned." He suggests *neḥelû,* from *ḥalâ,* "adorned with fine jewels, clothes." McKane, p. 467, also adopts this view. The change is unsupported and unneeded.

20 The poor is hated even of his own neighbour: but the rich hath many friends.
21 He that despiseth his neighbour sinneth: but he that hath mercy on the poor, happy is he.

20-21 We find here another practical observation drawn from life. The poor man (*raš*, cf. 10:4) is "hated" (*sana᾽*, cf. 11:15) by his friend (cf. *reaᶜ*, 6:1). The word *sana᾽* has a lighter sense. Friends view their poor acquaintances as a burdensome thing rather than a detesting thing. By his very presence, the poor man serves to restrain others since he cannot afford to do what they do.

The reverse is also true. Those who are "rich" (*ᶜašîr*, cf. 3:16) in material wealth "have many friends." The last half is better translated, "those who love [cf. *᾽ahab*, 9:8] the rich are many." We should also take *᾽ahab* in a light sense. These people are "attracted" to the wealthy rather than having a deep-seated love for them. Human nature is such that we like the company of those who are wealthy or famous. We bask in their reflected glory and feel that we also have achieved a measure of success, v. 20.

Verse 21 follows v. 20 naturally, giving the divine view of one who rejects his neighbor. One who "despises" (*baz*, cf. 1:7) his neighbor is guilty of "sin" (*hôte᾽*, cf. 1:10). The noun *hôte᾽* is the primary word for sin. It has the root meaning of "to miss the mark." Spiritually, *hôte᾽* refers to the failure to achieve God's standards for life. In 21*b*, *hanan*, "mercy," is "to be gracious, show favor," normally indicating a compassionate response to one who is in need. The noun *ᶜanayîm*, "poor," is not so much "poor" as "distressed," suffering in some way from an affliction or need. The suffering may be in any area—physical, material, emotional, social, or spiritual. It can also refer to the lowly or humble. One who shows "mercy," *hanan*, to the "poor," *ᶜanayîm*, is "happy" (better "blessed," *᾽ašrayw*, cf. 3:13).[14]

---

[14]The *qərê* gives *ᶜanawîm*, "humble," for the *kətîb* *ᶜanayîm*. Although Plaut, p. 162, and Greenstone, p. 154, follow the *qərê*, there is no need to abandon the MT. In v. 21*a*, AB, p. 97, emends *larᵉᶜehû*, "his neighbor," to *larāᶜēb*, "a hungry man." The change adds nothing significant and has only weak textual support.

22 Do they not err that devise evil? but mercy and truth shall be to them that devise good.
23 In all labour there is profit: but the talk of the lips tendeth only to penury.
24 The crown of the wise is their riches: but the foolishness of fools is folly.

22 The maxim contrasts the results of the two ways in life. Those who "devise [*ḥaraš,* cf. 3:29] evil" will "go astray" (*taʿâ,* cf. 10:17), pointing themselves into a morass of mental and moral perversions that will surely bring ruin. But those who "devise [also *ḥaraš*] good" will receive "mercy [*ḥesed,* cf. 2:8] and truth [*weʾəmet,* cf. 3:3]." They reap the benefits of their well-laid plans. Although the saying is introduced by the *he-*interrogative, the compound *həlôʾ* makes it the equivalent of a strong assertion: "Surely, those who devise evil go astray, while those who devise good *receive* kindness and truth." Cf. G.K. 150e.[15]

23 It is the work, not merely the talk, that produces gain. The verb form of "labour" (*ʿeṣeb,* cf. 10:10) refers to physical pain or to emotional sorrow. The idea of intensified discomfort extends to intensified work. As such, *ʿeṣeb* here has the idea of intensive labor or toil. It occurs here appropriately since this is the kind of work that produces gain for the worker.

"Penury" (*maḥsôr*) comes from the verb meaning "to need, lack." It may refer to material or immaterial things. The noun often expresses the idea of poverty that comes from a lack of wisdom. This may indicate a slothful or foolish condition. Here, there is much talk but little action. This results in poverty.

24 The maxim is similar in truth to v. 23. The "crown [*ʿaṭeret*] of the wise," i.e., their reputation, their honor, is found in their wealth. The word *ʿaṭarâ* most often has a poetical sense, representing honor, authority, or reward. The idea here, a general principle, is that the wise will become prosperous and thus will be held in esteem by others.

---

[15]While the majority of commentators and modern translations take 22a as a question, I feel that the *həlôʾ* requires an assertion. Along with the AV, NASB, and NIV, Plaut, Muenscher, French and Skinner, and Greenstone, among others, understand it as a question. Toy, McKane, Cohen, and the *Targum* accept it as an assertion.

25 A true witness delivereth souls: but a deceitful witness speaketh lies.
26 In the fear of the Lord is strong confidence: and his children shall
*   have a place of refuge.*
27 The fear of the Lord is a fountain of life, to depart from the snares of
*   death.*

Verse 24*b* is Hebrew poetry at its best. The phrase consists of three nouns, all of which relate to "folly." Literally, the phrase reads, "the folly [*ʾiwwelet,* cf. 1:7] of fools [*kəsîlîm,* cf. 1:22] is folly [*ʾiwwelet*]." Solomon draws a contrast with 24*a*. Whereas the wisdom of the wise results in prosperity and a good reputation, the foolishness of the fool simply remains foolishness. He gains nothing by his foolishness.[16]

25 The word "witness" (*ʿed*) strongly suggests that this observation comes from the courtroom. The verb *ʿûd* means "to repeat." A *ʿed,* "a witness," is one who repeats what he knows. A true witness will deliver the defendant who has been falsely accused of some wrong. A deceiver, however, speaks lies in his testimony. He misleads the judge of the case. The implied thought is that he causes the defendant to be wrongly convicted.[17]

26-27 Both of these precepts teach an aspect of the "fear of the Lord" (*yirʾat yəhwah,* cf. 1:7). This gives one a "strong confidence." This is more than mere physical safety. It also includes the sense of eternal

---

[16]Some would like to see a more direct contrast, e.g., "the crown of the wise is their prudence; the reputation of the fool is their folly." To this end, then, various emendations have been suggested to strengthen the parallelism. Reider, *VT* 2:125 linguistically emends *ʿašar,* "riches." He suggests that it must have had a meaning "to be clever, smart." Similarly, he forces the first *ʾwl* to come from a suggested root meaning "be in front, lead," and thus signifying "prominence." Linguistic emendation is always suspect. AB, p. 97, emends "riches" (*ʿošrām*) to "virtue" (*yošrām*) and the first "folly" to *liwyat,* "garland," with no textual support. Dahood, *PNWSP,* p. 32, relates *ʾiwwelet* to Ugaritic and translates, "the throne of fools." More commonly accepted is a change based on the LXX, *ʿarmatam,* "prudence," for *ʿašram,* "riches," and something like *wəliwyat,* "but the wreath . . . ," for the first "folly." These are all ingenious exercises but do not improve the verse. The MT is acceptable with no need of change.

[17]There is no real disagreement with the intent of the verse. Some, however, emend the MT to smooth it out. AB. p. 97, emends *mirmâ* (cf. 14:8) to *mərammeh* and translates, "one who spreads lies is a betrayer." Toy, p. 302, proposes *mədimmah* for *mirmâ* and translates, "he who utters lies destroys." Guillaume, *JRAS* (1940), 120, proposes *mərammeh.* He preserves the consonantal text by interpreting it as a magical incantation capable of bringing destruction. McKane, p. 469, takes *yapiaḥ,* "speaketh," as a noun, and understands *yapiaḥ kəzabîm* as "a perjurer" (literally, "false witness"). He then reads *mərammeh,* "deceiver." The changes do not improve the MT.

*28 In the multitude of people is the king's honour: but in the want of
people is the destruction of the prince.
29 He that is slow to wrath is of great understanding: but he that is
hasty of spirit exalteth folly.*

well-being, a spiritual dimension not possible from any other source.
The children of such a man similarly have a "refuge" (*maḥseh*). This
often speaks poetically of the protection given those who place their
trust in God. One who walks with a reverential attitude toward God,
then, has the hope that his godly example will benefit his children.
They, too, will come to faith in the Lord, v. 26.

Further, one who maintains a right relationship to the Lord has "a
fountain of life." This phrase occurs in the wisdom literature with a
poetical sense to describe a source of full, abundant life. This allows its
possessors to "depart from the snares of death," i.e., to escape those
areas of life that would produce premature judgment from God, v. 27.

28 A king who rules over a large group of people possesses a great
amount of "honor" (*hadrat*). The word *hadar* widely indicates the splendor and honor of man or God. When the number of the people declines,
however, there is the "destruction" (*məḥittat,* cf. 10:14) of the royal
leader. The term "want," *ʾepes,* indicates "cessation, non-existence." It
refers to the "cessation of the large number," i.e., the diminishing of the
nation's population for some reason. The noun *məḥittâ* often occurs
poetically in the book to represent some form of ruin. A foolish decision
by the king, an unpopular or unwise war, increased taxation that leads
many to flee the country, or even a natural catastrophe beyond the king's
power to control may cause the king to lose his power to lead the
people. His reign may come to an abrupt end. Coming back to the parallelism of the verse, at the very least some such calamity would mean the
end of the king's honor in the eyes of the people.[18]

29 That patience is a virtue to the biblical writers is no surprise. We
find here one more statement of its value. One who is "slow to wrath"
(*ʾerek ʾappayim*) has "great understanding," unusual discernment. The
phrase *ʾerek ʾappayim,* "long of nostrils," contrasts with *qəṣar ʾappayim*

---

[18]Coates, p. 63, comments, "This piece of worldly wisdom is quite contrary to the
spirit of Israel's inspired historians." He misses the point. Solomon here makes a perceptive comment on life. The reign of a king is not guaranteed to succeed when the times of
his people are troubled.

30 A sound heart is the life of the flesh: but envy the rottenness of the bones.
31 He that oppresseth the poor reproacheth his Maker: but he that honoureth him hath mercy on the poor.

in v. 17. Here, the idea of patience is in view, thus the man is slow to lose control of himself. In contrast, the one who is "hasty of spirit," *qəṣar rûaḥ,* exalts folly. The phrase *qəṣar rûaḥ* almost perfectly parallels *ʾerek ʾappayim.* The shortness of spirit is best understood as shortness of "breath," reflecting the quick, shallow breathing of an angry person.[19]

30 A "sound [*marpeʾ,* cf. 4:22] heart" is a "heart of health," i.e., a composed or controlled spirit that is at ease with whatever situation it faces. This is the "life [cf. *ḥayâ,* 4:4] of the flesh," i.e., it produces a fullness of life here on earth.[20] The plural "flesh," *bəśarîm,* is a plural of local extension, indicating the expanse of skin. On the other hand, "envy" (*qinʾâ*) is the "rottenness of the bones" (*rəqab,* cf. 10:7). The noun *qinʾâ* is a strong emotional feeling of jealousy, either wholesome when directed toward godliness or good things, or evil when selfish or directed toward wickedness or bad things. Envy destroys the body. It eats it emotionally until some physical disease comes to complete the destruction.

31 The theme of mercy toward the poor is common in the OT. Just as God has been merciful toward men, so He expects that men will be merciful toward one another. The one, therefore, who "oppresses" (*ʿošeq*) the poor (*dal*) at the same time "reproaches" (*ḥerep*) God. The root *ʿašaq* has to do with the abuse of power, taking advantage of those who are unable to defend themselves. The action is vigorously condemned throughout the OT. The *dal* is someone who is low, either in material possessions or in social influence (which would probably include the former idea). The idea of reproaching God is serious. The word *ḥerep*

---

[19]Toy, p. 302, with his usual lack of respect for the text, suggests that we read *marbeh,* "to increase," for the MT's *merîm,* "to exalt." The *hipʿîl* of *rûm,* causative of "to lift up," is a frequent idiom in the OT. It very naturally fits here as the angry man exalts folly, bringing it to the forefront of his life.

[20]McKane, p. 472, derives *marpeʾ* from *rph,* "to relax," and thus "tranquil." This gives a good sense, yet I doubt that the derivation can hold up. The word *marpeʾ* is not uncommon, and it allows for a reasonable interpretation.

*32 The wicked is driven away in his wickedness: but the righteous hath
hope in his death.*

carries with it the thought of showing scorn or of dishonoring someone.
Clearly, such an attitude would pit one directly against God.[21]

The parallel thought is in direct contrast with the initial phrase. The
suffix "him" refers to God. The one who has "mercy" (*ḥonen,* cf. v. 21)
on the "poor" (*ʾebyôn*) gives "honour" (cf. *kabed,* 3:9) to Him. The
ʾebyôn is a needy person, lacking in material possessions. The Mosaic
law obligated the Jews to care for such persons. This showed God's concern that men be merciful to one another. To do so brings "honour" to
God. This accepts His authority by showing obedience to His will.

32 The phrase "driven away," *yiddaḥen,* from *daḥâ,* here has the sense
"to thrust down." The wicked is "thrust down" as the direct result of his
"wickedness" (cf. *raʿ,* 1:33).[22] The comparison with the second half of
the verse makes it likely that this refers to his ultimate destiny, the eternal "casting down" of the wicked.

In opposition to this, the righteous has "hope" (*ḥoseh*) in the day of his
death. The word *ḥoseh* is literally "to seek refuge, protection," and thus
metaphorically "to put trust in, hope in (God)." This last is phrased a bit
awkwardly in Hebrew, but it is still best to hold to the text without
adopting another reading.[23]

---

[21] J. A. Emerton, "Notes on Some Passages in Proverbs," *JTS* 20:203-6, argues for the
meaning "to slander" for *ʿašaq.* Still, he admits that in some contexts the meaning "to
oppress" cannot be denied. He ends by suggesting a *"double entendre,"* that the reader
was naturally to think of both oppression and slander. This idea goes contrary to the natural use of the double entendre, which normally plays on the ambiguous meaning of
words to suggest some pun. But we cannot expect the Holy Spirit to use such forms of
speech in the inspired revelation of the Bible. The single meaning "oppress" serves well
to express the thought.

[22] KD I, 312, understands *baraʿatô* in the sense of "misfortune" and takes the verse as
referring to the overthrow of the wicked by the calamities into which he stumbles. This
is possible but a more exact parallelism comes by taking *baraʿatô* as discussed above.

[23] A literal translation reads, "the righteous seeks refuge in his death," a statement
that does not make much sense unless taken metaphorically. For this reason, various
suggestions have been made as to how the Hebrew should read. Some emend "his
death" (*bamôtô*) to *batummô,* keeping the same radicals but interchanging their order.
This, then, would read, "the righteous seeks refuge in his integrity." McKane, p. 475;
AB, p. 98; Jones, p. 139; Whybray, p. 82, and others follow this view. The MT, however,
is defensible.

*33 Wisdom resteth in the heart of him that hath understanding: but that
which is in the midst of fools is made known.*
34 Righteousness exalteth a nation: but sin is a reproach to any people.

33 Wisdom rests comfortably in the heart of one who has understanding. This is natural, for his heart has an affinity for wisdom. The word
"midst" is *qereb,* "inward part, midst." It refers to the seat of emotions
or thought. In the "midst" of fools, literally, "it is made known." This
refers to the contrasting response of each to the "wisdom" that resides
within them. In the man of understanding, wisdom rests quietly, not
bursting out at every provocation. But the fool is all too quick to speak
his mind, to give forth what he thinks is wise. The proverb is similar to
10:19 and 13:3.[24]

34 This is one of the more familiar proverbs. It is as well one of the
more misapplied proverbs. Righteousness does lift up a people (*gôy*).
The noun *gôy* refers to a body of people, often the Gentile nations but
also used of people in general. In stark contrast, sin is a "reproach"
(*ḥesed*) to a people (*ləʾummîm*). The word *ḥesed* here is *ḥesed* II, "to reproach, shame." The noun *ləʾummîm* refers to people in general, with no
distinction between Gentile or Jewish groups. The misunderstanding of
the verse lies in applying it to national groups. Neither *gôy* nor *ləʾom*
should be restricted to a nation. With each word, the context must determine the group. It is reasonable to apply the proverb to miscellaneous
groups of people, a city, a church, and so forth. In every case, righteousness exalts the group, while sin is a reproach to the group.[25]

---

[24]The LXX added the negative οὐ and this is followed by some, e.g., AB, p. 99;
Gemser, p. 51. Others suggest emending *tiwwadeaᶜ,* "it is made known," to *ʾiwwelet,* "but
folly in the midst of fools," e.g., Jones, p. 139; Martin, p. 95. Thomas, *JTS* 35:302-3, argues on the basis of an Arabic cognate for the meaning *ydᶜ = wdᶜ,* "to put or place," and
thus "to submit," i.e., wisdom is made submissive to folly in the heart of a fool. This
multiplying of suggestions tells us that any interpretation must be tentative. It also tells
us that changing the MT is not going to improve the situation. Since it is possible to
make sense of the MT, it is best to remain with that.
[25]AB, p. 98, follows the LXX in reading *ḥeser* for MT *ḥesed* II, and so translates, "sin
leads to the impoverishment of peoples," but this is unnecessary since the MT is clear.
There is no need to explain *ḥesed* II as an Aramaism (e.g., Frankenberg, p. 90; Toy, p.
302). It is rather an infrequent Hebrew word that occurs only three times (also Lev.
20:17; Prov. 25:10) in all of its forms.

35 The king's favour is toward a wise servant: but his wrath is against him that causeth shame.

35 This draws upon another perceptive observation of life. The king very naturally extends his favor (*raṣôn,* cf. 11:1) toward a "wise" (cf. *śakal,* 1:3) servant. Just as naturally, the king's "wrath" (cf. *ʿabar,* 11:4) is directed against "him that causeth shame" (*mebîš*). The word *mebîš* is the *hipʿîl* participle from *bôš,* thus "one who causes shame" or "acts shamefully." In this context, it is more likely "one who causes disgrace" to the king through his intemperate or imprudent actions.

Practical Applications from Proverbs 14

1. Contrast between wise and foolish wives 1
2. Contrast between the righteous and evil 11, 19, 22, 32, 34; cf. also 6, 14
3. Contrast between proud and wise speech 3
4. Value of investing 4
5. Contrast between trustworthy and perjured testimony 5, 25
6. Contrast between the wise and foolish 7, 8, 9, 15, 16, 18, 24, 33, 35
7. Difficulty in feeling another's emotion 10
8. Eternal punishment 12
9. Burdens of life 13
10. Contrast between patience and anger 17, 29
11. Contrast between wealth and poverty 20, 23
12. Relationships with others 21, 31
13. Fear of the Lord 2, 26, 27
14. Contrast between success or failure in ruling 28
15. Contrast between patience and envy 30

1 A soft answer turneth away wrath: but grievous words stir up anger.
2 The tongue of the wise useth knowledge aright: but the mouth of fools poureth out foolishness.

PROVERBS 15

1-2 The chapter begins with practical advice on the subject of speech. A "soft [*rak,* cf. 4:3] answer turneth away wrath [*ḥemâ*]." The adjective *rak* is "tender," or "soft." When referring to speech it denotes "gentle" or "conciliatory" words. In contrast, *ḥemâ,* "hot," refers to heated emotions, i.e., anger, wrath, rage, and generally expresses a strong emotional state. The idea is that conciliatory speech can calm an angry person. In contrast, "grievous [*ʿeṣeb,* cf. 10:10] words" actually cause "anger" (*ʾap*). When *ʿeṣeb* is used of speech, it describes "grievous" or "harsh" speech. The potential for this is seen in the use of "words," (*dabar,* cf. 11:13). This is singular in form, indicating that a single word can do irreparable harm; cf. James 3:5, 8. "Anger," *ʾap,* literally refers to the nose. Since the nose often dilates in response to anger, the word came to stand as well for the emotion, v. 1.

The second statement of the chapter regarding speech contrasts wise and foolish individuals. The wise man uses his knowledge "aright" (cf. *ṭôb,* 12:14). The word relates to the active practice of doing good, "to be well, be good, be pleasing." It produces good in others. The idea here is that the wise person speaks responsibly, accurately, and perceptively. His speech makes knowledge pleasing to others. Thus, "the tongue of the wise makes knowledge agreeable."[1]

The fool, however, "poureth out [*nabaʿ,* cf. 1:23] foolishness." The fool does not consider his words carefully. He speaks even when he has nothing worth saying, making his foolishness evident. Verse 28 expresses a similar idea, v. 2.

---

[1]Driver, *Biblica* 32:181, emends *têṭîb* to *taṭṭeb* or *taṭeb.* He postulates a Hebrew root *ṭabab* cognate with Syriac *ṭab(b),* "made clear, announced," thus, "the tongue of the wise announces knowledge." Hulst, p. 124, gives *taṭṭîp,* "to drop" (also adopted by Gemser, p. 52; Oesterley, p. 118; McKane, p. 478; Jones, p. 140). These are attempts to force direct parallelism on the verse. While parallelism in Hebrew may be direct, it is just as often elusive. There is no need to force the contrast.

3 The eyes of the Lord are in every place, beholding the evil and the good.
4 A wholesome tongue is a tree of life: but perverseness therein is a
breach in the spirit.
5 A fool despiseth his father's instruction: but he that regardeth reproof
is prudent.
6 In the house of the righteous is much treasure: but in the revenues of
the wicked is trouble.

3 This maxim is one of the more familiar proverbs of the book. It makes a direct statement about God's omniscience. The first half makes a broad statement that God sees man's actions; the second fills in the details, noting that God sees both evil and good. The nature of "evil and good" is not specified. It is left general so as to include both thoughts and actions, major and minor matters. God sees them all; cf. 5:21; 22:12.

4 A "wholesome [*marpe*ʾ, cf. 4:22] tongue" is a tongue that brings healing, i.e., a conciliatory or soothing tongue. It is speech that "pours oil on troubled waters" to bring peace. This is compared to a "tree of life" (ʿeṣ ḥayyîm, cf. 3:18), the emblem of a full and blessed present existence. The expression occurs again in 3:18; 11:30; and 13:12.

On the other hand, a man who is "perverse" (*selep,* cf. 11:3), or perhaps more accurately, "deceitful," in his speech will produce a "breach [*šeber,* cf. 6:15] in the spirit" of those who hear him. The term denotes the crushing wound dealt to another person's spirit by one's speech.[2]

5 Foolish and wise children differ in their response to parental guidance. The foolish child "despises" (*yinʾaṣ*) his father's instruction, spurning that which would assist him. The verb *naʾaṣ,* "to despise, abhor," refers to a conscious and deliberate rejection. The prudent child takes the "reproof" (*tôkaḥat,* cf. 1:23) of his parents seriously. He "regards" (cf. *šamar,* 2:8) it and changes his behavior and attitudes as necessary.

6 Literally, the first phrase reads, "the house of the righteous *is* much ḥosen." The word ḥosen occurs only twice in Proverbs (also at 27:24). It is "treasure" or "store." Here, it refers to the great resources that the righteous can draw upon, e.g., peace, confidence, hope, and so forth. It

---

[2]AB, p. 100, emends *bah šeber bərûaḥ,* "therein *is* a breach in the spirit," to *bəhiššābēr rûaḥ.* He translates, "falsity betrays a disturbed mind." There is no textual support for the suggestion and we may disregard it.

*7 The lips of the wise disperse knowledge: but the heart of the foolish
doeth not so.*
*8 The sacrifice of the wicked is an abomination to the Lord: but the
prayer of the upright is his delight.*
*9 The way of the wicked is an abomination unto the Lord: but he loveth
him that followeth after righteousness.*

is true that the righteous often gains material blessings in this life. But
the greater application relates to the immaterial blessings that he gains
from God's blessings upon him.

In contrast, the wicked finds "trouble" (cf. *ᶜakar*, 11:29) in his "revenues" (*təbûʾat,* cf. 3:9). Since he often gains his resources by evil
means, he will eventually reap the fruit of his wickedness.[3]

7 The wise person speaks "knowledge" (*daᶜat,* cf. 1:4) that has come
from his experience. The fool, however, "doeth not so." The interpretation here rests upon the phrase "not so" (*loʾ ken*). The simplest view
treats it literally, "not thus." This would indicate that the heart of the
fool, antithetically parallel to the lips of the wise, does not disperse
knowledge abroad. The "heart" and "lips" are paralleled since the lips
speak what is from the heart.[4]

8-9 The phrase "abomination to the Lord" joins these two proverbs.
The import of the two statements is that the righteous man pleases God
in all of his ways, while the godless pleases God in none of his ways.
Initially, the author focuses on worship. The wicked man's sacrifice is
an "abomination [*tôᶜabat,* cf. 3:32] to the Lord." Since the worship
comes from one who has not repented of his sin, it is ritualistic. It does
not come from one who truly loves God. The Lord therefore rejects it.
In opposition, the righteous person offers his prayer freely, willingly.

---

[3]In the first half, Toy, p. 309, omits the *b*-preposition from *təbûʾat* and inserts it before
bêt, thereby creating a prepositional phrase, "in the house. . . ." This is true, but unnecessary since the house (including not only his family but also his material and immaterial
possessions) of the righteous is itself a great resource. In the second half, he reads *nikrat*
for *neᶜkaret,* and translates, "the revenues of the wicked are cut off." The change again is
unnecessary since the MT makes reasonable sense.

[4]KD I, 319-20, forces the phrase to mean "direction is wanting," i.e., the heart of the
fool has no affinity for wisdom. Muenscher, p. 158, erroneously reads *ʾalˉkeʾn.* He translates, "is not right." Toy, p. 309, emends *ken* to *yabin,* "without intelligence." Jones,
p. 142, emends the same way. These attempts to understand the verse ignore the simpler
approach, which also yields good sense.

10 Correction is grievous unto him that forsaketh the way: and he that hateth reproof shall die.

This prayer comes from one who truly wants God's favor. This pleases the Lord. It is His "delight" (*raṣôn,* cf. 11:1), v. 8.

In like manner, the manner of life of the wicked is "an abomination" to the Lord. God requires the blood of Christ to be accepted as the only means for receiving forgiveness of one's sins. Until this is done, one's good works are of no value to God. They come from a heart that is sinful. The motivation is as important as the result. God rejects this way of life.

It is different with the righteous. God "loves" (*yeʾəhab,* cf. 9:8) the one who "follows" (*məraddep,* cf. 12:11) righteousness. The form of the verb here conveys the idea of intensity; thus the godly man here eagerly pursues righteousness, v. 9.

God's Reaction to Man

I. Man's Worship of God 8

II. Man's Works in Life 9

---

10 The initial part is better translated, "Severe correction is for him that forsakes the way." One who abandons the right "way" (*ʾoraḥ,* cf. 12:28) of life will receive this kind of "correction" (*mûsar,* cf. 1:2). It is "severe" (*raʿ,* cf. 1:33) in that it is "bad," difficult to bear up under. The word *raʿ* can mean "grievous, sharp," and, by extension, "severe." Parallel to this is the added penalty of death to the one who hates "reproof" (*tôkaḥat,* cf. 1:23).

Nothing in the verse requires this to be more than physical death. In fact, the idea of physical death gives the broadest possible application to the verse. Physical death is the natural outcome of the wicked man's sins. The righteous man who refuses to yield himself to the will of God may also receive the punishment of premature physical death (cf. I Cor. 11:29-30; I John 5:16). The verse thus gives a stern admonition to heed correction in spiritual matters.

11 Hell and destruction are before the Lord: how much more then the
*   hearts of the children of men?*
12 A scorner loveth not one that reproveth him: neither will he go unto
*   the wise.*
13 A merry heart maketh a cheerful countenance: but by sorrow of the
*   heart the spirit is broken.*

11 The phrase "Hell and destruction" is more accurately "Sheol and
Abaddon." The word "Sheol" (*šə'ôl*, cf. 7:27) is parallel here with
"Abaddon" (*'əbaddôn*) and must therefore have a parallel meaning. The
word *'əbaddôn* comes from *'abad*, "to be destroyed." It indicates the
"place of destruction."[5] The "place of destruction" is thus the place of
the living dead, the place of eternal separation from God. The distinction between *'əbaddôn* and *šə'ôl* lies in the emphasis of *'əbaddôn* upon
the nature of the afterlife as being a place of destruction. The word *šə'ôl*
simply refers to the fact that there is a place to which the dead go in the
afterlife.[6]

The teaching here has nothing to do with the afterlife. This is merely
an illustration. If God knows what is going on in the minds of those
who are beyond the grave, how much more does He know the thoughts
of living men! God is omniscient.

12 We return to the familiar theme of the "scorner" (*leṣ*, cf. 1:22). The
leṣ has no love for one who "reproves" (*yakaḥ*, cf. 3:12) him. The word
yakaḥ often has a forensic sense, rebuking someone for violations of the
covenant. It implies a call to repentance and often parallels the thought
of instruction in righteousness. The scorner will have nothing to do with
the wise, since their very presence likely rebukes him for his conduct.
Compare 9:7-8 and 13:1 for the similar thought.

13 Solomon makes another practical observation based on his experience in life. The countenance reflects the attitude of the inward man. A
"merry" (*samaḥ*, cf. 10:1) heart, one that is filled with joy, will be

---

[5]The word *'əbaddôn* occurs just six times, always in the Wisdom Literature. Job 31:12
is inconclusive concerning the meaning. Job 26:6 parallels the present passage in
thought. Job 28:22 parallels *'əbaddôn* and "death" (*mût*, cf. 2:18), the context suggesting
the realm of the dead. In Psalm 88:11, it parallels "grave" (*qeber*), again the realm of the
dead rather than merely a grave. Both times *'əbaddôn* occurs in Proverbs, here and
27:20, it parallels *šə'ôl*. This also suggests the realm of the dead.

[6]Irwin moves the verse to follow v. 3. This allows the two verses both to touch on the
omniscience of God. There is, however, no need for the change. It is normal in this part
of the book for proverbs to deal randomly with topics.

*14 The heart of him that hath understanding seeketh knowledge: but the
mouth of fools feedeth on foolishness.
15 All the days of the afflicted are evil: but he that is of a merry heart
hath a continual feast.
16 Better is little with the fear of the Lord than great treasure and trouble therewith.
17 Better is a dinner of herbs where love is, than a stalled ox and hatred
therewith.*

reflected in the face. To speak proverbially, "the face is the mirror of the
soul." There is a parallel work of grief. "Sorrow" (*ʿeṣeb*, cf. 10:10)
breaks (*nakaʾ*) a person's spirit. The verb *nakaʾ* means "to smite,
scourge." Joy lifts a person up, filling him so that the joy overflows on
his face. Grief smites a person, beating him down with sorrow.

14 The fool and the wise have an affinity for different things. The man
of "understanding" (cf. *bîn*, 1:2) avidly seeks (*yəbaqqeš*, cf. 2:4) knowledge. The *piʿel* of *baqaš* conveys a sense of intensity. The "mouth" of
fools feasts upon more foolishness, becoming further entangled in the
web of foolishness that controls him.[7]

15 Verse 13 introduced the effect of the emotions. We have here another perceptive observation of the impact that emotions have in a person's life. The word "afflicted" (*ʿanâ*, cf. 14:21) indicates the "poor,
weak, afflicted, humble," i.e., one undergoing some personal distress.
The word *ʿanâ* often occurs with the theological sense of contrition or
self-abasement or in describing the moral and spiritual condition of the
godly. The word "merry" translates *ṭôb; cf.* 12:14. When used of the
emotions, *ṭôb* is "glad" or "happy." For these who are "afflicted," every
day is "evil" (or "bad," *raʿ*, cf. 1:33). But the person whose heart is
"merry" has a "continual feast." This poetically indicates that all is well
with him.[8]

16-17 These two comparative proverbs teach the preeminence of a
right attitude over great possessions. It is better to have a small number

---

[7]The word "mouth" comes from the *qərê pî* rather than the *kətîb pənê*, "face" (so AV).
Thomas, *VTS* III, 285, emends "feedeth," *yirʿeh*, to *yidʿeh*, "seeks" or "desires." He cites
an Arabic cognate in support of this meaning. The Hebrew, however, is a familiar word
supported by the versions.

[8]Chaim Rabin, "Hittite Words in Hebrew," *Orientalia* 32:139, suggests that *leb* in
Proverbs normally refers to one's understanding; thus, he gives "one of ample understanding" for *ṭôb⁻leb*. While his view is possible, *leb* often refers to the emotions, e.g.,
14:13; 15:13, 30; 17:22; 27:9, 11. We best understand it so here.

18 A wrathful man stirreth up strife: but he that is slow to anger appeaseth strife.

of possessions while also having "the fear of the Lord" (*yir³at yəhwah,* cf. 1:7) than to have "great treasure" accompanied by "trouble." "Trouble" (*məhûmâ*) is "confusion, tumult, disturbance." It indicates a strong emotional disturbance that may even border on "panic," v. 16.

Verse 17 is the only verse of the book that directly comments on the love within a family although 13:24 refers to discipline as a necessary component of love for the children. The nature of the book is such that we would not expect much emphasis in this area. The book stresses the practical side of life. It brings wise conduct into the everyday arena of contact with the world about us. This practical orientation excludes stress on the emotional aspect of relationships between members of a family.

This lack of emphasis does not mean that love is not important. The emphasis is on the husband and wife carrying out their special roles in the home. The authors tacitly assume a strong foundation of love, which underlies the interaction of the husband and the wife.

Verse 17 comparatively expresses the need for love. A simple home with love far excels an elegant home with hatred between the wife and husband. The "dinner of herbs" is a meal of "greens," vegetables. The "stalled ox" (better "fattened ox") is an ox that has been fattened in preparation for a banquet. Metaphorically, it represents lavish food served at a sumptuous feast. Without love, such food has no lasting purpose.

18 The verse picks up the theme of v. 1, drawing a contrast between angry and patient persons. The "angry [*hemâ,* cf. v. 1] man" stirs up "strife" (*madôn,* cf. 6:14). In 18*b,* the verb is from *šaqat,* "to cause quietness, pacify." This has the general idea of producing tranquility or a sense of calm. "Strife" (*rîb,* cf. 3:30) refers to physical, verbal, or legal controversy. He that is "slow to anger" (*³erek ³appayim,* cf. 14:29) "appeaseth strife," calming the situation by a self-controlled spirit.[9]

---

[9]McKane, p. 482, understands *madôn* and *rîb* as legal terms. The angry man is thus quick to take another to court, while the patient man seeks to resolve conflicts without recourse to the judicial system. I would prefer to leave the statement as a general one, including the legal idea but also applying to other conflicts as well.

19 The way of the slothful man is as an hedge of thorns: but the way of the righteous is made plain.
20 A wise son maketh a glad father: but a foolish man despiseth his mother.

19 In general, the slothful man has a troubled way in life, while the righteous man travels a less difficult path. We cannot identify the "thorns" (or "briers") with certainty. More than two hundred species of plants in Palestine bear thorns. This must be a plant large enough to form an impassable hedge. The metaphor of the "hedge of thorns" pictures opposition and barriers to progress. The "plain" (*səlulâ,* cf. 4:8) path of the righteous likewise is a metaphor. The *səlulâ* is a "lifted up" path, a road that has been built on dirt or something similar, heaped up above the surrounding territory. In modern terms, it is a "highway" that allows for easy travel. This is the path of the "righteous" (*yəšarîm,* cf. 2:21).[10]

20 This is the counterpart to v. 5, contrasting the wise and foolish sons in their relationship to their parents. The wise son brings joy to his parents, while the foolish child "despises" (cf. *bûz,* 1:7) them. For the emphasis on "son" and the poetic variation of "father" and "mother," see the discussion at 1:8. The contrast between the wise and foolish children implies that wise children respect and honor their parents. This is the attitude that produces joy in the heart of the parents.

The perverse child is a "fool" (*kəsîl,* cf. 1:22). He rejects his parents' guidance. With this tension existing between him and his parents, he naturally scorns them.[11] The foolish child is *kəsîl ʾadam,* "a fool of a man." The genitive relationship indicates that this is a man who is of the foolish kind, i.e., has a foolish nature.

---

[10]Toy, p. 312, emends *yəšarîm,* "righteous," to *ḥaruṣîm,* "diligent," based on the LXX. McKane, p. 482, and Gemser, p. 52, follow this suggestion. But the parallelism is adequate since the "slothful" man is always unrighteous, and the diligent man is often a "righteous" man. There is no need to depart from the MT.

[11]Irwin, p. 123, omits the verse as a repetition of 10:1. While 10:1a and 15:20a are identical, 10:1b and 15:20b differ substantially. Oesterley, p. 122, suggests that the idea of a child despising his mother would have been "repugnant" in Israel. He consequently proposes that *bôzeh* should be emended to *tôgat,* after the parallel thought in 10:1. He supports this with the rather bold statement that the two words are "not very dissimilar." Jones, p. 144, also follows this approach and suggests that 20b be read at 10:1b. The two roots share only a common *h;* the remaining consonants differ considerably. The suggestion therefore has little merit.

21 Folly is joy to him that is destitute of wisdom: but a man of under-
standing walketh uprightly.
22 Without counsel purposes are disappointed: but in the multitude of
counsellors they are established.
23 A man hath joy by the answer of his mouth: and a word spoken in
due season, how good is it!
24 The way of life is above to the wise, that he may depart from hell be-
neath.

21 The man who is "destitute of wisdom" is more literally one who "lacks heart" (*ḥasar⁻leb,* cf. 6:32), i.e., he does not have understanding. He therefore delights in folly. If we draw the obvious comparison with 21*b,* he walks along a crooked path. He strays from that path that brings God's blessings. The "man of understanding" (cf. *bîn,* 1:2) walks "up-rightly" (*yašar,* cf. 2:21). This is a picture of one who stays on the path in which God directs him.

22 A person who fails to seek and receive counsel will have his plans "disappointed" (*haper*). He will not reach his goals. The word *haper,* from *parar,* "to break, frustrate," most often occurs with reference to the covenant and thus it has moral overtones. Normally, the self-sufficient person who relies upon himself will see his plans frustrated. But in the "multitude of counsellors," where one seeks advice and reaction from others, one may avoid many pitfalls. These plans will be "established" (*taqûm*). The verb *qûm* normally means "to rise up, stand." Figuratively, it means "to confirm, establish." This is the potential of wise counsel.

23 The "answer of his mouth" is a right answer, one that speaks cor-rectly to the moment. It is a source of satisfaction to the one who has spoken as he realizes the weight of his words. In like manner, a word spoken "in due season," neither early nor late but at the proper time, is "good" (*ṭôb,* cf. 12:14). Taken as a whole, the maxim teaches the value of both the content and the timing of speech, each one bearing upon the effectiveness of what is said.

24 For the "wise" (cf. *śakal,* 1:3), the "way of life" is "above," allow-ing him to escape "hell [*šəʾôl,* cf. 7:27] beneath." The statement extends the concepts of death and life beyond the purely physical area into the eternal. Proverbs 10:16 and 12:28 do this as well. The understanding man follows a way that leads to eternal life, a way that leads above this

25 The Lord will destroy the house of the proud: but he will establish the border of the widow.
26 The thoughts of the wicked are an abomination to the Lord: but the words of the pure are pleasant words.

temporal existence. In so doing he escapes the punishments of *šə'ôl,* the unblessed abode of the wicked that is below this present life.[12]

25 There is an implied contrast between the "proud" (cf. *ge'â,* 8:13) and the humble, illustrated by the widow for whom God cares. The widow who seemingly has no resources has in fact the great resource of divine help. The haughty self-sufficient individual lacks the greatest resource of all. He will one day have his house destroyed (*yissaḥ,* cf. 2:22). The verb *nasaḥ* is "to pull, tear away." This leads to the idea that the wicked will have his house torn down. For the widow, however, God will "establish the border." In OT times, the ownership of land was important since it made up the basis for life as well as an inheritance for the family. The Lord protects the defenseless widow. We may extend the thought further to make this idiomatic for protecting the widow's sphere of life. Compare 23:10-11.

26 The "thoughts" (*maḥšəbôt,* cf. 6:18) of wicked men are "abomination" (*tô'əbat,* cf. 3:32) to the Lord. No matter what their end may be, they come from hearts that oppose God. They cannot please Him. In contrast, "pleasant [*no'am,* cf. 3:17] words" are "pure" (*təhorîm*) in God's sight. "Pleasant" refers to that which is "sweet, delightful, beautiful, pleasant, or lovely." The word *təhorîm* widely indicates ritual or moral purity. The phrase literally reads "and pure *are* pleasant words." Thus, while the wicked concoct plans that nauseate God, pleasant speech is pure, acceptable in God's sight.[13]

---

[12]Toy, p. 314, argues that "life" here is physical life and *šə'ôl* physical death. Thus, "above" merely refers to life on upper earth while "below" refers to the grave in lower earth. He specifically rejects the "intimation of a doctrine of happy immortality." W. A. L. Elmslie, *Studies in Life from Jewish Proverbs* (n.d.) (hereafter cited as Elmslie), p. 190, likewise holds that the verse refers "to the character of a good man's life on earth." Whybray, p. 24, states that the Hebrew "need mean no more than 'above ground,' that is, in the 'land of the living' as contrasted with the underground 'land of the dead.'" This limited view, however, ignores the general teaching of eternal life elsewhere in the OT. See the comments on "tree of life" at 3:18, and on *šə'ôl* at 7:27 and the subject study on eschatology.

[13]Toy, pp. 315, 319, tentatively suggests reading *raṣonî* for *təhorîm,* exchanging one word for its synonym. This gives something like "pleasant words are pure," a direct parallel to 26a. Toy concludes, "the line seems to be out of place as well as formally corrupt."

27 He that is greedy of gain troubleth his own house; but he that hateth gifts shall live.
28 The heart of the righteous studieth to answer: but the mouth of the wicked poureth out evil things.
29 The Lord is far from the wicked: but he heareth the prayer of the righteous.

27 This brief statement warns against greed. The phrase "greedy of gain" is *bôṣeaᶜ baṣaᶜ*, both words from *baṣaᶜ*, "to cut off." This is used of one who tries to cut off something that is not his own; thus, he is "greedy, covetous." The repeated word intensifies the action, "one who is greatly greedy." This person brings trouble (*ᶜoker,* cf. 11:29) upon his family. From the parallelism, it is entirely possible that he expresses greed by his willingness to solicit and accept bribes. When found out, this places a blot upon his house under which his family must live. The man who hates bribes will "live," enjoy a fulness of life unhampered by the blemishes that sin brings.

28 We return to the theme of speech. The righteous person "studieth" (or "meditates," *hagâ,* cf. 8:7) before he answers. This practice of thinking before speaking lets him consider his speech, weighing it carefully before delivering it.[14] The wicked person, however, "poureth out" (cf. *nabaᶜ,* 1:23) his wicked speech. He follows the impulses of his wicked heart and therefore gives bad advice.

29 The word "far" has a metaphorical sense. It is not that God is physically far removed but that He has withdrawn Himself so that He does not respond to the requests of the wicked. Compare Isaiah 59:1-2; Ezekiel 39:23-24; and Micah 3:4. But God "heareth," i.e., effectually hears, the prayers of the righteous. Compare Psalm 145:18; I Peter 3:12.

Martin, pp. 98-99, suggests something similar. Hulst, *OTTP,* p. 124, mentions the possibility of a metathesis in the word order, reading *ᵓimrê ṭahorîm,* "the words of the pure," instead of the MT *ṭahorîm ᵓimrê.* Sense can be made of the MT and it is therefore best to accept it as it stands.

[14]Following the LXX, Toy, p. 319, suggests *ᵓamunâ* for MT *laᶜanôt,* "the hearts of the righteous meditate faithfulness." Martin, p. 99, likewise accepts this reading. But the MT makes a good contrast between 28*a* and 28*b*, and there is no need for a drastic change in the consonants.

*30 The light of the eyes rejoiceth the heart: and a good report maketh
the bones fat.
31 The ear that heareth the reproof of life abideth among the wise.
32 He that refuseth instruction despiseth his own soul: but he that
heareth reproof getteth understanding.*

30 The phrase "light of the eyes" (*məʾôr ʿênayim*) lends itself to differing interpretations. The phrase occurs only here in the OT and can be understood as objective or subjective, the light seen by the eye or the light belonging to the eye. This has given rise to such suggestions as the sparkling look in the eye of someone who brings good news (Aitken, Toy), the sparkle in your own eye as the result of hearing good news (Jones, Alden), the nature of light being a joy to one's eyes (Martin), and a pleasant sight (Greenstone, Muenscher).[15]

Almost everywhere else *məʾôr* is a physical source of light—the sun, moon, stars, burning lamps. Only at Psalm 90:8 is there a similar phrase, *məʾôr panêkâ,* the light of (God's) face. It is reasonable to understand *məʾôr ʿênayîm* in the same way, as the light is given off by another's eye. The parallelism with 30*b* strongly supports the notion that this is the cheerful look in the eye of one who is about to deliver good news. This brings joy to the heart.

The second phrase of the verse also uses an interesting idiom to state its message. The good report makes "the bones fat" (cf. *dašan,* 13:4). Fatness in the OT represents prosperity, good health, or blessing. Thus, the good message brings with it an accompanying sense of satisfaction and delight.

31-32 These two maxims show the need for accepting correction. The "ear" poetically represents the person. One who effectually hears the "reproofs" (*tôkaḥat,* cf. 1:23) that come to him throughout life "abideth" (*talîn*) among the "wise" (cf. *hokmâ,* 1:2). "Abideth," *lûn,* "to lodge, spend the night," often refers to staying overnight in a place. It also metaphorically denotes the presence of a moral condition. It has this sense here, referring to the wisdom gained by one who receives correction, v. 31.

---

[15]Thomas, *VTS* III, 287, suggests on the basis of the LXX that "light," *məʾôr,* be emended to *marʾeh.* The phrase then would indicate "what is seen (and enjoyed) by the eyes." The LXX, however, is more probably an interpretation of the Hebrew phrase rather than a translation of a different text.

33 The fear of the Lord is the instruction of wisdom; and before honour is humility.

Verse 32 draws a picture of the results of accepting or rejecting correction. One who refuses "instruction [*mûsar,* cf. 1:2] despiseth [cf. *ma²as,* 3:11] his own soul." He treats it as though it were of little worth and so follows the path that leads to eternal rejection by God. But the one who effectually hears "reproof" (*tôkaḥat*) acquires "understanding" (*leb,* "heart," here referring to the understanding, cf. 3:5), v. 32.

33 The "fear of the Lord" (*yir²at yəhwah,* cf. 1:7) is the foundation upon which a godly life rests. Therefore, that which fosters the "fear of the Lord" can properly be labeled "the instruction of wisdom," i.e., the instruction that leads to wisdom.[16] In the same way, "humility" (*ᶜənawâ,* cf. 14:21) leads to "honor" (*kabôd,* cf. 3:9). This attitude is essential to one who reverences the Lord.

---

[16]AB, p. 102, arbitrarily emends *mûsar* to *mûsad* and translates, "Reverence for the Lord is the foundation of wisdom." While the thought is correct, it is arbitrary to correct the MT.

Practical Applications from Proverbs 15

1. Comments on speech 1, 2, 4, 7, 23, 28, 30
2. Omniscience of God 3, 11
3. Parent-child relationships 5, 20
4. Contrast between the righteous and the wicked 6, 8, 9, 26, 29
5. Accepting or rejecting advice 10, 12, 22, 31, 32
6. Contrast between joy and grief 13, 15
7. Contrast between wisdom and folly 14, 21
8. Importance of right attitudes 14, 21
9. Contrast between anger and patience 18
10. Contrast between slothfulness and righteousness 19
11. Relationship between wisdom and eternity 24
12. Comments on pride and humility 25, 33
13. Comments on accepting bribes 27

1 The preparations of the heart in man, and the answer of the tongue,
is from the Lord.
2 All the ways of a man are clean in his own eyes; but the Lord
weigheth the spirits

PROVERBS 16

1 This is the first of seven consecutive verses to mention "the Lord."
He is mentioned again in v. 9, and many authors group these verses together. I have chosen to treat them individually since the focus of the
separate verses varies. Yet it does seem clear that these were grouped together in the initial gathering of the proverbs. Verses 10-15 likewise
group proverbs dealing with the king.

The AV translation wrongly implies God's sovereign control over
man's thoughts. The verse better reads, "The plans of the heart belong to
man, but the answer of the tongue is from the Lord." The "preparations"
(*ma^{c}ərak*) of the heart are the organized thoughts of a person. The word
ma^{c}ərak has the idea of an orderly array. The verb elsewhere describes
troops drawn up for battle. It should be translated "plans." Man may reflect upon an issue, considering and discarding options. When ultimately he has thought it through and given his decision, his ability to
express his thoughts is a gift from God.[1]

2 The thought of the verse is repeated in 21:2, although the phrasing is
different there. The word "clean" (or "pure," *zak*) occurs four times in
the Pentateuch describing the pure oil or frankincense used in Israel's
worship. The word *zak* also occurs seven times in Job and Proverbs,
most often relating to moral purity in one's actions. Here, it describes
one's moral judgment of his own conduct. This rests upon his accomplishments. God, however, bases His judgment upon the attitude that underlies the actions. He tries the "spirits." The abstract plural sums up the

---

[1]The verse is open to differing interpretations, most of which are possible. Coates, p. 68,
relates it to prayer, with man thinking his plea and God giving His answer. Perowne,
p. 113, warns that the wisest plans will fail unless God guides the tongue. Kidner, p. 118,
lays the stress on God's sovereignty, noting that while man has freedom to plan, he nevertheless "advances God's designs." Ross, *EBC*, p. 1002, notes that God "confounds
even the wise," leading them to say something different from what they planned.
McKane, p. 496, states that man can expect his plans to come to pass when they follow
along with God's will in the matter. Other views are also possible, but this sampling is
enough to show the variety in interpretations.

3 Commit thy works unto the Lord, and thy thoughts shall be established.
4 The Lord hath made all things for himself: yea, even the wicked for the day of evil.

various inward qualities comprised by man's spirit, e.g., his motivation, his goals, his temper.

3 The phrase "commit . . ." is idiomatic, literally reading "roll . . ." in the sense of rolling one's troubles upon someone else. The idiom occurs elsewhere at Psalm 22:8 and 37:5. Here, the picturesque idea is that of rolling our responsibilities upon the Lord. When we do this, He will "establish" (*kûn,* cf. 12:3) our thoughts, settling them and giving us a sense of confidence that allows us to act upon them.[2]

4 The maxim sets forth the sovereign control of God over mankind. It is very close in thought to Romans 9:21-22. A more literal translation of 4a is "The Lord has made everything for its answer." The thought here seems to be that the whole of creation has been divinely ordained for the "answer" that it gives to the various situations of life. Our word "purpose" admirably expresses the thought conveyed idiomatically by the MT.[3] The parallelism agrees with this in that even the wicked have been created "for the day of evil," better, "the evil day." God allows the wicked to have their day in this world for His own purposes. They serve as a black backdrop against which the righteousness of the righteous shines forth. Further, the wicked serve to test the righteous, and one day they will allow God to show His holiness in judgment.

---

[2]Jones, p. 148, takes *kûn* as "to be sincere" and suggests that we avoid insincerity by bringing God into our thought process. The basic sense of *kûn,* however, in the nipᶜal, is "firm, stable, fix, secure." Nowhere is the idea of sincerity clearly seen.
[3]Gerhard Lisowsky, *Konkordanz zum Hebraischen Alten Testament* (1958) (hereafter cited as Lisowsky), p. 841, understands *lammaᶜănehû,* "for himself," from *maᶜaneh,* "purpose," distinct from *ᶜană,* "to answer." BDB, p. 775, derives it from *ᶜană,* "to answer," as "that for which it *answers,*" i.e., "for its purpose." KD I, 336, derives it from *maᶜan,* cognate to Arabic *maʾanyn,* "aim, intention." McKane, p. 497, repoints to *lǝmaᶜănehû,* "for what answers to it or "in relation to its counterpart." The verse then teaches "a self-contained, self-regulating order." This is possible but I would prefer to understand as above, based on the parallelism of the verse.

5 *Every one that is proud in heart is an abomination to the Lord:
though hand join in hand, he shall not be unpunished.*
6 *By mercy and truth iniquity is purged: and by the fear of the Lord
men depart from evil.*
7 *When a man's ways please the Lord, he maketh even his enemies to
be at peace with him.*

5 We turn here to a more familiar theme, the judgment of the proud.
The word "proud" (*gəbah*) has the basic meaning of "height" in a physical sense, e.g., a high mountain. Figuratively, it indicates "height" of position, either good or bad depending upon the context. This attitude is an
"abomination" (*tôʿabat,* cf. 3:32) to the Lord. As in 11:21, the phrase
"*though* hand *join* in hand" refers to a formal agreement between two
individuals. Despite such agreement, the haughty will "not go unpunished" (*loʾyinnaqeh,* cf. 6:29). The word *naqâ* means "to be clear, free,
innocent." It is used primarily of ethical or moral matters. Here, there is
a forensic use of going unpunished; cf. also 19:5, 9.

6 God does not merely require sacrifice for atonement; cf. Hosea 6:6;
Micah 6:6-8. The prophets regularly railed against ritualism, going
through only the motions of worship. Solomon here speaks in accord
with this teaching, noting that it is by "mercy" (*ḥesed,* cf. 2:8) and
"truth" (*ʾəmet,* cf. 3:3) that iniquity is "purged" (or "atoned for,"
yəkuppar). The verb *kapar* means "to make an atonement, reconcilia-
tion." It most often occurs in connection with the sacrifice, but it may
also be found generally with the idea of atonement. The atonement sacrifices showed the faith of the OT saints and allowed God to withhold
judgment on them until the great atoning sacrifice of Christ; cf. Romans
3:25. The phrase "depart from evil" describes the result of godliness, the
turning away from wickedness. Compare v. 17; 3:7.[4]

7 The verse states a general principle that is often true. An individual
whose ways "please" (*raṣôn,* cf. 11:1) the Lord will likewise gain the
favor of man. Man generally enjoys the company of wholesome people.
Even the "enemies" (*ʾôybayw*) will be brought into a state of peace with
such a one. The word *ʾayab* indicates a general state of hostility with the
degree determined by the context. Sometimes the word indicates ethical

---

[4]McKane, p. 498, relates "evil" (*raʿ,* cf. 1:33) to physical evil or injury, a possible
view. It is true that the righteous will experience fewer physical problems than the
wicked. If so taken, the proverb is a general statement that is usually true. I feel, however, that the parallelism favors the above view.

8 Better is a little with righteousness than great revenues without right.
9 A man's heart deviseth his way: but the Lord directeth his steps.

hostility, those who oppose godliness, rather than personal or national
hostility. The thought of the verse is broad enough to include both ethical or personal hostility.

The only real debate with the verse is with the word "he." Is this the
Lord? Or is this the man himself? There is no question but that man's
actions are the direct influence upon others, that they will respond to the
individual himself. But the aphorism here is set in the middle of a passage that clearly recognizes the sovereignty of God in the affairs of man.
It is therefore best to relate "he" back to "the Lord" in the opening
phrase.[5]

8 This is the only one of the first nine verses to omit the name of the
Lord. Yet it clearly states a divine principle—that man should live righteously. To this end, a little material wealth gained by a righteous method
is desirable. It is better to have this than to have vast amounts of wealth
that have been earned by unrighteous means. The poetical books develop the principle elsewhere, e.g., Psalm 37:16; Proverbs 15:16;
Ecclesiastes 4:6.

9 "Heart" (*leb,* cf. 3:5) here refers to the mind. Man carefully plans his
way of life, considering various options, goals, and methods. In the final
analysis, however, it is the Lord who gives the direction in life that man
needs. The word "directeth" (cf. *kûn,* 12:3) denotes the activity of God
in establishing the way of man in life.

> Verses 1-9 can be roughly outlined as follows with every
> point related back to God:
>
> | | |
> |---|---|
> | 1. Gift of Speech 1 | 5. Certainty of Judgment 5 |
> | 2. Judgment of Attitudes 2 | 6. Purity of Life 6 |
> | 3. Guidance of Thoughts 3 | 7. Favor of Man 7 |
> | 4. Purpose of the Wicked 4 | 8. Value of Righteousness 8 |
> | 9. Guidance of Actions 9 | |

---

[5]Among others, McKane, p. 491; Cohen, p. 104; and Jones, p. 149, specifically make
man the subject of the verse.

10 A divine sentence is in the lips of the king: his mouth transgresseth not in judgment.
11 A just weight and balance are the Lord's: all the weights of the bag are his work.

10 The verse introduces a section (vv. 10-15) that deals with kings. Only v. 11 fails to mention the king. As with the preceding section, the verses have differing emphases. For this reason, they will be dealt with separately.[6]

To begin the section, the thought lies on the judicial role of the king. He renders "a divine sentence" (*qesem*). Properly, *qesem* indicates "divination." Throughout the OT, this practice is outlawed as ungodly. There are passages, however, to show that "divination" was not limited to satanic practices. Balaam is described as a "soothsayer" (or "diviner," Josh. 13:22). Isaiah 3:2 includes the office of "prudent" (better "diviner") in a list of other offices, including the proven hero, the warrior, the judge, the prophet, and the elder. The focus of the word, then, lies on the practice of divination, a practice that was in itself neutral. It was objectionable only when done outside the will of God. Here, the king apparently practices divination in discerning the truth of a legal matter.[7] The maxim admonishes, "his mouth should not transgress in judgment." The imperfect verb with the negative *lo᾿* expresses an emphatic injunction.

11 Elsewhere the Lord shows His concern with honesty in business (cf. Lev. 19:36; contra. Hos. 12:7). Honesty in weighing out the purchase is a divine concern since it shows truthfulness and trustworthiness. The "just

---

[6]Toy, p. 325, arbitrarily makes the passage postexilic, from the time of "non-Jewish monarchs of the Greek period." The view is not supported by any evidence. Further, the emphases of the passage agree with the spirit of other monarchial injunctions found in the OT.

[7]We do not know the means by which the king accomplishes this. This has given rise to various speculations. Eryl W. Davies, "The Meaning of *qesem* in Prv 16, 10," *Biblica* 61:554-56, suggests that it involved the casting of lots. Aitken, p. 212, mentions the possibilities of divinely given wisdom or of extreme perceptiveness, which made it seem as if his judgments were from the Lord. Toy, p. 324, states that the term is used "figuratively." French and Skinner, pp. 53-54, conclude that the decisions of the king are "framed with more than ordinary divine assistance" since he has been ordained to his position by God. R. N. Whybray, "Poverty, Wealth, and Point of View in Proverbs," *ET* 100:333, 336, thinks that the verse is one of several that "naively attribute supernatural powers or knowledge to the king." Following the practice of divination elsewhere, it would seem as if Davies has the correct explanation here. Any conclusion must be tentative since the text does not give us the method used by the king.

12 It is an abomination to kings to commit wickedness: for the throne is established by righteousness.
13 Righteous lips are the delight of kings; and they love him that speaketh right.

weight and balance" is better a "just balance and scales." These are "the Lord's" in that He is concerned with honesty. The "weights" (cf. ʾeben, 11:1), or "stones," of the bag are the work of God in that they reflect the standard by which one demonstrates his honesty. Compare 11:1; 20:10.[8]

12 God has ordained human government. He raises up kings and puts them down, and to all He gives the standards of righteousness by which they must govern. A king, therefore, who places himself above the law and practices wickedness in his reign does "abomination" (tôʿabat, cf. 3:32), that which God despises. The implied warning is that he jeopardizes the stability of his reign by his actions, very possibly bringing divine judgment upon himself.[9] Only righteous actions can establish his throne; cf. 20:28; 25:5.

13 Undoubtedly, every king has experienced the hypocrisy of those who tell him what they think he wants to hear. In contrast, "righteous lips" are a refreshing change. They give true speech, impartial and ethically correct. This is the "delight" (raṣôn, cf. 11:1) of the king. "He [not "they"] loves [cf. ʾahab, 9:8] him who speaks right." "Love" here refers to the friendship of the king.[10]

---

[8]Much has been made of the supposed lack of parallelism in the verse. Driver, *Textus* IV, 92 (1964), suggests that "just . . . balance," moʾznê mišpaṭ, is a misreading of moʾzǝnayim, "balances," with the concluding m being misunderstood as an abbreviation for mišpaṭ. Toy, p. 326, omits "just," mišpaṭ, as a gloss. These suggestions give too much weight to the form of the sentence rather than to its teaching. In another area, Martin, p. 102, without textual support, emends "the Lord's" to "the king's." This is so drastic as to be rejected out of hand. We cannot change the well-known yǝhwah to melek simply because the surrounding verses mention the king. The verse belongs in this section because the Lord is also a King.

[9]Among others, Zöckler, p. 155, and Greenstone, p. 175, understand the verse to say that the king will not tolerate evil among his subjects, that this is an abomination to him. This also is a possible way to understand the verse.

[10]Dahood, *ETL* 44:40, understands the plural "kings," mǝlakîm, in 13a, as a genitive singular with an enclitic mem. Further, on the basis of the chiastic parallelism, he repoints wǝdober yǝšarîm, "speaketh right," as a plural wǝdibrê yǝšarîm, "and the words

14 The wrath of a king is as messengers of death: but a wise man will pacify it.
15 In the light of the king's countenance is life; and his favour is as a cloud of the latter rain.
16 How much better is it to get wisdom than gold! and to get understanding rather to be chosen than silver!

14 The "wrath" (*ḥəmat,* cf. 15:1) of the king "is as messengers of death." The plural "messengers" sums up the means by which the king communicates his wrath, e.g., his verbal abuse, his anger, perhaps even his sentence of judgment. For this reason, a wise courtier will employ great tactfulness in opposing the king or in approaching him with unpleasant news. He will seek to do all in his power to "pacify" (cf. *kapar,* v. 6) the wrath lest he should be caught in its fury.

15 This is the converse of v. 14. "The light of the king's countenance" figuratively expresses his favor; cf. Job 29:24; Psalm 4:6; 89:15. This brings "life," i.e., the fulness of life that follows the blessing of the king. The king's favor is compared to a cloud that signals the "latter rain." In Palestine, the long summer drought is followed by the heavy *early rains* of October and mid-November. These prepare the ground for the fall plantings. Throughout the winter months of December, January, and February, the rains are frequent and light, with the cumulative amount being the major part of the yearly total. In March and April, the heavy *latter rains* fall. These are important since they fill out the fruit of the harvest. Further, they abate to some extent the severity of the summer drought. To compare the king's favor with the "latter rain," then, is to use a figure of that which gives fruit, growth, even life itself.

16 In the remainder of the chapter, we return to the more normal potpourri of topics, with no special organization or focus. Initially, we find the exaltation of wisdom. It is better to have wisdom than to possess gold! And it is likewise better to get understanding than to gain silver.[11]

---

of an upright man," again understanding an enclitic *mem.* The change does not affect the interpretation of the verse. It does, however, place too much emphasis on the form of the Hebrew, giving this precedence over the MT.

[11]The Hebrew is syntactically difficult. This has led to different suggestions for smoothing it out. McKane, p. 489, omits "than gold," *meḥarûṣ,* as an insertion to balance "than silver," *mikkasep,* in 16*b.* Toy, p. 330, and Gemser, p. 55, choose to omit "how much," *mâ,* as a dittography, repeating the *-mâ* ending on *ḥokmâ.* Although the Hebrew may be difficult, it is clear in meaning. These changes to the MT are not needed.

*17 The highway of the upright is to depart from evil: he that keepeth his
way preserveth his soul.
18 Pride goeth before destruction, and an haughty spirit before a fall.
19 Better it is to be of an humble spirit with the lowly, than to divide the
spoil with the proud.
20 He that handleth a matter wisely shall find good: and whoso trusteth
in the Lord, happy is he.*

This does not condemn the possession of silver and gold. It places the
priority on the possession of wisdom and understanding.

17 The "highway" (cf. *salal,* 4:8) of the righteous individual is the path
that departs from evil. The wise person will "keep" (cf. *naṣar,* 2:8) himself on that pathway as he engages in the various activities of life.[12] In
so doing, he "preserves" (cf. *šamar,* 2:8) himself. He avoids both the
premature judgment that might terminate his opportunity for service and
the lesser existence, the lack of a full life that sinners experience.

18-19 These two proverbs focus on pride, one of the more familiar
themes of the book. "Pride" (cf. *geʾâ,* 8:13) logically leads to "destruction" (*šeber,* cf. 6:15) since proud men rely upon themselves. Such self-
sufficiency is a resource that will surely fail. A "haughty [*gobah,* cf.
v. 5] spirit" will likewise lead to a "fall" (*kiššalon*). The word *kiššalon,*
"stumbling, calamity," occurs metaphorically elsewhere to indicate a departure from the successful way of life, v. 18.

The contrast with pride in v. 18 emphasizes the teaching of humility in
v. 19. It is good to have a "humble [*šəpal*] spirit" and to company with
others of a "lowly [*ʿənayîm,* cf. 14:21] spirit." The word *šəpal* means "to
be low, to crouch," but it regularly describes poetically those who are
"humble" or "abased." Similarly, the word "lowly" refers to one who is
"humble," either in spirit or in possessions. It is better to be a friend to this
person than to enter into some endeavor with the proud that will let you
gain a portion of spoil (or "plunder"). The contrast in the verse suggests
that the spoil would come from exploiting the poor in some way, v. 19.

20 This is the first of four verses that take up the theme of wise living,
each with a different emphasis within the area. Only v. 22 does not use
the word *ḥokmâ.* The phrase "handleth . . . wisely" is better "pays atten-

---

[12]Toy, p. 327, limits "evil" (*raʿ,* cf. 1:33) to misfortune and specifically rejects the
thought that it denotes "moral evil." This view is too restrictive as it avoids the familiar
use of *raʿ* with moral contexts elsewhere, e.g., 3:7; 6:24.

*21 The wise in heart shall be called prudent: and the sweetness of the
lips increaseth learning.
22 Understanding is a wellspring of life unto him that hath it: but the
instruction of fools is folly.
23 The heart of the wise teacheth his mouth, and addeth learning to his
lips.*

tion to" (cf. *śakal*, 1:3). Since one pays attention to it, "matter" (*dabar*,
cf. 11:13) is better "word." The first phrase says, "He who pays attention
to the word will find good." The parallelism suggests that this is the divine Word. When followed, this brings "good" (*ṭôb*, cf. 12:14). The one
who trusts the Lord will likewise be "happy" (or "blessed," cf. *ʾašrê*,
3:13).

21 The wise person will acquire a reputation for his wisdom. He will
be called "prudent" (cf. *bîn*, 1:2), discerning and perceptive. At the same
time, the "sweetness" (*meteq*) of his speech increases "learning" (*leqaḥ*,
cf. 1:5). "Sweetness," *meteq*, is parallel elsewhere with "honey," e.g.,
Judges 14:18; Psalm 19:10; Ezekiel 3:3. It indicates something sweet or,
figuratively, something desirable or attractive. With regard to speech,
this describes wholesome speech, speech that is gracious and pleasing in
nature. This will increase "learning" on the part of the hearers.

22 A "fountain of life" is a source of full and abundant life. "Life" is
an intensive plural, indicating that this life is more than mere existence.
It is a complete life, filled with all of the abundance that is potential for
it. This comes from having "understanding" (cf. *śakal*, 1:3). In contrast,
the "instruction" (or "correction," *mûsar*, cf. 1:2) of "fools" (*ʾawilîm*, cf.
1:7) is "folly" (cf. *ʾawîl*, 1:7). In other words, since the fool will not accept correction (cf. 15:5; 27:22), it is folly to persist in giving it to him.

23 The "heart of the wise" is his mind, the reservoir of his wisdom.
This "teacheth his mouth," more literally, "makes his speech wise." The
verb "teacheth" (cf. *śakal*, 1:3) is causative, suggesting that the mind directs the speech to cause it to display wisdom. In turn, this "addeth
learning" to his speech, i.e., it promotes "learning" (*leqaḥ*, cf. 1:5) in
those who hear him.[13]

---

[13]Following BH, McKane, p. 490, emends "to his lips," *waʿal śapatayw*, to *ûbaʿal
śapataw*, making the phrase parallel to *meteq śapatayim* in 21*b*. He translates, "an expert
speaker promotes learning." There is no textual support for the suggestion, and it adds
nothing to the understanding of the verse.

24 Pleasant words are as an honeycomb, sweet to the soul, and health to the bones.
25 There is a way that seemeth right unto a man, but the end thereof are the ways of death.
26 He that laboureth laboureth for himself; for his mouth craveth it of him.
27 An ungodly man diggeth up evil: and in his lips there is as a burning fire.
28 A froward man soweth strife: and a whisperer separateth chief friends.

24 This continues the thought of wholesome speech, describing it in attractive terms and mentioning its accomplishments. Such speech is as a "honeycomb," a source for honey and thus here a figure of speech indicating a source of sweetness and blessing. Compare 15:26. These are "sweet" (*matôq*, cf. v. 21) to those who hear them. Further, they bring "health" (*marpeʾ*, cf. 4:22), renewal, to others.

25 The verse is identical, in Hebrew and in interpretation, to 14:12.

26 Solomon draws another practical lesson from life. A man's hunger is a powerful motivation. It causes him to do even menial tasks in order to satisfy this craving. The first phrase, "he that laboureth laboureth for himself," would be better translated "the appetite [*nepeš*, cf. 7:23] of the laborer labors for him." Both the verb and the noun "laborer" come from *ʿamal*, a root that connotes the drudgery of work, the lack of fulfillment that comes from menial or physical labor. The idea, then, is that man's inner desires urge him to undertake that which would normally be undesirable and avoided. "His mouth craveth it of him," i.e., his hunger urges him to undertake the work.

27-28 The passage takes up the subject of evil speech once more. The "ungodly man" is literally a "man of Belial [*bəlîyaʿal*, cf. 6:12]," i.e., a worthless individual who draws his pleasure from bringing others into difficulty. He "diggeth up" (*koreh*) evil in the sense of causing trouble for the righteous person.[14] The verb *karâ* is "to dig" a hole of some kind,

---

[14] AB, p. 105, and Gemser, p. 55, propose *kur*, "furnace," for *koreh*. BH tentatively proposes *qarâ roʿeh*, "encounters evil," for *koreh raʿâ*, "diggeth up evil." Neither of these suggestions has textual support, and there is no reason to abandon the MT at this point. McKane, p. 494, refers 27*a* to digging up scandal, which he can then spread. While this is possible, I would prefer the broader view of digging up evil, encompassing scandal or anything else that would cause trouble for the target.

*29 A violent man enticeth his neighbour, and leadeth him into the way
that is not good.
30 He shutteth his eyes to devise froward things: moving his lips he
bringeth evil to pass.*

a pit, grave, or well. It figuratively refers to digging up difficulty for
someone else. From the parallelism, this difficulty comes from his
speech as he gossips or spreads rumors with the intention of causing
trouble for another. His lips are as "burning" (or "scorching") fire, consuming the individual at whom his words are aimed, cf. James 3:5-6, v. 27.

The "froward man" is a "perverse man" (*tahpukôt,* cf. 2:12). He delights in sowing strife. The parallelism in the verse relates his activities
to his speech. This can include gossip, spreading rumors, lying, slander,
or other evil forms of speech. As he does this, his words have an effect
upon friends (*ʾallûp,* cf. 2:17). The "whisperer" (or "murmurer") separates friends, turning one against another with his malicious words, v. 28.

29 The "violent man" (*hamas,* cf. 3:31) is an aggressive man, an oppressor. He "entices" (*yəpateh*) his "neighbour" (cf. *reaᶜ,* 6:1) by means
of his forcefulness. "Enticeth," *patâ,* "to be spacious, wide, open," is
figuratively "open to harm" and thus "naive" or "immature." This leads
to the verbal idea "to seduce, entice, persuade." The violent man causes
his friend to follow a "way *that is* not good," i.e., a way that is potentially destructive.

30 One who "shutteth his eyes" is rather one who "winks his eyes,"
giving the familiar sign of deceptiveness. He does this as he devises
"froward" (or "perverse," *tahpukôt,* cf. 2:12) matters. Further, "moving
[*qaraṣ*] his lips," he accomplishes his evil. The verb *qaraṣ* means "to be
narrow," and thus "to pinch, compress." The reference here is to pursing
the lips, compressing them in contemplation of the wickedness he is
about to commit.[15]

---

[15]*TWOT* II, 817, takes *ᶜoṣeh* as a "shutting" of the eyes, parallel to *qaraṣ,* the "barring"
of the lips. These mark one who closes his eyes to the problems of others and who shuts
his mouth in "hard cruelty." This ignores the verb *hašab,* which regularly refers to devising or planning a matter. McKane, p. 494, takes *lahsob,* "devise," as the 3ms imperfect
with a prefixed *l.* Driver, *Biblica* 32:196, sees the form as the infinitive preceded by a *l*
with the sense "is likely to." G.K. 114i simply locates the form as an infinitive with the
prefixed *l,* a view that accords nicely with the above discussion. There is no need for
Gemser's emendation to *yahṣob.* Compare also the note on Glendon Bryce's comments at
10:10.

31 The hoary head is a crown of glory, if it be found in the way of righteousness.
32 He that is slow to anger is better than the mighty; and he that ruleth his spirit than he that taketh a city.
33 The lot is cast into the lap; but the whole disposing thereof is of the Lord.

31 Throughout the OT, old age is seen as a sign of God's blessing. The elderly are to be treated with respect and dignity. Here, the gray hair of a person, a mark of his old age, is regarded as a "crown of glory," a distinctive sign of a long life of godliness. The verb "be found" (*timmaṣeʾ*) is the imperfect form of *maṣaʾ*. This represents the righteousness of this person as his customary way of life.

32 The word "mighty" (*gibbôr*) denotes a "mighty man," often a warrior or valiant individual. Here, it refers to a soldier, one who distinguishes himself in battle. As admirable as this is, one who has conquered his own spirit has achieved a greater victory. Patience, being "slow to anger" (*ʾerek appayim,* cf. 14:29), is "better than" heroic accomplishment in battle. The parallel phrase restates this thought. One who "rules [*mašal,* cf. 12:24] his spirit," i.e., gains the victory over himself, is greater than the warrior who captures another city.

33 Individuals used the lot to determine God's will in important decisions. Both private (I Sam. 14:40-42; Prov. 18:18; Jon. 1:7) and public matters (Lev. 16:8ff; Num. 26:55; Josh. 18:10; Obad. 11) were settled in this way. The details of casting lots are obscure. They may have differed from time to time. Here, however, the thought is of one who casts the lots into his "lap" ("hollow," thus the fold of the garment at the breast, cf. *ḥêq,* 6:27) or "breast pocket." Although man may make the arrangements for casting the lots, the Lord directs the final outcome of his actions.[16]

---

[16]McKane, p. 499, arbitrarily limits this to the decisions reached by means of the Urim and Thummim; cf. Exod. 28:30; Lev. 8:8. The lot here is cast into the breast pocket of the priestly garment. This certainly would be included within the thought of the verse. The Book of Proverbs, however, rarely mentions the priestly ritual. In addition, the lot was used by individuals and private groups. It is therefore better to adopt a broader interpretation at this point.

Practical Applications from Proverbs 16

1. Comments on speech 1, 13, 21, 23, 24, 27, 28
2. Divine judgment 2, 5
3. Divine guidance 3, 9, 33
4. Purpose for the wicked 4
5. Purity of life 6
6. Favor of man 7
7. Value of righteousness 8
8. Human judgment 10
9. Need for righteousness 12, 17
10. Power of the king 14
11. Favor of the king 15
12. Comments on wisdom and foolishness 16, 22
13. Comments on pride and humility 18, 19
14. Trust in the Lord 20
15. Danger of self-sufficiency 25
16. Motivation to work 26
17. Danger of violence 29
18. Nature of deception 30
19. Glory of old age 31
20. Comments on patience 32

1 Better is a dry morsel, and quietness therewith, than an house full of sacrifices with strife.

2 A wise servant shall have rule over a son that causeth shame, and shall have part of the inheritance among the brethren.

3 The fining pot is for silver, and the furnace for gold: but the Lord trieth the hearts.

PROVERBS 17

1 A "dry morsel" was the food of a poor person; cf. Ruth 2:14; I Kings 17:11. The word "sacrifices" (*zebaḥ*) occurs regularly in connection with the slaughtering of animals for the sacrifices. The phrase "sacrifices with strife" refers to the meat given back to the family to eat after the peace offering in its various forms—the thank offering, vow offering, or freewill offering, Leviticus 7:12-16. Here, the participants in this feast have a spirit of bitterness and ill-will flavoring the occasion. First Samuel 1:3-6 gives us an example. The peaceful conditions of a more common meal elevate it in value. It is better than an elaborate meal marked by strife. Compare 15:17.

2 Wise behavior is better than shameful conduct. The servant who serves with wisdom (cf. *śakal*, 1:3) will be elevated to a position of authority over a son whose conduct is shameful (*mebîš*, cf. 14:35). We have, in principle, an example of this in the elevation of Joseph from slavery to a position of great authority in the royal court.

Further, the wise servant will even receive "part of the inheritance" to reward his faithful service. The law did not provide for this. The Mosaic law set down principles that had to be interpreted on a case-by-case setting. There may well have been a development that allowed a worthless child to be disinherited in favor of other children or servants who had proved faithful.[1]

3 The phrase "fining pot" glosses *maṣrep*, from *ṣarap*, "to smelt, refine," metaphorically "to test." The *mem*-prefix denotes the place of

---

[1] KD I, 354, interprets the verb "have part" (*yaḥăloq*) as "distributing" the inheritance to the other sons. He specifically rejects the idea that the servant himself shares in the patrimony. The verb, however, normally denotes a sharing rather than a distribution. This is true the only other times it occurs in the book (16:19; 29:24). Further, we mute the point of the statement if the wise servant is given the position of executor and not that of heir.

4 A wicked doer giveth heed to false lips; and a liar giveth ear to a naughty tongue.
5 Whoso mocketh the poor reproacheth his Maker: and he that is glad at calamities shall not be unpunished.

activity, i.e., the "crucible." The "fining pot" was the instrument in which silver ore was purified in the smelting process. The worker would skim the dross from the melted ore. Similarly, the "furnace" (*kûr*) was the furnace where smelting took place. This allowed gold to be refined, eliminating its impurities. Each time *kûr* occurs, it has a figurative sense, picturing the heat of testing. These two figures are emblems of the refining process that God carries on as He rids mankind of his impurities. Compare Job 23:10.

4 The sentence draws upon the practical experience of life. A person who delights in wicked speech marks himself as evil. The verb "giveth heed" (cf. *qašab,* 2:2) indicates that this is more than just casual curiosity. This is the giving of close attention, even obedience to pernicious speech. The person is thus "evil" (cf. *raʿ,* 1:33).

Literally, 4*b* reads, "a lie pays attention to a destructive tongue." The word "lie" (*šeqer,* cf. 6:17) is abstract, dealing with a general subject. Here, however, the abstract phrase "a liar" represents a concrete individual. This representation is not unusual in Hebrew (G.K. 83c).[2] He "pays attention" (*mezîn*). The word *ʾazan* denotes the giving of close attention rather than casual listening. The "naughty tongue" is better a "destructive tongue," i.e., a tongue that speaks words that promote "destruction" (*hawwot,* cf. 11:6). There is no specific object of the destruction. This is a generalized destruction of friendships, of tranquility, of reputation, and so forth.

5 God is the Creator of all mankind, rich and poor alike. Therefore, to mock the poor "reproacheth" (*ḥerep,* cf. 14:31) God for His creative work. Further, one who delights in the calamities (*ʾêd,* cf. 1:26) that befall another will "not be unpunished" (*loʾ yinnaqeh,* cf. 6:29). From the

---

[2]There is no denying that the Hebrew is difficult here. Oesterley, p. 138, and AB, p. 108, want to read the participle form *mašaqqer* for the MT *šeqer.* Greenstone, p. 182, suggests supplying "man," i.e., "a man of lies." Martin, p. 107, simply concludes that the text is corrupt without making a specific correction. The easiest solution is to take the abstract *šeqer* as concrete.

6 Children's children are the crown of old men; and the glory of children are their fathers.
7 Excellent speech becometh not a fool: much less do lying lips a prince.

parallelism with 5a, it is clear that God is the one who will punish this person.

6 The phrase "children's children" is idiomatic for descendants. It embraces grandchildren and so forth. In the great majority of cases, the children of children are a "crown" (*ʿaṭeret,* cf. 14:24) to the elderly. They represent the pinnacle of life's experiences, signaling the blessing of God upon an individual; cf. Psalm 128:6. The family unit was more important in Israel than it is today, a sad commentary on modern life. It was therefore of great personal importance to see one's descendants flourishing.

At the same time, the children "glory" (*tipʾeret*) in their fathers. The verb *paʾar,* "to glory," has a distinct nuance of "boast," or "pride." The term "fathers" here includes the ancestors, not merely one's own father. The idea is that a son looks back on his line of ancestors and takes a healthy pride in his heritage.

7 "Excellent" (*yeter*) speech is that which offers so much as to be "excellent" or "fine." The adjective comes from *yatar,* "to remain over, leave," thus the noun "rest, remnant, abundance," leading to the idea of a smaller, excellent part.[3] We do not expect excellent speech from a "fool" (*nabal*). The word *nabal* occurs only four times in Proverbs[4] but it occurs widely elsewhere. It roughly corresponds to the *leṣ;* cf. 1:22. Both describe a hardened sinner, one who steadfastly opposes God's authority. We would also not expect to hear "lying" (*šeqer,* cf. 6:17) from a "prince," one of noble position. Such a person should speak with the character that befits his position.

---

[3]Nahum M. Waldman, "A Note on Excessive Speech and Falsehood," *JQR* 67:143-45, does not argue persuasively that *yeter* is "arrogant, overbearing speech" with an additional component of "false speech." Gemser, p. 56, and AB, p. 108, emend to *yošer,* "honest," an unnecessary change. The MT is sensible and should be retained.
[4]Prov. 17:7, 21; 30:22, 32.

PROVERBS

*8 A gift is as a precious stone in the eyes of him that hath it: whither-
soever it turneth, it prospereth.*
*9 He that covereth a transgression seeketh love; but he that repeateth a
matter separateth very friends.*

8 The statement does not approve bribery. It merely observes the effect
of giving a bribe successfully. The "gift" is, without any question, a
bribe given to gain some desired end. The one who gives the bribe finds
that it is as a "precious stone," literally, "a stone of grace," best understood as a jewel. It is highly desirable to those to whom he would give
it.[5] As a result, he prospers wherever "he," not "it," turns since he is able
to influence authorities and others who have the ability to meet his
needs.

The difficulty with the verse lies in the moral contradiction of seeming
to approve a bribe. Compare 18:16; 19:6; and 21:14. We must consider
the cultural context. In many parts of the world, a gift to a public official is accepted as a matter of course. In a sense it is similar to the tip
we give one who has given us good service. The fact that our culture
does not openly practice the giving of gifts to public officials does not
change the fact that the practice exists. The verse does not approve the
practice. It rather comments on it, noting that such a gift does promote
success in one's endeavors.

9 This is similar in thought to 10:12. Real love will cause a person to
cover a "transgression" (*pešaᶜ*, cf. 10:12). The verb "seeketh" (cf. *baqaš,*
2:4) refers to an earnest search, a diligent pursuit of an object. The statement about covering transgressions is general and should be understood
as referring to any kind of impropriety. One who uncovers such a thing
acts to destroy friendships. His willingness to gossip causes a breach in
the friendships of others with the object of his attack. Compare 16:28.

---

[5]Among others, KD I, 358, and Zöckler, p. 161, understand the phrase "him that hath
it" to refer to the one who receives the gift, rather than the giver of it. The second half of
the verse, however, favors the position above, that the giver is "him who hath it." Toy,
pp. 340-41, understands the "stone of favor" as a magic stone, an amulet that brings
good luck. McKane, p. 502, likewise understands it as an amulet, even relating it to a
"string of blue beads" often seen in Israel as a charm. The view is unlikely. It is far more
probable that the giver would regard his gift as more than a lucky charm.

10 A reproof entereth more into a wise man than an hundred stripes into a fool.

11 An evil man seeketh only rebellion: therefore a cruel messenger shall be sent against him.

12 Let a bear robbed of her whelps meet a man, rather than a fool in his folly.

10 A wise man responds well to correction. We best see his response by comparing it with the correction of a fool (*kəsîl*, cf. 1:22). The man of understanding will respond to a single "reproof" (cf. *ga'ar*, 13:1). The fool, however, hardens himself against rebuke. He will not respond to a "hundred stripes." This last is idiomatic, representing a large number. The "fool" does not respond to correction, not even to drastic punishment. The wise man (cf. *bîn*, 1:2) responds readily to reproof.

11 The AV is correct in making *ra'*, "an evil *man*," the subject.[6] All that the wicked man does leads to "rebellion," *mərî*. The word *mərî* overwhelmingly refers to rebellion against God. Only a few exceptions involve rebellion against someone else. Since rebellion against authority is fundamentally rebellion against God, the word occurs properly. Inevitably, this person stirs up such trouble that a "cruel messenger" will be sent against him. This cruel messenger represents civil or royal authority and is sent to execute judgment. He is "cruel" in that he is pitiless and without mercy, bent upon his task of punishing the one who stirs up the wrath of authority.

12 The emblematic she bear shows the danger of companying with a fool. The concern of a mother bear for her cubs is well known; cf. II Samuel 17:8; Hosea 13:8; possibly II Kings 2:24. The *Ursinus syriacus* at one time ranged throughout Palestine but today lives primarily in the mountainous northern regions. Despite the danger from a mother losing her cubs, it would be better to meet with her than to encounter a "fool" (*kəsîl*) engaged in his foolishness. The unspoken practical teaching

---

[6]Commentators divide over the choice of the subject. Among others, KD, *PC*, Toy, AB, Greenstone, and Plaut adopt *mərî* as the subject. While this is the majority position, a significant minority, including McKane, Zöckler, Conant, and Frankenberg, accept *ra'* as the subject. The Hebrew word order favors the choice of *ra'*, particularly in view of the fact that *mərî* is abstract, not concrete. Toy, p. 344, recognizes the problem and emends to *'îš mərî* in order to introduce a concrete subject. The change, however, is not required if *ra'* is the subject.

13 Whoso rewardeth evil for good, evil shall not depart from his house.
14 The beginning of strife is as when one letteth out water: therefore
leave off contention, before it be meddled with.
15 He that justifieth the wicked, and he that condemneth the just, even
they both are abomination to the Lord.

is that a man should choose his friends carefully, avoiding those who could involve him in foolish behavior.

13 Gratitude is of major concern throughout the Bible. A person who returns evil for good will reap a harvest of judgment. He has done evil (*ra⁶â*, cf. 1:33) to others; evil (*ra⁶â*) will therefore not depart from his house. "Evil" here has its broadest sense. It could include physical infirmities, financial reverses, or anything of an undesirable nature. Nothing limits it to moral wickedness. Notice that his "house" is involved as well. What the man as head of the home has done returns to the family. It involves them as well in the judgment that follows his wickedness. This is one of many illustrations of the *lex talionis,* e.g., Job 4:8; Proverbs 1:31; Jeremiah 6:19; Hosea 8:7; 10:13; Romans 2:6; II Corinthians 9:6; Galatians 6:7-8.

14 The beginning of "strife" (*madôn,* cf. 6:14) is potentially dangerous. Although the conflict may be small at the beginning, it may rapidly get out of hand and become an explosive situation. Thus, it is compared here with one who lets out water. The trickle that comes from the hole in a dam may be small when it starts. As the seepage wears away the surrounding area, the water flow increases until it becomes an uncontrollable torrent. Therefore, one should avoid "contention" (cf. *rîb,* 3:30) before it "be meddled with" (*gala⁶,* better, before it "discloses itself," i.e., develops into a violent confrontation). The root idea of *gala⁶* is "to break out," as in contention and strife. The word occurs only at 17:14; 18:1; and 20:3. It is related to an Arabic cognate, "to show one's teeth," as in a snarl.[7]

15 The maxim speaks directly concerning corruption by a judge. Having accepted a bribe, he perverts the sentence, either declaring the guilty person innocent or the innocent person guilty. In either case, his

---

[7]McKane, p. 505, suggests that the verse has special reference to litigation, the attempt to secure legal victory being only a way of perpetuating a quarrel. The words *madôn* and *rîb,* however, are general terms for conflict and therefore should not be limited to legal wrangles. Applying the verse to conflict in general gives it a wider and more practical application.

*16 Wherefore is there a price in the hand of a fool to get wisdom, seeing
he hath no heart to it?*
17 A friend loveth at all times, and a brother is born for adversity.
*18 A man void of understanding striketh hands, and becometh surety in
the presence of his friend.*

actions are wrong and he makes himself an "abomination" (*tôᶜəbat*, cf.
3:32). The principle here includes all who pronounce a wrong verdict,
even those outside a courtroom. It often happens in life that people
make decisions based on such things as friendships, expediency, or reputation. When matters that have nothing to do with a situation lead to
wrong decisions, the person is abominable to the Lord.

16 An old proverb may be paraphrased: "you can bring a student to
the fountain of learning, but you can't make him think!" The picture is
of a fool who has come with a gift of money to a wisdom teacher. To
what end? The "fool" (*kəsîl*, cf. 1:22) has no "heart" (*leb*, cf. 3:5), i.e.,
no capacity, for learning.[8] The lesson, however, goes deeper than this.
The fool will not gain wisdom. His whole character is such that he turns
from that which could make him wise (vv. 10, 24).

17 Friends rely upon one another. For this reason, it is wise to make
friends with those who have a wholesome influence. By the pure logic
of the matter, a good friend is more apt to be reliable than an evil friend.
Evil men live for themselves and so do not seek for opportunities to
help others.

Solomon here comments that true friends act consistently, no matter
what circumstances arise. A true friend, more than a casual acquain-
tance, will show his love "at all times." The mention of "adversity"
gives a specific example of a time when a friend is faithful. The
"brother" is synonymous with the "friend." He shows his steadfast, consistent affection even in troubled times.

18 Only a man "lacking in sense" (*həsar leb,* cf. 6:32) will enter into a
surety agreement with a "friend" (cf. *reaᶜ,* 6:1). The "striking hands" is
the sealing of the agreement with a handshake. This is done in the
"presence of his friend," no doubt because the friend is the one for

---

[8]Gemser, p. 56, and Toy, p. 346, view the offering of money as metaphorical, not as a
literal purchase price. First Samuel 9:7-8 shows that it was customary to make a gift to
the wisdom teacher in return for his services. It makes sense to so view this here.

*19 He loveth transgression that loveth strife: and he that exalteth his
gate seeketh destruction.
20 He that hath a froward heart findeth no good: and he that hath a
perverse tongue falleth into mischief.
21 He that begetteth a fool doeth it to his sorrow: and the father of a
fool hath no joy.
22 A merry heart doeth good like a medicine: but a broken spirit drieth
the bones.*

whom he assumes financial responsibility. The *rea^c* is apparently a casual friend, not one for whom there is a deep-seated bond of friendship.
Therefore, it would not be wise to accept a relationship that holds the
potential of financial harm. See the discussion of surety bonds at 6:1-5.

19 I prefer to reverse the subject and verb in the first phrase, translating instead "he who loves strife loves transgression." The Hebrew will
allow either this or the traditional rendering. The thought here is that
one who finds delight in quarreling shows his love for "transgression"
(*pesa^c*, cf. 10:12). He has a rebellious spirit.

In like manner, one who "exalteth his gate" actively seeks his own destruction. The phrase "exalteth his gate" is an idiom. It denotes pride.
The idiom comes from the practice of showing wealth by building an
ostentatious home with an ornate entry. One who has pride prepares the
way for his personal "destruction" (*šaber*, cf. 6:15).[9]

20-22 The next three proverbs focus on the emotions. One whose
heart is "froward" (or "perverse," *^ciqqeš*, cf. 2:15) will not accomplish
good. His attitudes and actions are evil, and his works are ultimately
evil. This is a general truth in this life, but it is a specific truth when
taken from an eternal view. Solomon no doubt draws upon his observations of others as well as the analysis of his own life.

The last half of the verse gives a specific example of the first half. A
man whose speech is "perverse" (*nehpak*) falls into "mischief" (cf. *ra^câ*,

---

[9]Toy, p. 350, emends *peša^c*, "transgression," to *peṣaṣ* and translates, "he loves wounds
who loves strife." He further adopts *pî* for *pithô*, "his gate," and translates 19*b*, "he who
talks proudly seeks destruction." Martin, p. 110, and Frankenberg, p. 105, make similar
changes to 19*b*. While these changes express biblical truths, there is no indication that
the MT is defective. It should be retained. AB, p. 111, understands 19*b* to refer to a man
whose doorway is inaccessible to others, thereby provoking their enmity. This is possible
but I feel the metaphorical view above is more likely.

1:33). The descriptive term *nehpak* is from *hapak,* "to turn oneself"; cf. 12:7. This occurs figuratively to denote perverse speech, speech that turns aside from proper speech. Here, then, is a man whose evil speech brings him into punishment, v. 20.

The sentence describes the grief of the parents both positively and negatively. The "fool" (*kəsîl,* cf. 1:22) causes sorrow (*tûgâ,* cf. 10:1), mental anguish over the way the son has chosen.[10] Further, we find that the "fool" (*nabal,* cf. v. 7) causes his parents to lack joy. Notice that there are no restrictions that limit the ability of the foolish child to cause grief. This heightens the seriousness of foolish behavior since even minor foolishness, defined from man's viewpoint, can cause the parents to grieve, v. 21.[11]

The noun *gehâ,* "medicine," occurs only here although the verb form occurs in Hosea 5:13. The Aramaic cognate signifies "to be free from pain or disease." It is appropriate to translate 22*a* "A joyful heart brings good healing."[12] The converse is also true: "a broken spirit dries the bones," i.e., robs the body of its vitality. The verse recognizes the psychosomatic relationship between the emotions and health. It is significant that the Bible notes this relationship since modern science has

---

[10]Dahood, *PNWSP,* p. 39, points out that the *l*-preposition in 21*a* "intensifies the notion of sorrow caused by the birth of a fool." It is true that the emphatic *l* occurs in the cognate language Arabic. This emphatic use, however, is not common in Hebrew. The preposition here more likely introduces the object of the unexpressed verb.

[11]Elmslie, p. 130, misses the point of the proverb. He explains the repetition of "fool" by saying, "the 'fool' of the first clause is in the Hebrew *Kasîl,* a coarse fool, and the 'fool' of the second is *Nabal; i.e.,* to have the first as a son will involve some regrets, but the second robs his father of all joy." This ignores the poetical nature of the proverb. Undoubtedly, *kəsîl* and *nabal* are interchanged in poetic variation. There is no contrast between their abilities to produce differing kinds of grief in the parents. McKane, pp. 237, 503, unnecessarily restricts the application of the verse. He translates *kəsîl* as "dolt" and describes him as one who will never "grow to maturity and the full exercise of his powers." While it is true that a mentally defective child will cause the parents to grieve, neither *kəsîl* nor *nabal* take this meaning elsewhere. Both refer to the individual who consciously chooses a life of rebellion.

[12]Perles, p. 102, understands *gehâ* as "countenance" on the basis of an Arabic cognate. He feels that this parallels 22*b* better since the face is a part of the body. Gemser, p. 57, on the basis of the Peshitta and Targum, emends to *gəwîyâ,* "body." Greenstone, p. 189, likewise accepts this reading. The fact that the noun *gehâ* occurs only here does not justify the change. The idea of "healing" fits nicely into the parallelism. The view of Perles is unlikely since this does not explain the verb form in Hosea 5:13.

23 A wicked man taketh a gift out of the bosom to pervert the ways of judgment.
24 Wisdom is before him that hath understanding; but the eyes of a fool are in the ends of the earth.
25 A foolish son is a grief to his father, and bitterness to her that bare him.

taken note of it only in comparatively recent times. Proverbs 12:25; 14:30; 15:13, 15; and 18:14 take up this same topic, v. 22.

23 The verse should rather be translated, "A wicked *man* receives a bribe out of the bosom to pervert the ways of judgment." The "bosom" (cf. *ḥêq,* 6:27) is the fold of the robe in which a bribe has been concealed, awaiting the appropriate time to give it. At a private moment, the giver takes it out and passes it to the unjust judge. This "gift," or "bribe," influences the judge to make an unfair judgment in the matter under consideration. He is therefore a "wicked *man,*" using his position for personal gain rather than for just causes.[13]

24 The discerning man (cf. *bîn,* 1:2) recognizes that wisdom is all about him. He pays attention to her, focusing on the opportunities she gives in the course of life. But the fool (*kəsîl,* cf. 1:22) fails to keep his attention fixed on the present. He rather allows it to skip to the "ends of the earth," to far-off places and times where he dreams of exploits. The contrast is stark. The understanding man takes advantage of everyday life; the fool loses himself in that which does not exist.

25 Once again, as in 10:1 and 17:21, we see the emotional impact of a foolish son upon his parents. He provokes them to "grief" (better, "vexation," *kaʿas,* cf. 12:16). They know that their wishes will best serve their child. When he spurns them and follows his own self-centered will, his response irritates them and brings an agitated response. At the same time, he causes "bitterness" (*memer*) to them. The word *memer* occurs only here in the OT. It is related to *marar,* "to be bitter," a verb that regularly expresses feelings of personal despair. It is likely that *memer* expresses the same idea, that of "despair."

---

[13]Among others, Muenscher, Greenstone, and Alden understand the "wicked man" as the one who gives the bribe rather than the judge who receives it. This is possible but I think the view above better reflects the meaning. The majority of versions understand the "wicked man" as the one who accepts the bribe.

26 Also to punish the just is not good, nor to strike princes for equity.
27 He that hath knowledge spareth his words: and a man of understanding is of an excellent spirit.
28 Even a fool, when he holdeth his peace, is counted wise: and he that shutteth his lips is esteemed a man of understanding.

26 As with v. 23, there is a forensic sense here. The "also" with which the verse begins lends emphasis. It is not limited to the following word but governs the entire phrase (G.K. 153).[14] "Punish," ʿanôš, is a legal term referring to monetary punishment and thus "to fine." It is not good to "punish" a just man. Likewise, it is not appropriate "to strike," to inflict stripes upon, to flog, a noble person who has been upright in his conduct. The word "noble" (nədîbîm) is from a root that means "to be willing." The "noble" is one who offers voluntary sacrifice or service to God. This can include both commoners and those of higher position. Thus the word focuses more on character than on position.[15] Once again, injustice toward the man is wrong.

27-28 These two proverbs extol the virtue of controlled speech, avoiding the temptation to talk without having something worthwhile to say. A man with knowledge will hold back his words, speaking cautiously and with purpose. Similarly, a man with understanding will have "an excellent" spirit. "Excellent," qar, from qarar, is "cold" and thus, figuratively, "calm, self-possessed." The phrase is better "a calm spirit." The AV has accepted the qərê reading yəqar, "excellent," which does not parallel 27a well, v. 27.

Even a foolish man can portray wisdom by remaining silent. The reserved, judicial appearance conveys a certain dignity of wisdom, no matter who is the actor. Thus, someone who keeps his mouth closed, concealing his foolishness, secures the respect of others. The thought of these two verses is seen elsewhere in 10:19; 15:2, 28; v. 28.

---

[14]McKane, p. 506, suggests that the *gam* indicates a previous statement on the topic that has dropped out. Martin, p. 111, likewise invents a similar explanation. In view of the regular use of *gam* to denote an intensive statement, it is not necessary to postulate a missing phrase or verse.

[15]Toy, p. 353, emends ʿal-yošer, "nor . . . for equity," to bal yašar and translates, "it is not seemly to oppress the upright." There is no need, however, to change the MT. McKane, p. 506, limits the nədîbîm to one of "rank and status," a possible view but one I have discarded because of the relationship of nadîb to moral character.

Practical Applications from Proverbs 17

1. Family relationships 1, 6, 21, 25
2. Contrast between wise and foolish behavior 2, 10, 12, 16, 24
3. Divine evaluation of man's works 3, 5, 15, 26,
   and the punishment of evil works 11, 13
4. Speech 4, 7, 9*b*, 20, 27, 28
5. Bribery 8, 23
6. True friendship 9*a*, 17
7. Warning against strife 14, 19
8. Surety 18
9. Emotions and health 22

1 Through desire a man, having separated himself, seeketh and inter-
meddleth with all wisdom.
2 A fool hath no delight in understanding, but that his heart may dis-
cover itself.

PROVERBS 18

1 The Hebrew reads something like "He who separates himself seeks desire; he breaks out to sound wisdom." This has been taken both in a bad sense and in a good sense.[1] The bad sense, however, fits the text better. The word "intermeddleth" (cf. *galaᶜ*, 17:14) is better "quarrels." The man who separates himself from conventional wisdom, following his own selfish desires, puts himself in the position of warring against sound wisdom. The verse warns against headstrong, self-centered decisions.[2] As 15:22 says, a "multitude of counsellors" helps to establish one's plans.

2 The foolish person does not "delight" (*ḥapeṣ*) in those matters that will give him greater understanding of life. The word *ḥapeṣ* describes a deep emotional involvement. The fool's antipathy toward understanding, then, comes from his emotional preoccupation with less important matters. He has no concern for wisdom. In particular, he concerns himself "that his heart may discover itself." He wants to reveal his own opinions. He has no concern with the ideas of others. His own thoughts are all-important to him; cf. v. 13.

---

[1] Matthew Henry, for instance, comments, "Our translation seems to take it as an excitement to diligence in the pursuit of wisdom. If we would get knowledge or grace, we must desire it, as that which we need and which will be of great advantage to us. . . . We must separate ourselves from all those things which would divert us from or retard us in the pursuit."

[2] There are several negative approaches. Zöckler, p. 166, emends *lətaʾəwâ* to *lətoʾanâ* and translates, "seeketh after an occasion (of strife)." Kidner, p. 127, follows the RSV and emends similarly. He applies it to one who seeks to break with a friend. Toy, p. 354, concludes, "it seems impossible to get a satisfactory sense from the Hebrew, and no good emendation presents itself." Plaut gives three Jewish interpretations: (1) a negative view, one who separates himself from God, Rashi; (2) a positive view, one who leaves his family in search of knowledge, Ibn Ezra; (3) another negative view, one who separates himself from the community, Hillel. Dahood, *PNWSP*, p. 42, understands *taʾawâ* as "ease, inactivity" on the basis of the Arabic cognate *ʾawa*, "to turn aside to lodge." He also appeals to 21:25, "his hands refuse to work," as defining the word. The support for the suggested emendations is weak and they are not necessary to understand the verse.

*3 When the wicked cometh, then cometh also contempt, and with ig-
nominy reproach.*
*4 The words of a man's mouth are as deep waters, and the wellspring
of wisdom as a flowing brook.*
*5 It is not good to accept the person of the wicked, to overthrow the
righteous in judgment.*

3 When the wicked person comes in, he is accompanied by "contempt" (*bûz*, cf. 1:7). Because this attitude characterizes the wicked person, we may say that it is with him wherever he goes.[3] "Ignominy" (or
"shame," *qalôn*, cf. 3:35) parallels "wicked," indicating that the wicked
is a shameful person. He is accompanied by "reproach" (cf. *ḥerep*,
14:31), the lack of honor that he directs toward those who oppose him.

4 This is a picturesque description of the value of wisdom. The parallelism requires that the "words of a man's mouth" be wise words. These
are "deep waters" (cf. 20:5), profound and providing an inexhaustible
supply of counsel and blessing.[4] Verse 4*b* explains 4*a*, the "wellspring
[or 'fountain'] of wisdom" being an emblematic portrayal of wise
speech. This is a "bubbling brook," a limitless source of wisdom.[5]

5 This adage argues for righteousness in the administration of justice.
This is a familiar theme in the book; cf. 17:15; 24:24. The phrase "to
accept . . ." is literally "to lift up the face of the wicked." The expression

---

[3]McKane, Gemser, Greenstone, Oesterley, and others read *rešaʿ*, "wickedness," for the
MT's *rašaʿ*, "wicked." This has the advantage of making the word abstract. There is no
support for the change. While this does not change the consonants, it is still unnecessary.
The thought of a wicked person being marked by contempt for others is very normal.

[4]Kidner, p. 128, follows 20:5 in understanding the phrase "deep waters" to refer to
concealment, i.e., that a man does not reveal his inward thoughts readily. Alden likewise
mentions the antithetical possibility that a man's thoughts are stagnant in contrast to the
flowing water that is pure. While these views are possible, the *waw* conjunction or *mem*
preformative normally signals antithetical poetry. These are absent here. Further, the
context includes synthetic and synonymous parallelism. For these reasons, I understand
the verse as synonymous poetry.

[5]KD, Plaut, McKane, and others treat the verse as synthetic poetry, "The words of a
man's mouth are deep waters, a bubbling brook, a fountain of wisdom." Toy, pp. 356-57,
varies this idea by emending *ḥokmâ* to *ḥayyîm*. He argues that "fountain" (*maqôr*), when
used metaphorically, always occurs elsewhere in connection with "life." He, however,
has overlooked such references as 25:26; Psalm 68:26; and Jeremiah 9:1. The word
"fountain" stands very nicely as a metaphorical representation of a "source." We may
take it generally as a source of life, wisdom, tears, etc. The context supports synonymous parallelism.

6 A fool's lips enter into contention, and his mouth calleth for strokes.
7 A fool's mouth is his destruction, and his lips are the snare of his soul.
8 The words of a talebearer are as wounds, and they go down into the innermost parts of the belly.

"to lift up . . ." occurs elsewhere to denote the showing of favoritism to someone, e.g., Genesis 19:21; Numbers 6:26; Psalm 4:6. Here, it is an obvious perversion of justice and so is condemned. The phrase "neither is it good" must be understood at the head of 5*b*. It is likewise evil to condemn the righteous.

6-7 Both of these maxims describe the results of foolish speech. In the first place, it stirs up "contention" (*rîb*, cf. 3:30).[6] Next, we see that the fool's speech cries out for "strokes," i.e., his words virtually demand that he be beaten by way of punishment. Most likely, in this OT setting, this would refer to a public flogging, v. 6. In addition, his speech brings about his downfall. "Destruction" (*məhittâ*, cf. 10:14) is too strong. "Ruin" more adequately conveys the thought. Finally, his speech figuratively sets a snare into which he himself will fall. This piling of phrase upon phrase gives a cumulative impact to the rebuke of foolish speech. It has no prospect of success, v. 7.

8 The "talebearer," *nirgan,* refers to a gossip, 16:28; 26:20, 22, or to one who complains about God, Deuteronomy 1:27; Psalm 106:25; Isaiah 29:24. The term "wounds" is misleading. While it may be true that words may hurt someone, this is not what the verse says. The word "wounds" comes from *laham,* "to swallow greedily," and thus "bits greedily swallowed" or, by interpretation, some "dainty morsels." The verse says, "the words of a talebearer are like dainty morsels." It is a commentary on man's insatiable desire to hear gossip. The gossip is as something tasty to eat. The man greedily takes it in. Proverbs 26:22 identically repeats the proverb.[7]

---

[6]Greenstone, Hulst, Oesterley, and others emend *yaboʾû,* "come," to the *hipʿîl yabiʾû,* "enter," citing the LXX and Targum variously as support. The sense then is that the fool's speech brings strife. This change is not required. The verb *bôʾ* occurs over twenty-five hundred times with the very general sense of "go, come, enter." The verb can readily be understood here in the sense taken above, that the fool's speech "enters into controversy."

[7]Zöckler, p. 167, takes *mitlahamîm* as "sporting words." He derives this from *lahâ,* "to play, sport." I feel the derivation discussed above is more likely.

9 He also that is slothful in his work is brother to him that is a great waster.
10 The name of the Lord is a strong tower: the righteous runneth into it, and is safe.
11 The rich man's wealth is his strong city, and as an high wall in his own conceit.
12 Before destruction the heart of man is haughty, and before honour is humility.

9 The word "waster" (*mašḥît*) is too weak. The verb *šaḥat* means "to destroy." By extension, the participle refers to "ruin" or "destruction." The strength of the word can be seen from its eschatological use in referring to Sheol, e.g., Psalm 16:10; 103:4. One who is lazy is a brother in spirit to one who destroys. Both of them have the same accomplishments, though, of course, the destroyer achieves his goal faster. The lazy man does not simply waste his opportunities. He destroys them since he can never regain lost time.

10-11 The phrase "name of the Lord" is here equivalent to the person of the Lord; cf. II Chronicles 6:7; Psalm 7:17; Isaiah 30:27. He is a "strong tower," a place of safety and defense. In times of crisis, then, the righteous person finds deliverance in the Lord, v. 10.

In contrast, the wealthy person relies on material riches. These are a "strong city," a refuge in which no one can touch him. Proverbs 18:11*a* repeats 10:15*a*. The word "conceit" (*maśkîtô*) is better "imagination." The word *maśkîtô* is "image, imagination, conceit," the context determining the sense. In his thoughts the rich man considers his wealth a "high wall," shielding him from all who would oppose him, v. 11.[8]

12 The contrast is between pride ("haughty," cf. *gəbah*, 16:5) and "humility" (cf. *ʿanâ*, 14:21). The man who lifts himself up in pride will be

Three Warnings
1. Warning against pride 1, 12
2. Warning against injustice 5
3. Warning against laziness 9

[8]AB, p. 112, emends *maśkîtô* to *massekatô*, from *sakak*, "to cover." He translates, "It shields him like a high wall." While this is supported by the early versions, it need not be adopted. The change is easily explained as a translator's attempt to understand 11*b*.

13 He that answereth a matter before he heareth it, it is folly and shame unto him.
14 The spirit of a man will sustain his infirmity; but a wounded spirit who can bear?
15 The heart of the prudent getteth knowledge; and the ear of the wise seeketh knowledge.

humbled with "destruction" (cf. *šabar,* 6:15) while the man who minimizes himself in humility will be lifted up with "honor" (*kabôd,* cf. 3:9). The verse expresses a principle that is generally true in life and, from an eternal perspective, always true.

13 Once more, Solomon addresses the theme of speech. A man who speaks without first considering all sides of an issue is foolish and will likely come to shame. It has often been noted that conversations often consist of two people who are talking and no one who is listening. How can you speak wisely without fully knowing the issue? Proverbs 15:2, 28, and 18:17 support this same theme.

14 This is one of several proverbs that note the influence of a man's emotions. Compare 12:25; 14:30; 15:13, 15; 17:22. Though illness or disease may afflict a man, his strong spirit enables him to bear the burden. In sharp contrast, who can bear a broken spirit? The rhetorical question requires a negative answer. There is an interesting play on words here. The first "spirit" is masculine and is intended to convey the idea of a strong, healthy spirit. The second "spirit" is feminine, conveying the thought of a delicate, weakened spirit.[9]

15 The word "heart" (*leb,* cf. 3:5) denotes man's mind, the seat of his understanding. A "prudent" (cf. *bîn,* 1:2) individual, a discerning person, is open to new sources of information. He considers new ideas and increases his knowledge as a result. The "ear of the wise" also represents the mind, the ear being the gate by which much information enters. The implication is clear. Man never knows everything. The wise man continually grows in his knowledge and understanding of matters.

---

[9]Jones, p. 161, misses the point of the alternating genders. He suggests that the first *rûaḥ* be omitted since "the usage of Proverbs is against two lines commencing with the same word." Aside from the fact that he is incorrect, e.g., 10:1; 16:16, 18; 18:12; 21:23, 30, he fails to deal with the change in gender between the two *rûaḥs.*

16 A man's gift maketh room for him, and bringeth him before great men.
17 He that is first in his own cause seemeth just; but his neighbour cometh and searcheth him.
18 The lot causeth contentions to cease, and parteth between the mighty.
19 A brother offended is harder to be won than a strong city: and their contentions are like the bars of a castle.

16 Solomon makes a practical observation on life. A gift to the right person can open doors of opportunity. This does not particularly refer to a bribe, although the thought includes that as well. Gifts are a way of expressing and maintaining good will, of cultivating a relationship that may well bring its reward later on.[10] The verse does not commend the practice. It simply notes the practice that has gone on through history.

17 Indirectly, this maxim argues for listening to both sides of an issue; cf. v. 13. In a controversy, the first to present his case (*rîb*, cf. 3:30) seems just. In 17*b*, the verb "searcheth" (*ḥaqar*) indicates a thorough and complete investigation. The idea is that one cross-examines the other and the matter is seen from a different perspective. The wise man hears all of the facts before making a judgment.

18 The casting of lots was an established way for determining God's will in obscure matters. See the comments at 16:33 for this practice. The word "mighty" (*ʿaṣûmîm*) denotes either physical strength or the power of position. Here, two "mighty men," men who are accustomed to forcing their wills upon others, have some conflict. To resolve the matter, the lot is cast and the dispute brought to an end.[11]

19 Literally, the Hebrew reads, "a brother who has been offended [or, who offends] is from a strong city, and contentions are like bars of a

---

[10]Toy, p. 363, notes that the practice of gifts to great men was common to the Greek period of Jewish history. The comment reflects his late date for the book and rejection of Solomonic authorship. In like manner, my feeling that the giving of gifts to influential men is common in all periods of history reflects my early date for the book and acceptance of Solomonic history. Plaut, p. 197, interprets the verse to mean that charitable giving gains public recognition of the giver, an idea that is certainly true but too restrictive for this verse.

[11]W. F. Albright, "The Copper Spatula of Byblos and Proverbs 19:19," *BASOR* 90:35-37 (see also his comments in *VTS* III, 10 and *JAOS* 67:159), has an interesting discussion of a bronze spatula from Byblos that apparently was used as a lot in settling a lawsuit between two parties. The inscription that is engraved on the spatula uses *našbît,* a cognate to "cease," *yašbît,* as it speaks of ending the dispute.

20 A man's belly shall be satisfied with the fruit of his mouth; and with the increase of his lips shall he be filled.

castle." The interpretation rests on deciding whether "offends" (*nipšaᶜ*, cf. 10:12) should be taken in a reflexive sense ("offends for himself") or in a passive sense ("has been offended"). Most commentaries and translations take the passive sense. In either case, a supplied verb connects the subject with the preposition preceding "strong city." Something like "an offended brother *is harder to be won* than a strong city" is appropriate. The thought is that this person has been separated from his friends through quarreling or some other sin against him. The friendship is broken, and to reach this one is compared to the conquest of a fortified citadel.[12]

The second half of the verse continues the thought: "and contentions are like the bars of a castle." The things that have come between the friends are like the bolts that secure the main entrance to a palace. Just as these are intended to keep the enemy out, so the contentions divide the friends from one another.

The practical application of the verse focuses on friendships. As Charles Bridges notes, "The thread once snapped is not easily joined." Friendships have great value. We must cultivate them, not abuse them. A broken friendship is almost impossible to restore to its former strength.

20 The phrase "fruit of his mouth" occurs elsewhere at 12:14 and 13:2, where it refers to good fruit. Here also it indicates the good fruit brought forth by a man's words. This brings an abiding satisfaction. The second half supports the idea that the fruit is that brought forth in the lives of others. It is an "increase" that comes as the result of his counsel and advice.[13]

---

[12]Lange, p. 168; French and Skinner, p. 58; and Conant, p. 89, all understand the verse as reflexive. Oesterley, p. 150, and Jones, pp. 162-63, follow the LXX in emending *nipšaᶜ* to *nôšaᶜ*, and translate, "a brother who helps is like a strong city." This, however, requires following the LXX in the second phrase: (a friend) "is as strong as a fortified palace." The fact that the first emendation requires the second (*mərûmîm* or *midwanîm*) suggests that this is not the right approach. Sense can be made from the MT. Samson Raphael Hirsch, *From the Wisdom of Mishlé* (1976) (hereafter cited as Hirsch), p. 190, relates the verse to an offended family member. While this might be included, the proverb is broader than this in its application.

[13]Among others, KD, *PC*, and Kufeldt relate the fruit to either good or bad results. Evil words, however, are apt to be destructive, to tear down rather than build up. The synonymous poetry of the section suggests that the fruit here is good fruit.

21 Death and life are in the power of the tongue: and they that love it
   shall eat the fruit thereof.
22 Whoso findeth a wife findeth a good thing, and obtaineth favour of
   the Lord.

21 The thought now broadens to include the possibility of evil fruit as
well as good fruit. The potential is stated poetically: "death and life are
in the hand of the tongue." The word "hand" (*yad*) often represents
"strength" or "power," e.g., Deuteronomy 32:36, Isaiah 59:1. It refers
here to the power of one's speech, able to bring about death or life according to whether its counsel is wicked or good. They who "love" (cf.
'ahab, 9:8) the tongue are those who enjoy using it. At every opportunity, they will give their opinion or offer advice to others.[14] The potential of the tongue is sobering, however, and it needs to be used with
great care. Compare Matthew 12:36 and James 3:5-8.

22 This is one of the most familiar of all the proverbs. Literally, 22*a*
says, "He finds a wife; he finds good." The AV correctly smooths this
out. The statement assumes that this is a "worthy woman"; cf. 31:10.
The man who has such a wife should thank the Lord for His gracious
provision.

Purely as a practical thought aside from the verse, this is the reason
that a young man should deliberately neglect the physical relationship
with a young woman in favor of the intellectual and spiritual relationships. The physical relationship is the least important of the three; however, in young people it often overshadows the other relationships.

Three Attractions Between a Man and a Woman

1. Physical—grows less important with age
2. Intellectual—normally grows in importance with age; note
   the number of adults who read news magazines and watch
   news programs on television
3. Spiritual—should grow in importance with age; note the age
   of most church leaders

---

[14]James G. Williams, "The Power of Form: A Study of Biblical Proverbs," *Semeia*,
17:53-54, relates the proverb to Eve offering fruit in the Garden of Eden, with the potential of offering the fruit of life or the fruit of death. This application of the proverb is too
narrow and loses sight of the practical application of the principle to life today.

23 The poor useth intreaties; but the rich answereth roughly.
24 A man that hath friends must shew himself friendly: and there is a
  friend that sticketh closer than a brother.

23 This statement is not particularly proverbial as we tend to think of proverbs. It is merely an observation on life. The poor man, because of his position of need, entreats the wealthy for assistance. The rich man, having been besieged by appeals from every side, answers "roughly" (ʿazzôt, cf. 7:13). The adverb "roughly" is "strong, mighty, fierce." This has the sense that the wealthy man is "curt," almost "rude," as he answers the plea of the poverty-stricken individual.

24 This is also one of the most familiar proverbs of the book. Unfortunately, because of the translation, it is also one of the most misunderstood of the proverbs. The first line literally reads, "A man of friends will come to ruin." The interpretation turns on understanding the word "ruin" (cf. raʿaʿ, 11:15). Since friendship does not normally cause harm to a person, obviously these must be unique friendships. The usual way of understanding the phrase is that this is a person who makes "*many* friends" and mistakenly relies upon these casual friendships. When he least can afford it, his friends let him down and he suffers harm as the result. The verse has been taken in many ways.[15]

The point of the proverb must be made in contrast with 24*b*, "there is a friend that sticketh closer than a brother." The contrast requires that the friend of 24*a* be one who does not stick closer than a brother, i.e., he is not reliable. The interpretation given above adequately supports this idea.

Verse 24*b* can have a messianic interpretation. Most probably, however, the sense is broader than this. In contrast with the unfaithful friend

---

[15]BDB, 950a, understands *hitroʿeaʿ* as from *raʿaʿ* II, "to break," and translates, "will be broken in pieces." Driver, Biblica 32:183-84, derives it from *ruaʿ*, "to shout," and translates, "a man of (many) friends (is a friend only) for chattering together." Gordon, *JBL* 49:408, notes that Rashi connected the word with *raʿ*, commenting, "Unto a man who makes friends will come a day when he needs them." Hulst, *OTTP,* p. 125, on the basis of ancient versions, suggests the reading *hitrâʿôt,* from *raʿâ,* with the sense "to feign friendships." He understands the text to mean "that there are 'so-called' friends who are not genuine, and to trust them can bring bitter disappointment." This also is the view of the RSV. Toy, pp. 365, 367, emends to *hitraʿot* and translates, "there are friends who only seek society," i.e., superficial friends. None of the emendations are compelling. The remaining variant interpretations are possible but I prefer the common view.

who will fail you in your need, there are those true friends who will prove to be reliable in your times of crisis. This view, of course, includes the messianic application.

Practical Applications from Proverbs 18

1. Warning against pride 1, 12
2. Contrast between the fool and the wise 2, 15
3. Character of the wicked 3
4. Comments on speech 4, 6, 7, 8, 13, 20, 21
5. Warning against injustice 5
6. Warning against laziness 9
7. Contrast between relying on God and relying on wealth 10, 11
8. Impact of the emotions 14
9. Influence of a gift 16
10. Seeing an issue from all sides 17
11. Casting lots 18
12. Comments on friendship 19, 24
13. Value of a good wife 22
14. Interaction between the poor and the rich 23

1 Better is the poor that walketh in his integrity, than he that is perverse in his lips, and is a fool.
2 Also, that the soul be without knowledge, it is not good; and he that hasteth with his feet sinneth.

PROVERBS 19

1 A poor man who lives his life with "integrity" (*tom,* cf. 2:7), though he has nothing of material value, is better than another man who is "perverse" (*ᶜiqqeš,* cf. 2:15) in his speech and is a moral fool (*kəsîl,* cf. 1:22). The proverb is very close to 28:6 but no compelling reason forces us to translate here as there.[1] While it is true that a righteous poor man is better than a perverse rich man, it is also true that a righteous poor man is better than a perverse poor man. Since the general statement of the MT has a broader application than the emended version, it is best to follow the MT.

2 As in 17:26, "also" (*gam*) gives emphasis to the statement.[2] The lack of knowledge is "not good." The "soul" (*nepeš,* cf. 7:23) represents a person with his normal vitality and desires. It does not have the sense of "zeal" or "drive." The context does not require this sense here (as at 23:2 or Eccles. 6:7).[3] It is not good for a person to lack practical knowledge (*daᶜat,* cf. 1:4).

A person who "hasteth with his feet" is one who acts without knowing his goal. He hurries into mindless activity with no clear end in mind. Such a person "sinneth" (*ḥoṭeʾ,* cf. 1:10), too strong an expression. The idea is rather that he "misses the mark."

---

[1]Toy, p. 368, emends *kəsîl* to *ᶜošer* on the basis that the parallelism requires the contrast between the poor and the rich individuals. AB, Greenstone, and Martin also follow this approach. An interpretation that is read into the text does not justify the emendation. KD II, 19, does not emend but interprets the one speaking perversely as a rich man who looks down on the poor. While this is possible, the verse does not require it.

[2]Oesterley, p. 153, calls *gam* a scribal addition and omits or emends it. Toy, p. 373, emends to *ᶜaśâ* or *ᶜaśat,* "to act." Neither change is justified. Cohen, p. 124, understands *gam* as introducing an argument from the lesser to the greater, i.e., if 2*a* is true, how much more so is 2*b*. This, however, would be a unique use of the particle.

[3]Perowne, p. 127; Whybray, p. 107; and WBC, 22, 142, interpret *nepeš* as desire. Marvin E. Tate Jr., "Proverbs," in *The Broadman Bible Commentary,* ed. Clifton J. Allen (1971) (hereafter cited as Tate), understands it as "zeal." AB, p. 117, and *EBC,* p. 1030, also interpret it this way. Not only does the use of *nepeš* elsewhere in Proverbs argue against this view, but also the use here of *daᶜat,* "experiential knowledge," does not agree with this sense.

3 The foolishness of man perverteth his way: and his heart fretteth against the Lord.
4 Wealth maketh many friends; but the poor is separated from his neighbour.
5 A false witness shall not be unpunished, and he that speaketh lies shall not escape.

3 A man's "foolishness" (cf. *ɔwîl,* 1:7) causes his way of life to go askew (cf. *selep,* 11:3). The last half of the verse requires that we understand "foolishness" here as moral foolishness, an ungodly attitude. When things go wrong in life, this person "fretteth" (*yizˤap*) against God. The word *zaˤap* is a strong word meaning "to storm, rage." Elsewhere, it portrays the turbulence in a man's heart (Gen. 40:6; II Chron. 26:19; Isa. 30:30). The idea of "fretting" is too gentle here; the thought is more that he "rages" against God, blaming his woes on Him.

4 Solomon makes another practical observation on life. The possession of wealth (*hôn,* cf. 3:9) attracts many "friends." Conversely, the "poor" (*dal,* cf. 14:31) finds that his "neighbour" (*reaˤ,* cf. 6:1, translated as "friends" in 4*a*, better translated here as "friend") distances himself, finding his poverty distasteful. Clearly, the "friends" of the verse are not real friends. They are those who respond to the prospect of material gain, pleasure, or the prestige of association.

5 The aphorism warns against perjury. The "false witness" is one who perverts the truth in giving testimony. When caught, and the verse

---

Punishment for Sin

The phrase "shall not go unpunished" (*loɔ-yinnaqeh*) occurs seven times in the book. The cumulative teaching is that you cannot get away with sin. God will punish those who break His commands!

1. The practice of adultery, 6:29
2. The rebellion of the wicked, 11:21
3. The manifestation of pride, 16:5
4. The joy over another's trials, 17:5
5. The act of perjury, 19:5, 9
6. The attitude of greed, 28:20

---

6 *Many will intreat the favour of the prince: and every man is a friend to him that giveth gifts.*

7 *All the brethren of the poor do hate him: how much more do his friends go far from him? he pursueth them with words, yet they are wanting to him.*

assumes this, he will not go "unpunished" (*lo> yinnaqeh,* cf. 6:29). He will not "escape" (*malat,* cf. 11:21), implying a divine judgment upon his wicked actions. Verse 9 of this chapter almost identically repeats the maxim.

6 We return to the thought of 4*a*, that there are those who are attracted by wealth. The phrase "intreat the favour" is literally "rub the face." This is a metaphorical picture of caressing the face in the attempt to cultivate a feeling of good will. The "prince" (*nadîb,* cf. 17:26) is here a liberal person, one willing to bestow his gifts and favor upon others.[4] Everyone is a "friend" to this kind of person, hoping thereby to receive personal gain. The idea of "friend" is again that of a sycophant, a self-seeking individual.

7 The statement of 7*a-b* repeats the thought of 4*b*, that the poor have difficulty in keeping friends. The word "brother" (*>ah*) denotes a blood relative, not just a brother but any relative. Even these "hate" (*śana>,* cf. 11:15), find it difficult to put up with, their relative who is poverty-stricken (cf. *ra>š,* 10:4). If his own family will not help him, how much more difficult is it for a "friend" to stand by him?

The phrase in 7*c* is literally "he who pursues words, not they." Something must be read into the phrase to make sense of it, and one person's guess is as good as another's, so long as the attempt is made to remain close to the MT. Something like "he pursues *them with* words, *but* they are *gone*" probably captures the idea. In others words, the poor man entreats his friends and relatives in vain. They reject his pleas for help.[5]

---

[4]Martin, p. 117, renders *nadîb* "prince," then concludes that the verse suggests the "atmosphere of the courts of the Greek period." This, of course, reflects his bias that the book was edited late, in the intertestamental period. It is, however, true that generosity has always attracted people who seek self-gain. Whether this is a prince or a liberal person, the principle is generally true.

[5]Toy, p. 370, rejects the phrase with the statement "The line appears to be the corrupt remnant of a lost couplet, but it is hardly possible, with our present means of informa

*8 He that getteth wisdom loveth his own soul: he that keepeth under-
standing shall find good.
9 A false witness shall not be unpunished, and he that speaketh lies
shall perish.
10 Delight is not seemly for a fool; much less for a servant to have rule
over princes.*

8 The phrase "he that getteth wisdom" is more literally "he who acquires heart" (*leb,* cf. 3:5). The parallelism with 8*b* shows that *leb* has a
mental sense here. One who has this delight in wisdom brings great
benefit to himself. His love for understanding shows love for himself.
He will gain the truly important things that life offers: peace, satisfaction, direction, and so forth. The parallel phrase in 8*b* restates the same
thought.

9 The verse is almost identical to v. 5. The only new thought occurs in
9*b*. It says there that the one who perjures himself will "perish" (cf.
ʾabad, 1:32). This may be a prediction of divine judgment upon one who
lies.

10 "Delight," *taʿanûg,* is from *ʿanog,* "to be soft, delicate." From this
comes the noun "daintiness, luxury." "Delight" therefore here is better
rendered "luxury." We would not expect to find a fool enjoying such a
rich atmosphere.[6] This picture serves as an emblem upon which the conclusion of 10*b* rests. If it is not fitting that a fool should indulge himself
with dainty living, it is even more unthinkable that a slave should rule
over princes. Compare 30:21-22. There is a natural order that should be

---

tion, to recover the original form." AB, pp. 115, 117, emends radically and translates,
"When he follows them they speak angrily to him," thereby paralleling 7*b* and 7*c* as
"different forms of the same saying." Coates, p. 78, assumes the phrase to be the "second half of a proverb, the first clause of which has been lost." The LXX conjectures,
"He who does much harm perfects harm; and he who uses provoking words shall not be
delivered." The NEB follows this: "Practice in evil makes the perfect scoundrel; the man
who talks too much meets his desserts." These treatments illustrate the variety in interpretations.

[6]D. Winton Thomas, "Notes on Some Passages in the Book of Proverbs," *JTS* 38:400-
401, derives *taʿanûg* from *ʿanog* II, related to an Arabic cognate "to draw, pull," thus "to
rule, manage." This parallels 10*b* more exactly. It is unlikely that we should explain the
phrase on the basis of a word that occurs nowhere else in Scripture.

*11 The discretion of a man deferreth his anger; and it is his glory to
pass over a transgression.
12 The king's wrath is as the roaring of a lion; but his favour is as dew
upon the grass.*

followed in life. We do not expect to encounter such violent exceptions
to this rule of life.

Absurdities in Proverbs

1. Social upheaval, 19:10
2. Undeserved honor, 26:1
3. Unexpected marriage and inheritance, 30:21-23
4. Indiscreet women, 11:22
5. False speech, 17:7

---

11 An individual's "discretion" (cf. *śakal*, 1:3) will lead him to restrain
his anger.[7] He understands that an angry reaction to a bad situation will
make it only worse. The word "glory" (*paʾar*, cf. 17:6) often occurs with
God as the subject. It is also used, as here, with a good sense of "boast-
ing." The individual considers it his "glory" to pass over some transgression committed against him. Compare 10:12*b*.

12 The king of a land is the ultimate source of both favor and punishment. Using a double word picture, Solomon illustrates this idea. The
wrath of the king is like the "roar" (*naham,* cf. 5:11) of a "lion" (*kəpîr,*
better "young lion"). The word *naham* is "growl, groan." Since the
growl of a lion may signal his intention to spring upon a victim, this is
an apt comparison, the king's anger signaling his intention to pronounce
some judgment. On the other hand, the king's favor is like the morning
dew, refreshing the "grass" (*ʿeśeb,* normally refers to "plants") each day.
Compare 16:14-15.

---

[7]Toy, p. 373, and Greenstone, p. 204, repoint the perfect *heʾərîk* to the infinitive
haʾərîk, understanding the verse to say that it is wise to restrain wrath rather than wisdom restrains wrath. While the difference is slight, there is no valid reason for departing
from the MT.

*13 A foolish son is the calamity of his father: and the contentions of a
wife are a continual dropping.*
*14 House and riches are the inheritance of fathers: and a prudent wife
is from the Lord.*
*15 Slothfulness casteth into a deep sleep; and an idle soul shall suffer
hunger.*

13 The proverb parallels two sources of disharmony in the home. The
word *hawwot,* cf. 11:6, indicates the result of one who falls into some
disaster.[8] So the foolish actions of the child bring his parents to this end.
The plural *hawwot* indicates that the child brings his parents into a series of calamities. The verse does not define the nature of these difficulties. We may generalize the destruction to include all of the problems
that come from a foolish child.

Similarly, a contentious wife brings multiplied grief to the home. This
is the first of six passages in the book that focus on this weakness of
character of the unworthy wife.[9] Contentiousness is the primary difficulty with a bad wife. She should bring harmony to the home. By failing in this, she introduces a contentious spirit that can destroy the home.
Her contentions are like the dripping of rain from the roof of a house.
The point of similarity in the metaphor is that her vexations repeat
themselves. Like the repetitive drops of rain, which fall one after another from the roof of a house, so the wife's contentions occur with an-
noying frequency.

14 A good wife is one of God's choicest gifts; cf. 18:22. It is certainly
fitting to have an attitude of praise and thankfulness to the Lord who
has given such a wife. One may acquire material wealth from an inheritance. But a "prudent" (cf. *sakal,* 1:3) wife, one with common sense,
comes from God.[10]

15 "Slothfulness" (cf. *ʿaṣel,* 6:6) puts a man into a "deep sleep" (cf.
radam, 10:5). We might say that slothfulness gives birth to more slothfulness. This is an unending cycle that eventually consumes a man with

---

[8]Guillaume, *JRAS* (1942), 111-15, argues for the meaning "binding curse" and attempts to prove the existence of sorcery and magic in Israel. The idea does not fit here.
[9]See also 21:9, 19; 25:24; 27:15-16; 30:21-23.
[10]McKane, p. 535, states that the choice of a wife "is a chancy business and that there
are no assured means of knowing beforehand how it is all going to work out." He concludes that no man would want to take the credit for a successful marriage. If it works

16 He that keepeth the commandment keepeth his own soul; but he that despiseth his ways shall die.

its poison.[11] It is only natural that the idle person will suffer hunger. His lazy efforts do not produce enough food to supply his needs.

16 The "commandment" (*miṣwâ*, cf. 3:1) is probably the commandment of God as mediated to the youth through his parents. One who guards this carefully, at the same time guards himself. In sharp contrast, a person who "despiseth" (cf. *bûz*, 1:7) his ways, i.e., treats the ways of morality with contempt, practicing unrestrained wickedness, will "die" (*yawmut*). The word *mût* refers to death in all of its forms, by natural means or by execution.

There are several questions here. Does the word "commandment" refer to God's commands (so most commentators), to the law of God (Aitken), or to general precepts regarding morality (Alden)? On the basis of the punishment stated in 16*b*, *yawmut,* "he will be put to death," implying a divine judgment, I refer this to God's will, most likely expressed through the parents.

What does it mean to "despise one's ways"? The awkwardness of treating one's own ways with contempt has led to several treatments of the phrase.[12] Treating oneself with contempt is not rare. Many do this regularly. A young man who regards his lifestyle with no more respect than to let himself indulge in evil practices certainly despises his own ways.

---

out, "he is inclined to believe that a higher wisdom had a hand in the match." This approach denies the doctrine of theodicy, i.e., that God guides His children through this evil world. A godly man and a godly woman who continually seek the blessing of God upon their marriage can have confidence in the success of their marriage relationship.

[11]Dahood, *PNWSP,* p. 40, argues from a Ugaritic parallel that *tardemâ* indicates rather a "place of sleep," i.e., a bedroom. Thus, slothfulness "will collapse a bedroom," picturing the barren results of inactivity. The word *radam,* however, is well established with the meaning of "deep sleep." This fits in well with the context here.

[12]On the basis of 13:13, Coates, Martin, Toy, and others propose to read *dabar,* "word," for *dərakayw,* "his ways." Dahood, *PNWSP,* p. 40, appeals to Ugaritic to find the meaning "dominion, authority" for *derek.* He translates, "despises His authority," i.e., the authority of God. This is unlikely in view of the lack of an antecedent referring to God. Van der Wieden, p. 131, follows Dahood. Emerton, *JTS* 20:206-9, takes the *waw* from *dərakayw* as a confusion for *yod,* an abbreviation for *yhwh.* He emends to *darkê yhwh* and

17 He that hath pity upon the poor lendeth unto the Lord; and that which he hath given will he pay him again.
18 Chasten thy son while there is hope, and let not thy soul spare for his crying.

Finally, should we adopt the *qərê yamût,* "shall die," or the *kətîb yawmut,* "shall be put to death"? Most translations adopt the *qərê* while commentators split on the decision. I follow the MT since it is sensible in the context. The phrase likely refers to premature death by way of divine judgment.

17 He who shows "pity" (cf. *ḥanan,* 14:21), better rendered "compassion," to the poverty-stricken individual (*dal,* cf. 14:31) places God in his debt. The idea is that God rewards such charitable actions. Until the reward is given in eternity, there is an unfulfilled debt owed by God. The proverb does not urge charity just for the sake of divine reward. It simply takes note of the fact that such a reward exists.

18 We must translate 18*b* something like "do not desire his death."[13] Parental neglect of proper discipline harms the child. The exhortation implies that the lack of discipline will cause a child to die prematurely. Compare 23:13. Verse 18*b* antithetically parallels 18*a*: discipline the child while hope remains for his correction, rather than bringing about his death by giving up on early discipline.

---

translates, "he that despises the ways of Yahwe shall die." While these approaches are fine exercises in academia, the results do not improve the MT.

[13]The Hebrew of 18*b* is idiomatic. The rendering of the AV cannot be upheld: "let not thy soul spare for his crying." More literally, the MT reads, "and to his death do not lift up your soul." KD II, 30, makes this refer to a parent who seeks revenge upon his child for violating parental standards. The verse cautions the parent not to turn correction into revenge. Cohen, p. 128, takes the idiom of lifting up the soul as an expression of despair, as though the parent despairs that the rebellious child will one day be put to death because of the ineffectiveness of the parent's discipline. Power, p. 136, takes the phrase as a warning against excessive chastisement since parental abuse can seriously harm the child. I have adopted the above position based on the following reasoning. The *hipʿîl* of *mût* occurs in Proverbs only here and in 21:25, where it means premature death. Outside of the poetical books, *mût* frequently refers to the putting of a person to death by some form of capital punishment, e.g., II Chron. 25:4; Jer. 26:15. The conclusion that it refers to premature death here, whether by means of God's judgment or by legal sentence, thus rests upon some evidence. The consideration that 23:13 parallels this sense also sustains the interpretation. Thomas, *VTS* III, 288, unnecessarily softens the force of *mût* by giving to it the meaning "to chastise him excessively." The *hipʿîl* of *mût* regularly refers to capital punishment or other forms of violent death.

19 A man of great wrath shall suffer punishment: for if thou deliver him,
yet thou must do it again.

This teaching regarding discipline answers the objection of some that
corporal punishment harms the child. This is false. Rather than discipline causing harm, it is the lack of discipline that harms the child.[14]

There is a time in the child's life during which his parents may mold
and shape his character and conduct into that which pleases them. The
use of the particle *yeš* ("there is") in the verse teaches that such a period
of time actually exists. That time is undoubtedly the younger years before his habit patterns of behavior become established. Parents who use
this period wisely will reap a harvest of personal satisfaction as their
child develops self-discipline.

The fact that this period exists suggests that a time will come when the
child will no longer receive training readily. The soft, pliable nature of
youth will be replaced with harder habit patterns of behavior that parents can change only with great difficulty. To take advantage of the period of time in which their child can be shaped easily, parents must
begin early in life to work toward producing desirable conduct.

To fail to do this gives the child time to develop undesirable behavior
patterns. His sinful nature leads him into ways that go contrary to the
godly ways of biblical wisdom. If these undesirable patterns develop
into established character traits, the parents may never be able to reori-
ent their child into acceptable patterns of personal behavior.

19 The *qərê gədal . . . ,* "great," followed by the AV, NASB, NIV, and
most versions is best here. The *kətîb gəral . . . ,* "portion," makes no
sense. A man with "great temper," i.e., a hot-tempered individual, must
bear his "punishment" (better "pay his fine," *ʿoneš,* cf. 17:26). If you, as
an influential person or someone willing to pay the fine in his place,
spare him by intervening, "thou must do it again." This last phrase is
subject to two interpretations. In the first place, his great temper shows
that he is incorrigible. Your kindness will have to be repeated (so

---

[14]Most authors who inveigh against corporal punishment cite studies concerned with
child abuse. This is no warrant, however, for concluding that all corporal punishment is
bad. It is the extreme in punishment that is harmful, an extreme in giving it as well as an
extreme in withholding it. The biblical requirement that discipline expresses the love of
the parents (13:24) rules out the use of excessive force. Any form of parental punishment must be reasonable as well as firm.

*20 Hear counsel, and receive instruction, that thou mayest be wise in
thy latter end.
21 There are many devices in a man's heart; nevertheless the counsel of
the Lord, that shall stand.
22 The desire of a man is his kindness: and a poor man is better than a
liar.*

Muenscher, Perowne, Phillott, Kidner). Another possible sense under-
stands the phrase as a warning. Your intervention will aggravate the
angry man, spurring him on to even greater anger (so McKane, *PC,*
KD). I lean toward this second view as explaining the text better. The
Hebrew gives something like "if you deliver him, you will add more."
This suggests that the charitable action increases the man's anger.

20 With words that remind us of c. 1-9, the maxim exhorts us to receive "counsel" (ᶜeṣâ, cf. 1:30) and "instruction" (mûsar, cf. 1:2) in
order that we may become "wise" (cf. ḥokmâ, 1:2). This willingness to
accept advice, to respond to reproof and correction, is a basic mark of
the wise man. Over and over again, wisdom exhorts the young man to
receive this guidance, e.g., 4:13; 8:33; 9:9. The wise person is teachable.
He grows in wisdom by responding to the insights and perceptions of
others.

21 The "devices" (maḥašabôt, cf. 6:18) of the man's heart are his
"plans," the many ideas and goals that course through his mind. These
are often ill-founded, sometimes at cross purposes with one another, and
perhaps shortsighted. As a result, the plans are normally transitory. In
contrast with this, the "counsel [cf. ᶜeṣâ, 1:30] of the Lord," i.e., those
plans that come from the Lord and thus belong to Him, shall "stand"
(cf. qûm, 15:22), established by the power of God.

22 Rendered literally, 22a says, "The desire of a man is his loyalty."
"Desire" (taᵊawat, cf. 10:24) refers to the inner cravings of a person.
One of those desires is that he should find "kindness" (ḥasdô, cf. 2:8),
better rendered "loyalty." This leads to the logical conclusion that it is
better to be poverty-stricken (cf. raᵊš, 10:4) than to be disloyal and untrustworthy, "a man of lies."[15]

---

[15]The phrasing of the MT has led to various attempts to understand the maxim.
Dahood, *PNWSP*, p. 42, relates taᵊawat to an Arabic cognate meaning "to dwell, lodge"
and derives the meaning of "ease, inactivity" for the noun. He then understands ḥasdô
from ḥesed II (cf. 14:34) and translates, "A man's inactivity is his reproach." While the
explanation is technically correct, it is unlikely that the correct sense is to be found in

23 The fear of the Lord tendeth to life: and he that hath it shall abide satisfied; he shall not be visited with evil.
24 A slothful man hideth his hand in his bosom, and will not so much as bring it to his mouth again.

23 The "fear of the Lord" is a familiar topic in the book.[16] As elsewhere (10:27; 14:27; 22:4), a right relationship to the Lord gives a fullness of life. Verse 23*b* is better translated "he shall spend the night satisfied, not visited with evil." The picture is of a man who is so at peace with God that he can sleep soundly, free from worries or other cares. He is able to enjoy life with no concern that calamity will overtake him.[17]

24 The same proverb occurs in a different form in 26:15, with the first halves identical and the second halves using different vocabulary and word order to express the same thought. The picture is clearly one of hyperbole. The sluggard (ʿaṣel, cf. 6:6) "hides" (or "buries," ṭaman, cf. 2:4) his hand in his "bosom" (ṣalaḥ). The word ṣalaḥ is cognate to Syriac and Aramaic words meaning "to scoop out, hollow out." The idea thus is of something hollowed out. The context here requires "dish" or "bowl." Having placed his hand in the dish, the customary way of eating in biblical times, the slothful person falls asleep, leaving it there and not bringing the food to his mouth.[18]

---

little-used and obscure meanings of the key words. Greenstone, p. 208, adopts the meaning of ḥesed II, "lust" or "greed." This is possible but it fails to parallel 22*b*. McKane, p. 532, follows the LXX and emends taʾăwat to təbuʾat, "productivity." He translates, "A man's productivity is his loyalty," as if a man's productivity should be based on the subjective standard of a man's attitude rather than his ability to assist. This is hardly less awkward than the MT. AB, p. 116, without support, emends ḥasdô to ḥosnô and translates, "It is human to desire gain."

[16]See 1:7, 29; 2:5; 3:7; 8:13; 9:10; 10:27; 14:26, 27; 15:16, 33; 16:6; 19:23; 22:4; 23:17; 24:21.

[17]Dahood, p. 41, makes the *bal* a positive force, "but he who sleeps to satiety will surely be visited by calamity." The word *bal*, however, is normally negative, often appearing in poetical contexts. Toy, p. 382, radically emends *šbʿ ylyn*, "shall abide satisfied," to *šbr ʿlyn* and translates, "who hopes in him." There is no support for this suggestion. The unusual phrasing does not justify the change in the MT.

[18]Toy, p. 380, rejects *ṭaman* as "hardly appropriate" and suggests *ṭabal*, "to dip," in its place. This adds nothing to the understanding of the verse and has no textual support.

25 Smite a scorner, and the simple will beware: and reprove one that
hath understanding, and he will understand knowledge.
26 He that wasteth his father, and chaseth away his mother, is a son that
causeth shame, and bringeth reproach.

25 The "scorner" (*leṣ,* cf. 1:22) will not learn from correction, 13:1;
15:12. Nevertheless, he should be punished since the correction will
help the "simple" (*petî,* cf. 1:22) learn. If a wise man is corrected, he
will benefit from the rebuke. He will learn that which will help him be
more consistent in his behavior and more discerning in his thinking. The
verse is very close in thought to 21:11.

26 This son "wasteth" (or "attacks," cf. *šadad,* 11:3) his parents. After
repeated encounters, he drives his parents away (*yabrîaḥ,* "to flee," is the
hipᶜîl of *baraḥ,* causative, "to drive away"), leaving them to fend for
themselves.[19] This wicked conduct of the child violates the spirit of
family obligations even though it may not break the law. Because his
conduct is contrary to the normal responsibility that a child bears toward
his parents, it reveals his shameful conduct. He shows no gratitude toward his parents for the sacrifices that they have made for him. He
brings "shame" and "reproach" upon himself.[20]

---

[19]The MT generalizes the situation without relating the experience to a particular life
setting. This has led some to restrict the verse in the effort of clarifying it. Oesterley,
p. 163, concludes that the verse describes a situation in which a son's aged parents depend upon him. He spurns his family obligations and fails to care for them. Thomas,
VTS III, 289, relates *məšadded* to an Ethiopian cognate *sadada,* "to expel." He makes the
word parallel to *yabrîaḥ* and sees the son as forcibly evicting his parents from their
home. Coates also follows this view. G. R. Driver, "Proverbs xix.26," *TZ* 11:373-74, explains *məšadded* from the Arabic *sadda,* "to silence." He further relates *yabrîaḥ* to Arabic
barraha, "to afflict." The sense is something like "He who silences his father distresses
his mother (like) a son who shames and disgraces his parents." These attempts to explain
the verse undoubtedly relate to the true situation. Yet, there is no reason to limit the application to a specific situation. A son who attacks his parents *in any way* shames and
disgraces himself.

[20]Both "shame" (*mebîš*) and "reproach" (or "disgrace," *maḥpîr*) are in the *hipᶜîl* theme.
This raises the question of whether the son causes his parents to be shamed or whether
he brings shame upon himself. Henry, III, 902, understands the first, that the son causes
his parents to bear shame as a consequence of their son's actions. This is possible. The
hipᶜîl, however, regularly expresses a condition of being in which the biblical writer sets
forth a condition periphrastically. It more often is inwardly intensive, especially when
there is no object of the verb expressed. In this case, the statement of the son's shame
and disgrace perfectly accords with the natural use of the verb in this theme.

27 Cease, my son, to hear the instruction that causeth to err from the words of knowledge.

27 Solomon gives a strong warning to his son. He should not turn aside from the instruction given by his parents. Children often listen carelessly to advice. They fail to consider the long-range implications of their conduct. They act without embracing the guidance that has been given them. Not only is this disobedience but also their actions cause them to turn aside from the path of true wisdom.

The translation "instruction that causeth to err" cannot be correct. It requires the "instruction" (*mûsar*, cf. 1:2) to be evil instruction that turns a young person away from the words of knowledge. In Proverbs, however, *mûsar* always has a desirable sense. It indicates the instruction that comes from a child's parents or from God Himself. Since it is natural to so understand *mûsar* here, there is no need for the supplied words. Adding the word "only" at the head of the second clause makes the sense clearer: "Cease hearing instruction, my son, *only* to go astray from the words of knowledge."[21]

The child thus has clear guidance as to his responsibility in the parent-child relationship. What the parents advise, the young person should accept. He should never receive parental guidance carelessly, with the

---

[21]The grammatical structure of the verse is important. The imperative *ḥadal* often takes an infinitive as its object with an attached *l*-preposition. The infinitive serves as the governing verb. Further, the infinitive construct with the *l*-prefix frequently introduces the purpose of an action. The construction of the verse thus supports the literal translation: "Cease hearing instruction, my son, to go astray from the words of knowledge." Other approaches to the verse have also been adopted. Toy, pp. 380-82, emends the text radically to read, "He who ceases to listen to instruction will wander from words of knowledge." Power, p. 138, follows a suggestion made by Hitzig and emends *smʾ* to *sms,* "to neglect." He then translates, "Cease, my son, to neglect instruction and stray not from the words of knowledge." Driver, *Biblica* 32:196, understands the *l*-preposition in the sense "is likely to." He changes the vowel pointing of several words and understands the verse to say that a son who stops hearing instruction is "likely to go astray from words of knowledge." Even though these views make good sense, there is no need to leave the MT here since it is sensible. McKane, p. 525, considers the verse as ironical, saying the exact opposite of what it means, in order to teach that neglect of the truth will result in serious consequences. The view is possible but it requires the reader to use the poetical device in order to understand the verse. Jim Alvin Sanders, "Suffering As a Divine Discipline in the Old Testament and Post-Biblical Judaism," *Colgate Rochester Divinity School Bulletin*, 28:37, reads the infinitive construct *hdl* as a *nomen verbale* (cf. G.K. 114a). He translates, "To cease, my son, to heed *mûsar* is to wander from the words of knowledge." Again, the view is possible but this is a rare use of the infinitive construct.

*28 An ungodly witness scorneth judgment: and the mouth of the wicked
devoureth iniquity.*
*29 Judgments are prepared for scorners, and stripes for the back of
fools.*

intention of choosing for himself whether he plans to follow it. The
verse strongly warns against this attitude.

28 The "ungodly" (bəlîyaʿal, cf. 6:12) witness is a "worthless witness,"
one whose testimony may be impugned. By his willingness to perjure
himself, he makes a mockery of justice. Verse 28*b* extends this thought
by noting that the "mouth of the wicked," the evil speech of the wicked
man, "devoureth iniquity." This is poetical, expressing the idea that the
wicked individual feasts upon evil (ʾawen, cf. 6:12). Verse 28*a* has a
forensic sense here, that the wicked person delights in perverting truth
in order to hurt the innocent.[22]

29 One who scorns the customs and laws of society will eventually
suffer judgment. This most likely refers to the justice of the court system, which will punish the scorner (leṣ, cf. 1:22).[23] One specific instance of this is the flogging of a foolish individual (kəsîlîm, cf. 1:22).
"Stripes" suggests the court-ordered punishment of this one who disregards the demands of society.

---

[22]Richardson, *VT* 5:165-66, follows Toy, Gemser, and others in emending yəballaʿ to
yabbîaʿ. This gives it the sense "to talk freely." The emendation is unnecessary. McKane,
p. 529, follows Driver in relating balaʿ to an Arabic cognate "to express." He translates,
"The mouths of wicked men enunciate evil," possible but requiring balaʿ to take a rare
sense.

[23]Among others, AB, Toy, Martin, and Greenstone follow the LXX and emend "judgments," šəpaṭîm, to šəbaṭîm, "rods," to improve the parallelism, an unnecessary change.
Dahood, *PNWSP*, p. 43, defends the MT but then explains šəpaṭîm as a dialectical form
chosen to create a pun on mišpaṭ of the preceding verse. He translates, "rods." This is
unlikely since the verses have no connection. KD II, 38, restricts šəpaṭîm to "the judgments of God, even although they are inflicted by human instrumentality." The restriction is not needed.

Practical Applications from Proverbs 19

1. Wealth and poverty 4, 6, 7
2. Comparison of righteous and unrighteous actions
   a. Righteous actions
      (1) Permanence of divine standards 21
      (2) Desirability of righteous actions 1, 16
   b. Unrighteous actions
      (1) Danger of immoral conduct 3
      (2) Punishment of those who scorn society 29
      (3) Value of punishment 25
3. Danger of lacking knowledge 2
4. Perjured testimony 5, 9, 28
5. Benefits of wisdom 8, 20 (negatively, warning against ignoring instruction, 27)
6. Natural order of life 10
7. Need for self-control 11 (negatively, punishment of anger, 19)
8. Power of the king 12
9. Family relationships 13, 14, 18, 26
10. Laziness 15, 24
11. A divine view of charity 17
12. Need for loyalty 22
13. Fear of the Lord 23

1 Wine is a mocker, strong drink is raging: and whosoever is deceived thereby is not wise.

2 The fear of a king is as the roaring of a lion: whoso provoketh him to anger sinneth against his own soul.

PROVERBS 20

1 "Wine" is the familiar *yayin;* cf. 9:5. Although fermented, the alcoholic content was minimal due to the ancient custom of mixing wine with water to reduce the likelihood of drunkenness. Still, uncut wine had the potential to produce drunkenness and a corresponding loss of control. Thus, "wine is a mocker" (*leṣ*, cf. 1:22), causing the drunkard to scorn things that are holy and decent.[1]

In like manner, "strong drink [*šekar*] is raging." The word *šekar* normally appears in conjunction with *yayin*. In light of the fact that distilled spirits with high alcoholic content were not discovered until the Middle Ages, it is not appropriate to identify *šekar* as whiskey or similar "strong drink." It is rather a grain or fruit wine, prepared from something other than grapes. As with *yayin,* it also had the potential to produce drunkenness. When under the influence of *šekar,* one was apt to become "raging" (or "boisterous," cf. *homâ,* 1:21). One who is "deceived thereby" (or "one who errs in them," *šagâ,* cf. 5:19) is not wise. Putting it bluntly, the drunkard is a fool. By letting the alcohol control him, he loses the self-control that allows him to move wisely in society.

2 The first phrase is similar to 19:12, excepting that "wrath," *zaʿap,* there is replaced by "fear," *ʾêmat,* here.[2] The word *ʾêmat* is strong, denoting "dread, fear, horror." The king can cause fear as he threatens or takes actual punitive steps. One who is the target of his power may well become as paralyzed with fear as if he had suddenly been confronted with the "roaring" (or "growling," *naham,* cf. 5:11) of an irritated young lion (*kəpîr,* cf. 19:12). The word "provoketh" is from *ʿabar* (cf. 11:4), "to go over, cross over." This occurs here in the sense of going beyond

---

[1]Rylaarsdam, p. 70, argues that wine mocks the "overindulgent user." This is a possible interpretation, but I feel that the parallelism with *homeh* better supports the view that the drunkard becomes a mocker.

[2]Frankenberg, p. 115, suggests *ḥemat,* "wrath," for *ʾêmat,* on the basis of the parallel in 19:12. Power, p. 138, accepts this change. It is not right, however, to forbid the biblical writers the free variation in vocabulary that is common to all authors.

3 It is an honour for a man to cease from strife: but every fool will be meddling.
4 The sluggard will not plow by reason of the cold; therefore shall he beg in harvest, and have nothing.

the boundaries of the king's will, thus provoking him. One who provokes the king "sinneth against his own soul." This is not to be taken in a spiritual sense, as of actual sin, but as of one who wrongs his "soul" himself.[3] The king punishes him for his actions.

3 It is honorable for a man to avoid strife. The phrase "cease from" is better to "remain apart from" (*šebet*). The root *yašab*, "to dwell, remain," joined here with the partitive *min*, indicates complete separation from strife. The wise man does not become entangled with the petty grievances that often characterize life. This is not to say that a godly man will avoid a matter when a spiritual principle is involved. Ample evidence from Scripture shows that God's people should vigorously defend the faith of Christianity. The godly man will not, however, become involved with the many neutral matters that give ground for quarreling and irritation. In contrast, the foolish man "will be meddling" (cf. *galaʿ*, 17:14). His lack of self-control leads him to focus on matters that would be best forgotten.

4 The lazy man wants to enjoy an abundant harvest, but he is not willing to work for it. He will not prepare the fields "by reason of the cold" (*ḥorep*). The word *ḥorep* is better "autumn" or "harvest" rather than "cold." This is the time when farmers in Palestine plow the fields and sow the seed. When harvest time comes, he will "beg [*šaʾal*] in harvest, and have nothing." The verb *šaʾal* means "to ask." Here it should be taken in a weakened sense, "to seek, desire." The idea is that he looks for the harvest, hoping to have a good crop, but instead he receives nothing.[4]

---

[3]Without support, Toy, p. 387, and Oesterley, p. 165, emend "sinneth," *ḥoteʾ*, to "angers," *ḥomes*. The MT, however, is sensible here and does not need the change.

[4]KD II, 41, and *PC*, p. 383, refer the verse to an indolent landowner who fails to have his laborers prepare the field. He asks about the harvest only to find that there has been none. This seems too narrow an interpretation to me although, of course, it is possible. Among others, Greenstone, p. 212, and Muenscher, p. 192, translate *šaʾal* as "beg," the lazy man being forced to seek help from his industrious neighbors. Once again, the interpretation is possible. The Jewish law, however, provided for charitable giving to help those in need; hence, it is unlikely that this person would have "nothing."

*5 Counsel in the heart of man is like deep water; but a man of under-
standing will draw it out.*
*6 Most men will proclaim every one his own goodness: but a faithful
man who can find?*
*7 The just man walketh in his integrity: his children are blessed after
him.*
*8 A king that sitteth in the throne of judgment scattereth away all evil
with his eyes.*

5 An unusual metaphor portrays the "counsel" (*ʿeṣâ*, cf. 1:30) of a
man. A man's counsel is like "deep water," difficult to plumb its depths
in order to find its extent; cf. 18:4. Still, a man of "understanding" (cf.
bîn, 1:2), by exercising his knowledge and discernment, can do exactly
that.

6 The word "goodness" (*ḥasdô*, cf. 2:8) is better "loyalty." Many men
will trumpet aloud their reliability; cf. Matthew 26:33, 35. But when the
crisis comes and they are needed, their boast proves itself hollow. Who
can find a "faithful man" (cf. *ʾaman*, 11:13)? The rhetorical question
implies that such a man is indeed difficult to find.

7 The example of a parent greatly influences the practice of the child.
We find here a "just *man*" who walks through life with "integrity" (*tom*,
cf. 2:7). The gender comes from the pronoun. His children acquire
godly habits from him that mark their lives as well. Thus, they are
"blessed after him," i.e., after the example that he sets before them day
by day.[5]

8 A throne of "judgment" (*dîn*) is a throne from which justice flows. It
is a place from which the king evaluates the rights and wrongs of the
cases before him and decides them on their merits. The word *dîn* is a
synonym of *šapaṭ* (cf. *mišpaṭ*, 1:3). Both words indicate governmental
action in the legal realm that brings about right. The chief distinction
lies in the greater use of *dîn* in poetical contexts. Such a king "scattereth
away all evil with his eyes," a unique description of the king's role. The
word "scattereth" (*zarâ*) elsewhere describes the winnowing of grain.

---

[5]Zöckler, p. 178, and Aitken, p. 160, understand "after him" as referring to the time
after his death. There is no reason, however, to limit the blessing. It begins during his
lifetime as his children adopt his upright ways, and it continues on into the future after
he has gone to be with the Lord.

9 Who can say, I have made my heart clean, I am pure from my sin?
10 Divers weights, and divers measures, both of them are alike abomi-
nation to the Lord.
11 Even a child is known by his doings, whether his work be pure, and
whether it be right.

The scoop or fork throws the grain into the air, where the wind can blow the husks aside and let the heavier kernels fall back on the threshing floor. The idea of "scattering" is thus related to "winnowing," and this is the thought here. As the king sits upon his throne of justice, his gaze takes in the whole situation. He catches a grimace here, a slight hesitation there, and he is able to discern the way of justice. Thus, he winnows "with his eyes" as he dispenses justice.

9 As in 6*b* and 24*b*, the author makes his point here with a rhetorical question. The question demands a negative answer. No one can pronounce himself morally pure, a victor over the sinful habits that strive for mastery over mankind. The proverb supports the doctrine of man's depravity, taught throughout Scripture (e.g., Eccles. 7:20; I Kings 8:46).[6]

10 The theme of honesty in business transactions is familiar in the book, e.g., 11:1; 16:8, 11; 20:23. Literally, 10*a* reads "a stone and a stone, an ephah and an ephah." The repetition in both cases indicates more than one kind. The stone was used as a weight to assist in weighing out an amount of something. With a stone that was slightly off, it would be possible to cheat someone, either selling less than he thought he was receiving or paying less than he thought he was getting. An ephah was a dry measure whose English equivalent is uncertain. Estimates range from less than half of a bushel to about nine-eighths of a bushel. Differing measures of the ephah could be used to defraud the other party in a business transaction. Either practice was an "abomination" (*tôʿăbat,* cf. 3:32) to the Lord.

11 This is the second of only two passages in the book that speak directly of a child's work responsibilities; see 10:4-5. The word "known," *nakar,* has a broad range of meanings related to the idea of "knowing,

---

[6]McKane, pp. 547-48, takes the verse to teach that man is unable to accurately assess the purity of his motives. He can never be certain that he has not deceived himself. The view is possible, but I prefer the more traditional interpretation expressed above.

12 The hearing ear, and the seeing eye, the Lord hath made even both of them.
13 Love not sleep, lest thou come to poverty; open thine eyes, and thou shalt be satisfied with bread.

recognizing." The initial *gam* applies to the whole sentence, and there is thus no need to move it to precede the *nakar*. It gives emphasis to the statement.[7] The child thus "makes himself known" by the quality of his work. In other words, even at an early age the child reveals his character. That a child shows his character through his actions is significant for the parents. Wise parents will carefully watch their child's work at an early age for signs of character weakness. Slipshod and careless work, or work left unfinished, shows weak character. Work with high quality, consistent with the child's maturity and training, should be praised since it shows the strength of his character.

12 That the Creator God has made both the eye that sees and the ear that hears seems at first glance almost trivial. But there is an implied lesson that goes far deeper and has practical value to it. That God has created seeing and hearing implies that God Himself sees and hears; thus, mankind's actions are not hidden from Him. We have therefore an obligation to live in a way that pleases Him; cf. 15:3.[8]

13 The association of sleep and poverty is a familiar theme; cf. 6:9-10; 10:4-5; 19:15; 24:33-34. "Sleep" poetically represents laziness. The person who gives in to this will become poor.[9] The command to "open thine eyes" urges the reader to awaken out of his lethargy in order to

---

[7]Toy, p. 388, asserts that the Hebrew demands an antithetical statement. He emends *yašar*, "right," to *rašaᶜ*, "bad." Martin, p. 124, accepts this change. Generally, an *ʾim...ʾim* construction does indicate contrast. The contrast, however, is not always drastic; cf. Deut. 18:3. Precedent, as well, does exist for using the construction without drawing a contrast; cf. Josh. 22:22. Since the *ʾim...ʾim* construction does not occur regularly in the poetical sections of the OT, and since poetical literature notably uses unique grammatical constructions, the absence of a sharp contrast here is not surprising. Any change in the MT is arbitrary. There is no textual support for emending the verse.

[8]McKane, p. 547, suggests that the lesson of the verse is rather to be found in the notion that our eyesight and hearing can be trusted. Since God made our eyes and ears, the evidence they produce is reliable. Toy, p. 388, notes that sight and hearing should be used in obedience to God. These views are also possible.

[9]McKane, pp. 541-42, understands *pen tiwwareš*, "lest thou come to poverty," as the loss of an inheritance. The *nipᶜal* of *yaraš*, however, expresses the meaning of poverty in general, without reference to inheritance (as in the *qal*). The proverb has a broader, more practical application when we apply it generally to poverty.

14 It is naught, it is naught, saith the buyer: but when he is gone his way, then he boasteth.
15 There is gold, and a multitude of rubies: but the lips of knowledge are a precious jewel.
16 Take his garment that is surety for a stranger: and take a pledge of him for a strange woman.

work. He will gain such reward as to be "satisfied" (śɔbaᶜ, cf. 3:10) with his "bread." "Bread" undoubtedly represents food in general.

14 Solomon here makes a practical observation. The repetition of *raᶜ* is an example of epizeuxis, the repetition of a word for emphasis. The buyer here haggles over the price of an item, a common practice in the Near Eastern markets. The item, he says, is *raᶜ raᶜ*, "bad, bad," i.e., "very bad," and thus not worth the asking price. After he has bargained the seller down to what he wants to pay, he brags to everyone about the good purchase he has made. As a practical application, statements made in negotiating a sale should be taken with a very large "grain of salt."

15 The verse develops the theme of speech, a theme touched on in the book over forty times. "Rubies" (pɔnînîm, cf. 3:15) should be taken as "jewels." Such objects of value as gold and jewels do indeed exist, even to the point at which they could almost be said to be common. But lips that speak only of knowledge are a greater treasure, very precious in value. The use of pɔnînîm as a standard of comparison occurs elsewhere in 3:13-15; 8:11; and 31:10. The phrase "precious jewel" is better "precious ornament" or "precious thing." God places a high valuation upon trustworthy speech.

16 The surety relationship occurs also in 6:1-5; 11:15; 17:18; 22:26-27; and 27:13. The verse here warns against financial dealings with one whose financial standing is precarious. Because he has entered into a surety relationship with a "stranger," he is on the brink of defaulting on his own loans. From the parallelism with 16*b*, it is likely that the "stranger" is a foreigner. He must therefore furnish security for what he has borrowed.

The outer cloak could be pledged as security (Exod. 22:26-27; Deut. 24:10-13; see also Amos 2:8). Because this was necessary for warmth at night, the creditor was to return it to the debtor for sleeping. This would be the last thing with which a person would part; anything else of value

17 Bread of deceit is sweet to a man; but afterwards his mouth shall be filled with gravel.
18 Every purpose is established by counsel: and with good advice make war.
19 He that goeth about as a talebearer revealeth secrets: therefore meddle not with him that flattereth with his lips.

would be pledged first. Taking this garment implies that this person has a shaky financial situation. Because he has become the surety for a "strange woman" (better, "foreigner," *nokrîyam,* cf. 2:16, note 15), his own financial well-being is questionable.[10]

17 Wealth, in and of itself, cannot satisfy. The verse notes that wealth gotten by deceitfulness will eventually be as gravel in the mouth, highly unsatisfying! The "bread of deceit" is that material gain that comes through lying or deceptive practices. Initially, it seems sweet, something upon which to congratulate yourself. But this reaction will not continue. Eventually, the deceit will be as a mouthful of sand. Calamity will come to one who feeds upon this diet.

18 The proverb moves from the general to the specific. Initially, we read that "every purpose" (or "plan," *mahašabôt,* cf. 6:18) "is established" (cf. *kûn,* 12:3) by "counsel" (*ᶜeṣâ,* cf. 1:30). This repeats the thought of 15:22, that effective planning requires reliance upon several wise counselors. War provides a specific example of such planning. To wage war successfully, it is necessary to consult others to develop the battle plan.[11] Compare 24:6.

19 Once again the thought turns to speech. The "talebearer" is better a "slanderer" (*rakîl,* cf. 11:13), a man who reveals to others things that have been spoken to him as "secrets" (*sôd,* cf. 3:32) in confidence. For

---

[10]The *kᵊtîb nokrîyam,* "foreigners," in 16*b* should be retained in preference to the *qᵊrê nokrîyâ,* which incorrectly reflects the influence of 27:13. The *qᵊrê* applies the verse to a "strange woman," a harlot. This misses the practical application to financial matters. There is no compelling reason to make the two verses identical. The AV; NIV; Plaut, p. 211; Power, p. 139; and others adopt the *qᵊrê.* The *kᵊtîb* referring to foreigners, however, nicely parallels 16*a.*

[11]Frankenberg, pp. 117-18, spiritualizes *milḥamâ* to the "Kriegslebens," the battles of life. He compares the verse to several from the Psalms that speak of life's trials in this sense, e.g., Ps. 27:3; 35:1ff; 109:3. While it is true that we are involved in a "holy war" against Satan and sin, *milḥamâ* routinely refers to the actual physical conflict of battle. Verse 18*b* is better a specific example of the principle stated in 18*a.*

20 Whoso curseth his father or his mother, his lamp shall be put out in obscure darkness.
21 An inheritance may be gotten hastily at the beginning; but the end thereof shall not be blessed.

this reason, one should not associate with "him that flattereth with his lips" (literally, "one who opens his lips," i.e., a gossip). The advice is practical: a man who slanders others to you will likely slander you to them. Have nothing to do with him!

20 Under OT law, a rebellious son could receive the punishment of death (see Exod. 21:17; Lev. 20:9). There is general agreement, however, that the Jews did not enforce this part of the law during the Solomonic and later kingdom periods. The death forecast in these proverbs, then, reflects a theological punishment rather than a legal punishment of the child.[12] God Himself intervenes to bring judgment upon the wicked child.

The passage picturesquely describes this death as the putting out of the child's lamp in "obscure [*ʾîšôn*] darkness." The word *ʾîšôn* normally has a figurative meaning. Here, the diminutive form refers to the "little man" that forms in the reflected image in the central part of the eye. By extension, it denotes the pupil itself and, metaphorically, the center of a thing. Thus, the lamp of this youth will be put out in the "center of darkness," the blackness that comes at the midpoint of the night. The picture vividly describes the judgment of death that God brings upon the youth for his sin.

21 There is broad support for the *qərê* "hastily," *məbohelet.* So AV, NASB, and NIV. The *kətîb,* "detested," *məbohelet,* makes no sense here. Accepting the *qərê,* the verse warns against greed, which tries prematurely to wrest the inheritance from the parents. In our day, this could be done by having the parents declared incompetent to handle their affairs or by deceiving them into signing over control of their affairs. Such greed will not be blessed by God. Compare the same thought in 28:22, 24.

---

[12]Proverbs 13:9 draws a contrast between "righteous" and "wicked" conduct. This also supports the idea of a theological punishment. Consistently, the word "lamp" has one of two figurative meanings. It represents the Lord's guidance (e.g., Job 29:3; Ps. 119:105) or an individual's life principle (e.g., Job 18:6; 21:17). The idea of divine judgment upon the life of an offending child comes naturally to mind here.

22 Say not thou, I will recompense evil; but wait on the Lord, and he shall save thee.
23 Divers weights are an abomination unto the Lord; and a false balance is not good.
24 Man's goings are of the Lord; how can a man then understand his own way?

22 The thought anticipates the fuller development of the NT, e.g., Romans 12:17; I Peter 3:9. When we suffer injustice, we should not try to get even. The verse does not forbid the making right of wrongs. It does, however, urge us not to do this with a self-reliant spirit. We rather "wait [or "hope," cf. *tiqwat,* 10:28] on the Lord," letting Him establish our thoughts and bless our actions. In so doing, we rely upon Him to "save" (*yošaᶜ,* cf. 11:14) us. The word *yašaᶜ* occurs broadly to express deliverance from physical and emotional trials. The word often refers to divine deliverance from trials. It occasionally takes the spiritual sense of salvation so often seen in the NT. Here, the idea is that we rely on the Lord to right the wrongs of this life that affect us.

23 Once more, the thought turns to the matter of honesty in business; cf. v. 10. The identical construction, "a stone and a stone," occurs in v. 10. It likewise here denotes stones of differing weights. These let others be defrauded in commercial transactions. Verse 23*b* parallels this with the example of a "false scale" used to defraud others. These actions are an "abomination" (*tôᶜəbat,* cf. 3:32) to the Lord. Verse 23*b* uses litotes, understatement by negating the positive, to make the point: this "is not good."

24 The aphorism takes up man's self-sufficiency. The "goings" (*misᶜad*) are better "steps." The word *saᶜad* refers to a cadenced pattern. The picture is of one walking step by step through life. In His divine grace, the Lord directs this one's path, "working all things together for his good" (cf. Rom. 8:28). Interestingly, the "man" (cf. *gəbûrâ,* 8:14) is a "mighty man," one that might well be thought of as able to control his way. Even this one, however, is subject to the direction of the Lord. The rhetorical question makes the point that no man understands the full significance of events that happen to him. We do not have the eternal perspective necessary for such conclusions.

25 It is a snare to the man who devoureth that which is holy, and after vows to make inquiry.
26 A wise king scattereth the wicked, and bringeth the wheel over them.
27 The spirit of man is the candle of the Lord, searching all the inward parts of the belly.

25 A man's vows to the Lord should be carefully considered. Here, the AV renders *yala^c* "to devour," but this yields no connection to 25*b*. It is better to take the verb as *yala^c* II, "to speak rashly." Stating that something was "holy" was to dedicate it to God, most likely a sacrifice given to the priests at the temple. To make such an ill-considered vow would be a snare, forcing a man to do what he, after reflection, did not wish to do. As Ecclesiastes 5:5 notes, it is better not to make a vow than to vow and not fulfill your promise.

The greater problem of the verse is *ləbaqqer,* "to make inquiry." The verb *baqar* occurs only seven times, most often in a worship context. In light of the rashness spoken of in 25*a*, I take the verb to indicate that this man is forced to seek some way to fulfill his vow, a vow whose full implications he did not consider before making.[13]

26 The wise king "scattereth" (or "winnows," *məzareh,* cf. v. 8) the wicked from among the righteous. At the same time, he brings the "wheel" over them. This is the "threshing wheel" of the cart as it is driven back and forth over the grain; cf. Isaiah 28:27. It thus separates the chaff from the kernel in preparation for further winnowing. Metaphorically, then, the picture is of the king's judicial work as he dispenses righteousness to the innocent and inflicts punishment upon the wicked.[14]

27 The "spirit," *nišmat,* is man's conscience. While *nəšamâ* normally refers to "breath," e.g., Genesis 2:7; 7:22, it also represents "spirit," Job 32:8; 33:4, and man's life principle, Job 26:4; Isaiah 57:16. The context

---

[13]Frankenberg, p. 119, takes this as considering how the vow can be fulfilled in an inferior way; cf. Lev. 27:33. Toy, p. 394, understands that the individual seeks a way out of fulfilling his vow. Kufeldt, p. 553, considers this a reflection upon whether the vow was necessary. None of these seems as suitable as the view expressed above. Toy and Frankenberg's views lead to a violation of the law. Kufeldt's approach requires the verb to have the sense "to reflect," a meaning that it never takes.

[14]Driver, *Biblica* 32:184, takes the "wheel" as figurative of the "wheel of fortune," which the king turns against the wicked men. This view, however, ignores the parallelism with 26*a,* which supports a winnowing theme.

*28 Mercy and truth preserve the king: and his throne is upholden by
mercy.
29 The glory of young men is their strength: and the beauty of old men
is the gray head.
30 The blueness of a wound cleanseth away evil: so do stripes the inward parts of the belly.*

must determine the exact sense. It is compared here with a "light" (or
"lamp," *ner*), an emblem of the conscience, which evaluates decisions
and actions. Just as the lamp drives away the darkness of a room, so the
"spirit" from God searches out the hidden crannies of our being. The
conscience, then, is a gift from God, given to prevent us from going on
in ignorance of our sin.

28 In both places, "mercy" is better "loyalty" (*ḥesed*, cf. 2:8). The twin
virtues of "loyalty" and "truth" (cf. *ʾemet*, 3:3) act as sentinels for the
king, watching over his reign. This may hint at God's faithfulness to His
covenant with Israel. With loyalty and truth He guards His relationship
to the nation by sustaining their king. Ultimately, of course, the Son of
God will take the throne as an everlasting King. In the meantime, the
king himself supports his rule by exercising "loyalty" to his people.[15]

29 Solomon here makes a perceptive observation upon life. Young
men glory in their physical strength, older men in their maturity. The
"gray head" here is the emblem of maturity and wisdom. In biblical
times, the leadership of the tribes rested with those who had proved
themselves over their lifetimes to be worthy of this trust. Having a
young man occupy a leadership role was rare. Thus, older men glory in
the dignity and experience of old age. Clearly, their choice of something
to exalt towers over that of the younger men.

30 The text here establishes the principle that discipline should hurt. Of
course, we must temper punishment with the observation elsewhere that
children should not be provoked unto wrath (cf. Eph. 6:4) and the numerous exhortations that Christians are to love at all times. The obvious

---

[15]Many commentators note that "loyalty" and "truth" act to support the reign of the
king. This is certainly true, but then why is there a need to repeat in 28*b* that loyalty
guards the throne? Whybray, p. 117; Greenstone, p. 220; and others (including the
NASB) solve the problem by emending the second *ḥesed*, "loyalty," to *ṣedeq*, "righteousness." This follows the LXX in making "righteousness" the third virtue necessary to sustain the reign of the king. The change is not necessary. The repetition is normal in
Hebrew.

conclusion is that the punishment of a child, while it is firm and definite and may bring pain, must always be tempered by the love of the parents for their child. A child can bear a great deal if he understands that it comes out of a loving concern for his well-being. Because of love, the parents must discipline; yet also because of love, they must not discipline in an unreasonable manner.

The statement here teaches that the parents must use corporal punishment as they shape the character of their child. The phrase "blueness of a wound" is better "stripes that wound." This stresses the firmness of the discipline. This cleanses the child from his evil tendencies, even affecting his innermost nature.[16]

---

[16]Toy, pp. 397-98, emends bəraʿ, "evil," to bašar, "body." Then, since it is difficult to see how stripes can cleanse the body, he omits peṣaʿ, "wound," as a gloss. He translates, "Cosmetics purify the body, and blows the soul." This linguistic contortion is not necessary. The MT is sensible as it stands.

Practical Applications from Proverbs 20

1. Influence of alcohol 1
2. Comments on royal justice 2, 8, 26, 28
3. Warning against strife 3
4. Comments on work 4, 11, 13
5. Value of understanding 5
6. Scarcity of reliability 6
7. Parent-child relationships 7, 20, 21, 30
8. Scarcity of purity 9
9. Comments on business 10, 14, 17, 23
10. Creative work of God 12
11. Value of knowledgeable speech 15
12. Comments on surety 16
13. Value of counsel 18
14. Warning against evil speech 19
15. Divine judgment of sin 22
16. Divine guidance 24
17. Finality of vows 25
18. Work of the conscience 27
19. Glory of mankind 29

*1 The king's heart is in the hand of the Lord, as the rivers of water: he
turneth it whithersoever he will.*

*2 Every way of a man is right in his own eyes: but the Lord pondereth
the hearts.*

*3 To do justice and judgment is more acceptable to the Lord than sac-
rifice.*

PROVERBS 21

1 While "rivers," *peleg,* may refer to an irrigation canal, it is also true
that it may indicate a natural stream, e.g., Psalm 46:4; Isaiah 30:25;
32:2. The point of the verse probably fits better a natural brook, mean-
dering across the pasture. A tree falling across it or the cave-in of a bank
to dam it may very likely set it along a new course. In exactly the same
way, the heart of a king is under the Lord's control. He guides the nation's government so as to give that nation what He decrees best. He
may send prosperity and freedom; He may send hardship and slavery. In
it all, the king's decisions are under the influence of a sovereign God.

It is reasonable that God gives a nation the rulers that it deserves. A
godly nation would expect godly rulers. An ungodly nation—such as
most nations have been in history—would expect ungodly rulers. In either case, God is in control. He gives the leadership that will direct the
nation to fulfill His will for it.

2 The verse is similar to 16:2. Man looks upon himself as doing what
is best for himself. His actions satisfy himself, i.e., are "right in his own
eyes." The Lord, however, looks more deeply than the mere external action. The Lord "pondereth" (*takan*) the heart. The verb *takan* can be
translated either "ponder" or "weigh" in the sense of measuring something against a standard. In this case, the standard is God's own standard
of righteousness. The Lord evaluates the motives behind the actions,
taking note of selfishness, pride, anger, and a host of other attitudes that
can affect behavior. The word "hearts," *libbôt,* cf. 3:5, is an abstract plural, embracing all of the various qualities of man's inner being.

3 This simple statement shows the relative importance of morality and
sacrifice. The Lord desires the morality of righteous living rather than
the ritual of sacrifice. "Justice [cf. *ṣedeq,* 1:3] and judgment [*mišpaṭ,* cf.
1:3]" is better "righteousness and justice." Proverbs 15:8, 17:1, and 21:27
express the same thought elsewhere. As well, we find the supremacy of
righteousness over sacrifice in I Samuel 15:22-23 and Micah 6:6-8.

4 An high look, and a proud heart, and the plowing of the wicked, is sin.

5 The thoughts of the diligent tend only to plenteousness; but of every one that is hasty only to want.

4 The difficulty here lies in determining how to take *nir*. Should it be "plowing" (as in AV) or "lamp"? If *nir* is from *nûr,* "light," we must re-point it to *ner;* cf. 20:27. Man's "lamp," then, would signify man's own spirit, alienated from God as evidenced by his proud, haughty attitude. If, however, we understand *nir* as from *nyr,* "plow," the indication is that whatever the wicked does is sin, even the breaking up of fallow ground (which is the precise significance of *nyr*). In this case, 4*b* does not parallel or complete 4*a*. It rather stands apart from the opening phrase, which refers to immaterial things. In addition, *ner* occurs in 20:20 and 24:20 to refer to the immaterial nature of the wicked. For these reasons, I accept the view that *nir* refers to "the lamp of the wicked."[1]

5 There is a contrast here between careful planning and impetuous action. The "thoughts" (better "plans," *maḥšabôt,* cf. 6:18) of the "diligent" produce "plenteousness." In 5*b,* the word "hasty" comes from *ʾaṣ.* This word occurs only ten times, but it consistently has the idea of "pressing, hurrying, haste." The word "want" (*maḥsôr,* cf. 14:23) refers to the poverty that comes from slothfulness or foolish behavior. In sharp contrast with the desirable result of 5*a,* the "hasty" actions of others bring them into "want."[2]

---

[1]The commentaries have gone in different directions. Toy, Jones, and Power conclude that the verse consists of two unrelated fragments and that there is no solution to the interpretation problem. AB, p. 123, emends to *neder* and translates, "the vow of evil men is a sin." These views can be rejected out of hand as unsupported and rejecting the concept of inspiration. Driver, *Biblica* 32:185, draws on an Arabic cognate *nuratu* and suggests that *nir* here means "mark." He translates, "having a high look and a proud heart, (which are) the mark of wicked men, is sin." The translation, however, is forced and there is no support for this elsewhere in Hebrew. Phillott, SPCK, takes *nir* as a symbol of the wicked man's prosperity, a metaphor not found elsewhere in Scripture. McKane, p. 559, takes the verse as though the plowing of the wicked man "(produces) only sin" since he will not submit to God. Zöckler, p. 185, understands *ner,* "light," as a symbol of pride.

[2]Toy, p. 401, emends *wəkal-ʾaṣ,* "everyone that is hasty," to *darkê ʿeṣel.* He translates, "the ways of the slothful." Martin, p. 129, agrees with this approach. There is, however, little support for the change, and the MT is sensible.

6 *The getting of treasures by a lying tongue is a vanity tossed to and fro of them that seek death.*
7 *The robbery of the wicked shall destroy them; because they refuse to do judgment.*
8 *The way of man is froward and strange: but as for the pure, his work is right.*

6 There is no disagreement on 6*a*. The subject is clearly the acquisition of wealth through deceitful means ("a lying tongue"). The major problem lies with taking 6*b* as two parallel predicate clauses (so NASB, "a fleeting vapor, the pursuit of death") or as a genitive relationship (so AV, "a vanity . . . of them that seek death"). The descriptive phrase "tossed to and fro" is too free. It is simpler and true to the MT to render "a fleeting vapor." Poetically, then, a person who uses devious methods to gain wealth follows a passing dream that will not last. Further, this "seeks death," a path that likely leads to his own premature judgment.[3]

7 The word "robbery" is better "violence" (*sod,* cf. 3:32). The godless conduct of the wicked will turn back on them, bringing them into the judgment that they had plotted for others. The word "destroy," *garar,* is better "drag them away." Habakkuk 1:15 graphically illustrates this: the Lord drags men away with a net. This takes place because "they refuse to do judgment" (*mišpaṭ,* cf. 1:3). The context requires this to be "justice." Their refusal to act justly drags the wicked into judgment.

8 Literally, 8*a* reads, "Crooked is the way of a *wazar* man." The word *wazar* occurs only here and therefore is open to various interpretations. The AV translators treated the *waw* as the copulative, translating the phrase "and strange." There is, however, an Arabic cognate that suggests another direction. The Arabic *wizru,* "crime," leads to the rendering "criminal" for *wazar;* thus, "the way of the criminal man" (or, more smoothly, "the guilty man") is crooked.[4] In contrast, the deeds (cf. *paʿal,* 10:16) of the pure are "right" (or "upright," *yašar,* cf. 2:21).

---

[3]Syntactically, it is easiest to make *hebel niddap,* "a fleeting vapor," and *məbaqšê mawet,* "pursuit of death," predicate clauses. While the genitive relationship is possible, the text does not clearly indicate it. Among others, Whybray, p. 120; Jones, p. 178; AB, p. 123; and Hulst, p. 126, follow the LXX in emending *məbaqšê* to *ûmoqšê* and translate, "a snare of death." While the thought accords well with the statement, there is no need to abandon the MT.

[4]Driver, *Biblica* 32:185, changes the word order and connects the *waw* with *derek,* reading "a man crooked of his way is false." AB, p. 123, and Gemser, p. 62, emend *wazar* to *kāzāb,* "the way of the liar is subversive." There is, however, no need to emend the text here. The MT is explicable.

9 It is better to dwell in a corner of the housetop, than with a brawling woman in a wide house.
10 The soul of the wicked desireth evil: his neighbour findeth no favour in his eyes.
11 When the scorner is punished, the simple is made wise: and when the wise is instructed, he receiveth knowledge.

9 A contentious woman makes life difficult for her husband. It would be better to live in the corner of the home's flat rooftop than to share the palatial surroundings of the home with a contentious wife. The word "wide" (*ḥaber*) in 9*b* causes variety in interpreting the verse. The idea of *ḥabar*, "to join, couple," is, by extension, that of "a partnership, a companionship." The phrase "house of joining" is very naturally that of a "shared house."[5] With minor variations, the verse is repeated in 25:24. See v. 19 for a second metaphor on this subject.

10 The verse summarizes the conduct of a wicked man. He "desireth" (cf. *taʾăwat*, 10:24) evil. The verb *ʾawâ* is a strong word that denotes "lust, desire, craving, covetousness." The context determines whether this is good or evil. Here, the wicked is not merely neutral toward sin. He craves it! For this reason, his neighbor "findeth no favour in his eyes." He continually looks for ways to gain an advantage over his neighbor. The implied thought is that the wicked is motivated by selfishness. He looks for the edge that will gratify his own desires, even to the extent of hurting his neighbors in some way.

11 Solomon here contrasts the "scorner" (*leṣ*, cf. 1:22), the "simple" (*petî*, cf. 1:22), and the "wise" (*ḥakam*, cf. 1:2). When the hardened

---

[5]KD II, 68-69, takes *pinnat-gag*, "corner of the housetop," as "the pinnacle of a housetop." This pictures the dwelling place as one of danger as well as one of inconvenience. This takes the metaphor to an extreme not required by the verse. The greater difficulty lies in *ḥaber*. Toy, p. 402, transposes the consonants to read *raḥab*, "a large house." The AV likewise adopts this view, which is supported by the LXX. J. J. Finklestein, "Hebrew חבר and Semitic *ḤBR," *JBL* 75:331, followed by Kufeldt, p. 555, derives the word from the Akkadian cognate "to be noisy." He translates, "a noisy household." Albright, *VTS* III, 10-11, derives it from the Akkadian *bit ḫubūri*, "a house of beer-vats," i.e., a "brewery." He translates, "a public house." Story, *JBL* 64:325-26, states that the equivalent Akkadian and Ugaritic words suggest "storehouse." Clearly, the verse has occasioned difficulty. Nevertheless, the Hebrew is straightforward and a reasonably literal translation gives good sense. This avoids the problems of justifying an emendation or of giving an unusual meaning to a relatively common word.

12 The righteous man wisely considereth the house of the wicked: but
   God overthroweth the wicked for their wickedness.
13 Whoso stoppeth his ears at the cry of the poor, he also shall cry him-
   self, but shall not be heard.

scorner is punished, the naive simpleton may learn from the example. It
is unstated but assumed that the *leṣ* himself rejects all correction; cf.
9:7-8; 13:1; 15:12; 19:28. The *petî* thus has the potential of learning
from someone else's punishment.[6] On the other hand, the "wise" person
will learn from "instruction" (cf. *śakal,* 1:3). Notice that this "instruction" is not necessarily correction for some faulty act of conduct. The
word *śakal* emphasizes the process of mental activity. The wise man
considers some aspect of life. Because he is wise, he discerns the right
path. He gains "knowledge" through the process.

12 From 12*b*, the subject of 12*a* must be God Himself; thus, it must
be read "The Righteous One." The all-knowing God considers the ways
of the wicked man; cf. 15:3. He judges them and "overthroweth the
wicked for *their* wickedness." The last phrase is better "into ruin."
"Wickedness" (*raᶜ,* cf. 1:33) has a general sense that may or may not
refer to eternal judgment. Ultimately, of course, all of the wicked will
come to eternal ruin, so 12*b* does include that thought.[7]

13 There is poetic justice in life. The focus here is on a person who
hardens himself against appeals for help from the poor. The day may
very well come in his own life when he will become poor. In that time,
however, his appeals will go unheeded by those to whom he calls. The
object of the call is left unstated and, thus, may refer either to God or to
man. The proverb is general, stating a principle that will often be true.

---

[6]Richardson, *VT* 5:172, argues for the meaning "babbler" for *leṣ.* He suggests that the
leṣ and the *petî* are the same person, i.e., that in punishing this one for his babbling, he
becomes wiser. His argument is weak.

[7]The lack of a clear reference to God has led to many interpretations. The AV relates
12*a* to a "righteous *man*" and supplies *God* as the subject to 12*b*. This leaves the two
halves without any clear connection between them. Power, p. 142, and Jones, p. 178,
suggest that the two phrases were independent lines joined by some editor. AB, p. 124,
follows the LXX and emends *labêt rašaᶜ,* "the house of the wicked," to *libbōt rašāᶜîm,*
"the thoughts of wicked men." These views are unlikely.

14 A gift in secret pacifieth anger: and a reward in the bosom strong wrath.
15 It is joy to the just to do judgment: but destruction shall be to the workers of iniquity.
16 The man that wandereth out of the way of understanding shall remain in the congregation of the dead.

14 The verse comments on life without attempting to pass judgment upon the morality of a bribe. Where the bribe interferes with the execution of justice, it is elsewhere pronounced evil, e.g., 17:23. Where, however, it is given simply to foster a feeling of good will, it may be acceptable, e.g., 18:16. The "gift in secret" and the "reward" carried in the "bosom" (cf. *ḥeq,* 6:27) are both bribes. These have the potential to subdue anger.[8]

15 It is a joy for the righteous man to do "judgment" (better "justice," *mišpaṭ,* cf. 1:3) since he delights in that which is right. When justice prevails, it brings "destruction" (*məhittâ,* cf. 10:14) for the workers of iniquity. "Destruction" is too strong for *məhittâ.* The idea here is better something like "ruin" or "harm." With this understanding of the verse, 15b reads, "*it is* ruin for the workers of iniquity." The practice of justice in 15a is the understood subject.

16 There are only two ways in life: the wise way of righteousness that leads to eternal life and the foolish way of wickedness that leads to eternal retribution. One, therefore, who wanders (*tôᶜeh,* cf. 10:17) from the "way of understanding" ends up in the way that leads to spiritual death. The "congregation of the dead" (*rəpaʾîm,* cf. 2:18) is the assembly of those who are on their way to spiritual judgment. This foolish person "shall remain" (*yanûaḥ*), adopting the way of death with no qualms about the direction of his life. The verb *nûaḥ* is better "rest," not the cessation of movement but rather the secure sense of settlement. The statement does not necessarily imply premature death, although that may occur to one who has this attitude; cf. I Corinthians 11:29-30.

[8]The verb *yikpeh,* "pacifieth," occurs only here. This has caused emendations to more familiar verbs. Frankenberg, p. 122, reads *yəkapper,* "cover." Symmachus, the Targum, and the Vulgate suggest *yəkabbeh,* "extinguish." The suggestions add nothing to the interpretation.

17 He that loveth pleasure shall be a poor man: he that loveth wine and oil shall not be rich.
18 The wicked shall be a ransom for the righteous, and the transgressor for the upright.
19 It is better to dwell in the wilderness, than with a contentious and an angry woman.

17 Once again Solomon makes a practical observation on life. The man who loves "pleasure" (cf. *śamaḥ*, 10:1) aims to gratify himself. His goal is to gain personal joy. The cost of such high living, however, is great, and he will become poor (*maḥsôr*, cf. 14:23). Verse 17*b* merely repeats the thought of 17*a*, giving a specific example of self-gratification.

18 The "ransom" (cf. *kapar*, 16:6) was "paid" for a specific punishment, e.g., Exodus 21:30. When animals were involved, the *koper* was the substitute of the innocent for the guilty. This leads to the conclusion that there is not a soteriological application here. The heathen are not innocent victims slain in place of the guilty. God does not cover the sins of His people on the basis of the sacrifice of the wicked. The verse must have another application. The most likely thought is that Solomon recognizes the sovereign activity of God as He works out His will for Israel through the heathen. The heathen are a "ransom" in the sense that they suffer on behalf of Israel. Compare Isaiah 43:3. Thus, God uses the heathen for the good of His people.[9]

19 This is the counterpart to v. 9. Here, a second metaphor pictures the problem of living with a contentious wife. It would be better to dwell in the parched economy of the barren wilderness regions of Palestine than to share the living space of a shrew. The phrase "than a contentious woman and vexation" indicates that vexation (*kaʿas*, cf. 12:16) and anger (*madôn*, cf. 6:14) mark the wife.

---

[9]Cohen, p. 141, relates the verse to a legal situation in which the innocent party is acquitted and the lawbreaker forced to pay the penalty. Plaut, p. 221, and, AB, p. 126, broaden this to include any trouble. The wicked gets into the same trouble he had planned for the innocent. Toy, pp. 405-6, suggests that when God punishes a community, it is the bad and not the good who suffer. These are possible views although I prefer the approach given above.

*20 There is treasure to be desired and oil in the dwelling of the wise;
but a foolish man spendeth it up.
21 He that followeth after righteousness and mercy findeth life, righteousness, and honour.*

20 The verse develops the thought of v. 17 still further. The wise man
has abundance in his home, while the fool squanders his resources.
"Oil" (*šemen,* generally olive oil) was used for food, cosmetics, and per-
fumes (e.g., II Sam. 14:2; Ps. 104:15; Amos 6:6). It was a very natural
symbol for prosperity. The wise man will have plenty to enjoy.[10] The
fool, however, "spendeth it up" (better, "swallows it," *yəballaᶜennû*). The
verb *balaᶜ,* "to swallow," refers to engulfing something, e.g., Exodus
15:12; Jonah 1:17. The fool here consumes his wealth.

21 "Mercy" is better "loyalty" (*ḥesed,* cf. 2:8). To "follow" (*rodep,* cf.
12:11) is to "pursue," a word that better conveys the intensity of the
chase. "Righteousness" is conduct that adheres to the standards of God's
Word, and "loyalty" is faithfulness to expected responsibilities that stem
from man's social interaction with others. Any person who makes these
his goals in life will be thrice rewarded. He will enjoy "life," a full and
abundant existence. He will gain "righteousness" before God and man.
And he will enjoy "honour" from others.[11] In summary, his reward is
material ("life"), spiritual ("righteousness"), and social ("honor").

---

[10]Toy, p. 406, considers "oil," *šemen,* an "incorrect scribal insertion" and so omits it.
AB, p. 124, suggests that oil may be original and "precious wealth" the insertion. Eitan,
pp. 62-63, followed by McKane, p. 553, relates *šemen* to an Arabic cognate "very dear,
precious." He translates, "A desirable and precious treasure." The MT's construction is
sensible and should be retained. A different problem comes from the LXX translation of
20a, "precious treasure will rest on the mouth of the wise," i.e., his words are of great
value while wisdom is swallowed up by the fool. Gemser, p. 62, emends to follow the
LXX, reading *yiškon,* "rest," for *šemen,* "oil," and *bəpî,* "mouth," for *binweh,* "dwelling."
Jones, p. 180, similarly adopts this suggestion. Again, the MT is explicable and need not
be changed.

[11]The awkwardness of seeking righteousness in order to gain righteousness has led
many to follow the LXX, which omitted *ṣədeqâ* from the list of rewards. McKane, pp.
556-57; Toy, pp. 406-7; and Whybray, p. 121, among others, omit the second *ṣədaqâ.*
Rightly understood, however, there is no need for this change. Adhering to a standard
produces a right standing before God. The word occurs with a different sense in each
phrase of the verse and there is no need to drop it.

*22 A wise man scaleth the city of the mighty, and casteth down the
strength of the confidence thereof.*
*23 Whoso keepeth his mouth and his tongue keepeth his soul from
troubles.*
24 Proud and haughty scorner is his name, who dealeth in proud wrath.

22 A combat situation illustrates the value of wisdom. The tactics by
which the wise soldier approaches a city overcome the defenses by
which it defends itself. A wise man "scaleth" (ʿalâ) the city. The AV has
interpreted the verb ʿalâ, literally "to go up, ascend," as "to scale," as
though the walls were climbed in the attack. It is just as reasonable to
assume that the wise man goes up into the strong city by stealth or by
some secret passage, e.g., II Samuel 5:8 ("the gutter"). In any case, his
tactics are such that he overwhelms the strength of the city's defenses
and it falls. "The strength of the confidence thereof" is better "the
strength in which they trust," i.e., the defenses of the fortress.

23 Those who guard (šomer, cf. 2:8) their speech protect themselves
from innumerable "troubles" (məṣṣarôt). The word ṣarar is "to bind, be
narrow," and thus, by extension, "to be in a tight place," i.e., "to be in
trouble." This strong word denotes intense anguish. This suggests that
the man who controls his speech delivers himself from particularly disagreeable troubles.

24 The translation can go in various directions, although the thought
remains clear in all of them. The NASB translates, "'Proud,' 'Haughty,'
'Scoffer,' are his names." The NIV reads, "The proud and arrogant
man—'Mocker' is his name." The problem lies in how we should understand "proud *and* haughty scorner," zed yahîr leṣ. The word zed, cf.
13:10, "proud," occurs twelve other times, always as an adjective. The
adjective yahîr, "haughty," occurs only here and at Habakkuk 2:5, where
it also is an adjective. It refers to arrogance. Since the two words are adjectives elsewhere, it is appropriate to take them as adjectives here: "A
proud, haughty scoffer is his name." He has this reputation because he
acts with "proud wrath" (bəʿebrat zadôn). The word ʿebrâ (cf. 11:4) is an
"overflowing," in this context, an "arrogance." The word zadôn, cf.
13:10, denotes "pride." Thus, this man acts with "arrogant pride."

25 The desire of the slothful killeth him; for his hands refuse to labour.
26 He coveteth greedily all the day long: but the righteous giveth and
  spareth not.

25-26 The "slothful" (*ᶜaṣel,* cf. 6:6) has his own dream world that he
lives in. His "desire" (*taʾǝwat,* cf. 10:24) is for wealth, prestige, and
mansions in faraway places. But, the reality of life being what it is, he
never gains any of these. His desires "kill him." By his refusal to work
at the day-to-day needs of life, he fails to gain his basic subsistence:
food, clothing, and shelter. The maxim uses hyperbole to make its
point.[12] The lazy man's lack of success is of his own making.[13]

Verses 25 and 26 are connected. Verse 26a literally reads, "Every day
he desires a desire." The repetition of "desire" conveys a thought something like "he covets greatly." The slothful man sees the blessings that
this world has to offer, and he intensely desires them. In contrast, the
righteous man liberally gives of his means to satisfy the needs of others.
The contrast is between the unfulfilled materialism of the lazy man and
the satisfied unselfishness of the righteous.[14]

---

[12]McKane, p. 550, suggests a literal death from frustration rather than from starvation.
Perowne, p. 140, suggests that (1) it is the slothful man's desire for ease that "kills" him
since his inactivity brings starvation or (2) his desire for comfort and the finer things of
life "wears him out with unsatisfied longings." These are possible ways of taking the
statement.

[13]Dahood, *PNWSP,* pp. 41-42, argues from selected passages that *taʾǝwat* means "ease,
inactivity." He translates, "The inactivity of the slothful will kill him." Barr, *CPTOT,*
p. 321, follows him in this position. The argument, however, rests upon a limited selec-
tion of passages. From the total number of occurences of *taʾǝwat,* the meaning of "desire" has better support.

[14]Since it is unusual in this section of the book for verses to connect up in thought,
some have given a different turn to the verse. Eitan, pp. 51-53, relates "desire," *ʾwh,* to
an Arabic cognate, "to rest." He further understands "gives," *ytn,* on the basis of an
Arabic cognate, to mean "perpetual" or "permanent," and by extension "ceaseless." He
applies the verse to the slothful man of v. 25 and translates, "All day long he rests and
reposes (= rests from work) while the righteous keeps watch (continues to work) inces-
santly." Cohen, p. 143, follows Eitan. The support for this is tenuous. Toy, p. 409, gives
up on the verse stating, "Text and meaning uncertain . . . No satisfactory emendation has
been proposed." AB, p. 125, radically emends *taʾǝwa* to *ḥoṭeʾ* and translates, "A sinner is
always selfish." BH similarly proposes *ḥaṭṭaʾ.* None of these proposals are convincing.
The MT is not difficult if we connect the verse to v. 25.

27 The sacrifice of the wicked is abomination: how much more, when he bringeth it with a wicked mind?
28 A false witness shall perish: but the man that heareth speaketh constantly.

27 God considers the sacrifice of the wicked an abomination; cf. 15:8. How much greater an abomination must this sacrifice be when it is brought with an evil motive. In our own day, we see this approach with people who attend church for the sake of business or professional contacts without any desire to worship the Lord. This is wicked and the Lord will not accept such worship. The verse does not diminish the value of sacrifice. It does, however, note that the ritual of sacrifice does not replace a repentant spirit on the part of the offerer.[15]

28 There is no problem with 28*a*: "a false witness shall perish" (*ʾabad*, cf. 1:32). Verse 28*b*, however, is difficult. Literally, it reads, "a man who hears will speak for *neṣaḥ*." The word *neṣaḥ* has multiple meanings, and this gives rise to differing interpretations. The word most often has the sense of "permanence, perpetuity." It as well can mean "glory, splendor." Taking the most frequent meaning, our statement here says that "a man who hears speaks forever." We must supply something to make sense of this. Apparently, the idea is that the man stops long enough to hear the opinions of others so that he cautiously determines the facts of a matter. He speaks, with no one successfully disputing his word.[16]

---

[15] An alternative view of the verse understands the wicked to bring his sacrifice as a ritual payment for sin. KD II, 78, and Perowne, p. 140, among others, take it this way. The word *zimmâ*, "wicked mind," refers primarily to evil plans rather than to the actual practice of wickedness. It is best to take the verse as above. Dahood, *PNWSP*, p. 44, proposes to translate *bəzimmâ* "with lewdness," a suggestion that has only weak support.

[16] AB, pp.125-26, reads *ləʾēṣāḥ* for *lanеṣaḥ* and translates, "A man who is well advised will speak up." He relates this to a witness in a legal matter. Greenstone, p. 231, takes *šômeaᶜ*, "heareth," in its alternative sense and translates, "the man that obeyeth shall speak unchallenged." Again, he relates it to the witness in a case. The man obeys God's command against giving false witness. Dahood, *PNWSP*, p. 45, proposes a meaning "to pursue" for *dabar*. He translates, "the man who listens [to false reports] will forever be pursued." Aside from its weak support, this proposal requires *dabar* to be repointed to a *puᶜal*. Jones, p. 181, follows the LXX and suggests, "he that guardeth his tongue will speak." Driver, *ZAW* 50:144-45, argues that on the basis of cognates *šômeaᶜ* is a rare word for "witness." He applies the verse to a courtroom scene where the "successful witness shall speak (on)," i.e., "speak on to the end without being put down." J. A. Emerton, "The Interpretation of Proverbs 21,28," *ZAW* 100:161-69, understands *yədabber* with a rare use, "to destroy." He translates, "He who listens will subdue (or destroy) (him) forever." These differing approaches illustrate the difficulty of the verse. We gain nothing, however, by going away from the MT, where some sense can be made.

29 A wicked man hardeneth his face: but as for the upright, he directeth
his way.
30 There is no wisdom nor understanding nor counsel against the Lord.
31 The horse is prepared against the day of battle: but safety is of the
Lord.

29 We have here a contrast between the wicked and the righteous. The
one boldly shows his defiant spirit by a hardened face. The other carefully prepares his way through life. The implication is that the wicked
man lives according to his own standards, resolutely pursuing his course
no matter what the opposition. The righteous man, on the other hand,
makes his way firm by carefully considering the ways he follows.[17]

30 This is a simple statement of philosophy. Nothing can stand in
place of the Lord. There is no human "wisdom" (*ḥokmâ*, cf. 1:2) nor
human "understanding" (cf. *bîn*, 1:2) nor human "counsel" (*ʿeṣâ*, cf.
1:30) that favorably compares with divine truth. Compare I Corinthians
3:19.

31 While man may prepare against the "day of battle," the ultimate
victory comes from God. This theme occurs broadly through the OT,
e.g., I Samuel 17:47; Psalm 33:16-17. "Safety" (cf. *yašaʿ*, 11:14) is better understood as "deliverance" or "victory."[18]

---

[17]Some set aside the *kətîb* reading *yakin*, "establishes," in favor of the *qərê yabîn*, "considers." KD II, 81; *PC*, p. 409; and Garrett, p. 185, among others, accept the *qərê*.
Zöckler, p. 188; Greenstone, p. 231; Conant, p. 98; and Muenscher, p. 203, accept the
kətîb. Either reading makes good sense but there is no compelling reason to depart from
the *kətîb*.

[18]Plaut, p. 224, makes the horse symbolic of Egypt or of foreigners in general. The
statement then warns Israel against relying upon methods or resources drawn from the
heathen. While it is true that Israel imported horses from Egypt, it is unlikely that there
is a symbolic meaning here.

Practical Applications from Proverbs 21

1. Divine control 1
2. Judgment of motives 2
3. Contrast between righteousness and ritual 3; cf. 27
4. Pride 4, 24
5. Contrast between laziness and diligence 5, 25
6. Judgment of the wicked 7, 12, 16
7. Contrast between the righteous and the wicked 8, 15, 18, 29
8. Contentious wife 9, 19
9. Contrast between selfishness and generosity 10, 13, 17, 26
10. Response to correction 11
11. Influence of gifts 14
12. Contrast between the wise and the foolish 20; cf. 22
13. Reward of the righteous 21
14. Control of speech 6, 23, 28
15. Deliverance of the Lord 30-31

1 A good name is rather to be chosen than great riches, and loving favour rather than silver and gold.
2 The rich and poor meet together: the Lord is the maker of them all.
3 A prudent man foreseeth the evil, and hideth himself: but the simple pass on, and are punished.

PROVERBS 22

1 The Hebrew is literally "A name is to be chosen [*baḥar,* cf. 1:29] rather than great riches." The familiar "*good* name" correctly interprets the phrase. The "name" of a person, his reputation, is far more important than material possessions. This is true with respect to man since our reputation determines what others think of us. And it is specially true with respect to God since He knows us by our "name" and grants eternal rewards based upon what we are rather than what we have done.[1] In like manner, "favor," a gracious spirit, is better than "silver and gold."

2 The idea here is that the "rich and poor" live side by side in society. This is so because the Lord is the "Maker of them all," the sovereign Creator, who has made all things for the accomplishment of His will.[2] Why this is so is not obvious, saving that it serves to bring about those events and attitudes that God knows are needed. Eternity alone will reveal the mystery of God's will.

There is no hint here that the poor should not better themselves. Knowing that poverty is not bad in and of itself, the poor person should remain content with his situation. At the same time he should work to improve his life.

3 The "prudent" (*ʿarûm,* cf. 1:4) hide themselves from "evil" (cf. *raʿ,* 1:33), those unpleasant matters that they would best avoid.[3] The "simple"

---

[1]Toy, p. 413, suggests that the value of our "name" lies in the advantage it brings, "respect, influence, material prosperity." Anyone, however, who cultivates a good reputation only for selfish purposes is in danger of losing that good reputation with man and has lost it already with God. A good name comes as an outgrowth of good character, not as a deliberate attempt to build a reputation.

[2]Greenstone, p. 233, translates *pagaš,* "together," as "to meet cordially." He treats the verse as though "the rich and the poor should meet in friendliness" because of their common Creator God. While the principle is true, it is not possible to find this nuance in *pagaš.* At best, the *nipʿal* is reflexive, "meet themselves."

[3]Dahood, *PNWSP,* pp. 45-46, derives *yistar* from *sûr,* "to turn aside." He translates, "the prudent man sees danger and turns aside," finding support for this in 14:16. If we read the *qǝrê* however, the form is *nistar* and is identically parallel to 27:12. The *qal* of *satar* does not occur elsewhere in the OT.

4 By humility and the fear of the Lord are riches, and honour, and life.
5 Thorns and snares are in the way of the froward: he that doth keep
  his soul shall be far from them.

(better, "naive," *petî,* cf. 1:22) are not deficient in intelligence. They
rather lack good judgment. They blissfully walk into difficulty without
realizing the pitfalls that await them.

4 The preposition "by" is from *ᶜeqeb*. We may as well translate this as
"reward," a sense that fits nicely. The phrase "fear of the Lord" (*yirʾat
yǝhwah,* cf. 1:7) stands alone, not connected to either "the reward of humility" or "riches . . . honor . . . life." We must supply something to
make a smooth connection to one of these phrases. If the verse is translated "the reward of humility *is* the fear of the Lord," then 4*b* will be in
apposition to "the fear of the Lord." But "riches . . . honor . . . life" is
not a good definition of the "fear of the Lord" (cf. 1:7). Further, humility results from the "fear of the Lord," not *vice versa.* It is therefore better to place it in apposition to "the reward of humility." This gives "the
reward of humility, *which is* the fear of the Lord, is . . . riches . . . honor
. . . life." Humility stems from a right relationship to the Lord. He rewards those who are faithful to Him.[4]

5 "Thorns" and "snares" normally are metaphors of trials and difficulties, often the judgments of God. Supplying the conjunction, the phrase
reads "thorns *and* snares." These come to the "froward" (better, "perverse," *ᶜiqqeš,* cf. 2:15) as the natural consequence of his foolish actions.
In contrast, the one who "doth keep his soul," or "guards himself," remains far from such problems.[5]

---

[4]Among others, KD, Barnes, Martin, and Plaut connect *yirʾat yǝhwah* with "the reward
of humility." Greenstone, p. 234, suggests transposing the subject and predicate and rendering, "Humility is the conseqence of the fear of the Lord." While it is true that humility follows "the fear of the Lord," it is unlikely that the construction should be so taken.
Dahood, *PNWSP*, pp. 23-24, proposes to derive *yirʾat* from *yaraʾ,* "to be fat" and thus
"blessing." He renders, "the reward of humility is the blessing of the Lord." It is unlikely, however, that such a familiar phrase as *yirʾat yǝhwah* should need reinterpretation.
Others (e.g., AV, AB, NIV, NASB) connect "the reward of humility" to "fear of the
Lord" by understanding (or inserting) the *wǝ*-conjunction, "and," before "fear of the
Lord." The statement thus becomes "the results of humility *and* the fear of the Lord are.
. . ." This is possible although it leaves the question of why the author mentions dual
sources of reward.

[5]The derivation of "thorns," *ṣinnîm,* is debated. Driver, *Biblica* 32:186, draws upon
Aramaic and Arabic cognates and understands it to mean "baskets" and, by extension, a
"basket trap." On the other hand, Toy, pp. 415, 420 emends *ṣinnîm* to *sammîm,* "traps."

*6 Train up a child in the way he should go: and when he is old, he will
not depart from it.*

6 Without doubt, v 6 is one of the most familiar of the proverbs. It is
also one of the most misunderstood and misapplied. The initial command, "train . . ." (*hənok*), states the need to prepare the "child" (*naᶜar*).[6]
The verb *hanak* occurs only five times, elsewhere all in connection with
buildings and meaning "to begin the use of" (or "to dedicate"). You do
not begin to use something that is unprepared. That leads to the meaning
here of "train."

The phrase "in the way that he should go" (literally, "according to his
way") is subject to differing interpretations. The word "way," *derek*, occurs seventy-five times in Proverbs. In only four cases does it denote an
actual road or path; in every other occurrence it poetically indicates "a
way of life or manner, actions." In addition, outside of v. 6, *derek* occurs
with the 3ms suffix only eleven times in the book. In every case, it represents a way of life. In several cases, parallelism demands that *derek*
denote one's way of life or actions. The word *derek* parallels God's
"works of old" (8:22) and "depart[ing] from evil" (16:17). A contrast
occurs between the careless keeping of one's ways and keeping the
"commandment" (19:16). Several times, *derek* parallels the thought of
walking uprightly (14:2; 28:6, 18). This leads, then, to the conclusion
that *derek* here refers to a way of life.[7]

The application most naturally refers to providing suitable instruction
to a child. His needs and potential guide the parents as they direct his

---

Martin, p. 136, and Greenstone, p. 234, similarly emend the word. The argument rests
upon the unlikelihood of parallelling "thorns" with "snares." The difficulty vanishes if
both words are understood as metaphors of hardships faced by perverse individuals.

[6]Ted Hildebrandt, "Proverbs 22:6a: Train Up a Child?" *GTJ* 9:10-14, argues that the
naᶜar is an upper-class adolescent or young man. The references to using a "rod" in
22:15; 23:13-14; and 29:15 suggest rather that this is a younger child. You do not normally use the rod in training a young man.

[7]Other interpretations have been adopted for "way": (1) the vocation for which the
child is naturally suited (so Nichol); (2) the vocation into which the parents of the child
wish him to enter (so Cohen, Hunter); (3) the "office" or "status-level" in life that the
child will occupy (so Hildebrandt); (4) the child's own way, i.e., his will (so Adams).
The metaphorical use of *derek* rules out the idea that it should be limited to the child's
"vocation" or "office," views that are too narrow. Further, the consistent symbolism of
the word does not permit it to be applied to the child's own will here. The most natural
view is that discussed above.

development. There is nothing in the verse that limits this to the spiritual area. The maxim rather suggests that the full scope of the child's training lies within the realm of parental guidance. This sphere naturally includes the spiritual within its boundaries. The guidance would embrace other areas as well.

The verse is both a command and a promise. Parents should provide individualized training, suitable to the needs of the child. His strengths and weaknesses, his temperament, his emotional needs, and a host of other attributes should be considered as the parents direct his way. As they remain faithful, they can have the assurance that their child will gradually adopt those ways and make them his own.[8]

There is no fatalistic view of maturity here. The child does play a part in forming his own character and in choosing the way in which he will walk. The child's parents do not sovereignly direct his choices; he retains his free will. The idea seems to be that the parents sovereignly determine the standards that their child will follow. The Lord honors their faithfulness by leading the child to freely choose those standards as his own.

One final objection holds that the proverbs express only general principles, not specific postulates that always hold true. In many cases, this cannot be denied. Righteous lips are not always a king's delight (16:13). One who digs a pit does not always fall into it (26:27). At the same time, however, there are many of the proverbs that express timeless truths that always hold true, no matter the specific situation. The man who trusts in the Lord will find that God always guides him through life (3:5-6). A man who has a worthy wife always has a treasure with more value than that of precious jewels (31:10). Christian parents who consistently show godly standards and who regularly seek the guidance of the

---

[8]We must note two additional points: (1) Nothing in the verse says that the child who turns aside from God and his parents for an extended period of time will later come back to a proper relationship. That may happen simply because God is gracious. But the verse promises that the child will never leave that path upon which he has been set by consistent training, a much greater promise! (2) Nothing in the verse says that the child will live in sinless perfection. The example of godly men in Scripture teaches us that even the best of men can fall into grievous sin. But throughout all of his foibles, the well-trained child will hold to a basic orientation, an underlying motivation, that will point him along the right way of life. Mistakes in his life will not take place with enough frequency to become settled habits of life.

7 The rich ruleth over the poor, and the borrower is servant to the lender.
8 He that soweth iniquity shall reap vanity: and the rod of his anger shall fail.

Holy Spirit will successfully achieve the goal of helping their children adopt godly standards as they mature.

The NT makes it clear that God wants the children of Christians to adopt godly standards, I Timothy 3:4-5, 12; Titus 1:6. We have many promises that God answers prayer. Knowing that God wants our children to live godly lives, we can pray that they will accept godly standards. When we begin to train our children from the earliest years, we can have the assurance that they will not turn from their training.

7 There is a frank recognition here of the borrower-lender relationship. The wealthy man "rules over" the poor in the sense that he has a claim on the poor man. The "borrower" (*loweh*) is a "servant" in the sense that his whole life revolves around his debt. Interestingly, *loweh* represents both the borrower and the lender. The *qal* meaning is "borrow." The *hipᶜîl* takes its usual causative sense, "causing to borrow," i.e., the lender. The "borrower" must refrain from the free use of his money in order to pay his debts. He faces the psychological pressure of knowing that failure to pay will result in personal loss. In biblical times, this could literally bring about slavery. He is a "servant" because of his debt.

8 The opening phrase reminds us of such verses as Job 4:8; Hosea 10:13; and Galatians 6:7-8. "Iniquity" (*ᶜawlâ,* cf. 12:8) is here perversion, a twisting aside from the path of righteousness. One who sows this will surely reap "vanity" (*ᵓawen,* cf. 6:12). The "rod of his anger" will "fail" (*kalâ*). The word *kalâ* occurs broadly to indicate the completion of some process or the consuming of something. The "rod of his anger" here represents the evil that he inflicts on others in his wickedness. When the judgment falls upon him, he will no longer brandish this "rod" before others.[9]

---

[9]The curious picture of a rod that "fail(s)" has led to alternative approaches. Toy, p. 421, follows Frankenberg, p. 126, in reading *ᶜᵃbodatô* for MT *ᶜebratô* and *šeber* for *šebeṭ,* "the produce of his work." This is a drastic change and unlikely, specially since *šeber* does not mean "product." Martin, p. 137, also adopts this same position. Jones, p. 184, follows Oesterley, p. 185, in accepting only *ᶜᵃbodatô* for *ᶜebratô.* He translates, "the rod of his labour will thresh him," i.e., he will be beaten with the same rod that was used in threshing the grain. AB, p. 127, emends *yikleh* to *yᵊkallēhû,* "the punishment he brings

*9 He that hath a bountiful eye shall be blessed; for he giveth of his
bread to the poor.
10 Cast out the scorner, and contention shall go out; yea, strife and reproach shall cease.
11 He that loveth pureness of heart, for the grace of his lips the king
shall be his friend.*

9 An interesting Hebrew idiom indicates the generous man. He is
ṭôb-ʿayin, "good of eyes" (contra. the covetous man who is "bad of
eyes," *raʿ ʿayin,* 23:6; 28:22). He looks on others with an unselfish
glance. Seeing needs, he gives of his means to help. The giving of his
bread to the "poor" (*dal,* cf. 14:31) represents the differing ways in
which his generosity might be seen. This charitable spirit is evidence of
a wholesome relationship with the Lord. Since this is the case, God
blesses him. The blessing is not stated since the blessing of God may
come in many ways; cf. 11:25.

10 The "scorner" (*leṣ,* cf. 1:22) is the hardened person who has no respect for spiritual matters. He is a source of strife and contention. The
statement advises on how to deal with such a person. He should be "cast
out [*gareš*]." The word *gareš* implies vigorous, even forcible, means to
bring about the expulsion. When this is accomplished, the "contention"
(*madôn,* cf. 6:14) will go out along with him. The "[legal] strife" (*dîn,*
cf. 20:8) and "reproach" (*qalôn,* cf. 3:35) brought by the scorner will
likewise "cease" (*yišbot*). The verb *yišbot* is from *šabat,* from which we
draw the word "sabbath." The idea of the verb is that of a total, complete rest.[10]

11 The opening phrase is generally agreed upon: "He who loves purity
[*ṭəhôr,* cf. 15:26] of heart."[11] The word *ṭəhôr* occurs broadly to refer to

---

on himself will be the end of him." This is a rather free translation, even after emending.
It is highly difficult to support. McKane, p. 570, follows Gemser, p. 64, and proposes
yakkehû for *yikleh,* "the rod of his wantonness strikes him." Once again, the variety of
directions taken shows the subjective nature of changing the MT.

[10]The word *qalôn* (cf. 3:35) has drawn attention here. Based on the LXX, H. A. Wolfson,
"Notes on Proverbs 22.10 and Psalms of Solomon 17.48," *JQR* 37:87, suggests *yaqlô* or
yaqlehû. He translates, "sitting in a court of justice, he dishonors it." Driver, *Biblica*
32:186 argues that *wəqalôn* should be emended to *wəyaqlennû.* He translates similarly.
The suggestions revise a text that makes good sense as it stands.

[11]Zöckler, p. 190, translates, "He that loveth with a pure heart, whose lips are gracious," taking the phrase *ṭahawrˈleb* as a prepositional phrase. The translation is unlikely
since the preposition is missing.

12 The eyes of the Lord preserve knowledge, and he overthroweth the
words of the transgressor.
13 The slothful man saith, There is a lion without, I shall be slain in the
streets.

ritual or moral purity. Verse 11*b* develops the thought of purity, noting first that his speech is gracious, then concluding with the idea that "the king shall be his friend." The conclusion flies in the face of probability. Most kings do not care about the moral purity and speech of the subjects of their realm. But there is one King who cares. The Lord Himself notes our speech and purity. It is well therefore to apply the proverb to man's relationship with God. The love of purity and graciousness of speech give evidence of a good relationship with God. In turn, God extends His friendship to those who so live.[12]

12 "Knowledge" (*da'at,* cf. 1:4) here refers to true knowledge. The Lord watches over this, preserving it in the face of attacks from evil and ungodly men; cf. 15:3.[13] In direct contrast, however, He distorts or perverts, i.e., ruins (cf. *salap,* 11:3) the words of the treacherous individual (*boged,* cf. 11:3), bringing their evil speech to naught.

13 The proverb is similar to 26:13. The saying uses exaggeration to make its point that the sluggard (*'asel,* cf. 6:6) makes excuses to justify

---

[12]Interpretations of the verse have gone in many directions. Driver, *JTS* 41:174, initially suggested that *re'eh* was a denominative verb from *rea'* or *re'â,* "friend," i.e., "makes him friendly with a king." Later, however, *Biblica* 32:186, he takes *melek* as the subject of the first clause. He alters *re'ehû* to *re'ahû* and translates, "The king loveth the pure of heart; the grace of his lips winneth his friendship," postulating that *re'â* is a causative *pi'el* from *ra'â,* "associated with." Still later, *Textus* IV, 89, he suggests that *'oheb* is an abbreviation for *'oheb yhwh.* Thus, "the friend of the Lord loves purity of heart. . . ." When I see something proposed and abandoned with such frequency, I get a little suspicious. The NEB follows the LXX, inserting "Lord" in 11*a.* AB, p. 127, translates similarly. The MT does not support the approach. Perowne, pp. 142-43, understands *hen šapatayw,* "that hath grace in his lips," as referring to fluency in speech. He will be able to make the king his friend. Again, this goes contrary to human experience. Toy, p. 421, transposes "king," *melek,* to 11*a* and emends *re'ehû,* "his friend," to *resonô,* "his delight." He translates, "the king loves the pure in heart, and grace of lips is his delight."

[13]D. Winton Thomas, "A Note on דַּעַת in Proverbs xxii.12," *JTS* 14:93-94, holds that *da'at,* "knowledge," has no satisfactory sense here. He concludes, on the basis of an Arabic cognate, that *da'at* has a forensic sense, "lawsuit." He translates, "The eyes of Yahweh watch over a lawsuit, and he subverteth the case of the deceitful." While his conclusion is correct, it is unlikely that such a common word as *da'at* needs to be reinterpreted. Martin, p. 138, concludes that "preserve," *nasarû,* cannot govern an abstract noun such as *da'at.* He supplies "*him that hath*" to make the object concrete instead of

14 The mouth of strange women is a deep pit: he that is abhorred of the Lord shall fall therein.
15 Foolishness is bound in the heart of a child; but the rod of correction shall drive it far from him.

his laziness. Because he is slothful by nature, he does not consider the logical ridiculousness of his self-defense; he simply speaks whatever comes into his mind. The word "lion," *ʾărî*, is from *ʾārâ*, "to pluck, gather." The lion thus is a "gatherer," speaking of his finding prey upon which to feed. The "lion" here, of course, represents all of the excuses that the sluggard can muster up.

14 The harlot's attractive appearance is a "deep pit," a trap to catch one who errs with her.[14] The Lord allows her treacherous nature to ensnare one who is "abhorred" (*zəʿûm*) or, better, one "with whom the Lord is angry." The word *zaʿam* occurs eleven times in the *qal*, always indicating "anger, indignation, wrath." The idea is that the harlot has the potential to bring man into judgment. As he responds to her sensual offerings, he falls into this "pit," a fall that results in his destruction.[15]

15 Solomon recognizes the sinful nature that all children have, "foolishness is bound in the heart of a child." In the book, folly expresses the contrast to wisdom. The one leads to life (8:35) while the other leads to death (9:18). This attitude is "bound in the heart," an appropriate description of mankind's sinful nature.[16]

---

abstract. Toy, p. 421, reasons similarly but rejects the supplied words. He proposes to emend *daʿat naṣārû*, "preserve knowledge," to *baṣṣaddiqîm*, "on the righteous," a radical change that lacks support. Zöckler, p. 193, looks favorably on changing *daʿat* to *raʿot*, taking the phrase in the sense, "Yahweh observes wickedness, and overthrows the words of the treacherous." None of these approaches are necessary since sense can be made of the MT.

[14]Aitken, p. 129, supposes that the reference to the harlot's "mouth" is meant to remind us that seductive speech is the primary weapon she uses to ensnare men. The suggestion is entirely possible.

[15]*PC*, p. 424, spiritualizes the passage to represent theological heresies rather than moral perversion. The comment stems from the presupposition that the adulteress in Proverbs pictures false doctrine (cf. p. 157). In view of the broad emphasis upon avoiding adultery, it is more reasonable to take this literally. The Lord here warns against involvement with immorality.

[16]Commentators generally divide along the lines of liberal and conservative in their treatment of the verse. Those who approach the Scriptures with a liberal philosophy tend to soften the teaching of the verse. Toy, p. 419, for instance, takes this as a reference to moral immaturity. McKane, pp. 564-65, speaks of "chaos in the mind of the youth" and thus the need for education. Cohen, p. 148, sees this as a reference to the child's "natural state in the early period of life." Conservatives take the verse as discussed above.

*16 He that oppresseth the poor to increase his riches, and he that giveth
to the rich, shall surely come to want.*

The sin nature imparts a self-centered attitude to everyone. This attitude leads children to gratify their own desires. Left to himself, the child
develops a selfishness that turns him aside from the Lord. A mark of
Christianity is love, and love has a self-sacrificing spirit that places the
good of others ahead of personal gain. But a self-sacrificing spirit and a
self-centered spirit oppose one another. The child must therefore have
his sinful nature curbed while he is young. Otherwise, he will develop
an undisciplined spirit that takes him after his own desires instead of
those that please the Lord. The "rod of correction," applied judiciously
during his youth, will keep this attitude from developing.

16 This is an uncertain statement with alternate interpretations apparently possible. We must take both of the *l*-clauses similarly, referring either to the subject or to the object. Everywhere else in Proverbs (11:24;
14:23; 21:5) *ʾak ləmaḥsôr,* "surely *come* to want," refers to the subject.[17]
Hence, it must here likewise describe the subject. He oppresses the poor
with the result that he himself becomes rich; he gives to the rich with
the result that he himself becomes poor. The verse is a general commentary on life. Those who oppress the downtrodden beat them down still
further while enriching themselves. Those who try to curry favor with
the wealthy by giving more to them cause themselves poverty by their
foolish actions.

---

[17]*PC,* p. 425, applies the *l*-clauses to the objects. He who oppresses the poor makes
him rich in that God will providentially bless him. At the same time, one who gives to
the wealthy encourages his indolence, bringing him into ruin. Zöckler, p. 193, treats
similarly, excepting that he explains 16*a* by stating that the oppression stimulates the
poor man to redoubled labors so that he becomes wealthy in the end. AB, pp. 128-29,
translates, "One who oppresses a poor man to make increase for him, will have to yield
to the rich and will end in poverty." This misses the parallelism while forcing the meaning of "yield" on the well-known verb *natan,* "give." While admitting that the suggestion
is "graphically not easy," Toy, pp. 420-21, emends ʿošeq, "oppresseth," to *noten,* making
16*a* commend benevolence and 16*b* condemn bribery. The suggestion is weak. Jones,
p. 186, and Martin, p. 139, follow Toy's flawed suggestion. Emerton, *JTS* 20:205-6
argues that ʿošeq has a meaning "to slander," the false accusation being made to bring
material gain to the accuser. His argument is not convincing.

Practical Applications of Proverbs 22:1-16[18]

1. True value 1
2. Comments on wealth and poverty 2, 7, 16
3. Contrast between the prudent and simple 3
4. Parent-child relationships 6, 15
5. Judgment of the wicked 5, 8, 10
6. Blessing of the charitable 9
7. Blessing of purity 11
8. Omniscience of God 12
9. Excuses of the lazy 13
10. Warning against the harlot 14

---

[18]The applications from 22:17–24:34 are at the end of c. 24.

EXCURSUS

The title "the words of the wise," from v. 17, applies to 22:17–24:34. The section is commonly extended to either 24:22 or 24:34. Due to similarities with the Egyptian writing *The Teaching of Amen-em-opet*, many have concluded that Proverbs draws upon the Egyptian document.[19] The view is widely accepted by both liberal and conservative critics.[20]

General Dependence of Proverbs upon Semitic Wisdom Literature

The dependence of Proverbs upon *Amen-em-opet* is part of an assumed wider dependence of the entire book upon Semitic wisdom literature in general. The nation of Israel did not exist in a vacuum; rather, they were influenced through trade and cultural interchange. Especially during Israel's early years, they were influenced by the older, more firmly established, neighboring countries. As a result, Israel adopted some of the literary forms of Egypt and the nearby Mesopotamian countries.

Evidence for this influence of neighboring countries can be seen within the pages of the Bible. There are numerous references to "wise men" or "wise women," e.g., Judges 5:29; Esther 1:13; Isaiah 19:11; Jeremiah 51:57. In addition, the poetical portions of the OT duplicate the style of gnomic literature. The wisdom literature of the Sumerians, Babylonians, and Assyrians often takes the form of collections of short proverbs and pithy sayings. This is much the same as in Proverbs. In both Egyptian and Mesopotamian writings, the stylistic feature of father-to-son instruction

---

[19]Kidner, p. 23, for instance, points out that almost all of 22:17–24:22 parallels portions of *Amen-em-opet*. Examples of this include the following: "Guard thyself against robbing the wretched and against being puissant over the man of broken arm," *Amen.* 2, lines 1-2; cf. 22:22. "Covet not the property of an inferior person, nor hunger for his bread. As for the property of an inferior person, it is an obstruction to the throat; it maketh a vomiting in the gullet," *Amen.* 11, lines 1-4; cf. 23:6. "As for the scribe who is experienced in his office, he shall find himself worthy to be a courtier," *Amen.* 30, lines 10-11; cf. 22:29. The translations are from J. M. Plumley, "The Teaching of Amen-em-ope," *DOTT*, pp. 176-85. Both *Amen-em-opet* and 22:17–22:34 have a common literary style. The form of instruction often uses a father-to-son motif. There is extensive use of wisdom in characterizing behavior. Both discuss common virtues and vices.

[20]Virtually all liberal commentators accept the hypothesis that Proverbs draws upon *Amen-em-opet*. Conservative authors who accept this view include such men as R. Laird Harris, *ZPBD*; and Derek Kidner. R. Laird Harris, *Proverbs*, in *The Wycliffe Bible Commentary*, ed. Charles F. Pfeiffer (1962) (hereafter referred to as *WBC*), also relies heavily upon *Amen-em-opet* for his exposition of Proverbs although he does not explicitly accept a connection between the two.

abounds. The writings use the imperative mode frequently. The authors normally address instructions to the individual rather than the nation.

Table 1[a]

Relationship of the Old Testament to Semitic Wisdom Literature	
Title	**Description**
The Instruction for King Meri-ka-Re (Egyptian)	Comments on morality and social justice; similar to the writing prophets
Counsels of Wisdom (Babylonians)	Moral exhortations, a portion of which are addressed to "my son," similar to Proverbs
The Words of Ahiqar (Assyrian)	Collection of Assyrian wisdom sayings, similar to Proverbs
Instruction of the Vizier Ptah-hotep (Egyptian)	Father-to-son instruction, comparable to Proverbs
Prayer to Any God (Sumerian)	Penitential prayer, containing many ideas and phrases similar to the Psalms
The Instruction of Ptaḥ-em-Djeḥoty, adapted by Sehetepibre (Egyptian)	Proverbial style; multiple similarities to Proverbs 25:2-27

[a]This selected list of wisdom literature has been compiled from Glendon E. Bryce, "Another Wisdom 'Book' in Proverbs," *JBL* 91:145-57; Whybray, W. C. Lambert, *Babylonian Wisdom Literature* (1960); *DOTT*; and McKane.

These Semitic gnomic writings are but a few of those similar to biblical writings. The broad scope of the relationship is beyond the limit of this excursus. This considers only the specific problem of the relationship of Proverbs to *Amen-em-opet*. There are many reasons that we reject the idea of a close relationship between the two. In principle, we may extrapolate these reasons to cover the entire subject of a relationship between Semitic wisdom literature and Israelite wisdom literature.

To begin, the connection is highly suspect, merely on the basis of the similar material. We are not considering lengthy passages, quoted almost verbatim from an Egyptian original. Rather, the similarities involve isolated phrases or verses, arranged in juxtaposition and freely edited to impart a distinctive Israelite character to them.[21]

There are similarities between Proverbs and *Amen-em-opet*. Within Proverbs, however, they are not extensive. Only 22:17–23:11 has clear parallels to *Amen-em-opet*. There are also similarities between *Amen-em-opet* and other parts of the Book of Proverbs and other books of the OT.[22] No one claims, however, that *Amen-em-opet* influenced the writing of other OT books.

In addition to the parallels between Proverbs and *Amen-em-opet*, there are significant differences between the two writings. In some cases, Proverbs has a distinctively different Israelite character to it that is not reflected in Egyptian writings.[23] There is a second clear contrast in the area of monotheism. *Amen-em-opet* contains polytheistic remarks while

---

[21]Even liberal critics admit this. McKane, p. 371, says, "the Israelite editor exercises freedom in his choice of Egyptian material, alters its order and imagery and inserts instructions of his own or from other sources." *WIP*, p. 24, states, "It is clear that their authors were not slavish imitators of their foreign models, and that they were aware of the necessity of adapting their teaching to suit the needs of their Israelite readers."

[22]For instance, *Amen-em-opet* 1, line 20, compares to Deut. 33:27; *Amen-em-opet* 4 to Ps. 1 and to Jer. 17:5-8; *Amen-em-opet* 6, lines 7-10, to Prov. 15:16-17 and 17:1; *Amen-em-opet* 13, line 6, to Jer. 8:8; *Amen-em-opet* 18, lines 1-2, to Prov. 27:1; and *Amen-em-opet* 25, line 1, to Lev. 19:14 and Deut. 27:18. *DOTT*, pp. 177-84.

[23]*Amen-em-opet* 2, lines 1-2, simply refers to the afflicted while Prov. 22:22 adds a reference to a "gate," the location of commerce and city government in Israelite towns. Proverbs 22:23 refers to the Lord and 23:14 to Sheol, both Israelite concepts. Both of these are in the middle of the section that supposedly shows the heaviest influence of *Amen-em-opet*.

Proverbs maintains a pure monotheism without references to the pagan gods.[24]

The haphazard nature of the similarities and the substantial nature of the differences forces me to conclude that there is no *direct* dependence of Proverbs upon *Amen-em-opet*. There may well have been an oral body of observations upon life that circulated in the Near East. This *may* have served to influence the written body of literature. This, however, is a far cry from direct influence. Conservatives, therefore, should reject the hypothesis that there is a direct influence by *Amen-em-opet* upon Proverbs.

As a matter of fact, wisdom writings were common in every Semitic country during OT times. Ample evidence shows that this style of literature pervaded ancient Near Eastern countries.[25] It is only natural that the biblical writers should adopt a similar style, consistent with the common cultural heritage that they shared with that section of the world. It is, however, unwarranted to assume that the biblical writers adapted their material from the writings of other nations.

The mere fact that the proverbs treat the same subjects does not mean that one of them drew from the other. The American proverb "Clothes make the man" is similar to the Chinese proverb "Change clothes; you cannot change the man." The familiar "Don't count your chickens before they are hatched" almost exactly translates the Irish proverb "Ná comhair do chuid sicíní go dtaga siad amach." The well-known "Too many cooks spoil the broth" parallels the Dutch proverb "Too many cooks make the porridge too salty." Despite the similarities, no one accuses the Americans of borrowing from other countries.[26]

---

[24]For example, *Amen-em-opet* 2, line 16, refers to the "moon," a symbol of Thoth, the Egyptian god who was concerned with the judgment of the dead. *Amen-em-opet* 4, line 12, mentions the "grove." This thought comes from the garden that the Egyptians associated with the realm of the dead who were blessed by the gods. In contrast, line 6 refers to "the flame" that served as a burial shroud for the wicked dead. *Amen-em-opet* 7, line 2, mentions the gods of fortune, "Shay and Renent." *DOTT*, pp. 177-79.

[25]The Bible mentions that wisdom characterized groups of men in several countries: Egypt, I Kings 4:30; Acts 7:22; Edom, Jer. 49:7; Obad. 8; Babylon, Isa. 47:10; Jer. 50:35; Dan. 2:48; Phoenicia, Ezek. 27:8; Zech. 9:2; Persia, Esther 1:13; 6:13; Israel, II Sam. 14:2; I Kings 4:34.

[26]The proverbs come from David Pickering, *Dictionary of Proverbs* (1997); Liam Mac Con Iomaire, *Ireland of the Proverbs* (1988); and Peter Beilenson, *Chinese Proverbs from Olden Times* (1956).

Within the Bible itself, there are many indications that wisdom practitioners were recognized in Israel.[27] It is logical that their writings would parallel, at least to some degree, the writings of other nations. With the writers living at the same time in history with parallel cultures, dealing with the same general themes, and following the same poetical style, occasional similarities would naturally occur.

Since the relationship between *Amen-em-opet* and Proverbs is generally accepted, *Amen-em-opet* is considered a reliable source for emendations. The religious tone of *Amen-em-opet* fosters this idea. Whereas Semitic wisdom literature often reflects the polytheistic society from which it came, *Amen-em-opet* is generally free from this. It emphasizes rather the virtue of piety without laying stress upon a multiplicity of gods. Numerous emendations have been proposed.[28] Many of these have found their way into newer translations, such as the Anchor Bible, the Jerusalem Bible, and the Dartmouth Bible. The critical notes of the Hebrew OT, edited by Georg Beer, and the major lexicons refer to *Amen-em-opet*.

As we have seen already, it is a misconception to perceive *Amen-em-opet* as monotheistic. Similarly, it is unwarranted to find a dependence of Proverbs upon *Amen-em-opet*. Any emendation that draws its support from *Amen-em-opet* rests upon a weak foundation. The two are independent works, related only as both draw upon the oral wisdom of the Near East. The MT should not be emended solely on the basis of *Amen-em-opet*.

---

[27] For example, see the counselors at court, I Chron. 27:32-33; the woman of Tekoa, II Sam. 14:2; the claim of the town of Abel, II Sam. 20:16-22; David's quote of the "ancients," I Sam. 24:13; Samson's riddle, Judg. 14:14; Jotham's fable, Judg. 9:8-15; Nathan's parable, II Sam. 12:1-4.

[28] For instance, 22:18*b*, *yaḥdaw*, "together," is emended to *kətated*, "tent peg"; 22:19*b*, *ʾap ʾattâ*, "even you," is emended partially on the basis of *Amen-em-opet* to *ʾorheteka*, "thy ways"; 22:21, *ʾimrê ʾəmet*, "the words of truth," are omitted on the basis of *Amen-em-opet*. *DOTT*, pp. 175-76. The most widely known emendation is that of 22:20. The difficult *šališiwm* (*qərê šališîm*) has been emended on the basis of *Amen-em-opet* 30, line 1, to *šəlošîm*, "thirty." Then, having concluded the similarity, this section of Proverbs is subdivided into thirty subsections, most of which have four verses each. Jones, p. 188, says, "When we examine the Egyptian work we find a precise reference to thirty chapters. . . ." He applies this to Prov. 22:17–24:34. There is, however, no general agreement on the actual arrangement of the thirty subsections in Proverbs.

*17 Bow down thine ear, and hear the words of the wise, and apply thine
heart unto my knowledge.*
*18 For it is a pleasant thing if thou keep them within thee; they shall
withal be fitted in thy lips.*
*19 That thy trust may be in the Lord, I have made known to thee this
day, even to thee.*
*20 Have not I written to thee excellent things in counsels and knowl-
edge,*
*21 That I might make thee know the certainty of the words of truth; that
thou mightest answer the words of truth to them that send unto thee?*

17-21 Much has been made of the phrase "the words of the wise,"
dibrê ḥakamîm; cf. 1:6. This is generally taken to indicate a separate
body of material incorporated into the book as an appendix to the main
body. It should, however, be noted that *dibrê ḥakamîm* parallels *ladaʿtî*,
"my knowledge," in 17*b*.[29] Solomon introduces material acquired from
"the wise men," other worthy teachers in the land, that follows along the
same lines as his own teaching. Solomon, however, is still the author of
the passage.

There is a stylistic change at this point. The passage consists of relatively clear paragraphs, one to seven verses in length. Solomon has already shown himself to adopt different styles (c. 1-9), depending upon
the nature of the material. We can readily accept the passage, then, as
Solomonic. Since he draws on the wisdom of other teachers, there is
variety in the structure of the paragraphs.

Verses 17-21 introduce 22:17–24:34. Initially, Solomon exhorts the
youth to "hear" (*šamaʿ*) the teachings that he has gained from the "wise
men." The word *šamaʿ* occurs over one thousand times in all sections of
the OT. It is translated many ways. In general, we may say that *šamaʿ*
denotes effective hearing. Verse 17*b* makes it clear that obedience will
follow this hearing. Solomon does not identify the group of "wise men,"
but it is reasonable to assume that they were noted teachers in Israel.
The young man is to apply his "heart" (or "mind," *leb,* cf. 3:5) to the understanding and application of the knowledge that he has received, v. 17.

---

[29]Among others, Aitken, p. 225, and Barnes, p. 62, take "the words of the wise" as a
title, originally placed before v. 17 as a heading to the whole section. This supposition
ignores the parallelism with "my knowledge" in 17*b* and is unsupported. The MT makes
good sense if we accept the explanation given above.

The result of such preparation is personal satisfaction. It will be "pleasant" (cf. no*am,* 3:17) to the youth. These principles, derived from the teaching, will become established within the youth. The truths are "fitted" (cf. *kûn,* 12:3) in his lips. The idea is that he will be prepared to speak of them at appropriate times (cf. I Pet. 3:15), v. 18.[30]

The final goal of instruction is a right relationship to the Lord. Solomon reminds the youth of this. He reminds the youth that he has given him instruction to this end. The phrase "even to thee" emphasizes the idea that it is to the son and to the son alone that he has spoken.[31]

Verse 20 is the crux so far as any connection with *Amen-em-opet* is concerned. The word "excellent things," *šališiwm,* is obscure, meaning "day before yesterday," or by extension, "heretofore." But this meaning requires the supply of *təmôl* (or *ʾetmôl*), "recently, before," which elsewhere always accompanies *šalšôm.* The *qərê* suggests *šališîm,* also a difficult word. The word *šališîm* is a military word, referring to army officers. Apparently, the reference was originally to the third man who commanded a chariot. The idea of a "commander" leads me to relate *šališîm* to the "chief, first" of something, i.e., something "excellent."[32]

Solomon thus reminds the youth that his words are "excellent." This implies that they are therefore to be accepted and followed. He further

---

[30]The word *yaḥdaw,* "withal," troubles some. Dahood, *PNWSP,* p. 46, relates it to an Arabic cognate, "to settle." He translates, "Let them be fixed, settled upon your lips." The suggestion is unnecessary and unsupported. A more prevalent suggestion is to emend *yaḥdaw* to *kəyātēd,* "tent peg." The words, then, are "fixed as a tent peg on your lips," e.g., Rylaarsdam, p. 76; AB, p. 135. This fails to improve the MT. The emendation is radical and unlikely.

[31]Among others, AB, p. 135, and Gemser, p. 64, read *ʾorḥoteka,* "thy paths," and *ʾorḥotayw,* "his paths," respectively, for MT's *ʾap-ʾattâ.* This follows the LXX, which probably interpreted the verse on the basis of the mention of the Lord in the opening phrase, v. 19.

[32]The prevailing view calls for *šališiwm* to be emended to *šəlošîm,* "thirty." This brings the verse into agreement with *Amen-em-opet:* "Have not I written unto thee thirty sayings?" So Patrick W. Skehan, "A Single Editor for the Whole Book of Proverbs," *CBQ* 10:117; Roth, *VTS* XIII, 88; most of the modern commentators; and NIV. But the Hebrew will not permit the number thirty to stand alone. Something must be supplied. Most commonly, *dəbarîm,* "sayings" is added. The simple emendation is thus not simple at all. It is complex and suspect on that basis. Taking a different approach, Coates, p. 89, accepts the *kətîb,* translating, "Have not I written unto thee the third time." While possible, this leaves unanswered the question of what the three times are. Coates applies it to "the third part of the book." KD II, 98, concludes that the idea of chief men is transferred to that of chief proverbs (cf. James 2:8, a "royal law") and translates, "choice proverbs." Zöckler, p. 196, derives *šališîm* similarly but translates, "excellent words." The AV and NASB follow this.

22 Rob not the poor, because he is poor: neither oppress the afflicted in the gate:
23 For the Lord will plead their cause, and spoil the soul of those that spoiled them.

describes them as words of "counsel [cf. *ʿeṣâ,* 1:30] and knowledge [*daʿat,* cf. 1:4]." The repetition intensifies the thought of their worth, v. 20.

The purpose of these instructions becomes clear in v. 21. They are to help the youth to know the "certainty" (*qošt*) of the "words of truth." He then will be able to respond properly to those who have sent him. On the basis of cognates, *qošt* relates to "truth." To avoid the redundancy, the phrase *qošt ʾimrê ʾəmet,* literally "the truth of the words of truth," is glossed "certainty of the words of truth."[33] The young man will then be able to return to the one who has sent him out, bringing back "the words of truth." The phrase is appositional, "words which are truth." The phrase "them that send unto thee" is better "him who sent thee," possibly referring to the parent who has commissioned the youth to learn the wisdom of Solomon.[34]

22-23 This begins the section of more-direct proverbial statements. Solomon exhorts the youth not to take advantage of the poor and afflicted. Although we might think that these are without recourse, in fact God is their Protector. He will plead their case and exact judgment upon those who persecute them. The "poor" is the *dal* (cf. 14:31), here one who has little to call his own. The "afflicted" is the *ʿanî* (cf. 14:21). The phrase "in the gate" suggests that he already endures some distress. He may have come to the gate hoping to receive some benevolence, v. 22. The youth needs to realize that the Lord will take up "their cause," the cause of the poor. "Spoil," *qabaʿ,* occurs again only in Malachi 3:8-9, where the context suggests the meaning "rob." Thus, here, Yahweh "robs

---

[33]Toy, p. 425, considers *qošt* "the gloss of an Aramaic-speaking scribe." He omits it (so Gemser, p. 66). AB p. 135, however, omits *ʾimrê ʾəmet* as a gloss on *qošt.* The MT is sensible, however, if we retain both *qošt* and *ʾimrê ʾəmet.*

[34]Among others, KD II, 99, and Frankenberg, p. 128, emend *lašolheka* to *lašoʾaleyka,* "to them that send thee," citing the LXX as support. The change is unnecessary. McKane, p. 377, states that the sender commissions an "apprentice-official" for the "task of acting as a go-between." While this is possible, it seems more natural to relate the matter to the commission that the young man's parents bestow upon him.

*24 Make no friendship with an angry man; and with a furious man thou
shalt not go:*
25 Lest thou learn his ways, and get a snare to thy soul.
*26 Be not thou one of them that strike hands, or of them that are
sureties for debts.*
*27 If thou hast nothing to pay, why should he take away thy bed from
under thee?*
28 Remove not the ancient landmark, which thy fathers have set.

[qabaᶜ] the life of those who rob [qobǝᶜêhem] the poor." The repetition
of qabaᶜ shows the application of the *lex talionis.*[35]

24-25 Friends influence one another; see 27:17. This influence can be
good or bad (13:20; 27:6). The influence depends upon the nature of the
friendship. Here, Solomon exhorts the youth not to make friends with a
quick-tempered person, v. 24. Because friends influence one another, the
youth will learn the angry ways of his evil friend. These will become a
"snare" (cf. *yaqoš,* 6:2), trapping him and holding him for some undesirable result, v. 25.

26-27 This paragraph has no parallel in *Amen-em-opet.* This strengthens the argument against claiming that this part of Proverbs comes from
the Egyptian writing. The statement warns against becoming surety for
another. The warning paints a bleak picture of what can happen. The guar-
antor does not have the resources to pay the debt. He therefore will have
his possessions seized, even to the extent of taking his bed from him.
Compare the similar teaching at 6:1-5; 11:15; 17:18; 20:16; and 27:13.

28 Proverbs 23:10 repeats the admonition. The command rests upon
Deuteronomy 19:14 and 27:17. There, Moses warned against removing
the stones that marked the boundaries of a plot of land. The root meaning
of "remove" (*sûg*) is "to turn back," thus here to push back the boundaries, making the parcel smaller than it should be. This would violate the

---

[35]Aelred Cody, "Notes on Proverbs 22, 21 and 22, 23b, *Biblica* 61:425-26, argues from
an Arabic cognate that qabaᶜ means "to squeeze." He concludes that God "will press the
life out of those who oppress them." It seems to me that the Malachi passage supports
rather the AV translation "spoil," or "rob."

29 Seest thou a man diligent in his business? he shall stand before kings; he shall not stand before mean men.

long-standing boundaries, agreed upon by the "fathers," the preceding generations who had entered into the ownership agreements.[36]

29 The first phrase gives the introduction. The second and third phases follow with both the positive and negative results. The whole effect is to encourage diligence in work. The word "diligent" (*mahîr*) has the root idea of "quick, prompt." Thus, here we must think of someone who does not put off his responsibilities. He will rise in his service until one day he will minister before the king himself. Clearly, there is unlimited potential in such service. The verse also describes his success negatively. He will not stand before "mean men [cf. *ḥošek,* 2:13]." This phrase is more literally "men of darkness." These are men who do not shine in this world, i.e., who have not achieved eminence.[37]

[36]Skehan, *CBQ* 10:121, omits the verse as a "verbal dittography of the present Prov. 23:10 in a damaged text." This is a subjective conclusion, not supported by evidence.

[37]The tristich form has led some to suggest changes in order to return to the more usual distich. AB, p. 138, brackets 29*c* and comments: "The third line appears to be a variant of the second." Gemser, p. 67, suggests the insertion of the phrase "aber einer, der träge (unbehend) ist in seiner Arbeit" ("but he who is sluggish [unhandy] in his work.") These suggestions have no support. Since tristichs are not that uncommon, 23:5, 7, 31; 24:14, 27, 31, we should retain the MT.

*1 When thou sittest to eat with a ruler, consider diligently what is be-
fore thee:*
2 And put a knife to thy throat, if thou be a man given to appetite.
3 Be not desirous of his dainties: for they are deceitful meat.
4 Labour not to be rich: cease from thine own wisdom.
*5 Wilt thou set thine eyes upon that which is not? for riches certainly
make themselves wings; they fly away as an eagle toward heaven.*

PROVERBS 23

1-3 The admonition is practical advice for one who will be entertained
at court. When he sits down for a meal, he should consider well "what"
(better "who") is before him. The likely purpose of such a state dinner is
as the preface to some negotiations. The youth must keep in mind the
eminence of his host and do all that is within his power to make a favorable impression on him, v. 1.[1] To this end, he must restrain his appetite.
The unusual phrase "put a knife to thy throat" is idiomatic. It suggests
that he should restrain himself, conducting himself in order to avoid giving an impression of greediness or a lack of discipline, v. 2.[2] The "deceitful meat" (literally, "bread of lies") leads you away from the
favorable impression that you must make, v. 3.[3]

4-5 Solomon here gives a proper philosophical view toward material
possessions. He exhorts the youth not to weary himself to become rich.
He should cease from considering wealth as an end in itself. For this reason, he should stop relying on man-made schemes to gain wealth, v. 4.[4]
The *hə*-interrogative at the head of v. 5 introduces a simple question: "Are

---

[1]The word *ʾăšer* can also be translated "what" (with the AV). So Conant, p. 101;
Greenstone, p. 242; and Bruce K. Waltke, "The Book of Proverbs and Ancient Wisdom
Literature," *BibSac* 136:237-38. It would seem, however, that the greater danger comes
from offending the host, rather than from the nature of the food. Still, the view is possible, especially if "what" is said to refer to the whole scene—ruler, guests, officials,
food, etc.

[2]AB, p. 139, completely loses the idiom by emending "to thy throat," *belocekâ,* to
bebilcəkâ, "in your swallowing." He translates, "Use a knife to eat with. . . ." R. Köbert,
"Zu Prov 23,1-2," *Biblica* 63:264, reads *wəśamtā ṣakîk biblᵒekā,* loosely paraphrased,
"Stop yourself." There is no textual support for either change.

[3]Toy, p. 428, and Oesterley, p. 198, omit v. 3 as out of place (see notes, vv. 8, 9). They
think it may have been picked up from v. 6*a,* where the thought is similar. Once again,
there is no textual support. Understood rightly, the verse fits nicely into the context of
vv. 1-2.

[4]Ludwig Keimer, "The Wisdom of Amen-em-ope and the Proverbs of Solomon," *AJSL*
43:16, misses the point when he objects to *mibbînatka* on the grounds that "its literal
translation would contain a warning to refrain from insight." Then, to compound the

6 *Eat thou not the bread of him that hath an evil eye, neither desire thou his dainty meats:*
7 *For as he thinketh in his heart, so is he: Eat and drink, saith he to thee; but his heart is not with thee.*
8 *The morsel which thou hast eaten shalt thou vomit up, and lose thy sweet words.*

you glancing with your eyes toward it, and it is gone?"[5] Verse 5b-c then explains this with a brief illustration. "*Wealth* will certainly develop wings; as an eagle, it flies away into the heavens."[6] The *kətîb waʿûp* in 5c is better read with the *qərê yaʿûp,* "and it flies. . . ," the subject referring to the riches (so AV).

6-8 One with an "evil eye" is a selfish person (see also 28:22), just as one with a "bountiful eye" (22:9) is a generous person. The warning here directs the youth not to become involved socially with such a person, v. 6.[7] Verse 7 notes the problem. He is what he is in his heart.[8] He

---

difficulty, he relies on *Amen-em-opet* to emend the phrase to avoid wealth gained through robbery. He follows Sellin in suggesting *mibbiṣṣateka,* "let go of thy robbery." This illustrates the danger of depending upon *Amen-em-opet.*

[5]Literally, 5a must read something like "Are you flying your eyes on it, and it is gone?" The use of *hətaʿûp* with "eyes" is puzzling. It must mean something like directing a fleeting glance toward wealth. The unusual idiom led the rabbis to adopt the *qərê* reading *hətaʿîp,* "are you causing your eyes to fly," still with the sense of glancing upon wealth. McKane, p. 383, suggests the notion "you take your eyes off it for an instant, and is it there any longer?" Less suitable is H. J. Byington's suggestion, "Hebrew Marginalia," *JBL* 64:348, that the *h* should be carried back to the end of v. 4 or that *hətaʿûp* be read as a *hithpaʿel.* The phrasing is unusual in English.

[6]Among others, Byington, p. 348, and Toy, p. 432, suggest that *ʿaśoh* be read *ʿošer,* "riches." This has the advantage of stating an explicit subject in the phrase. The subject, however, is clear already and the change causes the emphasis supplied by "certainly make themselves," *ʿaśoh yaʿaśeh,* to be lost.

[7]There is no real grammatical problem in v. 6. Something must be supplied to connect *raʿ ʿayin,* "evil eye," with the earlier part of 6a. Considering the poetical nature of the passage, this is not a surprising construction. The thought of the phrase is clear. Despite this, Driver, *Biblica* 32:187, transposes *ʾet* and *lehem,* taking *ʾet* as the preposition "with" to introduce *raʿ ʿayin.* BH suggests deleting *lehem,* again allowing *ʾet* to act as a preposition. While these proposals smooth out the grammar, there is no real need to change the text.

[8]The verb *šaʿar* occurs only here with the meaning "to calculate, reckon." The word is supported by Aramaic and Arabic cognates. Toy, p. 432, tentatively suggests emending to *yaʿaśeh,* "as he deals with himself." Dahood, *PNWSP,* p. 47, relates the word to Ugaritic, "to serve," and translates, "like one serving his own appetite." AB, p. 139, inserts *ləkâ* after *ken-hûʾ* and translates "as he estimates his own appetite, so he will yours." Keimer, *AJSL* 43:16, attempts to relate this to *Amen-em-opet.* He follows Gressmann and Sellin in emending *šaʿar bənapšô* to *śaʿar bənepeš,* and translates, "like a storm in thy

9 Speak not in the ears of a fool: for he will despise the wisdom of thy words.
10 Remove not the old landmark; and enter not into the fields of the fatherless:
11 For their redeemer is mighty; he shall plead their cause with thee.

may appear outwardly generous and gracious with his invitation to eat and drink. His invitation, however, has a selfish motive lying behind it, v. 7. When his real purposes become revealed, you will feel like vomiting up that which you have eaten. You will "lose" all of your complimentary words of thanks, i.e., they will have been wasted, v. 8.

9 This is a practical observation that has been seen before in different forms; cf. 9:7-8; 13:1; 15:12. The *kəsîl* (cf. 1:22) is haughty, a self-sufficient individual who has no concern for what others think. It is a waste of your time to give him wise instruction since he will reject your efforts.[9] There is no clear parallel to v. 9 in *Amen-em-opet*.

10-11 The paragraph makes the general admonition of 22:28 more specific, applying it particularly to the fields of orphans.[10] As there, so here the verb "remove" is to move back, to make the plot of land smaller than its actual size. To "enter" here is to go with an evil intention to move the boundary markers of the land, v. 10. The "redeemer" is a *goʾel,* the kinsman-redeemer, which has such important typical significance when applied to the Lord Jesus Christ. This is the only time this notable theological word occurs in the book. Basically, there were five considerations in the *goʾel* relationship:

> (1) an impoverished condition, Leviticus 25:47, such as man has spiritually without Christ;

---

soul is he." McKane, p. 385, follows the LXX in reading *śeʿar*. He translates, "He is like *a hair* in *the* throat," a disgusting thing. The lack of agreement shows the futility of emending the verse. Although the word is rare, the MT is sensible.

[9]Skehan, *CBQ* 10:122-23, considers this a place where there is damage to the text. He suggests that v. 9 is an introductory line for 9:7-9. Toy, pp. 430-31, mutilates v. 8, combining 8*a* with 3*b* and making the exhortation "a caution against indiscriminate dining out." He moves 8*b* after v. 9 to create a ternary saying. None of these suggestions have merit.

[10]Among others, Toy, p. 432, and Greenstone, p. 245, alter *ʿôlam* to *ʾalmanâ,* "the landmark of the widow." This makes the passage agree more closely with *Amen-em-opet,* a tenuous basis for the emendation. There is no textual support for the suggestion. In addition, *ʿôlam* occurs in the parallel in 22:28. There is no need to emend.

12 Apply thine heart unto instruction, and thine ears to the words of knowledge.
13 Withhold not correction from the child: for if thou beatest him with the rod, he shall not die.
14 Thou shalt beat him with the rod, and shalt deliver his soul from hell.

(2) a kinsman relationship, Leviticus 25:48-49, such as the Lord established by His birth as the son of Mary;

(3) the willingness of the redeemer, cf. Ruth 4:6, such as Christ demonstrated by coming into this world;

(4) the ability of the redeemer, Leviticus 25:50-52, such as Christ proved by resisting Satan's temptation;

(5) the resulting relationship of the redeemed, Leviticus 25:53, such as we acquire when we place our faith in Christ as Savior.

In this case, God Himself becomes the Redeemer of the ones who have been defrauded. He is "mighty" and thus well able to argue their case against the oppressor, v. 11.

12 This general exhortation to wisdom is similar to 22:17. It is widely taken as an introduction to the following section although there is no general agreement as to how far the section goes.[11] The "heart" (*leb,* cf. 3:5) has its customary meaning referring to the thinking process. The "ears" are the gateway by which speech enters into the mind. The youth, then, should focus his thoughts on that which is truly wise.

13-14 The book emphasizes the need for consistent discipline of the child by his parents (13:24; 19:18; 22:15; 29:15, 17). The child who cannot accept the discipline of his parents will not likely submit his will to the discipline of a heavenly Father. The punishment of his parents must be adequate to break the child's will. During his early years, he cannot understand reasoning or anticipate the consequences of an undisciplined life. He can, however, understand pain. Punishment that hurts communicates clearly to the young and immature mind of a child. Slowly but surely, the child learns to submit his will to the will of his parents.

---

[11]Zöckler, p. 201, says it introduces the proverbs only as far as vv. 16 or 18. AB, p. 143, thinks it introduces 22:13–24:22. Ross, *EBC* V, p. 1069, suggests it is a variant of 22:17 added later to the text. Coates, p. 91, states that the "verse marks the transition from miscellaneous maxims to an elaborate lesson in the form of those in i.-ix." Cohen, p. 154, suggests that the verse "may mark the beginning of a separate collection of sayings."

This prepares him to submit his will to God. In this way, the physical punishment that his parents apply helps deliver the youth from death and hell (so vv. 13-14). His actions, if not restrained, will naturally bring him to a premature death.[12] The corporal punishment that his parents apply allows him to escape this fate, v. 13.

There is one additional motivation for the parents. Disciplinary correction of the child will enable him to escape "hell," *šə'ôl;* cf. 7:27. The word *šə'ôl* often indicates the spiritual consequences of wickedness, divine judgment in hell. Left to himself, the child will end up with this as his destiny. Consistent discipline, administered under the guidance of the Holy Spirit, has the potential of delivering the child from this.

Corporal punishment thus has an immense importance to the child. It not only affects the temporal realm of this present life but also the eternal domain of the child's soul. A well-disciplined youngster has the preparation necessary to let him receive those spiritual truths that will result in his salvation, v. 14.

Discipline of a Child

1. Command of God, 19:18

2. Evidence of love, 13:24

3. Training of the child

    a. Negatively—Correcting the child, 22:15

    b. Positively—Imparting wisdom, 29:15

4. Results of the training

    a. Reward of the parents, 29:17

    b. Salvation of the child, 23:13-14

---

[12]A second view of this passage holds that it is a superlative, expressing the idea that corporal punishment will not harm the child. So Thomas, *VTS* III, 288-89. The only parallel to the verse is in 19:18, which supports the above view, that early discipline will turn the child aside from premature death. Cohen, p. 154, makes the death that of later punishment for some crime. There is no need, however, to restrict it so severely. The broader view of premature death, from any cause, better explains the verse.

15 My son, if thine heart be wise, my heart shall rejoice, even mine.
16 Yea, my reins shall rejoice, when thy lips speak right things.
17 Let not thine heart envy sinners: but be thou in the fear of the Lord
*   all the day long.*
18 For surely there is an end; and thine expectation shall not be cut off.

15-16 Solomon expresses his feelings regarding the wisdom of his
son. One of the marks of maturity is wise conduct. If the son demonstrates wisdom, Solomon will rejoice, v. 15. If the speech of the son is
proper, Solomon will likewise rejoice in that. The word "reins," *kilyôt,*
refers literally to the "kidneys." These organs poetically represent the innermost being, thus the seat of the emotions. When the son shows wisdom in his speech, he becomes a source of joy to his father, v. 16.

17-18 In this life, the sinner often seems to prosper while the righteous often struggle for their existence. The sinner flaunts his enjoyment
of this world's pleasures as he appears to live an exciting and stimulat-
ing life. There is, therefore, a natural appeal for a godly youth to give up
his self-controlled way in order to accompany evil men in their hedonistic pursuits. Solomon warns the youth not to envy those whose conduct
violates God's standards.

Verses 17*b* and 18 give two separate arguments to justify this warning.
In the first place, the youth should remain with his heart directed continually toward the "fear of the Lord" (*yirʾat yǝhwah,* cf. 1:7). The "fear
of the Lord" here is in antithetic parallelism with the wicked acts of
"sinners." The youth who goes after one will simultaneously depart from
the other. Solomon therefore urges the youth to fill his life with the
Lord and to turn from those individuals who would draw him from this
position.[13] The charge implies that this attitude will compensate for the
loss of the pleasures and material gain that comes to those who follow
an evil way of life. One who stays his mind on the Lord will not have
time for thoughts of this world, v. 17.

---

[13]Many have offered suggestions to try to explain the relationship between the two
halves of the verse. KD II, 113, makes *ʾal yǝqannehʾ,* "let not . . . envy," in 17*a* govern
the actions in 17*b*. The son should not "envy" sinners, but he should "envy," i.e., eagerly
desire, the fear of Yahweh. Driver, *Biblica* 32:196, followed by Thomas, *VT* 15:274, suggests that the abstract noun "fear," *yirʾat,* is a "collective term for a concrete subject,"
"fearers of Jehovah," antithetic to "sinners." Again, the verb *qanâ* governs both halves of
the verse. The youth should not envy sinners, but he should envy those who fear the
Lord. It is unlikely, in my judgment, that such a widely used phrase as "fear of Yahweh"

19 Hear thou, my son, and be wise, and guide thine heart in the way.
20 Be not among winebibbers; among riotous eaters of flesh:
21 For the drunkard and the glutton shall come to poverty: and drowsi-
ness shall clothe a man with rags.

Verse 18 gives the second justification for the warning. A time will come when God will correct the perverted ethics and experiences of this world. The "end" (ʾaḥărît, cf. 14:12) and the "expectation" (or "hope," tiqwâ, cf. 10:28) are parallel. Both refer to that glorious experience of life after death, when believers will inherit those blessings that God stores up for them in heaven.[14] The promise is doubly assured in its certainty by the Hebrew construction. The kîʾim introduction to the verse implies certainty, a positive affirmation of fact, "surely." The particle yeš, cf. 19:18, follows, implying existence with emphasis, "there is." The coupling of the two Hebrew terms emphatically emphasizes the certainty of the statement. These vigorously assert the actual existence of a coming time when the wise youth will experience the blessings of God.

19-21 A specific example of the wrong kind of friends immediately follows the admonition regarding the envy of sinners. The youth should

---

should have a specialized meaning in this verse. Toy, pp. 434, 438, objects to allowing the verb to govern both objects. He asserts that the verb, when elsewhere used in the sense of envy, always has a bad connotation. He suggests that yirʾat be emended to the imperative yəraʾ followed by the sign of the accusative ʾet. While the command "fear the Lord" makes a nice contrast with 17a, there is no textual support for this suggestion. The AV supplies the verb "be" in the second half. Jones, p. 193, supplies the verb "continue." While there is no general agreement regarding the treatment of the verse, the suggestions give the same understanding. The omission of the verb allowed Solomon to balance the rhythm of the verse (both vv. 17 and 18 are 3:3 in form). Since the sense is clear, there is no great loss by omitting the verb. We should supply something such as "be" or "remain" for smoothness.

[14]McKane, p. 388, sees the "end" only as the climax of a full life, one that attains its potential without being shortened by disaster or judgment. Walther Zimmerli, "Zur Struktur der alttestamentlichen Weisheit," *ZAW* 51:198, similarly infers that the word has a qualitative sense, that it denotes "gutes Ende," a good end. He bases this on the parallelism of ʾaḥărît and tiqwâ. These views do not adequately explain the context of v. 17. The whole point of the passage is that the wrongs of this life will one day be made right. Sinners may prosper now but God will vindicate His children in the time to come. Such passages as 14:32; 16:4; and 24:12 clearly indicate that the book anticipates a future judgment. In view of this, 23:18 and 24:14, 20 all naturally refer to the "end" of the blessed life after death. AB, pp. 140-41, softens yirʾat yəhwah in 17b to "religious faith." He then supplies māṣāʾtâ in 18a from 24:14, where 18b is repeated. He translates, "If you possess that, there is a future [for you]." The well-known yirʾat yəhwah does not need any change and there is no need for the insertion.

not associate with gluttons and drunkards. The initial statement is very general. The son should show his wisdom by following his father's instructions, v. 19.[15]

The caution of vv. 20-21 fits well into the spirit of the book. Young people often yield to the lusts of the flesh. Because of its seriousness, sensual lust receives more emphasis in the book. Drunkenness (*saba'*) and gluttony (*zalal*), however, fall into this same category of sins that appeal to the flesh. The word *saba'* refers to those who overindulge themselves in alcohol. The word *zalal,* "to be light, worthless," suggests "wastefulness" or "profligacy." Elsewhere it may refer to "worthlessness." The context here, however, suggests gluttony. Children should restrain themselves in these areas, not giving in to their natural inclinations.

The admonition parallels drunkenness and gluttony. By implication, this teaches that the one sin equals the other in importance. Both excesses go against the biblical principle of self-control (Gal. 5:23). A person who does not restrain himself in these areas has a character flaw. The lack of self-control here may develop into a lack of self-control in other areas as well. The exhortation guides the child to develop the self-discipline of one who walks in the ways of wisdom, v. 20.

The end of riotous living is want. Those who waste their substance in gluttony or drunkenness come to poverty (cf. *yaraš,* 20:13, note).[16] The parallel thought of "drowsiness" comes from the practical observation that eating and drinking frequently lead to sleepiness. This kind of person will likely end up wearing rags, an indication of his meager resources, v. 21.

---

[15]AB, p. 141, arbitrarily emends the MT *'attâ* to *'attâ,* translating, "Hear, now. . . ." While the suggestion fits very nicely, there is no intrinsic reason that "Hear, now . . ." is better than "Hear thou. . . ." In a different vein, Toy, pp. 435, 438, argues that since "way" (*derek*) does not elsewhere occur in Proverbs "in this absolute (undefined) sense," it must be changed to better parallel 19a. He suggests *libbeka* be changed to *binâ,* the "path of prudence." The argument is weak. Since the "way" parallels the exhortation to the "wise," the nature of the way is clear.

[16]As in 20:13, so here McKane, p. 388, applies *yiwwareš* to the poverty caused by disinheritance. There is nothing inherent in this word to require so limiting the thought. The *nip'al* of *yaraš* simply refers to poverty.

22 Hearken unto thy father that begat thee, and despise not thy mother when she is old.
23 Buy the truth, and sell it not; also wisdom, and instruction, and understanding.
24 The father of the righteous shall greatly rejoice: and he that begetteth a wise child shall have joy of him.
25 Thy father and thy mother shall be glad, and she that bare thee shall rejoice.

22-25 Initially, the charge directs the youth to obey his parents. The terms "father" and "mother" occur here in poetic variation, with no significance attached to their position in the verse. The unspoken thought is that the parents have gained wisdom through their experience. As the youth follows their guidance, he will gain wisdom, v. 22. Solomon builds on this foundation, urging the lad to buy and not sell truth. Compare 4:7. The verb "buy" governs 23*b* also, making 23*b* parallel the thought of 23*a*. The thought of "buying truth" suggests that a person should give up personal wealth, ease, and time for the sake of growth in understanding. At the same time, the youth must make every effort to see that truth is not snatched away because of carelessness or worldliness, v. 23.[17]

The parents of such a child rejoice over his righteous conduct. The spiritual maturity of the child is clear to others. What rests in the heart shows itself in life through speech and actions. This brings joy to the parents, v. 24.[18] The paragraph points back to v. 22. There the youth was charged with obedience to his parents. The result will be the rejoicing of the parents as they see their child develop righteousness and wisdom, v. 25.

---

[17]Oesterley, p. 206, states that the verse "is clearly out of place here." He suggests relocating it and coupling it to v. 19. Toy, p. 438, and Jones, p. 194, make similar suggestions. AB, p. 143, transposes the verse with v. 22. None of these suggestions have textual support.

[18]Toy, p. 436, mangles the passage, justifying his changes on the basis of parallelism. He emends v. 24 to read, "The mother of a wise son will rejoice," thus paralleling v. 25. Then, in order to parallel 25*a* with 25*b*, he emends to read, "Let thy father rejoice, let thy mother be glad!" This is all highly arbitrary since there is no textual support. Further, the MT is already parallel. Verse 24 emphasizes the father and v. 25 adds the mother. There is no need for the change. The *qərê*, "greatly rejoice," *gîl yagîl,* in 24*a* is more natural than the *kətîb gôl yagûl,* although the meaning is not changed.

26 My son, give me thine heart, and let thine eyes observe my ways.
27 For a whore is a deep ditch; and a strange woman is a narrow pit.
28 She also lieth in wait as for a prey, and increaseth the transgressors
*   among men.*

26-28 The father not only calls for his son's obedience but for his willing assent as well.[19] The word "observe" (cf. *raṣôn*, 11:1) denotes the son's attitude, one of "delight" toward his father's directions, v. 26. The charms of the adulteress are characterized as a "deep ditch" (*šûḥâ*) and as a "narrow pit" (*bəʾer*), a trap for one who becomes involved with her. Both *šûḥâ* and *bəʾer* draw on a literal pit or well to picture a place of entrapment. These metaphors occur elsewhere to indicate a place of entrapment (Jer. 18:20, 22; Lam. 3:53, 55). They describe here the trap that awaits those who dally with the whore, v. 27.[20] She is compared further with one who "lieth in wait as for a prey," i.e., a "robber." This is apt since she seeks to rob men of their virtue. Through her actions, she "increases the transgressors [better, "treachery," cf. *bagad*, 11:3] among men." This broad term includes sons who are unfaithful to the teaching of their parents and husbands who are unfaithful to their wives. Above all, it would include the treachery of all who through their wicked actions are unfaithful to God, v. 28.[21]

---

[19]The *kətîb,* "delight," *tiroṣnâ,* is acceptable and there is no need to read the *qərê,* "observe," *tiṣṣornâ,* as does the AV. The versions and commentaries divide between the two readings.

[20]Consistent with her view on the *nakrîyâ* and *zonâ* in earlier chapters, Farmer, p. 111, understands these references here in a figurative sense. She refers them to cultic practices. The view is forced. The passage occurs in the middle of a series of warnings that guide the son in his behavior in life. The more natural application here is as a warning against sexual misconduct.

[21]Gemser, p. 67, proposes to read *ûbəgudîm* or *ûbəgadîm,* "deceiver." Toy, p. 438, gains better parallelism with 28*a* by emending similarly. He translates, "Many are they she plunders." AB, p. 142, takes the verse similarly. Mitchell Dahood, "To Pawn One's Cloak," *Biblica* 42:363, vocalizes the MT as *bəgadîm,* "cloaks from men she snatches." None of these suggestions have textual support, nor do they improve the sense of the passage.

*29 Who hath woe? who hath sorrow? who hath contentions? who hath
babbling? who hath wounds without cause? who hath redness of
eyes?
30 They that tarry long at the wine; they that go to seek mixed wine.
31 Look not thou upon the wine when it is red, when it giveth his colour
in the cup, when it moveth itself aright.
32 At the last it biteth like a serpent, and stingeth like an adder.
33 Thine eyes shall behold strange women, and thine heart shall utter
perverse things.
34 Yea, thou shalt be as he that lieth down in the midst of the sea, or as
he that lieth upon the top of a mast.
35 They have stricken me, shalt thou say, and I was not sick; they have
beaten me, and I felt it not: when shall I awake? I will seek it yet
again.*

29-35 Verse 30 answers the six questions in v. 29. In the final question, *haklilôt* is better "dullness" (of eyes) rather than "redness."[22] This is the dullness produced in one who has imbibed too much alcohol, v. 29. These difficulties fall upon "those who give themselves to drink. They "tarry long" over the wine and "seek mixed wine." This last is literally "those who go to search [i.e., taste] mixed wine." Apparently, this refers to wine mixed with spices to enhance its flavor. See the discussion at 9:2, v. 30.[23]

Since the wine can produce such bad effects, the young man should avoid it. He should not be overcome by its attractive appearance, described as "red." The undiluted wine can have a deep, rich red color, attractive to the eye.[24] The phrase "colour in the cup," *bakos ʾênô* (reading

---

[22]Byington, *JBL* 64:351, proposes "black eyes," parallel to "wounds without cause." The parallelism already exists with the six questions all dealing with the same topic. The connection with alcohol argues for "dullness."

[23]Dahood, *PNWSP*, p. 49, argues on the basis of Ugaritic that *mimsak* means "mixing bowl." He takes the phrase as referring to those who come to inspect the bottom of the bowl (by drinking heavily). While this is possible, the root idea of *masak* supports "mixed wine."

[24]Driver, *Biblica* 32:187 and "Review of the Assyrian Dictionary, Vol. XVI," *JSS* 9:349, vigorously opposes the common translation "look . . ." as "absurd." He takes *raʾâ* as *ruah*, "to drink," making the proverb an admonition "not to drink deeply of unmixed wine." This misses the whole point of the phrase, which is to warn the youth against allowing the attractive appearance to deceive him into drinking too deeply. Athalaya Brenner, *Colour Terms in the Old Testament* (1982), pp. 77-78, suggests a meaning of "be pleasant, attractive," for *ʾadam*. She bases this on the Ethiopic cognate *ʾdm*. While the sense fits here, it is unlikely that a common word like *ʾadam* would have such a restricted meaning.

the qərê), is literally "eye in the cup." The word ʾênô is metaphoric for "appearance." The eye is the window to the soul, a barometer of inner feelings, and here, so applied to the wine, the vehicle for conveying its attractiveness.[25] The final phrase, "when it moveth itself aright," is better rendered "when it goes [down the throat] smoothly," v. 31.[26]

Though the wine may be attractive because of its appearance, there is a disastrous end to those who indulge in it. The verb "stingeth," yapriš, occurs only here. There are Akkadian and Aramaic cognates that refer to a staff or an ox goad. The Hebrew term may refer to the prick that comes from poking with the goad. The wine "pricks" like the serpent's bite, v. 32. Further, it may cause one to hallucinate, to see "strange things" (rather than "strange women," AV). The mind will bring forth "perverse things" (tahpukôt, cf. 2:12), v. 33.

The passage closes with two illustrations. The intoxicated person is like a person lying down on a ship in the midst of the sea. The swells passing under the ship cause him to move back and forth, a disagreeable feeling to one who is drunk. He is also like a man lying on top of a "mast," ḥibbel. The word ḥibbel probably comes from ḥabal, "to bind," and thus relates in some way to a "rope." Since the context relates to the sea, "rigging" expresses the sense well. Sleeping on a pile of rope, the man is uncomfortable, v. 34.[27]

---

[25]Driver, JSS 9:348-49, correctly notes that modern sparkling wines were not known in ancient times. He argues for the translation "and it forms its droplets on the cup." He supports this with a technical argument concerning the formation of condensation droplets on the inner surface of the cup and also from the Arabic cognate to "colour," ʿênô. I am not convinced that this sense can be carried over into Hebrew; hence, I prefer to take ʿênô in its figurative sense, something that occurs elsewhere in Proverbs, e.g., 22:9; 23:6; 30:17.

[26]To balance the verse, Gemser, p. 68, inserts dobbeb śəpatayim wəšinnayim, "gliding over the lips and teeth," comparing it to Song of Sol. 7:10c, where a similar phrase occurs. Conversely, Toy, p. 439, omits the phrase as not in accord with the rest of the couplet. Neither suggestion has support.

[27]Dahood, PNWSP, pp. 49-50, relates ḥibbel to Ugaritic, "mountain." The drunk man, then, feels one moment as if he were on the sea, then next as though he were on a mountain. Toy, p. 442, radically emends bəroʾš ḥibbel to basaʿar gadol, "a violent storm." AB, p. 142, accepts "mast" for ḥibbel but emends ûkəšōkēb bəroʾš to ûkəšōkēr kərōʾš. He translates, "who rolls drunkenly like the top of the mast." Other suggestions as well have been made. The word is difficult; however, sense can be made of the MT.

To show the incoherent thinking process of the drunkard, Solomon pictures him as talking to himself of his recent experience. He has been struck by someone, but he has not become "sick" (cf. *ḥalâ*, 13:12); he has been beaten, yet he did not know it. So enslaved is he to drink that he expresses his longing even before he is fully awakened, v. 35.

> **The Influence of Alcohol**
>
> 1. The aftereffects of alcohol 29-30
>
> 2. The avoidance of alcohol 31-32
>
> 3. The accomplishments of alcohol 33-35
>
>   a. Hallucinations 33
>
>   b. Hangover 34
>
>   c. Habit 35

1 Be not thou envious against evil men, neither desire to be with them.
2 For their heart studieth destruction, and their lips talk of mischief.
3 Through wisdom is an house builded; and by understanding it is es-
tablished:
4 And by knowledge shall the chambers be filled with all precious and
pleasant riches.

PROVERBS 24

1-2 Once more, as in 3:31 and 23:17, Solomon warns the youth not to envy evil men. The warning occurs again in 24:19-20. Wicked men may prosper in this life. Their way of life may look attractive with its blatant appeal to the flesh. But the wise youth will not be seduced by this. He will avoid prolonged or intimate contact with the godless. There is a subtly stated inference to the fate of the evil one. The phrase is literally "men of evil." The word "man" *(ʾanôš)* often emphasizes man's frailty or mortality. The choice of *ʾanôš* here reminds the youth of the undesirable end of the sinful, v. 1. Verse 2 gives representative reasons, not a complete listing of all of the sins of the wicked. Their thoughts and their speech focus on ways that go contrary to the ways of God. The youth should therefore avoid them, v. 2.

3-4 In a beautifully poetic passage, Solomon describes the building of a godly home.[1] "Wisdom," "understanding," and "knowledge" are synonyms, making the point that the successful family develops through the wise conduct of the family members.[2] The verb *kûn,* cf. 12:3, "builded," has a metaphorical sense. The house is "built" in that it is successfully established. Wholesome family relationships exist, and the family faces routinely the obstacles and challenges of life, v. 3. In the normal course of life, this home will prosper as God blesses it with His bounty, v. 4.

---

[1]Skehan, *CBQ* 10:122, 126, suggests that 24:3-7 is misplaced from c. 25 because of the nature of its contents. These three paragraphs are not proverbial (in a traditional sense); rather, they are more philosophical, a reflection upon the godly way of life. Skehan lacks textual support for his views. It is difficult to see how so many transpositions could have occurred as he requires to support his theory of the book's organization.

[2]Toy, p. 442, specifically rejects any application to the family. He holds that the synonyms express "practical sagacity, without reference to moral or religious qualities." This is a trite view and, to me, misses the point of the passage.

5 A wise man is strong; yea, a man of knowledge increaseth strength.
6 For by wise counsel thou shalt make thy war: and in multitude of
  counsellors there is safety.
7 Wisdom is too high for a fool: he openeth not his mouth in the gate.

5-7 The word "man" (cf. *gibbôr,* 16:32) has the connotation of a
"strong man." The term *geber* denotes a mature man at the fullness of
his strength, so it is appropriately used here of one who walks in wisdom. The definite article with "strong" (*ᶜôz,* cf. 7:13) is unusual but
may be explained on the basis of wisdom's certainty in the mind of the
author.[3] The idea is that the wise man is marked by the inner strength
that comes from his wisdom. Further, his possession of knowledge leads
to additional strength for the challenges of each day, v. 5.

The waging of war illustrates the need of wisdom. Someone must plot
the tactics carefully. Counsel taken with others helps to avoid mistakes
in the plans; cf. 11:14; 15:22; 20:18. This is necessary for the successful
conquest of an enemy. The situation illustrates the value of seeking
counsel, v. 6.

In contrast, wisdom (*ḥokmôt,* cf. 1:2; written intensively here, cf. 1:20)
is "too high" (better, "*as* corals," *raʾmôt*) for the fool (*ʾawîl,* cf. 1:7). The
idea is that wisdom's value is too great for the fool. He cannot attain it.[4]
The gate of the city is the place where city government, the buying and
selling of goods, and assemblies took place. As such, it was a natural
place for the gathering of news, for the debating of topics of interest,
and for general gossip. The fool, however, because of his lack of wisdom, cannot join these conversations. His lack of wisdom hinders his
participation, v. 7.

---

[3]McKane, p. 397, concludes that the Hebrew is impossible and emends to *gabar ḥakam
meᶜaz,* "a wise man has more strength than a strong man." This has the support of the
LXX and other ancient versions. AB, p. 144, and Toy, p. 446, treat the phrase similarly.
Whybray, p. 139, comments that "the Hebrew makes no sense here." He notes that the
NEB "attempted a reconstruction along the lines of the ancient Versions." He translates,
"Wisdom prevails over strength, knowledge over brute force." The MT has adequate parallelism without changing the text.
[4]The plenarily written *raʾmôt* is "corals" elsewhere, Job 28:18; Ezek. 27:16. Some accept *raʾmôt* as an alternative spelling of *ramot,* "high." So, among others, Kidner, p. 154;
Alden, p. 173; French and Skinner, p. 82; NIV; NASB. While this is true, *ruʾmôt* occurs
in this sense only when referring to the "heights" of a place. The AV normally transliter-
ates the word, e.g., "Ramoth in Gilead," Josh. 20:8. Martin, p. 150, and Toy, p. 443,
emend to *ramot,* "high," and interpret as the AV. Oesterley, p. 207, emends to *ʾêmôt,* "terrors," although he admits that *ʾêmôt* never applies to wisdom elsewhere.

8 He that deviseth to do evil shall be called a mischievous person.
9 The thought of foolishness is sin: and the scorner is an abomination to men.
10 If thou faint in the day of adversity, thy strength is small.
11 If thou forbear to deliver them that are drawn unto death, and those that are ready to be slain;
12 If thou sayest, Behold, we knew it not; doth not he that pondereth the heart consider it? and he that keepeth thy soul, doth not he know it? and shall not he render to every man according to his works?

8-9 The individual who plans out his evil will be known as a "mischievous person" (better, a "schemer," *məzimmôt,* cf. 1:4). The description is picturesque. The phrase *baᶜal⁻məzimmôt* is a "lord of plans," i.e., a master of intrigues. Though he may think that he hides his evil, others know his character, v. 8. Such devising of folly is sin. This individual is surely a "scorner" (*leṣ,* cf. 1:22), and, as such, he is an "abomination" (*tôᶜəbat,* cf. 3:32), v. 9.[5]

10-12 The "day of adversity" in v. 10 connects very nicely with the time of crisis referred to in v. 11. For this reason, I take vv. 10-12 as a paragraph dealing with a single theme as opposed to allowing v. 10 to stand by itself.[6]

The opening statement makes the point that one is strong only if he is strong in the crisis. Negatively, if you "faint" (*rapâ*) in the time of distress, you have limited strength. The *hitpaᶜel* of *rapâ,* "to sink down," is "become disheartened," v. 10.[7] Verse 11 is a command, not a conditional statement. The phrase "if thou forbear," expresses a wish: "O that you would spare *them.*" Rather than failing in the crisis, the strong man should face it successfully. He should deliver those who are being taken away to

---

[5]Richardson, *VT* 5:175-76, cites v. 9 in support of his theory that *leṣ* should be glossed "babbler." The context of vv. 8-9 rather favors the view that the *leṣ* is a "scorner." The word is broadly used in this sense throughout the poetical and prophetical portions of the OT.

[6]Among others, Muenscher, pp. 218-19; Kufeldt, p. 567; French and Skinner, p. 83; and Garrett, p. 199, take v. 10 by itself. In this case, the crisis reveals a lack of inner strength.

[7]Dahood, *PNWSP,* p. 50, takes "the day of adversity," *bəyôm ṣarâ,* as "hard times." He then redivides the consonants of "thy strength is small," *ṣar kohekâ,* to *ṣarek hek,* translating "your palate will hunger," supporting this from Ugaritic. This does not do justice to the phrase. This is a crisis, not merely a time of failure to sow the seed properly. Additionally, there is no textual support for the suggestion.

13 My son, eat thou honey, because it is good; and the honeycomb,
which is sweet to thy taste:
14 So shall the knowledge of wisdom be unto thy soul: when thou hast
found it, then there shall be a reward, and thy expectation shall not
be cut off.

face death and those who are "ready to be slain" (*ûmaṭîm,* cf. 10:30).[8]
The verb *môṭ,* "to totter, shake" (better, "staggering to the slaughter"),
denotes a general insecurity, v. 11.[9]

The all-wise God knows man's opportunities (cf. 15:3). If a man tries
to pretend ignorance of his opportunities for helping his fellow man, he
goes against the omniscient God.[10] The God who "pondereth" (better,
"weighs," *token,* cf. 21:2) the heart of man considers his excuses. The
God who "keepeth" (or "guards," *noṣer,* cf. 2:8) the soul of man knows
the opportunities that have come his way. He will one day repay man according to his works, v. 12.[11]

13-14 Verse 13 sets forth an emblem of the truth conveyed more fully
in v. 14. Honey is good in that it serves as food (II Sam. 17:29). It is
suitable as a gift (Gen. 43:11), it refreshes (II Sam. 14:29), it adds a
sweet flavor (Ezek. 3:3), and it has monetary value (Ezek. 27:17). The

---

[8]Perles, *JQR* 2:126, and AB. p. 145, arbitrarily propose *muttîm* for the MT's *matîm.*
AB translates, "protect those who are prostrate from being slain." This applies the
phrase to the wounded after a battle. There is no textual support for the change. Driver,
ZAW 50:146 and, again, *Biblica* 32:189, argues that *matîm* is from an Arabic root. He
most recently translates, "do thou preserve those ready for execution," a sense that is
possible. Dahood, *PNWSP,* p. 51, revocalizes *matîm* to *mattîm,* "rods." He translates, "do
restrain the rods from killing." To me, this is strained.
[9]There is no agreement on how to treat *ʾim.* McKane, p. 400, and Gemser, p. 69, give
it a negative force: "do not hold back help. . . ." KD II, 131, and Toy, p. 446, take it as
hortatory, "Save those. . . ." Cohen, p. 161, takes it as introducing a question, "wilt thou
forbear . . . ?" No compelling argument forces one sense above another. I arbitrarily take
ʾim to indicate a wish.
[10]The expected singular *yadaʿtî* is rather a plural *yadaʿnû.* This reflects the attempt by
the individual to group himself with others who have also failed to take action to rescue
the innocent victim from his circumstances. Martin, p. 151; Gemser, p. 69; and
Oesterley, p. 212, emend with the LXX to the first person singular rather than the third
person plural. The MT, however, needs no correction at this point.
[11]Greenstone, p. 256, considers the entire verse a scribal interpretation of v. 11. The
versions argue against this view. Farmer, p. 113, considers v. 12 an independent statement, separate from vv. 10-11. The *zeh,* "it," then is much broader than the preceding
verses. The view is possible but I feel it is more natural to take it as the conclusion to
the passage.

*15 Lay not wait, O wicked man, against the dwelling of the righteous;
spoil not his resting place:
16 For a just man falleth seven times, and riseth up again: but the
wicked shall fall into mischief.*

"honeycomb" is the source of honey and is also good to eat. These are
appropriate tokens to represent wisdom, v. 13. Just as honey is pleasant
to the taste, so wisdom brings its desirable reward to those who partake
of it.[12] Rather than taking "knowledge" (cf. *yadaᶜ*, 10:32) as a noun, it
should be understood as an imperative, "so know that wisdom is for
your soul." The "reward" (*ʾaḥărît*, cf. 14:12) is literally the "end." This
refers to the "future." Proverbs 23:18 uses the term similarly, indicating
the blessed hope of a heavenly life after death. This hope will never be
"cut off," v. 14.[13]

15-16 The wicked man should not attack the dwelling of the righteous.[14] The "dwelling of the righteous" undoubtedly represents the
righteous man himself, his home being the place where he can reasonably anticipate rest. The parallel "resting place," *ribṣô*, literally denotes a
place where animals lie down (so Isa. 35:7; 65:10). By extension, it is a
resting place, as here, v. 15. The number seven has its symbolic sense of
completeness, i.e., the righteous man will stumble over and over again
into difficulties, yet he will rise each time. The verb "falleth," *napal*,
often has a metaphoric sense of falling into undesirable circumstances.
It is never a fall into immorality. The unstated but implied sustaining
grace of God lets the man rise above his circumstances. The wicked
man, on the other hand, will "fall" (*yikkašlû*, cf. 16:18) into "mischief"

---

[12]Thomas, *JTS* 38:401, argues that *dəᶜeh* comes from an Arabic cognate meaning "to
seek, desire." He translates, "So seek wisdom for thyself. If thou find it. . . ." Barr,
CPTOT, pp. 24, 216, reasons similarly. Gemser, p. 69, reads *deᶜâ*. He inserts several
words to gain better metrical balance. The form *dəᶜeh* is unusual but explicable so need
not be repointed. The argument of Thomas and Barr is possible but adds nothing to our
understanding of the verse.

[13]Toy, p. 447, deletes the last half of the verse, "then there shall be a reward, and thy
expectation shall not be cut off," as being hardly appropriate here. Jones, p. 199, basically follows Toy. The suggestion is radical and unsupported and need not be considered
seriously.

[14]Jones, p. 199, and Toy, pp. 447-48, omit *rasaᶜ*. Jones states that it makes the line too
long, and Toy rejects it on stylistic grounds, since the son is normally addressed. Martin,
p. 152, also calls it out of place and suggests that it is a late insertion. The objection,
however, is unwarranted. It forces the pattern into a stylistic straightjacket, not allowing
for variation. The MT makes good sense.

*17 Rejoice not when thine enemy falleth, and let not thine heart be glad
when he stumbleth:*
*18 Lest the Lord see it, and it displease him, and he turn away his wrath
from him.*
*19 Fret not thyself because of evil men, neither be thou envious at the
wicked;*
*20 For there shall be no reward to the evil man; the candle of the
wicked shall be put out.*

(better, "calamity," cf. *raʿ*, 1:33). The verb *yikkašlû* refers to actual
falling, but it also has a figurative sense of destruction or ruin, many
times relating to a divine judgment upon sin. Here, it refers to one who
"stumbles" into judgment, v. 16.

17-18 The maxim is similar to 25:21-22. We must not gloat over the
plight of our "enemy." The word "enemy" should be read with the *qərê*
ʾôyibəka since the verbs suggest but one enemy (so the AV). The use of
the verbs "falleth," *napal,* and "stumbleth," *kašal,* suggests that the passage closely connects to vv. 15-16, where they also occur. When the
time comes that your enemy falls into calamity, do not rejoice over his
predicament, v. 17. Such an attitude displeases the Lord. By way of punishment upon you, He might well withdraw His wrath from the wicked
enemy, v. 18.

19-20 This completes the set of three paragraphs coupling the righteous man and the evildoer. We should not "fret," *tithar,* because of evil
men or "envy" (*qanâ,* cf. 14:30) the wicked. The verb *tithar* is from
hara, "to burn, kindle." Figuratively, it indicates burning oneself with
vexation and thus "to fret, worry." The contrast of the wicked man's
prosperity and the lack of success by the righteous might lead to jealousy or worry, v. 19. But the day will come when the Lord will make
right the topsy-turvy nature of this world. The wicked man has no "reward" (or "future," *ʾahərît,* cf. 14:12). This refers to the blessed hope of
a heavenly future since the wicked man clearly does have a future here
in this life. The "lamp" represents the life of the person; it will be "put
out" as God exercises judgment upon it. See the discussion at 20:20 of a
similar phrase, v. 20.[15]

---

[15]Among others, McKane, p. 405; Greenstone, p. 258; and Toy, p. 449 (cf. pp. 434-35),
deny that the verse refers to life beyond the grave. They refer it only to a full, abundant
life, or to the continuation of life through posterity. These are shallow views that do not
do justice to the promise of the verse.

*21 My son, fear thou the Lord and the king: and meddle not with them
that are given to change:
22 For their calamity shall rise suddenly; and who knoweth the ruin of
them both?*

21-22 Solomon admonishes the child to support both God and the
monarchy. In doing this, he must turn away from those who agitate for
change in these areas. There is no serious controversy over the positive
exhortation to "fear the Lord and the king."[16] This is a straightforward
challenge to revere both the Lord and the Lord's representatives to the
nation. The maxim implies that the individual has a solemn obligation to
carry out his civil responsibilities as taught in the decrees and laws of
the head of state. The passage foreshadows the apostle Peter's comments
on religious and civil obedience, I Peter 2:17.

The fact that religious and civil obedience are parallel in the verse
suggests that both aspects of life are important to wise conduct. A person generally shows religious obedience through the adoption and practice of the high standards taught in God's Word. The focus of civil
obedience is on the monarchy as continuing David's line of authority.
God Himself had decreed this authority (II Sam. 7:13-16). Civil obedience was but an extension of religious obedience. In Israel, the king
served as the representative of God to the nation. It was fitting, then,
that godly individuals in the land should obey him.

In principle, this obligation possesses a wider degree of application
than merely the obedience of the Israelites to their king. The command
is general. It suggests that godly individuals everywhere have a responsibility to practice civil obedience to the authorities of their nation. The
book makes it clear that rulers carry out the will of God (8:15; 21:1).
Thus, in every land, it is right for citizens to support secular govern-
ments as an extension of religious obedience.

---

[16]Toy, p. 450, comments: "*God*, as the more familiar word, may be substituted for
Yahweh." He gives no textual justification for the change nor any logical reason compelling it. In view of the well-established use of the expression "fear of Yahweh"
throughout the book (1:7, 29; 2:5; 8:13; 9:10; 10:27; 14:2, 26, 27; 15:16, 33; 16:6;
19:23; 22:4), it is highly unlikely that the MT needs correction. Emerton, *JTS*, 20:210-
11, points *melek*, "king," as a verb and translates, "Fear Yahweh, my son, and thou wilt
rule." Once again, there is no textual support.

The order of v. 21 is instructive. The command to fear the Lord precedes the command to fear the king. Obedience to the Lord takes precedence over other responsibilities. Obedience to the king, therefore, can continue only as long as the king himself demonstrates obedience to God. If the time comes that the decrees of the king depart from the ways of godliness, obedience to the Lord supersedes obedience to the king; cf. Daniel 3:16-18; 6:10.

The precept also warns the youth against associating with "those who are given to change," the *šûnîm*. The root *šanâ*, "to change," occurs frequently with this sense. Despite the rarity of the participle form, the basic meaning of the verb is not in doubt. For this reason, the translation "those who change" is here acceptable.[17] The youth should avoid "those who change" with respect to the Lord and the king. Since this antithetically parallels 21a, the presumption is that these changeable ones do not fear the Lord or the king. They do not submit to any authority. They are rebellious and unwilling to follow any authority higher than themselves, v. 21.

Following the warning of v. 21, Solomon states generally what will be the outcome of civil and religious rebels. They will come into "calamity" (*ʾêd*, cf. 1:26). The rhetorical question "Who can know the ruin of them both [*šənêhem*]" makes the point that no one can visualize the extent of the judgment.

There are varying interpretations for *šənêhem*, depending upon whether it stands for "years" or for "two." Taking the phrase as "the destruction of their years" creates fewer difficulties and nicely parallels the first half of the verse. In this case, the translation would be "who

---

[17]D. Winton Thomas, "The Root: שָׁנָה = سني in Hebrew," *ZAW* 52:236-37, connects *šûnîm* with an Arabic cognate and translates, "meddle not with them of high rank," i.e., the nobility. J. A. Montgomery, "שָׁנָה = سني," *ZAW* 53:207-8, follows Thomas and supports his work from Ugaritic parallels. Hulst, *OTTP*, p. 127, suggests the reading of the LXX: "do not disobey either of them." Toy, p. 450, and Eitan, pp. 10-11, suggest either of two possibilities, that of the LXX and that presented in a Targum, in which the word denotes "fools." It is likely that the LXX confused *šûnîm* with *šənêhem* in v. 22. The suggestions of Thomas and Toy are possible but I see no reason to abandon the classic understanding of the Hebrew word.

23 These things also belong to the wise. It is not good to have respect of persons in judgment.
24 He that saith unto the wicked, Thou art righteous; him shall the people curse, nations shall abhor him:
25 But to them that rebuke him shall be delight, and a good blessing shall come upon them.

knows the destruction of their years."[18] Without designating the specific nature of the judgment, the statement predicts that these wicked individuals will come into certain destruction as the years of their lives come under the judgment of God, v. 22.

23-25 The brief subtitle, "these also are the words of the wise," indicates that Solomon quotes from an existing body of wisdom. Following customary usage of his day, he adapts this to his own ends. The section, therefore, is part and parcel of the overall body of material in c. 10-24.[19]

The opening verse lacks parallelism, no doubt because of its nature as an introduction to the section. The point is that fairness is expected of a judge. To do otherwise is an abomination to God. The phrase "respect of persons" is more literally "to know faces." This is idiomatic for showing preference to one person over another, v. 23.

Verses 24-25 develop the idea introduced by v. 23. The unrighteous judge will arouse the hatred of the people, e.g., I Samuel 8:1-5. They

---

[18]Among others, Zöckler, p. 208, understands the construction to refer to "the destruction of them both," i.e., to those who rebel against God and against the king. This meets with the objection that the previous verse does not distinguish two classes of individuals but only one group that manifests their wickedness in two areas. Others, including Cohen, p. 163, take this as a genitive of source, referring to the punishment that proceeds from God and from the king. It is doubtful, though, that the phrase would embrace both God and man under one term. Oesterley, p. 215, emends to *šûnîm,* as in v. 21, and translates, "who knows the destruction of those who are given to change?" Thomas, *ZAW* 52:237, and H. Wheeler Robinson, *Record and Revelation* (1938), p. 393, emend on the basis of an Arabic cognate meaning "to be high." Driver, *Biblica* 32:189, emends on the basis of the same cognate to *haššonîm.* Both of these suggestions lead to the sense "Who knows when calamity will come upon the noblemen?" There is no textual support for this. Job 36:11, where *šanêhem* also occurs, supports taking the MT as I have done above.
[19]Verses 23-34 are customarily taken as a separate appendix, contributed by "the wise," probably the same group who wrote 22:17–23:22. The work of Kitchen, *TB* 28:70-71, however, has shown that this section is an integral part of the main body of the book, in c. 10-24. I believe that Kitchen's analysis contributes significantly to our understanding of the structure of Proverbs.

26 Every man shall kiss his lips that giveth a right answer.
27 Prepare thy work without, and make it fit for thyself in the field; and
afterwards build thine house.

will "curse" him, pronouncing imprecations upon him for his evil work.
The nation will "abhor" (cf. *za͑am*, 22:14) him, v. 24.[20] Conversely, the
righteous judge will stimulate "delight" (*na͑am*, cf. 3:17). There will be
a favorable attitude toward him among the people; cf. 28:23. He will be
exalted by the people, and they will render blessings to him as they
honor him for his work, v. 25.

26 An answer that is forthright and truthful is a thing of worth. To
show the value of speaking truth, Solomon picturesquely describes its
reward as a kiss. While the kiss on the cheek may show affection, the
kiss on the lips shows intimacy and love. Thus, an honest answer is a
sign of deep-seated love, appreciation for frankness and candor.[21]

27 Preparing the outside work and getting it ready in the field speaks
of economic preparation. In Solomon's times, an agricultural community was the norm. The principle, however, would include an industrial-
ized society such as we have today. Certainly, financial readiness is
necessary before one builds a house. The word "build" (*banâ*) in all of
its derivatives occurs only four times in the book (9:1; 14:1; 24:3, 27).
In every case, it has a metaphorical sense. In 9:1, wisdom is the subject.
Here and in 14:1 and 24:23, the verb refers to the building of a family
rather than the literal erection of a building. The practical application of
the maxim, then, lies in the mandate that it gives for fiscal preparation
before marriage.[22] Financial problems are one of the greatest difficulties

---

[20]Guillaume, *JRAS* (1942), p. 124, argues that *za͑am* means "curse" rather than
"anger" or "indignation," supporting his case from Arabic and Syriac cognates. The
close relationship between "to be hot" and "to be so angry that you curse someone" is
obvious. This, however, does not mean that we should abandon the classical meaning of
za͑am.

[21]Plaut, p. 251, understands the verse to refer to God's kissing the lips of those who
speak truth. This is possible but puzzling as to why the subject is not made more clear.
To improve the meter of the verse, Gemser, p. 70, proposes to add *kəmerea͑*, "as a
friend," to the end of the first phrase. The suggestion is unsupported. Jones, p. 201,
states that the idea of kissing in the context of a law court (vv. 24-25) is "incongruous."
He suggests taking *našaq* in the sense "to equip," i.e., equipping the lips with the words
for a right answer. The suggestion is possible although the idea of equipping the lips to
give a right answer is no clearer than the accepted translation.

[22]Toy, pp. 453, 456, on rhythmic grounds, inserts *tiqqaḥ lak ʾiššâ* after *ʾaḥar*, translating,
"Then thou mayest (take a wife)." AB, p. 148, transfers *lak* from 27*b* to 27*c*, following

28 Be not a witness against thy neighbour without cause; and deceive not with thy lips.
29 Say not, I will do so to him as he hath done to me: I will render to the man according to his work.
30 I went by the field of the slothful, and by the vineyard of the man void of understanding;
31 And, lo, it was all grown over with thorns, and nettles had covered the face thereof, and the stone wall thereof was broken down.
32 Then I saw, and considered it well: I looked upon it, and received instruction.
33 Yet a little sleep, a little slumber, a little folding of the hands to sleep:
34 So shall thy poverty come as one that travelleth; and thy want as an armed man.

for young married couples. It makes good sense that they should ready themselves financially before marriage.

28-29 The saying warns against bearing testimony in court against a neighbor "without cause," i.e., without having adequate grounds to speak. Verse 28*b* is rhetorical: "and should you deceive with your lips?" The word "witness," *ʿed* (cf. 14:25), suggests that this is a courtroom matter and that the testimony is perjured, v. 28.[23] The underlying reason for the perjury is now revealed. At some time in the past, the neighbor had committed some wrong. The subject of the proverb now takes revenge by bearing false witness. This is wrong since it usurps the authority of God who alone should punish for sin; cf. 20:22; 25:21-22, v. 29.

30-34 Solomon draws a practical lesson out of a routine experience that he has had.[24] He had passed by a field owned by a slothful man (*ʿaṣel,* cf. 6:6). This man is also a "man void of understanding" in that

---

ʾaḥar, and reads *lēk.* He translates, "After that, go, and build your house." Gemser, p. 70, basically parallels the AB. Neither of these suggestions has textual support.

[23]The interrogative particle also follows the *waw*-consecutive in II Sam. 15:35. Toy, p. 456, suggests that it be omitted and the negative continued from 28*a*. Martin, p. 155, who understands the word as an imperative, translates, "and deceive not. . . ." McKane, p. 574, follows the MT excepting that he omits the *waw.* Driver, *Biblica* 32:189, radically emends to *ûtəputehû,* retaining the consonants but changing their order substantially. Gemser, p. 70, emends with the LXX to *wəʾal-təpat,* "und solltest du täuschen," "and should you deceive?" Admittedly, the interrogative with the *waw*-consecutive is rare, but it does occur elsewhere. There is no need to alter the MT.

[24]Without giving any reasons, Whybray, p. 143, calls the illustration "fictitious," included as a "teaching device." While such a practice is possible, nothing in the story suggests that it is contrived.

he does not realize the consequences of his laziness, v. 30. The field is overgrown with "thorns" and "nettles," words at whose specific meaning we can only guess. Further, the stone wall around the field has been broken down; cf. Isaiah 5:5, v. 31. After reflecting upon this scene, he saw its practical application, v. 32. The final two verses are almost identical with 6:10-11 with only the spelling differing in poetical variation. The lesson is the same. With just a little more laziness, poverty will enter into the life of the sluggard. In 34a, "travelleth" is from *halak;* cf. 6:11. "One that travelleth" most likely refers to a vagabond, one who would likely walk into a place and pick up things of value for his own use. Similarly, his poverty will come as an "armed man" (see comments, 6:11), vv. 33-34.[25]

[25]Toy, p. 456, and Martin, p. 156, suggest that *mithallek* be emended to *mahallek,* "robber" (or "highwayman"). This adds nothing to the word picture painted by Solomon. As in 6:11, Albright, *VTS* III, 9-10, suggests that *magen* be repointed to *mogen* or *maggan,* "beggar." He supports this from Ugaritic. There is no need for the change.

Practical Applications from Proverbs 22:17–24:34

1. Exhortation to hear the truth, 22:17-21; 23:12, 22-25; 24:13-14
2. Warning against oppressing the poor, 22:22 23
3. Command to avoid evil friends, 22:24-25; 23:6-8, 17-18, 19-21, 26-28; 24:1-2, 19-20, 21-22
4. Advice regarding surety, 22:26-27
5. Commands regarding property boundaries, 22:28; 23:10-11
6. Advice regarding diligence, 22:29; 24:30-34
7. Advice regarding the home, 24:3-4, 27
8. Influence of wisdom, 24:5-7
9. Sinfulness of the evil schemer, 24:8-9
10. Guidance in international affairs, 23:1-3
11. Attitude toward material wealth, 23:4-5
12. Comments on the fool's attitude toward wisdom, 23:9
13. Comments on the discipline of a child, 23:13-14
14. Advice regarding proper speech, 23:15-16
15. Influence of wine, 23:29-35
16. Responsibility to assist others, 24:10-12
17. Warning against wickedness, 24:15-16
18. Attitude toward the wicked's judgment, 24:17-18
19. Guidance for administering justice, 24:23-25, 28-29
20. Comments on the value of truth, 24:26

SECOND COLLECTION OF SOLOMONIC PROVERBS

PROVERBS

25:1–29:27

1 These are also proverbs of Solomon, which the men of Hezekiah king of Judah copied out.
2 It is the glory of God to conceal a thing: but the honour of kings is to search out a matter.

PROVERBS 25

1 There is no reason to deny Solomon's authorship of c. 25-29 by stating that the collection was ascribed to him since he was looked at as the founder of wisdom literature.[1] The title agrees with the introduction to other Near Eastern writings of that time. Hezekiah's own writing, Isaiah 38:9-20, shows his interest in literature. We may also infer Solomon's authorship from such passages as II Chronicles 29:30 and 31:2, where he involves himself with Israel's liturgy in worship. In addition, the Talmud records that the men of Hezekiah edited the Song of Solomon, Ecclesiastes, Proverbs, and Isaiah. Hezekiah's interest in the collected wisdom of Solomon agrees with both Scripture and tradition.[2]

2-7 This passage centers on the theme of the king. Initially, we see a contrast between deity and royalty. The transcendent God veils Himself in mystery. The incomprehensible God remains distinct from His creation by virtue of His nature and attributes, the full understanding of which finite man does not grasp. The wisdom of God continues to lie outside of man's perception. Through this, God reveals Himself to man as a being worthy of worship. This is His glory. In contrast, the king's glory lies in providing wise leadership to his nation. He investigates, determines the ramifications of decisions, and correctly directs his country. As the people see progress and prosperity, the leader gains respect and honor from them, v. 2.

---

[1]Toy, p. 457, argues that the verb "copied," ʿateq, belongs to late Hebrew. The argument, however, is weak since this is the only place ʿateq occurs with the sense of copying something. The basic sense of the verb is "to remove." It is used here since the "men of Hezekiah" were removing Solomon's words from one document (or oral tradition) to another document. In the sense "to remove," ʿateq occurs in older parts of the OT, e.g., Gen. 12:8; 26:22.

[2]Skehan, *CBQ* 10:127, rejects any involvement by Hezekiah in the collection. He considers the name to have been attached to the collection only to indicate that the man was "a fountainhead of tradition." Therefore, the use of the name may not be used to date the collection. The view is subjective, unsupported by any evidence. There is no reason to reject the statement of the MT.

3 *The heaven for height, and the earth for depth, and the heart of kings is unsearchable.*
4 *Take away the dross from the silver, and there shall come forth a vessel for the finer.*
5 *Take away the wicked from before the king, and his throne shall be established in righteousness.*
6 *Put not forth thyself in the presence of the king, and stand not in the place of great men:*

At the same time, there is a sense in which no one knows why a king acts as he does. He receives information, he takes into account possible political implications, he considers the financial aspects, and he makes the final decision. As it is impossible to search out the height of the heavens or the depth of earth itself, so it is impossible to know the mind of the king; cf. I Corinthians 2:11*a*, v. 3.[3]

Verse 4 serves as the emblem to illustrate the conclusion of v. 5. The sense is clear although the details are debated. The "dross" is the impurity that limits the malleability of the silver. When this is skimmed from the molten metal, the "finer" (or "refiner," i.e., the silversmith) produces a fine vessel. Literally, 4*b* reads, "and a vessel comes out for the refiner." The verse speaks of what the silver is capable of becoming under the care of the silversmith, v. 4.[4] In the same way, the dross (the "wicked") should be taken away from the presence of the king. This will allow him to escape their corrupting influence through the counsel that they offer. The outcome will be the grounding of his rule in righteousness, v. 5.

Verses 6-7 give practical advice, focusing on the need for humility rather than pride. While the scene is a court setting, the application re-

---

[3]Dahood, *PNWSP*, p. 52, and Aitken, p. 216, take "earth," *ʾereṣ,* to refer to the "netherworld" ("underworld"). It is more reasonable that 3*a* is a simple illustration of the opaque thinking of the king.

[4]Toy, pp. 458-59, 462, emends the phrase *wayyeṣeʾ laṣṣorep kelî,* "there shall come forth a vessel for the finer," to follow the LXX. He reads *wayyeṣeʾ niṣrap kullô,* "it comes forth perfectly pure." Martin, p. 157, and Frankenberg, p. 139, follow the same general position. This, however, is an interpretation based on v. 5 rather than a faithful representation of the MT. Driver, *Biblica* 32:190, argues from cognates that *yaṣaʾ* should take a secondary sense, "to shine." Removing the dross enhances the brightness of the metal. Dahood, *PNWSP*, p. 52, reasons similarly, based on an Arabic cognate. AB, p. 153, adopts this view in the translation. It is unlikely, in my judgment, that we should trade an obvious meaning for a more obscure sense.

7 *For better it is that it be said unto thee, Come up hither; than that thou shouldest be put lower in the presence of the prince whom thine eyes have seen.*
8 *Go not forth hastily to strive, lest thou know not what to do in the end thereof, when thy neighbour hath put thee to shame.*
9 *Debate thy cause with thy neighbour himself; and discover not a secret to another:*
10 *Lest he that heareth it put thee to shame, and thine infamy turn not away.*

lates to any area of life. Rather than assuming a place of honor for oneself, it is better to take a position of humility, v. 6.[5] Those whom the king delights to honor will be brought forward openly, in front of the other nobles and dignitaries. Those who have thought too highly of themselves will be publicly degraded by being asked to move to a lower position.

Verse 7c naturally closes out the discussion of v. 7. The "prince" here is the one who has been exalted over the proud person. The shame is therefore greater. This haughty individual had seen the "prince" but had arrogantly assumed a position of greater honor than him. Now he is abased before the one whom he had judged to have less honor than himself; cf. Luke 14:8-10, v. 7.[6]

8-10 The verb *rîb* (cf. 3:30) occurs generally here, not particularly referring to a courtroom scene.[7] The admonition cautions against entering too hastily into an argument with your neighbor. You have the facts distorted, or perhaps you do not have all of the facts, and your neighbor easily vanquishes you in the dispute, v. 8.[8]

---

[5]Skehan, *CBQ* 10:123-24, relocates vv. 6-7b to follow 22:29 and 25:7c-10 to follow 24:28. He feels that the nature of the subject matter fits better there. His argument for this is subjective and unsupported by any Hebrew text.

[6]Among others, Alden, Coates, Kufeldt, and Kidner make 7c the beginning of v. 8: "what your eyes have seen, do not bring hastily to court. . . ." While the phrase does leave an element of ambiguity to v. 7 (does it refer to a lesser noble or is "prince" synonymous with the "king" of v. 6?), it does not clearly belong to v. 8 either. Placing 7c with v. 8 is forced.

[7]Cohen, pp. 167-68; Alden, p. 182; Greenstone, p. 265; and others see this as a courtroom situation. This is possible, but I prefer to take a broader view that would include the courtroom as well as neighborhood conflicts. The advice is practical in every situation.

[8]The conjunction "lest," *pen,* causes difficulty. The function of *pen* is to negate a dependent clause, in this case, "lest what will you do in the end when your neighbor puts you to shame." This has led to several treatments of the clause. Toy, p. 461, states that

11 A word fitly spoken is like apples of gold in pictures of silver.
12 As an earring of gold, and an ornament of fine gold, so is a wise re-
prover upon an obedient ear.
13 As the cold of snow in the time of harvest, so is a faithful messenger
to them that send him: for he refresheth the soul of his masters.
14 Whoso boasteth himself of a false gift is like clouds and wind without
rain.

Should you be involved in a confrontation with your neighbor, you should not reveal secrets that have been entrusted to you. This is a breach of faith and reflects upon your character. When the one you have betrayed hears of your actions, he will form a bad opinion of you, an opinion that will not easily pass away, vv. 9-10.

11-14 These four maxims use emblems. The opening proverb compares words to an object of art for their beauty. The AV reverses the order of the Hebrew for no apparent reason. The "apples of gold" are cast objects, set in a frame of beautifully worked silver.[9] The beauty of this artistic creation is like the beauty of words spoken at the right time and under the right circumstances. The word "fitly" in Hebrew is awkward. Literally, *ʾal ʾopnayw* refers to "upon his wheels," but the concept of a word spoken upon "his wheels" doesn't make sense. James 3:6 uses the notion of a "wheel" representing the round of life. It may well be that this idea is carried as well by *ʾopnayw*.[10] Thus, Solomon refers to a "word spoken in its time," i.e., the appropriate time, v. 11.

"lest" should be changed to "for" or omitted. Driver, *Biblica* 32:190, takes *mah*, "what," as the indefinite pronoun governing the verb. He translates, "lest thou do aught at the end of it." Frankenberg, p. 140, and Gemser, p. 71, suggest reading *kî*, "for," for *pen*. Dahood, *PNWSP*, p. 53, argues from Ugaritic that *pen* should be considered as a conjunction *pa*, "and," together with a suffix *-n*. He translates "for. . . ." Zöckler, p. 216, takes the expression as elliptical and supplies a verb, "lest (it be said to thee) 'what wilt thou do. . . .'" The AV likewise supplies a verb, "lest *thou know not* what to do. . . ." On the whole, this seems the easiest solution to the problem.

[9]KD II, 158-59, and Kidner, p. 158, interpret the "apples of gold" as some yellow orange fruit, such as apricots or oranges. The lofty nature of the comparison argues for something of greater value, as the work of art suggested. AB, p. 153, emends the word "apples," *tappûḥê*, to *pittûḥê*, "gold inlay," a change also proposed by BH. The MT, however, is sensible and does not need the change.

[10]AB, p. 153, emends *ʾopnayw* to *ʾōzen* and translates, "a secret which has been whispered in the ear." Cohen, p. 168, understands *ʾopnayw* as "its revolvings," i.e., the seasonable revolution of time. Muenscher, p. 225, derives the word from *ʾopen*, "time, season," a meaning that does not occur elsewhere. Perowne, p. 157, makes the sense equal to "smoothly and without hesitation." KD II, 156-57, makes this refer to "circumstances." The sense of the passage is clear, whichever view we follow.

Once more, Solomon extols the virtue of wise speech by comparing it to objects of value. The "earring" and the "ornament" go nicely together, enhancing the appearance of the one wearing them. "Earring," *nezem* (cf. 11:22), can mean either "nose-ring" or "earring." It is more properly associated with the ear here as the symbol of the obedient student. The "ornament" (*ḥalî*) is either a breast pin or a necklace. There is no clear distinction between the "gold" of the earring and the "fine gold" of the ornament.

In like manner to the attractive ornaments, the wise teacher and the student who opens his mind to receive learning go well together. The teacher is a "reprover" (cf. *yakaḥ*, 3:12), instructing the youth in the ways of righteousness.[11] The youth responds positively, obeying the instruction, v. 12.

The third simile likens the faithful messenger to the refreshing cold that comes from snow in the heat of the summer. The "cold of snow" is not the fall of snow. This would not happen during harvest season and, in fact, would be disastrous should it happen.[12] Rather, the "cold of snow" is that coldness that comes from snow that has been preserved in a cleft in the mountains and is now brought down to cool beverages.[13] In like manner, the reliable messenger who carries out his assigned task is a source of mental refreshment to his master, v. 13.[14]

---

[11]Toy, pp. 463, 466, emends *môkîaḥ* to *tôkaḥat*, "reproof," to achieve better parallelism with *dabar* in v. 11. There is adequate parallelism as the text stands. Since there is no textual support, the change is unnecessary.

[12]BH suggests *bəḥom*, "heat," for the MT's *bəyôm*, "day" (of harvest). AB, p. 154, adopts this without comment. This follows the interpretative paraphrase of the LXX, a weak basis for the change.

[13]Greenstone, p. 266, understands the "cold of snow" to be a refreshing breeze that comes off the snowcapped mountains of Israel. Plaut, p. 260, thinks that the verse is hyperbole, snow in harvest being the "height of imaginable pleasures." Cohen, p. 169, takes the phrase as referring to the "thought" of snow being pleasurable if it were available. AB, p. 155, compares the phrase with a change from the heat "to abnormally cold weather (though not snow!)." The views of Cohen and AB are weak. The positions of Greenstone and Plaut are acceptable.

[14]McKane, p. 586; Toy, p. 464; and Martin, p. 159, omit 13c as an unnecessary explanatory gloss added by some unknown scribe. This is an arbitrary correction to force the verse into a more normal distich form. The tristich, however, though occurring less frequently, is not rare in this part of the book, e.g., 25:20; 27:22; 28:10.

*15 By long forbearing is a prince persuaded, and a soft tongue breaketh
the bone.
16 Hast thou found honey? eat so much as is sufficient for thee, lest
thou be filled therewith, and vomit it.
17 Withdraw thy foot from thy neighbour's house; lest he be weary of
thee, and so hate thee.*

The final comparison focuses on a man who boasts falsely about giving a gift. Compare Acts 5:1-2. Or perhaps, more apt to the figure employed, he boasts about what he will give. All, however, is deceptive; he brings only disappointment. He is like the dark clouds and rushing winds that promise rain but bring none, v. 14.

15-17 The next three proverbs teach moderation. The first points out the virtue of patience and a conciliatory attitude. The term "long forbearing" is picturesque. Literally, it is the idiom *ʾorek ʾappayim,* "long of nostrils"; cf. 14:29. The "prince" (*qaṣîn*) is the leader of a group.[15] Though this one is the leader, it is possible to win him to your position through patient persuasion.

In 15*b*, the "bone," *gerem,* has a figurative sense of "strength," as in Genesis 49:14. The "soft tongue" is one that is not abrasive. This is speech that appeases, that smooths over the rough spots and persuasively wears down the strength of the adversary. The familiar proverb is apt: "You can catch more flies with honey than with vinegar," v. 15.

Earlier, Solomon had commended the eating of honey, 24:13. Its sweetness and nourishing qualities make it desirable. Now, however, he notes that the honey must be taken with restraint. Too much of a good thing can become unwholesome. This is the case with the sweet fruit of the honeycomb. It can cause sickness; cf. v. 27*a*, v. 16.

The word "withdraw" (literally, "make rare," *hoqar,* cf. 12:27) is an idiom.[16] The idea is that you should not become burdensome to your

---

[15]Oesterley, p. 225, and Frankenberg, p. 141, change *qaṣîn* to *qoṣep* and translate, "he that is wrathful is persuaded." Toy, pp. 464, 466, emends *yəputteh qaṣîn,* "is a prince persuaded," to *yasqaṭ qeṣep,* "by forbearance anger is pacified." He reasons that "one does not show forbearance to a prince." This misses the point of the proverb, showing the power of patience to change even the most autocratic of leaders.

[16]Thomas, *JTS* 38:402, argues from an Arabic cognate that we should translate *hoqar* "make heavy (your foot)," still with the sense of restraining the number and length of your visits to your neighbor. The suggestion does not change the sense of the verse.

18 A man that beareth false witness against his neighbour is a maul, and a sword, and a sharp arrow.
19 Confidence in an unfaithful man in time of trouble is like a broken tooth, and a foot out of joint.
20 As he that taketh away a garment in cold weather, and as vinegar upon nitre, so is he that singeth songs to an heavy heart.

neighbor by spending too much time in his presence. Otherwise, he will grow tired and "hate" (cf. *śanaʾ*, 11:15) you. As always, *śanaʾ* must be interpreted from the context. Here the neighbor will become exasperated from having you around so much. Actual hatred is not in view. The proverb "Familiarity breeds contempt" expresses the sense here, v. 17.

18-20 These three axioms are negative, using emblems to describe undesirable men. The first is one who testifies falsely in court against his neighbor. His perjury has the potential to ruin his neighbor. It may bring irreparable harm to his reputation; it may cost him financially; it may destroy any chance for advancement. It is no wonder that this man is described with a threefold emblem. He is compared to a "maul" (or "club"), a "sword," and a "sharp arrow." He beats his neighbor down with his words, cuts him to the heart, and pierces him deeply, all by what he says. The Hebrew reverses the order of the phrases given by the AV. Literally, it says "a club and a sword and a sharp arrow is a man who bears false witness against his neighbor." This emphasizes the destructive effect of perjured testimony, v. 18.

Once more the MT emphasizes the icon by listing it first before developing its meaning. "*Like* a bad tooth and an unsteady foot is an unfaithful man in a day of trouble." The "broken tooth" of the AV is better the "bad [*raʿâ*, cf. 11:15] tooth." Whether it is broken or simply decayed, a bad tooth can bring pain. The foot "out of joint" (*mûʿadet*, "to slip, slide") is better "an unsteady foot," one that is slipping or sliding, perhaps from a problem such as neuropathy or from an accident that has harmed it. The point is that it is unreliable, not trustworthy. In the same way, you cannot count on an unfaithful man in a crisis, v. 19.[17]

---

[17]Toy, pp. 465-66, followed by Martin, p. 161, understands "confidence," *mibṭaḥ*, as the bad man's "ground of hope," that which he relies upon, most probably his wealth. This will fail him in the day of trouble. The word *mibṭaḥ*, however, is not construct to "unfaithful man," *bôged*. It is modified by a prepositional phrase, "in the unfaithful man." Beer, BH, and Gemser, p. 72, omit *mibṭaḥ* with the LXX. In this verse, the LXX interprets rather than translates. It is therefore unreliable.

21 If thine enemy be hungry, give him bread to eat; and if he be thirsty, give him water to drink:
22 For thou shalt heap coals of fire upon his head, and the Lord shall reward thee.

The proverb uses three inappropriate figures, the first two prefacing the last, which makes the practical application. One who removes his garment when the weather is cold is foolish. In the second figure, the "nitre," or "soda," is sodium carbonate, widely used as a cleansing agent in both ancient and modern times. The hydrogen ion in vinegar combines with the carbonate radical to form the unstable hydrogen carbonate, carbonic acid. This immediately breaks down into water and carbon dioxide, producing effervescence. The process destroys both the sodium carbonate and the vinegar. One who spreads vinegar over "nitre" creates havoc without accomplishing anything useful. Similarly, one who sings cheerful songs to a heavy-hearted person shows himself insensitive, callously disregarding the other's feelings, v. 20.[18]

21-22 There is no greater teaching of love to be found elsewhere in Scripture. It is one thing to love your friends and family members. It is something entirely different to love those who hate you. Rather than returning evil for evil, we are commanded to return good in place of the evil that others direct toward us. The examples of feeding and giving

---

[18]The proverb is elliptical. The words of comparison are wanting, and the application is not very clear. McKane, p. 589, makes the application that one who sings, though he himself has a heavy heart, merely exacerbates his discomfort. This is a possible view. The awkward nature of the proverb has led some to change the text. Coates, p. 100, omits 20*a* as being a repetition of 19*b* (*ma͑ădeh beged bəyôm qarâ*, 20*a*, compared with *mibṭaḥ bôged bəyôm ṣarâ*, v. 19*b*). So Irwin, p. 153. Martin, pp. 161-62, likewise omits 20*a*. He follows the LXX in reading *neteq*, "wound" (literally, "scab"), for *nater*, "nitre." The vinegar has medicinal value for a wound; so the singing of songs cheers the heavy heart. Toy, p. 467, also omits 20*a* but does not clearly restore 20*b-c*. Driver, *VT* 4:241, argues from the LXX and Symmachus that *nater* occurred twice in the original text. He reasons that the original text was

[mayim ͑al-neter] ma͑ădeh beged bəyôm qarâ
ḥomeṣ ͑al neter sar bassarîm ͑al-leb ra͑,
which he translates,

"(like) water on natron is (one) removing a garment in cold weather;
"(like) vinegar on a wound is (one) singing among singers with heavy heart,"
to which he adds, from the LXX,

"Like a moth in a garment or rot in wood, so is a man's grief making the heart sick."
As is characteristic of the LXX, this is more of an interpretation than a translation. This does not justify such liberties with the MT.

drink to the enemy are clearly representative, not meant as an exhaustive list of our obligations. The point is that we should show Christian love in a practical way to those who are naturally unlovely. Paul quotes from the LXX rendering of vv. 20-21 in Romans 12:20-21, v. 21.

The phrase "heap coals of fire on his head" most naturally refers to the judgment that takes place upon those who reject our offer of love.[19] When we act in a loving way to our enemy, he has only two responses. If he is brought to remorse over his actions, he can respond in a kindly manner and the breach will be healed. If, however, he rejects our kindly actions, he puts himself in a position in which the wrath of God will overtake him. God's judgment, the "coals of fire," will rain down upon his life by way of punishment for his evil actions and attitude.

The kindness is not undertaken as a deliberate attempt to increase the judgment upon an enemy. It is always appropriate to show Christian love to another person, no matter whether friend or enemy. The verse simply states a logical result of the kindness. There is no attempt to exalt evil motives. The Lord's "reward" is for the godly response, not for an ungodly attitude of revenge, v. 22.

---

[19]The phrase "heap coals of fire on his head" most often is taken as the pain of contrition as the enemy is brought to realize his wrong. In deepest repentance, he turns from his evil actions and restores a friendly relationship. I object to this on two grounds. Such pain would be more aptly represented by something such as the "burning of fire" rather than "coals of fire." The "coals" produce the pain; they are not the pain itself. Second and more important, the phrase "burning coals" elsewhere in the OT is an emblem of divine judgment, e.g., Ps. 18:8, 12, 13; 140:10; Ezek. 10:2. Nowhere does it represent the pain of contrition. The majority of the commentators disagree with this position. Among others, Irwin, Whybray, Muenscher, Kufeldt, Greenstone, and Plaut all consider this phrase in some way referring to the shame or contrition to which the enemy is brought. Garrett, Perowne, French and Skinner, and Coates understand it as referring to vengeance. Mitchell Dahood, "Two Pauline Quotations from the Old Testament," *CBQ* 17:19-23, argues that the participle "heap," *hoteh,* here means "remove." He translates, "you will remove coals of fire from his head," i.e., in giving your enemy food and drink, you remove the pains of his physical affliction. God will reward you for your kindness. This approach goes contrary to the Greek in Romans 12:20 and thus cannot be correct. Gaster, pp. 805-6, concludes that *hoteh* means "shoveling *off,*" i.e., removing the flames of enmity. The meaning is difficult to defend in view of the NT quote. William Klassen, "Coals of Fire: Sign of Repentance or Revenge?" *NTS* 9:344, 349, interprets the "coals of fire" as having its "locus in an Egyptian repentance ritual" in which the carrying of coals of fire on the head was evidence of a repentant spirit. The coals of fire here are thus a sign of a change of heart, the enemy being made into a friend by the kindly actions. This goes contrary to the OT symbolism for "coals of fire." In addition, there is only strained evidence relating the verse to Egyptian tradition.

23 The north wind driveth away rain: so doth an angry countenance a backbiting tongue.
24 It is better to dwell in the corner of the housetop, than with a brawling woman and in a wide house.
25 As cold waters to a thirsty soul, so is good news from a far country.

23 The initial phrase is better "the north wind brings forth rain." The phrase serves as an emblem for the second half of the verse, that an angry spirit produces caustic speech. The north wind in Israel is not particularly associated with rain. Solomon most likely speaks generally here, including the northwest wind with his statement. The northwest wind generally dominates the weather pattern in Israel from late September to early November. It is during this time that the "early" (or "former") rain falls, preparing the soil for planting.

The phrase "backbiting tongue" is literally a "tongue of secrecy," a phrase that is vague. In view of the context of anger, I take this as vitriolic speech, bitter words spoken secretly about another. The somewhat archaic "backbiting" probably catches the sense about as well as any other word.[20] Under the influence of anger, a person may say many stabbing words about another.[21]

24 The verse is virtually identical with 21:9, with only a couple of minor spelling variations. It is likewise similar in thought to 21:19. For the commentary, see the discussion at 21:9.

25 The word "thirsty" (better "weary," *ᶜayepâ*) denotes one who has become physically drained through exertion. A drink of cold water refreshes this person.[22] This is an emblem to illustrate the effect of good news from a far-off land. That this news comes from a distant location implies that it was unexpected, a total surprise. Its impact is therefore

---

[20]McKane, pp. 582-83, understands the sense of *lašôn sater* to be "slander, gossip." This produces an enraged look upon the subject of the gossip when he finds it out. This view is also possible. I have taken a slightly different sense, feeling that harsh speech is more in accord with anger.

[21]Guillaume, *JRAS* (1942), 125, has a different view. He understands "secret tongue" as the subject that produces "a face bewitched" by means of the curse that is uttered. The meaning of "indignation" for *zaᶜam* (cf. 22:14; 24:24) is, however, well established. It is unlikely that we should abandon it here.

[22]McKane, pp. 589-90, takes "soul," *nepeš*, as "throat," true in Akkadian and Ugaritic but rare in Hebrew. McKane understands "tired throat" as idiomatic of the place where fatigue is most keenly felt. It is simpler to give *nepeš* its normal sense of "soul" or "man," referring to the whole person (cf. 7:23).

26 A righteous man falling down before the wicked is as a troubled
* fountain, and a corrupt spring.*
27 It is not good to eat much honey: so for men to search their own
* glory is not glory.*

even greater than if the news were from nearby, where it might have
been anticipated. The proverb is similar to 15:30.

26 Solomon uses still another emblem to make his point. The "troubled
fountain, and a corrupt spring" is more aptly "a fouled spring and a corrupt well." These should be pure. To pollute them is to make them unus-
able and unproductive. In like manner, when a righteous man submits to
a godless individual, he becomes useless and unproductive. The implied
lesson in this is that the righteous person should not willingly yield to
the opposition of the ungodly. Otherwise, his testimony and influence
will become nil. Elsewhere, e.g., 2:21-22; 10:25, 30; 12:3, the promise
of final victory over the wicked is expressed. There is no need to yield
to the wicked.

27 There is a reasonably clear parallel between the two clauses. For a
person to eat too much honey is not good. The excess of sweetness leads
to sickness. There is no need to gorge oneself with such a large amount
of food. In like manner, for persons to "search" (cf. *ḥaqar,* 18:17), i.e.,
investigate, those things that produce "honor" (*kəbodam,* cf. 3:9) is not
an honorable act. The subject must be plural since the -m suffix in
kəbodam requires one. The AV supplies "for men." One can, as well,
simply translate, "so to search out their glory is *not* glory."[23]

---

[23]KD II, 171-72, understands *kəbodam* in its root sense, "to be heavy." He takes the
proverb as antithetic, teaching that the investigation of difficult (heavy) things is honorable. While this is possible, none of the other emblems in the chapter are antithetic. Toy,
p. 470, gives up on the verse, calling the second half "obviously corrupt." Martin,
p. 164, says similarly, "the original text is beyond our reconstruction with any certainty."
AB, p. 155, emends *ḥeqer kəbodam kābôd,* "*for men* to search their own glory *is not*
glory," to *ḥaqor dəbar məkabbdekâ,* "So consider the words of one who compliments
you." Without giving the text, Aitken, p. 239, follows this same position. The emendation is not likely since it involves substantial changes in the MT. Kufeldt, p. 573, follows
Melville Scott, *Textual Discoveries in Proverbs, Psalms, and Isaiah* (1927) (hereafter
cited as Scott), p. 77, changes the word division to *kbd mkbwd,* and translates, "it is not
good to eat too much honey or to search out honor above (in addition to) honor," a
warning against unbridled ambition. Thomas, *JTS* 38:402, and Driver, *Biblica* 32:191,
understand *ḥeqer* as "despise." Verse 27*b* thus reads, "to despise honor is honor." Kidner,
p. 161, follows Thomas. While this makes good sense, it is an unlikely meaning for
ḥeqer. Byington, *JBL,* 64:348, changes the word division as above and also emends *ḥeqer*

28 He that hath no rule over his own spirit is like a city that is broken down, and without walls.

28 This statement is one of the most penetrating commentaries on the danger of an uncontrolled spirit. In OT times, cities defended themselves with an impenetrable wall. Unless the enemy could mount a siege of long duration, often difficult because of the need to supply the troops, a walled city was safe from attack. But if the wall were breached, or if the city had not erected a wall for defense, the enemy could come in at will. So it is with the human heart. One who has not learned to control himself can be defeated readily by a skilled opponent. His lack of self-control makes him think and act irrationally. His defenses are down, and the enemy can control him. Compare 16:32; 19:11.

---

to a *hipᶜîl* from *yaqar.* He translates, "making grandeur a rarity is better than grandeur." It is unlikely that such contortions are necessary to understand the verse. The verse is difficult but it is possible to make sense of it.

Practical Applications from Proverbs 25

1. Comments on royalty
   a. Leadership of the king 2
   b. Inscrutability of the king 3
   c. Counsel for the king 4-5
   d. Humility before the king 6-7
2. Relationships with a neighbor 8, 9-10, 17
3. Comments on speech 11, 12, 15, 18, 23
4. Comments on reliability 13, 19
5. Deceptive promises 14
6. Need for moderation 16
7. Insensitivity 20
8. Practical example of love 21-22
9. Husband-wife relationship 24
10. Emotional impact of unexpected good news 25
11. Opposition to the wicked 26
12. Pride 27
13. Self-control 28

1 As snow in summer, and as rain in harvest, so honour is not seemly for a fool.
2 As the bird by wandering, as the swallow by flying, so the curse causeless shall not come.

PROVERBS 26

This part of the book has an organization that is often lacking elsewhere. One of the "men of Hezekiah" (cf. 25:1) has grouped the maxims. The impact is cumulative, with proverb after proverb making similar points. The first part is the longest paragraph. It includes verses 1-12, with the theme of the passage being the "fool." Only v. 2 fails to mention the *kəsîl*.

Emblematic poetry marks this part of the book. Although emblems are common in Proverbs, the use here goes beyond that seen elsewhere. Almost every verse uses some comparison to make the point. Some of the comparisons are clearly humorous (e.g., vv. 13, 14, 15); others are pungent (e.g., vv. 6, 24). Some are dramatic (e.g., vv. 7, 11, 22), while others are commonplace (e.g., vv. 1, 28). Some seem contradictory (e.g., vv. 4-5, 10), though with some thought you will find that the contradiction resolves itself. In any case, the chapter is rich in similes.

Comments About Fools (vv. 1-12)

1 There are definite seasons when Palestine expects rain. After a hot, dry summer, the "former rains" begin in mid-October and last until early November, preparing the ground for sowing the seed. The main season for rain begins in December and lasts through February. Before the summer months, the "latter rain" falls in March and mid-April, nourishing the crops so that they are full and ready for the harvest. Rain after April is rare. In particular, rain is unwanted in the harvest since it can cause the crops to spoil. See the discussion at 16:15.

Just as you would not expect snow in the summer or rain during the harvest, so you would not expect a fool to acquire honor (*kabôd*, cf. 3:9). The idea is inconsistent with reality.

2 The parallelism with "swallow" suggests that *ṣippôr* be translated as "sparrow" rather than the generic "bird." The noun *ṣippôr* comes from the unused root *ṣpr*, "to peep, twitter." Just as the sparrow flitters to and fro in flight, and the swallow gracefully coasts in flight, neither of them

3 *A whip for the horse, a bridle for the ass, and a rod for the fool's back.*

4 *Answer not a fool according to his folly, lest thou also be like unto him.*

5 *Answer a fool according to his folly, lest he be wise in his own conceit.*

lighting to rest, so the undeserved curse will not come to light either. The verse does not teach that the sparrow and swallow remain aloft indefinitely. The statement simply focuses on them during that time when they are aloft. Just as they are in the air, so the curse that is made without a cause goes into the air, not coming upon the person who is its object.[1]

Clearly, this is a general adage, normally true. It is possible that an innocent person might be hurt by the curse of another. That does not, however, set aside the principle that the wicked will not normally prevail against the righteous.

3 In an amusing observation, Solomon makes the point that a fool requires physical punishment to restrain his actions. Just as you might use a whip on a horse to change his gait, or just as you would bridle a mule to control the direction of his travel, so the fool requires corporal punishment to bring about a change in his behavior.

While the verse does not mention children, it is reasonable that the discipline of children is the most appropriate application. You cannot reason with a foolish child. You can, however, make him uncomfortable to the point that he will change his behavior. Compare 10:13 for a similar proverb.

4-5 These two verses must have been deliberately placed side by side to make a play on words. The admonitions seem contradictory but, when taken naturally, they reinforce one another. Initially, the exhortation forbids responding to a fool in kind. If you become like the fool, you are no better than the fool. The following adage, however, warns us

---

[1]I prefer the kətîb *loʾ*, the negative particle, rather than the qərê *lô*, "to him." The parallelism requires the negative particle rather than the personal pronoun. The Jewish commentators Plaut, p. 265, and Greenstone, p. 273, follow the qərê and conclude that the undeserved curse will return upon the one who utters it. In general, however, commentators accept the text of the MT here.

6 *He that sendeth a message by the hand of a fool cutteth off the feet,*
and drinketh damage.

to deal with the fool's folly, to rebut it so that you can overcome his
false sense of self-worth. The phrase "wise in his own conceit" is literally "wise in his own eyes." The fool has a wrong view of himself. By
dealing with his foolishness, you can cut this short.

The Jewish rabbis did not understand the apparent conflict. *The*
Babylonian Talmud applied v. 4 to foolish views on secular subjects and
v. 5 to religious matters.[2] The first could be ignored while the second
needed promptly to be dealt with.

6 Solomon uses hyperbole to make his point here. One who sends a
fool to carry out a commission is asking for trouble. It is as though he
were cutting off his feet and drinking violence. He has sent the fool as
his messenger, thinking that this would save him time. In reality, the
situation develops so that he might as well cut off his own feet for all of
the good that is accomplished. Rather than solving the problems, the
fool stirs up such difficulty that his master must drink up the violence
that his emissary has created.

The passage is obscure due to its unfamiliar idiom. The phrase "cutteth off the feet" must refer to the hindrances caused by the fool. He
does not save his employer time. Far from it, he delays the completion
of the task. Similarly, the phrase "drinketh damage" denotes the difficulties that return upon the head of the employer.[3]

Literally, the verse says, "He who cuts off *his* feet *and* drinks violence
sends a message by the hand of a fool." Although it does not change the
meaning, the AV reverses the order of the two halves of the verse. This
smooths out the sentence.

---

[2]Shabbath I, 137, in *The Babylonian Talmud.*
[3]The unusual idiom in 6*a* has led some to emend the text. Toy, p. 481, suggests
maqaṣṣeh raglê malaʔkê, "he cuts off his messenger's legs." Joseph Reider, "Etymological
Studies in Biblical Hebrew," *VT* 4:285, adapts a suggestion by Torczyner and reads
ḥomes šatoh, "he who cuts off his own feet violates his very foundation." Neither suggestion has significant textual support.

7 *The legs of the lame are not equal: so is a parable in the mouth of fools.*

8 *As he that bindeth a stone in a sling, so is he that giveth honour to a fool.*

7 The word "equal," *dalyû,* is better "hang down."[4] Roughly, 7*a* says, "the legs of the lame hang down." This refers to a lame person whose legs are limp, unable to carry him. They are of no use to him. In the same way, a proverb in the mouth of a foolish person is of no value. He cannot use it skillfully to resolve issues or differences with another.

8 There are difficulties in the verse but again the meaning is clear. One of the problems lies with *margemâ,* which occurs only here. The root means "to stone." But does this derivative have the meaning "sling" or "heap of stones"?[5] The stone is bound into the *margemâ.* This rules

---

[4]There is a wide disparity in the treatment of *dalyû.* KD II, 179, concludes that the ending must be modified into *dilûy,* "the hanging down of the legs. . . ." Driver, *Biblica,* 32:191, accepts the view of Delitzsch but also redivides *šoqayim mippisseaḥ* into *soqê mappassəhîm,* "the loose hanging of the legs that limp." Emerton, *JTS,* 20:211, calls *dalyû* an "impossible form." He emends it to *dalǝlû* or *dallû.* He translates, "the legs of the lame hang loose." G.K. 75u suggests that the context requires an intransitive verb, *dallû.* Gemser, p. 73, reads *dallû,* from *dal,* "to hang down." Although the *he* in the *lamed-he* verb normally assimilates to the afformative, there are many places in which these verbs appear written fully, with the *yod* retaining its place, e.g., Deut. 32:37; Ps. 73:2 (*qərê*), both with the 3mp form as here. I would therefore retain the MT. I cannot see any way of deriving the verb from *dalal* though it has the same meaning in this context. It would also be possible to take the verb in its more customary meaning "to draw up," translating, "The legs of the lame draw up," thus becoming useless to him. The emblem is the same in this case as if the traditional translation is taken. Oesterley, p. 232, suggests that the two lines of a parable composed by a fool are as useless as the two legs of a cripple. The view is interesting but unlikely.

[5]The unusual figure in 8*a* has led to numerous suggestions as to how it should be understood. Cohen, pp. 174-75, takes *margemâ* as a "heap of stones." He applies the verse to a tenderhearted person at the stoning of an individual. Since the tenderhearted one does not want to hurt the other person, he wraps up his stone in some soft material as though this will keep the person from dying under the impact of the other stones. So, it is futile to give honor to a fool. While he arrives at the right place, Cohen takes a wrong turn somewhere in reaching for his goal. The view requires too much supposition. Phillott, *SPCK,* also understands *margemâ* as a "heap of stones." The verse describes one who places a precious stone on a stone heap where it will be lost. So he who honors a fool will find his honor wasted. It is unlikely that *ʾeben,* "stone," should be taken as a "precious stone." Greenstone, p. 275, takes *ṣərôr* as a chip, which, when tossed onto a pile of stones, remains unnoticed. So honor given a fool will be unnoted by others. This meaning for *ṣərôr,* while possible, is not so common as the verbal sense "to bind." *The Babylonian Talmud* understood *margemâ* as an altar to the Roman god Mercury, and the casting of a stone onto the altar as an ancient custom. As this is a waste of energy, so is

9 As a thorn goeth up into the hand of a drunkard, so is a parable in the mouth of fools.

10 The great God that formed all things both rewardeth the fool, and re- wardeth transgressors.

out the translation "stone heap" and forces the emblem to be that of a person who ties his stone into the pouch of a sling. How foolish! And that is exactly the point. In the same way, it is ridiculous to bestow honor upon a fool.

9 The picture is of yet another incongruous figure. "Thorn," *ḥôaḥ,* is best understood as "brier," or "bramble." This goes up into the hand of the drunkard. It doesn't belong there; it doesn't do any good there; and, if the drunkard pursues his normal reckless course of life, it will proba- bly do some harm there. So is the proverb in the mouth of a fool. It is incongruous to hear a fool spouting forth an encapsulated pellet of truth. It won't do any good for a fool to advise others. In fact, it may create harm since the fool will undoubtedly misapply the proverb when he advises others.[6]

10 The verse sets forth still one more improbable thing to make the point. I would translate, "*As* the archer who wounds everyone, so is he who hires a fool or who hires those who pass by." "The great *God,*" *rab,* is better "archer."[7] It is improbable that an archer would attack everyone.

---

the giving of honor to a fool. It is unlikely, however, that this Roman custom existed in Solomon's day. Byington, *JBL,* 64:348, emends *margemâ* to *marqemâ,* "variegated mate- rial." Just as a common stone should not be wrapped in precious material, so honor should not be given a fool. While the sense of this is right, there is no need to emend the text. KD II, 182, takes the giving of honor as the placing of a stone in a sling. Just as the stone will soon be slung away, so the fool will someday lose his honor.

[6]As in vv. 7, 8, so the figure here is not as clear as we would like it. This has caused variant interpretations of the maxim. McKane, p. 599, sees in this the comic picture of a drunk waving a thorn branch in his hand. So is the fool who attempts to use the speech of a wise man. Emerton, *JTS* 20:214, reads *ḥaḥ* for *ḥôaḥ,* and translates, "A proverb in the mouth of fools is a ring which has come into the possession of a drunkard." The drunkard, then, has a prize that he is too drunk to appreciate. There is no need, however, to depart from the MT. Robert Gordis, *The Word and the Book* (1976), p. 353, suggests that a proverb spoken by a fool irritates like a thorn used by a drunkard to harass his neighbor. Regardless of how the figure is taken, it is clear that a wise saying has no place in a fool's speech.

[7]Few verses have been taken in so many different directions. KD II, 184, translates, "Much bringeth forth from itself all; but the reward and the hirer of the fool pass away," an unusually inferior treatment for Delitzsch. AB, p. 157, mutilates the verse with emen- dations and changes in the word order. He translates, "To hire a fool or a drunkard is to

11 As a dog returneth to his vomit, so a fool returneth to his folly.
12 Seest thou a man wise in his own conceit? there is more hope of a
fool than of him.

It is equally improbable that one would hire a fool or a casual wayfarer. The point of the proverb is to compare the folly of the archer who attacks both friend and foe to the actions of one who employs a fool or those who casually pass by. Both actions are nonsensical. The warrior would not attack indiscriminately. Neither should a person hire an employee without carefully evaluating his ability to perform the work.

11 Solomon uses vivid imagery to portray the extent of the fool's folly. Just as the dog returns to lap up its own vomit, so the fool continues in his foolishness. He fails to heed the warnings that have been given him. The parallelism of "vomit" and "folly" graphically shows the nature of life lived apart from divine wisdom. Peter quotes this verse in II Peter 2:22 as a commentary on false teachers who ignore the gospel in favor of their ungodly teachings.

12 This final verse in the section dealing with fools is unusual. Rather than rebuking foolish conduct, it holds out a small hope that a fool might be reached. When compared to the self-sufficient man who is "wise in his own conceit" (literally, ". . . in his own eyes"), there is more hope for the fool. This is not so much meant as encouragement for the fool as it is to show the impossibility of correcting the pride of one who accepts his own importance.

---

wound all passersby with a sword," and explains the verse as a conflation of two popular sayings on the same theme. Phillott, SPCK, more reasonably translates, "A great man grieveth all, and he hireth the fool, he hireth also transgressors." He explains this as the actions of a tyrant who uses all sorts of men for his purposes. Perowne, p. 164, strains the Hebrew by translating, "A master workman formeth all things; but he that hireth the fool is as he that hireth them that pass by." Jones, p. 212, freely renders, "oft times doth a fool and a drunkard wound passersby," making the verse a comment on v. 9. Plaut, p. 268, loosely renders, "a master performeth all things; but he that stoppeth a fool is as one that stoppeth a flood." Cohen, p. 175, follows the RV margin: "A master-workman formeth all things; but he that hireth the fool is as one that hireth them that pass by." The point is that you should hire a qualified person; to hire a fool is the same as hiring casual wayfarers without investigating their qualifications. Byington, *JBL* 64:348, emends to get "fool and drunkard are more numerous than sand; fool and drunkard are transient."

*13 The slothful man saith, There is a lion in the way; a lion is in the
streets.*
*14 As the door turneth upon his hinges, so doth the slothful upon his
bed.*
*15 The slothful hideth his hand in his bosom; it grieveth him to bring it
again to his mouth.*
*16 The sluggard is wiser in his own conceit than seven men that can
render a reason.*

Comments About the Slothful (vv. 13-16)

The second section of this chapter focuses on the slothful person.
Although the AV translates with both "slothful" and "sluggard," the
Hebrew ʿaṣel (cf. 6:6) occurs in each of the verses. By the cumulative
impact of the verses, the writer forcefully makes his point that slothfulness is wrong, that God's people should fight against the natural tendency of human nature to be lazy.

13 Initially, Solomon uses hyperbole to establish the point that the
sluggard makes excuses to justify his laziness. The thought of the verse
is identical to that of 22:13 although the Hebrew differs. There is no dis-
cernible distinction drawn in the OT between "lion" (ʾarî, 22:13) and
"lion" (šaḥal, 26:13a). As before, the "lion" represents the various excuses brought up by the sluggard.

14 Once again, a humorous word picture illustrates the laziness of the
sluggard. The double-hinged door swings back and forth, not going anywhere but simply repeating the same pattern of movement as it opens
and closes. In the same way, the lazy man rolls from side to side on his
bed, going nowhere but repeating the same pattern of movement as he
indulges himself in his indolence.

15 The verse parallels 19:24 with which it is almost identical. As
there, ṣallaḥat signifies a "dish" rather than "bosom." Having reached
for the food, the indolent man "grieveth" (laʾâ) to bring it back to his
mouth. The verb laʾâ denotes weariness. This can be physical or psychological. Here, the thought is of a psychological weariness since the man
has done nothing to bring about physical weakness. His laziness leads
him simply to drop off to sleep with his hand remaining in the dish.

16 The final adage of this section notes the conceit of the sluggard.
He smugly justifies his actions (or, lack of actions). He esteems himself

17 He that passeth by, and meddleth with strife belonging not to him, is like one that taketh a dog by the ears.

wiser than others who may give discerning reasons (*ta‘am,* cf. 11:22) for hard work. The number seven here has its usual symbolic sense of "completeness"; cf. 9:1; 24:16. It refers to the united judgment of an indefinite number of men.[8]

Comments About General Matters (vv. 17-28)

The final section of the chapter begins with v. 17. The division is more general, without a clearly defined theme to characterize it. Perhaps it may be marked more by what it lacks than by a theme. While vv. 1-12 were marked by the fool, and vv. 13-16 by the sluggard, there is no characteristic word in this part of the chapter. Whether discussing foolish behavior (v. 17), unneighborly conduct (vv. 18-19), gossip (vv. 20-22), or deceitful words (vv. 23-28), the proverbs are negative. They illustrate wicked conduct.

17 The words "passeth by" refer to the dog: "he who takes by the ears a dog that passes by."[9] While you might take your own dog by the ears, you would never want to try this with a strange dog.[10] In biblical Palestine, packs of dogs roamed freely both inside and outside the walls of cities (e.g., I Kings 14:11; 16:4; 21:19, 23-24). Someone who tried to grasp one of these by the ears was apt to find himself with a snarling dog attempting to bite him. In like manner, a person who interferes with someone else's strife is likely to bring conflict upon himself.

---

[8]Toy, p. 477, tentatively suggests that the proverb "has in mind some form of Epicureanism," that the sluggard cannot comprehend these "higher pleasures of life." While the general meaning of the proverb might include this, there is no reason to so limit the meaning. We should apply the proverb in its broadest sense.

[9]Taking "passeth by," *‘ober,* with the first phrase improves the balance of the verse to 3-3, rather than 2-4 and solves the puzzle of what to do with the two consecutive participles. Oesterley, pp. 234-35, and Martin, p. 169, follow the LXX in omitting *‘ober.* This is, however, an arbitrary treatment. There is no compelling reason to turn from the MT.

[10]AB, p. 158, without justification, inserts the adjective "mad" to describe the dog. He further follows the LXX and translates, "by the tail," rather than, "by the ears." The MT is clear at this point and there is no reason to accept either of these changes.

18 As a mad man who casteth firebrands, arrows, and death,
19 So is the man that deceiveth his neighbour, and saith, Am not I in
sport?
20 Where no wood is, there the fire goeth out; so where there is no tale-
bearer, the strife ceaseth.
21 As coals are to burning coals, and wood to fire; so is a contentious
man to kindle strife.
22 The words of a talebearer are as wounds, and they go down into the
innermost parts of the belly.

18-19 The phrase "mad man," *mitlahleah,* occurs only here and is
quite unclear. The word comes from *lahâ,* "to exhaust." The context demands that it provide a negative description of some sort. The excuse
"Am I not in sport?" in v. 19 suggests foolish behavior of some kind.
The word, then, denotes one who has exhausted his own reason, i.e., a
"fool."[11]

The word picture is vivid. A man who deceives (*rimmâ*) his neighbor
is like one who throws firebrands, arrows, even bringing death by his
"joke." The verb *rimmâ* regularly indicates "beguile, deceive, mislead."[12]
In what he thinks is humorous, the man misleads his neighbor and tragic
consequences occur.

20-22 With three picturesque comparisons, Solomon now deals with
the topic of malicious gossip.[13] This is the fuel that fires contention. Just
as the fire will go out where the wood is removed, so the spirit of ani-
mosity will die down when gossip comes to an end, v. 20. Solomon repeats and expands the same figure. The *peham* is the glowing coal (cf.
Isa. 44:12; 54:16).[14] These were used to ignite the wood ("burning
coals," *gehalîm*) for such things as cooking. Similarly, wood was used as

---

[11]Jones, p. 214; Oesterley, p. 235; and Toy, p. 478, all suggest that a slight change is
preferable. The word they are thinking of is *holelâ,* which is similar but occurs elsewhere
only as a plural.

[12]Guillaume, *JRAS* (1942), 120, relates *rimmâ* to "slander." Martin, p. 169, refers the
verb to malicious gossip. The verb, however, elsewhere relates to deception.

[13]McKane, pp. 602-3, takes "talebearer," *nirgan,* cf. 18:8, as "slander," and interprets
the verse accordingly. This is too strong a sense and limits the broad application. Many
people who gossip would never think of slandering another. But their gossip has the
same potential for destroying a life as does slander.

[14]Among others, Gemser, p. 74, and Greenstone, p. 280, emend "coals," *peham,* to
"charcoal," *mappuâ,* changing the order of the consonants. The change, however, adds
nothing to an already clear simile.

23 Burning lips and a wicked heart are like a potsherd covered with silver dross.
24 He that hateth dissembleth with his lips, and layeth up deceit within him;

fuel to sustain the fire. In the same way, the "contentious" (cf. *madôn*, 6:14) causes the strife to burn, v. 21. For the commentary on v. 22, cf. 18:8. The two verses are identical in Hebrew, v. 22.

23-28 The last part of this third chapter division focuses on deceitful words. The initial verse gives a graphic illustration. "Silver dross" is a silver-colored substance used to cover a common clay vessel.[15] While this might make the vessel appear valuable, in reality it would be worth less than it seemed. "Burning lips" are lips that are fervent in their proclamation of friendship. When coupled, however, with a "wicked heart," they have much less value than that which they appear to possess. As is often the case in this section, the AV has reversed the two clauses to clarify the simile. Literally, the verse says "As silver dross covering an earthen vessel are burning lips and a wicked heart," v. 23.

The following three verses make a practical observation on life. A person whose heart is filled with hate will generally hide his feelings in his speech. Rather than saying what he feels, he "dissembleth" (*yinnaker*) in his speech. The verb *nakar* is "to disguise, make unrecognizable." The adversative *waw* sets forth a clear contrast. While he hides his hatred in his speech, he plans some deceptive act to satisfy his wrath, v. 24. Though he may speak "fair" (or "graciously"), he cannot be trusted. His

---

[15]The phrase "silver dross," *kesep sîgîm,* is obscure. The significance of the phrase turns on whether *sîgîm* can be understood as a glaze. Elsewhere, it is the impurity that is removed from silver, e.g., 25:4; Isa. 1:22, 25; Ezek. 22:18. In no place does it have value or is it used to coat something as a glaze to impart beauty. Zöckler, p. 225, represents the older commentators. He considers *kesep sîgîm* as impure silver that has been spread over a potsherd. Just as this is worthless, so are hypocritical words. H. L. Ginsberg, "The North-Canaanite Myth of Anath and Aqhat," *BASOR* 98:21, and Albright, *BASOR*, 89:24, suggest that the two words be combined, the consonants *kspsg* thus paralleling the Ugaritic *spsg,* "glaze." The *mem* is taken as an enclitic *mem.* The suggestion has been widely adopted, e.g., Driver, *Biblica,* 32:191, although there is little evidence to support it. Albrecht Goetze, "Contributions to Hittite Lexicography," *JCS,* 1:314, also combines the words but renders them "fine bowl." James L. Kelso, "The Ceramic Vocabulary of the Old Testament," *BASOR* Supplementary Studies Nos. 5-6 (1948), p. 44, bridges the gap between these views by translating "glazed vase." These views adequately explain the simile although the older view is simpler.

25 When he speaketh fair, believe him not: for there are seven abominations in his heart.
26 Whose hatred is covered by deceit, his wickedness shall be shewed before the whole congregation.
27 Whoso diggeth a pit shall fall therein: and he that rolleth a stone, it will return upon him.
28 A lying tongue hateth those that are afflicted by it; and a flattering mouth worketh ruin.

heart is filled with "seven abominations" (cf. the discussion of the number seven in v. 16 above), completely taken over with wickedness in his desire to gain superiority, v. 25. The rare forms in v. 26 do not affect the sense of the verse. The verb *tikkasseh* is from *kasâ* (cf. 10:6), "to cover" and thence "to hide." The verb *maššaʾôn* is unusual but clearly derived from *našaʾ*, "to deceive, beguile." Though his hatred may conceal itself by means of his deceitful words, others will eventually discover it.[16]

While v. 27 is generally true, the context forces us to make its primary application to deceitful speech. The two tableaus represent the same teaching. In the first, a man digs a pit to trap his enemy but falls into the pit himself. In the second, he rolls a stone toward the top of a hill, intending to send it down upon his opponent. He slips, or loses his balance, and the stone rolls back over him. The point in both cases is that one's evil intentions toward others will rebound with harm upon the person who plans the evil. While this is often true in life, it is always a theological truth. The final judgments will bring to light the evil intentions of men toward others.

The most natural sense of v. 28 applies the evil to the harm wrought upon others by wicked speech. One who speaks deceitfully hates those who are "afflicted" or, better, "crushed." The adjective *dakkayw*, "crushed, bruised," is a plural form with the masculine suffix. The construction that the evil speaker hates those who are crushed of him is awkward but not impossible.[17] The parallel thought is much clearer. Through his

---

[16]Zöckler, p. 225; Oesterley, p. 236; and Toy, p. 480, all relate the discovering of the man's sin to a judicial assembly of the congregation, a trial. This is possible, but the sense more likely is general, that others will eventually discover the hatred of the individual. There is no need to follow Oesterley's suggestion of reading *məkasseh* for "covered," *tikkasseh*, after the LXX. The MT is sensible as it stands.

[17]The awkwardness of *dakkayw*, coupled with the context of v. 27, has led some to apply the verse reflexively. Toy, p. 481, followed by Oesterley, p. 237, emends *yiśnaʾ dakkayw*, "hates *those that are* afflicted by it," to *yabîʾ šeber*, "brings to destruction."

speech, the flatterer works "ruin" (*midḥeh*). The word *daḥâ,* "to cast down," normally indicates a serious calamity. Evil speech, then, has serious potential to harm others.

This is an unlikely change of the radicals. AB, p. 158, suggests *dərakaw,* and translates, "A lying tongue is man's own worst enemy." Zöckler, p. 226, follows an earlier suggestion by Ewald and emends to *ʾədonayw,* "the lying tongue hates its own master." Gemser, p. 74, treats the phrase similarly, accepting *ʾədonayw* or, perhaps more likely, *bəʿalaw.* Driver, *JTS* 41:174-75, takes a different tack. He derives the word from an Aramaic root, "purity." Thus, "a false tongue hateth purity." While difficult, the MT can be construed sensibly.

Practical Applications from Proverbs 26

1. Comments about Fools 1, 3-12
   a. Will not be honored 1, 8
   b. Needs punishment 3
   c. Avoid his example 4
   d. Correct his foolishness 5
   e. Danger in relying upon 6
   f. Unable to use wisdom 7, 9
   g. Warning against hiring 10
   h. Continues in his foolishness 11
   i. Better than a proud person 12
2. Comments about the Slothful 13-16
   a. Makes excuses 13
   b. Practices indolence 14, 15
   c. Displays pride 16
3. Comments about General Matters 17-28
   a. Strife 17, 21
   b. Deception 18-19, 24-26
   c. Gossip 20, 22, 23
   d. Self-inflicted harm 27
   e. Harm inflicted on others 28

1 Boast not thyself of to morrow; for thou knowest not what a day may bring forth.
2 Let another man praise thee, and not thine own mouth; a stranger, and not thine own lips.
3 A stone is heavy, and the sand weighty; but a fool's wrath is heavier than them both.
4 Wrath is cruel, and anger is outrageous; but who is able to stand before envy?

PROVERBS 27

1-2 These two verses focus on boastfulness. Initially, the text warns us against a presumptuous attitude toward the future. While we may anticipate future needs and opportunities and should certainly plan for the coming days, we must not assume that we know the future. This is foolish since it is God who holds the future. The text may be the basis for the parable in Luke 12:16-21. Compare also James 4:13-14. Paul displayed the right attitude, accepting God's will over his own (Rom. 1:10; 15:32; I Cor. 4:19; 16:7; Phil. 2:24), v. 1.

Self-praise displays pride. For this reason, Solomon advises that we should not praise ourselves. We should let others recognize the value of our accomplishments and let them praise us. The "another" (*zar*, cf. 2:16) and the "stranger" (*nakrî*, cf. 2:16) occur in poetic variation, as do the negatives, *lo'* and *'al*. The *zar* and the *nakrî* point to another person, not involved with our accomplishments, who thus can praise us objectively, v. 2.

3-4 The next pair of maxims deal with negative emotions. Two vivid illustrations introduce the first. A great stone is heavy to carry, and a mass of sand has substantial weight. The emotional burden imposed by the wrath (*ka'as*, cf. 12:16) of a fool (*'ewîl*, cf. 1:7), however, is greater than both of these. The proverb has in mind the wrath imposed on one person by another, rather than the burden imposed by one's own anger, v. 3.[1]

---

[1]Zöckler, p. 229, understands this as the burden a fool must bear because of his own anger. The context, however, argues that this is a burden imposed by another. Just as the sand and the stone are external burdens, and as the jealousy in v. 4 is external, so the wrath must be from without. Toy, p. 482, misunderstands the figure. He comments, "*heavy* is not a proper epithet of anger—it is the fool himself that is burdensome." He therefore omits *ka'as*, "wrath," as a gloss. There is no textual support for his suggestion. Further, the figure makes excellent sense as it stands.

5 *Open rebuke is better than secret love.*
6 *Faithful are the wounds of a friend; but the kisses of an enemy are deceitful.*

The illustration here comes from the wicked emotions that plague men. The wrath of another is cruel, caring not for those it hurts. The anger of another is "outrageous" (*šeṭep*). The verb *šaṭap* is "to wash, overflow, engulf," and thus a "flood." Anger is an overflowing torrent, sweeping over those in its path. Difficult as these are to bear, jealousy is worse. The flood is short-lived, here a while and then gone. But jealousy smolders within a person until it breaks forth to consume its object. It is satisfied only when it harms another person.[2] The illustrations here occur in poetic variation with no significant difference meant between "wrath" (cf. *ḥemâ*, 15:1) and "anger" (cf. *ʾap*, 15:1), v. 4.

5-6 The next pair of proverbs sets forth principles relating to the love of friends for each other. By its very nature, love is giving, concerned for the well-being of its object. It must, therefore, be open, interacting with the other. It would be better to be the object of open correction than the object of concealed love. The openness of the correction would at least have the opportunity of bringing about change; the hidden love would do nothing at all, v. 5.[3]

The "wounds" of a friend are corrections to our behavior that come from our friends. Though these may hurt, they are for our good and are given out of a faithful spirit. The kisses of an enemy are the flatteries and words of praise that come from those who oppose us. These may make us feel good, but they come from one who wants to harm us and therefore are not trustworthy.

---

[2]There is no reason to limit jealousy here to the jealousy of a husband toward his wife; cf. Toy, p. 482, and Oesterley, p. 239. The jealousy of another is difficult to bear, no matter who is the source.

[3]Oesterley, p. 239, suggests reading "deceitful," *tarmît,* for "hidden," *məsuttaret,* an obvious misunderstanding of the verse. Toy, p. 483, tentatively proposes that "hate" be read for "love," again reflecting a misunderstanding of the verse. Zöckler, p. 229, interprets "secret love" as love that conceals another's faults. Martin, pp. 171-72, also supports this view. I cannot agree with this. The *puᶜal məsuttaret* is passive, "love that is concealed," rather than the active "love that conceals."

7 *The full soul loatheth an honeycomb; but to the hungry soul every bitter thing is sweet.*
8 *As a bird that wandereth from her nest, so is a man that wandereth from his place.*

The difficulty of "deceitful," *naʿtarôt,* has led to numerous approaches to 6b.[4] In form, the word is the *nipʿal* plural participle from *ʿatar.* There are three roots with these radicals. The word *ʿatar* I is "to pray." The word *ʿatar* II is "to be abundant." The word *ʿatar* III is "to give off an odor, smell." Of these, the second best suits the verse: "profuse [or "multiplied"] are the kisses of an enemy." The "wounds" of a friend will be few and always directed for your good. The kisses of your enemies may be many as they try to make you fall.

7 We have here another practical observation on life. A person (or "soul," *nepeš,* cf. 7:23, here clearly representing the person himself) who is satisfied with what he has eaten disdains the sweetness even of honey. His rejection is picturesque. He "loatheth," *tabûs,* "to trample under foot."[5] In sharp contrast, however, the hungry person delights even in what is bitter.

8 The home is a place of security and peacefulness. To be homeless is to be without roots, without assurance, to be in a state of apprehension. Such a man is in a state of exile from his family. Solomon pictures this here with the *ṣippôr,* the "bird." A man who wanders from his home, not establishing a wholesome relationship with other members of his family, is like a bird that flies away from its nest. He exposes himself to danger,

---

[4]AB, p. 161, proposes to read *kitaʿarot,* "like knives are the kisses of an enemy." Oesterley, p. 239, suggests *ʿiqqəšot,* "perverted." Eitan, pp. 59-60, accepts the MT but interprets *naʿtarôt* as "false" on the basis of an Arabic cognate. Toy, p. 485, suggests either the *nipʿal* participle of *ʿaqas* or *ʿawâ,* "deceitful." Driver, *JTS* 41:175, accepts the MT but relies on an Arabic cognate to interpret as "unruly, turbulent." Perles, *JQR* 2:107, accepts the MT but interprets *naʿtarôt* as "vapor-like." Waldman, *JQR* 67:142-43, cites an Akkadian cognate to support the meaning of "false" for *naʿtarôt.* Gemser, p. 75, emends to *nəʿôtôt,* "deceptive, treacherous." Frankenberg, p. 148, concludes that the root *ʿatar* is an Aramaic equivalent to the Hebrew *ʿašar* and thus accepts the MT as "numerous." It is clear that no textual change is persuasive. Similarly, linguistic emendations of the standard meaning of *ʿatar* are not convincing. While the contrast is not as clear as we might like, there is no rule that states that antithetic poetry must present a clear contrast. Numerous exceptions prove this.

[5]Georg Beer, in BH, suggests that *tabûs* be emended to *tabûz,* "to despise." While this fits nicely into the proverb, it adds nothing to our understanding and lacks textual support.

9 *Ointment and perfume rejoice the heart: so doth the sweetness of a man's friend by hearty counsel.*

10 *Thine own friend, and thy father's friend, forsake not; neither go into thy brother's house in the day of thy calamity: for better is a neighbour that is near than a brother far off.*

lacks the support and protection of his family, and may adopt principles and standards that go contrary even to those taught him by his parents.

9-10 The next two proverbs focus on friendship. Initially, the maxim notes the value of the "friend" (cf. *rea^c*, 6:1). "Ointment," *šemen,* cf. 21:20, was used in cosmetics and perfume, e.g., Song of Solomon 4:10; Isaiah 57:9; Amos 6:6. "Perfume," *qətoret,* denotes a sweet-smelling fragrance. It most often refers to burning incense but is also used once of perfume, Song of Solomon 3:6. There is no significant difference meant here. The two words both portray the desirable fragrant aroma of perfume. They illustrate the desirability of friendship.

The problem in the verse stems from the lack of a verb in 9*b* and the awkwardness of the phrase "hearty counsel." Literally, the phrase is "counsel of the soul."[6] We have no exact English equivalent. This is counsel that comes from the heart, i.e., sincere, even impassioned advice; cf. Psalm 13:2. This produces a sense of satisfaction in the one who receives it. Reversing the clauses and supplying the verb "is" gives a smoother reading: "The counsel of a man *is* sweet to his friend," v. 9.

Verse 10 teaches friends to rely upon one another (cf. 17:17). We should not ignore our responsibilities as a friend. The bond of loyalty that binds friends together is reciprocal. The son should therefore prepare himself to accept his responsibilities in this area. Not only his own friend but also a family friend should be able to count on him for assistance.

To illustrate the value of a good friend, Solomon poses the prospect of some unexpected crisis, v. 10*b*. At this time, it would be better to call upon a nearby friend who could quickly help than to appeal to one's

---

[6]Thomas, *VT* 15:275, calls 9*b* "untranslatable as it stands." He emends to *waᶜəṣat reaᶜ mamtîqâ nepeš,* "and the counsel of a friend makes sweet the soul." AB, p. 161, emends *meᶜəṣat* to *məhazzeq* and translates, "a friend's cordiality strengthens one's spirit." McKane, p. 613, emends 9*b* to *raᶜəwâ meᵓammeṣ,* obtaining a verb for 9*b*. He translates, "The sweetness of friendship strengthens the spirit." While these efforts make sense of a difficult verse, there is no need to abandon the MT.

*11 My son, be wise, and make my heart glad, that I may answer him
that reproacheth me.
12 A prudent man foreseeth the evil, and hideth himself; but the simple
pass on, and are punished.*

own brother who lived far away. The brother has a family responsibility
to help but the distance at which he lives prevents effective aid. For this
reason, the young man should go to his nearby friend to find the help
that he needs.[7]

11 The joy of the father rests upon the conduct of the son. The father
apparently anticipates criticism from others because of the methods or
standards he follows in the rearing of his child. For this reason, he urges
the son to conduct himself wisely. This will give the father the perfect
rebuttal to any who would condemn his child training. By holding the
son's conduct up to the light of examination, he justifies the methods he
has used. At the same time, his heart is made "glad," experiencing the
deep-seated satisfaction that comes from seeing a child go in the ways
in which he has been directed.[8]

12 The proverb is similar in word order to 22:3, but it is not identical
in the forms of the words used. The changes are insignificant and do not
greatly affect the interpretation. That two such proverbs exist argues
strongly that the sayings circulated orally in the nation for some time
before being written down. Minor differences can readily be explained

---

[7]Toy, p. 486, asserts that the verse contradicts the teaching of 17:17. He concludes that
the text here is defective. McKane, p. 614, views 17:17 and 27:10 as an "example of . . .
two apparently conflicting points of view . . . both have to be asserted in order to produce a balanced expression of opinion." Oesterley, p. 241, asserts that the author
wrongly constructed the proverb from the *Proverbs of Ahikar* (2:57 and 2:49). These
suggestions solve a problem that does not exist. There is no inherent disagreement between 17:17 and 27:10. This proverb considers a specialized case—the brother lives too
far away to provide quick assistance. Even if we understand 17:17 to refer to a family
member, 27:10 does not conflict with it.

[8]KD II, 208, assumes that the child is presently walking afar off from the standards in
which he has been trained. He therefore translates, "Become wise, my son. . . ." Others
have criticized the father because of the son's waywardness. He therefore urges the son
to come back to the ways of wise conduct so that he may be able to respond to his critics. The view is possible. It is more natural, however, to translate *ḥǝkam,* "be wise," as a
simple imperative. The father exhorts the son to continue his present wise conduct. I do
not see it as urging a change in the son's way of life.

*13 Take his garment that is surety for a stranger, and take a pledge of
him for a strange woman.*
*14 He that blesseth his friend with a loud voice, rising early in the
morning, it shall be counted a curse to him.*

as variations that occurred through the process of the oral preservation
of the statements. See 22:3 for the discussion.

13 The parallelism to 20:16 is extremely close. In 20:16, the *nakrîyam,*
"foreigner," is mentioned. Here, it is the *nakrîyâ,* the "strange woman"
(cf. 2:16). In 20:16, the emphasis is purely on financial matters; here,
moral issues are also in view. Just as one would give his outer garment
in pledge for a loan he had received, so he must give a pledge of some
kind for his involvement with the "strange woman." Her allurements
have led him to waste his resources. Anyone who would loan him
money should be careful to receive some form of security.[9]

14 Solomon now warns against being carried away by false friendliness. Here is an individual who, for some reason of his own, sees the
need to cultivate the friendship of another. He is so eager to do this that
he comes out early in the morning to offer compliments at the first of
the day. The wise person will see through this tactic and will count it as
a curse to the false friend. Rather than treating him as a close friend and
risking disappointment, the wise man will recognize the flattery for
what it is and will reject the proffered friendship.[10] The verse illustrates
well the teaching of v. 6.

---

[9]KD II, 208, accepts the *kətîb nakrîyâ* but interprets it neutrally, "strange matter."
Among others, McKane, p. 616; Oesterley, p. 242; and AB, p. 162, follow the LXX,
emending the verse and interpreting as in 20:16. Sense can be made of the MT and there
is no need to leave it at this point.

[10]Toy, p. 488; Martin, p. 173; and Gemser, p. 75, delete "rising early in the morning" on
the grounds that it makes the phrase too long, overbalancing the verse. AB, pp. 162-63,
suggests that the words vary the phrase "in a loud voice." He translates, "rousing him in
the morning." Neither of these views is necessary. The phrase picturesquely describes
the eagerness of the false friend to ingratiate himself into the favor of the other. Zöckler,
p. 230, offers a possible alternate interpretation. He suggests that this flattery, if accepted, will bring the person into judgment from others. This is an older rabbinic view.
Alden, p. 192, misses the significance by saying that early risers "should be sensitive to
others who may be still sleeping." While true, this is a trivial application of the proverb.

*15 A continual dropping in a very rainy day and a contentious woman
   are alike.*
*16 Whosoever hideth her hideth the wind, and the ointment of his right
   hand, which bewrayeth itself.*
*17 Iron sharpeneth iron; so a man sharpeneth the countenance of his
   friend.*

15-16 We have here a fuller expression of the thought first introduced
in 19:13b. The word *sagrîr* is "steady, persistent rain"; thus, the water is
running steadily off the roof. There is a repetitive dripping of water that
furnishes the picture of the woman's repetitive contentions, v. 15. Verse
16 completes the description. Just as a man cannot conceal the wind
with his hand, and just as the effort to grasp oil firmly in the hand meets
with frustration, so any effort to cover the contentious nature of a shrew
will also fail.

There are several interpretations of the verse.[11] The verb "hideth,"
ṣapan, cf. 2:1, means "to hide, store" and here carries the sense of trying
to conceal the contentions of the woman. To do this is like trying to conceal the wind, an impossible task. In 16b, the verb "bewrayeth," *qara',*
"encounter, meet," leads to the sense "to grasp." This carries the picture
further, comparing it to the futile attempt to grasp oil with the hand.
Contention, by its very nature, will show itself in some way. An attempt
by a husband to conceal this quality in his wife will fail.

17 In sharpening metal, you may rub one piece against another. In
particular, you may sharpen iron by rubbing it against another piece of

---

[11]Oesterley, p. 243, gives up by saying, "the text is in too hopeless a condition to do
anything with it." Coates, p. 105, follows tortuous reasoning to arrive at an interpretation. He reads "oil," *šemen,* as *šemâ* and interprets the verb *ṣapan,* "hideth," as a "pun"
for the direction "north." He translates, "The North holds wind, therefore why call it the
South?" This teaches that trouble is trouble even though it be renamed as something
else. Kidner, p. 167, follows the RSV, "to restrain her is to restrain the wind, or to grasp
oil in his right hand." This paraphrases *ṣapan,* which does not mean "restrain." Toy, p.
488, notes the impossibility of this translation and calls the interpretation "obscure, unnatural, and improbable." He concludes that "no satisfactory construction of the couplet
has been suggested." Cohen, p. 182, follows the AV in 16a but translates 16b, "and the
oil of his right hand calleth." He follows a rabbinic tradition that a person who anointed
himself first poured the oil into his right hand. Just as the odor of the oil disclosed what
had been done, so the nature of the vitriolic woman discloses itself. AB, p. 163, understands 16b idiomatically, "his hand is slippery," as though the man cannot hold on to
what he has grasped.

*18 Whoso keepeth the fig tree shall eat the fruit thereof: so he that wait-
eth on his master shall be honoured.
19 As in water face answereth to face, so the heart of man to man.*

iron. In the same way, one man influences the attitudes, intelligence,
character, and personality of another as he has continued contact with
him.[12]

Nothing is said here as to one's choice of friends, but it is clear that
this is the concern behind such verses as 4:14-15 and 13:20. The ancient
proverb observes, "He who lies down with the dogs will rise up with
fleas." And he who chooses wrong friends will have his character torn
down. Conversely, good friends build up a person.

```
                     Friendship
   1. Satisfaction from the counsel of friends 9
   2. Obligations of true friends 10a
   3. Value of the help of friends 10b
   4. Impact of close friends
        a. Value of correction 5
        b. Nature of correction 6
        c. Influence of friendship 17
```

18 Faithful labor brings a reward. The husbandman who diligently
tends the fig tree receives his reward when he samples the fruit. In the
same way, the servant who cares for his master's good will receive
honor. The word "honoured," *kabed* (cf. 3:9), is passive, "to be honored."
It refers here to a person who receives honor from others because of his
work. "Honor," in this sense, parallels the idea of reputation, a good
standing in the eyes of one's fellow man.

19 Because of the idiomatic construction of the verse, we must supply
something to make the thought clear. Literally, the verse reads, "As in

---

[12]AB, p. 162, and McKane, p. 615, limit the sharpening process to the mind, the person's perception. Experience suggests, however, that the proverb applies to the total person. This includes his perception but also his values, emotions, etc. Without warrant,
Toy, p. 492, and Coates, p. 105, omit "countenance," *panê*. The "face," however, is the
window to the soul and will likely reflect changes in mood, desires, goals, etc. It stands
here for the whole being.

20 Hell and destruction are never full; so the eyes of man are never satisfied.

the water, the face to the face, so the heart of the man to the man." We would naturally understand the verbs, "the face *is* to the face, so the heart of the man *is* to the man," but this still leaves the sense questionable.

The use of water suggests the mirrorlike reflection in which the face of one peering into the water would reflect back to him. In the same way, the "heart of man," e.g., his thoughts, his desires, his goals, reflects back to him. As he ponders the world about him, he finds support for what he himself is and what he is striving to become or accomplish.[13]

20 The adage uses eschatological truth to illustrate the selfish nature of man. By drawing a parallel between "hell" (*šǝʾôl*, cf. 7:27) and "destruction" (*ʾăbaddoh,* cf. 15:11), Solomon implies a future existence for the dead (cf. 15:11). This is no superstitious concept voiced by one who wants to understand the future life. This is the assured statement of one led by the Holy Spirit to express the truth of a place of future judgment. In a casual, offhand manner, the statement reveals the eschatological view of its author.[14]

Just as hell will never fill up, so the "eyes" of wicked men are never satisfied. Abaddon, *ʾăbaddoh,* here is a synonym for Sheol, *šǝʾôl.* Both refer to the region of the dead, a place with inexhaustible room for the wicked. The "eyes" are the gate through which man tantalizes his covetous nature; cf. the "lust of the eyes," I John 2:16. Man's nature is such

---

[13]There is a question as to whether 19*b* refers to one or two men. Among others, Greenstone, Zöckler, and Kidner see two people, the first seeing himself reflected in the other. Nothing requires this second person although the view is possible. It is natural to think of one person who finds himself reflected in the world about him. Toy, p. 490, states that the first line makes "no sense," the phrase "as water" probably being an error in the text. With only weak support, he deletes the phrase. Martin, p. 175, gives no support to his conclusion that the correct reading should be "as face answers to face, so does mind to mind." Though something must be supplied to make sense of the MT, it is defensible.

[14]McKane, p. 617, sees the verse as a reference to the mythological belief that man entered the throat of the god Mot at death. Through this, he descended into the netherworld. Since Mot's appetite was incapable of being satisfied, all mankind must inevitably pass through his mouth. While the heathen peoples of the biblical world undoubtedly held beliefs similar to this, the inspiration of the Holy Spirit preserved the biblical authors from such error. It is wrong to read heathen beliefs into Scripture.

*21 As the fining pot for silver, and the furnace for gold; so is a man to
his praise.
22 Though thou shouldest bray a fool in a mortar among wheat with a
pestle, yet will not his foolishness depart from him.*

that he always wants a little more. What he already has and what he has
already experienced never satisfy him.

21 The refiner's pot was used to change metal ore to a molten state.
Blowpipes were used to oxidize impurities that could then be blown
away or skimmed from the surface. The furnace was used similarly in
the purification of gold. Proverbs 21*a* exactly repeats 17:3*a*.

Verse 21*b* lends itself to differing interpretations.[15] The phrase is literally "and a man according to his praise." The parallelism suggests that
this is the praise given a man by others. It is his reputation. Just as the
refining process reveals impurities, so the reputation of a person shows
him for what he is.

Many of the proverbs are generally true although specific deviations
may exist. This is the case here. A man may establish his reputation with
others while he is in truth something very different. Normally, however,
a man's reputation accurately reflects his character.

22 This is one of the more vivid portrayals in the book. The "fool" is
the *ʾəwîl* (cf. 1:7), the hardened individual who has deliberately chosen
his course, not merely stumbled into it through ignorance. A mortar and
pestle crushes and pulverizes substances. Should the fool receive the
same bruising treatment as the wheat when it is crushed in the mortar, it
would change nothing.[16] He would still hold to his foolishness. The
verse holds out no hope that the hardened fool will ever change his
ways.

---

[15]Martin, p. 175, and Zöckler, p. 231, suggest that the character of a man is revealed
by that which he praises, a view that does not agree with 21*a*. AB, p. 163, translates,
"flattery will show what a man is," presumably by how he receives flattery. But *mahalalô*
is not "flattery." On the whole, the above view seems best.

[16]Toy, p. 491, objects to the phrase "among wheat with a pestle" in that it makes 22*a*
too long. Gemser, p. 76, and Jones, p. 220, similarly omit the three Hebrew words that
make up the phrase. The omission is arbitrary and forces the Hebrew into an unnecessary pattern.

23 Be thou diligent to know the state of thy flocks, and look well to thy herds.
24 For riches are not for ever: and doth the crown endure to every generation?
25 The hay appeareth, and the tender grass sheweth itself, and herbs of the mountains are gathered.
26 The lambs are for thy clothing, and the goats are the price of the field.
27 And thou shalt have goats' milk enough for thy food, for the food of thy household, and for the maintenance for thy maidens.

23-27 This is an extended passage that departs from the usual form of the proverb. The theme of it is typical of other extended passages; cf. 6:6-11; 24:30-34. The verses here differ from the other two passages cited in that they are positive rather than negative. They focus on the fruits of diligent labor rather than rebuking the negligence of the slothful.

The opening verse exhorts care for the flocks and herds. The *ṣoʾn,* "flocks," are the smaller grazing animals—including both sheep and goats. The *ʿădarîm,* "herds," embrace all of the grazing animals, sheep, goats, oxen, and cattle. The doubled opening verb, "be thou diligent to know" (*yadoaʿ tedaʿ,* cf. 10:32), makes the exhortation emphatic, v. 23.

The justification for this responsibility is both negative and positive. It is first set forth negatively, noting that possessions do not continue forever. One must continue working to insure that he has sufficient resources to supply his needs. Not even a royal position will automatically continue on without work. The king must serve as a good ruler or he stands the chance of an uprising overthrowing him, v. 24.[17]

The positive justification for diligence lies in the results of one's labors. The verb "appeareth" of the AV (*galâ*) is better "disappear." The word *galâ,* "to uncover, remove," leads naturally to the meaning "to depart, disappear." This refers to the spring harvesting of hay in the lower pastures and its subsequent storage in the barns. This lets a second crop

---

[17]Among others, Oesterley, p. 247; Toy, p. 494; Martin, p. 176; and AB, p. 162, emend *nezer,* "crown," to *ʿoṣer,* "treasure," better parallel to 24a. The change is unnecessary since the parallelism of the MT is adequate, noting that both wealth and position are transitory. Several authors take the "crown" as emblematic of the dignity of position, e.g., Zöckler, p. 231; KD II, 219. This is possible although I prefer the more direct interpretation given above.

grow, which may later be harvested and stored against the needs of winter. The "herbs of the mountains" are the grasses of the upper meadows on the mountains, v. 25.

Having supplied his needs for fodder throughout the winter months, the farmer may now enjoy the fruits of his labors. The *kəbaśîm* are sheep less than a year old. The thought cannot be of wool taken from the lambs and spun into yarn for clothing. More probably, the lambs are sold and the money used to purchase clothing. In the same way, the price of the goats makes possible the purchase of additional land, v. 26. In addition, the flocks will furnish milk for the owner, for his household, and for his serving maidens.[18] The picture is complete, showing that diligence brings its rewards, v. 27.

---

[18]Toy, p. 494, and Gemser, p. 76, omit the phrase "for the food of thy household," reading the verse with the LXX. This is not compelling evidence since the LXX is only a loose translation of Proverbs. The MT presents a very natural picture of the individual, his family, and his servants.

Practical Applications from Proverbs 27

1. Comments on pride 1, 2
2. Danger of negative emotions 3, 4
3. Comments on friendship 5, 6, 9, 10, 14, 17
4. Contrast between the full and the hungry man 7
5. Comments on the homeless 8
6. Obedience of a son 11
7. Contrast between the prudent and the fool 12
8. Financial advice 13
9. Comments on the contentious wife 15-16
10. Reward of faithful service 18
11. Perceptions from life 19
12. Comments on greed 20
13. Comments on reputation 21
14. Difficulty of correcting the fool 22
15. Comments on diligent labor 23-27

1 The wicked flee when no man pursueth: but the righteous are bold as
a lion.
2 For the transgression of a land many are the princes thereof: but by
a man of understanding and knowledge the state thereof shall be pro-
longed.

PROVERBS 28

1 The chapter begins with a beautiful picture of the confidence possessed by the righteous. The wicked often are fearful, giving in to conscience or to an instinctive knowledge that they stand condemned before
a holy God.[1] The righteous, however, are "bold" (*baṭaḥ*, cf. 1:33). The
verb means "to trust"; thus, the "righteous are confident as the lion."
The "lion" (*kəpîr*, cf. 19:12) here is the "young lion," who has not suf-
fered the ravages of old age and therefore has no fear of enemies.

2 The general sense of the verse is clear. A land that falls into wickedness will have many princes. The multiplication of authority shows
God's judgment upon a land. This is true when there are many rulers,
one after another, with a resulting lack of stability in the leadership of
the nation. The contrast with 2*b* suggests that the thought here is of a
succession of rulers rather than with many levels of authority.

The converse is also true. The phrase *mebîn yodeaᶜ*, "understanding
knowledge," involves two participles. We must supply *and* to join them:
"understanding *and* knowledge."[2] Thus, if an individual with ability
arises, right prevails in the land.[3] Presumably, such a ruler will lead the

---

[1]"Wicked," *rasaᶜ*, is a collective singular and therefore the plural *nasû*, "flee," is appropriate. Perles, *JQR* 2:126, explains *nasû* as a copyist's error, the singular *nas* being located immediately above the plural *yibṭaḥû*. The word *yibṭaḥ* now is written defectively.
The explanation is contrived, especially since it requires the *first* word of the verse to be
located above the *last* word. In any case, it is unnecessary since there is no grammatical
problem with a collective singular being paired with a plural verb.

[2]AB, p. 164, with no support, omits *yodeaᶜ* as a variant of *mebîn*. Oesterley, p. 248, follows the LXX and suggests *pešaᶜ ʾariṣ rîbim yeᶜoru* for *pesaᶜ ʾereṣ rabbîm śareyha*,
"through the transgression of the violent quarrels arise." He then joins *yodeaṣᶜ* and *ken*
into a single word in 2*b*, *yid̲ᶜakûn*, "to quench." The reasoning is difficult and unnecessary. Driver, *Biblica* 32:191-92, corrects *ʾereṣ* to *ᶜariṣ* and reads *rabbîm* as *rîbim* with the
LXX. He then emends *śareyha* to *yirseh* and translates 2*a*, "through transgression, a violent man raises suits, stirs up strifes." This is more awkward than the MT and solves
nothing of the uncertainties in 2*b*.

[3]The NASB, NIV, and AV take *ken* in different directions. The AV translates it as
"state." The NASB takes it as the adverb "so," possible only by ignoring the parallelism.
The NIV interprets it as "order," a paraphrase of "right." The parallelism suggests,

3 *A poor man that oppresseth the poor is like a sweeping rain which leaveth no food.*
4 *They that forsake the law praise the wicked: but such as keep the law contend with them.*

country into economic stability and prosperity. There will then be no reason to overthrow him.

3 The interpretation revolves around *raš* (cf. 8:26): whether to translate as "poor" and explain how a man comes to oppress other poor, or whether to emend the word in some way.[4] The statement apparently refers to a poor individual who through some means rises to a position of power. He seizes the opportunity to oppress those who are as he once was. He takes from them since they are in no position to resist him. His actions are compared to a "sweeping rain." The sweeping rain is a hard, driving rain that beats down the crops and spoils the harvest, leaving no grain for the people to eat.

4 The law (*tôrâ*, cf. 1:8) of Israel is in view here. The law is the only standard that held authority over all Jews. Those who do not accept it "forsake it" (*ʿazab*, cf. 2:13). This action "praises the wicked" by agreeing with their lifestyle. It compliments them by imitating their evil way of life. On the other hand, those who keep (*šamar*, cf. 2:8) the law "contend" (*yitgarû*) against the wicked.[5] The verb *garâ*, "to be stirred up, contend, strive," often refers to war but also to general strife.

---

however, that *ken* is used as a noun rather than the adverb, "thus, so." Wickedness brings much rule; little rule helps to preserve right.

[4]KD II, 225, reads *roʾš*, "head," on the grounds that Proverbs never uses *ʾîš raš* but always *raš* alone. Prov. 19:22, however, uses the expression *raš meîš*. The argument has no merit since the word for "man" here is *geber* rather than *ʾîš*. AB, p. 164; Frankenberg, p. 152; and Toy, p. 497, emend to *rašaʿ* and translate, "wicked ruler," an arbitrary conclusion. Driver, *JTS* 31:278, derives *raš* from an Arabic root, "to walk proudly," and so translates "wicked braggart." It is difficult, however, to see why "braggart" is an improvement over "poor." Further, *raš* occurs several times in the book; hence, we would not expect an uncommon root here. Jones, p. 222, and Oesterley, p. 248, emend *raš* to *ʿašir*, "a rich man," a radical change involving the transposition of two letters and the addition of the guttural. The MT needs no change here since it is explicable as it stands.

[5]McKane, p. 623, reads *bô* for *bam*, preferring the singular "against him." This agrees with the singular "wicked," *rašaʿ*, 4a. If we take *rašaʿ* as a collective singular, the plural *bam* is acceptable. The MT states a general truth. Oesterley, p. 250, in keeping with his idea of a late date for the book, makes the "wicked" here the Hellenizers that arose among the Jews during the Greek period of dominance. Keeping to Solomonic authorship, the late date is not possible.

5 Evil men understand not judgment: but they that seek the Lord un-
derstand all things.
6 Better is the poor that walketh in his uprightness, than he that is per-
verse in his ways, though he be rich.
7 Whoso keepeth the law is a wise son: but he that is a companion of
riotous men shameth his father.

5 There is a clear contrast between the wicked and the godly. Evil men do not understand "judgment" (or "justice," *mišpaṭ*, cf. 1:3).[6] Even a casual glance at the world about us reveals that this is a perceptive observation on life. Against this, however, is the position of the righteous man who diligently seeks (cf. *baqaš*, 2:4) to know more of the Lord. This man has understanding of all things; cf. I Corinthians 2:14; I John 2:20.[7]

6 The initial phrase is identical with 19:1*a* and presents the same teaching, that it is good to retain one's integrity. The comparison here is with a perverted (cf. *ʿiqqeš*, 2:15) wealthy man who tries to walk in two ways at once, the outward way of righteousness and the inward reality of wickedness. The word "ways," *dərakayim* (cf. 22:6), is a dual form (occurring again in v. 18) and requires a double path of some kind.[8] It lends itself to the idea of an outward display of righteousness and an inward possession of wickedness. The practical value of the proverb is to note that integrity has more value than that of mere riches. It is better to remain poor with integrity than to become wealthy without it.

7 The "law," *tôrâ* (cf. 1:8), here returns to its normal usage in the book, the father's "instruction."[9] This deals with the subject of friends. The son accepts this guidance away from the wrong types of friends.

---

[6]Jones, p. 222, refers *mišpaṭ* to the Jewish law, a possible view but, in my judgment, too restrictive.

[7]Dahood, *PNWSP*, p. 56, suggests that *kol*, "all *things*," should be derived from *ky/wl*, "to measure" (in the sense of moderation). Thus, the godly "understand moderation." The suggestion is unsupported and unnecessary since the MT is not difficult at this point.

[8]Toy, p. 500; McKane, p. 622; and Martin, p. 179, read the plural *dərakîm* for the dual *dərakayim*, "ways," an unnecessary simplification of the MT. The dual naturally refers to a dual way, both of which exist at the same time, rather than of a way that is now this and then that.

[9]Tate, pp. 87-88, and McKane, p. 462, argue that the *tôrâ* here is the Jewish law. The view is possible although I feel the context of 7*b* argues for the meaning of parental instruction.

*8 He that by usury and unjust gain increaseth his substance, he shall
gather it for him that will pity the poor.*
*9 He that turneth away his ear from hearing the law, even his prayer
shall be abomination.*

Presumably, the parents also guide him toward those who will be helpful
friends.

The son who keeps this instruction is a "wise son" (or "discerning,"
cf. *bîn,* 1:2). Conversely, a son who makes friends of "riotous *men*"
(*zôllîm,* cf. 23:20) brings shame upon his family. The *zôllîm* are probably
gluttonous individuals (cf. 23:20-21) although there is no mention of
food here. The discerning son will avoid close friendships with this kind
of person.

8 According to the Mosaic law, the Israelites were not to collect usury
from their fellow Israelites; cf. Leviticus 25:35-37; Deuteronomy 23:19-
20. They were to use their resources to help others in need, not to increase the burden on them. Nevertheless, the practice existed; see
Nehemiah 5:7, 10-11; Ezekiel 22:12. It most likely developed as Israel
grew commercially in addition to their agricultural pursuits.

Although "usury," *nešek,* and "unjust gain," *tarbît,* generally occur
without distinction, Leviticus 25:37 makes a difference between them.
There, *nešek* is connected with the loan of money, and *tarbît* with the
loan of food. The combination of the two words, then, signifies that the
people should take no advantage of any kind in loans to fellow
Israelites.

There is an implied divine judgment. One who violates the rule regarding interest will find that his own wealth will go to another who is
more charitable toward the poor. Through unnamed means, the Lord will
cause him to lose what he has gained. Others will acquire it as God rewards their practical example of love for others.

9 Once more, the "law," *tôrâ* (cf. 1:8), is the Jewish law. The person
who violates this is here a deliberate offender, one who will not "hear"
its voice. The prayer of this person will be an "abomination" (*tô'ebâ,* cf.
3:32) to God. The lesson is clear. Even prayer, one of the marks of godliness, has no value unless the sacrifice of an obedient life accompanies
it; see 15:8-9; I Samuel 15:22; Psalm 66:18.

10 Whoso causeth the righteous to go astray in an evil way, he shall fall himself into his own pit: but the upright shall have good things in possession.

11 The rich man is wise in his own conceit; but the poor that hath understanding searcheth him out.

10 This verse varies 26:27*a*. There, the emphasis was on deceitful speech; here, it is on evil conduct in general. The "evil way" is an evil manner of life, the usual sense of *derek* (cf. the discussion at 22:6). The "righteous" man is here a morally pure individual whose conduct is generally blameless. One who entices another away from this position will himself fall into the "pit" he has dug for the other, i.e., into ruin. The verb "go astray" (*šagâ*, cf. 5:19) normally denotes inadvertent sin rather than deliberate and willful rebellion. Here, the upright man is unthinkingly led away from the standards of God.

In contrast, the man who remains morally pure will "inherit good." By implication, he will have the blessing of God upon his life. The "upright," (cf. *tom*, 2:7) are upright individuals who turn away from wickedness. These will receive divine favor.[10]

11 The contrast here is not between the rich and the poor but between the self-sufficient and the discerning. The concepts of wealth and poverty serve to heighten the contrast. Here is a wealthy person who is "wise in his own conceit" (better, ". . . in his own eyes"), no doubt due to his material possessions. He may have inherited these, he may have been fortunate in an investment, or he may have genuinely earned his wealth. In the end, however, he allows this to make him self-sufficient and correspondingly proud.

In sharp contrast with the proud person is the poor man (*dal,* cf. 14:31). While he may struggle to make ends meet, he has acquired discernment (cf. *bîn,* 1:2). For this reason, he "searcheth" (*ḥaqar,* cf. 18:17) out the self-sufficient one. This denotes a thorough investigation. In the

---

[10]Among others, Toy, p. 499; Gemser, p. 77; and Oesterley, p. 251, hold that 10*c* is either an explanatory gloss or the remnant of a distich in which one member has been lost. This is highly arbitrary. While it is true that most proverbs in this section have two lines, it is also true that other forms occur. The three-line proverb occurs in 25:7; 25:8; 27:10, 22. The four-line proverb occurs in 26:18-19 and 28:25-26. A five-line proverb occurs in 25:6-7. The author uses variety. We cannot force the poetry into a preconceived pattern.

*12 When righteous men do rejoice, there is great glory: but when the
wicked rise, a man is hidden.*
*13 He that covereth his sins shall not prosper: but whoso confesseth and
forsaketh them shall have mercy.*

context here, it refers to the discerning man's ability to see through the
pretentiousness of the other.[11]

12 The righteous rejoice because of some success in their life. The
NASB and NIV translate, "when the righteous triumph," correctly giving the sense of the phrase.[12] In contrast with this "in the rising up of
the wicked a man is searched for," i.e., men hide themselves. The idea is
that the success of the wicked causes men to hide for fear that they will
be the next victims of the wicked man's oppression. For the same principle, cf. v. 28; 29:2.[13]

13 The proverb shows the basis upon which God forgives sin. A guilty
person who covers his sin, refusing to acknowledge it to God, will not
prosper. He forfeits spiritual prosperity, the blessing of God. This will
not come to those who hide their sins.

In contrast, the one who confesses his sin will prosper spiritually. This
is one of several verses in the OT that relate the mercy of God to confession alone.[14] See Leviticus 26:40-42; II Samuel 12:13; I Kings 8:47-49;

[11]Thomas, *JTS* 38:402-3, followed by Barr, *CPTOT*, 258, suggests the meaning "to despise" for *ḥaqar*, based on an Arabic cognate. The word *ḥaqar*, however, is not rare. It
occurs twenty-one times in the *qal*, primarily in the poetical sections but also in the historical and prophetic portions of the OT. The meaning of "search, investigate" is well established.
[12]With no justification, AB, p. 164, emends *baᶜaloṣ*, "rejoice," to *baᶜalot*, "ascend."
Oesterley, p. 251, relies upon the LXX in emending to *baᶜazor*, "to give help, succour,
come to the rescue." Toy, p. 500, followed by Jones, p. 224, emends to *bahéᶜalot*, "exalt."
Emerton, *JTS* 20:216, postulates *ᶜalaṣ* II, "to be strong, prevail," and translates, "when
the righteous prevail." None of these suggestions add materially to the MT.
[13]Driver, *Biblica* 32:193, relates "hidden," *ḥapaś*, to an Arabic cognate, "to prostrate,
be trampled upon." He translates, "when the wicked arise, (ordinary) men are prostrate,
trampled down." It is difficult to accept that such a common verb as *ḥapaś* (occurs
twenty-five times, although only here and Psalm 64:6 in the *puᶜal*) has such an uncommon meaning. The poetical nature of the passage adequately explains the unusual sense
given to the verb here. Gemser, p. 77, suggests that the *hitpaᶜel* be read. While this
smooths out the verse, it is unnecessary.
[14]Oesterley, p. 252, states that this is the only place in the OT in which the *hipᶜil* participle of *yadâ* has the meaning of "confess." Elsewhere, it is the *hitpaᶜel* that has the
sense of "confess." He mistakenly states that the *hitpaᶜel* occurs only in post-exilic passages. On this basis, he concludes that this verse must be a late addition by some scribe.

14 Happy is the man that feareth alway: but he that hardeneth his heart shall fall into mischief.

Psalm 32:5; Hosea 14:2. Nothing here requires sacrifice although, in the OT economy, sacrifice would naturally follow confession. The sacrifice showed the willingness of the offerer to obey God. It is in the attitude of the heart that God delights. He extends His mercy to those who confess their sins. Showing that the confession is genuine, the individual also forsakes his sin, turning from it to a godly manner of life.

> **The Response to Sin**
>
> 1. Covering the sin—leads to a lack of spiritual blessing
> 2. Confessing the sin—leads to an abundance of mercy
>   a. Confession—acknowledges failure
>   b. Forsaking—shows sincerity

14 The verb "feareth" (*paḥad*, cf. 1:26) here has the sense of "awe," or "reverence," toward God (see Hos. 3:5; cf. also Ps. 119:161). This feeling of reverence toward God leads naturally to accepting His Word and its standards.[15] He therefore follows the way of life that God can bless. As always, the word "happy" (*ʾašrê*, cf. 3:13) is better taken as "blessed," referring to the blessings that come upon the man who lives his life with a wholesome attitude toward God.

In sharp contrast, the one who does not "fear" God will harden himself toward the standards of God. Caring nothing for the limits set down by God's Word, he spurns them in his self-centered pursuits. He consequently falls into "mischief" (cf. *raʿ*, 1:33), better taken here as "evil."

Oesterley, however, has drawn his conclusion based on an inadequate sample size. The *hipʿîl* participle occurs only twice, here and I Chron. 29:13. The *hipʿîl* of *yadâ* refers to confession in I Kings 8:33, 35; Job 40:14; and Ps. 32:5, all pre-exilic passages. In addition, the *hitpaʿel* occurs widely in the historical and poetical portions of the OT, pre-exilic books. In the *qal, yadâ* frequently means "confess." It often occurs in the older historical parts of the OT. His argument that this is a post-exilic addition is not valid.

[15]KD II, 231; Plaut, p. 285; and Toy, p. 501, understand the object of "fear" as sin rather than God. The man fears the punishment that he will encounter if he does wrong. This is a possible view.

*15 As a roaring lion, and a ranging bear; so is a wicked ruler over the
poor people.
16 The prince that wanteth understanding is also a great oppressor: but
he that hateth covetousness shall prolong his days.
17 A man that doeth violence to the blood of any person shall flee to the
pit; let no man stay him.*

15-16 These two aphorisms both relate to the rule of wicked kings. A "roaring lion" is one that is ready to spring upon his prey. He roars to paralyze his victim with fright. A "ranging bear" is one that prowls in search of his prey.[16] So is the wicked ruler who oppresses his people. They are justly titled "poor people," no doubt a reflection of the state to which they have been brought by the pillaging of their ruler, v. 15.

The interpretation of v. 16 depends on the grammar, although the sense of the passage is clear no matter what solution we choose.[17] Literally, the verse reads, "a prince lacking understanding and great in extortions; he who hates unjust gain prolongs days." There is a sharp contrast here. On the one hand is a foolish prince who extorts gain from his people; on the other is a wise ruler who prolongs the days of his rule by exercising justice in his dealings with the people.

17 The first phrase is literally "one who is burdened with the blood of the soul," referring to a murderer, one who has taken the blood of another. He is "burdened" in the sense of bearing his guilt. It is further an

---

[16]Toy, p. 503, and Martin, p. 180, suggest that we read *dob saqul,* "bear robbed of her whelps," for *dob šôqeq,* "ranging bear," following the pattern of 17:12. The textual evidence does not support this, and it is highly arbitrary to deny the author poetic license. We should retain the MT.

[17]There are solutions to the problem that show respect for the MT. KD II, 232, and Zöckler, p. 236, understand the first part as an appeal to the ruler: "O prince lacking in. . . ." Cohen, p. 189, treats the verse as a continuation of v. 15: "(He is) a governor lacking. . . ." It is unusual, however, to find proverbs continued over multiple verses in this section. The easiest solution appears to me to supply the copulative and to understand the *waw* as lending emphasis: "A prince lacking in understanding (is) also great in extortion." The second half is then in antithetic parallelism: "(but) he that. . . ." Other solutions show little concern for the text. Toy, pp. 502-3, omits *nagîd,* "prince," and the first *waw* but inserts another *waw* before *šoneʾ (qərî).* He translates, "he who is oppressive is lacking in intelligence, he who hates unjust gain will live long." McKane, pp. 629-30, reads *yereb* for *wərab* and translates, "an undiscriminating ruler piles oppression upon oppression." Oesterley, p. 254, makes wholesale changes. Martin, pp. 180-81, omits *nagîd* and translates, "he who is a great oppressor lacketh understanding." AB, p. 165, also omits *nagîd* and translates, "A great oppressor lacks perception." Since the MT is explicable, it should be retained.

18 Whoso walketh uprightly shall be saved: but he that is perverse in his ways shall fall at once.

act of premeditated murder since he is fearful that the avenger of blood (see Num. 35:19; Deut. 19:6, 12) will kill him. He flees for his life to the "pit." The pit speaks of the grave, death. Because of his guilt, he never finds peace in this life. Instead, he continually flees as he tries to escape potential revenge for his actions. No one should "stay him," i.e., no one should assist him in his flight. Taking these thoughts into account, a better translation is "a man who is burdened with murder will flee to the grave; let no one support him."[18]

18 The "upright" (cf. *tom,* 2:7) is better a "blameless" man who walks in godly ways. His manner of life will deliver him from all sorts of evil. In contrast, however, the "perverse" (*neᶜqaš,* cf. 2:15) individual lives a life of ungodliness. As in v. 6, the dual form of "ways," *dərakayim* (cf. 22:6), indicates the attempt to follow two ways at once.[19] The perverse man tries to clothe his evil goals with an outward form of righteousness. He will, however, fall "at once," suddenly being overtaken by judgment.[20]

---

[18]The passage has caused difficulty. Cohen, p. 189, understands *bôr* as "uncultivated land." The guilty party is advised to flee from the city to an unoccupied region of the land. While this is possible, it is doubtful that Solomon would so advise a murderer. Toy, p. 502, thinks that it is prose, inserted here from some law book by mistake. AB, p. 167, suggests that ᶜ*ad bôr* is a corruption from "*mēhreb*" (*sic*), "[will free] from the sword." Greenstone, p. 300, concludes that the "pit" is the place where criminals were kept until punishment could be meted out. He suggests that there is no escape, that the guilty one should go directly to the dungeon until he could be punished. This is improbable advice. Driver, *Biblica* 32:192, relates ᶜ*asuq* to one of several cognates. He suggests that this is a man who is addicted to bloodshed and who thus is headed toward the "pit." Plaut, p. 288, thinks that *ʾadam* should be read as *ʾim,* and the verse translated, "if a soul is laden with blood. . . ." These views lack significant textual support and do not materially improve the MT.

[19]Among others, McKane, p. 622, and Oesterley, p. 255, repoint *derek* as a simple plural rather than the dual form. The dual, however, is sensible and does not need the change.

[20]Several authors object to *baʾeḥat.* Toy, p. 503, and Martin, p. 181, omit the word altogether. Hulst, p. 129, and Oesterley, p. 255, emend the word to *bašaḥat,* "pit," or *bəpaḥat,* also "pit," and compare it to v. 10. AB, p. 165, emends to *bəpaḥat,* "destruction." None of these improve upon the MT. While *baʾeḥat* is unusual, it is clear in meaning, predicting the sudden judgment that will fall upon the perverse man.

*19 He that tilleth his land shall have plenty of bread: but he that fol-
loweth after vain persons shall have poverty enough.
20 A faithful man shall abound with blessings: but he that maketh haste
to be rich shall not be innocent.
21 To have respect of persons is not good: for for a piece of bread that
man will transgress.*

19 The verse is identical with 12:11, excepting that the final two
words there, *ḥasar‑leb,* "lacks heart," are replaced here with *yiśba‑rîš,*
"shall have poverty enough." The verse is a tribute to hard work, with
the diligent man seeing the reward of his labors. The one who pursues
"vain *persons*" will wind up destitute, in abject poverty (*rîš,* cf. 10:4).
As in 12:11, the supplied word "persons" is too specific. "Vain *things*"
is more likely the correct thought.[21]

20 The implied thought here is of a man who is faithful to God and
who receives blessings from God. Since the area of faithfulness is not
stated, the verse applies generally to every walk of life. For the believer,
there is no difference between secular and sacred matters. Every area of
life is an area that should be devoted to God. As Bob Jones Sr. often
said, "There is no difference between the secular and the sacred. For the
Christian, all ground is holy ground and every bush a burning bush." A
man who is faithful in carrying out his responsibilities will receive
blessings from God as the fruit of his labors.

One whose chief end in life is wealth will find it impossible to be
faithful to God. He will have the wrong standards, the wrong goals, and
the wrong focus for his life. This naturally puts him at cross-purposes
with God. The phrase "will not be innocent" (*lo᾿ yinnaqeh,* cf. 6:29) is
better "will not be unpunished." He has no hope of escaping the judgment of God.

21 The verse is a polemic against injustice; cf. 18:5; 24:23-25. It is not
good to have "respect of persons." The Hebrew idiom is picturesque:
hakker panîm, "to regard faces," setting one before another. It is precisely for this reason that the emblem for justice shows her blindfolded,
extending equal treatment to all. The "man" (*gaber,* cf. 16:32) in 21*b* is

[21]McKane, p. 631, limits the verse to warning against occupations that are a poor economic risk, e.g., "mercantile and financial transactions." This seems unnecessarily restrictive since there is nothing inherently vain in such professions. It is more natural to
apply the verse to the contrast between hard work and vain pursuits in general.

*22 He that hasteth to be rich hath an evil eye, and considereth not that
poverty shall come upon him.
23 He that rebuketh a man afterwards shall find more favour than he
that flattereth with the tongue.*

a "strong man," one who is in a position of strength over another. This
strength may come from an occupation, from information that he possesses, from his position, or from some other area. In any case, when
the judiciary is partial in its decisions, it leads to society becoming partial in its relationships. Here, the *gaber* sells himself cheaply, the "piece
of bread" representing a very small payment given in exchange for his
using his "strength" wrongfully.[22]

22 The grasping, greedy, miserly individual whose only goal in life is
money has an "evil eye." This expression occurs elsewhere only at 23:6,
where the context again suggests a greedy person. Related phrases in
Deuteronomy 15:9 and 28:54, 56 also suggest greed. While money is
not inherently evil, a covetous lust for it is evil. It is a wrong emphasis
in life. This person ignores the fact that God may judge him. The
"poverty" (cf. *maḥsôr*, 14:23), or "lack, want," likely represents the
chastisement of God for his wrong motivation in life.

23 The book speaks elsewhere about rebuke, 9:8; 24:25; 27:5. The
thought occurs also in Paul's statement to the Galatians: "Am I therefore
become your enemy, because I tell you the truth?" Clearly, rebuke that is
given in love is desirable. While the initial impact may sting, reflecting
on the rebuke will "afterwards" produce a favorable reception.[23] One
who cares for others will rebuke them when necessary in order to help
them. This will bring him more appreciation than one who tries to curry
favor through flattery.

---

[22]Martin, p. 182, suggests that 21*b* is the second half of some proverb relating to
poverty and that it has been wrongfully associated with 21*a*. There is no evidence to
support his suggestion. Further, the thought of 21*b* follows very nicely the predicate laid
in 21*a*. The suggestion should be rejected.

[23]The word *ʾaḥəray*, "afterwards," must be taken with *ḥen yimṣaʾ*, "shall find more
favor." Toy, p. 506, and Oesterley, p. 257, omit the word. On the basis of Ugaritic,
Mitchell Dahood, "Hebrew-Ugaritic Lexicography I," *Biblica* 44:293, understands it as
"with," translating, "finds more favor with him." KD II, 237, awkwardly translates,
"reproveth a man who is going backwards." He refers this to one who goes backward
morally. It makes good sense to understand the form as a rare adverb and to interpret it
as above.

24 Whoso robbeth his father or his mother, and saith, It is no transgression; the same is the companion of a destroyer.
25 He that is of a proud heart stirreth up strife: but he that putteth his trust in the Lord shall be made fat.
26 He that trusteth in his own heart is a fool: but whoso walketh wisely, he shall be delivered.

24 The wayward child steals from his parents but justifies his theft. Apparently, he thinks he can take the valuables of his parents because they will become his one day by right of inheritance; cf. 20:21. The end, however, never justifies the means. The youth is like one who forms a friendship with a "destroyer."

His character is no better than that of the "destroyer." There is no object expressed for "destroyer"; cf. *šaḥat,* 18:9. It is a general description of those who bring misery and ruin to others through their evil actions. The young person who pits himself against his parents by greedy actions destroys the family harmony as well as the security that his parents have laid by for their older years.[24]

That the Mosaic law did not condemn this sin is understandable. No law code could fully embrace all of the deviant behaviors that man can devise. Nevertheless, the general principle of love and respect for parents as expressed in the fifth commandment would preclude such action. The sin falls into the category of gross moral turpitude rather than being a violation of a specific legal standard. The denial of guilt by the youth compounds the extent of his depravity.

25-26 These two aphorisms focus on trust—trust either in self or in God. The word "proud" (*raḥab*) has at its root the idea of "storming" against something or someone. This is an arrogant person who tries to run roughshod over others. He has no concern for the feelings or opinions of others. It is no wonder that his actions stir up strife as others resist his efforts to dominate them.

---

[24] Cohen, p. 191, concludes that the son "allies himself with those who undermine the social order." This is a possible interpretation. Martin, p. 182, concludes that the phrase "and saith it is no transgression" is an explanatory note by some scribe. He feels it disturbs "the metrical form of the verse." Oesterley, p. 257, omits *waʾimmô wa,* "and his mother, and," to achieve better balance. Toy, p. 506, achieves the same goal by omitting *waʾomer ʾên pašaʿ,* "and saith, It is no transgression." Neither of the suggested omissions is necessary. While the 5:4 meter is unusual, it is not improper.

27 He that giveth unto the poor shall not lack: but he that hideth his
eyes shall have many a curse.
28 When the wicked rise, men hide themselves: but when they perish,
the righteous increase.

The antithesis of this person is the man who "trusts in the Lord." The
idea of "trust" (*bôṭeaḥ,* cf. 1:33) is that of a feeling of security that
comes from trusting God. The idiomatic expression "shall be made fat"
denotes prosperity. This is understandable. Others gravitate to him because of his character and, as well, because he has the blessing of God
upon his actions, v. 25.[25]

The self-sufficient man who trusts himself is a hardened fool (*kəsîl,* cf.
1:22). The one who walks "wisely" (better, "in wisdom") follows divinely given directions. He will be delivered from the world and from
the problems that the world brings, v. 26.[26]

27 The person who shows a charitable spirit by giving to supply the
needs of the poor will himself never lack. This general principle follows
from God's willingness to bless those who are compassionate toward
others.[27] On the other hand, a miserly person who shuts his eyes to the
needs of others will find himself cursed. The curses undoubtedly come
from those he has scorned.

28 The interpretation must parallel that of v. 12. When wicked individuals "rise," i.e., come to positions of prominence, ordinary men hide
themselves. Fearing oppression from these evil men, they avoid their attention. When, however, the wicked fall from power, the righteous "increase." With the opposition to their position gone, the righteous now
openly show themselves and join with others of similar character. They
prosper and wield more influence upon society.

---

[25]The book makes it clear that the righteous trust only in the Lord. See the subject
study on Trust.

[26]Toy, p. 506; Greenstone, p. 303; and Plaut, pp. 287-88, consider these verses as dis-
located phrases. Toy suggests that 26*a* and 25*b* go together while 25*a* and 26*b* have lost
their counterparts. Greenstone and Plaut rearrange the verses to 25*a*, 26*b* and 25*b*, 26*a*.
There is no textual support for these suggestions. The synonymous parallelism of the
MT is adequate.

[27]The theme of charity receives broad stress throughout the book. See 11:24-25; 14:21,
31; 19:17; 21:13; 22:9; 28:8; 29:7; 31:9, 20.

Practical Applications from Proverbs 28

1. Contrast between the wicked and the righteous 1, 4, 5, 10, 11, 14, 18
2. Comments on government 2, 12, 15-16, 28
3. Contrast between poverty and wealth (3), 6, 19, 20, 22
4. Contrast between the obedient and the rebellious child 7, (24)
5. Usury 8
6. Prayer 9
7. Forgiveness of sin 13
8. Murder 17
9. Injustice 21
10. Contrast between rebuke of a friend and flattery 23
11. Trust 25, 26
12. Charity 27

*1 He, that being often reproved hardeneth his neck, shall suddenly be
destroyed, and that without remedy.*
*2 When the righteous are in authority, the people rejoice: but when the
wicked beareth rule, the people mourn.*

PROVERBS 29

1 The phrase "he that being often reproved" indicates that this person
has been reproved many times.[1] Despite the opportunities to change his
ways, he hardens his heart against the reproofs. He refuses to listen to
the voice of wisdom. There will come a time when he will be "suddenly" (*peta^c*) destroyed. The word *peta^c*, "suddenly, surprisingly," occurs most often in connection with an act of destruction or judgment.
The word "destroyed" (*šabar,* cf. 6:15) is strong, indicating complete destruction. For this, there is no remedy.

> **Judgment of the Wicked**
> 1. Rejection of Reproof 1*a*
> 2. Judgment of the Sinner 1*b*
> 3. Hopelessness of the Lost 1*c*

2 The thought is similar to that of 28:12, 28. The people rejoice over
the rule of a righteous leader. They grieve over the rule of a wicked
man. The verb "are in authority" (*birbôt*) is literally "in the increase."
The word *rabâ* is "to increase, multiply." Here it refers to a time when
there are many righteous.[2] By implication, these are then able to influence government and there is a general spirit of rejoicing among the
people. The word "mourn" is *ye^{3}anah,* "to groan." The word *^{3}anah* often
indicates general sorrow, e.g., Exodus 2:23; Joel 1:18. It also occurs
elsewhere, as here, to refer to mental anguish over the sad state of spirituality in Israel, Ezekiel 9:4; 21:6-7.

---

[1]On the basis of 12:1, AB, p. 168, reads *śōne^3*, "one who resents rebukes," for *^{3}iš,*
"men." With no justification, this forces the biblical author into a pattern of writing and
denies him the freedom of expression that authors should have. We should retain the
MT.

[2]Martin, p. 183; Oesterley, p. 259; and Toy, p. 509, read a form of *radâ,* "to rule," as
being better parallel to 2*b*. The change is unnecessary since the MT makes good sense.
Emerton, *JTS* 20:215, suggests that *rabâ* means "to become powerful, come to power."
His argument, however, is not persuasive.

3 *Whoso loveth wisdom rejoiceth his father: but he that keepeth company with harlots spendeth his substance.*
4 *The king by judgment establisheth the land: but he that receiveth gifts overthroweth it.*

3 Solomon reminds the son that the love of wisdom will bring joy to his father. The wise conduct advocated here refers to self-control in the realm of sexual relationships. With practical words of advice, the father points out that loose sexual conduct leads to poverty. If the son avoids such practice, he will bring joy to his father. The teaching parallels that of 5:9-10 and 6:26. Solomon points out in those passages that the indulgence of sexual lusts leads to financial loss. Economic harm naturally follows rebellion against parental guidance.[3]

4 Once again, as in v. 2, the verse speaks of the influence of government upon the nation. Where the king exercises "judgment" (*mišpaṭ*, cf. 1:3), better taken here as "justice," he will "establish" (*ᶜamad*, cf. 12:7) the land. The word *ᶜamad* here is causative, "to cause to stand," i.e., to impart stability to the land. Such a sense of well-being is natural when people know that right will prevail and that wickedness will be put down.

There is a significant difference, however, when the king is more interested in his own wealth than in the well-being of the country. The phrase "he that receiveth gifts" is *ʾiš tərûmôt*, "a man of contributions," i.e., bribes. The *tərûmôt* were most often given to the priests as offerings. The word also refers to offerings made to idols (Isa. 40:20) and to a tax levied upon the people for religious purposes (Num. 31:29). The occurrence here is the only clear noncultic use.[4] The sense, however, is clear.

---

[3]Cohen, p. 193, suggests that these resources are those that would naturally be expended in caring for the man's aged father. By wasting his wealth, he brings both himself and his father to destitution. This view reads into the verse what is not stated. Nothing here requires that the parents be financially dependent upon their son. I take the verse as a simple warning. Promiscuous sexual activity will cause problems with the young man's financial resources.

[4]With no textual support, AB, p. 168, emends *tərûmôt* to *rəmîyâ* and translates, "a deceitful one." Thomas, *JTS* 38:403, explains *tərûmôt* on the basis of an Aramaic cognate, "to desire." He translates, "a man of desires," i.e., a "covetous man," overthrows the country. The word is well-enough established in Hebrew usage that the appeal to Aramaic is suspect. We would not expect a cultic context in the Book of Proverbs. The sense of "gift" is appropriate here. Without emending, Toy, p. 507, translates as "exactions." He broadens the meaning to include taxes as well as bribes. While it is true that excessive taxes can cause the overthrow of a government, it is unlikely that *tərûmôt* has that meaning here.

5 A man that flattereth his neighbour spreadeth a net for his feet.
6 In the transgression of an evil man there is a snare: but the righteous doth sing and rejoice.

This ruler solicits gifts from the people, bribes to influence the decisions he renders. Righteousness no longer prevails and the land rapidly loses its stability.

5 The verb *maḥălîq,* cf. 2:16, "to cause to be smooth, slippery," regularly indicates flattery. One person flatters his neighbor. The flattery becomes a net, a snare that will trap the neighbor if he believes the flattery. Whether the flattery is intentional or not, a man who overvalues himself on the basis of flattering words sets himself up for a great fall.[5]

6 The evil man lays a snare (*môqeš*) for himself by means of his transgressions (*pešaʿ,* cf. 10:12). The verb *yaqôš,* cf. 6:2, occurs often with the meaning of "snare, trap." This can be a literal trap but it normally has a metaphorical sense of entrapping people. It has that sense here. In contrast, however, the righteous man avoids such snares to his path. His conduct gives him a sense of confidence and satisfaction. He therefore sings and rejoices. The distinction between these two actions lies in the duration of the act. To "sing" (*yarûn*) is "to cry out, shout for joy," a brief indication of exultation. To "rejoice" (*śamaḥ,* cf. 10:1), however, is a stronger attitude of joy, which may continue for a prolonged period of time.[6]

---

[5]D. Winton Thomas, "The Interpretation of Proverbs xxix. 5," *ET* 59:112, follows the LXX in referring the phrase "his feet" back to the "man," the one who has flattered his neighbor. This is a possible view. Thomas, however, also explains *maḥaliq* from an Arabic root and translates, "A man who lays a snare for his neighbor spreadeth a net for his own feet." Since *ḥalaq* refers to flattery also at 2:16; 7:5; 28:23, and three other times outside Proverbs, it is best to explain the verse as above.

[6]The verse does not parallel the two halves explicitly. Driver, *Biblica* 32:193, emends *môqeš* and *yarûn* to *mûqaš* and *yadôn* respectively. He translates, "in transgression an evil man is snared, but a righteous man abides and rejoices." Among others, Toy, p. 508; Oesterley, p. 260; and Jones, p. 230, emend *pešaʿ* to *pešaʿ,* "path," and *yarûn* to *yarûṣ,* "to run." Irwin, p. 164, makes only the first of these changes. Kidner, p. 173; McKane, p. 638; and Greenstone, p. 306, adopt only the last half of the suggestion, emending *yarûn* to *yarûṣ.* While these changes do not materially change the sense of the verse, I fail to see a serious problem with the MT. The thought of the second half contrasts with that of the first in a sensible and practical observation on life.

7 The righteous considereth the cause of the poor: but the wicked regardeth not to know it.
8 Scornful men bring a city into a snare: but wise men turn away wrath.
9 If a wise man contendeth with a foolish man, whether he rage or laugh, there is no rest.

7 The righteous shows concern for the poor. Throughout the OT, God shows His concern for "widows and orphans," the defenseless and those without resources. Extending this same care to the "poor" (cf. *dal,* 14:31) is a natural step. The wicked, however, does not have this care. The phrase "regardeth not to know it" refers to "the cause of the poor" in 7*a*.[7] The wicked are often self-centered and, consequently, selfish in their actions. They do not see concern for the poor as something necessary for them.

8 There are social consequences to wisdom and scorn. The "scornful" (cf. *lēṣ,* 1:22) bring "a snare" upon their city. The verb "bring . . . into a snare" (cf. *pûaḥ,* 14:5) means "to breathe, blow" and occurs most often to refer to "breathing lies." Here, however, the verb has a metaphorical sense of "blowing up a storm," i.e., bringing strife into the city. In clear distinction, the wise men calm the city by turning away "wrath" (*ʾap,* cf. 15:1).

9 A wise man who embroils himself in a controversy with a fool (*ʾəwîl,* cf. 1:7) will face exasperating conduct. The verb "contendeth" (cf. *mišpaṭ,* 1:3) often denotes a legal controversy. The statement here, however, can possibly include any matter that requires logical arguments to decide. The fool responds with rage or laughter, not careful reasoning. In either response, there will be no rest from these extremes in conduct. You cannot sensibly prove the point to settle the controversy.[8]

---

[7]Thomas, *JTS* 38:401-2, derives *daʿat* from an Arabic root denoting a lawsuit. He translates, "The wicked man regardeth not (his) suit." Toy, pp. 508, 509, followed by Oesterley, p. 260, emends to *yadîn ʿənî,* "The wicked man . . . does not plead for the needy." On the other hand, AB, p. 168, emends *ṣaddîq* in 7*a* to *ṣédeq,* and translates, "One who knows what is right pleads the case of the poor." These approaches have weak textual support and do not improve the MT.

[8]Henry III, 959, mentions the possibility that the subject in 9*b* who laughs or rages is the wise man himself. This, however, does not agree well with the thought of wisdom. It is best to take the subject as the fool.

10 The bloodthirsty hate the upright: but the just seek his soul.
11 A fool uttereth all his mind: but a wise man keepeth it in till after-
wards.

10 The verse describes the social consequences of evil and good. The
"bloodthirsty" are literally "men of bloods," violent men who believe in
making their way by means of physical force. These "hate" (*śanâ*, cf.
11:15) the "upright." The word *śanâ* here has its strongest sense of actual hatred. The "upright" (cf. *tōm*, 2:7) are the morally upright, the
blameless.

Some think that the second half indicates that the just show careful
concern for the upright. The phrase "seek his soul," *yəbaqšû napšô*, and
its variations elsewhere, however, regularly indicate the seeking of a life
with the intention of taking it. Only Esther 7:7 differs and the grammar
is slightly different there. For this reason, the subject of the phrase cannot be the "just" (*yašar*, or "upright," cf. 3:6). Such an action would violate the nature of uprightness. It is unlikely that the construction here
will vary from the norm established elsewhere in the OT. The only other
way to understand the MT is to refer the subject of "seek," *yəbaqšû*,
back to the "bloodthirsty." The bloodthirsty men seek the life of the just.
The 3ms suffix "his" is a collective singular, referring back to the "just."
While the construction is unusual, it is explicable.[9]

11 The idea of 11*a* is that the "fool" (*kəsîl*, cf. 1:22) gives vent to his
spirit. He is an angry man who gives in to explosive outbursts of wrath.
Verse 11*b* is literally "but a wise man stills it back." The idiom is clear.

---

[9]There are numerous attempts to explain the verse. Driver, *JSS* 12:108 and *Biblica*
32:194, relates *baqaš* to the Akkadian *baqašu*, "to be large." He translates, "The upright
amply esteem, i.e., make much of . . . his life." It is unlikely that such a common root
will have such an uncommon meaning. Kufeldt, p. 587, understands *baqaš* as "request,
intreat," and translates, "the upright make entreaty for his life." Again, it is unlikely that
such a common construction will take this unusual meaning here. Hulst, *OTTP*, 129,
suggests either that *wîšarîm* be emended to *ūrəšaʿîm*, "the wicked seek his life," or that
baqqer be read for *baqqeš*, "the upright seek his life" in the sense of caring for it. Among
others, Plaut, p. 296; Greenstone, p. 308; and Jones, p. 231, adopt the first of these suggestions. Martin, p. 185; Gemser, p. 78; Whybray, p. 168; and AB, p. 168, accept the
second change. Muenscher, p. 247, supplies something such as *naṣar* or *šamar* and translates, "the righteous seek (to preserve) his life." While the Hebrew construction is unusual, it is unlikely that any change is necessary.

12 If a ruler hearken to lies, all his servants are wicked.
13 The poor and the deceitful man meet together: the Lord lighteneth both their eyes.
14 The king that faithfully judgeth the poor, his throne shall be established for ever.

A wise man does not give free course to his angry spirit. He quiets it in the background, hiding it in the recesses of his heart.[10]

12 The word "hearken" (cf. *qašab*, 2:2) indicates that the ruler follows the deceitful advice that he receives. The practice spreads to other advisors and they soon all become wicked. Verse 12*b* requires that something be supplied for the verb. The verse supports the idea of "become." The comment has practical value. The leader is responsible for the people who advise him. If he fails to stop deceit among them, deceit will soon become a way of life in his realm.

13 The first phrase has two extremes. "Poor" (cf. *ruš*, 10:4) describes a poverty-stricken individual. The "deceitful" is better "oppressor." The plural *təkakîm* is intensive, "a man of oppressions," i.e., a great oppressor who likely is the cause of the poor man's condition. Despite the difference in their conditions, both dwell together in the same society. That God "lighteneth both their eyes" is idiomatic for the fact that He gives life to both of them. The "light of the eyes" is the light of life; cf. Job 33:30; Psalm 13:3. The thought is similar to that of 22:2; Psalm 145:9; and to the teaching of Matthew 5:45.

14 A kingdom rests upon its moral character. If the king deals justly (*beʾəmet*, "in truth," cf. 3:3) with the poor, his throne, the emblem of his kingdom, will be established "forever" (*ʿad*). Strictly speaking, *ʿad* does not mean "forever." The idea is that the king will rule a long time. The

---

[10]The idiom has suggested different translations. The AV takes *bəʾaḥôr* in the possible sense of "afterwards." This requires that *yəšabbəḥennâ* have the unlikely sense of "keeps." The use elsewhere dictates a meaning "to quiet, calm, still." Toy, p. 512, followed by Oesterley, p. 261, reads *yaḥsok* for *yəšabbəḥennâ* and *ḥərono* for *bəʾaḥôr*. He translates, "a wise man restrains his anger." While the emendation catches the sense of the verse, it is unnecessary. Dahood, *ETL* 44:36, argues that *bəʾaḥôr* contains an assimilated *nun*. He relates the word to *nəḥirâ*, "nostrils," and translates, "the wise man suppresses it in his nostrils." This does not clarify the verse. In view of the well-established usage of *ʾaḥar*, the translation is unlikely. Driver, *JTS* 33:42, relates *bəʾaḥôr* to Arabic cognates, "at the end, ultimately." He understands 11*b* as saying that the wise man ultimately appeases his anger. The suggestion is possible since the idiom fits well with the customary meaning of *bəʾaḥôr*.

15 *The rod and reproof give wisdom: but a child left to himself bringeth his mother to shame.*
16 *When the wicked are multiplied, transgression increaseth: but the righteous shall see their fall.*

thought behind this is that of divine blessing upon the king because he is just.

15 The maxim states that corporal punishment helps, rather than hurts, a child. It helps him develop a responsible character. Appropriate discipline helps the child practice right actions that show his wisdom. The logical conclusion is that the child learns from punishment. He learns the family standards. He learns that the practice of these standards brings approval while the flouting of these standards brings punishment.

The parents have two options as they work with their child.[11] They can use corporal punishment, the "rod," here understood to refer to some type of physical chastisement. Or they may use verbal rebuke, the "reproof" of their child's actions. A combination of these two, exercised with wisdom by the parents, guides the child to develop habits of wise conduct.

Verse 15b literally reads, "a child sent off causes shame to his mother." The phrase pictures the mother who does not concern herself with the supervision and guidance of her child. She permissively lets him determine his own choices as she sends him away, outside the immediate sphere of her influence. Left to himself, the child's sinful nature guides him into ways that will shame his family.

The fact that the mother is mentioned here does not mean that she provided discipline in biblical times. This is poetical variation, similar to what is found elsewhere in the book, e.g., 1:8; 10:1; 17:21. The principle applies equally to both parents.

16 In its own way, the proverb notes that the day is coming when the wrongs of this life will be righted. So long as the wicked increase in number, we can expect that "transgression" (*pešaᶜ,* cf. 10:12) will likewise multiply. The verb "multiplied" (*birbôt,* cf. v. 2) appears widely

---

[11]Ross, *EBC* V, 1115, understands the "rod and reproof" as a hendiadys, "the rod of correction." The identical grammatical construction occurs at 20:28 and 27:9, where it is not possible to understand a hendiadys. Since a literal understanding of the phrase makes sense, I refer it to two methods of discipline.

17 Correct thy son, and he shall give thee rest; yea, he shall give delight unto thy soul.
18 Where there is no vision, the people perish: but he that keepeth the law, happy is he.

with the meaning "to multiply, become many." Akkadian and Aramaic cognates have this same sense.[12] In the end, however, righteousness will prevail. The implied thought of 16*b* is that God will vindicate Himself upon the wicked. The day will come when the righteous will see the fall of the wicked.

17 The parents experience "rest" (*wînîheka*) when the natural waywardness of their child has been corrected. The word "rest" is from *nûah* (cf. 21:16), "to rest, settle down." It indicates "to be at rest, experience security." This child will "delight" (*maʿădannîm*) them. Elsewhere, Genesis 49:20; Lamentations 4:5, the word indicates "delicacies" that are eaten. Here, the "delicacies" are metaphoric. They refer to the inward joy that the parents receive from their child's conduct.

The Discipline of a Child
1. Correction of the Child 15*a*
2. Failure of the Parents 15*b*
3. Results of the Discipline 17

18 The word *hazôn* has here the meaning of "revelation, a divinely given vision." This is not, as is so often understood, the sense of "a vision for the future" with the idea of setting goals. Solomon notes the relationship between divine revelation and morality. Where the Word of God is absent, the people "perish" (*yipparaʿ*).[13] The verb *paraʿ* has as its root idea "to let loose, let go." Metaphorically, it denotes the lack of re-

---

[12]Emerton, *JTS* 20:215-16, suggests that *rabâ* has the meaning "come to power." Toy, pp. 511-12, argues similarly but emends *birbôt* to *birdot* to support his conclusion. Oesterley, p. 262, follows the same reasoning as Toy. The MT, however, is sensible and does not require the change.

[13]Toy, pp. 512-13, argues that *hazôn* cannot be correct since the worst period of Israelite history was the period when prophecy flourished. He suggests something like *tahbulot,* "guidance," on the basis of 11:14. This is a drastic change and unlikely. Toy misses the point of prophecy. The rebellion of the people was precisely the reason that God sent prophets. The people needed reproving. With continued rebellion by the people, God withdrew His gracious provision of divine revelation. Where revelation does not exist, then, we would expect to find undisciplined people.

19 A servant will not be corrected by words: for though he understand he will not answer.
20 Seest thou a man that is hasty in his words? there is more hope of a fool than of him
21 He that delicately bringeth up his servant from a child shall have him become his son at the length.

straint of the people. Without revelation, the people are "unrestrained, undisciplined." The implication is that this is bad, that people need the restraint of God's Word. As at 28:4, 9, "law" refers to the Mosaic law. The contrast develops this by stating that those who follow divinely given revelation will be "happy" (better "blessed," cf. ʾašrê, 3:13).

19 You cannot correct a foolish or rebellious servant by verbal reproof alone. Even though he may understand what you say, he will not "answer" or, better, "respond." The principle that Solomon develops here is that punishment must hurt in some way. For a child, it may be the matter of spanking or restriction. For an employee, it is the possibility of not getting a raise or, worse, of losing his job. For a student, it is the fear of a low grade. Mere words may give guidance, but effective discipline demands a potentially greater harm.

The statement makes a general observation of servants. While there may have been many servants who did their best as a matter of personal pride, there were many others who did only what they were forced into doing. This practice of servants remains true today.

20 Solomon compares the danger of impetuous speech with that of foolish behavior and concludes that there is more hope for one who acts foolishly. "Hasty," ʾaṣ, cf. 21:5, means "to hurry, urge," and refers naturally to rash speech, speech that is not well thought out. One who develops this habit will likely harm himself and others. There is a chance, however, that a "fool" (kəsîl, cf. 1:22) may simply be uninstructed. Occasionally, such a man can be helped. As in 26:12, the purpose of the proverb is not to show hope for the fool. Rather, it shows the danger of unrestrained speech.

21 The initial phrase describes one who "delicately bringeth up" his servant from childhood. The phrase "bring up," məpanneq, occurs only here. Arabic and Aramaic cognates give us the meaning "to indulge, pamper." "Son," manôn, in the second half, also occurs only here. A

411

22 An angry man stirreth up strife, and a furious man aboundeth in transgression.
23 A man's pride shall bring him low: but honour shall uphold the humble in spirit.
24 Whoso is partner with a thief hateth his own soul: he heareth cursing, and bewrayeth it not.

master who coddles a servant from the time the servant is a youth will eventually wind up with someone that is *manôn.*

The AV and NASB conjecture "son" for *manôn,* a translation with little support. In view of the close context of vv. 19, 20, and 22, something negative should be adopted here. Several translations suggest something like "he will come to grief." Is the subject of the second clause the master or the servant? Grammatically, either one will fit. I take the verse as a warning to the master. It cautions him that indulgence of a servant will lead him eventually to grief as the servant takes advantage of his kindness.[14]

22 The proverb focuses on the undesirable results of an explosive temper. The phrase "angry man" is picturesque. The phrase *ʾîš ʾap* is "a man of nostrils." The image rests on the fact that an angry person dilates his nostrils. By his anger, this man stirs up "strife" (*madôn,* cf. 6:14). The parallelism with 22*b* makes it clear that this is sin. His quick temper causes "transgression" (*pešaʿ,* cf. 10:12) to multiply. See the discussion of 14:17.

23 The same thought occurs in 18:12; Luke 14:11; and 18:14. The basic sense of "pride," *gaʾâ,* is "to lift up." The proud man lifts himself up. When he falls, he will be brought "low," humbled. In direct contrast, the man who humbles himself will obtain honor; cf. 3:9.

24 The situation in view here is similar to that of Leviticus 5:1. The thief has stolen, and someone in the community has shared in the ill-gotten spoils. A leader of the community gathers the people and asks

---

[14]KD II, 255-56, understands the master as the subject of 21*b*. He, however, interprets *manôn* in the sense of a nursery, a house filled with children of his spoiled servant. Toy, p. 516, suggests that the word is miswritten. He does not, however, have anything better to suggest. Hulst, p. 129, follows the Vulgate *contumax,* "unmanageable." This requires that the servant be the subject of 21*b*. Reider, *VT* 4:286, relates it to an Arabic verb, "to be weak," and refers it to the servant. He translates, "shall become a weakling." The word is obscure. The sense of the verse, however, is clear. Indulgence brings an evil reward.

25 The fear of man bringeth a snare: but whoso putteth his trust in the Lord shall be safe.
26 Many seek the ruler's favour; but every man's judgment cometh from the Lord.

anyone knowing of the crime to step forward with his testimony. The "cursing" is the public charge, an "oath." The person who has shared the spoil with the thief hears this but does not respond. When he fails to do this, he is as guilty as if he had committed the theft himself. He "hateth his own soul" in that he brings harm upon himself.

25 This is one of the most practical observations of the book. Real peace of mind comes only from faith in the Lord, from trusting in His loving care and guidance. In a day when men search almost pathetically for some emotional crutch to sustain them, the proverb gives a simple solution to the problem: total abandonment of self to the will of God.

The fear of man can bring only a "snare" (cf. *yaqoš,* 6:2). We fear men when we allow their opinions and pressures to turn us away from right conduct. The fear of others may trap us literally when we are caught in evil actions. Most often, it traps us emotionally as we worry or face depression. In contrast, whoever places his trust in the Lord will be "safe" (*yəśuggab*). The predicate adjective is from *śagab,* "to be inaccessibly high." Metaphorically, it is "to be unreachable by others, to be safe."

Who Influences You?

1. Man 25*a*

2. God 25*b*

---

26 The way of man is to seek the favor of a highly placed official or an influential person. In this way, men try to advance to levels that agree with their self-evaluation. Real "judgment" (*mišpaṭ,* cf. 1:3), better understood as "justice," comes from the Lord. As 21:1 notes, He turns the heart of the king to do His will. He is well able to bring about the promotion of a person within the framework of His purposes for mankind.

27 An unjust man is an abomination to the just: and he that is upright in the way is abomination to the wicked.

27 There is a mutual antithesis between just and unjust men. The righteous look upon the wicked as "abominable" (*tôʿăbat,* cf. 3:32), while the wicked look upon those who walk in the ways of righteousness in the same way. It is interesting to note that both groups draw the same conclusion with regard to the others, that they are "abominable." If you use a crooked stick as your standard, straight appears wrong. If you use a straight stick as your standard, crooked appears wrong. The key is to have the right standard by which to evaluate others.

414

Practical Applications from Proverbs 29

1. Comments on reproof 1
2. Contrast between righteous and wicked rulers 2, 4, (12, 14, 26)
3. Advice to the son 3
4. Flattery 5
5. Contrast between the righteous and the wicked 6, 7, 16, 27
6. Contrast between the scorner and the wise 8, (9)
7. Murder 10
8. Speech 11, 20
9. The poor man and the oppressor 13
10. Discipline of a child 15, 17
11. Influence of God's Word 18
12. Correction of a servant 19, 21
13. Anger 22
14. Contrast between pride and humility 23
15. Associating with a thief 24
16. Contrast between the fear of man and trust in God 25

PROVERBS
30:1–31:31

1 The words of Agur the son of Jakeh, even the prophecy: the man spake unto Ithiel, even unto Ithiel and Ucal,

PROVERBS 30

1 While we cannot identify Agur with any OT character, there is no reason to identify him with Solomon as did the older Jewish rabbis. Whoever he was, his writings had stature enough to find acceptance with the Jews. He is the son of Jakeh, also an unknown character, and he writes to Ithiel and Ucal, likewise unknown persons. From the kind of instruction in the chapter, it is reasonable to suppose that these are sons or grandsons and that Agur writes to give them some practical advice.[1]

There is debate as to how much of the chapter should be given to Agur. Various suggestions have been made, giving him vv. 1-4, vv. 1-9, and so forth.[2] Any attempt to divide the chapter into independent sections results in a writing of Agur that is impossibly short. For this reason, I assign the entire chapter to Agur.

The word "prophecy," *maśśaʾ*, occurs in prophetic literature with the only exceptions here and 31:1. It refers to a "burden, a heavy weight,"

---

[1]The lack of identification has led to attempts to translate the words rather than taking them as proper names. Revocalizing the text and dividing *laʾîtîʾel* as *laʾîtî ʾel*, McKane, p. 644, translates, "I am weary O God, I am weary O God and exhausted." Gemser, p. 79, suggests reading *loʾeh ʾet-haʾel loʾeh ʾet-haʾel wayyûkal*, "der ich abmühte mit Gott, abmühte mit Gott und siegte," "I have struggled with God, I have struggled with God, and have prevailed." AB, p. 175, also divides *laʾîtîʾel* and assumes a negative particle, translating, "There is no God! There is no God, and I can [not know anything]," a particularly radical treatment. Charles C. Torrey, "Proverbs, Chapter 30," *JBL* 73:95, vocalizes the text *loʾ ʾanî ʾel loʾ ʾanî ʾel waʾukal*, and translates, "I am not a God, I am not a God, that I should have power." Eva Strömberg Krantz, "'A Man Not Supported by God'": On Some Crucial Words in Proverbs XXX 1," *VT* 46:548-52, revocalizes and divides the text as *naʾum haggeber loʾ ʾittô ʾel lâʾîtî ʾel waʾekel*, "The words of a man not supported by God: 'I am weary O God, and exhausted.'" The man "not supported by God" and Agur are different persons. Toy, p. 520, calls the text "corrupt beyond possibility of restoration." Other suggestions have also been made. Historically, however, the oldest treatments of the verse take Ithiel and Ucal as proper names. This gives the fewest problems with the text although it leaves us unable to identify the main characters of the chapter.

[2]Horace D. Hummel, *The Word Becoming Flesh* (1979), pp. 452-53, makes the opening verses a dialogue between skepticism and orthodoxy, with Agur playing the role of "devil's advocate." Elmslie, p. 192, attributes vv. 1-4 to Agur and vv. 5-6 to "another and a happier man than Agur." Oesterley, p. 267, understands vv. 1-14 as an independent collection, separate from the remainder of the chapter. Rylaarsdam, pp. 90-91, limits the first independent collection of proverbs to vv. 1-4. These divisions of the chapter into independent sections are subjective and fail to understand the nature of it.

419

2 Surely I am more brutish than any man, and have not the understanding of a man.

3 I neither learned wisdom, nor have the knowledge of the holy.

4 Who hath ascended up into heaven, or descended? who hath gathered the wind in his fists? who hath bound the waters in a garment? who hath established all the ends of the earth? what is his name, and what is his son's name, if thou canst tell?

metaphorically a message of judgment. Here, then, it indicates that the message that follows is principally one of reproof.[3]

2-4 Agur begins by exalting God. Agur himself is "more brutish" (*baʿar,* cf. 12:1) than other men. The word *baʿar* here does not have the evil connotation it so often takes. Agur rather abases himself in comparison to others in their profession of understanding God. Others may claim to know what God will do in certain situations, how He will judge another, or how He will supply a need. Agur, however, disclaims any such understanding, v. 2.

Agur states this more directly in v. 3. He has not learned "wisdom" (*ḥokmâ,* cf. 1:2), clearly referring to the wisdom possessed by God. In addition, he does not have an experiential knowledge (cf. *yadaʿ,* 10:32) of God.[4] The name "holy," rather "Holy One" (*qədošîm,* cf. 9:10), is a plural of majesty. It describes God in His role as the holy God, the standard for all that is right and good in creation, v. 3.

Agur now asks six questions to show the glorious nature of God; cf. Job 38-39. The questions are rhetorical, with each one suggesting God as the answer. Who has ascended into heaven, or descended from heaven to the earth? Only God has done this in His many theophanies; cf. Judges 2:1. For the NT counterparts to the thought, cf. John 3:13 and Ephesians 4:8-10.

---

[3]Referring to Gen. 25:13-14 (cf. I Chron. 1:29-30), some identify Massa as a location in northern Arabia, where some of the descendants of Ishmael settled. Among others, KD II, 261-67; Greenstone, pp. 314-15; Whybray, p. 172; and Kidner, p. 182, so understand the word. Farmer, p. 119, assumes that Massa refers to a tribe descended from Ishmael; cf. Gen. 25:14. These identifications introduce the problem of a non-Israelite author, something that would have been abhorrent to the Jews. For this reason, I take *maśśaʾ* in its more usual sense.

[4]The *waw* introduces a final clause that continues the negative thought of 3a. The NASB contrasts 3b with 3a but the context does not favor this idea.

420

The next three questions refer to the creative work of God. Who has gathered the wind in His hands so as to control its currents?[5] Who has wrapped the waters of the earth up in His garment so as to prevent them from falling on the earth? The "garment" (*śimlâ*) here has its only metaphorical use in the OT, referring to the clouds, which hold the waters above the earth; cf. Job 26:8. Who has established the uttermost parts of the earth?

The final questions have occasioned controversy because of the potential for Christian interpretation.[6] The questions are straightforward: What is the name of the one who has done these things just mentioned? What is "his son's name?" The notion of a person's "name" is closely bound with his nature in OT writing; cf. Exodus 3:14; 6:3. The first question, then, asks that the nature of such a glorious God be revealed.

To relate the "son" directly to Jesus Christ goes too far. We would not expect to see this much development in OT revelation yet. There does appear in the OT the doctrine of God as having a Son. See Psalm 2:7, 12; the other messianic psalms; the numerous theophanies; the hypostasis of c. 8; and the Servant of the Lord passages in Isaiah. It is well,

---

[5]Kevin J. Cathcart, "Proverbs 30,4 and Ugaritic HPN, 'Garment'," *CBQ* 32:419, argues from Ugaritic that "in his fists," *bəhapnayw,* means "in his garments." Meir Malul, "כַּפִּי (Ex 33,22) and בְּחָפְנָיו (Prov 30,4): Hand or Skirt?," *ZAW* 109:361, follows Cathcart. Later, *VT* 48:264-65, Cathcart is tentative regarding his previous suggestion. The root *ḥapan,* however, is not rare, occurring six times in a wide variety of contexts. There is no need to make the change on such tenuous grounds.

[6]Numerous suggestions attempt to explain the final question. Greenstone, pp. 316-17, understands all of the questions to refer to man. What man can do these things? What is his name, or the name of his son? Muenscher, p. 251, takes the question ironically, teaching man's ignorance when compared to God. Toy, p. 521, likewise understands all of the questions to refer to man, "a sarcastic description of a man who controls the phenomena of the universe." Perowne, p. 180, interprets the "son" as "any other who may in any sense be called His 'Son.'" Coates, pp. 112-13, suggests that the term refers to the conception of Wisdom, in c. 8, or that it may be taken generally "to amplify the idea of familiarity with God which seems so impossible to the questioner." Zöckler, p. 248, relates the idea to "other manifestations of God's nature, e.g., to His hypostatic wisdom," seen in c. 8. Martin, p. 191, thinks the question is proverbial for full knowledge of God. Kufeldt, p. 589, holds that these are sarcastic questions, meant to show that no one compares with God. This sampling shows the difficulty of the passage. AB, pp. 175-76, emends with the LXX to make the word plural and refers to "the divine beings of the heavenly host." This is wrong since the heavenly host are not divine. Gaster, pp. 806-7, suggests that each of the previous questions refers to mythological tales. The concluding questions are riddles, teaching "that special knowledge of which the writer professes himself ignorant." These last suggestions are clearly wrong.

5 Every word of God is pure: he is a shield unto them that put their trust in him.
6 Add thou not unto his words, lest he reprove thee, and thou be found a liar.
7 Two things have I required of thee; deny me them not before I die:
8 Remove far from me vanity and lies: give me neither poverty nor riches; feed me with food convenient for me:
9 Lest I be full, and deny thee, and say, Who is the Lord? or lest I be poor, and steal, and take the name of my God in vain.

then, to say that the question touches on the relationship between the Father and His Son, asking for additional information on the nature of this one.

5-6 Although Agur does not comprehend the nature of such a glorious God, he does understand the nature of God's revelation to mankind. His Word is "pure" (*ṣarap*, cf. 17:3). The word *ṣarap* refers to metallurgy. It describes the refining of metals to eliminate the dross. Metaphorically, it indicates purification from wickedness. It appropriately describes God's Word as being free from all wrong and therefore trustworthy.

Agur also understands that this glorious God will "shield" (*magen,* cf. 2:7) those who place their faith in Him; cf. Psalm 18:30. From the parallelism, placing one's trust in God is equivalent to receiving and obeying His Word. Nothing in the statement limits this to the Mosaic law. Agur likely has in mind the whole revelation of God to that time, v. 5.

We should not add to this revelation. Agur does not rule out the possibility of additional revelation. Rather, he limits the application to the revealed Word of God. We should not add to it nor modify it in order to justify wicked practices; cf. Revelation 22:18-19. We accept it and let it naturally guide our doctrines and conduct. To do otherwise is to put ourselves in the position in which God Himself will bring judgment and reveal our false position, v. 6.[7]

7-9 Agur prays briefly for God's guidance throughout his life. He asks specifically for two things, v. 7. In the first place, he desires that God will keep him from "vanity and lies," both terms referring to deceitfulness. "Vanity" (*šaw'*) refers to "emptiness," and thus anything that is

---

[7]Martin, p. 192, and Toy, p. 523, argue that the paragraph may have been written as late as 132 B.C. See the Introduction for a discussion of the dating of the book.

10 Accuse not a servant unto his master, lest he curse thee, and thou be found guilty.

without value. The most widely known use of the word is in the third commandment, "Thou shalt not take the name of the Lord thy God in vain," Exodus 20:7; Deuteronomy 5:11. The phrase refers to words that are wasted, words without value. "Lies" (*kazab*) are untruthful words. The act of lying is not compatible with a wholesome relationship to the Lord.

The second request receives most of the emphasis in the prayer. Agur asks that God will supply his material needs. He does not want too much or too little, but rather that God would meet his needs in an adequate way. The phrase "food convenient for me" is better "bread that is my custom," i.e., the daily allotment of food necessary to sustain life, v. 8.

The motivation for this request is godly. Agur is fearful that an imbalance in meeting his material needs will lead him away from God. Too much may cause him to become independent of God; too little may cause him to violate God's standards of honesty and lead him even to blaspheme God. In this last phrase, "take" (*tapaś*) means "to seize, take hold of." It often has a metaphorical sense, referring to the wicked who are "caught" in their schemes or to those who have "seized the law," i.e., become skillful in it. Here, it refers to "laying hold of the name of God," i.e., using it in a blasphemous way, v. 9.[8]

10 Agur now begins his advice to Ithiel and Ucal. He warns them against slandering another man's servant. This, of course, is a general truth as well. Agur, however, limits it here to servants, perhaps because of some local situation of which we are unaware. When the servant finds out what has been said of him, he will "curse" (*yəqallelka*) you. The verb *qalal* means "to be slight, light, trifling." It has the sense of placing one in a lower state, i.e., "to vilify, disgrace." The outcome of this is that you will "be found guilty," i.e., your wicked actions will be found out.

---

[8]Toy, p. 525, suggests that vv. 5, 9 are by different authors. He rests this suggestion on the use of the differing names of God in the verses. This, however, ignores the fact that *ʾəlôah* belongs in v. 5, where the omnipotent God gives His standards to man by means of divine revelation. Likewise, *yəhwah* fits the context of v. 9*a*, where the denial is of the need for a gracious God. The names of God have theological significance in the OT. The Book of Proverbs is no exception to this.

11 There is a generation that curseth their father, and doth not bless their mother.

12 There is a generation that are pure in their own eyes, and yet is not washed from their filthiness.

13 There is a generation, O how lofty are their eyes! and their eyelids are lifted up.

14 There is a generation, whose teeth are as swords, and their jaw teeth as knives, to devour the poor from off the earth, and the needy from among men.

11-14 The word "generation" (*dôr*) standing at the beginning of each of these verses is interesting. It comes from the verbal root *dûr,* "to heap up, pile." This idea comes from the circular shape at the base of a pile. The noun *dôr* represents the circle of life, a generation, encompassing the birth, the life, and the death, and then beginning again with a new generation. By extension, *dôr* represents a group of mankind characterized by a particular morality. This is its use here as Agur describes four evil groups of people.[9]

The first group shows no respect for their parents. The "curse" (cf. *qalal,* v. 10) parallels the negative "doth not bless" (*loʾ yəbarrek,* cf. 11:25). Both terms refer to the children's disdain toward their parents, to the failure to honor them.

Agur does not pronounce any divine judgment upon this group, or on any of the groups mentioned in the passage. He merely classifies some of the sins so rampant in his day, sins that have characterized wicked individuals throughout time. There is an implied rebuke of these actions, though he says nothing explicitly, v. 11.

The second group are the self-righteous, those who consider themselves "pure" (*ṭahôr,* cf. 15:26) when in reality they still wallow in their own "filthiness." The verb "they have not been washed" (*ruḥaṣ*) normally refers to ritual washing. From this, it extends naturally to washing from sin. The word "filth," *ṣoʾâ,* indicates literal filth, then metaphorically the filth of sin, v. 12.

---

[9] C. F. Kent and Millar Burrows, *Proverbs and Didactic Poems* (1927), p. 109, insert a numerical introduction to the passage: "There are three kinds of men whom the LORD hates, And four that are abhorrent to him." This follows the pattern of vv. 7-9, 15*b*-17, 18-19, 21-24, 25-28, and 29-31. Roth, *VTS* XIII, 38, and Oesterley, p. 274, interpret similarly. There is, however, no textual evidence to support this. That Agur is not slavish in following a pattern can be seen from vv. 1-6, 10, 15*a*, and 32-33. We do not need to force him into the common pattern in these verses.

*15 The horseleach hath two daughters, crying, Give, give. There are
three things that are never satisfied, yea, four things say not, It is
enough:*
*16 The grave; and the barren womb; the earth that is not filled with
water; and the fire that saith not, It is enough.*

The next group includes the proud, a class of people often singled out
for rebuke in the book.[10] They are "lofty" as they look down on others.
The "eyelids" (ᶜapᶜap, cf. 4:25) are "lifted up," arrogantly considering
others lesser than themselves, v. 13.

The final group focuses on the insatiable nature of man as each tries
to take advantage of others who cannot defend themselves. To heighten
the picture of rapacity, Agur picturesquely describes the teeth as swords
and knives. "Jaw teeth" (matalləᶜotayw) are probably the incisors, distinguished from šinnayw, a more general word for teeth. These individuals
spoil the poor and needy.[11] They devour them, taking advantage of them
so as to actually cause them to disappear.[12]

15a In a vivid word picture, Agur describes the greedy man by comparing him to a leech. The "two daughters" are the suckers on either end
of the leech. Just as the leech attaches itself to its victim and begins to
suck in as much blood as it can, so these two daughters poetically portray their greed by crying, "Give! Give!" i.e., "give us more."[13] The
leech and its suckers illustrate the greed that so often consumes men in
this life.

15b-16 The emblem of greed leads naturally into the second numerical proverb of the chapter. Agur sets forth four things that are never satisfied, things that display a rapacious hunger for more.

---

[10]See the subject study on Pride and Humility.

[11]Roth, *VTS* XIII, 38, omits the final phrase on the grounds that interpretation does not
normally occur in this chapter. Martin, p. 194, and Oesterley, p. 274, agree with this.
Once again, this forces the poet into a mold, an action that has no warrant. We should
expect individuality in poetical passages.

[12]AB, p. 178, emends meʾadam, "from man," to meʾadamâ, "from the earth," to gain
better parallelism with meʾereṣ. Dahood, *PNWSP*, pp. 57-58, argues unconvincingly from
Ugaritic that ʾadam can mean "land." The MT, however, makes good sense and adequately parallels the thought of meʾereṣ.

[13]A wide variety of interpretations have been given to the leech and the two daughters.
Oesterley, p. 275, identifies the "leech," ᶜalûqâ, as "the flesh-devouring ghoul of the
Arabs," with the two daughters two diseases whose "names were not pronounced."
Jones, p. 240, and Gaster, p. 807, follow this view. Plaut, pp. 304-5, understands the

The numerical saying of the type x / x + 1 is common in the OT. It is also duplicated in nonbiblical poetical writings of that age.[14] It clearly is a poetical form, although we do not know its origin and exact sense. It is clear, however, that the numerical summary calls attention to the points about to be made, v. 15*b*.

The "grave" (*šəʾôl*, cf. 7:27) is never satisfied, always making room for one more dead person. The word *šəʾôl* occurs here in its normal sense to refer to the place of burial. The "barren womb" is also unfulfilled, always hoping to give birth to at least one child; cf. Genesis 16:2; 25:21; 30:1.[15] The earth itself has not been filled with water since the days of the Flood. It manages to drink up all that is poured out upon it. The fire rages as long as it has fuel. Agur does not draw any spiritual lesson from these similes. The implied lesson, however, is that greed can never be satisfied, v. 16.

Hebrew as naming the author of these sayings, "(the sayings) of Alukah." Stuart, p. 412, understands the *ʿalûqâ* as a vampire, an imaginary creature that sucks the blood from men. The names of the two daughters are proper names that reveal the character of those who, like vampires, are insatiable. The Babylonian Talmud identifies the leech as hell, and the two daughters those who cry from Gehenna to this world, "Bring, Bring." *Babylonian Talmud, Abodah Zarah,* trans. A. Mishcon and A. Cohen (1935), p. 86. J. J. Gluck, "Proverbs XXX 15*a*, *VT* 14:369-70, strains in his argument that *ʿalûqâ* means "erotic passion," with the two daughters loving "(carnal) pleasures." Francis Sparling North, "The Four Insatiables," *VT* 15:282, refutes Gluck. The word occurs only here and is therefore difficult. An Aramaic cognate supports the meaning of "leech."

[14]Roth, *VTS* XIII, identifes many biblical and nonbiblical numerical proverbs. Among these are nonbiblical proverbs that take the form x / x + 1: e.g., Ecclus. 23.16-17 and Ugaritic *Baal II* iii.16-19. Biblical passages with this form include Job 5:19-22; Prov. 6:16-19; 30:15-16, 18-20, 21-23, 29-31; and Amos 1:3-5, 6-8, 9-10, 11-12, 13-15; 2:1-3, 4-5, 6-8.

[15]Thomas, *VTS* III, 290, suggests that *raḥam* refers to the vulture (*raḥam,* translated "gier eagle" in the AV) mentioned in Lev. 11:18; Deut. 14:17. The phrase "barren womb," *ʿoṣer raḥam,* then, refers to "the voracity of the carrion-vulture." Both *ʿoṣer* and *raḥam* occur broadly, and their meanings are not in doubt. Since the "barren womb" fits nicely into the proverb, no change is necessary. McKane, p. 656, suggests that death, the thirsty land, and the raging fire are all metaphors of "the insatiable appetite of the god Mot . . . for sexual intercourse, for the fierce urge to remove the reproach of her barrenness." This rather bizarre suggestion has no support.

*17 The eye that mocketh at his father, and despiseth to obey his mother,
the ravens of the valley shall pick it out, and the young eagles shall
eat it.
18 There be three things which are too wonderful for me, yea, four
which I know not:
19 The way of an eagle in the air; the way of a serpent upon a rock; the
way of a ship in the midst of the sea; and the way of a man with a
maid.*

17 A single verse rebukes a child's attitude of scorn toward his parents.[16] The "eye" here is the window to the soul, revealing the innermost
attitudes of the heart. The verb "mocketh," *til⁽ag,* is strong, indicating
"mocking" or "derision." The parallel suggests that this shows itself in
rebellion, refusing to obey the directions of the parents.[17] Poetic justice
will be received. The eye had mocked; the eye will be pecked out.
Undoubtedly, this is poetical, picturing the fact that the rebellious child
will receive appropriate judgment.

18-19 Repeating the numerical formula, Agur now cites four things
that are beyond his comprehension, v. 18.[18] The soaring of an eagle in
the air, hundreds of feet above the ground, perplexes him. Likewise, the
motion of a snake is difficult to understand. Twisting its body one way
and yet moving in another, the serpentine motion requires mathematical

---

[16]Skehan, *CBQ* 10:123, argues unconvincingly that v. 17 should be moved after 23:22.
This would develop the idea suggested there. His suggestion is arbitrary and unsupported, made only to lend weight to his equally unconvincing ideas regarding the struc-
tural form of the book.
[17]Toy, p. 532, emends *yiqqəhat* to *ziqnât* to make the MT conform to the LXX. The
suggestion has only weak textual support. D. Winton Thomas, "A Note on לִיקֲהַת in
Proverbs xxx. 17," *JTS* 42:154-55, argues that *yîqqəhat* is from *lhq,* "to be hoary, old."
Thus, the child despises "the hoary age of his mother." H. H. Rowley, *The Old
Testament and Modern Study* (1951) (hereafter referred to as *OTMS*), p. 243, and Jonas
C. Greenfield, "Lexicographical Notes I," *HUCA* 29:212-14, argue similarly. This argument has the support of the LXX. The word *yîqqəhat* occurs only here and at Gen. 49:10.
In both places, however, the idea of "obedience" is satisfactory. The Arabic cognate supports the meaning of "obedience."
[18]Several commentators find the point of connection in that the four examples are all
trackless, failing to leave any sign behind. The eagle's flight, the serpent's slithering, the
ship's path, and the bond of love are all without a physical trace that can be identified.
Among others, Garrett, Phillott, Muenscher, and Perowne take this view. The ship, however, does leave a short-lived track in the water. The serpent may leave its track as it
passes over sand. The formation of the emotional tie of love leaves very clear signs behind. It is better to stress the incomprehensibility of the actions.

20 Such is the way of an adulterous woman; she eateth, and wipeth her mouth, and saith, I have done no wickedness.

analysis to understand it. Similarly, the mighty ship plowing through the sea raises questions. How is it that the wind can blow one direction while the ship moves in another?

Agur meditates on these thoughts and then introduces the final and climactic thought. The first three are illustrations of the amazing relationship that forms between a man and a maiden. What magnetism causes a bond of such strength that a man can claim the "virgin" as his own?

The word "maid" (*ᶜalmâ*) has long been considered a *crux interpretum* at Isaiah 7:14. In my judgment, the word should be rendered "virgin." The NT's use of παρθενος at Matthew 1:23 is decisive. In addition, this sense fits nicely at every OT use, v. 19.

Agur makes no application of these incomprehensible things. It is an easy step, however, to see these as illustrations of the marvelous creation in which we live. God's handiwork shows a wonderful variety. What God has done for the creation as a whole, He can do as well for individuals as He works out His will in their lives.

20 The last statement of v. 19 leads Agur to consider the incomprehensibility of an amoral woman. Eating and wiping her mouth are euphemistic for her adultery, following the same figure as used in 9:17. The love relationship in marriage is marvelous. How can this woman turn her back on this wonder and enter into an adulterous relationship? How can she treat it as nothing more than eating a meal, with no sense at all of sin?[19]

---

[19]E. J. Dillon, *The Skeptics of the Old Testament* (1973), p. 141, treats v. 20 as a scribal comment, which "was afterwards removed from the margin to the text where it now figures as the twentieth verse." Martin, p. 197; Oesterley, p. 277, and KD II, 298, treat the verse similarly. There is, however, no textual support for this view. The MT should be retained.

*21 For three things the earth is disquieted, and for four which it cannot
  bear:*
*22 For a servant when he reigneth; and a fool when he is filled with
  meat;*
*23 For an odious woman when she is married; and an handmaid that is
  heir to her mistress.*

21-23 The next group focuses on four situations in which people have
been elevated suddenly into a high social position. This causes the earth
to be "disquieted" (*ragzâ,* "to tremble, become agitated," and so here "to
quake"). This is hyperbole, indicating the turmoil caused in society
when such events transpire, v. 21.

While a servant in ancient times might gradually rise in position until
he held significant authority, this is not the case here. The idea here is of
a slave who suddenly rises to a position of rule. Not being accustomed
to authority, he offends everybody with his newfound power. The fool
who becomes "filled with meat" is one who has stumbled into prosperity. Once again, he does not know how to draw upon such resources and
he becomes an irritant to others, v. 22.

The final two examples come from family relationships. The first
woman has been an old maid with a sour disposition. By some chance
of fate, she finds a husband. She immediately shows her contentious
spirit by bringing misery upon those with whom she was formerly associated. The final illustration draws upon the serving maiden who becomes her mistress's "heir" or, better, "displaces" her mistress in the
affections of the husband. This could happen after her mistress's death
or after a divorce.[20] She no doubt flaunts her authority over those who
were formerly her associates, v. 23.

These examples of things that cause social upheaval have a practical
application. Order is desirable in life. Things that seem unlikely are
probably not for the best. There is simply too much chance that they
will cause difficulty.

---

[20]While "heir," *yaraš,* may refer to inheriting, in the normal situation the husband controlled the estate. For this reason, it is better to view the phrase as reflecting social upheaval. The servant takes her mistress's place in the husband's affections.

24 There be four things which are little upon the earth, but they are exceeding wise:
25 The ants are a people not strong, yet they prepare their meat in the summer;
26 The conies are but a feeble folk, yet make they their houses in the rocks;
27 The locusts have no king, yet go they forth all of them by bands;
28 The spider taketh hold with her hands, and is in kings' palaces.

24-28 We have here four unexpectedly wise creatures. At first glance, no one would anticipate great accomplishments from these creatures. And yet, in their own ways, each performs feats that are extraordinary. The *puᶜal* participle of *ḥakam;* cf. 1:2, coupled with the adjective *ḥəkamîm* gives emphasis: "making wisdom, they are wise!" or "they are exceedingly wise," v. 24.[21]

The ant has been used before as a positive illustration of work; cf. 6:6. Although they are feeble creatures, easily crushed, through diligence the colony stores sufficient food to sustain them through the winter months, v. 25. The word "conies" (*šəpannîm*) refers to the Syrian hyrax, a small mammal with short legs, ears, and tail and reddish brown fur. These animals have large front teeth and heavy, broad nails on their feet, which are also padded. Though not a particularly strong animal, they make dwellings for themselves in crevices among the rocks, and even on the sides of cliffs, v. 26.

The locusts have no king or queen to lead them. Yet, instinctively, they move in bands without leadership, ravaging their way across the fields of a country and wreaking great havoc as they do so, v. 27. The "spider" (*śəmamît*) is a kind of lizard. Verse 28*a* is better "You may grasp the lizard in your hands." Despite its ease of capture, this animal uses its climbing ability to go everywhere, even on the walls of the king's palace, v. 28.

The passage implies a moral lesson again rather than stating it explicitly. None of these creatures have any intrinsic strength or ability that

---

[21]Dillon, pp. 144-45, relies on the form of the proverb to conclude that vv. 24-28 are the work of an editor, added as a companion to vv. 29-31. He notes the different numerical formula, the differing number of lines in the strophe, and the lack of an important moral point. The argument is not impressive. It fails to allow for poetical variation, clearly seen elsewhere throughout the chapter. As for the moral point, see the discussion above.

29 There be three things which go well, yea, four are comely in going:
30 A lion which is strongest among beasts, and turneth not away for
any;
31 A greyhound; an he goat also; and a king, against whom there is no
rising up.

would fit them for great accomplishments. Yet by using their God-given abilities, they accomplish significant tasks: storing food for the winter, dwelling safely in what might be thought as an inhospitable place, working cooperatively with others, and residing in the palace of a king! So it is that we, though not greatly gifted, using our God-given talents, can accomplish significant tasks, the will of God for us as individuals.

29-31 Agur follows the pattern here seen previously in vv. 18-19, with the first three examples serving to introduce the fourth. All four illustrations deal with stately bearing, a regal attitude that stems from the mastery of their individual realms, v. 29. With his great strength, the lion serves as the master of his domain, fearless of lesser animals, v. 30.

The "greyhound" (*zarzîr matnayim*) is puzzling and must remain, at best, an educated guess. From the context, it must refer to something with a regal bearing. The phrase means something like "girded about the loins." The phrase is clearly idiomatic but the idiom is now lost. There is no reason for departing from the LXX and Vulgate here. I translate "strutting cock," thinking of the array of feathers as the girding about the loins.[22] The "he-goat" (*tayiš,* which possibly refers to the goat's "butting") also serves as the master of his world, tolerating no interference with his plans.

The final phrase is also difficult due to the presence of *ʾalqûm,* a word that occurs only here. The AV takes this as two words, *ʾal* and *qûm,* in the sense of "no rising up." The NASB and NIV have paraphrased with the same sense, "no uprising," equivalent to having his army with him. This also takes into account the existence of an Arabic cognate meaning "army, militia." This is sensible as it allows the first three examples to lead naturally into the regal leader of the army, v. 31.[23]

---

[22]Zöckler, p. 252, argues for the translation "greyhound." He takes *zarzîm matnayim* as "slender in the loins." *PC*, p. 578, and KD II, 309, argue similarly. Henry III, 970, and French and Skinner, p. 111, suggest the horse. Phillott, SPCK, offers "courier." The phrase is awkward to translate; however, the versions lend most support to "cock."
[23]Thomas, *VTS* III, 291, argues that the first three examples make it necessary that the fourth example be an animal also. He suggests that *melek ʾalqûm* is a dittography of

These four examples illustrate the practical lesson of regalness. Just as these animals maintain a stateliness, so the child of God should manifest a royal manner to the world. By avoiding that which degrades him and practicing those habits that are appropriate to one who is the child of the King of kings, we show forth the regalness of our position in Christ.

For three . . . for four . . .

1. Four Examples of Greed 15-16

    a. Grave, barren womb, earth and water, fire

    b. Greed is never satisfied; greed will never satisfy.

2. Four Incomprehensible Things 18-19

    a. Eagle, snake, ship, man and a woman

    b. God's creation is wonderfully varied; we serve a great God.

3. Four Social Problems 21-23

    a. Servant who assumes power, fool who becomes prosperous, shrew who marries, servant who replaces her mistress

    b. Order is desirable in life; disorder causes problems.

4. Four Wise Creatures 24-28

    a. Ant, coney, locust, lizard

    b. God uses small things in His will; are you small enough to be used?

5. Four Regal Examples 29-31

    a. Lion, strutting cock, he-goat, a general

    b. Christians are children of the King; we should so live.

---

melek ʾeyn laʾarbeh in v. 27 with the final two words there being abbreviated to *ʾ* and *l.* If the phrase is omitted, this leaves *qûm ʿimmô* as the name for some animal. The explanation is contrived. Julius A. Bewer, "Two Suggestions on Prov 30 31 and Zech 9 16," *JBL* 67:61-62, understands *qûm* as a corruption from *qadam.* Following the patterns of participles used earlier, he turns this into *məqadam.* For *ʾal* he reads *ʾayil,* "leader," and translates "the leader marching in front of his people." Again, the explanation is forced. Driver, *Biblica* 32:194, reverses the word order and emends to *ʿimmô loʾ-qam,* translating, "against whom there is none rising up." This is better but the emendation is without textual support. These suggestions offer nothing more plausible than the MT.

32 If thou hast done foolishly in lifting up thyself, or if thou hast thought evil, lay thine hand upon thy mouth.

33 Surely the churning of milk bringeth forth butter, and the wringing of the nose bringeth forth blood: so the forcing of wrath bringeth forth strife.

32-33 The final bit of advice given to Ithiel and Ucal warns them against self-exaltation and the plotting of evil. Such wickedness stirs up strife. There is no object of the verb "thought," *zammôta*. The root *zamam* occurs widely referring to the thoughts of both God and man. When used of man, it normally refers to evil plans. The parallelism of the verse suggests that something like "evil," *rašaᶜ*, be supplied (so AV). The omission is perhaps due to the attempt to parallel the meter of the first phrase, v. 32.[24]

The two word pictures illustrate the strife that follows the stirring up of anger. "Butter" (*hemʾâ*) is better "curdled milk," still a common food in the Middle East. "Churning," *mîṣ*, refers to "pressing" or "squeezing." Curdled milk is squeezed or pressed to drain off the liquid and then the remainder is dried until ready to be eaten. When the nose is squeezed (*mîṣ*), it bleeds. In the same manner, when one "forces" (or "presses," *mîṣ*) anger, he stirs up strife (*rîb*, cf. 3:30). The translation partially obscures the poetic repetition of "pressing . . . brings forth," *mîṣ . . . yôṣîʾ*, in each of the three phrases, v. 33.[25]

---

[24]Toy, p. 537, objects to "done foolishly," *nabalta*, on the grounds that this sense does not occur elsewhere. The verb, however, occurs only four other times, all in the *piᶜel*; hence, his argument is not conclusive. The widespread use of *nabal* in the noun form supports the traditional sense for the *qal* here.

[25]AB, p. 182, understands the pressing of the nostrils as a rude gesture. This is possible although it is less direct than taking the phrase to refer to a blow on the nostrils. He also suggests that the final phrase is a variant of the second, an unlikely suggestion with no textual support. Zöckler, p. 252, curiously understands the dual "wrath," *ʾappayim*, as indicating "the wrath of two whose sharp pressing upon each other leads to the development of strife." The dual, however, normally occurs when referring to the two nostrils as they dilate in anger (see the discussion in 14:17).

Practical Applications from Proverbs 30

1. Incomprehensibility of God 4
2. Comments on God's Word 5-6
3. Prayer for purity 8*a*
4. Reliance on God 8*b*-9
5. Slander 10
6. Four unrighteous groups 11-14
7. Four illustrations of greed 15-16
8. Judgment of a rebellious child 17
9. Four incomprehensible things 18-19
10. Adultery 20
11. Four actions causing social upheaval 21-23
12. Four wise creatures 24-28
13. Four regal examples 29-31
14. Warning against evil 32
15. Anger 33

1 The words of king Lemuel, the prophecy that his mother taught him.

PROVERBS 31

GUIDANCE FOR KING LEMUEL 31:1-9

1 We have the same problem here as with Agur in c. 30. There is no way to identify Lemuel as one of Israel's kings. There is no individual named Lemuel among the kings of nearby countries. He may have been a lesser member of the royal family, cf. v. 4, with the potential of becoming king. While we cannot identify him with certainty, he was well known enough that the Jews accepted his writings.[1]

The "prophecy" (*maśśaʾ,* better, "oracle" or "burden," cf. 30:1) actually has words of instruction taught Lemuel by his mother. We catch a glimpse here of the broad spectrum of responsibilities borne by the mother; cf. 1:8-9. She discusses briefly three topics. First, she exhorts her son to avoid the destructive ways of promiscuity (v. 3). Then she guides him with respect to the use of alcoholic beverages. Drunkenness would cause him to forget his own laws. This, in turn, would cause him to make wrong decisions that would bring additional difficulty to the oppressed. Rather than this, he should give wine to cheer those who were undergoing various difficulties (vv. 4-7). Finally, she admonishes him to act on behalf of the downtrodden and unfortunate. As an official of the land, Lemuel undoubtedly held the legal responsibility to maintain

---

[1]A variety of approaches have attempted to identify Lemuel. Several commentators understand *maśśaʾ* as a country on the border between Edom and Arabia; cf. Gen. 25:14. The place is also associated with Agur, 30:1. Lemuel supposedly is the king of this region. This view, however, disregards the accents in the verse. A. Jirku, "Das n. pr. Lemu'el (Prov 31 1) und der Gott Lim," *ZAW* 66:151, translates the name as "Lim ist Gott." He cites the Mari texts as containing names in which Lim forms the second part. Henry III, 971, mentions the possibility that Lemuel and Solomon should be identified. He understands the name as "for God," i.e., one devoted to God. Cohen, p. 209, likewise understands the name as representing Solomon. Cohen, Plaut, and Greenstone all relate a story from the *Midrash.* Supposedly, Solomon remained up all night in revelry with an Egyptian bride. The following morning, he slept in late. Because the keys to the temple were kept under his pillow, the morning sacrifice was delayed by several hours. The exhortation of vv. 1-9 from his mother supposedly followed this incident. Martin, p. 201, suggests that the name is a dittography corrupted from *melek.* Oesterley, p. 281, simply makes the name the result of a corrupted text. AB, p. 183, emends *ləmōʾēl* to *ləhiwwāʾēl* and translates, "Words [of advice] to a king acting foolishly." These suggestions are not convincing. As with Agur, the lack of identification of Lemuel is not a barrier to accepting the passage as part of the Word inspired by God. The Jews so understood it.

2 What, my son? and what, the son of my womb? and what, the son of my vows?

3 Give not thy strength unto women, nor thy ways to that which destroyeth kings.

justice. As he wisely exercised this control, he insured that the afflicted would receive their legal rights and fair treatment (vv. 8-9).

2-3 The threefold question catches Lemuel's attention. Clearly, something must be supplied to complete the ellipsis. Most likely, something such as "What shall I say to you, my son?" is appropriate here.[2] The two repetitions heighten the call to attentiveness.

An Aramaism occurs here, with *bar* rather than *ben* denoting the son each time.[3] The phrase "son of my womb" is a term of endearment, indicating that this is the son that she has carried within her, that she is indeed his mother.[4] Likewise, the phrase "son of my vows" relates back to his origin, that she has made vows concerning him; cf. I Samuel 1:11.

The first of the instructions follows. This warning concerns the possibility of promiscuous behavior. Lemuel's mother warns him against allowing adulterous behavior to control him. The word *ḥayil* often refers to virtue or worth; cf. 12:4. It as well denotes strength or power, the basis underlying the AV here. The context here, however, argues for a meaning more in the first sense, the idea of honor. Should Lemuel give in to the temptation to engage in sensual conduct, he would destroy his honor, something that could very well destroy his ability to reign. The effective leader must have the respect of his followers or else he will find it difficult to lead.

---

[2]Dahood, *PNWSP*, p. 60, suggests, "What ails my son," arguing from Ugaritic parallels. The parallels, however, are coincidental. The context calls for something relating to speech or advice.

[3]The use of *bar* does not warrant an extreme late dating of the passage. Plaut, p. 311, suggests a date of 400 B.C.E. or later. Toy, pp. xxx-xxxi, cites these Aramaisms as supporting a second century B.C. date. The word *bar,* however, occurs elsewhere in older settings: Ezra 5:1; Dan. 3:25; and especially Ps. 2:12. The use of the foreign word may suggest that the passage is later than c. 1-29. There is no reason to place it later than Hezekiah.

[4]Ferdinand Deist, "Prov. 31:1: a Case of Constant Mistranslation," *JNSL* 6:3, argues that the phrase is a figurative term of affection and that it should be translated "my own son"; cf. Job 19:17 (MT). This makes the instruction come from Lemuel to his own sons rather than from Lemuel's mother. The view goes against the virtually unanimous understanding of the ancient versions.

4 It is not for kings, O Lemuel, it is not for kings to drink wine; nor for princes strong drink:
5 Lest they drink, and forget the law, and pervert the judgment of any of the afflicted.
6 Give strong drink unto him that is ready to perish, and wine unto those that be of heavy hearts.
7 Let him drink, and forget his poverty, and remember his misery no more.

The "ways" (cf. *derek,* 22:6) are activities of a sensual nature.[5] The word *derek* occurs widely to refer to a way of life. Should Lemuel give himself to these pursuits, he may destroy himself as a leader. "Destroyeth," *lamḥôt,* is a strong word. The verb *maḥâ* means "to blot out, extinguish." It appropriately describes what will happen to Lemuel as the king of the land should he allow licentious conduct to control him.[6]

4-7 The second warning focuses on the need to abstain from alcoholic beverages. The leaders of the people should not be addicted to "wine" (*yayin,* cf. 9:5) or "strong drink" (*šekar,* cf. 20:1). The word *rôznîm* is better "rulers" than "princes." The word *razan* is "to be weighty, commanding." Four of the six times it occurs in the OT, it parallels "king," *melek.*

The only real textual problem in v. 4 is *ʾew.* The form must be an infinitive construct from *ʾawâ,* "to desire." The final consonant assimilates, which should cause the verb to lengthen to a *pathaḥ.* With this repointing, the translation becomes "nor for rulers to desire strong drink."[7]

---

[5]AB, p. 183; Gemser, p. 82; and McKane, p. 409, emend *dərakeyka* to *yərekêka,* "loins," on the ground that it gives better parallelism to "strength," *ḥêleka.* The argument is without value if *ḥêleka* is understood in the sense of "honor." Even, however, if the sense of "strength" is taken, the parallelism of the MT is adequate.

[6]Perles, *JQR* 2:105, relates *lamḥôt* to the Greek μοιχαω, "to commit adultery." The view is unlikely since it requires the passage to have been written extremely late. Reider, *VT* 4:287, relates both *lamḥôt* and *məlakîm* to Aramaic and translates, "destroyers of counsel," referring to evil women. This ignores the common meanings of the words, meanings that satisfactorily fit here.

[7]The *qərê ʾey,* "where," does not suit the parallelism. KD II, 322, however, accepts the *qərê.* This creates an ellipsis for which he supplies the verb "to ask." It is not right, then, for kings to eagerly seek after strong drink, asking, "Where is mead?" Greenstone, p. 331, takes a similar view. Driver, *Biblica* 32:195, understands *ʾew* as either an infinitive absolute written defectively for *ʾawwô* or an Aramaicizing similar to *reaᶜ,* "purpose."

Indulgence in alcoholic beverages dulls the senses and causes good judgment to fail. Such a leader would be unable to carry his responsibilities well. He would forget his obligations to the law of the land, and he would render unfair judgments of the people. While "judgments" (məhuqqaq) occurs only here in a judicial sense, its meaning is not debatable. The noun ḥoq occurs widely with the sense of "statute, decree." Similarly, the expression "pervert the judgment," wîšanneh dîn, is not doubtful. The verb šanâ, cf. 24:21, means "to change." The expression therefore refers to the changing of a decree. This is not merely a perversion of justice. It is the altering of a correct decree, most likely due to bribery or the accommodation of friends with whom the ruler has caroused, v. 5.

Lemuel's mother points out the stupefying effects of alcoholic beverages. Their impact is such that they can ease the pain of one who is dying (cf. Matt. 27:34; Mark 15:23; and the Lord's desire not to minimize in any way the pangs of death). They also can cheer those who are "heavy of heart," literally "bitter of soul," speaking of the emotional pains caused by sorrow.

The change from the singular to the plural in v. 6 and the change back to the singular in v. 7 is not serious. Plural words often express abstract ideas. Even if, however, we translate "heavy hearts," ləmarê napeš, as "those who have bitter spirits," there is no reason that v. 7 cannot have a singular subject, v. 6.[8]

Lemuel's mother notes that alcoholic beverages will cause the poverty-stricken individual (cf. ra'š, 10:4) to forget his poverty. He will forget "his misery" ('əmalô, cf. 16:26), the unfruitful nature of his labor. The

---

AB, p. 183, and Hulst, *OTTP*, p. 130, read the word as 'awwē(h), "to desire." Toy, p. 541, suggests reading msk or sbo', a radical departure from the MT. D. Winton Thomas, "אי in Proverbs XXXI 4," *VT* 12:499, suggests that 'ew is a scribal error for r'ô = rəwô, "to drink deeply." Without support, Thomas and Toy as well omit ləmu'el 'al lamlakîm as unsuitable to the rhythm of the verse. Zöckler, p. 256, understands the word as 'ô, "or." The phrase then would be translated, "it is not for kings to drink wine, and rulers *to drink wine* or strong drink." This requires the supply of the phrase "to drink wine." The accents argue against this but it is possible, v. 5. The repointing suggested above does the least damage to the MT.

[8]Dahood, *Biblica* 56:241, argues that the plural verb in v. 6 must agree with the singular verbs in v. 7. He suggests that *marê* must be repointed to *marî*, with the final -î an archaic genitive ending, following the usage in Ugaritic. While this does not alter the sense of the verse, the change in the MT is unnecessary.

8 Open thy mouth for the dumb in the cause of all such as are appointed to destruction.
9 Open thy mouth, judge righteously, and plead the cause of the poor and needy.

noun is from ʿamal, "to labor, travail, be in misery." The stress is on the struggle and travail of labor rather than on the accomplishments of work, v. 7.

8-9 The final admonition reminds Lemuel of his need to defend the helpless. The word "dumb" figuratively refers to those who for various reasons are not able to speak effectively on their own behalf.[9] The king should take up their cause.

The king should as well speak for those who are "appointed to destruction" (bᵊnê ḥᵊlôp). The phrase is obscure and various suggestions have been offered. Literally, the phrase is "sons of change," not a clear expression. The verb ḥalap may also mean "to pass away," Job 9:26; Isaiah 8:8; 21:1. This suggests that the phrase refers to those who are transitory, passing away. Lemuel should assist those who are in such dire straits, v. 8.[10]

Paralleling the thought of v. 8, Lemuel should render righteous judgment to those who come before him in his role as judge. He should not be swayed by the eminence of those who press their cases. Rather, he should treat fairly the unfortunate of the land, v. 9.

---

[9]Among others, KD II, 323, and McKane, p. 411, understand ʾillem, "dumb," to refer to an actual physical infirmity that results in the inability to speak. While this is possible, the context suggests the figurative use to me. Toy, p. 541, suggests the emendation to ʾᵊmet, "truth," on the grounds of better parallelism with 9a. The change is radical and unneeded.

[10]Driver, *Biblica* 32:195-96, relies on an Aramaic cognate. He takes the phrase to refer to "adversaries," i.e., legal opponents. Lemuel should defend the dumb against the suit of his adversaries. Thomas, *VT* 15:277, rejects this in favor of an Arabic cognate, "stupidity, want of intellect." Lemuel should defend those who have no understanding. Plaut, p. 312, connects ḥᵊlôp with another Arabic word and translates, "victims of circumstance." McKane, p. 412, relies on a parallel from the Nabateans and also translates, "victims of circumstance." Without offering a specific suggestion, Dahood, p. 60, states that the parallelism with ʾillem forces the phrase to describe some physical infirmity. Oesterley, p. 283, emends to ḥolî, and translates, "sickness." While the verse is open to differing suggestions, we should maintain the MT here since some sense can be made of it.

DESCRIPTION OF THE WORTHY WOMAN 31:10-31

The remaining passage is an acrostic poem in which the unknown author paints a vivid picture of the worthy woman. He describes her labors on behalf of the family. The poem pays tribute to the faithful wife for the nature and extent of her influence on the home.[11] The somewhat erratic nature of the passage is explained by its poetical nature, with the author bound by the acrostic structure, which he has imposed upon himself.

Surprisingly, Proverbs mentions the general responsibilities of the wife in the home far more than it does the husband's obligations. She acts as a business manager, overseeing various economic enterprises carried out in connection with the home (31:10-29). She sets an example of industriousness by her actions (31:13-27). She shares the responsibility for training the children (1:8-9; 6:20; 31:1, 26). She takes charge of extending charity to the unfortunate (31:20).

This emphasis reflects the natural division of responsibilities in the home. The husband normally worked at some distance away while his wife stayed at home. There are only a limited number of occupations mentioned in the book: judge (8:16); nobility and king (mentioned over a dozen times, e.g., 16:10, 12-15); ambassador (13:17); farmer

---

[11]Some older commentators allegorized the woman of the passage. *Saint Augustine: Treatises on Marriage and Other Subjects, the Fathers of the Church*, ed. Roy Deferrari (1955), XXVII, 280, notes that Augustine equated the woman with the church. Deane and Taylor-Taswell, *PC*, p. 597, state, "The spiritual expositors see in this description of the virtuous woman a prophetic representation of the Church of Christ in her truth and purity and influence." On the other hand, Margaret B. Crook, "The Marriageable Maiden of Prov. 31:10-31," *JNES* 3:139, suggests that the passage was designed to assist in the instruction of young married women in Israel. Plaut, p. 312, says that the passage is customarily recited by the husband and the children at the Friday evening meal that begins the Sabbath ritual. In this sense, the passage does provide instruction. There is no warrant, however, for going as far as Crook to make the passage a poem composed expressly for this formal instruction. Otto Eissfeldt's view, p. 472, can be rejected out of hand. He states that the passage is "an independent poem," ascribed to the mother of Lemuel and placed here only because in v. 3 she had warned Lemuel against "improper relations with women." Some late editor felt the need for a positive statement to counter the negative warning. Ross, *EBC* V, 1128-29, views the poem as a personification of wisdom and not at all "a portrayal of an ideal wife." While there is no question concerning the wisdom of the woman, to take the poem merely as a personification misses the valuable practical application.

10 Who can find a virtuous woman? for her price is far above rubies.

(10:5; 12:11; 24:30-31); and herdsman (27:23-27). The general picture of the OT shows Israel as an agricultural society. Most men were away from home during the day, involved in some way with the fields or herds. Responsibilities within the household naturally fell to the wife to carry out.

The passage poetically presents the picture of an ideal wife. Though the passage is ideal, the description should not be taken lightly as not practically possible. The passage gives God's standards for the wife, standards that a worthy woman will strive to meet. In her accomplishments, the godly woman finds the fulfillment of her role as a wife and mother. Both the woman and her husband benefit from reaching these goals. This benefit lies chiefly in the personal satisfaction that they gain. It also includes the economic well-being and harmony of the family.

Incidentally, the passage reveals an important principle concerning the role of the woman and work. The Bible does not forbid the wife from working. Rather, it shows her as working at such work as naturally complements that of her husband. She helps to meet the needs of the family. The arrival of children will normally demand that she remain at home to guide them. The example of the worthy woman in this passage, however, establishes the fact that the wife may hold some work responsibilities.

10 The opening question justly expresses admiration for the "virtuous [*ḥayil,* cf. 12:4] woman." With the question, the author implies that such a wife is rare. The question is rhetorical. It expresses esteem for a woman who has such valued qualities of virtue and industriousness. The question implies the great value of this wife. In view of the scarcity of such character, a man who possesses this kind of wife has a rare jewel (*pənînîm,* cf. 3:15).[12]

---

[12]Perles, *JQR* 2:105, repoints *mikrah,* "her price," to *mikreha* to satisfy the normal meaning of *raḥoq,* normally relating to distance. He translates, "the place where she may be found is more distant than that where corals are found." The change is unnecessary. Not only is this a poetic context, where unusual meanings are sometimes found, but *raḥoq* has the same sense of comparison in Jer. 2:5.

*11 The heart of her husband doth safely trust in her, so that he shall
have no need of spoil.*
12 She will do him good and not evil all the days of her life.

11 The woman has the esteem of her family. Her husband trusts her
without reservation.[13] In and of itself, this relationship serves as sufficient reward for the diligence and consistency of the woman. A harmo-
nious home avoids the contention that the book so often warns against
elsewhere. Moreover, it brings a high degree of personal satisfaction to
those who gain this emotional benefit.

As a result of her labors, the wife achieves financial success. Through
her work, she earns enough so that she can materially assist her husband. He has no need of "spoil" (*šalal*). The noun *šalal* frequently refers
to booty or plunder. Here, it has a broader sense of gain apart from the
context of war.[14]

12 The worthy woman performs good works rather than evil ones.
These works characterize her over the course of the entire marriage as
she seeks to please her husband. Nothing here requires that we limit the
thought just to those good works performed outside of the immediate
household. In fact, the woman's husband is the object of the verb. She
shows her love for him by positive actions. No specific description of
these actions limits them to any one area of the husband-wife relationship. The thought is general, indicating that the godly wife cares for her
husband in a variety of ways, all of which receive the characterization
"good."[15]

---

[13]Cohen, p. 211; McKane, pp. 666-67; and Toy, p. 543, all limit the husband's trust to
his confidence in his wife's business acumen. The expansion of the thought in v. 12,
however, supports a broader application of the thought. In every area of life, the worthy
woman consistently benefits her husband. He therefore trusts her in all areas.

[14]Thomas, *VTS* III, 292, proposes that *šalal* be glossed "wool" rather than "spoil" or
"gain." Perles, *JQR* 2:127, suggests that *šalal* was originally *šalom*. This was abbreviated
in some texts to *šalʾ*, which was later interpreted as *šalal*. While these suggestions are ingenious, they are unnecessary. It is reasonable that *šalal*, apart from a war context, has
the broad general sense of gain. *PC*, p. 597, translates, "he shall not lack gain," and sees
this as foreshadowing the church winning souls away from Satan. Such allegorical interpretation has no value for understanding the meaning of the text.

[15]Toy, pp. 543-44, limits the woman's goodness to her ability to secure the economic
prosperity of the household. His position is arbitrary. In view of the wider scope of her
good works also presented in this same context (charity, v. 20; kind and wise speech,
v. 26), it is better to take the woman's goodness more broadly, including all of her
actions toward her husband.

13 She seeketh wool, and flax, and worketh willingly with her hands.
14 She is like the merchants' ships; she bringeth her food from afar.
15 She riseth also while it is yet night, and giveth meat to her house-
hold, and a portion to her maidens.

13 By far the greatest emphasis in this description is on the nature and extent of the woman's industriousness. She gathers raw materials for the spinning operations that her servants conduct. She herself enters into the labors, working "willingly" (*ḥepeṣ,* cf. 18:2) with her hands. The root *ḥapeṣ* means "to take delight in, be pleased with." The idea is that she takes personal pleasure in her work.[16]

14 The wife gathers the needed household materials, both for the daily routine and for the diverse economic enterprises of the home. She trades with traveling merchants as they pass by. The verse does not demand that she have formal business ventures involving trade with foreign nations. The author compares her with "merchant ships" to make the point that she provides for her household by drawing upon distant resources. These sources would not be options for a typical wife who relied only upon local suppliers to meet her needs.[17]

15 The worthy woman uses her time wisely. She rises "while it is yet night," early each morning, in order to distribute food to her family and household servants. "Meat" (*ṭerep*) is from a verb meaning "to tear, rend," an action often associated with eating. The word is best translated "food," a more accurate meaning in our day.[18]

---

[16]Toy, p. 544, objects to this interpretation, calling it "unnatural" to personify the hands, i.e., to attribute emotions to this part of the body. He suggests that the phrase be translated, "she works in (or 'according to') the pleasure of her hands," indicating that she performs such work as seems best to her. Dahood, *PNWSP*, pp. 60-61, takes an alternative approach in rendering the phrase "which her hands turn into a thing of beauty." This, however, ignores the preposition that dictates that her hands work "with pleasure."

[17]McKane, p. 667, understands the simile in a broader sense. Just as merchant ships range to far-off ports to gain their increase, so the wife goes beyond the immediate production of her husband's agricultural endeavors. She gains wealth for the home through manufacture and trading. While this view is possible, the more obvious comparison lies in the woman's trade with others rather than in her secondary production of wealth.

[18]Toy, p. 544, notes that *ṭerep* normally means "prey" rather than "food." Without support, he suggests that v. 15c is a gloss, a scribal explanation of v. 15b. Hebrew poetry, however, has this freedom and Toy is incorrect in attempting to dictate the structure here. Crook, *JNES* 3:139, and McKane, p. 668, understand the word as a corruption from *ṭorah,* "work." These explanations overlook the full scope of the word's use. While the word normally means "prey," it can also take the meaning "food," e.g., Job 24:5; Ps. 111:5; Mal. 3:10.

*16 She considereth a field, and buyeth it: with the fruit of her hands she
planteth a vineyard.*
17 She girdeth her loins with strength, and strengtheneth her arms.
*18 She perceiveth that her merchandise is good: her candle goeth not
out by night.*

16 In addition to her household responsibilities, the wife uses her
spare time productively. She undertakes agricultural activities. Again,
the picture of the wife does not limit her work to that performed at
home. She labors outside of the home, the presumption being that her
children are older and that her work meets with her husband's approval.[19]

17 In these labors, the wife diligently exerts herself, not merely dele-
gating the work to others. She "girdeth her loins," tying up her robe to
keep it from interfering with her labors. This pictures her readiness to
begin her work. Further, she "strengtheneth her arms." This idiom pictures her power to perform the tasks at hand; cf. Psalm 89:10; Isaiah
44:12; 51:9; Hosea 7:15; contra. Job 26:2.

18 All in all, the results of her productivity bring satisfaction to this
wise woman. The verb "perceiveth" (*ṭaʿămâ,* cf. 11:22) is literally "to
taste." Here, it figuratively indicates that she "experiences," or "perceives," the good results from the sale of her produce.[20] This moves her
to diligence, even leading her to remain up late at night to finish some
project.[21]

---

[19]Oesterley, p. 284, asserts that "all this verse is a rhetorical exaggeration" since such
matters lay outside the domain of women. He misunderstands the divinely ordained role
of the wife. She is a complementary assistant to her husband, perfectly filling out his
being so as to let the home gain its full potential (Gen. 2:18). The two jointly lead the
activities of the home. There is abundant evidence in the OT to show that women were
involved with agricultural and pastoral duties. They tended the flocks (Gen. 29:6; Exod.
2:16) and watered the camels (Gen. 24:19-20). They worked with raw materials from the
fields (Josh. 2:6), kept the vineyards (Song of Sol. 1:6; 8:12), and gleaned in the fields
(Ruth 2:9; note the female pronoun indicating that Ruth was to work after the female
servants of Boaz). They directed servants (I Sam. 25:18-19). The OT does not give us a
complete description of the woman's role. There is enough information, however, to
show that they were involved with a broad range of activities.
[20]McKane, p. 668, understands *ṭaʿămâ* in the sense that the woman concludes that trading conditions are good. She therefore labors diligently to take advantage of them.
While this fits the spirit of the passage, the more natural sense does not suggest the activity of trade but rather the outcome of it.
[21]Greenstone, p. 335, thinks that the lamp burning at night marked a prosperous house.
Cohen, p. 213, and Oesterley, p. 285, suggest that it was a custom to keep a lamp

19 She layeth her hands to the spindle, and her hands hold the distaff.
20 She stretcheth out her hand to the poor; yea, she reacheth forth her
*   hands to the needy.*
21 She is not afraid of the snow for her household: for all her household
*   are clothed with scarlet.*

19 As part of her responsibilities, this wife involves herself with spinning operations. She prepares the yarn that will eventually be made into cloth. The AV has reversed "spindle" (*kîšôr*) and "distaff" (*palek*). The word *kîšôr* more likely comes from *kašer,* "to be straight, erect." This suggests the staff upon which the flax, tow, or wool is held for spinning operations. The Akkadian cognate *pallukku* suggests that the Hebrew *palek* is "round, circular." From this, we draw the meaning "spindle," the rounded stick used to form and twist the yarn in spinning operations. Neither word is particularly clear excepting that both have something to do with the drawing out and twisting of fibers into yarn.[22]

20 In addition to her work on behalf of the family members, the worthy woman also shows her concern for others outside of the home. She is charitable, reaching out to those in need. In this way, she helps to relieve their suffering. Her example demonstrates the practical love that Christianity has always showed toward the less fortunate.[23]

21 The future holds no fear for this woman, for she has wisely anticipated the needs of her household. The "snow" here represents many such needs that might be set forth as examples. She has clothed her household with "scarlet" (*šanîm*). The word *šanî* occurs widely with the sense of "scarlet." The word occurs in II Samuel 1:24, where Saul provides for the women of Israel. It was used with reference to the curtains (Exod. 26:1) and veil (Exod. 26:31) of the tabernacle, and the priestly robe (Exod. 28:33). The association with the king and with the

---

burning night and day. Whybray, p. 185, mentions the Arab custom of burning a lamp at night to keep away the power of darkness. The more natural view relates the burning lamp to diligence in work, making it possible to use the evening hours wisely.

[22]Kufeldt, p. 595, understands the terms as symbolic of "true womanhood." Despite her hard work, the woman does not lose her "feminine charm." His argument is weak. The context deals with the labors of the woman and is not symbolic.

[23]Oesterley, p. 285, notes that the context of the verse refers to the making of garments. He suggests that the gifts to the poor may involve clothing that was made in the household. The suggestion has merit. The poetical nature of the passage, however, makes it unlikely that we should limit her charity. More probably, her charity is general, adapted to the needs of those about her.

22 She maketh herself coverings of tapestry; her clothing is silk and
purple.
23 Her husband is known in the gates, when he sitteth among the elders
of the land.

tabernacle suggests that this was high-quality material. This is probably the sense in which it occurs here, clothing of such quality and weight that it warms the wearers.[24]

22 The phrase "coverings of tapestry" (*marbaddîm,* cf. 7:16) is difficult. The parallelism both here and at 7:16, the only other occurrence in Proverbs, suggests that some sort of fabric is in mind. I have translated "decorated spreads" in 7:16 and I will stay with that here.[25] Her own clothing is from the best of cloth. She has garments of *šeš,* an Egyptian loan word referring to byssus, fine Egyptian linen. Purple garments were expensive. The purple dye was obtained from the secretion of a mollusk found in the eastern parts of the Mediterranean Sea. The word *ʾargaman,* "purple," is an Aramaic loan word well established by cognates.

23 In keeping with the overall picture of an above-average financial setting for the household, the husband of the family exercises community leadership. He holds a position of responsibility and trust, sitting "in the gates" with other elders of the city. The gates were the place where business, legal, and governmental matters were carried on. The context suggests that his ability to devote himself to these matters rests upon his knowledge that his wife carefully oversees the household. He is able to devote himself to community matters outside of the family.

---

[24]It is difficult to understand how scarlet clothing would afford any special help in cold weather. For this reason, various suggestions have been made to explain the verse. Toy, pp. 543, 545, rearranges the passage to read 21*a*, 22*a*, 22*b*, 21*b*. This makes good sense but has no textual support. The LXX reads *šᵊnayim,* "double clothing" (so also AB, p. 185; Oesterley, p. 285; and Whybray, p. 186, among others). S. R. Driver, "On a Passage in the Baal Epic (IV AB iii 24) and Proverbs xxxi 21," *BASOR* 105:11, supports this reading from Ugaritic. Brenner, p. 229, takes the final *mem* as a dittography with the initial *mem* of v 22. She recommends emending to *šānî,* "scarlet," a suggestion with weak textual support. The MT is sensible and is supported by the references to fabric and color in v. 22.

[25]The word is uncertain. Whybray, p. 186, offers "coverlets." Without discussion, McKane, p. 261, gives "bedspreads." KD II, 335 holds out for "pillows." Zöckler, p. 91, suggests "variegated coverlets." Coates, p. 118, suggests "silk." Any translation must be, to some extent, an educated guess. I rely on the parallelism in relating the word to some sort of fabric.

24 She maketh fine linen, and selleth it; and delivereth girdles unto the merchant.
25 Strength and honour are her clothing; and she shall rejoice in time to come.
26 She openeth her mouth with wisdom; and in her tongue is the law of kindness.
27 She looketh well to the ways of her household, and eateth not the bread of idleness.

24 As part of her involvement with the economic affairs of the household, the worthy woman oversees the manufacture and sale of "fine linen" (*sadîn*) and "girdles" (*ḥəgôr*). The *sadîn* was an outer linen wrap worn by both men and women; cf. Judges 14:12-13; Isaiah 3:23. The *ḥəgôr* was a belt, again worn by both men and women; cf. I Samuel 18:4; Isaiah 3:24.

25 Through her many accomplishments, this woman covers herself with "strength and honour." This alludes to the financial stability of the household under her leadership.[26] For this reason, she faces the future with confidence. She "rejoic(es) in time to come," i.e., laughs at concerns over future problems. In light of v. 30, we should be careful not to make this attitude one of self-reliance. She has confidence in God and, therefore, has a confident spirit about the future.

26 As she instructs her family, the godly wife carries out her responsibilities in "wisdom" (*ḥokmâ*, cf. 1:2) and in "kindness" (*ḥesed*, cf. 2:8). This moral example in her instruction likely makes more of an impact on the children than the formal teaching that she gives them. It is important that godly character shine forth in every situation. This woman has a consistent example before her family.

27 What has been illustrated before is now stated directly. This wife is diligent. She keeps herself busy in order to use the precious opportunities of each day. She does not eat "the bread of idleness" through indolence.[27] Rather, she works long hours in order to establish the well-being of the home.

---

[26]Henry III, 977, understands these terms to refer to the woman's own virtue, a quality that gives her a "firmness and constancy of mind" that enables her to bear up under the adversities of life. The context, however, supports the association of this phrase with the results of the woman's economic endeavors. Moreover, ʿoz, "strength," occurs twice elsewhere in the book with the same economic association; see 10:15; 18:11.

[27]AB, p. 186, emends *toʾkel*, "she . . . eateth," to the *hipʿîl taʾakîl*. It then translates, "and permits no one to eat food in idleness." This relates the phrase to the household rather

*28 Her children arise up, and call her blessed; her husband also, and he
praiseth her.
29 Many daughters have done virtuously, but thou excellest them all.
30 Favour is deceitful, and beauty is vain: but a woman that feareth the
Lord, she shall be praised.
31 Give her of the fruit of her hands; and let her own works praise her
in the gates.*

28-29 In addition to the praise of her husband, the immediate family
of the worthy woman also praises her. Her children bless her, and her
husband expresses his appreciation for her accomplishments. Other
women may have performed nobly, but this woman has exceeded them
all.[28] It may well be that the children follow the example set by their father as he praises his wife for all she has done. The father's example has
a teaching function, setting the proper way of life before his children.

30-31 The final two verses are general although they clearly draw
upon the pattern of the worthy woman established in the earlier verses
of the poem. Mere self-adornment is not worthy of praise. There are two
grounds for this conclusion. In the first place, the external appearance
of a woman changes throughout life. It is a transitory thing and, therefore, unsubstantial, with no enduring quality to it.

More importantly, the woman's appearance is vain because it is an external quality only. What meets the eyes does not necessarily reflect the
orientation of the soul. As Matthew Henry perceptively noted, "There
may be an impure deformed soul lodged in a comely and beautiful
body." Beauty, then, does not guarantee character. In fact, beauty may
indicate the weak character of one who overemphasizes the development
of the external appearance at the expense of the inward development of
the soul. The surface may be an illusion, a mirage that detracts from the
far more important quality of character.

---

than to the woman herself. There is no support for the change and the verse does not require it.
[28]Thomas, *VT* 15:278-79, relies on the Arabic version and adds *wayyodeha* in 28*b*: "her
husband lauds and praises her." He sees the need for a 3 + 3 rhythm in the verse. There
is no other textual support. It may well be that the Arabic expanded upon the Hebrew at
this point.

Positively, however, the godly woman "feareth the Lord" (*yirᵓat yǝhwah,* cf. 1:7).²⁹ She demonstrates the godly qualities of life that mark one who has a wholesome relationship with the Lord. As the result of this outward testimony before others, they praise her, v. 30. The author ends the theme by pronouncing a blessing upon such a woman. May she receive the abundance that comes forth as the result of her work. Moreover, may these works testify of her praiseworthiness to others outside of the immediate family, v. 31.³⁰

²⁹Crook, *JNES* 3:137, considers *yirᵓat yǝhwah* a late emendation. Toy, pp. 549-50, similarly emends to *ᵓešet bînâ,* "a woman of intelligence, she will have praise." While it is true that there is no stress on the religious aspect of the woman's character elsewhere, this does not justify eliminating the reference to her religious beliefs. The diligence of the woman, her compassion toward others, her kindness of speech, and her wisdom, are all evidences of a godly spirit. It is natural that the poem should end on the crescendo of a direct statement of her relationship to God.

³⁰Oesterley, p. 287, suggests that the verse cannot be taken literally since the works of the woman would hardly be discussed in a public assembly. He concludes that this is exaggerated praise. This conclusion ignores the fact that the gates of a city served as the center of a wide variety of activities in the OT. Not only were they the place for legal actions (Deut. 21:19-20; 25:7) and prophetic oracles (Jer. 17:19-20; Amos 5:10), but they also served as places for the gathering of news (II Sam. 15:2) and gossip (Ps. 69:12). Ruth received praise in the gates and the people pronounced a blessing upon her there (Ruth 4:11-12). Since the passage poetically describes the ideal woman, the "gates" may well be meant metaphorically, signifying public praise. A literal understanding of the word, however, fits well with the use of the word elsewhere.

The Worthy Wife, v. 12

1. Importance of Trustworthiness
   a. Scripture condemns trust in anything other than the Lord
   b. Scripture commends trust in the Lord
      (1) Requires the wife to develop character
      (2) Cf. here, she "does good . . . evil"
2. Evidence of Trustworthiness
   a. Positively
      (1) Industrious 17 (gathers raw material 13*a*; trades 14; agricultural activities 16; spins 19; sews for the household 21; for others 24; for self 22)
      (2) Consistent 12
      (3) Trains her children 1, 26
      (4) Charitable 20
      (5) Joyful 13
      (6) Prepares for emergencies 21
      (7) Invests 16
   b. Negatively
      (1) Avoids self-adornment 30
      (2) Avoids laziness 15*a*, 18*b*
      (3) Avoids idleness 27
3. Results of Trustworthiness
   a. Internal attitude
      (1) Satisfaction 18*a*
      (2) Confidence 25
   b. External esteem
      (1) Husband 11, 28*b*
      (2) Children 28
      (3) Others 31

SUBJECT STUDIES

PROVERBS

CHARITY

Charity, a practical love for others, has long been considered a mark of the godly man. It is no less so in the Book of Proverbs. The book mentions the subject eleven times. This emphasis shows the obligation that God's people have toward others in need. The statement "When it comes to giving, some folks stop at nothing" should not describe Christians.

The only command to show charity comes in the mother's instructions to her son, King Lemuel, 31:9. Elsewhere, the book assumes that godly people will show concern for others. Proverbs 29:7 clearly states that charity is one of the differences between a righteous and a wicked person. The "virtuous woman" in 31:20 shows her interest in supplying the needs of others. This attitude honors God, 14:31.

In response, God promises to bless those who demonstrate charity toward others, 22:9. The blessing here is left unstated and may thus come in many areas. The specific nature of the blessing is not important. It is enough that God pledges to favor those who show charity to others. In addition, the one who shows mercy to the poor will be "happy," ʾašrê, 14:21. This word occurs widely. It is more than mere happiness. It is rather a blessedness given to those who walk closely with God. One specific blessing given to the merciful is the right of prayer, 21:13. The passage states it negatively. Those who refuse to hear the cries of others will themselves not have their cries heard. The clear implication is that God will hear the cries of those who listen to the voices of others in need.

There are also material blessings promised. In several places, the Lord promises to provide concrete blessings to the charitable. In 11:24-25, the description is picturesque. The generous person will "be made fat." This is idiomatic for blessings that will return to the one who provides the needs of others. He waters others; he himself will be watered, again an idiom describing the physical blessings that God will provide. Proverbs 19:17 pictures charity as a loan to the Lord that He will repay. Proverbs 28:8 warns that the wealth of the one who takes advantage of the needy will be given to those who are merciful to them. Proverbs 28:27 simply states that the charitable "shall not lack." All these parallel the NT promises of Luke 6:38 and II Corinthians 9:6.

There is no indication of how these blessings come to the charitable. We do not give to the poor simply to gain blessings from God. That motivation would negate the charity. Further, experience proves that giving resources away does not particularly increase a person's wealth. The conclusion, then, is that God gives the promised blessings in an eternal reward. God will reward the act of giving to others in eternity just as He does any other form of faithful service.

God gives the light, Genesis 1:3; the seed, Genesis 1:11; and the rain, Genesis 27:28. He gives physical life, Job 33:4; riches and honor, I Chronicles 29:12; and grace for this life, I Peter 5:5. He gives repentance, II Timothy 2:25, and eternal life, I John 5:11. He gives the Scriptures, II Timothy 3:16, and the Holy Spirit to guide us, John 16:7. He gives wisdom, James 1:5. Should He not expect that we would be willing to give back to Him? Walter B. Keffries summed up charity with his statement: "Some folks give their mite, others give with all their might, and some don't give who might."[1] Which category do you fall into?

---

[1] Walter B. Knight, ed., *Knight's Treasury of Illustrations* (1963), p. 139.

EATING AND DRINKING

The words "eat" and "drink" occur in Proverbs in twenty verses. In half of these, the words have a symbolic application. These refer to partaking of different actions. These actions may be good or bad. Proverbs 1:31 refers to those who have rejected Wisdom's call. Proverbs 4:17 speaks of eating "the bread of wickedness" and drinking "the wine of violence." On the other hand, 9:5 gives Wisdom's invitation to eat of her food. Proverbs 13:2 and 18:21 contrast the partaking of good and bad works. Proverbs 13:2 contrasts good with violence. Proverbs 18:21 mentions the power of the tongue to bring life or death and then states that we eat whichever we love.

The American proverb is apt: "Great rivers come from little brooks." A single taste of wickedness may lead to a life of unrestrained sin. This is why the book admonishes us to eat that which is pure. Proverbs 5:15 is a direct command to maintain sexual purity. Proverbs 23:6 urges us to avoid the fruit of those who have "an evil eye," i.e., are selfish. We should return good for evil from our enemies. In doing this, we bring additional judgment to them and we gain reward from the Lord, 25:21-22; cf. Romans 12:20. When we build on a diet of godliness, it makes us spiritually healthy.

Eating and drinking also refer to judgment. When evil men deceive us into eating of their wicked ways, that which we have eaten becomes distasteful. We vomit it up, 23:7-8. Those who mistreat their parents will find that the eagle plucks out their eye to eat, a poetical picture of judgment, 30:17. When Ethel and Julius Rosenberg were on trial in 1952 for passing on U.S. secrets to the Soviets, they said to the judge, "Give us justice, that's all we ask for. That's what we're after." The judge responded, "No, what you're after is mercy. But this court can't give mercy, only justice. And what you've got is justice."[1] So it is that those who partake of wickedness will one day find that its end is justice.

The ancient proverb says, "You are what you eat." This is true spiritually as well as physically. If we regularly partake of godliness, that reveals a godly nature. If we regularly partake of ungodliness, that reveals an ungodly nature. May God help us to develop proper diets.

---

[1]Roy B. Zuck, ed., *The Speaker's Quote Book* (1997), p. 216.

THE ESCHATOLOGY OF PROVERBS

Many commentators view the Book of Proverbs as relating to this life alone.[1] There is no life after death. There are no glories of heaven or judgments of hell. I vigorously disagree with this view. As I read the book, I find a simple but clear view of life after death. The wicked will receive judgment from a holy God, and the righteous will receive blessing as God rewards their faithfulness.

Sheol is the abode of the wicked dead, 5:5-6; 15:24. This never fills up, 27:20. It is a place of destruction, 15:11, not a place of reward, 24:20. The wicked there receive punishment for their sin, 24:12. Those who have no spiritual understanding join others of a like mind on the path that leads to judgment, 21:16. God will not allow them to continue unchecked in their wickedness, 10:30. One's earthly possessions will not help him, 11:4. The judgment will be a "day of wrath." 11:4. At great cost to himself, the sinner will receive that which he has loved, 8:36. "In this day, when law and order seem on the way out and criminals get only a slap on the wrist, it is well to remember that the wages of sin remain the same and what men sow they still reap."[2]

In contrast, the righteous person faces death with hope, 14:32. His righteousness leads him to eternal life, 12:28, and allows him to escape the judgment of hell, 10:2; 15:24. He has a glorious "end" awaiting him, 23:18; 24:14. He will never die, 12:28. The righteous possess wisdom. This is a "tree of life," a source of eternal life, 3:18; 11:30a; cf. Genesis 2:9; 3:22; Revelation 2:7. There is a hint of millennial blessing in the book. The wicked will be cut off from "the land" while the righteous will continue to dwell there, 2:21-22. As well, the righteous will rule with Christ during the Millennium, 14:19. It has well been pointed out

---

[1] Elmslie, p. 190, says, "No traces of [human immortality] have made their appearance in the proverbs." Plaut, p. 149, commenting on 12:28, states, "There is no reference here to immortality, a concept foreign to Proverbs." Greenstone, p. 136, commenting on the same verse, concludes, "The concept of immortality in the theological sense is not found elsewhere in this book." In one of the strongest statements, Toy, p. xvi, says, "The eschatology is of the simple and primitive sort that is found in the greater part of OT.: Sheol, the abode of all the dead, has no moral significance; there is no judgment after death, and the position of men in Sheol has no relation to their moral character: . . . The divine judgment is manifested in the last moment of life . . . The idea of ethical immortality was either unknown to the sages or was regarded by them as unimportant for practical life."

[2] Vance Havner, *The Vance Havner Quote Book*, ed. Dennis J. Hester (1986), p. 125.

that we cannot cash checks on heaven's bank until we have first opened an account. For the righteous, the account is opened when we place our faith in Christ. We then have the hope spoken of in Proverbs.

There are at least two practical consequences of this eschatology. In the home, parents should discipline their children wisely, knowing that their discipline will help their child avoid God's judgment in hell, 23:13-14. In their associations with others, the righteous should try to convince them to adopt their beliefs. In modern terms, they should seek to win lost souls and gain the "tree of life" that comes to the righteous, 11:30.

THE FEAR OF THE LORD

The "fear of the Lord" is one of the main themes in Proverbs. The phrase and its variations occur seventeen times. The "fear of the Lord" is important both for what it is and for what it does. It is important to note that this "fear" (*yir'at*) is not "terror." It is rather a reverential submission to the Lord. It is an attitude of worship.

Solomon describes the "fear of the Lord" in its importance. It is the "beginning of knowledge [*da'at*]," 1:7, and wisdom, 9:10; 15:33 ("instruction," which leads to wisdom). Thus, a right attitude toward the Lord is the first step in gaining true spiritual knowledge. Further, God rewards the search for wisdom with an increased "fear of the Lord," 2:1-5. In v. 5, the "fear of the Lord" parallels "knowledge," *da'at*, a personal experiential knowledge of God. It is no wonder that Solomon commands his son to "fear the Lord," 24:21. The attitude has great value.

The "fear of the Lord" opposes wickedness. This attitude hates "evil," 8:13. The verse divides evil into three categories: an evil attitude of pride, an evil way of life, and an evil use of words. Proverbs 16:6 states this generally. The "fear of the Lord" leads us to actively avoid evil. Proverbs 3:7 singles out pride as one form of evil to avoid. Rather than envying the wicked, we should seek a right relationship with the Lord, 23:17. Positively, the man who walks uprightly, in a godly manner, shows that he fears the Lord, 14:2.

The major emphasis in Proverbs is on the rewards that come to those who fear the Lord, 22:4 (see commentary). As the old proverb says, "God is no man's debtor." He will reward those who honor Him. The "fear of the Lord" gives you access to God, an access not given to the wicked, 1:28-29. This attitude gives a fullness of life, 14:27, with all of the days God desires you to have, 10:27. You will enjoy a confident attitude toward life, 14:26. You will experience contentment, 15:16; 19:23. The modern proverb states, "Peace rules the day when Christ rules the heart." Our right relationship with the Lord gives us this peace.

THE ROLE OF THE PARENTS

Proverbs emphasizes the responsibilities of parents toward their children. At the heart of these responsibilities lies the guidance that they give during the child's formative years. During this time, the parents assert their will. Through this means, they build the patterns that will likely guide the child through life. Parents therefore have a great responsibility to set the right guidelines for their child.

The Responsibility of Discipline

The major responsibility of parents developed in Proverbs is discipline. God commands this, 19:18; 23:13-14. The book develops this in such a way as to show the desirability of consistent parental discipline, 13:24; 22:15; 29:15, 17. This focus on discipline imparts a sense of obligation to the parents. They must train their children properly!

The words "chasten" and "correction" normally translate *mûsar*. This has a broader meaning than just the simple thought of discipline. There is often an underlying sense of chastisement. In 13:24; 22:15; and 23:13, Solomon associates chastening with the "rod." In 3:11; 10:17; 13:18; and 15:10, the word parallels reproof (*tôkaḥat,* cf. 1:23).

The word *mûsar* also refers to instruction. This may be teaching of a moral nature, 4:13: 5:23; 15:33. It may be neutral teaching, 24:32, or a summary of teaching, 13:1. Mental chastisement is necessary in learning. The root idea of chastisement is still a part of the word's meaning.

Self-discipline of this kind does not come naturally to a child. Man's sinful nature tends toward laziness and self-pleasing, 22:15a. Left to himself, the child will develop evil habits of life. These will turn him away from God and from that which is good, 9:18. Parents therefore have the responsibility to train their child. During the formative years, they help him develop good habits. In particular, he must learn to discipline himself. This will help him overcome the influence of his own sinful nature. Parents have the major responsibility for guiding their child in this area.

The parents may use corporal punishment to train their child. Several verses charge the parents to use the "rod of correction," 13:24; 22:15; 23:13-14; 29:15. Despite the fact that many reject authoritative discipline in favor of a permissive approach, the Bible is clear. Corporal punishment helps parents to train their child to adopt wise practices of living. As we suit the punishment to the child's misbehavior, we train him to adopt right habits for life.

The Lord Himself used a variety of methods as He chastened His children for their sins. Proverbs does not relate anecdotal accounts of historical events. The book, however, does give many illustrations of this principle of retributive judgment. The young men who seek the life of another will forfeit their own life, 1:11-18. Those who spurn God's appeal in times of prosperity will find that God spurns them when they turn to Him in times of adversity, 1:24-29. The adulterer who sins with his body will find that his body pays the price, 5:11. The sluggard becomes poverty-stricken as the result of his laziness, 6:9-11. Generally, those who err shall "eat of the fruit of their own way, and be filled with their own devices," 1:31.

In some cases, the child's conduct does not lend itself to punishment that teaches. Likewise, a younger child might not fully understand the significance of punishment that parallels his disobedience. In these cases, spanking may well be the best discipline. On the whole, however, parents should follow the biblical pattern of conforming the punishment to the misbehavior.

In the light of modern educational theories, we must ask, "Will spanking harm my child?" Proverbs answers this question with a resounding No! Corporal punishment does not hurt the child. Rather, it helps him develop a responsible character. At the first, corporal punishment helps the child develop godly wisdom, 29:15a. Ultimately, it turns him away from the eternal punishment of hell, 23:13-14.

Proverbs 19:18 bears on the question of permanent harm. The verse encourages parents to apply discipline rather than to desire the child's death (see commentary). This implies that it is the lack of discipline that brings death to the child; cf. 23:13. The two halves of the verse contrast with each other: discipline the child while hope remains for his correction rather than giving up on discipline and bringing about a premature death.

We may now draw a logical conclusion about discipline. Permissiveness is not the godly ideal for parents. Inconsistent or weak discipline does not adequately show God's standards to the child. Rather, this leads a child to develop a character that lacks self-control. Since self-control is essential in serving God, parents must not ignore misbehavior in a child. Judge Franklin Jonah Goldstein wisely observed that "the place to stop crime is at the high chair and not the electric chair."[1]

Proverbs 29:15b warns against permissiveness. Parents have the potential to train their child to live wisely. If they neglect this opportunity, he will shame them by his undisciplined life. The permissiveness of the parents causes the child to develop a character that does not please God. The verse literally says, "a child sent off causes shame to his mother." The idea is that the mother sends her child away, beyond her guidance. This lets him determine his own behavior. Left to himself, he goes in ways that shame his parents. Leonardo da Vinci's comment is apt: "He who does not punish evil commands it to be done."[2]

Many modern educators teach permissive child training. They think that freedom of choice lets the child develop wisdom. He learns to weigh the options and to consider the consequences of his actions. This thinking, however, goes contrary to the biblical teaching of authoritative direction by parents. Of course, parents must exercise their authority with love. Parents who love their children will discipline them for their ultimate good. When wisely given, discipline becomes a valuable part of the total home atmosphere that the child needs.

There are practical reasons for parents to discipline a child. Discipline has two purposes. It punishes and it trains. Knowing this, parents should apply such discipline that most effectively brings about these two goals.

In the first place, parents punish their child for bad behavior. Solomon established the principle that discipline should hurt, 20:30. One of the purposes of discipline is to establish in the child's mind that his rebellious behavior will bring punishment. As the parents wisely apply corporal punishment, they show the child the principle that God eternally punishes those who disobey Him.

Of course, we must understand the principle that discipline hurts in the light of New Testament teaching. Paul advised parents to control themselves lest they should actually drive the child away from them, Ephesians 6:4; Colossians 3:21. The controlling element in discipline

---

[1]Zuck, p. 217.
[2]Zuck, p. 321.

must always be the love that the parents have for their child. Because of their love, they must punish him, 13:24. Yet, because of their love, they must not punish him unreasonably.

A child who cannot accept the discipline of his parents will not likely accept the discipline of a heavenly Father. The punishment given by his parents must therefore be adequate to break the child's will. During his childhood years, he cannot understand reasoning or the eventual consequences of an undisciplined life. He can, however, understand pain. Punishment that hurts communicates to the immature mind of a child. Slowly but surely, the punishment leads him to submit his will to that of his parents.

This prepares a child to submit his will to God. In this way, physical punishment delivers the child from hell, 23:13-14. Corporal punishment therefore has an immense importance. It does not merely relate to this present life. It as well applies to the eternal domain of the child's soul. Proper discipline prepares a child to receive the truths of salvation. Parents represent God in the home. Either they represent Him well and draw their child to Christ for salvation or they represent Him poorly and drive their child away from God.

A second purpose for discipline is to educate a child in proper standards of conduct. As the parents punish the child, he learns that certain actions violate the family's standards. As the parents wisely discipline him, he comes to the point at which he adopts standards of behavior that please his parents. With time, he will personalize these standards as he realizes the reasons for them.

Several verses express the principle that discipline should train. Proverbs 19:18a teaches that there is a period in the child's life during which his parents may mold his conduct into that which pleases them. This time involves the early years before the child's habits become established. Parents who take advantage of these years to train their child will reap a harvest of personal satisfaction as he develops self-discipline.

The fact that this period exists implies that a time will come when the child will no longer readily receive training. His soft, pliable nature will harden. Parents will be able to change him only with difficulty. For this reason, parents must begin early, during the formative years, to guide their children toward right behavior.

How long is this period of time? The Bible does not define the length so we may not be dogmatic. The fact that the length is indefinite argues that the parents should begin their training in the earliest years. Only in this way can they use the full period wisely as they rear their child.

During these early years, parents should use corporal punishment to help shape the character of their child, 20:30. The verse stresses the firmness of punishment (see commentary). Such punishment cleanses the child from his evil tendencies. It affects even his inner nature. This agrees with the biblical principle that firm punishment has a wholesome effect on a child's behavior.

The clearest indication that punishment should teach comes in 29:15. Punishment brings wisdom. When the child receives firm but reasonable chastisement for his bad actions, he learns what standards he must keep. His willingness to adopt these standards shows his wisdom.

The parents have two options as they guide their child. They may use corporal punishment, the "rod," here representing some type of physical chastisement. They may also use verbal rebuke, the "reproof" of their child's actions. The combination of these two, exercised in wisdom by the parents, will help the child develop habits of wise living.

The responsibility of the parents to train their child is an important part of the disciplinary program of the home. The training that they give goes beyond the mere reproof of a child's actions. This training develops all of the child's life. The discipline of the parents helps educate him, set his moral standards, develop his attitude toward life, establish his basic character, and more.

The key verse that expresses this responsibility is 22:6. When the parents train their child properly, he will not depart from the "way" in which he has been trained. Parents should give their child instruction that is suitable to his needs. This includes spiritual training, but we must not limit the verse to the spiritual. The full scope of training lies within the realm of the parents' guidance. Parents should concern themselves with academic matters, with character development, with courtesy, with practical matters, with everything!

The promise of 22:6 should move the parents to carry out their responsibilities. Naturally, they rely on God's Word and the Holy Spirit to guide them in the decisions they face. With this supernatural direction giving them wisdom, they can have the confidence that their work will succeed. As the child matures, he will adopt right ways of life.

Parents may be confident regarding the basic character of their child as he grows. The parents have the resource of prayer to guide them as they train their child. Further, the Bible emphatically states the principle that the submission of the child is necessary if the parents wish to render maximum service to God, I Timothy 3:4-5, 12; Titus 1:6. This principle shows that God wants the parents to be successful in their child training. Christian parents who themselves walk according to biblical principles and who make the future walk of their children a matter of regular prayer can be certain that they have a godly goal. In the light of many promises that show God's desire to answer prayer, parents can confidently anticipate that their child will adopt godly standards for himself.

The Responsibility of Love

Proverbs says little about the obligation of the parents to love their child. Except for the rather general statement of 10:12 and the more direct comments of 13:24 and 15:17, love receives little attention. The nature of the book gives us the reason for this. The book stresses the practical side of life. It speaks of bringing wise conduct into the everyday arena of life. In general, emotions do not receive much emphasis. The practical nature of the book leaves no room for emotional relationships.

Love shows itself in a proper relationship between individuals. Parents who carry out their responsibilities to their children actually show their love by performing these duties. This display brings valuable benefits to the child. Through no other means can parents so effectively build the love relationship with their child.

Proverbs 13:24 illustrates this principle. Solomon notes that the discipline of the child shows the parent's love. Conversely, a parent who fails to chasten his child acts as though he hates him. This is the same principle that God follows with His children. He disciplines those whom He loves, 3:12. Discipline thus is a positive manifestation of the love of concerned parents for their child.

The lack of emphasis on love in Proverbs does not imply that the emotion is not important. Discipline can influence a child properly only when love is present. In the same way, a child can show love for his parents only by his obedience. Love therefore underlies the parent-child relationship in every aspect. It is the emotional bond that lets the complex interpersonal relationships of the home blend smoothly together.

Results of Obedience

The submission of a child has benefits that go beyond the child himself. In particular, his parents will enjoy blessings that come from his obedience. Seven passages deal with these blessings, 10:1; 15:20; 23:15-16, 24-25; 27:11; 29:3, 17. A remarkable unity marks these verses. Over and over, joy stands out as the great benefit that the parents receive from their child's obedience. Only 29:17 does not stress this directly. There, a specific aspect of joy receives the emphasis. The verse focuses on the comfort the parents receive from their child's obedience.

Six passages describe the result of a child's obedience as "joy" (śamaḥ). In Proverbs, this word describes the feeling of personal satisfaction that parents have as they reflect on the growth and maturity of their child. It is a wholesome emotion that rewards parents who have devoted themselves to the development of their child.

In each case, the wisdom displayed by the child serves as the source of his parents' joy. The child displays wisdom by his practical response to the various situations of life. The book does not give a complete list of possibilities. Rather, it gives several representative areas of life. These include his relationship to his parents, 10:1; 15:20; 27:11; his speech, 23:15-16; and his choice of companions, 29:3. He is righteous in these matters, 23:24-25.

Proverbs 10:1 gives the basic contrast between the wise and foolish child. While the wise son causes his parents to rejoice, the foolish son causes them to grieve. The stark contrast heightens the desirability of the joy gained by the parents through the obedience of their child.

A similar contrast occurs in 15:20. There the wisdom of the child contrasts with the contempt shown his parents by the foolish child. There is a clear implication that the wise child respects and honors his parents. This attitude produces joy in the heart of the parents. Once again, the contrast between the wise and foolish actions of the child brings attention to the results gained by the parents. With options of joy or shame, the joy is desirable.

Both passages in c. 23 relate the joy of the parents to the actions of their child. They rejoice over the godly speech of a wise child, 23:15-16. They likewise rejoice over his righteous conduct, 23:24-25. In both areas, the spiritual maturity of the child displays itself to others. What rests in the heart shows itself in life, both by speech and actions.

In 27:11, the father's joy rests upon his son's conduct. The father expects criticism from others concerning the methods he has used in rearing his family. By holding his son's conduct up to the light of examination, he justifies his approach. At the same time, he gains the deep satisfaction that comes with seeing his child mature properly.

One additional passage urges the son to bring joy to his father through wise behavior. Proverbs 29:3 stresses the friends of the son. The wise conduct urged here refers to self-control in the area of sexual relationships. The father takes a practical approach. He points out to his son that loose sexual conduct leads to poverty. If the son will avoid this conduct, he will be a source of joy to his father.

Proverbs 29:17 speaks of the comfort (*nuah*) received by the parents when they correct the waywardness of their son. The word *nuah* refers to relief from some burden such as weariness, Exodus 17:11 ("let down"); war, Deuteronomy 3:20; or enemies, II Samuel 7:11. Here, the son's response brings "relief" to his parents from their burden of worry.

The responsibility for correction lies with the parents. The benefits of correction likewise come to the parents. The responsibility and the reward thus go hand in hand. Unless the parents carry their responsibility faithfully, they cannot expect the reward. When they take up their parental obligations, they do so with the confidence that God will reward them with the proper development of their child.

Proverbs speaks of several undesirable results that come to the parents of a disobedient child. These include the emotional attitudes of both the child and his parents. There are two categories. In the first group, the parents are the target of their child's emotions. In the second group, the parents themselves have unpleasant emotions. Practically speaking, of course, these responses intertwine with one another.

When a child and his parents disagree over the child's conduct, a natural emotional barrier grows between them. The child develops bitter feelings toward his parents as he tries to justify himself. The parents, unfortunately, bear the brunt of his feelings. They are the natural object of his emotions. Two verses develop this aspect, 15:20 and 19:13.

The first result experienced by the parents is the scorn of their child, 15:20. Solomon describes this child as a "fool." The idea is that a child who rejects the guidance of his parents is foolish. As evidence of his foolishness, he scorns his parents. He scorns them and, therefore, scorns their guidance. They can point out his willful conduct. They can reason with him and tell him of the tragic outcome of his actions. In all likelihood, their efforts will fail. His basic attitude is self-centered and he rejects anything that differs from what he wants.

The second result of the willful child is the "destruction" (*hawwot*) of his parents, 19:13. Figuratively, *hawwot* indicates a severe calamity. The foolish actions of the child bring his parents to such an end. In the verse, the word is a numerical plural. The foolish child brings his parents into calamity after calamity.

Several emotions plague the parents as the result of their child's actions. In reality, these emotions occur together. Proverbs describes them separately to show the breadth of the parents' emotional response to their child. This serves as negative motivation, encouraging parents to be faithful in carrying out their responsibilities to their child. Failure here will bring these undesirable emotional responses.

The foolish son provokes his parents to anger, 17:25 ("grief," better "vexation," *ka'as*). They know that their wishes will best serve their child. When he spurns their will, his response vexes them. His stubbornness irritates them and stimulates an agitated response. The book says nothing about whether this vexation is right or wrong. Normally, anger expresses the old nature. Their vexation may indeed be a wrong reaction to their child. It may be a wholesome expression of their feelings as they fret over their child's lack of obedience. The point is that they become angered in response to their child.

The same passage, 17:25, speaks of the "despair" that the parents feel when their son goes in his foolish ways. "Despair" comes from the verb *marâ*, "to be bitter." This verb regularly expresses the feeling of personal despair. The noun likely has this same idea.

Proverbs 10:1 and 17:21 speak of the grief that a foolish child causes. Proverbs 10:1 contrasts the feelings of grief with joy. A wise son brings joy while a foolish child brings grief. Proverbs 17:21 expresses the grief both positively and negatively. The fool causes "grief" (*tûgat*, better "despondency") and robs his parents of joy. In both 10:1 and 17:21, Solomon does not relate the grief to any specific conduct. This heightens the seriousness of foolish behavior since even minor foolishness can cause the parents to grieve.

Proverbs 28:7 and 29:15 point out the humiliation that the parents receive from their child's foolish behavior. Proverbs 28:7 gives a specific situation in which the child becomes friends with gluttonous companions. His choice of friends shames his parents. Proverbs 29:15 is more general. The child goes his own way in preference to that of his parents. The results bring shame to his parents.

The impact of the teaching regarding the emotional impact of a rebellious child is great. The failure of the parents to gain their child's obedience brings vexation, despair, grief, and shame. These are bad when experienced apart from one another. The realization that they will likely come together gives emphasis to the results that parents face from their child's disobedience.

Self-discipline is a worthy goal. The parents should work to gain this end. Failing to obtain success brings highly undesirable emotional responses. Gaining success brings personal satisfaction. The knowledge of these two results should prompt parents to make the training of their child a priority matter. They should exercise wise and consistent guidance as they train him in the way he should go.

PRIDE AND HUMILITY

The book stresses the attitudes of pride and humility, sometimes contrasting them and sometimes dealing with them singly. Since every person has the potential to adopt these attitudes, it is important that we have a right view toward them. Is it right to be proud when we accomplish something worthwhile? Must we always be humble? What does the book teach about these attitudes?

Pride

Pride is natural. All of us can find some reason for self-praise. Someone has said, "The human body is very sensitive. Pat a man on the back and his head begins to swell."[1] Bob Jones Sr. used to talk about men who walked around as though they were "waiting for a vacancy in the Trinity." This is the norm. Small men can cast long shadows. Unfortunately, we let the size of the shadow determine our opinion of ourselves.

The book deals briefly with the *evidences of pride*. The person who stirs up trouble as he tries to get his own way is proud, 21:24. Agur describes four groups of people—children with a wrong view toward their parents, those who are self-righteous, the proud, and those who prey upon others, 30:11-14. From the association with the other groups, it is clear that pride is undesirable. "None are so empty as those who are full of themselves."[2]

It is logical that the *results of pride* should also be undesirable. Pride causes shame, 11:2. The proud person speaks proudly. The "rod of pride," his tongue as it engages in proud speech, brings forth proud words, 14:3. It is no wonder that the proud person stirs up contention. He can't see any other way or attitude than his own. This leads to strife, 13:10; 28:25. Inevitably, the proud person will be found wrong. He will be brought "low," humbled, but not in a good sense, 29:23. For this reason, the book warns against self-exaltation, 30:32. As the mother whale said to her baby, "When you go up to the surface and start to blow, that's when you get harpooned."[3]

---

[1]Zuck, p. 313.
[2]Benjamin Whichcote, quoted in Zuck, p. 314.
[3]Zuck, p. 313

One who persists in pride will encounter the *judgment of pride*. God hates this wicked attitude, 6:17; 8:13. It is sin, 21:4, and therefore not good, 25:27. Though the proud might band together against God, they will be punished, 16:5. He promises to "destroy the house of the proud." This undoubtedly refers to the eternal loss inflicted upon those who have gloried in themselves in this life, 15:25. Pride now prepares for judgment then, 16:18. As has been aptly stated, "Pride shall have a fall, and it always was and will be so!"[4]

Humility

Humility is not natural. We like to think well of ourselves. It has been well said, "The rarest man in the orchestra of God is the saint who knows how to play second fiddle."[5] Despite its rarity, it is important. "Humility is the mother, root, nurse, foundation, and center of all other virtues."[6] Dwight Moody noted, "Moses spent forty years thinking he was somebody; then he spent forty years on the back side of the desert realizing he was nobody; finally, he spent the last forty years of his life learning what God can do with a nobody!"[7]

The book states its *approval of humility*. Proverbs advises humility, 25:6-7. It is better to be poor and humble than rich and proud, 16:19. It is a mark of wisdom, 11:2. There is a *value of humility*, positive results that come from its display. This attitude, equivalent to the fear of the Lord, brings "riches, honour, and life," 22:4. Such an attitude can have practical value, delivering a person from an unwise financial agreement, 6:3. Over and over, the book speaks of the honor that comes to the humble. While there is no mention of the source of the honor, presumably it comes from both men and God, 15:33; 18:12; 29:23. By far the greatest *result of humility* is God's reward. He gives special grace to those who humble themselves. This promise is general, no doubt applied to the areas in which grace is needed, 3:34.

There is a clear contrast between pride and humility. Pride always antagonizes God and humility always pleases Him. We do well then to keep our natural emotions in check, confessing the sin of pride when we

---

[4]Charles Dickens, *Dombey and Son* (1816).
[5]Havner, p. 113.
[6]John Chrysostom, quoted in Zuck, p. 201.
[7]Zuck, p. 202.

see it in ourselves. At the same time, giving God the glory for what we are and what we accomplish helps to keep a right view of ourselves.

Some of the old master composers finished their musical works with the abbreviation *S.D.G.* These initials stood for *soli deo gloria*, Latin for "To God alone be the glory." This should be the attitude of every believer. In every achievement, in every goal that we reach, in every award that we gain, "To God be the glory, great things He hath done!"

TRUE TREASURE

Several of the individual proverbs in Proverbs compare life to valuable materials. The book uses such words as "silver," "gold," "rubies," "oil," and "treasures" to describe the attributes of man. By using these in both positive and negative senses, the authors establish certain things as desirable and certain things as undesirable.

Godly Wisdom

The greatest emphasis is on the need for godly wisdom. The gain from wisdom far exceeds that which comes from silver, gold, jewels, or "all the things thou canst desire," 3:14-15. Proverbs 8:10-11 repeats this same idea. The "fruit" of wisdom, that upon which others may feed, is more valuable than silver or gold, 8:19. Rhetorically, Solomon asks if it is better to get wisdom than gold? Clearly, the answer is yes, 16:16. In contrast with the fool, the wise man will prosper in this life, 21:20. When John D. Rockefeller said, "The poorest man I know is the man who has nothing but money,"[1] he spoke the truth. We have all we need when we gain the wisdom that comes from God.

Righteous Speech

Several verses deal with the value of righteous speech. Such speech is "as choice silver." This is silver that has been purified of its impurities and thus has the highest value possible for the metal, 10:20. Lips that speak knowledge are compared to "a precious jewel," 20:15. In like manner, a person who wisely reproves another is as "gold," 25:12. The beautiful expression of 25:11 sums up the value of wholesome speech: "A word fitly spoken is like apples of gold in pictures of silver." The proverb says, "See no evil, hear no evil, speak no evil." That's true. Our speech should be wholesome, helpful, and godly.

The book also deals negatively with speech. A person who tries to gain "treasures" by lying follows "a vanity," a fleeting vapor that will not last, 21:6. "Burning lips" that falsely proclaim friendship are like a clay pot covered with the dross from silver. While it may outwardly appear beautiful, it has little value, 26:23. The English proverb notes that "the tongue is not steel, yet it cuts." We should control our speech, limiting it to that which pleases God.

---

[1]Knight, p. 326.

Wholesome Actions

Three maxims show that random actions have value. The person who practices righteous actions has "much treasure," 15:6. A good reputation has more value than wealth, and a favorable demeanor is good. What we are is far more important than what we have, 22:1. The "virtuous woman" of Proverbs 31 demonstrates this. She is hard working, reliable, concerned for others, generous, wise, and kind, and she fears the Lord. The value of such a wife is "far above rubies," 31:10.

Wicked Behavior

Two passages approach this theme negatively. Treasures gained through wicked means have no eternal profit. What a misplaced effort to spend one's life seeking that which has no lasting value. As the familiar proverb says, "All that glitters is not gold." Temporal pursuits are just that, temporary! Treasures that come from wicked behavior have no lasting value. Only righteousness has eternal worth. We need to place our efforts in eternal goals, 10:2. Inappropriate behavior is likewise of no value. We would think it ridiculous to place a gold nose ring into a pig's snout. So the inappropriate behavior of a woman is as well without value, 11:22.

Rather than placing a high value on material wealth, the Christian should focus on spiritual wealth. The well-known statement of Jim Elliott is appropriate: "He is no fool who gives that which he cannot keep, to gain that which he cannot lose." Riches and position in life are temporary, 27:24. Instead of trying to lay up "treasures on earth," we should lay up true treasures, treasures that will never pass away, in heaven.

TRUST

Proverbs translates *baṭaḥ* as "trust," or "confidence." The word *baṭaḥ* refers to a feeling of confidence with regard to one's situation in life. Specifically, it is the security that comes from trusting God. There are several other bases that might be thought adequate to give security. A person might look at himself, his personality, or talents. The book does not mince words with regard to trust in self. This man is a "fool," 28:26. Similarly, a person might look at his resources as a basis for confidence. These are inadequate, 11:28. Finally, a person might look to others— friends, officials, relatives—for his security. Apart from a wholesome relationship with God, these also will fail him, 25:19.

There is only one adequate basis for a confident approach to life. Over and over, Proverbs mentions God as this basis. One of the most familiar commands in the book highlights this thought both positively and negatively: "Trust in the Lord with all thine heart; and lean not unto thine own understanding," 3:5. The idea of trusting "with all [the] heart" is that the whole inner being—mind, emotions, and will—relies on the Lord. At the same time, we reject our own natural ability to understand the various situations that we face in life.

The book mentions seven specific benefits that we gain when we trust the Lord. The first of these is the "understanding" (*bîn*) mentioned in 3:5-6. The word *bîn* refers to discernment or insight. Knowing that our sinful nature has marred our ability to reason correctly, we look to the Lord for the guidance we need. In response, He "directs our steps." The knowledge that God guides His children gives us "strong confidence," 14:26. We are surrounded by a world that lacks confidence in the ways they have chosen. We, however, have the assurance that God works all things together for the good of His own; cf. Romans 8:28. This lets us face the future with confidence, both for this life and for the life to come. Frances Ridley Havergal illustrated this attitude with her words: "Great is God's faithfulness and I will fear no evil about the future. There is no room for the word disappointment in the happy life of entire trust in Jesus and satisfaction with His perfect and glorious will."[1]

As we follow the instructions given us by God's Word, we come into a right relationship with Him, 22:19. We begin by trusting Him in small

---

[1]Knight, p. 418.

matters, move on to trusting Him for greater issues, and end by trusting Him in all things. As we do this, we develop an ever-closer relationship with Him. Although this relationship may not be put clearly into words, it can be experienced by the children of God. It is no wonder that the Bible speaks of the blessedness given to those who trust God, 16:20. The word "happy" (ʾašrê) refers to the blessing given to those who walk uprightly. This leads naturally into the fifth benefit to those who trust God, the spiritual prosperity that He gives them, 28:25-26. The idea of being spiritually "fat" pictures the spiritual growth of the believer. The world will never seduce us into its way of life. We shall be "delivered" from its enticements and from the problems that await those who follow the ways of the world. It has well been said, "Faith sees the invisible, believes the incredible, and receives the impossible."[2] Our trust in God brings us untold gain.

The final two benefits are practical, relating to this life. There is financial security to gain, 31:11. The book sets this idea forth in the context of the family. The man has a godly wife. He trusts her because she trusts the Lord. She contributes to the family in such a way that "he will have no need of spoil." Nothing is specific as to how this is done. She may be frugal; she may bring income into the family by her work at home. In some way she contributes to bring financial stability to the home.

Finally, those who trust God are "safe" from the attacks of the world, 28:1; 29:25. The world follows the ways of Satan. For this reason, it hates those who walk with God. Believers may face attacks from an ungodly world for no other reason than that they belong to God. Because we are close to Him, however, the world cannot do more than God desires; cf. John 10:28-29.

Augustine said, "Trust the past to the mercy of God, the present to His love, and the future to His providence."[3] Corrie ten Boom said, "Never be afraid to trust an unknown future to a known God."[4] Daniel Webster said, "Faith puts God between us and our circumstances."[5] These and many other statements illustrate the glorious truth that we can place our confidence in the unfailing God.

---

[2]Eleanor Doan, ed., *The Speaker's Sourcebook* (1960), p. 101.
[3]Zuck, p. 400.
[4]Zuck.
[5]Zuck, p. 143.

WORK

The Book of Proverbs has little positive teaching about work. The bulk of its teaching is negative, warning against the results of laziness. There is enough teaching, however, to establish the fact that work done in the right manner pleases God.

The Nature of Godly Work

The book urges the "sluggard" to learn the lesson of hard work from the ant. Even though no higher authorities guide his work, the ant labors diligently to supply the food he will need later, 6:6-8. Benjamin Franklin agreed: "None teaches better than the ant, and she says nothing."[1] There is a reason for diligence. Neither one's position in life nor his crops will remain forever. We must work to meet our needs, 27:23-27. At the same time, we need God's blessing on our work. To this end, we rely on Him, 16:3. Literally, the word "commit" is "roll." We roll our responsibilities over on the Lord so that He can guide our thoughts.

We should be honest in our work, 16:8, not taking advantage of others who are poor or distressed, 22:22-23. The book gives several exhortations drawn from the use of a balance scale, 11:1; 16:11; 20:10, 23. In this, two pans were balanced against each other. Both stone and metal weights were used. If the seller used false weights, or if his scale had arms of unequal length, he could cheat the buyer. In addition to being honest in work, we should follow regular labors rather than speculative methods to gain wealth, 13:11.

Such work establishes our reputation before others, 20:11; 31:28. The acrostic poem of 31:10-31 mentions the diligence of the worthy woman, 31:13. It is a mark of wisdom, 10:5a, and a characteristic of purity, 21:8.

The Nature of Ungodly Laziness

Several passages describe the lazy person. He is so slothful that he leaves his hand in the dish of food (see commentary on "bosom") rather than lifting it to his mouth, 19:24; 26:15. He is like a double-hinged door that swings back and forth. He rolls from side to side on his bed but goes nowhere, 26:14. Despite his obvious laziness, he is wise in his own eyes. He justifies himself, thinking himself more wise than others

---

[1]Benjamin Franklin, *More of Knight's Timely Illustrations,* Walter B. Knight, ed. (1984), p. 327.

who give reasons for hard work, 26:16. These descriptions use hyperbole, conscious exaggeration for the sake of making a point. Taken together, they support the saying that "A lazy man is good for two things: good for nothing and no good."[2]

Because of his laziness, the slothful person makes excuses. Proverbs 22:13 and 26:13 use hyperbole again to make this point. He expresses his fear that a lion might attack him if he goes outside. More realistically, he allows cold weather to keep him from plowing his fields, 20:4. He prefers comfort to crops, and he will be forced to beg because he lacks a harvest. With Ben Franklin, we can say, "He that is good at making excuses is seldom good at anything else."[3]

The end result of the sluggard is a lack of accomplishments. He is wasteful, 18:9. He will pay tribute rather than receive it from others, 12:24. He will fail to find game to eat, 12:27; cf. 19:15b. He is self-destructive, 21:25. He will irritate others, likely his employers, 10:26. He will live in poverty, 6:9-11; 24:30-34. Several verses contrast the success of the diligent with the poverty of the slothful, 10:4; 13:4; 14:23. We can sum up his life by saying he will have a troubled path, 15:19. Many proverbs recognize the outcome of laziness. "No sweat, no sweet!" "No pain, no gain!" "He that wad eat the kernel maun crack the nut!" "The dog in the kennel barks at his fleas; the dog that hunts does not feel them."[4]

One of the great dangers of laziness is that it reproduces itself. Proverbs 19:15a, "slothfulness casteth into a deep sleep," indicates that laziness gives birth to more laziness. The lazy person moves through life in a stupor so that he does not realize what he does to himself. It has been widely observed that there are three kinds of people: those who make things happen; those who watch things happen; and those who have no idea what happened. The danger of laziness is that it leads to membership in this third group.

The greatest application of these principles is spiritual. While it is sad that a man may have a troubled life in poverty because of his laziness, it

---

[2]Doan, p. 141.
[3]Benjamin Franklin, *Sourcebook for Speakers,* Eleanor Doan, ed. (1968), p. 146.
[4]These four proverbs come from *PC,* p. 463.

is far more tragic that Christians fail to work at their Christianity. We have excuses for not participating in spiritual activities. We fail to bring the full dish of God's Word to our mouth. We say that we believe in prayer but we don't pray. We say that we believe in evangelism but we don't witness. Many say that they believe in Christ but they fail to receive Him. The importance of faithfulness is seen in James 2:20, "faith without works is dead."

In the Cathedral of Lubeck, in Germany, are the following words:

> Ye call Me Master and obey Me not;
> Ye call Me Light and see Me not;
> Ye call Me Way and walk Me not;
> Ye call Me Life and desire Me not;
> Ye call Me Wise and follow Me not;
> Ye call Me Fair and love Me not;
> Ye call Me Rich and ask Me not;
> Ye call Me Eternal and seek me not;
> Ye call Me Gracious and trust Me not;
> Ye call Me Noble and serve Me not;
> Ye call Me God and fear Me not.[5]

May God help us to be diligent in the daily practice of our Christianity.

---

[5]Zuck, p. 113.

SELECTED BIBLIOGRAPHY
COMMENTARIES AND OTHER BOOKS ON PROVERBS

Aitken, Kenneth T. *Proverbs.* In *The Daily Study Bible.* Ed. John C. L. Gibson. Philadelphia: Westminster Press, 1986.

Alden, Robert L. *Proverbs.* Grand Rapids, Mich.: Baker Book House, 1983.

Clarke, Adam. *Commentary on the Holy Bible.* Vol. III. New York: T. Mason & G. Lane, 1840.

Coates, J. R. *The Book of Proverbs.* Cambridge: Cambridge University Press, 1911.

Cohen, A. *Proverbs.* London: Soncino Press, 1946.

Conant, Thomas J. *The Book of Proverbs.* New York: Sheldon & Company, 1872.

Dahood, Mitchell. *Proverbs and Northwest Semitic Philology.* Rome: Pontificium Institutum Biblicum, 1963.

Deane, W. J. and S. T. Taylor-Taswell. *Proverbs.* In *The Pulpit Commentary.* Ed. H. D. M. Spence and Joseph S. Exell. New York: Funk & Wagnalls, n.d.

Delitzsch, Franz. *Biblical Commentary on the Book of Proverbs.* In *Commentary on the Old Testament.* Trans. M. G. Easton. 2 vols. 1875. Reprint. Grand Rapids, Mich.: William B. Eerdmans Publishing, 1978.

Farmer, Kathleen A. *Who Knows What Is Good? A Commentary on the Books of Proverbs and Ecclesiastes.* In *International Theological Commentary.* Ed. Fredrick Carlson Holmgren and George A. F. Knight. Grand Rapids, Mich.: William. B. Eerdmans Publishing, 1991.

Frankenberg, W. *Handkommentar zum Alten Testament.* Göttingen: Vandenhoeck & Ruprecht, 1898.

French, William and George Skinner. *A New Translation of the Book of Proverbs.* London: John Murray, 1831.

Fritsch, Charles T. *Proverbs.* In *The Interpreter's Bible.* Ed. George Arthur Buttrick. New York: Abindon Press, 1955.

Garrett, Duane A. *Proverbs, Ecclesiastes, Song of Songs.* In *The New American Commentary.* Ed. E. Ray Clendenen. Nashville: Broadman Press, 1993.

Gemser, B. *Sprüche Salamos.* Tübingen: J. C. B. Mohr, 1937.

Gill, John. *An Exposition of the Old Testament.* 1810. Reprint.
Streamwood, Ill.: Primitive Baptist Library, 1979.

God's Word to the Nations—Proverbs. Cleveland: NET Publishing,
1991.

Greenstone, Julius H. *Proverbs.* Philadelphia: Jewish Publication
Society of America, 1950.

Harris, R. Laird. *Proverbs.* In *The Wycliffe Bible Commentary.* Ed.
Charles F. Pfeiffer. Chicago: Moody Press, 1962.

Healey, John F., trans. *The Targum of Proverbs.* Collegeville, Minn.:
Liturgical Press, 1991.

Henry, Matthew. *Commentary on the Whole Bible.* Vol. III. 1910.
Reprint. New York: Fleming H. Revell Company, 1935.

Hirsch, Samson Raphael. *From the Wisdom of Mishlé.* New York:
Feldheim Publishers, 1976.

Irwin, Nora. *Solomon and Proverbs.* New York: Carlton Press, 1973.

Jones, Edgar. *Proverbs and Ecclesiastes.* New York: Macmillan, 1961.

Kidner, Derek. *Proverbs.* Downers Grove, Ill.: InterVarsity Press, 1964.

Kufeldt, George. *The Book of Proverbs.* In *The Wesleyan Commentary.*
Vol. II. Ed. Charles W. Carter and Lee Haines. Grand Rapids,
Mich.: William B. Eerdmans Publishing, 1968.

McKane, William. *Proverbs.* Philadelphia: Westminster Press, 1970.

Martin, G. Currie. *Proverbs, Ecclesiastes, and Song of Songs.* In *The
Century Bible.* Ed. Walter F. Adeney. Edinburgh: T. C. & E. C. Jack,
1908.

Muenscher, Joseph. *The Book of Proverbs.* Gambier, Ohio: Western
Episcopalian Office, 1866.

Oesterley, W. O. E. *The Book of Proverbs.* In *Westminster
Commentaries.* Ed. Walter Lock and D. C. Simpson. London:
Methuen & Co., 1929.

Perowne, T. T. *The Proverbs.* Cambridge: Cambridge University Press,
1916.

Phillott, W. H. *The Proverbs.* In *Commentary on the Old Testament.* Vol.
II. London: Society for Promoting Christian Knowledge, 1880.

Plaut, W. Gunther. *Book of Proverbs.* New York: Union of American
Hebrew Congregations, 1961.

Power, A. D. *The Proverbs of Solomon.* New York: Longmans, Green &
Co., 1949.

Ross, Allen. *Proverbs*. In *The Expositor's Bible Commentary*. Vol. V. Ed. Frank E. Gabelein. Grand Rapids, Mich.: Zondervan Publishing House, 1991.

Rylaarsdam, J. Coert. *The Proverbs, Ecclesiastes, the Song of Solomon*. In *The Layman's Bible Commentary*. Ed. Balmer H. Kelly. Richmond, Va.: John Knox Press, 1968.

Scott, Melville. *Textual Discoveries in Proverbs, Psalms, and Isaiah*. London: Society for Promoting Christian Knowledge, 1927.

Scott, R. B. Y. *Proverbs, Ecclesiastes*. In *Anchor Bible*. Ed. W. F. Albright and D. N. Freedman. Garden City, N.Y.: Doubleday & Company, 1965.

Stuart, Moses. *Commentary on the Book of Proverbs*. Andover, Mass.: Warren F. Draper, 1860.

Tate Jr., Marvin E. *Proverbs*. In *The Broadman Bible Commentary*. Ed. Clifton J. Allen. Nashville: Broadman Press, 1971.

Thomas, D. Winton. "Textual and Philological Notes on Some Passages in the Book of Proverbs." In *Wisdom in Israel and the Ancient Near East, Vetus Testamentum Supplements*. Vol. III. Ed. M. Noth and D. Winton Thomas. Leiden: E. J. Brill, 1960.

Toy, Crawford H. *The Book of Proverbs*. In *The International Critical Commentary*. Ed. S. R. Driver, A. Plummer, and C. A. Briggs. 1899. Reprint. New York: Charles Scribner's Sons, 1970.

Van der Wieden, W. A. *Le Livre des Proverbes*. Rome: Biblical Institute Press, 1970.

Whybray, R. N. *The Book of Proverbs*. In *The Cambridge Bible Commentary*. Ed. P. R. Ackroyd, A. R. C. Leaney, and J. W. Packer. Cambridge: Cambridge University Press, 1972.

―――. *Wisdom in Proverbs*. Naperville, Ill.: Alec R. Allenson, 1965.

Zöckler, Otto. *The Proverbs of Solomon*. Trans. Charles Aiken. In *Commentary on the Holy Scriptures*. Ed. John Peter Lange. 1871. Reprint. Grand Rapids, Mich.: Zondervan Publishing House, n.d.

GENERAL WORKS

Albright, W. F. "Canaanite-Phoenician Sources of Hebrew Wisdom." In *Wisdom in Israel and the Ancient Near East, Vetus Testamentum Supplements*. Vol. III. Ed. M. Noth and D. Winton Thomas. Leiden: E. J. Brill, 1960.

Barr, James. *Comparative Philology and the Text of the Old Testament.* Oxford: Clarendon Press, 1968.

Brenner, Athalaya. *Colour Terms in the Old Testament.* Sheffield, England: JSOT Press, 1982.

Dillon, E. J. *The Skeptics of the Old Testament.* New York: Haskell House Publishers, 1973.

Driver, G. R. "Abbreviations in the Massoretic Text." *Textus.* Vol I. Jerusalem: Magnes Press, 1960.

—. "Once Again Abbreviations." *Textus.* Vol. IV. Jerusalem: Magnes Press, 1964.

—. *Words and Meanings.* Ed. Peter Ackroyd and Barnabas Lindars. Cambridge: Cambridge University Press, 1968.

Eissfeldt, Otto. *The Old Testament: An Introduction.* Trans. Peter R. Ackroyd. New York: Harper & Row, Publishers, 1965.

Eitan, Israel. *A Contribution to Biblical Lexicography.* New York: AMS Press, 1966.

Elmslie, W. A. L. *Studies in Life from Jewish Proverbs.* London: James Clarke & Co., n.d.

Gaster, Theodor H. *Myth, Legend and Custom in the Old Testament.* New York: Harper & Row, Publishers, 1969.

Gordis, Robert. *The Word and the Book.* New York: KTAV Publishing House, 1976.

Hailperin, Herman. *Rashi and the Christian Scholars.* Pittsburgh: University of Pittsburgh Press, 1963.

Hulst, A. R. *Old Testament Translation Problems.* Leiden: E. J. Brill, 1960.

Hummel, Horace D. *The Word Becoming Flesh.* St. Louis: Concordia Publishing House, 1979.

Kelso, James L. "The Ceramic Vocabulary of the Old Testament." In *BASOR* Supplementary Studies Nos. 5-6. New Haven, Conn.: American Schools of Oriental Research, 1948.

Kent, C. F. and Millar Burrows. *Proverbs and Didactic Poems.* New York: Charles Scribner's Sons, 1927.

Pedersen, Johannes. *Israel, Its Life and Culture.* 4 vols. 1940. Reprint. London: Oxford University Press, 1953.

Robinson, H. Wheeler. *Record and Revelation.* Oxford: Clarendon Press, 1938.

Roth, Wolfgang M. W. "Numerical Sayings in the Old Testament." In *Vetus Testamentum Supplements*. Vol. XIII. Leiden: E. J. Brill, 1965.

Rowley, H. H. *The Old Testament and Modern Study*. Oxford: Clarendon Press, 1951.

Scott, R. B. Y. "Solomon and the Beginnings of Wisdom in Israel." In *Wisdom in Israel and the Ancient Near East, Vetus Testamentum Supplements*. Vol. III. Ed. M. Noth and D. Winton Thomas. Leiden: E. J. Brill, 1960.

Thomas, D. Winton, ed. *Documents from Old Testament Times*. New York: Harper & Row, Publishers, 1958.

———. "בְּלִיַּעַל in the Old Testament." *Biblical and Patristic Studies in Memory of Robert Pierce Casey*. Ed. J. Neville Birdsall and Robert W. Thomson. Freiburg, West Germany: Herder, 1963.

LINGUISTIC AIDS

Brown, Francis, S. R. Driver, and C. A. Briggs. *Hebrew and English Lexicon of the Old Testament*. Oxford: Clarendon Press, 1974.

Harris, R. Laird, ed. *Theological Wordbook of the Old Testament*. 2 vols. Chicago: Moody Press, 1980.

Holladay, William L. *A Concise Hebrew and Aramaic Lexicon of the Old Testament*. Grand Rapids, Mich.: William B. Eerdmans Publishing, 1971.

Kautzsch, E., ed. *Gesenius' Hebrew Grammar.*, Trans. A. E. Cowley. Oxford: Clarendon Press, 1970.

Koehler, Ludwig. *Lexicon in Veteris Testamenti Libros*. 2 vols. Grand Rapids, Mich.: William B. Eerdmans Publishing, 1953.

Lisowsky, Gerhard. *Konkordanz zum Hebraischen Alten Testament*. Stuttgart: Wurttembergische Bibelanstalt, 1958.

Richardson, Alan. *A Theological Word Book of the Bible*. London: SCM Press, 1950.

Waltke, Bruce, and M. O'Connor. *An Introduction to Biblical Hebrew Syntax*. Winona Lake, Ind.: Eisenbrauns, 1990.

Weingreen, J. *Introduction to the Critical Study of the Text of the Hebrew Bible*. New York: Oxford University Press, 1982.

PERIODICALS

Ahlstron, Gosta W. "The House of Wisdom." *Svensk Exegetisk Arsbok* 44 (1979): 74-76.

Albright, W. F. "An Archaic Hebrew Proverb in an Amarna Letter from Central Palestine." *BASOR* 89 (February 1943): 29-32.

———. "The Copper Spatula of Byblus and Proverbs 18:18." *BASOR* 90 (April 1943): 35-37.

———. "The Phoenician Inscriptions of the Tenth Century B.C. from Byblus." *JAOS* 67 (1947): 153-60.

———. "The Oracles of Balaam." *JBL* 63 (1944): 207-33

Barr, James. "באריץ ~ ΜΟΛΙΣ: Prov. XI. 31, I Pet. IV. 18." *JSS* 20 (1975): 149-64.

Bewer, Julius A. "Two Suggestions on Prov 30 31 and Zech 9 16." *JBL* 67 (1948): 61-62.

Blocher, Henri. "The Fear of the Lord As the 'Principle' of Wisdom." *TB* 28 (1977): 3-28.

Bratcher, Robert G. "A Translator's Note on Proverbs 11.30." *BT* 34 (1983): 337-38.

Bryce, Glendon E. "Another Wisdom 'Book' in Proverbs." *JBL* 91 (1972): 145-57.

———. "Omen-Wisdom in Ancient Israel." *JBL* 94 (1975): 19-37.

Burney, C. F. "Christ As the APXH of Creation." *JTS*, 27 (1926): 160-77.

Byington, H. J. "Hebrew Marginalia." *JBL* 64 (1945): 339-55.

Cathcart, Kevin J. "Proverbs 30,4 and Ugaritic ḤPN, 'Garment'." *CBQ* 32 (1970): 418-20.

———. "Short Note $B^EHOPN\bar{A}W$ in Proverbs XXX 4." *VT* 48 (1998): 264-65.

Cody, Aelred. "Notes on Proverbs 22,21 and 22,23b." *Biblica* 61 (1980): 418-26.

Crenshaw, James L. "Impossible Questions, Sayings, and Tasks." *Semeia* 17 (1980): 19-34.

Crook, Margaret B. "The Marriageable Maiden of Prov. 31:10-31." *JNES* 3 (1954): 137-40.

Dahood, Mitchell. "Canaanite-Phoenician Influence in Qoheleth." *Biblica* 33 (1952): 30-52, 191-221.

———. "Immortality in Proverbs 12,28." *Biblica* 41 (1960): 176-81.

———. "To Pawn One's Cloak." *Biblica* 42 (1961): 359-66.

———. "Qoheleth and Northwest Semitic Philology." *Biblica* 43 (1962): 349-65.

———. "Hebrew-Ugaritic Lexicography I." *Biblica* 44 (1963): 289-303.

———. "Honey That Drips: Notes on Proverbs 5,2-3." *Biblica* 54 (1973): 65-66.

———. "The Archaic Genitive Ending in Proverbs 31, 6." *Biblica* 56 (1975): 241.

———. "The Hapax in Proverbs *ḥārak* 12,27." *Biblica*, 63 (1982): 60-62.

———. "Two Pauline Quotations from the Old Testament." *CBQ* 17 (1955): 19-24.

———. "Proverbs 8,22-31." *CBQ* 30 (1968): 512-21.

———. "Ugaritic and the Old Testament." *ETL* 44 (1968): 35-54.

Davies, Eryl W. "The Meaning of *qesem* in Prv 16, 10." *Biblica* 61 (1980): 554-56.

Deist, Ferdinand. "Prov. 31:1, a Case of Constant Mistranslation." *JNSL* 6 (1977): 1-3.

Della Vida, G. Levi. "El 'elyon in Genesis 14:18-20." *JBL* 63 (1944): 1-9.

Driver, G. R. "Problems in the Hebrew Text of Proverbs." *Biblica* 32 (1951): 173-97.

———. "On a Passage in the Baal Epic (IV AB iii 24) and Proverbs xxxi 21." *BASOR* 105 (February 1947): 11.

———. "Witchcraft in the Old Testament." *JRAS* (1943): 6-16.

———. "Review of the Assyrian Dictionary, Vol. XVI." *JSS* 9 (1964): 346-50.

———. "Review of the Assyrian Dictionary, Vol. IIB." *JSS* 12 (1967): 105-9.

———. "Some Hebrew Verbs, Nouns, and Pronouns." *JTS* 30 (1929): 371-78.

———. "Studies in the Vocabulary of the Old Testament." *JTS* 31 (1930): 275-84.

———. "Studies in the Vocabulary of the Old Testament." *JTS* 33 (1932): 38-47.

———. "Hebrew Notes on Prophets and Proverbs." *JTS* 41 (1940): 162-75.

———. "Proverbs xix.26." *TZ* 11 (1955): 373-74.

———. "Hebrew Notes." *VT* 1 (1951): 241-50.

———. "Problems and Solutions." *VT* 4 (1954): 225-45.

———. "Problems in 'Proverbs.'" *ZAW* 50 (1932): 141-48.

———. "Hebrew Notes." *ZAW* 52 (1934): 51-56.

Emerton, J. A. "A Note on the Hebrew Text of Proverbs i.22-3."
JTS 19 ns (1968): 609-14.

———. "Notes on Some Passages in Proverbs." *JTS* 20 ns (1969):
202-20.

———. "A Note on Proverbs II. 18." *JTS* 30 ns (1979): 153-57.

———. "A Note on Proverbs xii. 26." *ZAW* 76 (1964): 191-93.

———. "The Interpretation of Proverbs 21,28." *ZAW* 100 (1988):
161-70.

Finklestein, J. J. "Hebrew חבר and Semitic *ḤBR." *JBL* 75 (1956):
328-31.

Fox, Michael V. "Aspects of the Religion of the Book of Proverbs."
HUCA 39 (1968): 60.

Gaster, Theodor H. "Short Notes." *VT* 4 (1954): 73-79.

Giese Jr., Robert L. "Strength Through Wisdom and the Bee in
LXX-Prov 6,8^{a-c}." *Biblica* 73 (1992): 405-6.

Ginsburg, H. L. "The North-Canaanite Myth of Anath and Aqhat."
BASOR 98 (April 1945): 15-23.

Gluck, J. J. "Proverbs XXX 15a." *VT* 14 (1964): 367-70.

Goetze, Albrecht. "Contributions to Hittite Lexicography." *JCS* 1
(1947): 307-20.

Gordis, Robert. "A Note on Yad." *JBL* 52 (1924, 1933 rv): 153-62.

Gordon, Cyrus H. "Rabbinic Exegesis in the Vulgate of Proverbs." *JBL*
49 (1930): 384-416.

Greenfield, Jonas C. "Lexicographical Notes I." *HUCA* 29 (1958):
203-28.

———. "The Seven Pillars of Wisdom (Prov. 9:1)—A Mistranslation."
JQR 76 (1985): 13-20.

Guillaume, Alfred. "A Note on the √בלע." *JTS* 13 ns (1962): 320-22.

———. "A Note on the Roots ריע, ירע, and רעע in Hebrew." *JTS* 15
ns (1964): 293-95.

———. "Magical Terms in the Old Testament." *JRAS* (1942): 111-31.

Habel, Norman C. "The Symbolism of Wisdom in Proverbs 1-9."
Interpretation 26 (1972): 131-57.

Halper, B. "The Notions of Buying and Selling in Semitic Languages."
ZAW 31 (1911): 261-66.

Hildebrandt, Ted. "Proverbs 22:6a: Train Up a Child?" *GTJ* 9 (1988):
3-19.

Irwin, William A. "Where Shall Wisdom Be Found?" *JBL* 80 (1961): 13-142.

Irwin, William II. "The Metaphor in Prov 11,30." *Biblica* 65 (1984): 97-100.

Jirku, A. "Das n. pr. Lemu'el (Prov 31 1) und der Gott Lim." *ZAW* 66 (1954): 151.

Keimer, Ludwig. "The Wisdom of Amen-em-ope and the Proverbs of Solomon." *AJSL* 43 (1926): 8-21.

Kitchen, Kenneth. "Proverbs and Wisdom Books of the Ancient Near East: The Factual History of a Literary Form." *TB* 28 (1977): 69-114.

Klassen, William. "Coals of Fire: Sign of Repentance or Revenge?" *NTS* 9 (1963): 337-50.

Köbert, R. "Zu Prov 23,1-2." *Biblica* 63 (1982): 264-65.

Krantz, Eva Strömberg. "'A Man Not Supported by God': on Some Crucial Words in Proverbs XXX 1." *VT* 46 (1996): 548-53.

Kruger, Paul A. "Promiscuity or Marriage Fidelity? A Note on Prov. 5:15-18." *JNSL* 13 (1985): 61-68.

Lambdin, Thomas O. "Egyptian Loan Words in the Old Testament." *JAOS* 73 (1953): 145-55.

Landes, George M. "The Fountain at Jazer." *BASOR* 144 (December 1956): 30-37.

Malul, Meir. כפי and כְּחָפְנָיו (Prov 30,4): Hand or Skirt?" *ZAW* 109 (1997): 356-68.

Montgomery, J. A. "שׁנה‎ = سنى ." *ZAW* 53 (1935): 207-8.

Murphy, Roland E. "The Kerygma of the Book of Proverbs." *Interpretation* 20 (1966): 3-14.

North, Francis Sparling. "The Four Insatiables." *VT* 15 (1965): 281-82.

Peels, Hendrik G. L. "Passion or Justice? The Interpretation of *bᵊyôm nāqām* in Proverbs VI 34." *VT* 44 (1994): 270-74.

Perles, Felix. "A Miscellany of Lexical and Textual Notes on the Bible." *JQR* 2 (1911-12): 97-132.

Rabin, Chaim. "Hittite Words in Hebrew." *Orientalia* 32 (1963): 113-39.

Reider, Joseph. "Miscellanea Hebraica." *JJS* 3 (1952): 78-86.

———. "Etymological Studies in Biblical Hebrew." *VT* 2 (1952): 113-30.

———. "Etymological Studies in Biblical Hebrew." *VT* 4 (1954): 276-95.

Renfroe, F. "The Effect of Redaction on the Structure of Prov 1,1-6." *ZAW* 101 (1989): 290-93.

Richardson, H. Neil. "Some Notes on לִיץ and Its Derivatives." *VT* 5 (1955): 163-79.

Sanders, Jim Alvin. "Suffering As a Divine Discipline in the Old Testament and Post-Biblical Judaism." *Colgate Rochester Divinity School Bulletin* 28 (1955): 1-135.

Skehan, Patrick W. "Proverbs 5:15-19 and 6:20-24." *CBQ* 8 (1946): 290-97.

———. "The Seven Columns of Wisdom's House in Proverbs 1-9." *CBQ* 9 (1947): 190-98.

———. "A Single Editor for the Whole Book of Proverbs." *CBQ* 10 (1948): 115-30.

———. "Wisdom's House." *CBQ* 24 (1962): 468-86.

Stein, Robert H. "Wine Drinking in New Testament Times." *Christianity Today* 19 (June 1975): 9-11.

Story, Cullen I. K. "The Book of Proverbs and Northwest Semitic Literature." *JBL* 64 (1945): 319-37.

Thomas, D. Winton. "The Interpretation of Proverbs xxix. 5." *ET* 59 (1948): 112.

———. "Note on נַל־יָדְעָה in Proverbs 9¹³." *JTS* 4 ns (1953): 23-24.

———. "A Note on דַעַת in Proverbs xxii.12." *JTS* 14 ns (1963): 93-94.

———. "Additional Notes on the Root ידע in Hebrew." *JTS* 15 ns (1964): 54-57.

———. "The Root ידע in Hebrew." *JTS* 35 (1934): 298-306.

———. "Notes on Some Passages in the Book of Proverbs." *JTS* 38 (1937): 400-403.

———. "A Note on לִיקָהַת in Proverbs xxx. 17." *JTS* 42 (1941): 154-55.

———. "אֻו in Proverbs XXXI 4." *VT* 12 (1962): 499-500.

———. "Notes on Some Passages in the Book of Proverbs." *VT* 15 (1965): 271-79.

———. "The Root שנה = سنى in Hebrew." *ZAW* 52 (1934): 236-38.

———. "The Root שנה = سنى in Hebrew II." *ZAW* 55 (1937): 174-76.

Torrey, Charles C. "Proverbs, Chapter 30," *JBL* 73: 93-96.

Trible, Phyllis. "Wisdom Builds a Poem, The Architecture of Proverbs 1:20-33." *JBL* 80 (1961): 509-18.

Van Der Toorn, Karel. "Female Prostitution in Payment of Vows in Ancient Israel." *JBL* 108 (1989): 193-205.

Waldman, Nahum M. "A Note on Excessive Speech and Falsehood." *JQR* 67 (1976-77): 142-45.

Waltke, Bruce K. "The Book of Proverbs and Ancient Wisdom Literature." *Bibliotheca Sacra* 136 (1979): 221-38.

Whybray, R. N. "Poverty, Wealth, and Point of View in Proverbs." *ET* 100 (1989): 332-36.

———. "Some Literary Problems in Proverbs I-IX." *VT* 16 (1966): 482-96.

Williams, James G. "The Power of Form: a Study of Biblical Proverbs." *Semeia* 17 (1980): 35-58.

Wolfson, H. A. "Notes on Proverbs 22.10 and Psalms of Solomon 17.48." *JQR* 37 (1946): 87.

Zimmerli, Walther. "Zur Struktur der alttestamentlichen Weisheit." *ZAW* 51 (1933): 177-204.

INDEX OF HEBREW WORDS

ʾ

ʾabad 1:32
ʾăbaddon 15:11
ʾebyon 14:31
ʾeben 11:1
ʾahab 9:8
ʾohel 14:11
ʾəwîl 1:7
ʾawen 6:12
ʾawen 11:7
ʾôṣor 8:21
ʾazan 17:4
ʾah 19:7
ʾaḥărît 14:12
ʾeṭûn 7:16
ʾayab 16:7
ʾêd 1:26
ʾêk 5:12
ʾayyalâ 5:19
ʾemet 3:3
ʾîšôn 20:20
ʾêtan 13:15
ʾakzar 11:17
ʾakzarî 12:10
ʾallûp 2:17
ʾalqum 30:31
ʾamôn 8:30
ʾaman 11:13
ʾêmat 20:2
ʾenôš 24:1
ʾanaḥ 29:2
ʾap 15:1
ʾapal 4:19
ʾopnayw 25:11

ʾepes 14:28
ʾaṣ 21:5
ʾarab 12:6
ʾargaman 31:22
ʾoraḥ 12:28
ʾarḥôt 1:19
ʾărî 22:13
ʾerek ʾappayim 14:29
ʾiššâ zarâ 2:16
ʾašûr 14:15
ʾašam 14:9
ʾešnab 7:6
ʾašrê 3:13

b

bəʾer 23:27
baʾaš 13:5
bagad 11:3
bəhemâ 12:10
bûz 1:7
bahar 1:29
baṭâ 12:18
baṭaḥ 1:33
beṭen 13:25
bîn 1:2
bêt 14:11
bəlîyaᶜal 6:12
balaᶜ 21:20
banâ 24:27
baᶜar 12:1
baṣaᶜ 15:27
baqar 20:25
baqaš 2:4

bar 11:26
baraḥ 19:26
barḥobôt 7:12
barak 11:25

g

gaʾâ 29:23
geʾâ 8:13
goʾel 23:11
gəbah 16:5
gibbôr 16:32
gəbûrâ 8:14
gehâ 17:22
gôy 14:34
gehalîm 26:22
galâ 27:25
galaᶜ 17:14
gəmûl 12:14
gaᶜar 13:1
garâ 28:4
gerem 25:15
garar 21:7
gareš 22:10

d

dəʾagâ 12:25
dabar 11:13
dibrê ḥăkamîm 1:6
dəbar šeqer 13:5
dôr 30:11
daḥâ 14:32
dîn 20:8
dakkayw 26:28
dal 14:31

dalyû 26:7
daᶜat 1:4
derek 22:6
daraš 11:27
dašan 13:4

h

hebel 13:11
hagâ 8:7
hadar 14:28
hôd 5:9
hôn 3:9
hawwat 11:6
halak 6:11
hamâ 1:21
hapak 12:7
hoqar 25:17

w

wazar 21:8

z

zebaḥ 17:1
zûd 13:10
zak 16:2
zalal 23:20
zamam 30:32
zaᶜam 22:14
zaᶜap 19:3
zar 2:16
zarâ 20:8
zarzîr matnayim 30:31

ḥ

ḥabal 1:5

ḥabar 21:9
ḥəgôr 31:24
ḥôaḥ 26:9
ḥôṭeʾ 14:21
ḥazôn 29:18
ḥaṭṭaʾîm 1:10
ḥəṭubôt 7:16
ḥoṭer 14:3
ḥîdâ 1:6
ḥayâ 4:4
ḥêq 6:27
ḥayil 12:4
ḥek 8:7
ḥaklilôt 23:29
ḥokmâ 1:2
ḥalâ 13:12
ḥallôn 7:6
ḥəlî 25:12
ḥalap 31:8
ḥalaṣ 11:8
ḥalaq 2:16
ḥemʾâ 30:33
ḥamad 6:25
ḥemâ 15:1
ḥamas 3:31
ḥen 3:4
ḥanak 22:6
ḥanan 14:21
ḥanep 11:9
ḥesed I 2:8
ḥesed II 14:34
ḥoseh 14:32
ḥosen 15:6
ḥəsar-leb 6:32
ḥapeṣ 18:2

ḥaper 13:5
ḥapaš 2:4
ḥaṣab 9:1
ḥaqar 18:17
ḥarâ 24:19
ḥarûṣ 3:14
ḥarak 12:27
ḥerep 14:31
ḥorep 20:4
ḥaraṣ 12:24
ḥaraš 3:29
ḥošek 2:13

ṭ

ṭəhôr 15:26
ṭôb 12:14
ṭaman 2:4
ṭaʿam 11:22
ṭerep 31:15

y

yad 18:21
yadaʿ 10:32
yaḥîd 4:3
yaḥîr 21:24
yayin 9:5
yakaḥ 3:12
yalaʿ 20:25
yaʿəlâ 5:19
yaʿaṣ 12:20
yapriš 23:32
yeqeb 3:10
yaqar 12:27
yaqoš 6:2
yareʾ 13:13

yirʾat yəhwah
1:7
yarûn 29:6
yaraš 20:13
yeš 19:18
yašab 20:3
yašaʿ 11:14
yašar 2:21
yatar 17:7

k

kəʾîšôn ʿêneyka
7:2
kabed 3:9
kəbaśîm 27:27
kûn 12:3
kûr 17:3
kazab 30:8
koaḥ 5:10
kalâ 22:8
kilyôt 23:15
keseʾ 7:20
kasâ 10:6
kəsîl 1:22
kaʿas 12:16
kəpîr 19:12
kapar 16:6
karâ 16:27
karat 2:22
kîšôr 31:19
kiššalon 16:18

l

laʾâ 26:15
loʾ yinnaqeh
6:29

ləʾom 14:34
leb 3:5
labaṭ 10:8
laham 18:8
loweh 22:7
lûz 2:15
liwyat ḥen 1:9
lûn 15:31
laḥem 9:5
leṣ 1:22
leqaḥ 1:5

m

məʾôr 15:30
maʾas 3:11
məʾerat 3:33
mebîš 14:35
məgôrat 10:24
magen 2:7
madôn 6:14
midḥeh 26:28
məhûmâ 15:16
mahîr 22:29
mûm 9:7
mûsar 1:2
mût 19:16
mawet 2:18
məzimmâ 1:4
maḥâ 31:3
maḥseh 14:26
maḥsor 14:23
məḥuqqaq 31:5
maḥšəbôt 6:18
məḥittâ 10:14
moṭ 10:30
mîṣ 30:33

ṣaʿad 20:24

ṣippôr 26:2

ṣapan 2:1

ṣarap 17:3

ṣarar 21:23

q

qabaʿ 22:23

qadôš 9:10

qedem 8:22

qûm 15:22

qûṣ 3:11

qəṭoret 27:9

qalôn 3:35

qalal 30:10

qinʾâ 14:30

qanâ 4:7

qesem 16:10

qaṣîn 25:15

qəṣar ʾappayim
14:17

qəṣar⁻rûaḥ 14:29

qaraʾ I 2:3

qaraʾ II 27:16

qereb 14:33

qaraṣ 16:30

qarar 17:27

qašab 2:2

qošt 22:21

r

raʾmôt 24:7

raʾš 10:4

roʾš 8:26

reʾšît 1:7

rab 26:10

rabâ 29:2

rabaṣ 24:15

ragzâ 30:21

radam 10:5

radap 12:11

rahab 6:3

rôznîm 31:4

rûm 11:11

raḥab 28:25

raḥam 12:10

ruḥaṣ 30:12

rîb 3:30

rak 4:3

rakîl 11:13

rimmâ 26:19

rəmîyâ 12:24

raʿ 1:33

reaʿ 6:1

raʿâ 10:21

raʿaʿ 11:15

repaʾîm 2:18

rapâ 24:10

rapas 6:3

raṣôn 11:1

raqeb 10:7

rešaʿ 8:7

ś

śabaʿ 3:10

śagah 29:25

śakal 1:3

śekel tôb 3:4

śamaḥ 10:1

śimlâ 30:4

śəmamît 30:28

śanaʾ 11:15

š

šəʾôl 7:27

šaʾal 20:4

šabar 6:15

šabat 22:10

šagâ 5:19

šadad 11:3

šawʾ 30:8

šûb 1:32

šûḥâ 23:27

šaḥâ 12:25

šaḥal 26:13

šaḥar 8:17

šaḥat 18:9

šeṭep 27:4

šît 7:10

šakaḥ 3:1

šekar 20:1

šalwâ 1:32

šalôm 3:2

šulḥan 9:2

šalal 31:11

šillamtî 7:14

šališiwm 22:20

šamad 14:11

šemen 21:20

šamaʿ 22:17

šamar 2:8

šanâ (noun) 5:9

šanâ (verb) 24:21

šenehem 24:22

šinnayw 30:14

šanîm 31:21

šaʿan 3:5

šəpal 16:19

šəpannim 30:26

šaqad 8:34

šiqqûy 3:8

šaqaṭ 15:18

šeqer 6:17

šoreš 12:3

šeš 31:22

t

taʾəwat 10:24

təbûʾâ 3:9

tabûs 27:7

tahpukôt 2:12

tûgâ 10:1

tôḥelet 10:28

tôkaḥat 1:23

tôʿəbat 3:32

tûr 12:26

tôrâ 1:8

taḥbulôt 1:5

tayiš 30:31

takak 29:13

takan 21:2

tilʿag 30:17

tom 2:7

tamak 4:4

taʿâ 10:17

tapaś 30:9

tiqwat 10:28

taqaʿ 6:1

tarbît 28:8

tərûmâ 29:4

tušîyâ 2:7